OUTLINES

OF

ENGLISH LITERATURE

BY

THOMAS B. SHAW, B.A.,

PROFESSOR OF ENGLISH LITERATURE IN THE IMPERIAL ALEXANDER LYCEUM OF ST. PETERSBURG.

A NEW AMERICAN EDITION,

WITH

A SKETCH OF AMERICAN LITERATURE,

BY

HENRY T. TUCKERMAN,

AUTHOR OF "CHARACTERISTICS OF LITERATURE," ETC.

NEW YORK:
SHELDON & COMPANY, PUBLISHERS,
498 & 500 BROADWAY.

1866.

STEREOTYPED BY J. FAGAN.

AMERICAN PUBLISHERS' NOTICE.

In presenting a new edition of the "OUTLINES OF ENGLISH LITERATURE," the publishers have thought that a brief sketch of what has been accomplished by the authors of this country would render it more complete and more suitable for the use to which it has been applied, as a class-book in many of our best seminaries and academies. They have, therefore, induced Mr. TUCKERMAN to undertake that task, which he has executed upon the same general plan as that adopted by the author. The present edition is therefore presented in the hope that it will be found even more worthy than the former of the wide popularity which the work has acquired.

PHILADELPHIA, *June*, 1852.

TO THE READER.

THE author of the following pages has been engaged, during some years, as Professor of English Literature in the Imperial Alexander Lyceum of St. Petersburg; and, both in the discharge of his duties there and in his private teaching, he has very frequently felt the want of a *Manual*, concise but comprehensive, on the subject of his lectures. The plan generally adopted in foreign countries, of allowing the pupil to copy the lecturer's manuscript notes, was in this case found to be impracticable; and the often-repeated request of the students to be furnished with some elementary book, as a framework or skeleton of the course, could only be met by a declaration, singular as the fact might appear, that no such work, cheap, compendious, and tolerably readable, existed in English. The excellent volumes of Warton are obviously inapplicable to such a purpose; for they only treat of one portion of English literature —the poetry; and of that only down to the Elizabethan age. Their plan, also, is far too extensive to render them useful to the general student. Chambers's valuable and complete 'Cyclopædia of English Literature' is as much too voluminous as his shorter sketch is too dry and list-like; while the French and German essays on the subject are not only limited in their scope, but are full of very erroneous critical judgments.

Induced by these circumstances, the author has endeavoured to produce a volume which might serve as a useful outline Introduction to English Literature both to the English and the foreign student. This little work, it is needless to say, has no pretensions whatsoever to the title of a complete Course of English Literature: it is merely an attempt to describe the causes, instruments, and nature of those great revolutions in taste which form what are termed "Schools of Writing." In order to do this, and to mark more especially those broad and salient features which ought to be clearly fixed in the reader's mind before he can profitably enter upon the details of the subject, only the *greater* names — the greater types of each period — have been examined; whilst the inferior, or merely *imitative*, writers have been unscrupulously neglected: in short, the author has marked only the chief luminaries in each intellectual constellation; he has not attempted to give a complete Catalogue of Stars.

This method appears to unite the advantages of conciseness and completeness; for, should the reader push his studies no farther, he may at least form clear ideas of the main boundaries and divisions of English literature; whilst the frequent change of topic will, the author trusts, render these pages much less tiresome and monotonous than a regular sytematic treatise.

He has considered the greater names in English literature under a double point of view: first, as glorified types and noble *expressions* of the religious, social, and intellectual physiognomy of their times; and secondly, in their own individuality: and he hopes that the sketches of the great Baconian revolution in philosophy, of the state of the Drama under Elizabeth and James the First, of the intellectual character of the Commonwealth and Restoration, and of the romantic school of fiction, of Byronism, and of the present tendencies of poetry, may be found — however imperfectly executed — to possess some interest, were it only as the first

1*

attempt to treat, in a popular manner, questions hitherto neglected in elementary books, but which the increased intelligence of the present age renders it no longer expedient to pass over without remark.

The work was written in the brief intervals of very active and laborious duties, and in a country where the author could have no access to an English library of reference: whatever errors and oversights it may contain on minor points will, therefore, he trusts, be excused. The only merits to which it can have any claim are somewhat of novelty in its plan, and the attempt to render it as little dry — as readable, in short — as was consistent with accuracy and comprehensiveness.

CONTENTS.

CHAPTER I.

The English Language.

CHAPTER II.

Chaucer and his Times.

CHAPTER III.

Sidney and Spenser.

CHAPTER IV.

Bacon.

CHAPTER V.

Origin of the English Drama.

CHAPTER VI.

Marlow and Shakspeare.

CHAPTER VII.

The Shakspearian Dramatists.

CHAPTER VIII.

The Great Divines.

CHAPTER IX.

John Milton.

CHAPTER X.

Butler and Dryden.

CHAPTER XI.

Clarendon, Bunyan, and Locke.

CHAPTER XII.

The Wits of Queen Anne's Reign.

CHAPTER XIII.

Swift and the Essayists.

CHAPTER XIV.

The Great Novelists.

CHAPTER XV.

THE GREAT HISTORIANS.

CHAPTER XVI.

THE TRANSITION SCHOOL.

CHAPTER XVII.

SCOTT AND SOUTHEY.

CHAPTER XVIII.

MOORE, BYRON, AND SHELLEY.

A SKETCH OF AMERICAN LITERATURE.

CHAPTER I.

PAGE

CHAPTER II.

CHAPTER III

POETRY.

OUTLINES

OF

GENERAL LITERATURE.

CHAPTER I.

THE ENGLISH LANGUAGE.

Britons—Their Oriental Origin—Cæsar's Invasion, B.C. 60—Traces of the Celtic Speech in English—Analysis of English—Saxon Tongue—Disuse of Saxon Inflections—The English *Th*—The English *W*—Pronunciation—Latin Element—Origin of English Language—Norman Conquest—William—Monasteries—Twelfth Century—Saxon Chronicle—Norman French—Layamon—Thirteenth Century—Robert of Gloucester—Neologism—Fourteenth Century—Mannyng—Wickliffe and Chaucer—Gower—Hermit of Hampole—Pleadings in English—Trevisa, Translation of Higden—Mandeville—Fifteenth Century—Lydgate—Statutes in English—Sixteenth Century—Reformation—Cheke—Skelton—Surrey and Wyatt—Berners—Ascham—Spenser—Chaucerism—Euphuism—Seventeenth Century—Protectorate—Gallicism—Restoration—Eighteenth Century—Proportion of Saxon in English.

THE most ancient inhabitants of the British islands were the Celts, Cymry, or Britons, as they are variously styled. That these rude and savage tribes were offshoots from the mighty race whose roots have struck so deep into the soil of most countries of Western and Southern Europe, there can be no doubt. Antiquaries may be undecided as to the origin of this venerable family of mankind, or as to the period at which it first migrated into Europe; but it is impossible not to believe that it formed one of the primary divisions of the human race; and there is very strong probability, from many noteworthy circumstances, that it originally came from the eastern regions of the globe.

In their mysterious and venerable system of theistic philosophy there are to be found so many points of resemblance with various recondite doctrines which we know to have been current from the remotest ages in the interior of India, that it is very difficult to believe such resemblances to be entirely accidental; particularly when we reflect that many of these dogmas—the transmigration of the soul, for instance—were parts of a creed not at all likely to have arisen spontaneously among so rude and savage a people as we know the Celts to have been. The extraordinary reverence paid by the Druids to the oak; their adoption of the mistletoe as an emblem of the immortality of the soul; the peculiar virtues which they attached to the number *three;* the magic powers which they imagined to reside in certain rhythmical and musical combinations; their addiction to the study of astronomy; and the singular peculiarity of a religious caste among them—these, among many other coincidences, would seem to claim for the Celts an evident, though perhaps remote, Oriental origin: an opinion further strengthened by the analogies which exist between some of the most ancient Indian dialects and the language of the Britons.

It was with this singular people that the Romans came in contact; and seldom had Cæsar's iron veterans encountered a more desperate and obstinate foe. With the history of that long contest we have nothing to do at present; it is sufficient for our purpose to sketch, as briefly and rapidly as possible, the results of the struggle. Such of the Britons as were spared by the Roman sword, by the not less fatal influence of Latin corruption, and the fierce intestine convulsions which decimated their ranks, were gradually driven back from the southern and central parts of Britain to take refuge in the inaccessible fastnesses of their mountains. A glance at the map will suffice to explain this; for we shall see the descendants of the ancient British race still occupying those parts of the country to which their ancestors had retired. In all districts of England and Scotland distinguished by any considerable tract of mountains, the Celtic blood has remained more or less pure, the Celtic language unchanged, and strong traces of the Celtic manners, language, and superstitions still prevail. It is, however, singular to remark how invariably the Celtic race has continued to diminish wherever it has been exposed to contact with the Teutonic tribes: thus the once purely Celtic population of Cornwall has gradually lost its individual character, and has almost ceased to exist; in Wales and in the Highlands of Scotland, two districts in which, and particularly in the former, the British blood has been least exposed to foreign admixture, the ancient race is yet slowly losing its marked peculiarities; and the day will probably come when the wild mountain fastnesses, which formed an insuperable barrier to the Roman sword and to the Saxon battle-axe, will have ceased to resist the silent spread of Teutonic commerce and Teutonic civilization.

The fate of the Celtic race in Britain has somewhat resembled that of the aboriginal tribes of the American continents: slowly but surely have they retired and contracted before the invading nations; and possibly in future ages the harp of the Bard and the claymore of the Sennachie will be picturesque but unsubstantial recollections, such as exist of the feathered tunic of the Mexitlan or the chivalric scalping-tuft of the Sioux.

Words are the pictures or reflections of things; and the genius, character, and capabilities of a nation can in no way be so well studied as in its language. From the earliest periods of our history the Celtic race has existed over the whole or a notable portion of the British islands; the British language, and, in some cases, no other, is spoken over a considerable extent of these countries—in Wales, in the Highlands of Scotland, in Ireland, and in the Isle of Man; some among these tribes possess large collections of very ancient and curious poems written in the respective dialects of the great Celtic speech; and yet, notwithstanding all this, the number of Celtic words which have taken root in the English language is so incrediby small that it can hardly be said to have exerted any influence whatever on the composite speech now used in the country. A large proportion, too, even of these scanty transplantations has taken place at a comparatively recent period, and the words so adopted have generally been transferred by poets and writers of fiction—Scott, for example—who found the Celtic expression either more picturesque and forcible than the equivalent which already existed in English (of Norman or Saxon origin), or else a lively and characteristic image for some object or idea peculiarly Celtic. Of the former kind we may adduce the words "*cairn*," "*cromlech*," and of the latter the word "*clan*." "Clan," it is evident, expresses an idea so exclusively Celtic that it forms a perfect and untranslatable sign of that idea; while "cairn," though by no means peculiar to the Celts, and defining a mode of honourable burial universal in former ages (as testified by the χαμος of the Greek heroic age, by the tumulus of the Etruscan peoples, and by the barrows of the Teutons), was nevertheless adopted as being a more local and exact image of the same hero-burial among the Celts.

With regard to the paucity of Celtic words which have retained a place in modern English, a Russian would remark something analogous in the history of his own language. The Tartars, in spite of two centuries and a half of complete and universal domination in Russia, have left hardly any traces of their language in the present Slavonic dialect of Russia; and the few words of Tartar origin that might be cited generally express articles of dress, equipment, food, &c., for which the Russians had no proper equivalent. In this case too we may note the difference of circumstances which tended to prevent any fusion between the conquered and conquerors: the abhorrence with which the Russian people—always extremely bigoted—regarded rapacious and haughty oppressors of a different religion, and of utterly barbarous habits. It is to be remarked, too, that the Tartar language is destitute of any literature at all comparable, in point of richness or antiquity, to the Celtic poems—a barrenness which the Russian must have contrasted with his own majestic, flexible, and abundant idiom. Compare with this scanty and meagre transfusion of Tartar words the immense and permanent influence of the Moors upon the language, sentiment, and character of Spain, during the glorious dominion of the Mahommedans in Granada, and we shall see that, while the Moorish or Arab element forms an integral, permanent, and essential ingredient in the language of the country, the communication between the conquering and conquered nations must be rated, in the case of Britain and of Russia, so much lower as to be considered comparatively insignificant.

During the Roman occupation of the isles of Britain—an occupation which extended over a period of 470 years, *i. e.* from 60 B.C. to A.D. 410—there can be no doubt but that a considerable part of the indigenous population submitted to the victorious invaders, and continued to occupy their estates in the Roman provinces of Britain, paying tribute, as was natural, to the Roman government. We know, too, that the officers and soldiers of the Roman legions permanently stationed in Britain freely intermixed, and even allied themselves, by marriage and otherwise, with the now half-civilized British population which surrounded their military posts; and we may consequently speculate upon what would have been the consequence had they continued to maintain their footing in Britain. In the process of time there would have arisen a new mixed population, partaking in some measure of the qualities, of the blood, and perhaps also of the vices, of its double origin; and, what is of more importance to our present subject, the language spoken at the present day by the descendants of such a *creole* race would have resembled the French or the Spanish; that is to say, it would have been a dialect bearing the physiognomic character of some one of the numerous ***Romanz*** languages, all of which are the result of efforts, more or less successful, of a rude Celtic or Gaulish nation to speak the Latin, with which they were only acquainted by practice and by the ear.

In this barbarous, but useful and improvable dialect, some words of the ancient Gaulish or Celtic would remain; and in point of proximity to the Latin—its fundamental element—it would resemble the language of classical Rome to a greater or to a less degree exactly in proportion as the communication with the Romans was closer or more relaxed. Further, if the language of the conquerors happened to be, as was the case with that of Rome, an inflected and highly artificial tongue, the new dialect would be distinguished, like the modern French or the Italian, by an almost universal suppression of all inflected terminations indicating the various modifications of meaning, which modifications would thereafter be expressed by independent particles—by prepositions, by pronouns, by auxiliary verbs.

But the supposition which has just been made was not to be verified in the modern language of the country: such a species of corrupt Latinity was not destined to become in our times the spoken dialect of the British islands; and, small as is the influence upon our present speech of the pure Celtic aboriginal tongue, the corruption of that tongue by the admixture of Latin (or rather the corruption of the Latin by the admixture of Celtic forms) was to be no less completely supplanted by new invasions, and by new languages originating in different and distant regions. It is undoubtedly obvious that a very large part of the modern English vocabulary, and even many forms of English grammar, are to be traced to the Romanz dialect, and therefore must be considered as having arisen from a corrupted Latinity, such as we have been describing as likely to have been employed by Gallic or Celtic tribes imperfectly acquainted with Latin. It would, however, be a fatal mistake to consider that these, or even any part of them, came from any such Romanz dialect or *lingua franca* ever spoken *originally* in Britain. They are, and without any exception, *not* of British growth, but were introduced into the English language after the Norman invasion of the country in 1066

We have said that the traces existing in the modern English of the aboriginal Celtic are exceeding few and faint: it is, however, proper to except one class of words—we allude to the names of places. In the long period of anarchy and bloodshed which intervened between the departure of the Romans and the arrival of the Saxon hordes in 449, and the gradual foundation in England of the Eight Kingdoms, the country must be conceived to have gone back rather than advanced in the career of civilization. The Saxons, we know, who were during a long period incessantly at war, as the Romans had been beforé them, with the Picts, the Scots, and the Welsh, strenuously endeavored to obliterate every trace of the ancient language, even from the geography of the regions they had conquered: and it is singular to observe an Anglo-Saxon king, himself the member of a nation not very far removed from its ancient rudeness and ferocity, stigmatising as barbarous the British name of a spot to which he had occasion to allude, as known "*barbarico* nomine Pendyfig," by the *barbarous*—this was the *British*—name of Pendyfig. National hatred is perhaps the longest-lived of all things: and it is curious to observe the mutual dislike and contempt still existing between the Celtic and the Saxon race, and the Irish peasant of the present day expressing, in words which 1300 years have not deprived of their original bitterness, his detestation of the Sassenagh—the Saxon. A moment's inspection of the map of England will show the immense number of places which have retained, in whole or in part, their original Celtic form: we may instance the terminating syllable *don* with which many of these names conclude, and which is the Celtic *dun*, signifying a fortified rock. The Irish *Kil*, which begins so many names of places, is nothing more than a corruption of the Celtic *Caille*, signifying a forest; and the *Caer*, frequently found in the beginning of Welsh, Cornish, and Armorican names, and which the

Bretons have so often preserved in the initial syllable *Ker* (as Kerhoët), is evidently nothing but *Caer*, the rock or stone.

From what has been suggested, then, upon the subject of the Celtic language, the reader will conclude that, for all practical purposes of analogy or of derivation, it has exerted no appreciable influence on the modern speech of the country. Some few words indeed have been adopted into English from the tongue of the aboriginal possessors of the country, but so few in number, and so unimportant in signification, that it will be found to have borrowed as much from the language of Portugal, nay, even from those of China and Hindostan, as it has derived from the ancient indigenous tongue.

The English language, then, viewed with reference to its component elements, must be considered as a mixture of the Saxon and of the Romanz or corrupted Roman of the middle ages: and before we can proceed to investigate the peculiar character, genius, and history of such a composite dialect, it will be essential to establish with some degree of correctness—first, in what proportions these two elements are found in the compound substance under consideration; and second, what were the periods and what were the influences during and through which the process of amalgamation took place.

In examining the relative proportions of two or more elements forming together a new dialect, it would certainly be a very simple and unphilosophical analysis which should consist of simply counting the various vocables in a dictionary and arranging them under the various languages from which they are derived, then striking a balance between them, and assigning as the true origin of the language the dialect to which the greater number should be found to belong. No; we must pay some attention to the nature and significance of the vocables themselves, and also to the degree of primitiveness and antiquity of their meaning; nor must we neglect, in particular, to take into the account the general form and analogies of the composite language viewed as a whole. It is evident that that dialect must be the primitive or radical one from which are derived the greatest number of vocables expressing the simpler ideas and the most universally known objects—such objects and ideas, in short, as cannot but possess equivalents in every human speech, however rude its state or imperfect its development.

Following this important rule, we shall find that all the primary ideas, and all the simpler objects, natural and artificial, are expressed in English by words so evidently of Teutonic origin—nay, so slightly varied from Teutonic forms—that a knowledge of the German will render them instantly intelligible and recognizable. Such for instance, are the words "man," "woman" (wif-man; *i. e.* female man), "sun," "moon," "earth;" the names of the simpler colours, as "green," "red," "yellow" (note that "purple"—a compound colour—is derived from the Greek), "brown," &c.; the commoner and simpler acts of life, "to run," "to fly," "to eat," "to sing," &c.; the primary and fundamental passions of our nature, and the verbs which express those passions as in activity, "love," "fear," "hate," &c.; the names of the ordinary animals and their cries, as "horse," "hound," "sheep," "to neigh," "to bark," "to bleat," "to low," &c.; the arts and employments, the trades and dignities of life, "to read," "to write," "seamen," "king," "miller," "earl," "queen," &c.; and the most generally known among artificial objects, as "house," "boat," "door." It is worthy of remark how universally applicable is this principle of antiquity or primitiveness: thus, those religious objects and ideas which are of the simplest and most obvious character are represented in English by words derived from the Teutonic dialects, while the more complicated and artificial—what we may call the scientific or technic—portion of the religious vocabulary, is almost in every case of Latin or Greek derivation: thus, "God," "fiend," "wicked," "righteous," "hell," "faith," "hope," &c., are all pure Saxon words; while "predestination," "justification," "baptism," &c., will generally be found to come from other sources. So generally, indeed, is this principle observable in the English language, that we may in most cases decide, *à priori*, whether the equivalent for a given object or idea be a Saxon or a Latin word, by observing whether that object be a primitive and simple or a complex and artificial one.

It must not, however, be inferred from this that the Saxon language was a rude and uncultivated mode of speech: such a notion would be in the highest degree unjust and unfounded. Like all the languages of the Teutonic stock, the Anglo-Saxon was distinguished for its singular vigour, expressiveness, and exactness, and in particular for the great facilities it afforded for the formation of compound words.

We may remark that most of the Saxon compound words have ceased to exist in the modern English: in short, the tendency of our remarks is to show, not that the Saxon was incapable of expressing even the most complex and refined ideas, but that, by a curious fatality, those words have generally given place, in the tongue of the present day, to equivalents drawn from the Latin and Greek origins. That this substitution (for which we shall endeavor to assign a reason) of Latin and Greek derivatives for words of Saxon stock has been injurious in some cases to the expressiveness, and in all to the vigour, of the modern idiom, no one can deny who compares the distinctness of the older words, in which all the elements would be known to an English peasant, with the somewhat pedantic and far-fetched equivalents: for instance, how much more picturesque, and, let us add, intelligible, are the words "mildheartedness," "deathsman," "moonling," than the corresponding "mercifulness," "executioner," and "lunatic"!

But perhaps the most singular transformation undergone by the Saxon language, in the course of its becoming the basis of the English is the annihilation of all, or nearly all, its inflections. The tongue of our Saxon ancestors was distinguished, like the modern German—one of the offshoots of the same great parent stock—by a considerable degree of grammatical complexity; it possessed its declensions, its cases, its numbers, and in particular its genders of substantive and adjective, indicated by terminations, as in almost all the languages ever spoken on the earth.

The whole of this elaborate apparatus has been rejected in our present speech, in the same manner as a great portion of it has been rejected by the Italian, Spanish, and French languages in their process of descent from the Latin. The English language presents, therefore, the singular phenomenon of a dialect derived from two distinct sources, each characterized by peculiarities of inflection, yet itself absolutely or nearly without any traces of the method of inflection prevalent in either the one or the other of those sources.

Among the singularities of the English pronunciation which place, as it were, upon the threshold of the language so many unexpected obstacles in the way of the foreigner, there are two or three always found peculiar difficulties by all, and particularly by Germans, who discover, in other respects, so many analogies between their language and our own. These are, among others, the sound, or rather the two distinct sounds, of the *th.* A very little explanation would suffice to render at all events the theoretical part of this difficulty very easy and intelligible to them; for they would then discover that the *th* which they so bitterly complain of represents the sound of two different and distinct letters in the Saxon alphabet, which were most injudiciously suppressed, their place being supplied by the combination *th*, which exists in almost all the European languages, but which is pronounced in none of them as in the English. The Saxon letters in question are ð and þ, and are nothing more than ꝺ and ꞇ (the Saxon *d* and *t*) followed by an aspirate, indicated by the cross line; and which are both most absurdly represented in English by *th*, the pronunciation of which varies, as in the words "*this*" and "*thin*;" to assign the right sound being an effort of memory in the learner. Now the Saxon words in which is found the character ð are almost invariably observed to exist in German with the simple 𝔡, and those containing þ, with either 𝔡 or 𝔱𝔥; a circumstance tending strongly to prove that it is the *Germans* who have lost the ancient aspirated sound of the two letters or combinations (for it is of no consequence whether they were anciently written by the Germans with one character or two), and that, consequently, the English alone, of all the Teutonic races, have preserved the true ancient pronunciation in this particular. The same conclusion may be arrived at, we think not unfairly, with reference to the English *w*, the letter corresponding to which in Ger man, viz. w, seems to have lost not only its true name, but also, which is of much more importance, even its correct sound.*

If the German pronunciation of w be the correct and original one, either the v or the f is a superfluous and unnecessary letter. We think it, therefore, not improbable that in this, as well as in the preceding instance, it is the English language alone which, in spite of a thousand fluctuations and a thousand caprices in orthography and etymology, has preserved the genuine pronunciation of these very important letters: we say very important, for it is only sufficient to reflect on the immense number of words in German, English, and, in short, all the Teutonic languages into the structure of which enter one or the other of these letters, to be convinced that the *th*, the *d*, and the *w* play a most considerable part.

The pronunciation of every language must obviously depend principally upon the sounds assigned to the various vowels, and consequently the learner, when he finds that in English almost all the vowels have a name and a power totally different from what they bear in all other tongues, is apt to lose all courage, and to despair of using, in the acquisition of English, the most powerful instrument with which he can be armed; namely, the analogy existing between the original and the derived dialects. He finds, for instance, that the English vowels *a*, *e*, *i*, and *u*, have quite different names and sounds from the same characters in French and German; and his ear, perpetually tantalised by analogies of sound which do not exist, is very apt to become incapable of perceiving those which do. So generally, indeed, is this difficulty experienced, that it may be laid down as an almost universal principle, that in all words derived from a foreign source, and naturalized in the English vocabulary, one of two results is invariably found to take place; viz. either the *pronunciation* of the original word is changed, or its *orthography:* in other terms, the word is made to submit either to the pronunciation of the English letters, when its original spelling is retained, or the spelling is altered, so as to make another combination of English letters express the original sound of the word. In the case, however, of derivatives from languages of the Teutonic stock, these changes of orthography ought by no means to be considered as involving such great difficulty as is generally attributed to them; and in a majority of cases they will be found much less capricious than is usually supposed. One considerable portion of the above difficulty arises from the circumstance that there exists in German a much greater number of dipththongal combinations than have been retained, in a written form, in the English; and thus we are frequently obliged to represent such combinations by means of our limited number of vowels, in giving

* The Germans pronounce *w* as *v* in English.

to the same vowels a different power, and consequently assigning to each letter a number of distinct and often very dissimilar sounds.

As an example of this, let us take the word Mann, which is so faithfully reflected in the English *man*, that the identity of meaning in the two cases is instantly and inevitably perceived; in the plural, however, of the English form, the *a* of the singular is changed into *e*, forming an exception to the usual manner of expressing the plural of a substantive by the addition of *s*. Now it is obvious that the *e* of the plural number of the word *men* is nothing else than an attempt to represent in English the somewhat complicated combination of vowels in the German plural Männer, i. e. *maenner*, of which sound the English *e*, though not an exact, yet is the best representation of which the case would admit. Of this kind of representation the examples are innumerable, and they will go far to explain, if not to palliate, the alleged caprice of the English pronunciation. Again, in that multitude of words which exist in nearly similar forms (though it must be confessed under great differences in point of pronunciation) in the French and English languages, and which have a common Latin origin, it will be universally found that, however great be the difference of pronunciation, the orthography in the English form is in general so little changed from the original Latin as to be immediately recognizable. Indeed, it is very curious to remark that the orthography of almost the whole of this large class of words is in English absolutely much more correct—that is, much closer to the Latin—than in the French, the Italian, or even than in the Spanish itself; so much so indeed as to induce a linguistic student unacquainted with the history of the language rather to suppose that these words came into modern English either directly from the Latin, or that they were incorporated into our speech through some separate and independent channel, than that they had been (as they undoubtedly were) first filtered, so to speak, through the French and Italian idioms. It is strange that this large stream of words seems to have purified itself from foreign admixtures as it descended from the antique Latin through the various Romanz idioms which have become the several languages of modern Europe; so much so, that the Latin words in our present speech may be said, at least as far as their orthography is concerned, to have reached among us a greater purity than they have in French, Italian, or even in Spanish.

"Nothing can be more difficult," says the judicious and accurate Hallam, "than to determine, except by an arbitrary line, the commencement of the English language; not so much, as in those of the continent, because we are in want of materials, but rather from an opposite reason—the possibility of tracing a very gradual succession of verbal changes that ended in a change of denomination. For when we compare the earliest English of the thirteenth century with the Anglo-Saxon of the twelfth, it seems hard to pronounce why it should pass for a separate language, rather than a modification or simplification of the former. We must conform, however, to usage, and say that the Anglo-Saxon was converted into English—1, by contracting or otherwise modifying the pronunciation and orthography of words; 2, by omitting many inflections, especially of the noun, and consequently making more use of articles and auxiliaries; 3, by the introduction of French derivatives; 4, by using less inversion and ellipsis, especially in poetry. Of these, the second alone, I think, can be considered as sufficient to describe a new form of language; and this was brought about so gradually, that we are not relieved of much of our difficulty, whether some compositions shall pass for the latest offspring of the mother, or the earliest fruits of the fertility of the daughter."

With respect to this excellent and comprehensive judgment, it is only necessary to remark, that in tracing practically the application to the English language of the first of these processes by which Hallam explains the gradual transition from the Anglo-Saxon into English, they are found universally taking place in the transformation of an inflected into an uninflected language, or even into one less completely and regularly inflected: a very long list has been made, nay, an almost complete vocabulary might be compiled, of words in the French language which differ from their Latin roots only in their having lost the final syllable, expressive in the Roman tongue, of case, of gender, or of tense. A very few instances will suffice: if we compare, for example, the old French *hom* and *homs* with the Latin *hom-o* and *hom-ines*, we shall find that only as much of the Roman inflection has been retained as was indispensable to the required distinction of singular and plural. In other respects the word was *truncated*—and it is of no consequence whether this contraction took place gradually or suddenly—until nothing remains but the significant or radical syllable *hom*.

In tracing from the momentous epoch of the Norman invasion the gradual developement of the English language, it will be by no means necessary to enter into any very minute details of philological archæology: our task will be more agreeably, and certainly not less profitably fulfilled, if we content ourselves with accompanying, with due reverence and a natural admiration, the advance of that noble language along the course of centuries: we shall see it, springing from the distant sources of barbarous and unpolished but free and vigorous generations, at one time rolling harshly, like a mountain streamlet, over the rugged bed of Saxon antiquity, then slowly and steadily gliding onward in a calmer and more majestic swell, receiving into its bosom a thousand tributary currents, from the wild mountains of Scandinavia, from the laughing valleys of Provence and Languedoc, from the storied plains of Italy or the haunted shores of Greece, from the sierras of Andalusia and the Moorish vegas of Granada—till, broadening and strengthening as it rolls, it bears upon its immeasurable breast the solidest treasures of human wisdom and the fairest harvests of poesy and wit.

It is by no means to be supposed that the invasion of the Normans under William was the first point of contact between the Saxon and French races in England, and that it is to that event that we must attribute the first fusion: on the contrary, it is well established that for a long time previous to this epoch the nobles and the court of England had affected to imitate French fashions, and even sent their youth to be partially educated in the latter country. Between the sovereign houses of Great Britain and Normandy, in particular, there were too many relations of blood and alliance of ancient standing to allow us to be surprised at this. This imitation of French customs, dress, and language was not likely to be very palatable to the English of the pure Anglo-Saxon stock, and we accordingly find that a good deal of ridicule was cast by the lower orders on such of their countrymen as showed too great a taste for the manners of the other side of the Strait of Dover. They had a species of proverbial saying with respect to such followers of outlandish fashions, which is not destitute of a certain drollery and salt: "Jacke," they said, "woud be a gentilman if he coud bot speke Frenshe." It is known, too, that in the first part of his English sovereignty William had in vain exhausted his patience and fatigued his ear in the attempt to learn the Anglo-Saxon language; and it was not until after his return from Normandy, after a nine months' absence from England, that he began to employ, for the suppression of the language and nationality of his new kingdom, those severe measures which have rendered his name so memorable. It would be superfluous to allude to these at any length; the institution of the curfew, the forced employment of the Norman language in all public acts and pleadings, the compulsory teaching of Norman in the schools—all these are well-known measures, and sufficiently prove William's conviction that no hope was left of subduing the national obstinacy by fair or gentle means, and that nothing remained but proscription and violence.

In spite of these ominous proceedings, however, the sacred flame of letters was still kept alive in the monasteries: the superiors of these institutions, it is true, were almost universally changed, the recalcitrant Saxons being displaced to make way for Norman ecclesiastics, but under the monk's gown there often beat the stern Saxon heart, and the labouring brain was often working with patriotic fervour under the unmarked cowl. The chroniclers of this period were in many cases Saxons, and in their rude but picturesque narratives we find the most ineffaceable marks of the hatred felt by the great body of the nation against the haughty conquerors. In these monasteries were taught rhetoric, theology, physic, the civil and canon law; and it is in them also that were nursed the school-divinity and dialectics which form so striking a feature in the intellectual physiognomy of the middle ages.

The year 1150 is generally assigned as the epoch at which the Saxon language began that process of transformation or corruption by which it was ultimately changed into English. This change, as we have specified above, was *not* the effect of the Norman invasion, for hardly any new accession of French words is perceptible in it for at least a hundred years from this time: it may be remarked that some few French words had crept in before this period, and also a considerable Latinising tendency may be remarked; but the changes of which we are speaking are rather of form than of matter, and are generally referable to one or other of the various causes which have been assigned a few pages back in the clear and emphatic words of Hallam.

In the year 1150 the Saxon Chronicle—that venerable monument of English history—comes to an abrupt conclusion. This chronicle (or rather series of chronicles, for it was evidently continued by a great number of different writers, and exhibits an immense variety of style and language) is intended to give an account of the English annals from A. D. 1; and though the earlier portion, as might be expected, is filled with trivial and improbable fables, the accuracy and importance of the work, as a historical document, becomes immeasurably greater as it approaches the period when it was discontinued; the description of the more recent events, and the portraits of contemporary personages, bearing in many cases evident marks of being the production of men who had been the eyewitnesses of what they paint.

The French language was still spoken at court; and there is a curious anecdote exemplifying the profound ignorance of our English kings respecting the language and manners of the larger portion of their subjects. We read that Henry II., who ascended the throne in 1154, having been once addressed by a number of his own subjects during a journey into Pembrokeshire, in a harangue commencing with the words "Good Olde Kynge!" he turned to his courtiers for an interpretation of these words, whose meaning was totally unknown to him.

Towards the latter end of this century, viz. in 1180, Layamon wrote his translation of Wace's metrical legendary romance of Brut; and nothing will give a more distinct idea of the difficulty encountered by philologists in fixing the exact period at which the Saxon merged into the English, than the great variety of decisions founded upon the style of this work; some of our most learned antiquarians, among whom is the accomplished George Ellis, deciding that the language of Layamon is "a simple and unmixed, though very barbarous Saxon," while others, who are followed by Campbell, consider it to be the first dawning or daybreak of English. Where so learned and accurate a person as Ellis has hesitated, it becomes every one to avoid anything like dogmatism; but the truth probably is, that the language of Layamon is to be considered either as late Saxon or as very early English, according as the philologist is inclined to attribute the change from one language into the other to a modification taking place in the form or in the matter of the Saxon speech.

At the beginning of the reign of Henry III., in 1216, the English language had made considerable progress, though it had not even yet begun to be spoken at court: and it must be regarded at this period as a harsh but vigorous and expressive idiom, containing in itself the seeds or capabilities of future perfection. This century, too, is characterised by the circumstance of Latin having begun to fall into disuse; the learned adopting their vernacular language as a medium for their thoughts. The increasing neglect of the Latin is to be attributed to the secret but extensive spread of those doctrines which afterwards took consistency at the Reformation. Recent investigations have assigned to one very curious monument of old English a different and much earlier date than had been previously fixed for it: we allude to the beautiful song beginning "Sumer ys ycumen in," &c. This venerable relic has been usually attributed to the fifteenth century, but there can be little doubt as to its being really the production of the thirteenth. It was probably composed about the year 1250, and the language, when divested of its ancient and uncouth spelling, differs so little from the English of the present day as to have caused the error to which we have alluded. About 1280 was written the work of Robert of Gloucester, and it is extraordinary to observe how great a change had taken place between this time and the appearance of Layamon, a hundred years earlier. We are now rapidly approaching a period when the language may be said to have acquired some solidity; for at the beginning of the following century we find complaints in a great multitude of writers against neologisms and innovations in language—an infallible sign that some standard, however imperfect, and some rules, however capricious, had begun to be applied to the idiom—now rapidly rising into a written, and consequently regular, language. In the year 1303, Robert Mannyng, in his 'Handlyng of Sinne,' an English translation of Bishop Grosteste's 'Manuel des Pes Peschés,' protests repeatedly against foreign and outlandish innovations: "I seke," says this venerable purist, "no straunge Ynglyss." In what consisted the innovations against which he desires to guard—whether the "strange English" was corrupted by an admixture of French words, of Latinisms, or of Grecisms—it is obviously very difficult to ascertain. This century is one of the most important in the history of the literature, and consequently in that of the language also. It was in this century that Wickliffe, in popularising religion, tended also so powerfully to popularise language: it was in this century, too, that the Father of

English Literature, the immortal Chaucer himself, introduced the elegance, the harmony, the learning, and the taste of the infant Italián muse, assimilating and digesting, by the healthy energy of genius, what he took, not as a plagiarist, but as a conqueror, from Petrarca and from Boccaccio. Gower, too, who was born shortly before the year 1340, mainly helped to polish and refine the language of his country; and though, for want of that vivifying and preserving quality, that sacred particle of flame, which we designate by the word *genius*, his works are now obsolete, and consulted less for any merit of their own than to illustrate his great contemporary, the smoothness and art of his versification had doubtless a considerable influence in developing and perfecting the language. It was in the reign of Edward III. that the Lombard character was first disused in charters and public acts, and to this reign also must be assigned the oldest instrument known to exist in the English language. In the middle of this century wrote Richard Rolle, the Hermit of Hampole, in whose dull ethical poem, the 'Prikke of Conscience,' 'Stimulus Conscientiæ'—we find the same dread of innovation that was expressed forty years earlier by Robert Mannyng, or Robert de Brunne, as he was otherwise denominated. The Hermit of Hampole exhibits the strongest desire to make himself intelligible to *lewed* or unlearned folk: "I seke no straunge Inglyss, bot lightest and communest." We cannot pass this epoch without an allusion to Langlande's 'Vision of Piers Plowman,' a long and rather confused allegorical poem, containing many striking invectives against the corruptions of the Romish priesthood, and in particular a most singular prophecy of the severities which were afterwards exercised against the monastic orders by Henry VIII. at the suppression of the religious houses. In 1350, or about that year, the character called Old English, or Black Letter, was first used; and though the language of this period was disfigured by the most barbarous and capricious orthography, it is surprising how similar it is, in point of structure and intelligibleness, to the English of the present day.

Twelve years after this, by the wisdom and patriotism of King Edward III., the pleadings before the tribunals were restored to the vernacular language — an irrefragable proof of the universal prevalence of the native speech, and of the diminished influence of the Norman French. It is curious to remark how absolutely identical has remained the speech of the mob even from so remote a period to the present day. The following is a passage from a species of political pasquinade disseminated in the year 1382, and gives a very fair specimen of the popular language of the day: we have modernized the spelling; and, with this precaution, there is not a word or an expression which differs materially from the language of the people in the nineteenth century:—"Jack Carter prays you all that you make a good end of that ye have begun, and do well, and still better and better; for at the even men near the day. If the end be well, then all is well. Let Piers the ploughman dwell at home, and dight (prepare) us corn. Look that Hobbe the robber be well chastised. Stand manly together in truth, and help the truth, and the truth shall help you."

In 1385 the Latin chronicle of Higden (attributed to the year 1365) was translated into English by John de Trevisa. It appears that, in the interval which had elapsed since the original was written, the custom of making children in grammar-schools translate their Latin into French had been, principally through the patriotic efforts of a certain Sir John Cornewaill, almost universally discontinued: "so that now," to use the words of Trevisa, "the yere of our Lorde 1385, in all the grammere scoles of Engelond, children leaveth Frensche, and construeth and lerneth in Englische."

Another strong proof of the growing spread and importance of the English language at this period is to be found in the circumstance that our earliest traveller, Sir John Mandeville, who had written in Latin and in French the interesting account of his long wanderings, should have thought fit to give to the world an *English* version of the same curious work.

In his translation of Higden, Trevisa avoids what he calls "the old and ancient Englische;" and the same author gives a most terrifying description of the barbarous dialects and pronunciation prevalent in the remoter parts of the country. "Some use," says he, in words ludicrously responsive to the sounds he describes, "strange wlaffing, chytryng, harring, garring, and grysbytyng. The languages of the Northumbres, and specyally at Yorke, is so sharpe, slytyng, frotyng, and unshape, that we sothern men may unnethe (hardly) undirstonde that language." And even to the present day the inhabitants (even in neighbouring counties) of distant and retired or "uplandish" districts can hardly understand each other's speech. According to the learned Ritson, the year 1388 was signalised by the restoration to the English language of parliamentary proceedings—a great and important advance for the vernacular idiom: and a singular circumstance, bearing a similar tendency, is to be remarked in the fact that both the present king, Henry IV., and his son and successor, Henry V., made their wills in English, a thing certainly not customary among the nobles of the period: the conduct therefore of the two sovereigns proves that they were desirous of setting an example of a more general use of the language of the people.

Henry V. ascendeded the throne in 1413, and he ever exhibited an enlightened care of the national language; a care worthy of the heroic sovereign who had so splendidly illustrated his reign by his achievements in France. The Victor of Azincour appears to have fostered and protected the language of his country. There still exists a letter addressed by this great sovereign to the Company of

Brewers in London, containing the following remarkable expressions: "The English tongue hath in modern days begun to be honourably enlarged and adorned, and for the better understanding of the people the common idiom is to be exercised in writing." It also appears by the same document that many of the craft to whom the letter is addressed "had knowledge of reading and writing in the English tongue, but Latin and French they by no means understood." Here, then, we see the revolution gradually becoming complete, and the English idiom finally succeeding in supplanting, at least for the common business of life, the French and the Latin.

In the following century, and at the beginning of the reign of Henry VI., flourished the poet Lydgate, and also the learned Sir John Fortescue, Chief Justice of the King's Bench, one of the first important prose-writers in the language. King James of Scotland, who holds an honourable place among English poets, was assassinated at Perth in the year 1437. The language must still be considered as advancing, in spite of the civil contentions which agitated England during a considerable part of this century. We may remark that the Gothic letters ceased to be used during this period; and in 1483, at the beginning of the reign of Richard III., the statutes were recorded in English, having been till now written in the Norman French. As an example of the gradual change that had taken place in the language, we may mention the fact that Caxton modernised Trevisa in 1487—Trevisa, who had himself, just a hundred years before, so strenuously endeavoured to avoid the old English: "thus the whirligig of time," as the Clown says in 'Twelfth Night,' "brings about his revenges."

In 1509 commenced the long and eventful reign of Henry VIII., and the recognition, on the part of the sovereign and the government, of the principles of the Reformation. The court, as well as the nation in general, was distinguished in this age for learning and intellectual activity; and we find a very considerable advance in the cultivation of the vernacular language. Among the remarkable men who adorned this period it would be impossible to omit mentioning Sir John Cheke, who first introduced into England a profound and enlightened study of the Greek language.

Cheke is also entitled to the grateful memory of after generations by the wise and accurate attention which he paid himself, and inculcated upon others, to the purity of his own language. One of the most curious and valuable specimens of the writing and criticism of this time is a letter written by him to his friend Hoby, containing remarks upon the latter's translation of the 'Cortegiano' of Castiglione, a very favourite book of this period. We cannot forbear quoting a few passages from this excellent composition of Cheke, as well on account of the weight and value of the sentiments, as on that of the language in which they are conveyed. It should be remarked that

Sir Thomas Hoby had requested Cheke's opinion of his work:—"Our own tongue should be written clean and pure, unmixed and unmangled with borrowing of other tongues; wherein, if we take not heed, by time, ever borrowing and never paying, she shall be fain to keep her house as bankrupt. For then doth our tongue naturally and praisably utter her meaning when she borroweth no counterfeitness of other tongues to attire herself withal; but used plainly her own, with such shift as nature, craft, experience, and following of other excellent, doth lead her unto; and if she wants at any time (as, being imperfect, she must), yet let her borrow with such bashfulness that it may appear that, if either the mould of our own tongue could serve us to fashion a word of our own, or if the old denizened words could content and ease this need, we would not boldly venture on unknown words. This I say not for reproof of you, who have scarcely and necessarily used, where occasion seemeth, a strange word so as it seemeth to grow out of the matter, and not to be sought for; but for my own defence, who might be counted overstraight a deemer of things if I gave not this account to you, my friend, of my marring this your handiwork." We find at this time innumerable complaints of the vast quantity of foreign words imported, from a thousand different sources, into the English tongue; and it is curious to observe the struggles made, and made in vain, by the purists of this period, to establish some model or standard of style. In spite (or, perhaps, even in consequence) of these difficulties, the language was undoubtedly fixed and consolidated in the sixteenth century more effectually, perhaps, than in any other period of equal duration; for we must reflect that in this age also is included the whole splendid reign of Elizabeth.

As specimens of the most familiar and idiomatic English—the English of the lower orders—we may cite the wild and witty pasquinades of Skelton, who attacked Wolsey with such persevering temerity. The translation of the Scriptures is by many supposed to have strongly and beneficially influenced the language of this age, but Barrington attributes (and in our opinion justly) a much greater power of purifying and fixing the idiom to the publication of the statutes in English. Those noble and illustrious friends, Lord Surrey and Sir John Wyatt, had a powerful influence in the adorning of their native tongue, no less than Lord Berners, the translator of the Chronicles of Froissart. In the works of Roger Ascham, the learned preceptor of Elizabeth, we find the same dread of neologisms; in short, almost every author of the times seems to be on his guard against that torrent of Italianisms, Gallicisms, and Spanish terms, which was soon to invade the language—"taffeta phrases, silken terms precise." Arthur Golding, who wrote in 1565, thus complains:—

> "Our English tongue is driven almost out of kind,
> Dismember'd, hack'd, maim'd, rent, and torn,
> Defaced, patch'd, marr'd, and made in scorn:"

and Carew, about 1580, informs us that, "within these sixty years we have incorporated so many Latin and French words as the third part of our language consisteth in them." Spenser, in order to give (as a multitude of poets, ancient and modern, have striven to do) an air of antiquity to the language of his 'Faery Queen,' in harmony with the romantic chivalry of its subject, set the example—unhappily followed by many writers who had no such excuse as the English Ariosto—of reviving the obsolete diction of Chaucer; and Shakspeare, with that intuitive good taste which characterises the higher order of genius, levelled the keen and brilliant shafts of his ridicule against the fantastic Euphuism or Italianated pedantry of the court, exactly as Rabelais has gibbeted in immortal burlesque the "Pindarizing" Latinity of the pedants of his day, and Molière has so cruelly immortalized the conceited jargon of the Hôtel de Rambouillet.

The influence, at this period, and even down to the end of the reign of James I., of Italian manners and literature, was very great; an influence which was occasionally mingled with the somewhat similar tone of Spanish society: but this was afterwards to give place to a decided tendency towards a French taste in language, dress, and so on. During the stormy interval occupied by the Republic and Protectorate, men were too much occupied with graver and more pressing interests to cultivate literature with great ardour or success; and even had this period been one of tranquil prosperity, the gloomy fanaticism of the times would have forbidden us to expect any improvement in the language. At a period when British senators would rise in Parliament to expound the Epistles of St. Paul, when the stage was suppressed, and serious propositions were made to paint all the churches black to typify the gloom and corruption that reigned within them, it was natural to find the style of writers as mean as was the condition of most of the rulers, as narrow as their intolerance, and as extravagant as their doctrines; and perhaps one of the true causes of Milton's adoption of the singularly artificial, learned, and involved way of writing which characterises his prose works, was his contempt for the ignorance of most of the republican party, whose political opinions he shared, while he abhorred their vices and despised their bigotry.

Phillips, the nephew and pupil of Milton, in the preface to his 'Theatrum Poetarum,' a work which is without doubt deeply tinged with the literary taste and opinions of the author of the 'Paradise Lost,' complains of the gradually increasing French taste which characterised our literature when he wrote, *i. e.* in 1675, in the reign of Charles II. "I cannot but look upon it as a very pleasant humour that we should be so compliant with the French custom as to follow set fashions, not only in garments, but in music and poetry. . . . . Now, whether the trunk-hose fashion of Queen Elizabeth's days, or the pantaloon genius of ours, be best, I shall not be hasty to determine." The cause of the great influx of Gallicisms which took place at the Restoration is undoubtedly to be found in the long exile of Charles II. during the stormy period of the Republic. Charles, and the few faithful adherents who composed his court, passed many of those years in France; he was indeed a pensioner of Versailles. He there naturally acquired a taste for the artificial and somewhat formal refinements of French literature, much more active and permanent than any which he might have retained for the vernacular literature of that nation which had brought his father to the block and compelled himself to encounter all the vicissitudes of poverty and exile. At his return to the kingdom of his ancestors, it was the court which gave, in a great measure, the tone to the rest of the nation; and it is from this epoch, consequently, that we must date the commencement of that long influence exerted on English by French manners and modes of thinking.

This influence is very perceptible in all our writers during the reigns of William, Anne, and the three first Georges: it is to this that we must attribute that faintness, dimness, and commonplace good sense which characterises, with occasional splendid exceptions, the prose; and that unimaginative and monotonous classicism which marks the *courtly* school of poetry, and which was not to be supplanted by anything truly national and vigorous, till the glorious outburst of new forms and modes of thought and expression in that splendid epoch illustrated by the contemporary names of Lord Byron, Scott, and Wordsworth.

As to the elementary constitution of the English language as spoken and written in the present day, the following calculations may be found curious and instructive, and perhaps they may give a better notion of the present condition of the language than more general description. It has been ascertained that the English now consists of about 38,000 words, of which 23,000, or nearly *five-eighths*, are Anglo-Saxon in their origin; and that in our *most* idiomatic writers about nine-tenths are Anglo-Saxon, and in our *least* idiomatic writers about two-thirds. As examples of the most completely idiomatic authors, we may instance the immortal De Foe, and among those who are least Saxon perhaps Gibbon may, without injustice, be adduced. There can be no doubt, however, that the Anglo-Saxon element is slowly but perceptibly diminishing; and the learned Sharon Turner considers that one-fifth of the Saxon language has ceased to be used.

CHAPTER II.

CHAUCER AND HIS TIMES.

Age of Chaucer — His Birth and Education — Translation in the Fourteenth Century — His Early Productions — His Career — Imbued with Provençal Literature—Character of his Poems—Romaunt of the Rose—Troilus and Cresseide — Anachronism — House of Fame — Canterbury Tales— Plan of this Work — The Pilgrims — Proposition of the Host — Plan of the Decameron—Superiority of Chaucer's Plan—Dialogue of the Pilgrims—Knight's Tale — Squire's Tale—Story of Griselda — Comic Tales — The two Prose Tales—Rime of Sir Thopas—Parson's Tale—Language of Chaucer—The Flower and the Leaf.

Neither the plan nor the extent of the present volume will permit us to give a detailed history of all the productions, nor, indeed, even a list of all the names, which figure in the annals of English literature. It will be our aim to direct the reader's attention upon those great works and those illustrious names which form, as it were, the landmarks of the intellectual history of the country, and which gave the tone and colour to the various epochs to which they belong; exerting also, according to circumstances, an influence more or less powerful on contemporary and succeeding generations. And by this method we hope to give a clearer idea of the scope and character of English literature than we could expect to afford them by a more elaborate and detailed work, the materials for which are so abundant, that it would require not a volume but a library to develop them as they deserve.

We consider, therefore, the age of Chaucer as the true starting-point of the English literature properly so called. In Italy letters appear to have revived after the long and gloomy period characterised by the somewhat false term of "the dark ages," with astonishing rapidity. Like germs and seeds of plants which have lain for centuries buried deep in the unfruitful bowels of the earth, and suddenly brought up by some convulsion of nature to the surface, the intellect of Italy burst forth, in the fourteenth century, into a tropical luxuriance, putting out its fairest flowers of poetry, and its olidest and most beautiful fruits of wisdom and of wit. Dante died seven years before, and Petrarch and Boccaccio about fifty years after, the birth of Chaucer, who thus was exposed to the strongest and directest influence of the genius of these great men. How great that influence was, we shall presently see. The great causes, then, which modified and directed the genius of Chaucer were—first, the new Italian poetry, which then suddenly burst forth upon the world, like Pallas from the brain of Jupiter, perfect and consummate in its virgin strength and beauty; second, the now decaying Romanz or Provençal poetry; and third, the doctrines of the Reformation, which were beginning, obscurely but irresistibly, to agitate the minds of men; a movement which took its origin, as do all great and permanent revolutions, in the lower depths of the popular heart, heaving gradually onwards, like the tremendous ground-swell of the equator, until it burst with resistless strength upon the Romish Church in Germany and in England, sweeping all before it. Wickliffe, who was born in 1324, only four years before Chaucer, had undoubtedly communicated to the poet many of his bold doctrines: the father of our poetry and the father of our reformed religion were both attached to the party of the celebrated John of Gaunt, and were both honoured with the friendship and protection of that powerful prince: Chaucer indeed was the kinsman of the Earl, having married the sister of Catherine Swinford, first the mistress and ultimately the wife of "time-honoured Lancaster;" and the poet's varied and uncertain career seems to have faithfully followed all the vicissitudes of John of Gaunt's eventful life.

Geoffrey Chaucer was born, as he informs us himself, in London; and for the date of an event so important to the destinies of English letters, we must fix it, on the authority of the inscription upon his tomb, as having happened in the year 1328; that is to say, at the commencement of the splendid and chivalrous reign of Edward III. The honour of having been the place of his education has been eagerly disputed by the two great and ancient universities of Oxford and Cambridge; the former, however, of the two learned sisters having apparently the best established right to the maternity—or at least the fosterage—of so illustrious a nurseling. Cambridge founds her claim upon the circumstance of Chaucer's having subscribed one of his early works "Philogenet *of Cambridge*, clerk." He afterwards returned to London, and there became a student of the law. His detestation of the monks appears, from a very curious document, to have begun even so early as his abode in the grave walls of the Temple; for we find the name of Jeffrey Chaucer inscribed in an ancient registar as having been fined for the misdemeanour of beating a friar in Fleet Street.

The first efforts of a revival of letters will always be made in the path of translation; and to this principle Chaucer forms no exception. He was an indefatigable translator; and the whole of many—nay, a great part of *all*—his works bears unequivocal traces of the prevailing taste for imitation. How much he has improved upon his models, what new lights he has placed them in, with what skill he has infused fresh life into the dry bones of obscure authors, it will hereafter be our business to inquire. He was the poetical pupil of Gower, and, like Raphael and Shakspeare, he surpassed his master: Gower always speaks with respect of his illustrious pupil in the art of poetry; and, in his work entitled 'Confessio Amantis' places in the mouth of Venus the following elegant compliment:—

"And grete wel Chaucer, when ye mete,
As my disciple and my poéte:
For in the flowers of his youth,
In sundry wise, as he well couthe,
Of ditees and of songés glade
The which he for my saké made," &c.

These lines also prove that Chaucer began *early* to write; and probably our poet continued during the whole course of his eventful life, to labour assiduously in the fields of letters.

His earliest works were strongly tinctured with the manner, nay, even with the mannerism, of the age. They are much fuller of allegory than his later productions; they are distinguished by a greater parade of scholarship, and by a deeper tinge of that amorous and metaphysical mysticism which pervades the later Provençal poetry, and which reached its highest pitch of fantastical absurdity in the *Arrêts d'Amour* of Picardy and Languedoc. As an example of this we may cite his 'Dream,' an allegorical composition written to celebrate the nuptials of his friend and patron John of Gaunt, with Blanche, the heiress of Lancaster.

Chaucer was in every sense a man of the world: he was the ornament of two of the most brilliant courts in the annals of England—those of Edward III., and his successor Richard II. He also accompanied the former king in his expedition into France, and was taken prisoner about 1359, at the siege of Retters; and in 1367 we find him receiving from the Crown a grant of 20 marks, *i. e.* about 200*l.* of our present money.

Our poet, thus distinguished as a soldier, as a courtier, and as a scholar, was honoured with the duty of forming part of an embassy to the splendid court of Genoa, where he was present at the nuptials of Violante, daughter of Galeazzo Duke of Milan, with the Duke of Clarence. At this period he made the acquaintance of Petrarch, and probably of Boccaccio also: to the former of these illustrious men he certainly was personally known; for he hints, in his 'Canterbury Tales,' his having learned from him the beautiful and pathetic tale of the Patient Griselda:—

"Learned at Padua of a worthy clerke
Francis Petrarke, the laureate poét,
Highte thys clerke, whose rhethorique sweet
Enlumined al Itale of poesy."

It was during his peregrinations in France and Italy that Chaucer drew at the fountain-head those deep draughts from the Hippocrene of Tuscany and of Provence which flow and sparkle in all his compositions. It is certain that he introduced into the English language an immense quantity of words absolutely and purely French, and that he succeeded with an admirable dexterity in harmonizing the ruder sounds of his vernacular tongue; so successfully, indeed, that it may be safely asserted that very few poets in any modern language are more exquisitely and uniformly musical than Chaucer. Indeed, he has been accused, and in rather severe terms, of having naturalized in English "a waggon-load of foreign words."

In 1380 we find Chaucer appointed to the office of Clerk of the Works at Windsor, where he was charged with overlooking the repairs about to made in St. George's Chapel, then in a ruinous condition.

In 1383 Wickliffe completed his translation into the English language of the Bible, and his death, in the following year, seems to have been the signal for the commencement of a new and gloomy phase in the fortunes of the poet. Chaucer returned to England in 1386, and, the party to which he belonged having lost its political influence, he was imprisoned in the Tower, and deprived of the places and privileges which had been granted to him. Two years afterwards he was permitted to sell his patents, and in 1389 he appears to have been induced to abandon, and even to accuse, his former associates, of whose treachery towards him he bitterly complains.

In reward for this submission to the government, we afterwards find him restored to favour, and made, in the year 1389, Clerk of the Works at Westminster. It is at this period that he is supposed to have retired to pass the calm evening of his active life in the green shades of Woodstock, where he is related to have composed his admirable 'Canterbury Tales.' This production, though, according to many opinions, neither the finest nor even the most characteristic of Chaucer's numerous and splendid poems, is yet the one of them all by which he is now best known: it is the work which has handed his name down to future generations as the earliest glory of his country's literature; and as such it warrants us in appealing, from the perhaps partial judgments of isolated critics, to the sovereign tribunal of posterity. The decisions of contemporaries may be swayed by fashion and prejudice; the criticism of scholars may be tinged with partiality; but the unanimous voice of four hundred and fifty years is sure to be a true index of the relative value of a work of genius.

Beautiful as are many of his other productions, it is the 'Canterbury Tales' which have enshrined Chaucer in the penetralia of England's Glory Temple; it is to the wit, the pathos, the humanity, the chivalry of those Tales that our minds recur when our ear is struck with the venerable name of Chaucer. In 1390 we find the poet receiving the honourable charge of Clerk of the Works at Windsor; and, two years later, a grant from the Crown of 20*l.* and a tun of wine annually. Towards the end of the century which his illustrious name had adorned, he appears to have fallen into some distress; for another document is in existence securing to the poet the protection of the Crown (probably against importunate creditors); and in 1399 we find the poet's name inserted in the lease of a house holden from the Abbot and Chapter of Westminster, and occupying the spot upon which was afterwards erected Henry VII's Chapel, now forming one of the most brilliant ornaments of Westminster Abbey. In this house, as is with great probability conjectured, Chaucer died, on the 25th of October, 1400, and was buried in the Abbey, being the first of that long array of mighty poets whose bones repose with generations of kings, warriors, and statesmen beneath the "long-drawn aisles" of our national Walhalla.

In reading the works of this poet the qualities which cannot fail to strike us most are—admirable truth, freshness, and *livingness* of his descriptions of external nature; profound knowledge of human life in the delineation of character; and that all-embracing humanity of heart which makes him, as it makes the reader, sympathise with all God's creation, taking away from his humour every taste of bitterness and sarcasm. This humour, coloured by and springing from universal sympathy, this noblest humanity—we mean humanity in the sense of Terence's: "homo sum; humani nihil a me alienum puto"—is the heritage of only the greatest among mankind; and is but an example of that deep truth which Nature herself has taught us, when she placed in the human heart the spring of Laughter fast by the fountain of Tears.

We shall now proceed to examine the principal poems of Chaucer, in the hope of presenting to our readers some scale or measure of the gradual development of those powers which appear, at least to us, to have reached their highest apogee or exaltation in the 'Canterbury Tales.'

In the first work to which we shall turn our attention, Chaucer has given us a translation of a poem esteemed by all French critics the noblest monument of their poetical literature anterior to the time of Francis I. This is the 'Romaunt of the Rose,' a beautiful mixture of allegory and narrative, of which we shall presently give an outline in the words of Warton. The 'Roman de la Rose' was commenced by William de Lorris, who died in 1260, and completed, in 1310, by Jean de Meun, a witty and satirical versifier, who was one of the ornaments of the brilliant court of Charles le Bel. Chaucer has translated the whole of the portion composed by the former, together with some of Meun's continuation; making, as he goes on, innumerable improvements in the text, which, where it harmonizes with his own conceptions, he renders with singular fidelity. "The difficulties and dangers of a lover, in pursuing and obtaining the object of his desires, are the literal argument of the poem. This design is couched under the allegory of a rose, which our lover, after frequent obstacles, gathers in a delicious garden. He traverses vast ditches, scales lofty walls, and forces the gates of adamantine castles. These enchanted holds are all inhabited by various divinities; some of which assist, and some oppose, the lover's progress." The English poem is written, like the French original, in the short rhymed octosyllabic couplets so universally adopted by the Trouvères, a measure well fitted, from its ease and flowingness, for the purpose of long narratives. We have said that the translation is in most cases very close; Chaucer was so far from desiring to make his works pass for original when they had no claim to this qualification, that he even specifies, with great care and with even a kind of exultation, the sources from whence his productions are derived. Indeed, at such early periods in the literature of any country, writers seem to attach as great or greater dignity to the office of translator than to the more arduous duty of original composition; the reason of which probably is, that in the childhood of nations as well as of men learning is a rarer, and therefore more admired, quality than imagination.

The allegorical personages in the 'Romaunt of the Rose' are singularly varied, rich, and beautiful. Sorrow, Envy, Avarice, Hate, Beauty, Franchise, Richesse, are successively brought on the stage. As an example of the remarks we have just been making, we will quote a short passage from the latter part of Chaucer's translation, *i. e.* from that portion of the poem composed by John of Meun: it describes the attendants in the palace of Old Age: we will print the original French beside the extract:—

"Travaile et douleur la hébergent,
Mais ils la lient et la chargent,
Que Mort prochaine luy présentent,
En talant de se repentir;
Tant luy sont de fléaux sentir;
Adoncq luy vient en remembrance,
En cest tardifve présence,
Quand il se voit foible et chenue."

"With her, Labour and eke Travaile
Lodgid bene, with sorwe and wo.
That never out of her court go
Pain and Distress, Sekenesse and Ire,
And Melancholie that angry sire,
Ben of her palais Senatoures;
Goning and Grutching her herbegeors.
The day and night her to tourment,
With cruel death they her present,
And tellen her erliche and late,
That Deth standith armid at her gate."

Here Chaucer's improvements are plainly perceptible; the introduction of Death, standing *armed* at the gate, is a grand and sublime thought, of which no trace is to be found in the comparatively flat original; not to mention the terrible distinctness with which Chaucer enumerates Old Age's *Senators*, Pain, Distress, Sickness, Ire, and Melancholy; and her grim chamberlains, Groaning and Grudging.

The next poem which we shall mention is the love-story entitled 'Troilus and Cresseide,' founded on one of the most favourite legends of the Middle Ages, and which Shakspeare himself has dramatized in the tragedy of the same name. The anachronism of placing the scene of such a history of chivalric love in the heroic age of the Trojan War is, we think, more than compensated by the pathos, the nature, and the variety which characterize many of the ancient romances on this subject. Chaucer informs us that his authority is Lollius, a mysterious personage very often referred to by the writers of the Middle Ages, and so impossible to discover and identify that he must be considered as the Ignis Fatuus of antiquaries. "Of Lollius," says one of these unhappy and baffled investigators, "it will become every one to speak with deference." The whole poem is saturated with the spirit not of the Ionian rhapsodist, but of the Provençal minstrel. It is written in the rhymed ten-syllabled couplet, which Chaucer has used in the greater part of his works. In the midst of a thousand anachronisms, of a thousand absurdities, this poem contains some strokes of pathos which are invariably to be found in everything Chaucer wrote, and which show that his heart ever vibrated responsive to the touch of nature.

Though we propose, in a future volume, to give such specimens and extracts of Chaucer as may suffice to enable our readers to judge of his manner, we cannot abstain from citing here a most exquisite passage: it describes the bashfulness and hesitation of Cressida before she can find courage to make the avowal of her love:—

"And as the newe-abashed nightingale
That stinteth first, when she beginneth sing,
When that she heareth any herdis tale,
Or in the hedgis any wight stirring,
And after siker doth her voice outring;
Right so Cresseide, when that her drede stent,
Opened her herte and told him her entent."

We may remark here the extraordinary fondness for the song of birds exhibited by Chaucer in all his works. There is not one of the English poets, and certainly none of the poets of any other nation, who has shown a more intense enjoyment for this natural music: he seems to omit no opportunity of describing the "doulx ramaige" of these feathered poets, whose accents seem to be echoed in all their delicacy, their purity and fervour, in the fresh strains of "our Father Chaucer:"—

"Sound of vernal showers
On the twinkling grass,
Rain-awakened flowers,
All that ever was
Joyous, and clear, and fresh, thy music doth surpass!"

We have mentioned the anachronism of *plan* in this poem; it abounds in others no less extraordinary. Among these, he represents Cresseide as reading the Thebaid of Statius (a very favourite book of Chaucer), which he calls 'The Romance of Thebis;' and Pandarus endeavours to comfort Troilus with arguments of predestination taken from Bishop Bradwardine, a theologian nearly contemporary with the poet.

The 'House of Fame,' a magnificent allegory, glowing with all the "barbaric pearl and gold" of Gothic imagination, is the next work on which we shall remark. Its origin was probably Provencal, but the poem which Chaucer translated is now lost. We will condense the argument of this poem from Warton :—"The poet, in a vision, sees a temple of glass decorated with an uncountable number of golden images. On the walls are engraved stories from Virgil's Eneid and Ovid's Epistles. Leaving this temple, he sees an eagle with golden wings soaring near the sun. The bird descends, seizes the poet in its talons, and conveys him to the Temple of Fame, which, like that of Ovid, is situated between earth and sea. He is left by the eagle near the house, which is built of materials bright as polished glass, and stands on a rock of ice. All the southern side of this rock is covered with engravings of the names of famous men, which are perpetually melting away by the heat of the sun. The northern side of the rock was alike covered with names; but, being shaded from the warmth of the sun, the characters here remained unmelted and uneffaced. Within the niches formed in the pinnacles stood all round the castle

'All manere of minstrellis,
And gestours, that tellen tales
Both of weping and eke of game;'

and the most renowned harpers—Orpheus, Arion, Chiron, and the Briton Glaskeirion. In the hall he meets an infinite multitude of heralds, on whose surcoats are embroidered the arms of the most redoubted champions. At the upper end, on a lofty shrine of carbuncle, sits Fame. Her figure is like those of Virgil and Ovid. Above her, as if sustained on her shoulders, sate Alexander and Hercules. From the throne to the gates of the hall ran a range of pillars with respective inscriptions. On the first pillar, made of lead and iron, stood Josephus the Jewish historian, with seven other writers on the same subject. On the second, made of iron, and painted with the blood of tigers, stood Statius. On another, higher than the rest, stood Homer, Dares Phrygius, Livy, Lollius, Guido of Colonna, and Geoffrey of Monmouth, writers on the Trojan story. On a pillar of 'tinnid iron clere' stood Virgil; and next him, on a pillar of copper, appeared Ovid. The figure of Lucan was placed upon a pillar of iron 'wrought full sternly,' accompanied by many Roman historians. On a pillar of sulphur stood Claudian. The hall is filled by crowds of minor authors. In the mean time crowds of every nation and condition fill the temple, each presenting his claim to the queen. A messenger is sent to summon Eolus from his cave in Thrace, who is ordered to bring his two clarions Slander and Praise, and his trumpeter Triton. The praises of each petitioner are then sounded, according to the partial or capricious appointment of Fame; and equal merits obtain very different success. The poet then enters the house or labyrinth of Rumour. It was built of willow twigs, like a cage, and therefore admitted every sound. From this house issue tidings of every kind, like fountains and rivers from the sea. Its inhabitants, who are eternally employed in hearing or telling news, raising reports, and spreading lies, are then humourously described: they are chiefly sailors, pilgrims, and pardoners. At length our author is awakened by seeing a venerable person of great authority; and thus the vision abruptly terminates." From the few lines we have quoted, it may be seen that this poem, like the 'Romaunt of the Rose,' is written in the octosyllabic measure. Though full of extravagances, exaggerations of the already too monstrous personifications of Ovid, this work extorts our admiration by the inexhaustible richness and splendour of its ornaments; a richness as perfectly in accordance with Middle Age art, as it is extravagant and puerile in the tinsel pages of the Roman poet. That multiplicity of parts and profusion of minute embellishment which forms the essential characteristic of a Gothic cathedral is displaced and barbarous when introduced into the severer outlines of a Grecian temple or a Roman amphitheatre.

It now becomes our delightful duty to speak of the 'Canterbury Tales;' and we can hardly trust ourselves to confine within reasonable limits the examination of this admirable work, containing in itself, as it does, merits of the most various and opposite kinds. It is a finished picture, delineating almost every variety of human character, crowded with figures, whose lineaments no lapse of time, no change of manners, can render faint or indistinct, and which will retain, to the latest centuries, every stroke of outline and every tint of colour, as sharp and as vivid as when they came from the master's hand. The Pilgrims of Chaucer have traversed four hundred and fifty years — like the Israelites wandering in the Wilderness — arid periods of neglect and ignorance, sandy flats of formal mannerism, unfertilised by any spring of beauty, and yet "their garments have not decayed, neither have their shoes waxed old."

Besides the lively and faithful delineation — *i. e. descriptive* delineation — of these personages, nothing can be more dramatic than the way in which they are set in motion, speaking and acting in a manner always conformable to their supposed characters, and mutually heightening and contrasting each other's peculiarities. Further yet, besides these triumphs in the *framing* of his Tales, the Tales themselves, distributed among the various pilgrims of his troop, are, in almost every case, masterpieces of splendour, of pathos, or of drollery.

Chaucer, in the Prologue to the 'Canterbury Tales,' relates that he was about to pass the night at the "Tabarde" inn in Southwark, previous to setting out on a pilgrimage to the far-famed shrine of St. Thomas of Kent — *i. e.* Thomas à Becket — at Canterbury. On the evening preceding the poet's departure there arrive at the hostelry —

"Wel nine and twenty in a compagnie
Of sondry folk, by avanture y-falle
In felawship, and pilgrimes wer they alle,
That toward Canterbury wolden ride."

The poet, glad of the opportunity of travelling in such good company, makes acquaintance with them all, and the party, after mutually promising to start early in the morning, sup and retire to rest.

Chaucer then gives a full and minute description, yet in incredibly few words, of the condition, appearance, manners, dress, and horses of the pilgrims. He first depicts a Knight, "brave in battle, and wise in council," courteous, grave, religious, experienced; who had fought for the faith in far lands, at Algesiras, at Alexandria, in Russia; a model of the chivalrous virtues:—

"And though that he was worthy, he was wise,
And of his port *meke as is a mayde.*
He was a veray parfit gentle knight."

He is mounted on a good, though not showy, horse, and clothed in a simple *gipon* or close tunic, of serviceable materials, characteristically stained and discoloured by the friction of his armour.

This valiant and modest gentleman is accompanied by his son, a perfect specimen of the *damoyseau* or "bachelor" of this, or of the graceful and gallant youth of noble blood in any period. Chaucer seems to revel in the painting of his curled and shining locks—"as they were laid in presse"—of his tall and active person, of his already-shown bravery, of his "love-longing," of his youthful accomplishments, and of his gay and fantastic dress. His talent for music, his short embroidered gown with long wide sleeves (the fashion of the day), his perfect horsemanship, his skill in song-making, in illuminating and writing, his hopeful and yet somewhat melancholy love for his "lady,"—

"So hote he loved, that by nightertale
He slept no more than doth the nightingale—"

nothing is omitted; not a stroke too few or too many.

This attractive pair are attended by a Yeman or retainer. This figure is a perfect portrait of one of those bold and sturdy archers, the type of the ancient national character; a type which still exists in the plain independent peasantry of the rural districts of the land. He is clad in the picturesque costume of the greenwood, with his sheaf of peacock arrows bright and keen stuck in his belt, and bearing in his hand "a mighty bowe"—the far-famed "long-bow" of the English archers—the most formidable weapon of the Middle Ages, which twanged such fatal music to the chivalry of France at Poictiers and Agincourt. His "not-hed," his "brown viságe," tanned by sun and wind, his sword and buckler, his sharp and well-equipped dagger, the silver medal of St. Christopher on his breast, the horn in the green baldric — how life-like does he stand before us!

These three figures are admirably contrasted with a Prioress, a lady of noble birth and delicate bearing, full of the pretty affectations, the dainty tendernesses of the "grande dame religieuse." Her name is "Madame Eglantine;" and the mixture, in her manners and costume, of gentle worldly vanities and of ignorance of the world; her gaiety, and the ever-visible difficulty she feels to put on an air of courtly hauteur; the ladylike delicacy of her manners at table, and her fondness for petting lap-dogs,—

"Of smale houndes had she, that she fed
With rosted flesh, and milk, and wastel-bread,
But sore she wept if on of hem were dead,
Or if men smote it with a yerde smert,
For al was conscience, and tender herte,"—

this masterly outline is most appropriately *framed* (if we may so speak) in the external and material accompaniments—the beads of "smale corall" hanging on her arm, and, above all, the golden brooch with its delicate device of a "crowned A," and the inscription *Amor vincit omnia.* She is attended by an inferior Nun and three Priests.

The monk follows next, and he, like all the ecclesiastics, with the single exception of the Personore or secular parish priest is described with strong touches of ridicule; but it is impossible not to perceive the strong and ever-present *humanity* of which we have spoken as perhaps the most marked characteristic of Chaucer's mind. The Monk is a gallant, richly-dressed, and pleasure-loving sportsman, caring not a straw for the obsolete strictness of the musty rule of his order. His sleeves are edged with rich fur his hood fastened under his chin with a gold pin headed with a "love-knot," his eyes are buried deep in his fleshy rosy cheeks, indicating great love of rich fare and potent wines; and yet the impression left on the mind by this type of fat roystering sensuality is rather one of drollery and good-fellowship than of contempt or abhorrence.

Chaucer exhibits rich specimens of the various *genera* of that vast species "Monachus monachans," as it may be classed by some Rabelœsian Theophrastus. The next personage who enters is the Frere, or mendicant friar, whose easiness of confession, wonderful skill in extracting money and gifts, and gay discourse are most humorously and graphically described. He is represented as always carrying store of knives, pins, and toys, to give to his female penitents, as better acquainted with the tavern than with the lazar-house or the hospital, daintly dressed, and "lisping somewhat" in his speech, "to make his English swete upon the tongue."

This "worthy Limitour" is succeeded by a grave and formal personage, the Merchant: solemn and wise is he, with forked beard and pompous demeanour, speaking much of profit, and strongly in favour of the king's right to the subsidy "pour la saufgarde et custodie del mer," as the old Norman legist phrases it. He is dressed in motley, mounted on a tall and quiet horse, and wears a "Flaundrish beaver hat."

The learned poverty of the Clerke of Oxenforde forms a striking contrast to the Merchant's rather pompous "respectability." He and his horse are "leane as is a rake" with abstinence, his clothes are threadbare, and he devotes to the purchase of his beloved books all the gold which he can collect from his friends and patrons, devoutly praying, as in duty bound, for the souls of those

> "Who yeve him wherewith to scolaie."

Nothing can be more true to nature than the mixture of pedantry and bashfulness in the manners of this anchoret of learning, and the tone of sententious morality and formal politeness which marks his language.

We now come to a "Serjeant of the Lawe," a wise and learned magistrate, rich and yet irreproachable, with all the statutes at his fingers' ends, a very busy man in reality, "but yet," not to forget the inimitable touch of nature in Chaucer, "*he seemed besier than he was.*" He is plainly dressed, as one who cares not to display his importance in his exterior.

Nor are preceding characters superior, in vividness and variety, to the figure of the "Frankelein," or rich country-gentleman, who is next introduced: his splendid and hospitable profusion, and the epicurean luxuriousness of the man himself, are inimitably set before us. "It *snewed in his house* of mete and drink."

Then come a number of burgesses, whose appearance is classed under one general description. These are a Haberdasher, Carpenter, Webbe (or Weaver), Dyer, and Tapiser—

> "——— Alle yclothed of o liverè,
> Of a solempne and gret fraternitè,"—

that is, they all belong to one of those societies, or *mestiers*, which play so great a part in the municipal history of the Middle Ages. The somewhat *cossu* richness of their equipment, their knives hafted with silver, their grave and citizen-like bearing—all is in harmony with the pride and vanity, hinted at by the poet, of their wives, who think "it is full fayre to be ycleped *Madame.*"

The skill and critical discernment of the Cook are next described: "Well could he know a draught of London ale," and elaborately could he season the rich and fantastic dishes which composed the "carte" of the fourteenth centnry. He joins the pilgrimage in hope that his devotion may cure him of a disease in the leg.

A turbulent and boisterous Shipman appears next, who is described with minute detail. His brown complexion, his rude and quarrelsome manners, his tricks of trade, stealing wine "from Burdeux ward, while that the chapman slepe," all is enumerated; nor does the poet forget the seaman's knowledge of all the havens "from Gothland to the Cape de Finistere," nor his experience in his profession: "In many a tempest had his berd be shake."

He is followed by a Doctour of Phisike, a great astronomer and natural magician, deeply versed in the ponderous tomes of Hippocrates, Hali, Galen, Rhasis, Averrhoes, and the Arabian physicians. His diet is but small in quantity, but rich and nourishing; "*his study s but little on the Bible*;" and he is humorously represented as particularly fond of gold, "*for gold in phisike is a cordiall.*"

Next to the grave, luxurious, and not quite orthodox Doctor enters the "Wife of Bath," a daguerreotyped specimen of the female *bourgeoise* of Chaucer's day; and bearing so perfectly the stamp and mark of her class, that, by changing her costume a little to the dress of the nineteenth century, she would serve as a perfect sample of her order even in the present day. She is equipped with a degree of solid costliness that does not exclude a little coquetry; her character is gay, bold, and not over rigid; and she is endeavouring, by long and frequent pilgrimages, to expiate some of the amorous errors of her youth. She is a substantial manufacturer of cloth, and so jealous of her precedency in the religious ceremonies of her parish, that, if any of her female acquaintance should venture to go before her on these solemn occasions, "so wroth was she, that she was out of alle charitee."

Contrasted with this rosy dame are two of the most beautiful and touching portraits ever delineated by the hand of genius—one "a pour Persoune," or secular parish priest; and his brother in simplicity, virtue, and evangelic purity, a Plowman. It is in these characters, and particularly in the "Tale" put into the mouth of the former, that we most distinctly see Chaucer's sympathy with the doctrines of the Reformation: the humility, self-denial, and charity of these two pious and worthy men, are opposed with an unstudied, but not the less striking pointedness, to the cheatery and sensuality which distinguish all the monks and friars represented by Chaucer. So beautiful and so complete is this noble delineation of Christian piety, that we will not venture to injure its effect by quoting it piecemeal in this place, but refer our readers to the volume of extracts, in which the whole of Chaucer's Prologue will be found at length.

Then we find enumerated a Reve, a Miller, a Sompnour (an officer in the ecclesiastical courts), a Pardoner, a Manciple, and "myself," that is, Chaucer.

The Miller is a brawny, short, red-headed fellow, strong, boisterous and quarrelsome, flat-nosed, wide-mouthed, debauched; he is dressed in a white coat and blue hood, and armed with sword and buckler.

His conversation and conduct correspond faithfully with such an appearance: he enlivens the journey by his skill in playing on the bagpipe.

The Manciple was an officer attached to the ancient colleges; his duty was to purchase the provisions and other commodities for the consumption of the students; in fact, he was a kind of steward. Chaucer describes this pilgrim as singularly adroit in the exercise of his business, taking good care to advantage himself the while.

Another of the most elaborately painted pictures in Chaucer's gallery is the "Reve," bailiff, or intendant of some great proprietor's estates. He stands before us as a slender, long-legged, choleric individual, with his beard shaven as close as possible, and his hair exceedingly short. He is a severe and watchful manager of his master's estates, and had grown so rich that he was able to come to his lord's assistance, and "lend him of his owen good." His horse is described, and even named, and he is described as always riding "the hinderest of the route."

Nothing can surpass the nature and truthfulness with which Chaucer has described the Sompnour. His face is fiery red, as cherubim were painted, and so covered with pimples, spots, and discolorations, that neither mercury, sulphur, borax, nor any purifying ointment, could cleanse his complexion. He is a great lover of onions, leeks, and garlic, and fond of "strong win as red as blood;" and when drunk he would speak nothing but Latin, a few terms of which language he had picked up from the writs and citations it was his profession to serve. He is a great taker of bribes, and will allow any man to set at nought the archdeacon's court in the most flagrant manner "for a quart of wine."

The last of the pilgrims is the "Pardonere," or seller of indulgences from Rome. He is drawn to the life, singing, to the bass of his friend the Sompnour, the song of "Come hither, love, to me." The Pardoner's hair is "yellow as wax," smooth and thin, lying on his shoulders: he wears no hood, "for jollité,"—that is, in order to appear in the fashion. His eyes (as is often found in persons of this complexion — note Chaucer's truth to nature) are wide and staring like those of a hare; his voice is a harsh treble, like that of a goat; and he has no beard. Chaucer then enumerates the various articles of the Pardoner's professional budget; and certainly there never was collected a list of droller relics: he has Our Lady's veil. a morsel of the sail of St. Paul's ship, a glass full of pigges bones,' and a pewter cross crammed with other objects of equal sanctity With the aid of these and the hypocritical unction of his address, h could manage, in one day, to extract from poor and rustic people more money than the Parson (the regular pastor of the parish) could collect in two months.

The number of the pilgrims now enumerated will be found by any one who takes the trouble to couut them to amount to thirty-one, including Chaucer; and the poet describes them setting out on their journey on the following morning. Before their departure, however, the jolly Host of the Tabarde makes a proposition to the assembled company. He offers to go along with them himself, on condition that they constitute him a kind of master of the revels during their journey; showing how agreeably and profitably they could beguile the tedium of the road with the relation of stories. He then proposes that on their return they should all sup together at his hostelry, and that he among them who shall have been adjudged to have told the best story should be entertained at the expense of the whole society. This proposal is unanimously adopted; and nothing can be finer than the mixture of fun and good sense with which honest Harry Bailey, the Host, sways the merry sceptre of his temporary sovereignty.

This then is the framework or scaffolding on which Chaucer has erected his Canterbury Tales. The practice of connecting together a multitude of distinct narrations by some general thread of incident is very natural and extremely ancient. The Orientals, so passionately fond of tale-telling, have universally — and not always very artificially—given consistency and connection to their stories by putting them into the mouth of some single narrator: the various histories which compose the Thousand and One Nights are supposed to be successively recounted by the untiring lips of the inexhaustible Princess Scheherezade; but the source from whence Chaucer more immediately adopted his *framing* was the Decameron of Boccaccio. This work (as it may be necessary to inform our younger readers) consists of a hundred tales divided into decades, each decade occupying one day in the relation. They are narrated by a society of young men and women of rank, who have shut themselves up in a most luxurious and beautiful retreat on the banks of the Arno, in order to escape the infection of the terrible plague then ravaging Florence.

If we compare the plan of Chaucer with that of the Florentine, we shall not hesitate to give the palm of propriety, probability, and good taste to the English poet. A pilgrimage was by no means an expedition of a mournful or solemn kind, and afforded the author the widest field for the selection of character from all classes of society, and an excellent opportunity for the divers humors and oddities of a company fortuitously assembled. It is imposible, too, not to feel that there is something cruel and shocking in the notion of these young luxurious Italians of Boccaccio whiling away their days in tales of sensual trickery or sentimental distress, while without the well-guarded walls of their retreat thousands of their kinsmen and fellow citizens were writhing in despairing agony. Moreover, the similarity of rank and age in the personages of Boccaccio produces an insipidity and want of variety: all these careless voluptuaries are repetitions of Dioneo and Fiammetta: and the period of ten days adopted by the Italian has the defect of being purely arbitrary, there being no reason why the narratives might not be continued indefinitely. Chaucer's pilgrimage, on the contrary, is made to Canterbury, and occupies a certain and necessary time; and, on the return of the travellers, the society separates as naturally as it had assembled; after giving the poet the opportunity of introducing two striking and appropriate events—their procession to the shrine of St. Thomas at their arrival in Canterbury, and the prize-supper on their return to London.

Had Chaucer adhered to his original plan, we should have had a tale from each of the party on the journey out, and a second tale from every pilgrim on the way back, making in all sixty-two—or, if the Host also contributed his share, sixty-four. But, alas! the poet has not conducted his pilgrims even to Canterbury; and the tales which he has made them tell only make us the more bitterly lament the non-fulfilment of his original intention.

Before we speak of the narratives themselves, it will be proper to state that our poet continues to describe the actions, conversation, and deportment of his pilgrims: and nothing can be finer than the remarks put into their mouths respecting the merits of the various tales; or more dramatic than the affected bashfulness of some, when called upon to contribute to the amusement of their companions, and the squabbles and satirical jests made by others.

These passages, in which the tales themselves are, as it were, incrusted, are called Prologues to the various narratives which they respectively precede, and they add inexpressibly to the vivacity and movement of the whole, as in some cases the tales spring, as it were, spontaneously out of the conversations.

Of the tales themselves it will be impossible to attempt even a rapid summary: we may mention, as the most remarkable among the serious and pathetic narratives, the Knight's Tale, the subject of which is the beautiful story of Palamon and Arcite, taken from the Teseide of Boccaccio, but it is unknown whether originally invented by the great Italian, or, as is far more probable, imitated by him from some of the innumerable versions of the "noble story" of Theseus current in the Middle Ages. The poem is full of a strange mixture of manners and periods: the chivalric and the heroic ages appear side by side: but such is the splendour of imagination displayed in this immortal work, so rich is it in magnificence, in pathos, in exquisite delineations of character, and artfully contrived turns of fortune, that the reader voluntarily dismisses all his chronology, and allows himself to be carried away with the fresh and sparkling current of chivalric love and knightly adventure. No reader ever began this poem without finishing it, or ever read it once without returning to it a second time. The effect upon the mind is like that of some gorgeous tissue, gold-inwoven, of tapestry, in an old baronial hall; full of tournaments and battles, imprisoned knights, and emblazoned banners, Gothic temples of Mars and Venus, the lists, the dungeon and the lady's bower, garden and fountain, and moonlit groves. Chaucer's peculiar skill in the delineation of character and appearance by a few rapid and masterly strokes is as perceptible here as in the Prologue to the Tales: the procession of the kings to the tournament is as bright and vivid piece of painting as ever was produced by the "strong braine" or mediæval Art: and in point of grace and simplicity, what can be finer than the single line descriptive of the beauty of Emilie — so *suggestive*, and therefore so superior to the most elaborate portrait— "Up rose the sun, and up rose Emelie"?

The next poem of a serious character is the Squire's Tale, which indeed so struck the admiration of Milton—himself profoundly penetrated by the spirit of the Romanz poetry—that it is by an allusion to the Squire's Tale that he characterizes Chaucer when enumerating the great men of all ages, and when he places him beside Plato, Shakspeare, Æschylus, and his beloved Euripides: he supposes his Cheerful Man as evoking Chaucer:—

> "And call up him who left half told
> The story of Cambuscan bold."

The imagery of the Squire's Tale was certainly well calculated to strike such a mind as Milton's, so gorgeous, so stately, so heroic, and imbued with all the splendour of Oriental literature; for the scenery and subject of this poem bear evident marks of that Arabian influence which colours so much of the poetry of the Middle Ages, and which probably began to act upon the literature of Western Europe after the Crusades.

In point of deep pathos—pathos carried indeed to an extreme and perhaps hardly natural or justifiable pitch of intensity—we will now cite, among the graver tales of our pilgrims, the story put into the mouth of the Clerke of Oxenforde. This is the story of the Patient Griselda—a model of womanly and wifely obedience, who comes victoriously out of the most cruel and repeated ordeals inflicted upon her conjugal and maternal affections. The beautiful and angelic figure of the Patient Wife in this heart-rending story reminds us of one of those seraphic statues of Virgin Martyrs which stand with clasped hands and uplifted, imploring eye, in the carved niches of a Gothic cathedral—an eternal prayer in sculptured stone,—

> "——— Patience on a monument,
> Smiling at Grief!"

The subject of this tale is, as we mentioned some pages back, invented by Boccaccio, and first seen in 1374, by Petrarch, who was so struck with its beauty that he translated it into Latin, and it is from this translation that Chaucer drew his materials. The English poet indeed appears to have been ignorant of Boccaccio's claim to the authorship, for he makes his "Clerke" say that he had learned it from "Fraunceis Petrarke, the laureat poéte." Petrarch himself bears the strongest testimony to the almost overwhelming pathos of the story, for he relates that he gave it to a Paduan acquaintance of his to read, who fell into a repeated agony of passionate tears. Chaucer's poem is written in the Italian stanza.

Of the comic tales the following will be found the most excellent: — The Nun's Priest's Tale, a droll apologue of the Cock and the Fox, in which the very absurdity of some of the accompaniments confers one of the highest qualities which a fable can possess, viz. so high a degree of individuality that the reader forgets that the persons of the little drama are animals, and sympathizes with them as human beings; the Merchant's Tale, which, like the comic stories generally, though very indelicate, is yet replete with the richest and broadest humour; the Reve's Tale, and many shorter stories distributed among the less prominent characters. But the crown and pearl of Chaucer's drollery is the Miller's Tale, in which the delicate and penetrating description of the various actors in the adventure can only be surpassed by the perfectly natural yet outrageously ludicrous catastrophe of the intrigue in which they move.

There is certainly nothing, in the vast treasury of ancient or modern humorous writing, at once so real, so droll, and so exquisitely *enjoué* in the manner of telling. It is true that the subject is not of the most delicate nature; but, though coarse and plain-speaking, Chaucer is never corrupt or vicious: his improprieties are rather the fruit of the ruder age in which he lived, and the turbid ebullitions of a rich and active imagination, than the cool, analysing, studied profligacy—the more dangerous and corrupting because veiled under a false and morbid sentimentalism — which defiles a great portion of the modern literature of too many civilised countries.

It is worthy of remark that all the tales are in verse with the exception of two, one of which, singularly enough, is given to Chaucer himself. This requires some explanation. When the poet is first called upon for his story, he bursts out into a long, confused, fantastical tale of chivalry, relating the adventures of a certain errant-knight, Sir Thopas, and his wanderings in search of the Queen of Faërie. This is written in the peculiar versification of the Trouvères (note, that it is the only tale in which he has adopted this measure), and is full of all the absurdities of those compositions. When in the full swing of declamation, and when we are expecting to be overwhelmed with page after page of this "sleazy stuff," — for the poet goes on gallantly, like Don Quixote, "in the style his books of chivalry had taught him, imitating, as near as he can, their very phrase,"—he is suddenly interrupted by honest Harry Bailey, the Host, who plays the part of Moderator or Chorus to Chaucer's pleasant comedy. The Host begs him, with many strong expressions of ridicule and disgust, to give them no more of such "drafty rhyming," and entreats him to let them hear something less worn-out and tiresome. The poet then proposes to entertain the party with "a litel thinge in prose," and relates the allegorical story of Melibœus and his wife Patience. It is evident that Chaucer, well aware of the immeasurable superiority of the newly revived classical literature over the barbarous and now exhausted invention of the Romanz poets, has chosen this ingenious method of ridiculing the commonplace tales of chivalry; but so exquisitely grave is the irony in this passage, that many critics have taken the 'Rime of Sir Thopas' for a serious composition, and have regretted it was left a fragment!

The other prose tale (we have mentioned Melibœus) is supposed to be related by the Parson, who is always described as a model of Christian humility, piety, and wisdom; which does not, however, save him from the terrible suspicion of being a *Lollard, i. e.*, a heretical and seditious revolutionist.

This composition hardly can be called a "tale," for it contains neither persons nor events; but it is very curious as a specimen of the sermons of the early Reformers; for a sermon it is, and nothing else—a sermon upon the Seven Deadly Sins, divided and subdivided with all the pedantic regularity of the day. It also gives us a very curious insight into the domestic life, the manners, the costume, and even the cookery, of the fourteenth century. Some critics have contended that this sermon was added to the Canterbury Tales by Chaucer at the instigation of his confessors, as a species of penitence for the light and immoral tone of much of his writings, and particularly as a sort of recantation, or *amende honorable*, for his innumerable attacks on the monks. But this supposition is in direct contradiction with every line of his admirable portrait of the Parson; and, however natural it may have been for the licentious Boccaccio to have done such public penance for his ridicule of the "Frati," and his numberless sensual and immoral scenes, his English follower was "made of sterner stuff." The friend of John of Gaunt, and the disciple of Wickliffe, was not so easily to be worked upon by monastic subtlety as the more superstitious and *sensuous* Italian.

The language of Chaucer is a strong exemplification of the remark we made in our first chapter respecting the structure of the English language. The ground of his diction will be ever found to be the pure vigorous Anglo-Saxon English of the people, *inlaid*, if we may so style it, with an immense quantity of Norman-French words. We may compare this diction to some of those exquisite specimens of *incrusting* left us by the obscure but great artists of the Middle

Ages, in which the polish of metal or ivory contrasts so richly with the lustrous ebony.

The difficulty of reading this great poet is very much exaggerated: a very moderate acquaintance with the French and Italian of the fourteenth century, and the observation of a few simple rules of pronunciation, will enable any educated person to read and to enjoy. In particular it is to be remarked that the final letter *e*, occurring in so many English words, had not yet become an *e mute;* and must constantly be pronounced, as well as the termination of the past tense, *ed*, in a separate syllable. The accent also is more varied in its position than is now common in the language. Read with these precautions, Chaucer will be found as harmonious as he is tender, magnificent, humorous, or sublime.

Until the reader is able and willing to appreciate the innumerable beauties of the Canterbury Tales, it is not to be expected that he can make acquaintance with the graceful though somewhat pedantic 'Court of Love,' an allegorical poem, bearing the strongest marks of its Provençal origin; or with the exquisite delicacy and pure chivalry of the 'Flower and the Leaf;' of which latter poem Campbell speaks as follows, enthusiastically but justly:—"The Flower and the Leaf is an exquisite piece of fairy fancy. With a moral that is just sufficient to apologise for a dream, and yet which sits so lightly on the story as not to abridge its most visionary parts, there is, in the whole scenery and objects of the poem, an air of wonder and sweetness, an easy and surprising transition, that is truly magical."

We cannot conclude this brief and imperfect notice of this great poet without strongly recommending all those who desire to know something of the true character of English literature to lose no time in making acquaintance with the admirable productions of "our father Chaucer," as Gascoigne affectionately calls him: the difficulties of his style have been unreasonably exaggerated, and the labour which surmounts them will be abundantly repaid. "It will conduct you," to use the beautiful words of Milton, "to a hill-side; laborious indeed at the first ascent, but else so smooth, so green, so full of goodly prospects and melodious sounds on every side, that the harp of Orpheus was not more charming."

CHAPTER III.

SIDNEY AND SPENSER.

Elizabethan Era—Ages of Pericles, Augustus, the Medici, Louis XVI.—Chivalry—Sidney—the Arcadia—His Style—Spenser—Shepherd's Calendar—Pastoral—Spenser at Court—Burleigh and Leicester—Settlement in Ireland—the Faery Queen—Spenser's Death—Criticism of the Faery Queen—Style, Language, and Versification.

In the history of most countries the period of the highest literary glory will generally be found to coincide with that of some very marked and permanent achievements in commerce or in war. Nor is this circumstance surprising. Those men who best can perform great actions are in general best able to think sublime thoughts. It was not a fortuitous assemblage, in the same country and at the same period, of such minds as those of Eschylus, Sophocles, and Euripides, that has made us assume the age of Pericles as the culminating point of Athenian literature. No! the defeat of the Persians cannot but be considered as having a great deal to do with the existence of that splendid period.

In the same way the far-famed age of Louis XIV. was undoubtedly prepared, if not produced, by the long religious wars of the Reformation, the national enthusiasm being also raised by the brilliant exploits of French arms in Germany and Flanders.

That period in the history of English letters which corresponds to the epochs to which we have alluded is the age of Elizabeth. It is the Elizabethan era which represents, among us, the age of Pericles, that of Augustus, that of the Medici, that of Leo, that of Louis; nay, it may be asserted, and without any exaggerated national vanity, that the productions of this one era of English literature may boldly be opposed to the intellectual triumphs of all the other epochs mentioned, taken collectively.

In this case, as in the others, a gigantic revolution had taken place, recent indeed, but not so recent as to leave men's minds under the more immediate action of party spirit and political enmity. The intellect of England had lately been engaged in a struggle for its liberty and its religion; it had had time to repose, but not to be enfeebled: it now started on its race of immortality, glowing, indeed, from the arena, but not weakened; its muscles strung with wrestling, but not exhausted. During the actual ardour of any great political struggle, men's minds are naturally too intent upon the more immediate and personal question, and their views too much narrowed and distorted by prejudice and polemics, for any great achievements in general literature to be expected; but it is in the period of tranquillity *immediately succeeding* such great national revolutions that the human intellect soars aloft with steadiest, broadest, and sublimest wing into the calmer empyrean of poetry or philosophy—

> "Above the smoke and stir of this dim spot
> Which men call Earth."

The great revolution to which we have been alluding is, we hardly need say, the Reformation; the doctrines of which were first solidly established in England under the sceptre of Elizabeth, and in whose vehement struggles was trained that generation which was to be adorned by Sidney, by Spenser, and by Raleigh.

The other condition, too, which we have specified as necessary to the production of a great and immortal era in literature, viz. a high degree of military glory, was certainly to be found in this reign: we need only mention the annihilation of the Spanish Armada.

In England, at all periods of our history, literature, speaking generally, has almost always emanated from the people, and consequently has always talked the language of the people, and addressed itself to the people's sympathies; and this is the reason of the greater *vital force* which it must be allowed to possess. Homer and Shakspeare will ever be read with increasing ardour and veneration, and this because their works reflect, not so much a period or a nation, as the universal heart of man—the same in every climate and in every age.

Besides this fortunate circumstance there were also certain influences at work, peculiar to that brilliant period, and calculated to produce and foster the rapid development which then took place. We have seen the tone of the Italian poetry first infused, so to speak, into English literature by Chaucer and Gower, and the immense influx of classic ideas and classic language which flowed in at that time. At first, however, the *crasis* (to use a term of the old medicine) between the dissimilar and discordant elements—the ancient Saxonism, the modern classicism, and the romantic spirit of the chivalrous literature—was not, as might have been expected, perfect or complete; and it was not till the time of Elizabeth that the amalgamation of these elements was sufficiently brought about to produce a harmonious and healthy result. The spirit of the Reformation, also—an inquiring, active, practical, and fervent spirit—was necessary to complete the union of these discordant ingredients.

Chivalry, indeed, as a political or social system, had ceased to exist at the period of Elizabeth: that is to say, chivalry no longer exerted any very perceptible influence on the relations of men with the state or with each other. But though it no longer existed as an active and energetic influence, modifying either social life or political relations; though it no longer gave any tone to the general physiognomy of the times, its moral influence still existed with powerful though diminished force: it still perceptibly modified the *manners* of the court and of the higher classes; the idol was indeed cast down from the altar, but a solemn and holy atmosphere of sanctity still breathed around the walls of the temple; the pure, the ennobling, the heroic portion of the knightly spirit yet glowed with no decaying fervour in the hearts of such men as Essex, Raleigh, Sidney; and found a worthy voice in the sweet dignity of Spenser's song.

Though the joust and tournament had degenerated from their ancient splendour (and this because they were no longer so necessary as of old), and had become the idle pageant of a magnificent court, many of the gallant tilters of Whitehall had not forgotten the principles of the chivalric character—"high thoughts, seated," to use the beautiful language of Sidney, "in a heart of courtesy."

Of this majestic period the brightest figure is that of Sir Philip Sidney, the most complete embodiment of all the graces and virtues which can adorn or ennoble humanity. He was at once the Bayard and the Petrarch of English history, a name to which every Briton looks back with pride, admiration, and regret. Noble of birth, beautiful in person, splendid and generous, of a bravery almost incredible, wise in council, learned himself, and a powerful and generous protector of learning — in him seem to be united all the solidest gifts and the most attractive ornaments of body and of mind. The throne of Poland, to which he was elected, could hardly have conferred additional splendour upon so consummate a character; and we almost approve of the jealous admiration of Elizabeth, who prevented him from mounting that throne, that she might not lose the "jewel of her court." Very brief, indeed, was the career of this glorious star of the Elizabethan firmament, but the brightness of its setting was well worthy of its rising and meridian ray; and the field of Zutphen was sanctified by those words which can hardly be paralleled in the history of ancient or modern heroism: "this man's necessity is greater than mine." But the hand which faintly motioned the cup to the lips of the dying soldier was the same which wrote the knightly pages of the 'Arcadia,' and touched the softest note of "that small lute" which "gave ease to Petrarch's pain," and drew from the sonnet a tender melody not unworthy of the poet of Arqua.

There are few productions of similar importance whose character and merits have been so much misrepresented by modern ignorance and superficial criticism as Sidney's great work, the romance of the 'Arcadia.'

Disraeli has collected, in his 'Amenities of Literature,' a large number of depreciating criticisms made by various authors on the 'Arcadia' of Sidney. Walpole pronounced it "a tedious, lamentable, pedantic, pastoral romance;" Gifford affirms "that the plan is poor, the incidents trite, the style pedantic;" Dunlop complains that it is "extremely tiresome;" yet this book was the favourite and model in the age of Shakspeare! Shakspeare has in a thousand exquisite places imitated the scenes, the manners, and even the diction of the 'Arcadia;' Shirley, Beaumont, and Fletcher turned to it as their text-book; Sidney enchanted two later brothers in Waller and Cowley; and the world of fashion in Sidney's age culled their phrases out of the 'Arcadia,' which served them as a complete 'Academy of Compliments.'

Disraeli then goes on to show that modern critics, misled by the title of this prose romance, which Sidney injudiciously adopted from Sannazzaro, have generally concluded, without taking the trouble of reading it, to consider it as a pastoral, similar to that multitudinous class of fictions so popular in the sixteenth and seventeenth centuries, and of which the 'Galatea' of Cervantes is a well-known specimen. The fact is, however, that the *Arcadian* or pastoral parts of Sidney's work are merely supplementary, forming no essential portion of the narrative; being, in short, merely interludes of shepherds introduced dancing and reciting verses at the close of each book. There can be no doubt but that the scenes and sentiments described with such a sweet luxuriance of beautiful language were reflections of true events in Sidney's own chivalrous life, and transcripts from his own gentle and heroic heart. We cannot better conclude our notice on this work than by a selection from the remarks of Disraeli:—"He describes objects on which he loves to dwell, with a peculiar richness of fancy: he had shivered his lance in the tilt, and had managed the fiery courser in his career; and in the vivid picture of the shock between two knights we see distinctly every motion of the horse and horseman. But sweet is his loitering hour in the sunshine of luxuriant gardens, or as we lose ourselves in the green solitudes of the forests which most he loves. There is a feminine delicacy in whatever alludes to the female character, not merely courtly, but imbued with that sensibility which St. Palaye has remarkably described as 'full of refinement and fanaticism.' And this may suggest an idea, not improbable, that Shakspeare drew his fine conceptions of female character from Sidney. Shakspeare solely, of all our elder dramatists, has given true beauty to woman; and Shakspeare was an attentive reader of the 'Arcadia.'"

Besides this romance, which, though in prose, partakes more markedly of the character of poetry, Sidney was the author, as we have hinted above, of a considerable number of Sonnets, some of very singular beauty, and of a short treatise entitled 'The Defense of Poesie,' the nature of which is perfectly expressed in the title. The beauty of our author's prose style is no less conspicuous in this work than the deep feeling which he exhibits for the value and the charms of poetry. The language, indeed, is itself poetry of no mean order, and in this work, no less than in the 'Arcadia,' we do find in every line reason to confirm the judgment of Cowper, who was keenly alive to Sir Philip's merits, and who thus qualifies his style:—

"Sidney, *warbler of poetic prose.*"

He was mortally wounded by a musket-ball in the left thigh at the skirmish at Zutphen, September 22, 1586, and died on the 15th of October following, in his thirty-second year, and was buried in St. Paul's. To do, in so short a life, so much for immortality, is the lot of few; of still fewer to excite, in dying, such universal sorrow as that which followed Sidney to the grave; for in him the court lost its chiefest ornament, learning its steadiest patron, genius its boldest defender and firmest friend, and his country her most illustrious child—

"The courtier's, soldier's, scholar's eye, tongue, sword:
The expectancy and rose of the fair state,
The glass of fashion, and the mould of form,
The observed of all observers."

The greatest English poet after Chaucer, Edmund Spenser, was born in London about the year 1553, that is, a year before Sidney, and educated at Pembroke College, Cambridge. On leaving the University he retired (it is supposed in the quality of a private tutor) to the North of England, in which retirement he composed the first production which attracted notice to his youthful genius. This was 'The Shepherd's Calendar,' a long poem divided into twelve parts or months, and consisting of pastoral dialogues of a plaintive and amatory character. The Italian taste then prevalent in Europe, and which filled the literature of every country with imitations, more or less frigid, of the Arcadianisms of Guarini and Sannazzaro, is perhaps more perceptible in Spenser than any author, even of the "Italianated" Elizabethan age; and it is singular to observe how universally this manner was adopted in the early essays of the young poets of the day. "Babes," says the Scripture, "are fed with milk;" and it seems natural that the romantic genius of youth should nourish itself on the pure but somewhat insipid delicacies of the poetical "Golden Age." Eager to give to the form of his work the originality which was necessarily wanting to its design, Spenser rejected the rather worn-out Corydons and Tityruses of the classical idyllists, and gave to his shepherds and his scenery as much of an English air as he could by adopting English names and describing English nature: the same result also was aimed at in the language, into which he strove to infuse the spirit of the antique, and at the same time of a rustic simplicity, by adopting a great deal of the now almost obsolete diction of Chaucer. His shepherds, however, are not much inferior in point of nature and probability to the general run of pastoral personages—to the disguised courtiers who pipe and sing in Virgil's Mantuan shades, or the masquerading pedants of the modern Italian school; in short, to none of these sham shepherds, always excepting the admirable rustics of Theocritus. The subjects of the various poems of the 'Shepherd's Calendar' are the same which form the *curta supellex* of ordinary pastorals: the hinds of Spenser are sufficiently "melancholy and gentlemanlike," and pour out their melodious complaints without exciting any very deep sympathy in the reader. They remind us of young, thoughtful scholars, who have, "for very wantonness," put on the garb of rustics, and whose elegant and graceful thoughts are breathed in the language not of the field but of the study.

This work, besides exercising the youthful poet's powers of diction and harmony, acquired for him the admiration and friendship of the learned Gabriel Harvey, who, though fantastical in his literary tastes, and though for a time infecting Spenser with his own enthusiasm for his metrical whimsies, was of the greatest use to his modest and sensitive friend. The projects to which we have alluded were, among others, nothing less than the employment of the classical or syllabic mode of versification in English poetry. He has left us some most inimitable specimens of dactylic and iambic measures, which furnish a ludicrous proof of the inherent absurdity of the project. Spenser, too, has perpetrated some monstrous "classicisms" of this nature; and these show that not even the exquisite ear of the most harmonious of our poets could render bearable the application of the prosody of quantity to a language essentially accentual in its metrical character.

This curious literary folly, however, was at this period exceedingly epidemic; for similar attempts were made, and with exactly as much success, to naturalize the Greek and Roman metres in the Italian, Spanish, and even the French languages. In German, however, the innovation has lasted (and with tolerable success) down to the present day.

It was to Harvey that Spenser is supposed to have owed his introduction to Sir Philip Sidney, at whose ancestral seat of Penshurst the poet passed perhaps the brightest years of his unhappy life. We have stood beneath "Spenser's Oak" in the beautiful park of that venerable place, and dreamed of the hero and the poet—both still so young, yet with the halo of immortality already on their front, seated, "in colloquy sublime," beneath those murmuring boughs. It was here that Spenser completed his 'Shepherd's Calendar,' dedicating it, under the title of 'The Poet's Year,' to his young patron, "Maister Philip Sidney, worthy of all titles, both of learning and chivalry." Through the medium of Sidney the poet obtained the protection of the great Earl of Leicester, the favourite of Elizabeth, and uncle of "Maister Philip;" and through Leicester Spenser acquired the notice of his royal mistress.

Our youthful poet now became a courtier, and forms one star—

and one of the brightest too—of that glorious galaxy which gave such splendour to the court of the "Maiden Queen."

But in leaving the green solitudes of Penshurst for the splendours of the court, Spenser was destined to exchange his freedom and his happiness for a chain only the heavier because it was of gold. He forgot the profound truth concealed in that oracular verse of the poet which so truly describes the proper atmosphere for a lettered life,—

"Flumina amem sylvasque, inglorius;"—

and he paid for his mistake, the heavy penalty of a life embittered by court disappointments, and finished in affliction.

Though early distinguished by the favour of Elizabeth, his life at court seems to have been a nearly uninterrupted succession of mortifications and disappointments. The very favour of the Earl of Leicester, powerful as it was, was not omnipotent, and in courts, as in the fairy tale, the talisman or charmed weapon, given to the adventurous knight by a friendly magician, often proves the very cause of his being attacked by a hostile enchanter. The very patronage and protection of Leicester naturally drew upon Spenser the dislike and suspicion of Lord Burleigh, then Chancellor and highly favoured by Elizabeth; and the poet, in innumerable passages of his works, has alluded to the discouragement and coldness he experienced at the hands of the great lawyer. One stanza, indeed, describing the miseries of court dependence, has passed ineffaceably into the memory of every reader of English poetry. It is so painfully beautiful and so evidently sincere—written, as it were, with the very heart's blood of the poet—that we cannot forbear quoting it here:—

"Full little knowest thou who hast not tried,
What hell it is in suing long to bide;
To lose good days that might be better spent;
To waste long nights in pensive discontent;
To speed to-day, to be put back to-morrow;
To feed on hope, to pine with fear and sorrow;
To have thy prince's grace, yet want her peers';
To have thy asking, yet wait many years;
To fret thy soul with crosses and with cares;
To eat thy heart in comfortless despairs:
To fawn, to crouch, to wait, to ride, to run,
To spend, to give, to wait—to be undone."

At length, however, Spenser received (in 1580) the appointment of secretary to Lord Grey de Wilton, whom he accompanied to Ireland, and under whose orders the poet seems to have distinguished himself as a man of business, for he was soon afterwards rewarded with a grant from the Crown of 3000 acres of land in the county of Cork, an estate which had previously formed part of the domains belonging to the Earls of Desmond, but which had been forfeited to the Crown. This is one of the numerous instances of Elizabeth's ingenious policy; for she thus rewarded a faithful servant with a gift of land which cost her nothing, and which the recipient (or "undertaker," as he was termed) was bound by his contract to inhabit and keep in cultivation. A territory, however, recently devastated by contending armies with fire and sword, was a gift rather splendid in appearance than profitable in reality; and perhaps the principal advantage derived by Spenser from this donation was the necessity it imposed upon him of residing on his estate, and the leisure which it enabled him to dedicate to his literary pursuits. He took up his abode in the ancient castle of Kilcolman, situated in the midst of his beautiful but unproductive domain, and it is here that he composed the greater part of his immortal work—the poem of 'The Faerie Queene.' The scenery by which he was here surrounded is remarked for its beauty even in beautiful Ireland; and it may not be fanciful to speculate how far the natural loveliness of the spot is reflected and reproduced in the rich pictures which fill the pages of the poem.

It was here that the poet was visited by Raleigh, then a young man, beginning, as Captain of the Guards, that extraordinary and brilliant career which has rendered his name so illustrious at once for learning and for enterprise. To Raleigh—a kindred spirit—Spenser communicated his literary projects, and read to him the unfinished cantos of the 'Faerie Queene.' Among the various friendships and meetings recorded among great men, there is perhaps none on which we reflect with such interest as this: how delightful is it to picture to ourselves the Ariosto of England and the colonizer of Virginia seated together on the banks of Mulla, exchanging thoughts bright with immortality,

> "amongst the coolly shade
> Of the green alders, by the Mulla's shore!"

The "Shepherd of the Ocean," as Raleigh was styled in Spenser's poetical nomenclature, replaced for the bard, in some degree at least, the irreparable loss inflicted by the early death of Sidney—perhaps the severest blow inflicted on the sensitive heart of the poet during the earlier part of his career: the death of his youthful patron cast a gloom over the whole of his too short existence.

In 1590 Spenser returned to England in order to present to Elizabeth the first part of the 'Faerie Queene;' and, insatiable as was that great sovereign in the matter of praise and adulation, with the exquisite tribute of Spenser's Muse she must have been profoundly gratified. All the learning and genius of an age remarkable for learning and genius were exhausted in supplying the Maiden Monarch with incessant clouds of elegant and poetical incense; and among all the worshippers in the temple none were certainly more devoted or more capable than Spenser. The annals of court adulation are in general among the most humiliating pages of human folly and absurdity; but the age of Elizabeth was singular and fortunate in one respect: the greatness of the sovereign's character was not unworthy of the sublimest strains of panegyric, and the greatest among poets—for Shakspeare and Spenser both praised, in deathless verse, this extraordinary ruler—found in the achievements and the wisdom of their patroness a subject which they could adorn, but hardly exaggerate. The queen expressed her approbation of the poem by conferring on the author a pension of 50*l.* per annum—in estimating which reward we must consider the much higher value of money at that period: and Spenser then probably returned to Ireland; for in 1595 he published his pastoral of 'Colin Clout,' and in 1596 the second part of the 'Faerie Queene.' It must not however be supposed that the poet had no occupation during this period excepting such as he found in the strenua inertia"—the laborious abstraction of a literary life: he was employed actively and uninterruptedly in the service of the state; for, after passing through many subordinate employments, we find him about this time, Clerk of the Council for the province of Munster, and exhibiting the knowledge he had acquired of the character and prospects of the conquered nation in his interesting prose work entitled 'A View of the State of Ireland.' This book, the production of one who was at the same time a poet and a statesman, bears every mark of its author's double quality: it gives a most curious and evidently faithful description of the manners of the Celtic inhabitants of the country, and contains many wise hints for the subjection and civilizing of that warlike race. It is true that some of the measures recommended by Spenser are of a violent and coercive character; but we should be unwise to expect in a writer of the sixteenth century a tone of mildness and toleration unknown in politics previous to the nineteenth.

During the whole of Spenser's residence in Ireland, he appears to have made frequent voyages to his own country, and seems to have been agitated by an incessant and feverish discontentment—dissatisfied probably with the very reward conferred upon him by the queen—a reward which condemned him to reside in a barbarous and disturbed country, and deprived him of the pleasures and society of the court. This honourable banishment under the disguise of advancement was perhaps an ingenious contrivance of the profound and tortuous policy of Spenser's great opponent, Burleigh, who thus removed the dangerous fascinations of Spenser's manners and genius far from the sphere of the court, and thus deprived the party of Leicester of a hold upon Elizabeth's capricious and impressionable vanity.

In 1597 Spenser retired for the last time to Ireland, and shortly afterwards the flame of popular discontent, communicated from the furious outburst which, under the name of "Tyrone's Rebellion," had been raging for some years in Ulster, swept over his retreat at

Kilcolman Castle, and drove Spenser, a heartbroken and ruined man, to die in sorrow and distress in London. In his offices of Clerk of the Council, and afterwards of Sheriff of Cork, Spenser had probably given but too much grounds for the accusation of injustice and oppression brought against him by the Irish, and exaggerated by the natural indignation of a proud and savage people uneasy under a recent yoke. In October, 1598, the Castle of Kilcolman was attacked and burned by the insurgents, and Spenser, with difficulty saving himself and his wife from the fury of the victors, escaped to England. In the hurry of leaving his blazing residence, however, either from the imminence of personal danger or from one of those frightful mistakes so likely to happen at such terrific moments, the poet's infant child was left behind, and perished with the house. Spenser reached London, ruined, heartbroken, and despairing, and, after lingering for three months, he died, in King Street, Westminster, on the 16th of January, 1599.

He was buried in Westminster Abbey, near the tomb of Chaucer.

The following is an account of the principal poems of Spenser, at least of such as are not alluded to in the foregoing pages: — 'The Tears of the Muses,' and 'Mother Hubbard's Tale,' published in 1591; 'Daphnaida,' 1592; The 'Amoretti' and 'Epithalanium' — two works descriptive of his courtship and marriage, the latter one of the noblest hymeneal songs in any language — in 1595; and the 'Elegy on Astrophil,' a lament on the death of the illustrious Sidney, at the same period. We have hinted that the 'Fairy Queen' was given to the world in detached portions and at long intervals of time: the dates of these various publications are nearly as follows: — Books I., II., and III. appeared together in January 1589–90; IV., V., and VI. in 1596.

The design of the whole poem, if completed, would have given us one of the most splendid works of romantic fiction in which Chivalry ever pronounced the oracles of Wisdom: and we may judge, by the unfinished portion of this Palace of Honour, what would have been the gorgeous effect of the whole majestic structure. Spenser supposed the Fairy Queen to appear in a vision to Prince Arthur, who, awaking deeply enamoured, resolves on seeking his unearthly mistress in Faery Land. The poet then represents the Fairy Queen as holding her solemn annual feast during twelve days, on each of which a perilous adventure is undertaken by some particular knight; each of the twelve knights typifying some moral virtue. "The first," to use the words of Chambers's abridgment of the plan, "is the Red-cross Knight, expressing Holiness; the second, Sir Guyon, or Temperance; and the third, Britomartis, 'a lady knight,' representing Chastity. There was thus a blending of chivalry and religion in the design of the 'Faery Queen.' Besides his personification of the abstract virtues, the poet made his allegorical personages and their adventures represent historical characters and events. The queen, Gloriana, and the huntress, Belphœbe, are both symbolical of Queen Elizabeth; the adventures of the Redcross Knight shadow forth the history of the Church of England; and the distressed knight is Henry IV. The Fourth, Fifth, and Sixth Books contain the legend of Cambel and Triamond, or Friendship; Artegal, or Justice; and Sir Calidore, or Courtesy. A double allegory is contained in these cantos, as in the previous ones: Artegal is the poet's friend and patron, Lord Grey; and various historical events are related in the knight's adventures. Half of the original design was thus finished; six of the twelve adventures and moral virtues were produced: but unfortunately the world saw only some fragments more of the work."

Even were we not fully aware of the great general influence exerted on the age of Elizabeth by the taste for Italian poetry, we should be easily enabled to trace its effect in modifying the genius of Spenser. The 'Faery Queen' is written in a peculiar versification to which we have given the name of the "Spenserian stanza." It is really nothing more than the Italian "ottava rima," or eight-lined stanza, to which Spenser, in order to give to the English the "linked sweetness long drawn out" of the "favella Toscana," most wisely added a ninth line, whose billowy flow admirably winds up the swelling and varying music of each stanza. This measure is as difficult to write with effect in English as it is easy in Italian, a language in which the rhymes are so abundant, and the rhythmic cadence so inherent, that it requires almost an effort to avoid giving a metrical form even to prose: and Spenser has wielded this complicated instrument with such consummate mastery and grace, that the rich abundant melody of his versification almost oppresses the ear with its overwhelming sweetness. Like the soft undulation of a Tropic sea, it bears us onward dreamily with easy swell and falls, by wizard islands of sunshine and of rest, by bright phantom-peopled realms and old enchanted cities.

The genius of Spenser is essentially *pictorial*. There are no scenes, soft or terrible, which ever glowed before the intellectual gaze of the great painters which have more reality than his; like the gallery so exquisitely described by Byron: —

> "There rose a Carlo Dolce, or a Titian,
> Or wilder group of savage Salvatore's;
> There danced Albano's boys, and here the sea shone
> With Vernet's ocean lights; and there the stories
> Of martyrs awed, as Spagnoletto tainted
> His brush with all the blood of all the sainted.
>
> There sweetly spread a landscape of Lorraine;
> There Rembrandt made his darkness equal light;
> Or gloomy Caravaggio's gloomier stain
> Bronzed o'er some lean and stoic anchorite."

"His command of imagery," says Campbell, the truth and beauty of whose criticisms will form our best apology for adopting them instead of our own, "is wide, easy, and luxuriant. He threw the soul of harmony into our verse, and made it more warmly, tenderly, and magnificently descriptive than it ever was before, or, with a few exceptions, than it has ever been since. It must certainly be owned that in description he exhibits nothing of the brief strokes and robust power which characterise the very greatest poets; but we shall nowhere find more airy and expansive images of visionary things, a sweeter tone of sentiment, or a finer flush in the colours of language, *than in this* ***Rubens*** of English poetry."

But perhaps the best and most comprehensive criticism upon Spenser's merit is that recorded by Pope in one of his letters to Spence:—"After my reading a canto of Spenser two or three days ago to an old lady between seventy and eighty, she said that I had been showing her a collection of pictures. She said very right."

The chief defect of this admirable poet is one almost inseparable from allegory in general, and particularly allegory so complicated as that of Spenser, where the feigned resemblance often represents several distinct and different types or objects. It cannot be denied that there is a great want of human interest in the 'Faery Queen,' and that the events of his drama have frequently no perceptible connection with each other or bearing upon the supposed catastrophe. Moreover, there is no bond of interest uniting the several cantos of the poem, for they are separate and detached adventures, performed by different and unconnected characters, and very feebly linked together by their being supposed to be undertaken at the command of Gloriana. Arthur is, it is true, the nominal hero, but he is soon forgotten by the reader; and his reappearance at the end of the poem would hardly suffice to incorporate into one living body the "disjecta membra poetæ" scattered through the various exploits of the twelve knights. In fact, criticism can only enlarge here the definition of Pope's old lady, and say that the cantos of Spenser, admirably beautiful as they are, glowing with the most varied colours of fancy and imagination, want, like the pictures in a gallery, a mutual dependence and connection.

Exquisitely diversified, too, as is the melody of Spenser's verse and *manner of treatment*, we cannot disguise from ourselves a feeling that it is injured by some tinge of that lusciousness and dilatation perceptible in the style of Tasso and Ariosto, whose writings it so much resembles. This over-sweetness and luxuriance seems inseparable from the genius of the Italian language, but harmonizes less naturally with the less *sensuous* character of our Northern poesy.

In the innumerable allegories which people the enchanted scenery of Spenser, we are sometimes shocked with those incongruous details which make us laugh in the engravings of the emblematic Otto

Venius, where either the attribute distinguishing the moral quality to be personified is so dark and far-fetched as to be absolutely unintelligible without explanation, or where it is of a nature unfit for the purposes of art. Those who are acquainted with the works of Rubens (the pupil of Venius), to whom Spenser has been so well compared by Campbell, will be at no loss to understand our meaning.

Like many great poets of ancient and modern times, Spenser sought to give vigour and solemnity to his language by a plentiful adoption of archaisms, words, and expressions consecrated by their having been employed by older authors. Virgil gave an air of antiquity and simplicity to the Eneid by using multitudes of venerable words employed by Ennius. Spenser imitated Chaucer; just as La Fontaine gave *naïveté* and edge to his sly satire by an infusion of the admirable expressions of Villon and Rabelais: and we hardly agree with those critics who have complained of our poet's freedom in this respect. If the rough but time-honoured stones taken from the Cyclopean walls of old Ennius be allowed to give dignity to the graceful Ionic edifice of Virgil, we do not see why the simple diction of Chaucer should not harmonize well with the rich elegance of the 'Faery Queen'—the rather that the latter work is, after all, a Tale of Chivalry—a Romance.

CHAPTER IV.

BACON.

His Birth and Education—'View of the State of Europe'—His Career—Impeached for Corruption—Death—His Character—State of Philosophy in the Sixteenth Century—Its Corruptions and Defects—Bacon's System—Not a Discoverer—The New Philosophy—Analysis of the Instauratio: I. De Augmentis; II. Novum Organum; III. Sylva Sylvarum; IV. Scala Intellectûs; V. Prodromi; VI. Philosophia Secunda—The Baconian Logic—Style—His Minor Works.

Francis Bacon, the Luther of Philosophy, was born in London on the 22d of January, 1561. He was the son of Sir Nicholas Bacon, a distinguished lawyer and Lord Keeper of the Privy Seal in the reign of Queen Elizabeth. The subject of our present remarks was sent, while yet a boy of thirteen, to the University of Cambridge; and though it appears to have been customary at this period to begin the public part of education much earlier than is now usual, we can hardly be wrong in deeming that Bacon must have given proofs of a most precocious intellect, when we learn that when hardly sixteen he had formed distinct notions respecting the defects of the Aristotelian system of philosophy, and had no doubt already conceived the outline of that gigantic plan of destruction and innovation which has made his name immortal. After remaining four years at Cambridge he went abroad, and travelled in France, probably intending to pass several years in acquiring practical experience in the various courts of the continent; but the death of his father, in 1579, suddenly recalled him to England; not however before he had given proof of the success with which he had employed his time in foreign countries, by the production of a most sagacious and valuable essay 'On the State of Europe.' The political knowledge exhibited in this little treatise, and the profound wisdom and acuteness displayed in it, would astonish us, as the work of one hardly entered upon the period of adolescence, if any manifestation of intellect could surprise us on the part of this astonishing person. It is obvious that he had already felt the mysterious vocation of genius—that secret oracle which points out to the highest order of minds the true path which Providence intended them to pursue, a path from which they never deviate with impunity. Bacon so strongly felt that the true bent of his character would lead him to consecrate his future life to sublime and solitary meditation, and was so proudly and justly confident in the yet unexercised strength of his intellect, that he entreated Burleigh, the powerful favourite and Chancellor, to procure him from the state some provision which would enable him to prosecute his studies in uninterrupted leisure.

Burleigh, however, refused to accede to a proposition which must have appeared then, as it would now, so extraordinary and unusual; and the young philosopher was obliged to devote himself to the study of the law, which he pursued with industry and success. Bacon's after career affords a melancholy example of the danger of neglecting that inward voice which calls, as we have said a few lines back, the sublimer intellects among mankind to the true sphere of their exertions, whispering to the mental, as the Dæmon of Socrates to the moral, ear the true direction of the course.

While studying the law in Gray's Inn, Bacon sketched out the first plan of the 'Instauration,' and probably had decided upon the general purport and arrangement of the great works which contain his conclusions. The rest of his personal career may be described in a few words: the task is a melancholy and humiliating one. He rapidly passed through the inferior dignities of the law and of the state, being appointed queen's counsel in 1590, and in 1593 chosen member of parliament for the county of Middlesex. Both in the courts of law and in the House of Commons he was distinguished for the vastness of his knowledge and for the brilliancy of his eloquence; but he was also notorious, even in that age, for his subserviency to the most iniquitous despotism of the court. Having on one occasion (we select a single example from among many) advocated before the Commons, with all the power which marked his mind, a measure of a popular tendency, he was weak enough, on the first intimation of his independence having displeased the sovereign, to renounce, with shameless facility, the convictions which he had just before been asserting, and even to apologise for having entertained them. But this great man was reserved for yet deeper degradation. His political conduct continued to present a worthy continuation to this lamentable commencement. Obeying every fickle current of court favour, he first deserted the party of the Cecils (*i. e.* of his first protector and kinsman Burleigh) for that of the unfortunate Essex, who, failing in obtaining for his new proselyte the dignity of attorney-general, rewarded his apostacy with the gift of an estate at Twickenham worth two thousand pounds.

Bacon's attachment to Essex was as mercenary as had been his adherence to Burleigh, and, on the disgrace and impeachment of the Earl, the great lawyer showed a base eagerness to aid the overthrow of the unhappy and illustrious victim, exhibiting a ferocious violence hardly exceeded in the long and black annals of mercenary tribunals and subservient advocates. In order to gratify the court, Bacon crowned his apostacy by composing a 'Declaration of the Treasons and Practices of the Earl of Essex.' In the foul descent from baseness to baseness which marks the whole of Bacon's political career, we cannot find any extenuating circumstances, except indeed such as transfer his guilt from deliberate depravity to a servile calculation of interest. It is consoling indeed to reflect that there has been in no part of human conduct so great an improvement in point of morality as in the change which has taken place in political relations from the sixteenth century to the present day. The fatal prevalence of that atrocious and infernal policy which is systematised with such a hideous minuteness in the pages of Machiavelli, had extended itself from the petty Italian states, where it first appeared, to all the countries of Europe; and that dreadful sophism that "we may do evil that good may come" had destroyed the natural barriers between right and wrong in public affairs. It is but a poor excuse to say that Bacon was no worse than many of his contemporaries; still less to attempt to palliate ingratitude and cowardice by alleging that Bacon deserted his benefactors and attacked the fallen without the inducement of passion and animosity: the avarice, the ambition, the cool calculation of profit, which was the cause of such wretched servility, is certainly not less able to excite our contempt, than a similar conduct dictated by sincere hatred or a natural depravity would be capable of inspiring us with detestation. The truth is that Bacon, though not personally avaricious, was cursed with that passion for state, splendour, and magnificence which is so frequently found in a highly imaginative character; and being always plunged in difficulties, he took, with that unscrupulousness too common at the period when he lived, the shortest way to supply his incessant needs.

In 1603, at the beginning of the reign of James I., Bacon was knighted, and appointed successively king's counsel, solicitor-general, and attorney-general (the last dignity having been attained in 1613), and he fully justified whatever confidence the court could have placed in his subserviency and pliability: so far indeed had he forgotten the great principles of the law whose unworthy minister he was, that he assisted in inflicting on a certain Paacham, an aged and obscure clergyman, accused of treason, the cruelties of the torture, in order to extort a confession by a means in no way countenanced by the English constitution. It was at this period that Bacon married the daughter of a wealthy alderman, and seems in this, as well as so many other acts of his life, to have consulted interest. He still continued to advance in his career of ambition, and in 1619 reached the highest dignity to which an English subject can aspire, having been named in that year Lord High Chancellor, with the title of Baron Verulam. This rank he afterwards exchanged, by the protection of Villiers — the vain and haughty favourite of James — for the still more exalted style of Viscount St. Alban's. In this advance he probably received from Villiers the hire for some new act of obsequiousness to the favourite's power, for he allowed the minister to interfere in and control the exercise of his high judicial functions — a crime of which he was accused before parliament, and of which (together with many minor instances of corruption) he proclaimed himself guilty in a confession written with his own hand. On being asked, by a committee sent for the purpose from the House of Lords, whether he confessed the authenticity and the truth of this humiliating avowal, he is reported to have said, with an expression of sorrow and repentance which under any other circumstances would have been deeply touching, "It is my act, my hand, my heart; I beseech your lordships, press not upon a broken reed." Being fully convicted of these grave charges, he was deprived by parliament of the office he had so unworthily prostituted, and sent, with the dark stain of a just condemnation upon him, to finish his life in retirement and disgrace.

He retired to his estates, and, devoting the remainder of his life to those grand speculations which have survived his follies and his crimes, and let us hope also to repentance for his past errors, he died in 1626, deeply in debt, leaving, as he says himself, with a noble sense of the services he had rendered to the human race, "his name and memory to foreign nations, and to mine own country after some time is passed over."

It is singular enough that the death of this great philosopher should have been caused by a cold caught in performing a physical experiment, and that he should have been, not the apostle only, but also the martyr of science. It is related that, travelling by Highgate, near London, ir wintry weather, he was struck with the idea that flesh might be preserved by means of snow as well as by salting: he bought a fowl, and, descending from his coach, assisted with his own hands in making an immediate trial of the project by stuffing the hen with snow; and in doing this he is said to have received a chill, which, aggravated by his being immediately put into a damp bed at Lord Arundel's house, caused his death in a very few days. But even when his end was approaching, the great philosopher, with "the ruling passion strong in death," could not forbear communicating to a friend, in a letter which he dictated, being too ill to write himself, that his experiment "had succeeded excellently."

A monument was erected over his grave by his faithful friend and disciple, Sir Thomas Meautys, who was buried at his master's feet: and this monument, executed after the design of Sir Henry Wotton, a man imbued with a taste for Italian art, has a peculiar interest as being a portrait of the philosopher, who is represented in his usual dress seated in an attitude of profound meditation; and the work bears the appropriate inscription, "Sic sedebat."

Of Bacon's personal manners and demeanour all that we know is calculated to give us a most extraordinary idea of the charms of his conversation and the amiability of his character. Ben Jonson, himself so remarkable for his own wonderful stores of learning and powers of conversation, and who was, too, no very indulgent critic, has expressed his admiration of Bacon's eloquence and ready wit. It is consoling to find that, while the conduct of the politician presents so many points for the severest reprobation of the moralist, the character of the *man* was as attractive as his intellect was sublime. Bacon was a most profuse and generous master to his dependants; and his flagitious avidity for money may be as justly attributed to an easiness of temper, preventing him from being able to say "no" to a petitioner, and to those habits of inattention to small matters which so often accompany the literary character, as to the darker vices to which they might be ascribed by severer judges. Osborn, a contemporary writer, most probably gives the result of personal experience in the following description of Bacon's conversational powers:—"In all companies he did appear a good proficient, if not a master, in those arts entertained for the subject of every one's discourse. His most casual talk deserveth to be written. As I have been told, his earliest copies required no great labour to render them competent for the nicest judgment. I have heard him entertain a country lord in he proper terms relating to horses and dogs; and at another time out-cant a London chirurgeon. Nor did an easy falling into argument appear less an ornament in him. The ears of his hearers received more gratification than trouble; and were no less sorry when he came to conclude, than displeased with any who did interrupt him." The learned and amusing Howell calls him "a man of recondite science, born for the salvation of learning, and, I think the eloquentest that was born in this isle." But of his eloquence we shall be able to give a more exact idea when we come to speak of the style of his writings.

In order to form even an approximative notion respecting the nature and importance of the immense revolution produced in science by the writings of Bacon, it is indispensable to have some general idea of the state of science when he wrote. Vague, general, and superficial eulogiums have done real injury to the fame of this great man; for they have propagated very false notions respecting the nature of the revolution he effected, and respecting the means by which that revolution was brought about. Among other vulgar errors of this nature, one of the most dangerous is that which consists in considering Bacon as a discoverer, and attributing to him the invention of analysis. This is degrading a great man to the level of a quack. "Bacon's philosophy," as D'Alembert profoundly says, "was too wise to astonish;" and as to the inductive method of discovering truth, that is as old as Aristotle, or rather as old as human reason itself.

The simple account of the great Baconian innovation will be substantially as follows. The Aristotelian method had reigned in all the schools and universities of Europe from the period of the revival of letters in the fourteenth century; nay, it may be considered as having existed during the whole period of the dark ages; and thus to have continued in action, with various degrees, it is true, of cultivation and extension, uninterruptedly from the time of Aristotle himself. The acute and disputatious spirit of the ancient Greeks, so ingenious, so inquisitive, so paradoxical, was calculated to abuse the opportunity for idle and fruitless speculation afforded by the general tone of the Aristotelian logic; and this word-catching and quibbling --in short, this habit of arguing to abstract conclusions on insufficient premises—was not likely to diminish among the schools of Alexandria and Byzantium. The perverted ingenuity of the Lower Empire was still further sharpened by the part which the Orientals now began to play in philosophy. The wildest fantasies and irregularities of Eastern subtlety were thus added to the Greek passion for paradox and sophistry, and it was in this state, debased with these admixtures, that the schools of the middle ages received the philosophy of the Stagyrite. Now the monastic spirit was characterised by all the various peculiarities together. It was as dreamy and fantastical as the Oriental genius, as subtle and disputative as the Greek, and as sophistical in its tone as the Alexandrian speculations: and to all these sources of corruption was added another, more dangerous than any we have mentioned, in the circumstance of the Aristotelian philosophy being made part of the ecclesiastical system—that is to say, the alliance between the theology of Rome and the philosophy of the Lycæum.

Orthodoxy having once taken under her fatal protection a particular system of philosophy, the consequences were equally injurious to the one and the other; for the Church of Rome was thus not only compelled to recognise by her adherence, and protect by her authority, the most false conclusions of the sophical system, but deprived herself (through her assumption of infallibility) of the power of ever renouncing any conclusion, however absurd, which she had once sanctioned. On the other hand, the philosophical system, thus unnaturally connected with religious orthodoxy, became at once timid and extravagant, appealing not to sense and reason for the support of its deductions, but to tradition and authority, and maintaining its supremacy, not by arguments, but by persecution and violence, by the sword, the dungeon, and the stake.

There are few episodes in the great drama of past ages more wonderful, and at the same time more melancholy, than the spectacle afforded by the intense mental activity of the middle ages. What laborious and powerful intellects were there, wasting their energies on the vainest of empty speculations! Incessantly they argued and concluded—but their arguments proved nothing, and their conclusions were but idle phrases:

> "They found no end, in wandering mazes lost."

We are not, however, to suppose that, at a period of such profound and universal agitation as that which preceded the Reformation, the Aristotelian philosophy, though defended by all the thunders of orthodoxy, could pass unquestioned, and meet with universal adhesion. No; there were bold spirits who dared to question the soundness of its principles, and examine their reasonableness on grounds of common sense. The great dispute between the Nominalists and Realists, by accustoming men to hear the boldest speculations upon abstract subjects, prepared the way for the ultimate overthrow of the system which had so long reigned triumphant over the mind. Luther, in attacking the Romish Church, most undoubtedly struck a heavy though indirect blow against the system of philosophy supported by that Church; and in the enormous outburst of activity which characterises that wonderful epoch many speculators had revolted against the tyranny exercised on human thought under the usurped and much-abused name of Aristotle. In the sciences particularly, there were many great men, who, "falling upon evil days and evil tongues," have come down to posterity as mountebanks, as visionaries, or as impostors, but who, had they lived at a more auspicious time would probably command our veneration as lights of science and benefactors to their kind: Cornelius Agrippa, Paracelsus, Roger Bacon, Giordano Bruno, Cardan, and Campanella.

A vain reliance on the supposed adequate power of human ratiocination kept the philosophers of the Middle Ages reasoning incessantly in a circle, or diverting their attention from the only rational object in philosophy; that is, as the very word implies, "a love for, or search after, truth." They knew not, or they despised, the immense practical and physical benefits which might flow from a well-directed inquiry into the laws of nature; and it was reserved for the intellect of an Englishman—"*divini* ingenii vir, Franciscus Bacon de Verulamio," as he is styled by Leibnitz—to show that science is only valuable in proportion as it is practical and productive.

The principal defect of the Aristotelian method was the habit which it encouraged of generalising too rapidly upon insufficient grounds: that is, of applying some principle or law of nature to phenomena of similar, but not identical, conditions. In short, its essential vice was a neglect of the great rule which teaches us to observe with particular care the points of resemblance and dissimilitude existing between individual phenomena, or classes of phenomena. The knowledge possessed by the ancients with respect to the true properties of bodies and the nature of physical operations was vague and limited enough; though we cannot be surprised at this imperfection of knowledge at a period when the mechanical aids to observation were in so primitive a state. For want of instruments they transferred to pure reason those duties which can only be effectually performed by accurate observation and patient experiment. These remarks will perhaps appear to possess more weight when we reflect that in those sciences independent of experiment, and whose deductions are to be arrived at by the sole exercise of the ratiocinative faculty unaided by practical trials, the intellect of the ancient world had advanced so far that modern ages have made little or no additions to the mass of human knowledge. In geometry, for example, a science which investigates abstract properties of space, and which consequently is independent of experiment, modern times have hardly, if at all, extended the frontiers beyond the limits reached by the schools of Alexandria.

But we have hitherto spoken of the ancient philosophy in its pure and normal state; we must not forget the corruptions to which it was in its very nature exposed, and under which it ultimately succumbed. The grand and sublime speculations of Aristotle, exhibiting, as we have seen, a noble but misplaced confidence in the omnipotence of human reason, degenerated in the Middle Ages, and under the influences which we have essayed to indicate, into a mere spirit of empty subtlety and ingenious trifling; a system at once of timid servility to precedent and prescription, and rash and illogical generalization: it was still

> "Uncertain and unsettled,
> Deep versed in books, and shallow in itself,
> Crude or intoxicate, collecting toys
> And trifles for choice matters, worth a sponge,
> As children gathering pebbles on the shore."

The old philosophy, which in its youth and vigour had never been fruitful, gradually fell into dotage as its age advanced, and its latest period of existence was characterized by the same weakness which accompanies in man extreme old age—a senile and senseless garrulity, a perpetual recurrence of the same worn-out topics, and a stiff and obstinate assertion of its own infallibility:—

> "Everlasting dictates crowd her tongue,
> Perversely grave or positively wrong."

Bacon has most profoundly and acutely compared old systems to children: "quippe qui," he says, "ad *garriendum* prompti sint, *generare* non possint."

Our great philosopher was the first to perceive clearly the two predominant vices of the older method—its sterility and its stationary character; and he was the first to discover a remedy for these defects. His own system is characterized above all its other merits by the qualities of utility and capability of progressive development. It is, in short, eminently and essentially practical; the great reformer rightly considering that utility is the only measure of excellence in any science. He never pretended to be a discoverer, and as invariably disclaimed that title, rendering ample justice to the merits of the great men who had devoted themselves to science, and expressing his conviction that the unproductive state of science was not to be attributed to any want of intellect in the philosophers who had preceded him, but simply and solely to a radical defect in their method. "Francis Bacon thought in this manner: The knowledge whereof the world is possessed, especially that of nature, extendeth not to *magnitude and certainty of works.*" This is the key to Bacon's whole system, and this must excite our gratitude for the eminently practical character of his mind. It is this circumstance which has given value and vitality to what he has produced. How fortunate is it for the destinies of science that Bacon was a man of active life, occupied during his whole existence with real interests! it was thus that he not only saw, with the clear and steady eye of common sense, the exact state of the disease which it was his aim to cure, but was enabled to avoid pedantry and vain speculations in the administering of the remedy. "There is not anything in being or action," to use his own comprehensive words, "which could not be drawn and collected into contemplation and doctrine."

It now remains to examine the means which he adopted to bring about this immense revolution in the empire of human thought. We shall find that his great principle was to show how universally the previous systems neglected the middle links in that vast chain of facts connecting the general principle or law of nature with the remote and individual phenomena. "Axiomata infima non multùm ab experientiâ nudâ discrepant: suprema verò illa et generalissima (quæ habentur) notionaria sunt et abstracta, et nil habent solidi. At media sunt axiomata illa vera et solida et viva, in quibus humanæ res et fortunæ sitæ sunt, et suprà hæc quoque, *tandem* ipsa illa generalissima, talia scilicet quæ non abstracta sint, sed per hæc media verè limitantur." The vice of the older philosophy was the passing from one of the extremes of this chain, abruptly, and "per saltum," to the other.

As we have already mentioned, Bacon has never preferred any claim to the character of a scientific discoverer; his mission was a more exalted and a vaster one: the object of his works was to "note the deficiency" in the various species of knowledge composing the philosophical systems of the world; to distinguish with accuracy which among the various lines taken by investigation were capable of leading to certain, useful, and productive results; then to establish the method to be pursued in following those preferable lines when once ascertained; and finally to give examples or specimens of his own method applied and put in action.

In contemplating this gigantic scheme, it is impossible to admire sufficiently the genius which has traced with prophetic accuracy the paths of sciences which were not then in existence; the union of good sense and enthusiasm in that mind, which, while limiting in one direction the advance of human knowledge, encouraged us to push on, in another, to a development so remote as to be even yet undefined; or the rich and masculine eloquence in which these sublime thoughts are communicated.

The great project which has immortalised the "Lord Chancellor of human nature" was conceived at a very early age. "Such noble ideas are most congenial to the sanguine spirit of youth," as Hallam justly remarks, "and to its ignorance of the extent of labour it undertakes." Bacon himself mentions, as one of his earliest productions, a work bearing the somewhat ambitious title 'Temporis Partus Maximus,' which is now lost to us, but which probably contained the germ or embryo of his system. We will now give a short account of his great productions, in the hope of thus rendering his philosophy more intelligible in its unity to our readers—a precaution which has been too much neglected by those who have written on the subject, and who have treated Bacon's works rather as separate and independent treatises, than as parts of one vast edifice or creation.

In 1597 appeared the first edition of his Essays, a little work on miscellaneous subjects, which contains perhaps more of wisdom, novelty, and profound remark than any book of equal size that was ever composed. The subjects of these short treatises are often of a most trite and ordinary kind, but yet it is impossible to read them, even for the fiftieth time, without being struck by some new and original remark, or seeing some thought placed in a new and original light. "The Essays," says Stewart, "are the best known and most popular of all his works. It is one of those where the superiority of his genius appears to the greatest advantage; the novelty and depth of his reflections often receiving a strong relief from the triteness of the subject. It may be read from beginning to end in a few hours; and yet, after the twentieth perusal, one seldom fails to remark in it something unobserved before. This, indeed, is a characteristic of all Bacon's writings, and is only to be accounted for by the inexhaustible aliment they furnish to our own thoughts, and the sympathetic activity they impart to our torpid faculties."

The best way which we can follow to give a clear idea of Bacon's gigantic plan for the restoration of philosophy will be to present our readers with a sort of programme of the whole system of works in which he develops the various parts of his project; and this, arranged in a tabular form, will, we think, avoid the danger so very natural for persons to fall into with respect to the details of Bacon's great intellectual temple. That so vast a design could ever have been projected by a single person is more wonderful than that some parts of the work were never executed. We have, however, enough to prove with what justice the learned men of all countries have united, during a period of nearly two centuries and a half, in considering Bacon as the father of experimental philosophy. Having given this *conspectus* or synopsis, we shall proceed to examine more in detail the various works composing the great Verulamian Cycle, and thus we hope to unite the advantages of brevity and distinctness. We shall see that, as these works appeared successively, though each forming, as it were, one stone of the Baconian edifice, there were necessarily to be expected many repetitions of ideas previously enounced, and many anticipations of future arguments.

Our synoptical arrangement will be as follows:

The Instauratio.

Instauratio Magna.

- I. De Augmentis Scientiarum.
- II Novum Organum.
  - i. De Prærogativis Instantairum.
  - ii. *Adminicula Inductionis.
  - iii. *Rectificatio Inductionis.
  - iv. *Variatio Inquisitionis pro naturâ subjecti.
  - v. *De Prærogativis Naturarum quâtenus ad Inquisit.
  - vi. *De Terminis Inquisitionis.
  - vii. *Deductio ad Praxin.
  - viii. *De Paracevis ad Inquisitionem.
  - ix. *De Scalâ Axiomatum.
- III. Sylva Sylvarum.
- IV. Scala Intellectus.
- V. *Prodromi.
- VI. *Philosophia Secunda.

[The articles marked with an asterisk were never executed.]

We will now make a few remarks on the nature and subjects of the above works, which together form the whole system of the Baconian philosophy. The author, before commencing the construction of his edifice, begins by what may be called clearing the ground on which it is to stand. The treatise 'De Augmentis' is mainly a Latin version of an English book 'On the Proficience and Advancement of Learning,' which had appeared in 1605. It contains the outline of the whole system, and points out the defects perceptible in the methods previously employed in the investigation of truth. It would however be a great mistake to consider the 'De Augmentis' as a mere translation of the treatise just alluded to; it is in many respects almost a new work; not more than two-thirds of the whole being translated, while the remaining third contains the result of fresh speculations. Much, however, as the 'De Augmentis' is superior to its English predecessor, Bacon did not intend it, at least in the form under which we have it, to form the first treatise of the 'Instauratio.' That place was to be occupied by a book, 'De Partitionibus Scientiæ,' intended to exhibit the actual state of human knowledge when he wrote, and to show its deficiencies. This general summary of human science must therefore be considered, though not as altogether wanting in the 'Instauratio,' yet as but very imperfectly supplied by the treatise 'De Augmentis.'

The second part was to discuss, as he himself expresses it, "the science of a better and more perfect use of reason in the investigation of things, and of the true aids of the understanding;" this being the new logic, the inductive method, in which what is eminently called the Baconian philosophy conists. This is very well expressed in the title which the author has given to his work, "Organum" signifying literally "instrument." The treatise which we possess under the title of 'Novum Organum' is rather ι collection of materials for the work than the book itself, as Bacon intended it to stand second in his list. He calls it 'Partis Secundæ Summa, digesta in Aphorismos;' and it contains the heads or propositions of the projected work. It is subdivided into nine distinct portions, of which Bacon has given us the titles and the general object, though only the first of these subdivisions contains any development of the idea. The first of these treated of what in his picturesque language he calls "prerogative instances," that is, of what phenomena are to be selected for investigation, as most likely to conduce, by the speculations to which they give rise, to the advantage of the human species. This singular term "prærogative," is not used in the ordinary English sense of the same word, but contains an allusion to the "prærogativa centuria" of the Roman people, *i. e.* the first tribes whose votes were taken at the elections of the Comitia, and whose decision was supposed to influence the suffrages of the rest of the citizens. Of these instances fifteen are used to guide the intellect, five to assist the senses, and seven to correct the practice. And here we may remark a striking instance of Bacon's wonderful mind. In all former theories of logic we had been taught to detect and guard against certain fallacies or false reasonings, arising from a wrong employment of words or a vicious arrangement of the various parts of an argument. Bacon goes farther than this, and has tracked, so to say, these fallacies to their true origin—not in the abuse or imperfections of language, but to the innate weaknesses of the human mind itself. The former dialecticians, like inexperienced physicians, contented themselves with applying local or topical remedies to the external and merely symptomatic efflorescence of the disease, while Bacon, gifted with a larger spirit and a deeper insight into nature, attacks the evil in its internal and invisible source, not cleansing the surface only, but purifying the blood. He has classed the general causes of logical error under four heads, in a passage universally quoted for its brilliancy and truth. These errors of reasoning he calls *idola*, a term often rather absurdly rendered in English by the word "idols," but which would be much more correctly represented by the expression "images," or, as Bacon himself phrases it, "false appearances"—phantoms of the mind, in short. These are idola Tribûs, idola Specûs, idola Fori, and idola Theatri; against all of which it behoves us to be upon our guard. By fallacies of the Tribe, Bacon indicates the natural weaknesses to which every human being is liable; those of the Den or Cavern are the errors into which we are betrayed by peculiar dispositions and circumstances; the fallacies of the Market-place are those false conclusions arising from the popular and current use of words which represent things otherwise than as they really are; and the *idola* of the Theatre, the errors proceeding from false systems of philosophy and incorrect reasoning. It will be seen, from this as well as from a thousand other instances, how high is the ground on which Bacon philosophises, not merely attempting, as all before him had done, to regulate and correct the expression of reason, but aspiring to purify the very atmosphere of thought itself. To proceed with our analysis of the 'Novum Organum,' the second subdivision treats of the aids to induction; the third, of the correction of induction; the fourth, of varying the investigation according to the nature of the subject; fifthly, of prerogative natures — *i. e.* what objects shall be first inquired into; sixthly, of the boundaries of inquiry; seventhly, on the application of inquiry to practice, and what relates to man; eighthly, on the preparations (paraskeuis) for inquiry; and lastly, on the ascending and descending scale of axioms.

The third division of the 'Instauratio' was to contain a complete system of Natural History; not however of that science to which the name of Natural History is at present confined, but Bacon implies in that term an inquiry into the properties of all physical bodies, and a faithful and accurate register of all the phenomena that have ever been observed in man's dealing with natural substances. In the title given to this part of the work, 'Sylva Sylvarum,' Bacon probably used the word *sylva* in the sense which the ancient philosophers of the Epicurean school attached to it—a sense originating in the similar signification assigned to its Greek radical ὕλη, that is, primary matter, capable of being modified by a plastic force. It would be absurd to suppose that the outline here sketched in by Bacon could be filled up by any single hand, during any single life, in any age of mankind. He had previously published as a separate work his 'Centuries of Natural History,' containing about a thousand miscellaneous facts and experiments: and he has given a hundred and thirty particular histories which ought to be drawn up for this great work. A few of these he has given in a sort of skeleton, as samples rather of the method of collecting the facts than of the facts themselves; namely, the History of the Winds, of Life and Death, of Density and Rarity, of Sound and Hearing.

The fourth part, called 'Scala Intellectûs,' is also wanting, with the exception of a few introductory pages. "By these tables," says Bacon, "we mean not such examples as we subjoin to the several rules of our method, but types and models, which place before our eyes the entire process of the mind in the discovery of truth; selecting various and remarkable instances."

We now come to the fifth part of the 'Instauratio,' in which Bacon had designed to give a specimen of the new philosophy which he hoped to raise after a due use of his natural history and inductive method, by way of anticipation or sample of the whole. He calls it 'Prodromi sive Anticipationes Philosophiæ Secundæ;' and though the work does not exist as he projected it, we possess various fragments of this part under the titles of 'Cogitationes de Naturâ Rerum,' 'Cogitata et Visa,' 'Filum Labyrinthi,' and a few more; being probably all that he had reduced to writing. The last portion of Bacon's colossal plan was to be a perfect system of philosophy, deduced by a legitimate, sober, and exact inquiry according to the method whose principles he had established. This consummation, however, of his new system Bacon well knew was beyond his own mighty powers to execute; indeed he expresses his conviction that it was altogether beyond the sphere of human thought. "To perfect this last part is above our powers and beyond our hopes. We may, as we trust, make no despicable beginnings; the destinies of the human race must complete it—in such a manner perhaps, as men, looking only at the present, would not readily conceive. For upon this will depend, not only a speculative good, but all the fortunes of mankind, and all their power." "And with an eloquent prayer," continues Hallam, from whose excellent view of the Baconian philosophy the foregoing remarks are condensed—"with an eloquent prayer that his exertions may be rendered effectual to the attainment of truth and happiness, the introductory chapter of the 'Instauratio,' which announces the distribution of its portions, concludes. Such was the temple, of which Bacon saw in vision before him the stately front and decorated pediments, in all their breadth of light and harmony of proportion, while long vistas of receding columns and glimpses of internal splendour revealed a glory that it was not permitted to him to comprehend."

As the reader will easily conclude from the titles of the various parts of the 'Instauratio,' the work was (with the few exceptions specified above) published in Latin; the original conceptions of its immortal author having been translated, under his immediate inspection, by Herbert, Hobbes, and other persons, "masters of the Roman eloquence." The Latin style in which it is written is admirably adapted to the subject, and a worthy vehicle for such majestic conceptions; it is in a high degree concise, vigorous, and accurate, though by no means free from obscurity, and of course in no way to be considered as a model of pure Latinity. In reading Bacon, either in his vernacular or more learned dress, we feel perpetually conscious of a peculiarity, inevitably accompanying the highest genius in its manifestations:—we mean that in him the language seems always the flexible and obedient instrument of thought; not, as it is in the productions of a lower order of mind, its rebellious and recalcitrant slave. All authors below the greatest seem to use the mighty gift of expression with a certain secret timidity, lest the lever should prove too ponderous for the hand that essays to wield it: or, rather, they resemble the rash student in the old legend, who was overmastered by the demons which he had unguardedly evoked. There is, perhaps, no author so metaphorical as Bacon; his whole style is saturated with metaphor; the very titles of his books are frequently nothing else but metaphors of the boldest character; and yet there is not one of these figures of speech by which we do not gain a more vivid, clear, and rapid conception of the idea which he desires to convey. With him such expressions, however beautiful, are never merely ornamental: like some of the most exquisite decorations of Grecian and of Gothic architecture, what appears introduced into the design for the mere purpose of adornment will ever be found, when closely examined, to give strength and stability to the structure, of which it seems to inexperienced eyes a mere unessential and unnecessary adjunct.

It would be superfluous here to devote more than a passing notice to one objection which has been brought against the originality of the Baconian system of philosophy, and against the importance of the reformation which it produced in human science. The methods recommended by Bacon, say the objectors, have always been more or less in use from the very infancy of human knowledge. The art of induction, and of advancing from particular to general cases in the investigation of the laws of nature, was certainly employed and repeatedly insisted on long before the Verulamiam method was in existence. We have in another place strongly insisted on the absurdity of considering Bacon as an inventor in the proper sense of the word: what he did was not to teach us *a philosophy*, but to show us *how to philosophise*; and the immeasurable importance of what he did will best be appreciated by a simple comparison of the progress made in real knowledge during the twenty-two centuries which have elapsed since the time of Aristotle, and the acquisitions made in the two hundred and nineteen years since the death of Bacon.

It is quite true that Bacon, as he was not a discoverer in the art of investigating truth in general, so neither did he make any specific discoveries in any particular department of science. He was not a mathematician, nor an astronomer, nor a naturalist, nor a metaphysician; and in this respect we might be disposed to echo the ironical criticism of his contemporary Harvey, who, competent enough himself to perceive Bacon's deficiency in the practical and technical parts of natural science, complained that the author of the 'Instauratio' "wrote philosophy like a Lord Chancellor." No! the true obligation which the human race must ever feel, to the latest generations, to Bacon is that he did what no man else perhaps was ever sufficiently gifted to do; that, seated as it were on the pinnacle of his sublime genius, he saw distinctly, and mapped out accurately, all that can ever be an object of human investigation; that his far-darting and all-embracing intellectual vision took in at once the whole expanse of the domains of philosophy; nay, that it penetrated into the obscurity which brooded over the distant and unexplored regions of the vast country of the mind, and traced, with prophetic sagacity, the paths that must be followed by future discoverers, in ages yet unborn.

With his own notions on physical subjects, there were mingled many of the prejudices and erroneous ideas prevalent in his day; but such is the essential and invariable justness of the rules which he has laid down for the conduct of investigation, that these false conclusions may be swept away, and replaced by facts more accurately observed, without any weakening of the system which he originated. To apply the admirable comparison of Cowley, Bacon, though himself not free from the errors of his time, yet clearly foresaw the gradual disappearance of those errors:—

"Bacon, like Moses, led us forth at last:
The barren wilderness he pass'd
Did on the very border stand
Of the bless'd promis'd land,
And from the *Pisgah-height of his exalted wit*
Saw it himself and show'd us it."

At the same time, gifted as he was with "the vision and the faculty divine," by which he could thus anticipate centuries, and behold "not as through a glass darkly, but face to face," sciences which had no existence when he wrote, nothing is more admirable than the *common sense* which distinguished Bacon's divine intelligence. The ruling and vital principle, the very life-blood of the new philosophy, is the indispensable necessity of accurate and complete observation of nature, *anterior* and *preliminary* to any attempt at theorizing and drawing conclusions. Yet, though he was the apostle of experiment, he has no less foreseen and warned us against the ill effects that would follow the rash generalization founded upon particular and imperfect observation — effects which have been very perceptible in modern science, and which have tended to give to the knowledge of later days an air of superficiality little less dangerous than the more visionary and sophistical tone which characterizes the ancient systems.

But above all, what strikes us as the most admirable peculiarity of Bacon's philosophy is the spirit of *utility* which runs through and modifies the whole design. We do not mean utility in the low and limited sense of a care for the development of man's merely physical comforts and advantages; the exercise and cultivation of the highest faculties of our being, the enlarging of our sphere of intellectual pleasures, the strengthening of our moral obligations, the refining and elevating of our perception of the beautiful — all these Bacon has treated, and would have exhausted, had they not been as infinite as the soul itself. On many of these subjects — on the *beau idéal*, for example — it will be hardly too much to say that he has left nothing for future speculators.

Another peculiarity which we cannot forbear noticing, as forming one of the striking features of Bacon's intellectual character, is the circumstance that his writings will not be found in any high degree *apophthegmatic*: that is, the reader will not be likely to meet with many of those short, extractable, and easily remembered sentences, or *gnomai*, which pass from mouth to mouth as weighty maxims, or separate masses of truth — the gold coins, if we may so style them of the intellectual exchange. Many such are undoubtedly to be found in his pages, but they are certainly less plentiful in Bacon than in other great writers; but we shall generally find these passages so embedded and fixed in the argument of which such propositions form a part, as not to be extracted without manifest loss to their value and significancy. In consequence of this, Bacon is one of those authors who must be *read through* to be correctly judged and worthily appreciated. Nor will any aspiring and truly generous mind begrudge the labour which will attend this exercise of the highest faculties with which God has endowed it; it is surely no mean privilege to be thus admitted into the laboratory and workshop of the new philosophy, and to behold—no indifferent spectator—the sublime alchemy by which experience is transmuted into truth.

Among the minor works of the illustrious Chancellor it may not be improper to mention two or three of the principal. We shall specify, first, a very curious treatise 'On the Wisdom of the Ancients,' being an attempt to explain the classical mythology, by a system of moral and political interpretation, much less founded on probability than calculated to elevate, in our eyes, the degree of knowledge possessed by the pagan world. The following is the judgment, respecting this work, attributed to Balzac, from one of whose letters it is supposed to be a quotation: "Croyons donc, pour l'amour du Chancelier Bacon, que toutes les folies des anciens sont sages, et tous leurs songes mystères; et de celles-là qui sont estimées pures fables, il n'y en a pas une, quelque bizarre et extravagante qu'elle soit, qui n'ait son fondement dans l'histoire, si l'on en veut croire Bacon, et qui n'ait été déguisée de la sorte par les sages du vieux temps, pour la rendre plus utile aux peuples." Another work is entitled the 'Felicities of the Reign of Queen Elizabeth;' and a third is a production of greater importance, a 'History of King Henry VII.,' written probably in a courtly desire to gratify King James, who was, as everybody knows, ambitious of the reputation of the pacific glories of a wise and tranquil administrator, and whose character in this respect would find a flattering parallel in the unwarlike reign of the politic Henry. Besides these, he is the author of a philosophical fiction entitled 'The New Atlantis.'

The glory of Bacon, as he himself had predicted, rose gradually but steadily on the literary horizon of Europe. It may however be complained (and this is not a circumstance to be wondered at) that his works were often rather vaguely eulogized than accurately studied: the profound nature of their subject, and the vastness of their design, were likely to have much limited the number of their readers; and in consequence many erroneous opinions became prevalent, not only respecting the true value of the Baconian revolution in science, but even respecting the nature of the system itself. It is unnecessary to say, that what the great philosopher gained in this way from vague and unintelligent praise he lost in true glory, which can only be founded on justice. It was reserved for various illustrious metaphysicians of the Scottish school "to turn," in Hallam's words, "that which had been a blind veneration into a rational worship." These profound and elegant writers, Reid, Stewart, Robison, and Playfair, by clothing the philosophy of Bacon in the language of the nineteenth century, have deprived it of whatever repulsive and difficult features it may have retained from its being written in a dead language, and from its somewhat complicated arrangement and subdivisions; while some of the greatest among modern experimental philosophers have been proud to draw, from practical observations and more recent improvements of astronomy and other branches of physics, new illustrations of the justness of Bacon's predictions, new conclusions clearing up obscure passages, and new proofs of the truth of his system. It is delightful to see experiment thus the willing handmaid of theory, and Herschel paying practical worship at the shrine of Bacon.

CHAPTER V.

ORIGIN OF THE ENGLISH DRAMA.

Comparison between the Greek and Mediæval Dramas — Similarity of their Origin—Illusion in the Drama—Mysteries or Miracle-Plays—Their Subject and Construction — Moralities — The Vice — Interludes — The Four P.'s — First Regular Dramas—Comedies—Tragedies—Early English Theatres — Scenery—Costume—State of the Dramatic Profession.

THERE are very few æsthetic subjects upon which more controversy has been raised than upon the respective merits of various schools of the Drama: and certainly there are not many which have excited more critical asperity than the long-vexed question as to the comparative merits of the two great dramatic schools, to which Schlegel has assigned the not inapposite titles of Classical and Romantic. But both parties seem to have forgotten the similar origin and history of the two schools which they represent as so different, nay, even as so opposed; and to have pretty generally overlooked the important fact that the peculiarities of structure which respectively characterise the two classes of productions, so falsely considered as *antagonistic*, are really not essential or inherent, but arise from merely technical or superficial circumstances. Thus, for example, the Greek tragic drama was originally a religious ceremony, and, however modified, never entirely lost that sacred character. The personages of the Attic stage were almost always to a certain degree mythic: that is, they were almost invariably *heroic;* invested, either by antiquity, by the greatness of their exploits, or their immediate relations with the deities, with something of a religious character; and it is easily conceivable that, with such a people as the Greeks, the boundary-line between the god and the hero was not very distinctly traced: Theseus, for instance, was very little less a god than Hermes, and Apollo very little more divine than Orestes; there were indeed many characters, frequently produced on the Athenian stage, who, like Hercules, obviously partook of the two qualities. Thus the Attic tragedy always retained a good deal of the historico-mythic character—a character which pervaded even the technical details of its construction, performance, and *mise en scène.*

Indiscriminate admiration, however, has discovered beauties in merely accidental and unimportant peculiarities, and has attempted to derive from the necessary laws of art rules which were founded upon circumstance or convenience. Thus, because the Greek theatres were of colossal dimensions, and consequently uncovered, enthusiastic critics have discovered beauty and grandeur in the contrivances employed to exaggerate the size of the actor and increase the sound of his voice:—because their construction, and also the imperfection of the arts of mechanism, together also perhaps with some prejudices connected with the gravity and even sacredness of these spectacles, precluded them from changing the scene, attempts have been made to prove that the fixed scene—or unity of place—is an essential law of the dramatic art, and that consequently the modern plays are necessarily and demonstrably barbarous. It is exceedingly curious to observe with what ingenuity the so-called classical critics have defended the adherence to the Three Unities in dramatic composition. Their reasoning has all along been founded upon the supposition, that in the dramatic art the source of pleasure is to be found in *illusion,* and that consequently the preservation of the unities is necessary. Now, we will not maintain in this place the very false and low view of the true nature and object of art involved in this supposition; we will not show its fallacy when applied to painting, to music, to sculpture, or show that illusion — or rather *delusion,* a cheating of the senses—is never at all contemplated in works of any degree of excellence; we will not repeat the obvious fact that illusion, properly so called, never was and never can be attained, or even approximatively reached, in any dramatic work whatever, and that, even could it be attained, the result would be precisely subversive of the only conceivable end of the drama, viz. the production of pleasure We will go at once to the point, and say that this principle of illusion, as an object to be attained by the dramatist, was never at all recognised by the Greeks themselves. It is true that the Apollo or the Venus might be rendered by a coating of rose-pink much more like a man and a woman; but the object of the sculptor was to elevate and gratify our imagination, and not to cheat our eye. Had the latter been the aim of sculpture, a wax doll would be a finer production than the noblest marble that ever breathed under the chisel of Phidias.

We have only to read a Greek play to see that nothing can be less artificial as a contrivance for producing mere illusion. The formality and regularity of the language, the simple and straightforward character of the dialogue, the lyric portion or chorus, written in a different dialect and more splendid imagery than the rest of the work, the total neglect of probability and even possibility in the arrangement of the events, time and space perpetually annihilated, and every conceivable rule of human conduct and prudence incessantly violated—all these things sufficiently prove to us that the great Greek dramatists never so much as contemplated the possibility of producing what we call illusion.

No man, we flatter ourselves, ever admired more fervently than we do the admirable genius and exquisite taste which characterise the Greek tragedies: their dignity, their pathos, the wonderful depth and acuteness of the remarks with which they are crowded, the dazzling splendour of the lyric portions so nobly contrasted with the pure marble-like severity of the dialogue, the rich descriptions (put into the mouth of the messenger in most of them) of the terrible catastrophe with which they conclude, and which the Greeks did not permit to take place on the stage, from a scruple founded, we are persuaded, not on a principle of taste, but of religion—these are merits which we can allow with enthusiastic readiness; but they are merits very distinct from that principle of illusion which has been considered as having guided the mighty art of Æschylus, of Sophocles, and of Euripides.

If we examine into the early history of that Romantic Drama which has become universal over the whole of modern Europe, and which has in our own century finally expelled the so-called Classicism from its last entrenchments on the stage of France, we shall see how singularly its origin and first development resembled the rise of the Grecian Tragedy. Both species of composition were at first purely religious; both were performed on solemn occasions in temples; both were distinguished for the simplicity of their structure, and for a total neglect of the much-vaunted principle of illusion; both were accompanied by a certain proportion of lyric declamation, executed by a number of persons who occupied a middle or intermediate position between the principal dramatic characters on the stage (the protagonists) and the audience who witnessed the solemn show.

The food, the *pabulum*, of the dramatic art was in the two cases as different as were the religion, the manners, the modes of thought and action at the two periods which we have thus contrasted. The Greek dramatist drew his materials from the rich storehouse of pagan mythology, the black annals of his ancient kings, and the legends of his national heroes: in these he found ample materials for his scenes; and the whole was bound together by one pervading principle, in the highest degree moving and sublime—the over-ruling and incessant action of the dramatic fate. These grand and awful events were familiar to the audience from their infancy; they were calculated to gratify to the highest degree the national vanity and patriotic enthusiasm: every Athenian felt himself the countryman, many the descendants, of Theseus or of Œdipus; and when we reflect upon the intensity of the patriotism which characterised the citizens of the little republics of Greece, together with the delicate sense of the beautiful which seemed peculiarly innate in the Hellenic character, we shall find that their dramatists were as amply provided with materials for their art as with rewards for its triumphant exercise.

In the Middle Ages the external manifestations of the art were all changed, but the art itself remained the same. The rude populations of chivalric Europe, the serfs of England, France, and Germany, could have felt but very imperfectly any sentiments addressed to their patriotism. Ignorant, barbarous, and oppressed, how could men love their country, who could not call their wives and children their own? How could men, reduced to a mere brutish state of animal obedience, feel their hearts swell within them at the mimic representation of great exploits? As to the mere abstract perception of the beautiful, such a feeling could not exist in their minds. What strings were left in the human heart undeadened and capable of responding to the touch of genius? We answer, the sense of wonder. Catholicism, with all its miracles, its legends, its enthusiasm, had supplanted the paganism of classical antiquity. We are not inclined to consider the credulity of the ancients, at least at the period when the Greek drama reached its highest pitch of splendour, as very deeply seated, or likely to modify very profoundly the character of the Athenian people. Their credulity was rather of the *imagination;* that of the Middle Ages was of the *heart.* What a difference between the airy grace and sensuous allegory of the pagan mythology, where belief was merely a matter of assent, involving no practical change of conduct, and offering no promises, or very faint ones, of a future existence, with that deep, all-pervading, and solemn religion which offered to the oppressed serf of the Middle Ages his only consolation in this life, together with his mighty hope and onlooking to the next! The very superstitions, too, of the time, the huge mass of striking and yet fantastic imagery which composed a world of legend, exhibit an example of the fact that in depriving the human mind of some of its senses (as takes place in those of the body) we only add intensity and power to those we leave behind.

The religious dramas of the Middle Ages were nothing but an embodiment of Christianity as it appeared to the simple imagination of those rude times. They were often little else but the narration of some biblical or legendary miracle, rudely dramatised, and often in the language of Scripture. They are supposed to have originated in the recitals of pilgrims, returning from their long wanderings in distant and unknown lands with an abundant stock of wonders, perilous adventures and hair-breadth 'scapes, gorgeous descriptions of the magnificence of the East, enthralling tales of persecution and wild idolatries. With these the "palmer graye" would collect a crowd about him, and keep his simple hearers listening with unwearied wonder hour after hour; just as the professed tale-teller of the East enchants his grave and bearded audience in the coffee-houses of Damascus, or the ragged improvvisatore of Naples enchains his circle of boatmen and lazzaroni. That such tales should have by degrees taken a dramatic form is not surprising; still less so that the Church should have very soon perceived the efficacy of such representations, not only as instruments of instruction for the people, but also as a means for extending the authority of the priesthood, and increasing the revenues of the ecclesiastical institutions. The people were unable to read, and their ideas respecting the Scriptural history were exceedingly imperfect; and the priests of the Middle Ages were far too well acquainted with the human heart not to know the truth of the Horatian precept—

> "Segniùs irritant animum demissa per aures,
> Quàm quæ sunt oculis submissa fidelibus."

The Church therefore encouraged, as far as possible, the strong taste early developed for the religious dramas, viewing them as at once a powerful medium of religious instruction, and as an inexhaustible source of profit and influence; and we find them used as a very important mechanism for raising the immense sums destined to the support of the crusades. At first they were of a purely religious character; the subjects were always either events of the biblical history itself, or else extracts from the legends of the saints. The representation of these dramas was very early taken, by the profound policy of the hierarchy, out of the hands of the laity; and the performance was carried on in the church itself, the actors being priests, and the splendour of the spectacle augmented by the use of the rich vestments and ornaments of the clergy.

Here we may clearly see the singular resemblance existing between the Greek tragedy and the religious plays of the Middle Ages. Both were performed in a sacred spot; the subjects of both were drawn from what was considered, at the respective periods, to be most holy and venerable; both were placed before the spectator with the greatest magnificence attainable; and the spirit of mingled patriotism and religion, which it was the object of the Greek theatre to excite, was certainly little inferior in intensity to the credulous and simple awe with which the rude audiences of Catholic times must have witnessed the great mysteries of their religion represented before the altar of a cathedral. In fact, we cannot but remark that the very name of this species of spectacle is strongly corroborative of the truth of our parallel; they were called "*mysteries*" and "*miracles.*" Even the division of the stage recalls something of the rigour and complexity of the Greek scene: it was divided into three platforms; the upper being reserved for the appearance of God, angels, and glorified spirits; the next below it, to the human personages of the drama; and the lowest, devoted to the devils, being a representation of the yawning mouth of hell — the "alta ostia Ditis"—a black and gloomy cavern, vomiting flames and sulphureous smoke, through which incessantly ascended the howling of the damned, and by which the evil spirits made their exits and their entrances, rising to tempt and torture humanity, or plunging back with the bodies of their victims. In all these peculiarities it is impossible not to be struck with the resemblance between the drama of the Middle Ages and that of classical antiquity. Nor can we fail to remark the innumerable traces left by the religious dramas upon the art of this period. The much-agitated question of the meaning of the singular title given by Dante to his great work could hardly have been raised had the critics remembered that the *commedia* of the "gran padre Alighier" is nothing else but a *mystery* in a narrative form; and that the three divisions of Hell, Purgatory, and Paradise correspond exactly with the three stages of the religious dramas.

The subjects of these dramas were generally taken from the most striking and pathetic passages of the Bible history: the Creation, the Deluge, the Fall of Man, the Sacrifice of Abraham, the Massacre of the Innocents, the Crucifixion; no subject appears to have been too solemn or too vast for the attempt of this bold but barbarous art. They never shrank from introducing upon the stage the most sublime personages; the Deity himself, the Saviour, the patriarchs, all figure in these singular dramas. They seem not to have felt that species of awe which would now prevent an author from presenting, in a visible form, such impersonations—an attempt which not even the genius of Goethe could succeed in rendering successful. At such early periods, when the critical faculty had not yet dried up in man the springs of wonder and belief, there could have been neither real nor imaginary disrespect in this freedom. They followed as closely as they could the march, and even the language, of the Scriptural narration, and would probably have felt it as derogatory to the dignity of their subject to omit any detail of the Bible history, as we should find it dangerous, or even reprehensible, to follow those details with too great a fidelity.

These compositions were for the most part written, as might be expected, in the popular metre of the various countries which produced them: for it must not be forgotten that such representations were the favourite amusement of mankind in all the countries of Europe during a very long period. Germany, France, Italy, Portugal, and Spain—in short, there is not any country which does not possess a large collection of these singular productions.

They were sometimes of inordinate length, and in many cases lasted even several days: there is one in existence, on the subject of the Creation, which occupied in the performance a period as long as the event which it represented, and consequently the spectators of this mystery gratified their wonder during a period of six successive days. We may inquire how the authors of these productions could have succeeded in introducing any thing ludicrous and comic into dramas whose principal action was so solemn and supernatural. Ludicrous scenes, however, they were obliged to have; for the people were in far too rude a state to be able to sit listening for so long a time to purely religious and moral declamation. To attain this end they hit upon the happy expedient of making the *Devil* the never-failing comic character in those cases where the nature of the subject precluded the possibility of introducing a mere human buffoon. The devil was the butt and clown of the performance, and, being generally represented in a light at once terrific and contemptible, this circumstance has probably originated the very curious part played in the popular legends by the Father of Evil. The malignant spirits, in all systems of mythology and popular belief, with the single exception of Christianity, are presented in colours darkly and tremendously sublime, and certainly their agency is never represented as accompanied by circumstances in any way mean or ridiculous. Christianity, however, the vital principle of which is the victory of truth over the powers of evil, has originated the popular character of a malicious and ugly fiend, whose machinations are defeated by a very moderate degree of ingenuity and address. How far the obscurer superstitions of paganism which still remained in the popular imagination may have conduced to this curious anomaly, it is not at present our object to inquire: it is not improbable that it arose in some measure from an ancient belief, propagated by many of the Christian fathers, that the deities of the various pagan mythologies were in reality evil spirits allowed for a time to mislead and delude the human race; and also the first propagators of Christianity, finding the notions of polytheism so deeply and ineradicably implanted in the mind of man, contented themselves with representing as malignant the nature of those beings whose existence they could not disprove, and were probably themselves very little inclined to deny. The devil, therefore, of popular belief—not the haughty and beautiful creation of Milton, but the hideous demon, the "lubber fiend," of Ariosto, with his horns and hoofs and tail—was the comic character of the mysteries; to which, wherever possible, they added other buffoons of a like ludicrous colour, generally selected among the wicked human personages of the drama. Thus, in the miracle-play of the 'Massacre of the Innocents,' the satellites of Herod—his *knights* as they are called with a laughable anachronism, and who are represented as swearing by "Mahound," or Mahomet—are exposed to the alternate laughter and detestation of the audience. Nor did these old authors neglect those broad and general subjects of satire presented by human weaknesses, and which are found in the writings of all periods. The quarrels of matrimony, and the miseries undergone by henpecked husbands, as they are subjects of all ages, and "come home to the business and bosoms of men," have excited the laughter of mankind in every epoch: undoubtedly there were scolding wives before the flood, but it is curious to see a virago forming one of the "dramatis personæ" in a miracle-play on the subject of the Deluge. In the very singular drama to which we have just alluded, "Noe's Wif" is a character of a purely comic nature, and is represented, in a scene by no means devoid of coarse drollery, as refusing to enter the ark unless she is allowed to bring with her "her gossips every one," whom she swears (*by St. John!*) that she loves with great affection. In a German mystery, which we believe has been printed, Cain and Abel are introduced as examined by the Almighty, in the presence of Adam, as to their proficiency in the "Lord's Prayer." Abel is prompted by our Saviour, and gets through his task pretty respectably; but Cain, who is secretly instigated by the devil standing behind him to say the prayer backwards, is very properly and condignly flogged, having previously received divers cuffs from his father for refusing to take his hat off! We see, therefore, that the humour of these pieces, however natural and *enjoué*, was of no very refined character; the pathetic passages, it is fair to add, sometimes reach a high degree of excellence. In an English mystery on the subject of Abraham's sacrifice, the scene between the father and the son is exceedingly tender and beautiful, and the speech of Isaac, in particular, of very great merit. In short, these works show that the heart of man, however imperfect be his civilization, has always some chords which vibrate responsive to the touch of nature.

We have hitherto been speaking of the mystery or miracle-play in its pure and original form, as a representation exclusively religious in its subject and in the mode and place of its performance. It will now be our business to trace, as rapidly as possible, the changes by which it was gradually transformed into the romantic drama of modern times. It may easily be conceived that so favourite and so profitable a species of entertainment as the stage could not long be monopolised by the Church. In the mind of man there has ever been an inherent taste for dramatic impersonations; there is no age so rude, no country so barbarous, as not to possess some amusement of a dramatic nature; indeed, it may be said that the very rudeness of an age is itself a measure of what may be called its dramatic sensibility. Children, as we see, are perpetually acting; and the childhood of nations is like that of individuals; at that period the imagination is in the highest degree excitable, while at the same time the judgment and the comparing faculty are not yet developed.

The mysteries then, from being a purely religious exhibition, gradually degenerated into the moralities, a species of entertainment which is one step farther towards the embodiment of imaginary personages. In these pieces the historical or theological characters of the Scripture were supplanted by personifications of abstract qualities —the virtues, the vices, the sentiments of human nature. In the morality, instead of Moses, of Adam, of the Holy Spirit, we have Justice, Mercy, Temperance, Folly, Gluttony, and Vice. In fact, this last character, whose language and costume were ludicrous, enters into the composition of every morality as the clown or buffoon. We are not, however, to suppose that the devil was dismissed: in spite of the less religious character of the morality as compared with the mystery, Satan was far too droll a personage to be thus cashiered — he is retained; and the greater part of the comic scenes consist of dialogues between the Devil and the Vice, the latter of whom is generally represented as baffling and beating his infernal antagonist, who, however, sometimes enjoys his revenge, and carries off the Vice at the end of the piece. It should be remembered that the Vice was habited in the motley, and wore the coxcomb, of the jester of this period, and armed with the wooden sword which figures on the stage even down to the present day as the wand of Harlequin.

Indeed, Harlequin himself, and that other pleasant Italian, Pulcinella — the universal type, under some name or other, of popular drollery and satire—are supposed by the learned to trace their pedigree to the moralities of the Middle Ages: so few in number are the forms under which the human mind embodies its creations. The old Italian comedy, the ancient Spanish comedy, in fact all the dramatic types of modern Europe, bear indisputable traces of a very high antiquity indeed; nay, some antiquaries have even gone so far as to see in Arlecchino, in Pulcinella, in the clown of the English stage, and in the Gracioso of the Spanish, the principal characters of the Atellan farces, which the Romans laughed at so heartily, and, not stopping even here, have considered this pleasant family of drolls as representing various personages in the celebration of the mysteries of Eleusis, and the yet remoter worship of the Cabiri!

The subjects of the moralities were, as the name implies, of an ethical nature, intended to inculcate principles of virtue; and however imperfect, as a means of exciting sympathy and interest in the spectator, were the cold impersonations of abstract ideas which composed their "dramatis personæ," these works are by no means deficient either in ingenuity of plot, or in the occasionally skilful delineation of character. They were generally performed either by students at the universities, or by the great municipal bodies in towns, to celebrate some solemn festival, or to do honour to some exalted personage. In the former case they were often in Latin; and in the latter—that is, when produced by the members of the trades, *mestiers*, or craft-corporations of the cities — they were either acted on a temporary stage erected in the open air, or on a moving platform on wheels; thus forming part of those splendid processions of which we read so much.

Among the more remarkable of these compositions which have come down in the English language to our times, it will be necessary merely to cite the titles of two or three; as the name of the piece will give us in general a pretty good idea of its subject and contents. 'Lusty Juventus,' in which the hero, a personification of the abstract idea of youth, is seduced by the various passions and vices, and protected by the opposing virtues. Other examples will be found in 'Impatient Poverty,' 'Hit the Nail on the Head,' 'The Hog hath lost his Pearl,' &c. &c. These moralities imperceptibly merged into another species of drama, less ambitious in its construction, less regular in its plot, and admitting a good deal more drollery and humour. These were the interludes, which formed a favourite entertainment in the days of Henry VIII., and which were much shorter and of a much merrier character than the solemn and scholastic morality. Of these a noted and most prolific author was John Heywood, a sort of jester at the court of the king just mentioned, and whose wild farces exhibit extraordinary powers of humour and even wit. Heywood was an enthusiastic Catholic, and his rude dramas bear innumerable marks of that great war of polemics and ridicule which preceded the Reformation. In times of religious dissension, every province of literature, even the least fitted to be made the scene of religious warfare, is invaded by the contests of theology; and a complete collection might be made of moralities and interludes of this time, written to maintain the opinions of the Catholics on one side, and of the Reformers on the other, in which plentiful volleys of ridicule and abuse are directed by the author against the partisans of the opposite Church. As the name implies, the interlude is properly a short dramatic scene, intended to be performed in the intervals of some greater ceremony or festival. It was originally represented in the pauses unavoidably occurring during the representation of the solemn morality, or, as a kind of *entr'acte*, in the vacant intervals which frequently took place in the long festivities of the Middle Ages. It is thus that at the present day dramatic representations are introduced in China to enliven the guests between the courses of their interminable banquets; and the interlude, we know, was frequently performed in the great halls of our ancestors on festival occasions. These representations were almost always of a broadly comic character, and were frequently, like the satiric dramas of the Attic stage, a species of parody or burlesque upon the graver action of the piece in the intervals of which they were performed. One of the drollest of these dramatic caricatures is entitled 'The Four P's:' it is in a rude kind of jingling, doggrel verse, and represents a species of match made by its four interlocutors—the four P's, from whence it takes its title—a pedler, a pilgrim, a 'poticary, and a pardoner—as to who can tell the greatest lie: after a good deal of astonishing mendacity, the pardoner asserts, as if accidentally, that he never saw a woman out of temper; and this being unanimously agreed to be the greatest lie ever heard, the prize is awarded to the assertor of so tremendous a falsehood.

It is obvious that the dramatic art was now upon the very verge of the regular Comedy and Tragedy; and the process of gradual improvement can be traced no farther from the allegorical personages of the morality to the creation of specific human characters and the representing of actual human life. We have now reached the period of the first regular comedies, properly so called; the excellence of which, it is but proper to remark, was such as to give noble earnest of the splendid triumphs in this way of writing which the English literature was destined afterwards to achieve. Probably in the reign of Henry VIII., but certainly not later than 1551, Nicholas Udall produced his 'Ralph Royster Doyster,' the first comedy in the language, in which the ingenuity of the plot, the nature of the characters, and the ease of the dialogue are all carried to a high degree of perfection. The dramatis personæ are all taken from middle life, and the play gives us a most admirable picture of the manners of the citizens of London at this period. It is written in a very loose and conversational species of rhymed couplet, and was probably performed by the scholars of Westminster, of which school the author was master. About ten years afterwards we meet with another comedy, long supposed to have been the earliest in the language: this is 'Gammer Gurton's Needle,' and is a rich piece of rustic drollery, the plot turning upon the loss of a needle with which Gammer (*commère?*) Gurton was mending the breeches of her man Hodge, and which loss is attributed by a beggar — the clever and rascally *intrigant* of the piece — to the dishonesty of a neighbour, between whom and Mistress Gurton there occurs a most admirable scolding scene. After a considerable period of consternation, misunderstanding, and quarrelling in all quarters (for we must think that a needle at this period, and in a remote village, was a serious loss), and after we have been amused with Hodge's terrors in a scene where the Beggar proceeds to call up the Devil in order to discover the needle, the missing article is found, sticking in the breeches, by Hodge, who roars out with mingled pain and delight when its prick announces the recovery of the long-lost little implement. This droll production is full of a real *verve* and rude richness of language, and the characters are delineated with broad strokes of truth and a rustic animation. It was the work of John Still, who ultimately became Bishop of Bath and Wells, and was probably acted at the university. Its versification — for it is, like its predecessor, in rhyme — is rather more loose and irregular than that of 'Ralph Royster Doyster,' and is an excellent vehicle for the rustic shrewdness and broad humour which distinguish it. This curious play has been compared to the famous comedy of 'Patelin,' which was one of the earliest comic efforts of the French stage, but we think the English piece superior in point of vigour and naturalness.

While comedy, as we have just seen, appears to have made a very striking and rapid advance in this period of English literature, it is singular enough that the earliest tragedies in our language should exhibit all the poverty, stiffness, and formality of manner consequent upon a close imitation of the classic models. The early dramatic authors, although they had sense and taste enough to look for the materials of their *comedy* into the abundant mine of oddity and humour offered by the domestic life of their own country, did not venture, in their *tragic* delineations, to cast off the rigid yoke of classic form and precedent. The tragedy of 'Ferrex and Porrex,' written by Thomas Sackville, afterwards Earl of Dorset, and Thomas Norton, was acted by the students of the Inner Temple before Queen Elizabeth in the year 1561. It is considered to be the earliest tragedy in the language. Its subject is founded upon a legend of the almost fabulous epochs of British history, and the leading incident resembles that of the story of Eteocles and Polynices, which has again been repeated by Schiller in his 'Braut von Messina;' a tale, singularly enough, found in the annals of various nations and distinct periods. 'Ferrex and Porrex' exhibits in all its details a servile adherence to the technical forms of the classic drama, in the fewness of the persons, the uniform gravity and philosophic stateliness of the language, and, above all, in the retention of the chorus. Nothing can be more striking than the contrast between the formal solemnity of the dialogue of this play—the perpetual severity of the style—the apophthegms with which it is crowded—

"Dry chips of short-lung'd Seneca—"

the intense care to preserve a tone of regal dignity which prevails throughout the work, and the freedom, richness, and idiomatic humour which distinguish the comedies written previous to its appearance—qualities which were afterwards recalled to tragedy by the great authors of the Shakspearian school.

After 'Ferrex and Porrex' we pass rapidly over a long list of works all more or less characterised by the same classical stiffness and adherence to dramatic dignity, and which were in almost every case either direct adaptations from other languages, or, when founded upon events in the early history of the country, always composed upon the same classical models. After enumerating a few of them we will proceed to give an idea of the mechanism of the theatres at the dawning of our dramatic literature, and the general condition of the art previous to the appearance of Shakspeare:—'Damon and Pythias,' written by Richard Edwards, and acted at Oxford in 1566; the comedy of 'The Supposes,' taken from 'I Suppositi' of Ariosto, and 'Jocasta,' a tragedy, imitated from Euripides; 'Tancred and

Gismunda,' acted in 1568; 'Promos and Cassandra,' ten years afterwards, written by George Whetstone; and a number of historical plays, as 'The Troublesome Reign of King John,' 'The Famous Victories of Henry V.,' 'The Chronicle History of Leir, King of England,' and a multitude of others, chiefly valuable as being the mine from which Shákspeare afterwards extracted his materials. These works were generally performed before the court, and must be considered as the first rude and imperfect essays of that grandest dramatic school which forms the chief literary glory of the reigns of Elizabeth and James I.

It is singular to remark that, while the theatres of this period were of the rudest construction and the appliances for producing the illusion of the scene were yet in a most imperfect state, the dramatic profession should have numbered in its ranks men who carried their art to a pitch of splendour which succeeding ages have neither equalled nor approached. It seems as though the very insufficiency of the material contrivances only tended to make these great men rely upon their own genius to produce impressions upon the imagination of their audience more vivid and intense than the rude theatre of the time could hope to make upon their senses. The actors of this time, who were in many cases dramatic authors also, generally associated themselves into a sort of joint-stock company, and either travelled about the country, performing in the houses of the nobility, and for the amusement of the people on temporary stages in the yards of inns, or established themselves in some of the numerous theatres of London. These latter buildings, though erected expressly for the performance of plays, retained many peculiarities traceable to the custom of acting in inns. They were uncovered, excepting over the stage; and the scenery, if it deserves the name, was of the rudest description, and consisted generally, till the time of Davenant at the Restoration, of nothing but a few curtains of tapestry or painted canvas, suspended so as to give the actors the power of making their exit and entrance, as if into a room, square, forest, street, &c. As the Elizabethan dramas are remarkable for the frequent supposed changes of scene which take place in them, the spot presented to the audience was indicated by the simplest expedient; a placard was fixed to one of the curtains, bearing the name of the city or country supposed, and this placard was changed for another at a change of scene: if, for example, the action was to be imagined in Padua, an inscription with the word "Padua" was suspended in view of the audience; should the scene be supposed to take place in a palace, a throne and canopy, called a "state," would be pushed forward; if in a tavern, the production of a table with bottles and glasses upon it —if in a court, a combination of the "state," with a table bearing pens and ink, were all that was necessary to give the hint or suggestion to the imaginative minds of an Elizabethan audience. We know, from innumerable passages of the old dramatists, that it was customary for the "gallants," dandies, or *raffinés* of the period, to sit during the performance on chairs placed on the stage in full view of the audience, smoking their pipes and exhibiting the splendour of their dress, and scrupling not to criticise aloud the drama which was going forward—a circumstance which must have still further injured the *probability* of the scene. At the back of the stage was erected a species of balcony or scaffolding of various platforms, on which appeared the persons who were supposed to speak from a window, from the wall of a besieged city, and so forth; and there were also permanent projections in various parts of the stage, behind which the actors might retire, in order unobserved to overhear and see what was going on—a dramatic expedient so much used in the theatre of every country and period.

It must not be forgotten, by any one who desires to form a correct idea of the Elizabethan stage, that the female parts were acted by boys, no woman having appeared as a performer in England until the Restoration, when the possibility that the other sex could represent fictitious characters seems first to have been demonstrated in Italy, whence the example was rapidly followed in England and elsewhere. This circumstance is calculated to immeasurably increase our wonder and admiration at Shakspeare's genius, the profoundest, most delicate, and most inimitable of whose delineations are often his female characters, and who has never fallen into that coarseness of allusion and indulgence in *double entendre* which defiles the scenes of even the greatest of his illustrious contemporaries. Mean as was the scenery of the Elizabethan theatre, it would be an error to suppose that the dresses were in the same degree poor and unvaried. The actors appear to have exhibited great splendour of personal decoration, wearing, in plays of all ages and countries, the costume of their own time and nation—a costume, however, the anachronisms of which were not likely to have greatly shocked the uncritical audiences of the day. It is true that the universal employment, on the stage, of a contemporary costume has led many of the authors into the commission of trifling breaches of chronological or geographical correctness, giving, in Massinger, *watches* to Spartan senators, and arming Romans with the Spanish rapier of the sixteenth century; but, after all, the importance of such errors is in general much overrated by the critics, and they make but little impression upon the truly imaginative and excitable spectator, who seldom stops to verify dates and judge the niceties of costume. Be this as it may, the manly, graceful, and splendid costume of the reign of Elizabeth appears to have been generally employed, as it still is retained (in our opinion with great propriety) in all those plays of imaginative character, the scene and age of whose supposed action is incapable of being strictly assigned and particularised.

The literary and even the personal career of most of the great dramatists of this period is in many respects so much the same, and also tends in so great a degree to throw light upon the true character of their works, that we will make a few general remarks on this subject before entering into any critical or biographical details: by so doing also we hope to give a clearer notion of our national stage at this vigorous and brilliant period of its existence. The immortal men who have illustrated this portion of our literature were, in a great majority of cases, persons of academical education—in some instances, as in those of Ben Jonson and Chapman, they were distinguished for their learning, even in a learned age. In a multitude of instances, too, they were young men of violent passions and desperate fortune, who rushed up to the capital from their academic retirement of Oxford or Cambridge, and thought to find in the theatre the source of a rapid and turbid glory, and perhaps the means for indulging, with little exertion to themselves, in the riotous pleasures of the town, elevated the while by the spirit of freedom and intellect which prevailed in the theatrical circle. They almost all of them began their career as actors, and it is to this circumstance that we must attribute some of the peculiar excellences of their way of writing. It made them consummate masters of what is called "stage-effect," the art of placing their characters in the most striking and picturesque situations, though at the same time it tended to increase that taste for violent exaggeration and inconsistent passion which forms one of their evident defects. They were not calm, contemplative scholars, building up, in the silence of their study, structures of elaborate and artificial character; but *men*—active, suffering, enjoying *men;* who had mingled in the serious business of life, and painted its smiles and its tears, its grandeur and its littleness, from incessant and personal observation. They wrote, too, for an audience eager for novelty, thirsting and hungering for strong, true passion—an audience composed, not of the court, but of the body of the people. On reading the dramas of this period we cannot understand how human sensibilities could bear the shock of such terrible pathos as we find in these wonderful works—agony piled upon agony till it becomes almost too powerful when *read;* what then must it have been when represented with all the graces of delivery! The truth is, that "there were giants in those days," and the spectators cared not how painfully their sympathies were awakened, provided they were moved strongly, naturally, and directly.

The language, too, in which these terrible or playful scenes were written, was a medium admirably suited to the purpose and to the time: it was in the highest degree rich, varied, tender, and majestic; adorned with all the graces of classical imagery, but without a trace of pedantry or formality. The great object of these writers was

Passion; as Dignity had been the principal aim of the Greek dramatists. They therefore directed all their efforts to a faithful delineation of Nature, and made their scene a true mirror of Life itself, mingling the grave and the merry, the serious and the comic, in the same play, the same scene, and even in the same speech. And thus they have produced a constellation of immortal works, which, like the creations of the greatest among them all, "were not for an age, but for all time;" and which, notwithstanding the great and grievous faults with which their excellences are contrasted, will be read with still increasing ardour and admiration through age after age, because in them Art has been but the interpreter and handmaid of Nature!

CHAPTER VI.

MARLOW AND SHAKSPEARE.

Marlow: his Career and Works — His Faustus — His Death— Contemporary Judgments on his Genius. Shakspeare: His Birth, Education, and Early Life—Traditions respecting Him — His Marriage—Early Studies—Goes to London—His Career—Death and Monument—Order of his Works—Roman Plays — His Diction — Characters.

The remark which we made in the preceding chapter respecting the general character and career of the great dramatists of the Elizabethan era will be found to apply so universally as to render it unnecessary for us to give biographical details of individuals whose life was, for the most part, a constant alternation of squalid poverty and of temporary success.

The profession of playwright at the period we are considering was held in but low esteem; in fact, was not raised in any perceptible degree above the occupation of the actor. It will be found, indeed, that most of the great authors we are speaking of were themselves actors, as well as writers for the stage; and this circumstance undoubtedly tended to give their productions some of those peculiarities which so strongly distinguish this school of dramatists from any other which ever existed in the world. The peculiarities so communicated were, as might naturally be expected, both good and evil. Writing for an audience of the most miscellaneous character, and addressing themselves at the same time to the learned and the ignorant, to the refined and to the illiterate, they were obliged to seek for matter adapted to every taste; now gratifying the most elegant tastes of the courtly and scholarlike noble, and then, in the same play — often in the same scene—tickling the coarser fancy of the rude and jovial artisan. It is in some measure, therefore, to the popularity of the drama as a favourite amusement, at this period, of all ranks, that we owe much of what is most grand, most airy, and most romantic, in the Elizabethan theatre, and also, it cannot be denied, a good deal of the irregularity that characterises these wonderful compositions — their strange mixture of elevated passion and mean buffoonery; much of their sublimity, and much also of their meanness.

It should be carefully borne in mind that the above remarks apply universally (though of course not in the same degree or proportion) to all the dramatists of the Shakspearian or Elizabethan school, some being distinguished for pathos, some for sublimity, others for sweetness of fancy and a "Sicilian fruitfulness" of beautiful diction and harmony. Passing, therefore, over John Lyly, the affected euphuist and fantastical innovator on the language of the court, but whose dramas are distinguished by an exquisite grace and Grecian purity of construction, and whose songs in particular are models of airiness and music, we come to Peele, Nash, Greene, and Lodge, the immediate predecessors of Marlow, who was himself, so to speak, the forerunner and herald of Shakspeare.

The luxuriant fancy of his 'David and Bethsabé,' and the kingly amplification of his 'Edward I.,' would have given Peele's name no mean place on the national Parnassus; the "gall and salt" of Nash's vigorous satire would have preserved his memory in the admiration of his country; Greene's "happy talent, clear spirit, and lively imagination" would have saved him from that oblivion whence his works are seldom recalled but by the painful commentator on Shakspeare; and the romantic spirit and woodland freshness of Lodge's graceful muse might have earned him a lasting niche in "Fame's proud temple." But all these bright intellects were quenched and swallowed up in the immeasurable splendour of their great successor. At noon we know, as well as at midnight, the stars are in the sky, but we can only see them in the absence of the sun.

The dates of the birth and death of the above dramatists are as follows: — Lyly, born 1554, died some time after 1600; George Peele, a fellow-actor and shareholder with Shakspeare in the Blackfriars Theatre, died before 1599; Nash, born in Suffolk, 1564, and died, "after a life spent," as he pathetically says himself, "in fantastical satirism, in whose veins heretofore I misspent my spirit, and prodigally conspired against good hours," also about 1600; Greene died in 1592; and Lodge, who at the end of his life is supposed to have renounced the stage, and become a physician of eminence, is reported to have died in London of the plague in 1625.

While these authors had been gradually but imperceptibly improving and developing the infant drama of England, we now come to the great writer who performed for our stage nearly the same offices as were rendered to that of Greece, according to the well-known dictum of Horace, by Æschylus:—

"Et docuit magnumque loqui, nitique cothurno."

This was Christopher Marlow. Born at Canterbury, about the year 1562, he received a learned education at Bene't College, Cambridge, and is supposed to have been attracted by the reputation he had obtained by his first dramatic essay, the tragedy of 'Tamburlaine,' to embrace the profession of actor. The play to which we have just alluded was calculated, from the wild oriental nature of its subject, to give a too free current to Marlow's natural tendency to bombastic fury of declamation, and gigantic monstrosity and exaggeration of sentiment. Jonson has left on record his admiration for "Marlow's mighty line," as he so nobly expresses the peculiar character of this dramatist's wild and swelling spirit; and the Æschylus of the English stage, like his great Athenian prototype, seems to have impressed his contemporaries with a most exalted respect for his sublime and irregular genius. Indeed it may easily be conceived that, as grandeur and force are the qualities most likely to strike the imagination of the public at a period when art is in its infancy, so the too often accompanying faults of tumidity and exaggeration are generally perceptible at such a period. The biting raillery of Aristophanes has shown no mercy to the extravagance, obscurity, and bombast of Æschylus; and we cannot, therefore, be surprised to find the deeper and more delicate raillery of Shakspeare fixing upon the absurdities of Marlow's gigantic dramas. The two greatest works of this powerful writer are undoubtedly the 'Faustus' and the 'Jew of Malta,' the latter of which was produced before 1593. We trust we shall be excused for attempting to give some account of the first of these extraordinary works, when we mention the obligations incurred by Goethe to the 'Faustus' of Marlow, obligations which the patriarch of Weimar never failed to acknowledge. As in the 'Faust' of Goethe, Marlow's hero is a learned man of Wittenberg, who, finding the vanity of those studies which have made him the glory and envy of all Germany, makes a compact with the Evil One that he may enjoy, in exchange for his eternal salvation, a certain period of youth, beauty, and sensual indulgence. It must be confessed that, in the grandeur and vastness of the satire on human follies, in the tenderness of the pathetic scenes, in the admirable conception of the character of Margaret—that daisy, dew-besprent with tears, and blooming so sweetly at the mouth of an infernal abyss of sin and misery which yawns to engulf it—and, above all, in the complete creation of that wondrous Mephistophiles, the German bard has shown a power not approached by the old English bard. In the pictures, however, of terror, despair, and unavailing remorse, and particularly in the terrific scene when Faustus is expecting the approach of the demon to claim performance of the dread contract,—in these, and in a rich glow of classic imagery, and in the appropriate colouring of gloom and horror thrown over the whole action, we must be pardoned if we think our countryman superior. The 'Jew of Malta' is the portraiture of revenge and hatred embodied in the common type of the Jewish character as it appeared to the popular imagination of the sixteenth century; that is, under a form at once terrific, odious, and contemptible. Not among the least astonishing proofs of Shakspeare's divine and prescient mind is the fact that, living at a period when the Jews were still persecuted, and when popular prejudice—that indestructible monster—still believed the calumnies of the Middle Ages, and fancied that the Jews sacrificed a Christian child at the Passover, and practised the forbidden arts of magic and necromancy, that Shakspeare should have been victorious over the prejudices which still enchained the mind even of the learned Marlow, and should have given us, in Shylock, the portrait, the living image, of "an Israelite indeed,"—not the absurd bugbear of the Elizabethan stage, with his red nose, his impossible riches, and equally impossible crimes, but a real breathing man, desperately cruel and revengeful it is true, but cruel and revengeful on what seem to him good grounds, and only so far a Jew as not the less to remain a human being like ourselves. Nothing can surpass the absurdity of Marlow's plot in this play—an absurdity hardly compensated by occasional passages of majestic though somewhat tumid declamation. Few things, for instance, can be finer than the dying speech of Barabas, the Jew—

"Die life, fly soul, tongue curse thy fill, and die!"—

or his comparison of himself to the ominous and obscene bird—

"The sad-presaging raven, *that tolls*
The sick man's passport from her hollow beak,
And in the shadow of the silent night
Doth shake contagion from her sable wings."

Marlow's life was as wild and irregular as his genius, and his death at once tragic and deplorable. It is related that in an unworthy brawl, in a place and with a person (according to some accounts a serving-man) as disreputable as the occasion, he endeavoured to use his dagger on the person of his antagonist, who, seizing Marlow's wrist, gave a different direction to the poniard; the weapon entered Marlow's own head, "in such sort," to use the words of Anthony Wood, "that, notwithstanding all the means of surgery that could be brought, he shortly after died of his wound."

He was buried at Deptford on the 1st of June, 1593; and many dramas have come down to us bearing the impress of his genius, and several, indeed, ascribed to his name: but such was the prevalence of his style when he wrote, and so universal at this period was the custom for several dramatists to work together or successively at the same piece, that it is very difficult to affiliate with certainty the dramas of the Elizabethan age, except those of Shakspeare.

The finest, perhaps, of these works is the 'Edward II.,' which contains many passages of deepest pathos. As a proof of the high reputation enjoyed by Marlow among his contemporaries, we will quote the spirited lines of Drayton:—

"Next Marlow, bathed in the Thespian springs,
Had in him those *brave translunary things*
That the first poets had; his verses were
All air and fire, which made his verses clear:
For that *fine madness* he did still retain
Which rightly should possess a poet's brain."

In taking our leave of this great and brilliant genius, we cannot but regret that his untimely death deprived his works of the regularity which time and experience would probably have given to them; and whether we speak of him as a man or as an author, we may very well apply to him the lines pronounced in his own tragedy by the scholar over the mangled limbs of Faustus:—

"Cut is the branch that might have grown full straight;
And burned is Apollo's laurel bough,
That sometime grew within this learned man."

There is a great deal of melancholy truth in that profound verse of the modern poet,

"The world knows nothing of its greatest men:"

and this verity will especially apply to that class of which we would desire the most minute details—the Poets. Of Homer we know so little that his very existence and personality have been brought in question; respecting Virgil we possess only a few vague and cold notices; of the private life, and, above all, the intellectual life, of Milton, we possess no information but what we can glean from his writings; and of a greater yet than these—Shakspeare—all the details which we possess may be condensed into a few lines, and are principally derived from the most frigid and unattractive of all sources, legal documents, the poet's will holding among these the most forward place.

William Shakspeare or Shakespeare was born, as everybody knows, in the little town of Stratford, on the Avon, in Warwickshire, in the month of April, 1564. He was baptized on the 26th, which has originated the poetical, and certainly not very improbable tradition, that the greatest of Englishmen was born on the 23rd of April, the anniversary of St. George, the tutelary saint of his country. His father was a dealer in wool (not a butcher, as was long ignorantly supposed), and had at one time been in flourishing circumstances, for he had occupied the office of high-bailiff, or chief municipal dignitary, in his native town, but he appears, notwithstanding his having married an heiress possessed of some little fortune, to have gradually sunk into great distress, and ultimately to have received charity from the corporation of which he had once been a prominent member. "Genius," as Washington Irving prettily says, "delights to nestle its offspring in strange places;" and it is a proud distinction of England that its literature should number among its brightest names so large a proportion of men born in the humblest ranks of society. It is beneath low roofs, and few are humbler than that venerable one at Stratford, that the cradles of our greatest men were rocked; it is by poor firesides that their genius budded and expanded; and this is the reason why our literature, more than that of any other country, echoes the universal sentiments of the human heart, and speaks a language intelligible to every country and every age.

Of Shakspeare's childhood and education nothing is accurately known; perhaps the poverty of his father, by preventing him giving his son more than very limited and rustic instruction, enabled the boy's intellect to develop itself naturally and gradually, unstiffened and uncrippled by the too early discipline of a schoolmaster—that discipline which, like the swathing and swaddling-bands of the injudicious nurse, so often cripples and deforms what it is intended to render strong and beautiful. His early years were probably passed amid the smiling scenery surrounding Stratford, marking, with prophetic eye, every tint of cloud and stream, every feature of external beauty, and laying up a store of observations on the passions, the sentiments, and the oddities of human character,—

> ——"While he was yet a boy,
> Careless of books, yet having felt the power
> Of Nature, by the gentle agency
> Of natural objects then led on to feel
> For passions that were not his own, and think
> (At random and imperfectly indeed)
> On man, the heart of man, and human life."

There can be little doubt of Shakspeare having at some early period of his life been employed as clerk to some country attorney; for he shows in all his works a technical acquaintance with the phraseology of the English law—an acquaintance, indeed, which could only have been acquired by actual practice: this circumstance is also further proved by some of the few passages in the writings of his contemporaries in which mention is made of the great dramatist. His life at Stratford, according to the vague and imperfect traditions subsisting after his death in his native place, was idle, and perhaps even riotous: careful investigation has shown the impossibility of the events assigned by the well-known anecdote of the deer-stealing in Sir Thomas Lucy's park at Charlecote, as the immediate cause of his quitting Stratford and first adventuring in the career of London life. However reluctant we may be, in our eagerness to know the details of such a life, we must resign this picturesque story of the youthful Shakspeare's woodland misdemeanour, and seek for some other cause of his leaving Warwickshire. This is to be found in the register of the poet's marriage with Anne Hathaway, the daughter of a small farmer residing at Shottery, a village about a mile from Stratford. On the 28th of November, 1582, Shakspeare obtained at Worcester a licence of marriage, permitting the ceremony to take place *with once asking of the banns*, a circumstance which shows that this important act of life was accompanied with great hurry and precipitation, the more obviously so as Shakspeare was at this time a minor, and consequently unable to enter legally into any contract for himself. In this document, therefore, we find the names of two persons as sureties for the bridegroom, who was, it must be observed, seven years younger than his wife. All this precipitation, however, is explained by the register of baptisms in the church of Stratford, by which it appears that the poet's daughter Susanna was christened on the 26th of May, 1583, or only six months after the marriage. In a year and a half two other children, twins, were born to the poet, who had no offspring afterwards. Finding himself thus, at the early age of nineteen, a husband and a father, and probably perceiving that the obscurity of a retired village was no sphere for his intellectual powers, our poet about this time betook himself to London, there to commence his brief career of glory. Educated so imperfectly as he must have been, it is only to solitary and intense, though perhaps desultory study, that he could have owed that extensive acquaintance with books which he undoubtedly possessed; and it is therefore fair to conclude that he had been a diligent reader before he left his native place. In the employment of classical images, for example, Shakspeare shows no inferiority to any of that great number of dramatists at this period who were men of academical education; many of them indeed men of distinguished learning. His writings abound in passages indicating a very extensive and accurate acquaintance with classical imagery, and at the same time his splendid imagination has imparted to such allusions a vivacity, a brilliancy, and a glory not to be found in any other author. Much controversy has been raised with respect to Shakspeare's scholarship, and minute and ingenious investigation has been employed not only to determine how far he was acquainted with the literature of Greece and Rome, with the Italian, Spanish, and French languages, but even to ascertain what books he had read; and while some have considered his acquirements as unusually great, others have thought to exalt his glory by denying him even moderate share of learning. The truth is, however, probably between these two extremes; and when we reflect that many of the great autnors of antiquity, with whose *thoughts* he was evidently familiar, were translated, when he wrote, into English, we may be justified in considering him to have had a tolerable acquaintance with Latin and French, two languages which enter largely (though in a comparatively impure state) into the legal phraseology of England.

Plutarch, for example, had been translated into English, and Chapman's grand version of Homer had doubtless rolled its majestic harmonies over the ear of Shakspeare: this was enough for such a mind, whose assimilative power was so immense. With such intellects the slightest hint is sufficient: from the mere ruins and imperfect fragments of the Beautiful, they can build up a perfect and complete edifice, even as the eye of Cuvier, from a tooth, from a fragment of bone of some antediluvian reptile, could reconstruct the whole system of animal life which had passed away for ever. Of all the attempts in modern literature to reproduce the manners and sentiments of the classical periods, Shakspeare's are by far the most successful: we need only refer to the characters of Coriolanus, of Cleopatra, of Cæsar, of Ulysses; while in the employment of classical imagery no poet has ever exhibited such mastery and grace.

Shakspeare's first introduction to London life and to the theatrical profession has been as much misrepresented by tradition as the cause of his leaving his native town. The legend goes, that the poet, on his first arrival in the metropolis, was reduced to such distress as to hold horses at the door of the theatres, and that he thus ultimately obtained his introduction "behind the scenes." This, however, like the story of the deer-stealing, is a tale totally without foundation. We have seen in a former chapter that the companies of actors were occasionally in the habit of going about the country, and performing at the houses of the nobility: it was very possible for Shakspeare to have gratified that youthful desire which so many of us have felt for a peep into the enchanted world of the stage, long before he even thought of going to seek his fortune in London. This is the more probable as Thomas Green, an actor of note at the time, was a native of Stratford, and, some have supposed, a kinsman of the poet; and Richard Burbage, the greatest tragedian of the day, and perhaps one of the greatest actors whom England ever produced, was a Warwickshire man. We know also that the actors were frequently in the habit of visiting Stratford, and the probability is, that it was by Green's invitation that Shakspeare first joined a troop of players. That he was possessed of poetical genius could not have been unknown even at this time, as it is difficult to believe that his first works—the 'Venus and Adonis' and the 'Lucrece'—were not composed during his residence at Stratford. These two works, though disfigured by that Italian taste which was prevalent at the time, and though containing passages of a somewhat too warm complexion for the stricter taste of the present day, are full of the softest harmony and the most luxuriant imagery: the youthful fancy of the poet seems to run riot in the richest profusion: these works bear all the marks, and exhibit all the defects, of youth — but it is of the youth of a Shakspeare.

Our poet, then, became a member (and of course a share-holder also) of the Blackfriars theatre, and seems to have steadily and rapidly risen in reputation among his comrades, for in November, 1589, Shakspeare's name is inserted eleventh in a list of fifteen proprietors; in 1596 his name is fifth in a list of eight shareholders; and in 1603 it was second in the new patent granted by James I. As he increased in fame and importance at his theatre he gradually became proprietor of the wardrobe and stage-properties, which, together with the shares he previously possessed, were valued at 1400*l.*, a sum equivalent to nearly 7000*l.* of our present money. He was also a large proprietor in the Globe theatre, and his annual income is calculated at at least 1500*l.* As an actor he is said not to have exceeded mediocrity, though this is hardly in accordance with the tradition of two or three of the parts which he is said to have performed, and which would by no means be intrusted to an indifferent actor. These are Hieronymo, in the 'Spanish Tragedy,' to which we have alluded in another place; the Ghost in his own 'Hamlet;' and Adam in 'As You Like It,'—characters, we repeat, which would now never be placed in the hands of inferior talent. Besides this, it is impossible to read the admirable directions to the players in the second scene of the third act of 'Hamlet' without being convinced that no man ever possessed so delicate and profound an appreciation for the true excellences of the histrionic art, or could so well communicate its precepts. From the list of characters just enumerated, it will be seen that Shakspeare's *line*, as it is called, was the old men of the mimic world, or what is denominated on the French stage the *pères nobles.*

It was in the interval between his coming up to London and the year 1611 that he produced the thirty-seven plays which form the first folio edition; and he appears to have always retained the intention of retiring, as soon as he had acquired a competency, to his native place. As he grew richer he purchased land in Stratford, and became the proprietor of New Place, the principal house in the town, in the garden of which there long was to be seen a mulberry-tree, said to have been planted by his own illustrious hand. Will our readers believe that this tree was actually cut down by order of a clergyman of Stratford, under the pretext of its attracting so many curious pilgrims to the spot, which had fallen into the possession of this clerical Vandal! Shakspeare continued during his whole residence in London to pay annual visits to Stratford, and about 1612 he retired altogether to New Place, to pass the evening of his glorious life in that calm and dignified retirement which he had so nobly earned. There is something touching in this desire of our great poet; something well in accordance with his divine genius in this tender recollection of his birthplace, this returning in honoured manhood to those well-remembered scenes of infancy which had greenly dwelt in his remembrance, and over which he was to cast, till time shall be no more, the magic of his name. In this retirement, so beautiful by nature, and so hallowed by the most tender recollections in the society of his childhood's friends, and among the quiet home-scenes of pastoral England, the poet passed four years of what must appear to us felicity as unmingled as ever fell to the lot of man; and on the 23d of April, 1616, he died, having just completed his 52d year. Who ever, in so short a life, did so much for immortality? His widow survived him seven years: his two daughters were married, and one of them had three sons, but these latter all died without issue, and consequently, as the poet's only son, Hamnet, died young, there now exists no lineal descendant of the poet. Shakspeare was buried in the parish-church of Stratford, and over the place of his interment there has been erected a mural monument in the Italian taste of the day, being a half-length of the poet, seated, with a pen in his hand, and bearing a laudatory inscription in Latin verse. This bust is undoubtedly a portrait, and was originally painted to imitate life, so that it gave an idea of the complexion, colour of the eyes, hair, &c., of the original. Malone, more barbarous than a churchwarden, however, covered this most interesting work with a thick coat of white paint, from which it has not been and cannot be rescued. Shakspeare appears in this portrait to have been singularly handsome: the outline of the face is regular and oval; the extraordinary height, breadth, and peculiar airy lightness of the forehead in particular makes it one of those heads which, once seen, never can be forgotten. This is perhaps the most remarkable peculiarity of the head, and this is perceivable in all the portraits. The forehead is really vast, and yet singularly light—a worthy temple for such lovely and majestic oracles. The hair, which is divided on the top of the head, is, like his beard, of an auburn or golden sunny brown; his complexion is healthy, and the expression of the whole face is in perfect accordance with what we learn of his generous, gentle character.

There is very little doubt but that Shakspeare's literary career as a dramatic author was in no respects different from what we have described as almost universal at the period. He began by the rearrangement of old plays, and it was probably while engaged in this mean and almost mechanical employment that he felt the first electric flash of that admirable genius which was afterwards to burn with such a steady splendour in his great dramas. Many of the works which came into the world with the passport of his name, nay, some which have found a place in the editions of his collected works, were, in reality, only *réchauffés* made by him, or older works to which his pen had only added some scene, character, or speech. Of the former of these two kinds we may instance the 'Yorkshire Tragedy,' and 'Arden of Feversham;' and of the latter, 'Pericles,' and 'Titus Andronicus.' A reference to any edition of Shakspeare will inform the reader that the two former plays are not included in the poet's works, and that the two latter are. We find then in this matter that the editors have acted with partiality; for whatever claims 'Pericles' and 'Titus' possess to the honour of being called Shakspeare's might be safely maintained by the two other dramas. Consequently either 'Pericles' and 'Titus' ought to be excluded from the list of our poet's productions, or the 'Yorkshire Tragedy,' 'Arden of Feversham,' and several others, ought to be admitted. The chronology of the plays has been investigated by the commentators with a painful and laudable minuteness; but we perhaps hardly possess sufficient data to enable us to demonstrate with any degree of certainty the order of their production. This is much to be regretted, as our ignorance deprives us of the pleasure and improvement to be obtained from tracing the gradual development of Shakspeare's genius and art. It seems to us probable that 'Othello' and the 'Tempest' were among the last of these wonderful productions, and the 'Two Gentlemen of Verona,' the 'Comedy of Errors,' and 'Love's Labour's Lost,' were among the first. It should be remarked, however, that our opinion is founded chiefly on internal evidence of style and treatment, a criterion not always to be depended on.

The sources from whence Shakspeare drew the materials for his works were in every respect the same as those to which we have already alluded. It would be highly interesting to read the old plays of which he made so copious a use, and to remark what were the rude hints of character, what the coarse draughts and outlines of passion, which he has transformed into such impersonations as Lady Macbeth, as Jaques, as Ariel. The most essential peculiarity of his genius appears that intuitive and instantaneous certainty with which he threw himself, so to say, into a character, and perceived all the limits of its personality. The personations of all other dramatists appear like bas-reliefs, or pictures, presenting but one surface to the eye of the intellectual spectator; those of Shakspeare resemble statues, which may be viewed from all points equally well, without losing any of their likeness to reality. But why should we limit our words? are they not rather living, moving beings, with flesh and blood and passions like our own? In reading the dramatic works of all other men, you may admire the truth with which the character is conceived, and the skill with which it is set in motion, but you feel that it is created for a particular purpose, and set before you in a particular light. In Shakspeare you seem, on the contrary, to perceive depth beyond depth of personal identity or individuality, stretching far beyond human ken, and losing itself in the unfathomed abysses of the heart of man. It is as when you fix your eyes upon the vastnesses of the summer sky, or upon the deeper purple of a tropic ocean,—your gaze seems to die away in the immeasurable profound. It will not seem too much to say of Shakspeare's characters, that there is not one, among the thousand figures which people his living scenes, to which you might not assign (from the elements given by the poet in any number of speeches, small or great, put into its mouth) a whole train of antecedent events, and possible development of character. And this is one of the most marked and admirable peculiarities of our poet In the works of other dramatists, the personages, conceived with what vividness you will, seem, so to say, *ready made*, and set in motion for the nonce; while Shakspeare's seem to be acted upon during the course of the events, and to be modified and changed just as real men and women perpetually are in their intercourse with the world and with each other. Where this wonderful creator gained the knowledge of human nature, and experience of human motives, which have presented him to posterity rather as something divine than as a mere mortal artist, it is impossible to learn.

The naturalist knows that the details of creation are inexhaustible; and Linnæus, when he told his scholars that there were more wonders and mysteries in turf covered by his foot than the longest life of the most laborious botanist would suffice to describe or to explain, but expressed the difficulty encountered by the critic who attempts to examine the vast and inexhaustible dominions of Shakspeare's creation. The three great subdivisions, then, may be stated as follows: —1, Plays founded on subjects of classical antiquity; 2, Plays founded on the history, either legendary or authentic, of modern countries; and 3, Dramas on romantic stories, such as the innumerable *novels* of Spain and Italy. Of the plays which take for their materials antique personages and manners, the most remarkable are 'Julius Cæsar,' 'Antony and Cleopatra,' 'Timon of Athens,' 'Coriolanus,' and 'Troilus and Cressida.' In these works the spirit and tone of thought of the antique world is most admirably seized, and delicate and subtle distinctions are made between the manners of different epochs of Roman history. For instance, the language, turn of thought, and local colouring are exquisitely and profoundly Roman, both in 'Coriolanus,' 'Antony,' and 'Julius Cæsar;' yet the reader is conscious that the Romans in 'Coriolanus' are as different from the Romans of the other two plays as was the Roman people at the two different epochs in question. In 'Coriolanus' every line breathes the simple, fervid patriotism of the republic, its rude manners, its severe virtues; while in the other plays we feel that the Roman republic has ceased to exist, and the monarchic, civilized, corrupt tone of manners has already come into existence.

'Timon of Athens' has been finely called "the Lear of private life;" and certainly never was there composed a grander or more impressive picture of profuse indiscriminate friendship punished by its natural offspring, ingratitude. The over-loving and over-confiding spirit of Timon, soft, effeminate, thirsting for universal attachment, degenerates into the bitterest misanthropy — like luscious wine, which, soured, becomes the sharpest vinegar; and what other poet but Shakspeare could have ventured to give, in one drama, two characters of misanthropy, like Timon and Apemantus, so alike externally, yet so strongly contrasting: the one a manhater from nature, the other made so by circumstances? If the misanthropy of Timon be (as we have just ventured to image it) the sweet and potent wine turned sour in the sunshine of a too luxuriant prosperity, that of the Cynic is rather the poor and acid fruit of a cold and barren and unloving nature, which no prosperity could render rich or generous.

We need not speak here of the wonderful life, fervour, and animation which pervade all these plays, and the lifelike reality with which the poet places us amid the stirring scene. Here is no idle declamation, no parade of classical propriety; and yet how admirably are the great characters delineated and relieved against the moving background of inferior interests and passions! How exquisite are those little glimpses into private life, afforded us, as if by accident, yet with such consummate skill, amid the tumult and fermentation of great events—the domestic scenes in 'Coriolanus,' the revelries, the quarrelling, and reconciliations of Cleopatra! The play of 'Troilus and Cressida,' though disfigured in parts by some singular anachronisms, is invaluable for the truly Homeric delineations of Ulysses and Agamemnon. Can anything in the way of pure rhetoric be finer, more skilful, than the speech of Antony over the body of Cæsar, or than the harangue of Ulysses in the 'Troilus?' We have here the very essence and soul of classicism, and we have too, what the ancients have not given us—the household and private physiognomy of their times. Shakspeare and Homer are absolutely the only men who have ever succeeded in representing what is *heroic* without once losing sight of what is truly *natural* and moving. As to the language of these and all his plays, it would be useless to speak of its beauty here; we could but repeat, and perhaps weaken in repeating, the enthusiastic admiration of all who have been able to judge of this kind of merit: of all authors Shakspeare is the most natural and unforced in his style, and yet there is none whose words are either so musical in their arrangement, so striking and picturesque in themselves, or contain so many thoughts. Sometimes, indeed, we meet with paragraphs in which every important word is not only admirable, as conveying, strengthening, or adorning the meaning, but is itself an image new, bold, true, and vigorous in the highest degree. We open our Shakspeare at hazard: for instance, the following—

> 'Thou desperate pilot, now at once run on
> The dashing rocks thy *sea-sick weary bark*''—

where the *bark*, by the "fine madness" of the poet, is made "weary" and "sea-sick." Again; where Æneas says to the trumpeter,

"Trumpet, blow loud,
Send thy *brass voice* through all these *lazy tents*" —

where the epithet "brass" is transferred from the instrument to its sound, and the "tents" said to be "lazy," instead of their inhabitants; or the "vagabond flag," that

"Goes to and back, *lackeying* the varying tide;"

and a thousand others in this—and in all the plays.

"the quick comedians
Extempore shall *stage* us; Antony
Shall be brought drunken forth, and I shall see
Some squeaking Cleopatra *boy* my greatness."

But why multiply examples? Every page of Shakspeare would furnish us with many instances of such intensifying of expression, where some happy word conveys to us a whole train of ideas, condensed into a single luminous point as it were—words so new, so full of meaning, and yet so unforced and natural, that the rudest mind perceives almost intuitively their meaning, and yet which no study could improve or imitate. It is this which constitutes the most striking peculiarity of the Shakspearian language; it is this point in which his treatment, his *manner*, differs from that of all other authors, ancient or modern, English or foreign, who ever wrote; it is this which, while it justifies the almost idolatrous veneration of his countrymen, makes him of all authors the most untranslatable.

All have observed the simplicity and homeliness which distinguish the images of this great poet, and particularly in passages of intense passion; and the time has arrived when critics of all countries unite in appreciating the true grandeur and nature of such images, which are precisely those most likely to suggest themselves in moments of the greatest agitation. The time, we say, is past when a false and artificial system of so-called *propriety* can find fault with Lady Macbeth's terrific image—

"Nor Heaven peep through the *blanket of the dark*,
To cry, *Hold, hold!*"—

or that admirable picture of tranquillity and silence, presenting itself, it should be remembered, to the imagination of a tired soldier: "not a mouse stirring."

What a terrible train of guilty thoughts, of horror and unavailing remorse, in that short dialogue between Macbeth and his wife, beginning with the words—

"*Macb.* I have done the deed:—Didst thou not hear a noise?
Lady Macb. I heard the owl scream, and the crickets cry.
Did you not speak?
Macb. When?
Lady Macb. Now.
Macb. As I descended?

Lady Macb. Ay.
Macb. Hark!—
Who lies i' the second chamber?

But we dare not trust ourselves to quote. In Shakspeare the various excellences of the art are so wonderfully mingled, that it is seldom easy to quote one passage as a specimen of mere beautiful imagery, another of grand declamation, another of wit, another of humour, and so on. Admirable as the passages are in themselves, they are still more so in their places, forming strokes of character and touches of truth and nature.

Of all authors Shakspeare is the one who has least imitated or repeated himself. All other dramatists—nay, all other men—conscious of successful power in some particular line of development, have failed to resist the natural temptation which leads us to do often what we know we do well. Let us imagine any other dramatist capable of conceiving such a character as Hamlet, as Lear, as Othello, or as Falstaff. Would he not assuredly have delighted to repeat such grand creations, and show us these admirable figures in different lights and attitudes? Yet in Shakspeare, when once these terrible or humorous personages have quitted the scene, and finished that long life of woe or of merriment, condensed, by the poet's art, into the three short hours of dramatic existence, they disappear for ever—we hear no more of them—they vanish as completely as real men would have done, and leave, like real men, no exactly similar beings behind them.

Dealing with the universal sentiments and passions of mankind, this author has given us, in many places, different portraits of the same passion; but these delineations are as distinct and as dissimilar in Shakspeare as they are in nature.

How many portraits have we of jealousy, for example! Yet who cannot distinguish the jealousy of Othello from that of Leontes, that of Posthumus from that of Ford, and a thousand other instances? The jealousy is as different as the man, yet always as true to reality. What an infinite multitude of fools are to be found in Shakspeare! yet no two are the least alike. We may follow an ascending scale of silliness through as many gradually and imperceptibly rising varieties of the *genus*, extending from almost complete imbecility to the highest degree of intellect, tinctured with that slight shade of fantastic mental distortion from which the human mind is hardly ever free. What a range of character from Audrey, Aguecheek, or Silence, to Jaques! And why stop here? Why not to Lear himself, to Hamlet, to Falstaff? It is absolutely impossible to ascribe any important speech in Shakspeare to the wrong person: and this is perhaps one of the most difficult points of the dramatic art—a point which has never been reached by any author but Shakspeare, and sometimes by Molière.

Wonderful, too, as is the individuality and originality of the more passionate or humorous characters, Shakspeare has succeeded in giving, by light, imperceptible, infallible touches, quite as much reality and personality to a class of personages which in the works of all other writers of fiction are generally found uniform, and even *fade* — we mean the delineations of young men and women, the heroes and heroines of comic or romantic adventures. Even Fielding, Scott, and Dickens, though possessing the far greater facilities afforded by narrative fiction, have seldom succeeded in rendering such characters interesting in themselves; that is, independently of the circumstances which surround them. Compare the Sophia and the Tom Jones of the first, the Waverley and the Miss Wardour of the second, the Nicholas Nickleby and the Miss Maylie of the third, with Rosalind and Orlando, with Helena, with Hero— nay, even with such secondary characters as Margaret, as Mariana, as Laertes, as Lorenzo — and we shall see that, while the elegant, and sometimes even delicate, creation of the romancer owes all its hold on our sympathies to the trials to which it is exposed, and to the patience and energy with which it undergoes them, the characters of the greatest of dramatists possess a real and distinct individuality, as subtly though not as strongly marked as that which divides Lear from Falstaff, or Isabella from Beatrice.

The great art of Shakspeare, as a portrayer of character and passion, seems to consist in his manner of making his personages, accidentally, involuntarily, nay, even in spite of themselves, express their own character, and admit us, as it were, into the inmost recesses of their hearts. And this is especially true of his *passion*. In the dramatists of the French classical school, in particular, the characters are very apt to give us — in noble and sounding verse, it is true, admirably reasoned and majestically harmonized — a description of the feelings which affect them. They, in short, *say*—"I am terrified," "I am angry," "I am in love." This Shakspeare's men and women, like real men and women, never do. Hamlet, asked by his mother what is the dreadful object on which his eyes are fixed, does not break out into a long *tirade* descriptive of it, but paints his own terror, and the spectre which causes it, in one line: —

> "On *him*, on *him!* Look you, how pale he glares!"

And this method (if it be not rather an intuition) is perceivable in every scene and every character: it is found in the lightest as in the most solemn, in the most splendid as in the most pathetic scenes.

The development of the fable in Shakspeare is generally conducted with that natural yet unrestrained coherence which is found in the real dramas of human life. The events, it is true, are often hurried towards the close of the drama, and trifling and unexpected circumstances, arising in the course of the action, often completely change what we should imagine had been the author's previous plan. But does not the same thing perpetually happen in the world? Is it not a profound truth that the most insignificant events perpetually modify the most important actions? Does not experience show us that truth is stranger than fiction, that no event can be called unimportant excepting according to its consequences, and that no intellect is sufficiently vast and penetrating to trace all the consequences springing from even the most trivial act of our lives?

In point of *art*, it cannot be denied that Shakspeare has sometimes hurried over the latter part of his dramas, and cut, with violence and improbability, the Gordian knot of an intrigue which he had not time or perhaps patience to untie; but this defect is principally observable in those plays which internal evidence induces us to assign to the early period of his career. In many of the greatest works the dramatic complexity is as skilfully and completely resolved as the catastrophe is morally complete. What, for example, can be more complete than the resolution of the fable in 'Lear' and in 'Othello'? The latter play, indeed, may be considered as a miracle of consummate constructive skill. There is not a scene, a speech, a line, which does not evidently bear upon and contribute to the catastrophe; and that catastrophe is in the highest degree terrible and pathetic.

Of all the thousand errors prevalent respecting the genius and the works of Shakspeare, and which the industry of a respectful and affectionate and loving criticism has not yet entirely dispelled, perhaps the most fatal was a spirit of patronizing admiration and wondering approval, which seemed to consider his dramas as astonishing productions of an irregular and barbarous genius. Let it be to the eternal honour of Coleridge that he was the first to lead the way to a truer and more just appreciation of the poet of humanity, and to have shown his countrymen that the criticism which considered these wonderful creations as the work of *accidental genius* (absurd and contradictory as must appear such a collocation of the two words) was the mere dream of pedantry and ignorance. "What!" he says with a noble indignation, "does God perform miracles in sport?" Is it conceivable that these wonders of intellect and imagination—these worlds of fancy, redolent of beauty, of life, of a glorified reality—

"All that is most beauteous—imaged there
 In happier beauty; more pellucid streams,
An ampler ether, a diviner air,
 And fields invested with purpureal gleams;
Climes which the sun, who sheds the brightest day
 Earth knows, is all unworthy to survey"—

that all this subtle music of humanity, all this deep knowledge of the human heart—its passions, its powers, its aspirations—could be the result of accident—of a happy genius in an age of barbarism?—that the woolstapler's son of Stratford could have created, by accident, Juliet and Cordelia, Imogen and Miranda, Katherine and Cleopatra, Perdita and Ophelia?—that it was accident which reflected on the never-dying page of the dramatist of the Blackfriars the thunderous gloom of Lear's moral atmosphere, the fairy-peopled sunshine of Prospero's enchanted isle, the moonlit stillness of the garden at Belmont, the merry lamp-light of the Boar's Head in Eastcheap, or the warm English daylight of Windsor? No! such an opinion would be no less absurd (we had almost written blasphemous) than the sceptic's fancy that this earth was the result of blind chance and a fortuitous concourse of atoms.

From the works of Shakspeare may be gleaned a complete collection of precepts adapted to every condition of life and to every conceivable circumstance of human affairs. The wisest and best of mankind have gone to him for maxims of wisdom and of goodness — maxims expressed with the artlessness and simplicity of a casual remark, but pregnant with the thought of consummate experience and penetration: from him the courtier has learned grace, the moralist prudence, the theologian divinity, the soldier enterprise, the king royalty: his wit is unbounded, his passion inimitable, his splendour unequalled; and over all these varied glories he has thrown a halo of human sympathy no less tender than his genius was immeasurable and profound, a light reflected from the most gentle, generous, loving spirit that ever glowed within a human heart: the consummate union of the Beautiful and the Good.

CHAPTER VII.

THE SHAKSPEARIAN DRAMATISTS.

Ben Jonson: The Humours — His Roman Plays — Comedies—Plots. Beaumont and Fletcher—Massinger—Chapman—Dekker—Webster—Middleton —Marston — Ford — Shirley.

We now come to a galaxy of great names, whose splendour, albeit inferior to the unmatched effulgence of Shakspeare's genius, yet conspires to glorify the reigns of Elizabeth and James. The literary triumphs of this wonderful epoch are principally confined to the drama, which "heaven of invention" was, to use the beautiful expression of one of these playwrights, "studded as a frosty night with stars;" and deeply indeed do we regret that our space will only permit us to give a very short and cursory notice of the individual members of this admirable class of writers —

"those shining stars, that run
Their glorious course round Shakspeare's golden sun."

The first of these illustrious dramatists whom we shall notice is Ben Jonson, a mighty and solid genius, whose plays bear an impress of majestic art and slow but powerful elaboration, distinguishing them from the careless ease and unpremeditated abundance so strongly characterising the drama of this period. He was born in 1574, ten years after Shakspeare, who honoured him with his close friendship and well-merited protection. He was undoubtedly one of the most learned men of this or indeed any age of English literature; and he brought to his dramatic task a much greater supply of scholastic knowledge than was possessed by any of his contemporaries. Educated at Cambridge, he adopted the stage as his profession when about twenty years of age, and when he had already acquired very extensive knowledge of the world, and experience in various scenes of "many-coloured life," in the university and even in the camp: for Ben had served with distinguished bravery in the wars of the Low Countries. As an actor he is reported to have completely failed, but it was at this period that he began to exhibit, in the literary department of his profession, that genius which has placed his name next to that of the greatest. Like all his contemporary dramatists, Jonson began by repairing and adapting older plays, and his name is connected, like that of so many of the dramatic *débutans* of this period, with several of such recastings; for example, with that of 'Hieronymo,' &c. It was not till 1596 that he produced his first original piece, the admirable comedy of 'Every Man in his Humour,' which gave infallible proof that a new and powerful genius had risen on the English stage. This comedy was brought out (considerably altered from its first sketch,) at the Globe theatre, in 1598, and in some degree, it is related, through the instrumentality of Shakspeare, who acted a principal part in the piece. It was soon evident that Jonson had cut out for himself a new path in the drama; and he rapidly attained, and steadily preserved, the highest reputation for genius and for art. In fact, Jonson, during the whole of his life, occupied a position at the very head of the dramatists of the day—a position perhaps even superior to that of Shakspeare himself. Nor is this wonderful. The qualities of Jonson's peculiar excellence were more obvious and appreciable than the delicate and, as it were, coy merits of the great poet, whose works, possessing all the depth and universality of nature, require no less study, subtlety, and discrimination in him who would understand them as they deserve. All, on the contrary, could admire Jonson's wonderful knowledge of real life, his vast and accurate observation of human vices and follies, his somewhat rough but straightforward and vigorous delineations of character, and the epigrammatic condensation of a strong and masculine style, armed with all the weapons of classic rhetoric, and decorated with the splendours of unequalled learning. Jonson was, in short, a great comic dramatist; and it will be found that the chief excellence even of his two tragedies is less of a tragic than of a comic kind, and that they please us rather by their admirable delineations of manners than by those pictures of passion and sentiment which it is the legitimate province of tragedy to present. The peculiar excellence of this great writer lay in the representation of the weaknesses and affectations of common and domestic life—in the delineation of what were then called the "humours," a word which may be explained to mean those innate and peculiar distortions and deformities of moral physiognomy with which nature has stamped the characters of individuals in every highly artificial and civilized state of society, and which are afterwards exaggerated and rendered inveterate by vanity and affectation. In delineating these obliquities of character Jonson proceeded philosophically, we may even say scientifically: he appears to have carefully and minutely anatomised the follies and foibles of humanity, and to have accumulated in his comic or satiric pictures (for his comedy is of the satiric kind) every trait and little stroke of the particular folly in question, with a most consummate skill and industry; frequently concentrating in one character not only all the moral phenomena which his own vast and accurate observation could supply, aided as that was by a systematic and elaborate classification, but often exhausting all the touches left us in the moral portraits of the historians and satirists of antiquity.

His Roman plays, indeed, 'Catiline' and 'Sejanus,' the two tragedies of which we have spoken, and the comedy of 'Poetaster,' may be considered as absolute *mosaics* of language, of traits of character and points of history, extracted from the works of Tacitus, of Sallust, of Juvenal, of Horace—in short, the quintessence of Roman literature. Yet such is Jonson's skill, and so perfect a harmony was there between the vigorous, majestic, ***Roman*** character of his own mind, and the tone of the literature which he studied so profoundly, that this mosaic, though composed of an infinite number of distinct particles, has the most absolute unity of effect. Nay, more, he has done the same thing in those comedies which have for their subject modern domestic life and modern manners; and he has managed to introduce, in the portraiture of the ludicrous and contemptible persons of English citizen life in the sixteenth century, the strokes of humour and character taken from the delineations of Roman manners executed by the great satiric artists of the time of the Cæsars. This is undoubtedly a point of consummate skill in rendering available the stores of a species of learning which we should at first sight consider rather as an encumbrance than a useful instrument; but it arises also in some measure from that *classical* tone of character which we have attributed to Jonson: he was, indeed,

> ' More an antique Roman than a Dane."

It must, however, be confessed that Jonson's characters are sometimes too elaborate, too scientific, and overloaded with details which, though individually true and comic, are never found concentrated in one person. He has therefore been accused, and not unjustly, of painting, not men and women, but impersonations of their leading follies and vices. And in this respect a parallel between Jonson and Shakspeare would be exceedingly unfavourable to the former. Both have given us admirable portraits, for example, of braggarts, of coxcombs, and of fools; but while Shakspeare's are real men and women with real individuality of their own, but in whom the bragging, the coxcombry, the folly happen to be remarkable features, the comic characters of Jonson cannot be separated from the predominant folly ridiculed. We might conceive Parolles becoming a modest and sensible man, Osric a plain-spoken and downright citizen, and Slender or Aguecheek transformed by some miracle into reasonable beings, and something of them would remain; but imagine Bobadil cured of his boasting, Sir Fastidious of his courtly puppyism, or the exquisite Master Stephen of his imbecility, and nothing would be left behind.

In the construction of his plots Jonson is immeasurably superior to all the other dramatists of the period. Naturally haughty and confident in his own genius, and entertaining, too, a much higher opinion than was common at the time of the gravity and importance of the dramatist's office, he scorned to found his plays upon the substructure of the Italian novelist or the legends of Middle Age history; and consequently we are never offended in his dramas with that improbability of incident, inconsistency of character, hurried and imperfect development, which is the principal *structural* defect of most of the dramatic works of this period — a defect, indeed, from which Shakspeare's productions are by no means free. His plots Jonson always invented himself; and some of them are perfect models of complicated yet natural intrigue. It has been justly said that the comedy of the 'Silent Woman,' of the 'Alchemist,' of 'Volpone,' are inimitable as series of incidents, natural, yet interesting, gradually and necessarily converging to a catastrophe at once probable and unexpected.

The language of this great dramatist is in the highest degree vigorous, picturesque, and lively: it possesses, it is true, little or none of that sweet and flowing harmony, that living and transparent grace, which makes the golden verses of our Shakspeare absolutely superior to the far-famed diction of the Greek poets; but it is an admirably strong and flexible medium for his acute and masterly exhibition of character; and though in general not much elevated above the level of weighty and powerful prose, sometimes rises to a considerable pitch of rhetorical splendour. It must be confessed that Jonson wants that deep sympathy with human nature which is the true source of grace of language, as it is of tenderness of thought;

but there is often to be found in him a kind of gallant bravery of language, a splendour of imagery, recalling to us the dusky glow of his great prototype Juvenal, with whose genius the literary character of Jonson has many points of resemblance. Both writers describe the follies of their kind in a contemptuous and sarcastic spirit, and their crimes with a powerful but somewhat too declamatory invective; and both appeared to have less sympathy with virtue than detestation for vice: they were both, too, inclined to treat with indifference, if not with contempt, the virtues and graces of the female character—a sure sign of hardness of mind. Jonson's two Roman plays, 'Catiline' and 'Sejanus,' are of course founded on the history, the former of Sallust, and the latter of Tacitus. Though presenting a noble and impressive copy of the terrible outlines of their subject, it may be objected that the principal characters in each are so unmixedly hateful or contemptible, that they are unfit for the purposes of the tragic dramatist. The senate scene in the latter, and the character of Tiberius, are very grandly conceived, and the assembly of conspirators in 'Catiline,' together with the description of the battle and the death of the hero, related by Petreius, are among the finest declamatory passages in English poetry. These two dramas are in verse.

Of the comedies the finest, in point of richness of character, are 'Every Man in his Humour,' the 'Alchemist' (the scenes of which are in London), and 'Volpone.' In the first the characters are numerous and admirably delineated; the interest of the second rests upon the jovial villany and cunning sensuality of the hero; and the third contains some richly-contrasted touches of vulgar knavery and self-deluding expectation, wrought up with astonishing vivacity. We have already spoken of the excellence of plot which characterises the 'Silent Woman,' though the chief personage is a character so rare as to be, if not impossible, at least so improbable that nothing but its exquisite humour can reconcile us to it. 'Bartholomew Fair' is full of satire and animation, but would have little interest for a reader of the present time, being a satire upon the Puritans; and of the other pieces some are merely local and temporary attacks on individuals, as the 'Poetaster,' 'Cynthia's Revels,' and the 'Tale of a Tub,' while others are generally considered inferior in merit: we may instance the 'Magnetic Lady,' the 'Staple of News,' and the 'New Inn.' The comedies are written, some entirely in prose, some in mingled prose and verse. It would be unjust not to state that, though the above remarks will be found to apply generally to Jonson, he has occasionally attained to a high degree of fanciful elegance of language and a singular delicacy of harmony. Many passages may be cited, particularly from his Masques, his unfinished pastoral comedy of the 'Sad Shepherd,'—a most exquisite fragment

—and all his songs, which have seldom been equalled for flowing elegance.

In spite, therefore, of his faults, both as a man and as an author—his arrogance, his intemperance, his sarcastic and sometimes coarse humour, his pedantry and his pride—we must ever hold him to have been a great and a good man; grateful, generous, valiant, free-spoken, with something of the old Roman spirit in him, a mighty artist, and a man of a gigantic and cultivated genius; and we may reverently echo the beautiful words of the epitaph which long remained inscribed upon his grave—

"O rare Ben Jonson!"

He died, in poverty, in 1637, and was buried, in a vertical position, in Westminster Abbey.

There is a far stronger resemblance between the leading features of Shakspeare's dramatic manner and that of the two illustrious authors of whom it is now our delightful duty to speak—Beaumont and Fletcher, the twin stars of the English literary sky. These two men, each of distinguished birth and considerable fortune, and bound by the closest ties of friendship, present the rare and admirable picture of a pair of friends, uniting, during a long period of authorship, their powers in the joint production of a multitude of admirable works, in which the respective excellences of each were so intimately mingled, that it is almost impossible to trace the pen of either separately from that of the other.

"They still have slept together,
Rose at an instant, learn'd, play'd, eat together;
And wheresoe'er they went, like Juno's swans,
Still they went coupled and inseparable."

And there are no works in the whole range of literature which give such noble pictures of the friendship of elevated and generous spirits as the twin-born dramas of these illustrious fellow-labourers.

They wrote under the immediate influence of the Shakspearian manner, and were obviously imitators of the great poet—not servile copyists, but free and enlightened followers. They were exceedingly prolific as authors, the editions of their works consisting of fifty-two pieces, the greater part of which were composed in partnership. This association was only dissolved by the death of Beaumont, who died, before he had completed his thirtieth year, in March, 1615; his companion Fletcher surviving him till 1625, when he died in the great plague, ten years after his brother dramatist, than whom he was ten years older. They appear, as we have said, to have set Shakspeare before them as their model, not however in his vaster and completer developments of tragic passion, or in his deep-searching analysis of character, nor even in his rich and genial creations of humour; but rather that phase of his dramatic art in which he has ventured into the airy world of graceful and imaginative fiction: not, in short, such characters as Macbeth, Othello, Falstaff, Hamlet, or Shylock; but rather the persons which people the fairy isle of Prospero, or the sunny gardens of Illyria. They are in particular admired for the fresh, and vigorous, and courtly pictures they have given of youthful generosity and friendship, and for the occasionally happy portraits of love and innocent confidence; nor must we forget the many admirable figures of loyal and military devotion to be found in many exquisite characters of war-worn veterans.

In their plots they are even more careless and irregular than Shakspeare; never scrupling to commit the most outrageous offences against consistency of character and probability of event, and appearing to rely mainly on their skill in presenting striking and picturesque situation, and their mastery over every varied tone of majestic, airy, and animated dialogue.

"There are," says Campbell, speaking of these two dramatists, "such extremes of grossness and magnificence in their dramas, so much sweetness and beauty interspersed with views of nature either falsely romantic or vulgar beyond reality; there is so much to animate and amuse us, and yet so much that we would willingly overlook, that I cannot help comparing the contrasted impressions which they make to those which we receive from visiting some great and ancient city, picturesquely but irregularly built, glittering with spires and surrounded by gardens, but exhibiting in many quarters the lanes and hovels of wretchedness. They have scenes of wealthy and high life, which remind us of courts and palaces frequented by elegant females and high-spirited gallants, whilst their noble old martial characters, with Caractacus in the midst of them, may inspire us with the same sort of regard which we pay to the rough-hewn magnificence of an ancient fortress."

The prevailing vices of these great but unequal writers are, first, the shocking occasional indelicacy and coarseness of their language, and, secondly, the frequent inconsistency of their characters. With respect to the former, it is no excuse to say that it is partly to be attributed to the custom of the female parts being at this period universally represented by boys; nor is it much palliation to consider this licentiousness of speech as the vice of the times. It is true that the charge of indecency may safely be maintained against nearly all the writers of this wonderful period, and we know that the stage has a peculiar tendency to fall into this error; but Shakspeare has shown us that it is very possible to avoid this species of pruriency, and to portray the female character not in its warmth only and its tenderness, but also in its purity. The most singular thing is, that many of the more indelicate scenes, and much of the coarsest language in Beaumont and Fletcher, will be found to have been composed with the express purpose of exhibiting the virtue and purity of their heroines. It cannot however be denied that it is but an inartificial and dangerous mode of exalting the triumph of virtue, to represent it as in immediate contact with the coarsest and most debasing vice. Nor is that Juvenalian manner of satire either to be imitated or approved which consists in elaborate description of immorality, however strong may be the tone of its invective, and however elevated the height from which its thunders may be hurled The precepts of good sense will coincide with the Duke's answer to Jaques in 'As You Like It:'—

> "*Jac.* Give me leave
> To speak my mind, and I will through and through
> Cleanse the foul body of the infected world,
> If they will patiently receive my medicine.
> *Duke.* Fie on thee! I can tell what thou wouldst do,—
> Most mischievous foul sin in chiding sin;
> For thou thyself hast been a libertine;
> And all the embossed sores and headed evils,
> That thou with licence of free foot hast caught,
> Wouldst thou disgorge into the general world."

The other main vice of Beaumont and Fletcher is the extraordinary and monstrous inconsistency of the characters. Nothing is more common in their plays than to see a valiant and modest youth become, in the course of a few scenes, and without any cause or reason, a coward and a braggart; and the devoted and loyal subject of the first act metamorphosed into the traitor and assassin of the third; the pure and high-born princess transformed into the coarse and profligate virago. In order to exalt some particular virtue in their heroes, these writers sometimes represent them as enduring indignities and undergoing trials to which no human being would submit, or the very submission to which would render impossible the existence of the virtue in question.

In spite of the general truth of the foregoing remarks, our readers must not be surprised to learn that the plays of these dramatists abound in many exquisite portraits of female heroism and magnanimity. Indeed, the principal defect of their female characters (at least of those which are really striking and attractive) is that they seem to be conceived in a spirit too romantic and ideal, and are, as Campbell well expresses it, "rather fine idols of the imagination than probable types of nature:" but it would be unjust to forget that the polluted stream of such base and monstrous conceptions as 'The Island Princess,' and 'Cupid's Revenge,' flows from the same source as the pure and sparkling fountain of 'Philaster,' of 'The Double Marriage,' of 'The Maid's Tragedy,' and of 'Bonduca.' We do not mean that even these latter works are free from objectionable passages; but what is revolting might easily be cleared away, and would leave much to elevate the fancy and to purify the heart. Beaumont and Fletcher have been justly praised by all the critics, from Dryden downwards, for their beautiful delineations of youthful friendship, and for the ease, grace, and vivacity which distinguish their dialogue, particularly such dialogue as takes place between high-spirited and gallant young men. In this they probably drew from themselves.

Their comic characters, though generally very unnatural, and devoid of that rich *internal* humour—that *luce di dentro,* as the Italian artists phrase it—which makes Shakespeare's so admirable, are written with a droll extravagance and fearless *verve* which seldom fails to excite a laugh. The Lieutenant, who has drunk a love-potion, and is so absurdly enamoured of the old king; Piniero, Cacafogo, La Writ, the hungry priest and his clerk, and a multitude of others, though fantastic and grotesque caricatures, are yet caricature executed with much freedom and spirit.

According to the ancient tradition, Beaumont is said to have possessed more judgment and elevation, Fletcher more invention and vivacity. How far this can be proved by comparing those works written conjointly by the two illustrious fellow-labourers, with those composed after Beaumont's death by his surviving friend, it is difficult to determine. We think it may be safely concluded that Beaumont possessed more markedly the tragic spirit, Fletcher the *vis comica*—one of the best of the comic pieces being Fletcher's 'Rule a Wife and have a Wife.'

We must now pass rapidly over a number of mighty yet less illustrious names, which in any other age, and in any other country, would have been secure of immortality. The works of these dramatists, so admired in their own day, and possessing all the qualities likely to render them permanently popular, have been long condemned (that is, during the whole period intervening between the civil wars and the beginning of the present century) to an obscurity and neglect incredible to those who are acquainted with their various and striking merits, and inexplicable to all who are ignorant of the capricious tyranny of popular taste.

Disinterred from the dust and cobwebs of two hundred years, and brought to light by commentators and philologists eager to explain the works of the greatest among their glorious army, these authors have gradually attracted the attention of the general reader in England, and may now be considered as finally and solidly established in popular and national admiration. Strange! that the very genius which eclipsed them all, and threw them as if for ever into the abyss of neglect and "the portion of weeds and out-worn faces," should have been, in an after age, the indirect means of restoring to them that heritage of glory which they appeared to have irredeemably forfeited!

The next name to which we shall invite the reader's attention is that of Philip Massinger, a man who passed his life in struggling with poverty and distress. He has left us a considerable number of dramas, the greatest part of them in that mixed manner so general at this time, in which the passions exhibited are of a grave and elevated character, the language rich and ornamented, and yet the persons and events hardly to be called heroic. Of these works the finest are 'The City Madam,' 'The Great Duke of Florence,' 'The Bondman,' 'The Virgin Martyr,' and 'A New Way to Pay Old Debts.' In the first and last mentioned of these plays the author has given a most striking and powerful picture of oppression, and the triumphant self-glorifying of ill-got wealth. The character of Sir Giles Overreach in the one, and that of Luke in the other, are masterpieces. In expressing the dignity of virtue, and in showing greatness of soul rising superior to circumstance and fate, Massinger exhibits so peculiar a vigour and felicity, that it is impossible not to conceive such delineations (in which the poet delighted) to be a reflection of his own proud and patient soul, and perhaps, too, but too true a memorial of "the rich man's scorn, the proud man's contumely," which he had himself undergone. In the tender and pathetic, Massinger had no mastery; in the moral gloom of guilt, in the crowded agony of remorse, in painting the storm and tempest of the moral atmosphere, he is undoubtedly a great and mighty artist; and in expressing the sentiments of dignity and virtue, cast down but not humbled by undeserved misfortune, he is almost unequalled. His versification, though never flowingly harmonious, is skilful and learned, an appropriate vehicle for the elevation of the sentiments; and in the description of rich and splendid scenes he is peculiarly powerful and impressive. The soliloquy of Luke in his brother's counting-house, when the long-despised "poor relation" suddenly finds himself the possessor of enormous wealth, and the gorgeous description in which he enumerates the gold and jewels and "skins of parchment" in which his newly-acquired power is condensed, and his long-desired vengeance on his oppressors—all this is conceived in a dramatic spirit of the highest order. Massinger was born about 1584, and died in great poverty in March, 1640.

In reviewing the long succession of squalid lives and early and obscure deaths which composes the biography of the dramatic school of Elizabeth, it is very gratifying to meet with an illustrious poet whose existence was as tranquil as his productions were excellent. This was George Chapman, one of the most learned men of his age, and the author of the finest translation of Homer in the English language. Deeply imbued with the spirit of Greek poetry, and baptised, so to say, in the fire of its earliest and most heroic inspirations—in the works of Homer and of Æschylus—Chapman has infused into his dramas, and particularly into those written on classical subjects, far more of the true Greek spirit than will be found in a thousand of those pale and frigid *centos* which go under the name of regular classical tragedies; and would be an unanswerable reply to the prejudices and ignorance of those foreign critics who so glibly accuse the British drama of irregularity and barbarism. The life of this great and learned man was worthy of his genius, "preserving," to use the words of Oldys, "in his conduct, the true dignity of poesy, which he compared to the flower of the sun, that disdains to open its leaves to the eye of a smoking taper." He died, at the age of seventy-seven, in 1634.

We will pass over Dekkar, a most prolific and multifarious dramatist, whose productions, however, are difficult to examine and appreciate, from his having generally written in partnership with other playwrights. He appears to have been by no means destitute of imagination, of pathos, or of humour; though his genius has always appeared to us rather lyric than dramatic. He was celebrated in his own day for his literary warfare with Jonson, whom he attacked in his 'Satiro-mastix;' his finest passages are marked by great felicity of idea, and a delicate music of expression. He died in 1638.

John Webster, a mighty and funereal genius, is the next author we shall mention. We can compare his mind to nothing so well as to some old Gothic cathedral, with its arches soaring heaven-ward, but carved with monsters and angels, with saints and fiends, in grotesque confusion. Gleams of sunlight fall here and there, it is true, through the huge window, but they are coloured with the sombre dyes of painted glass, bearing records of human pride and human nothingness, and they fall in long slanting columns, twinkling silently with motes and dusty splendour, upon the tombs of the mighty; lighting dimly up now the armour of a recumbent Templar or the ruff of some dead beauty, and now feebly losing themselves amid the ragged coffins and scutcheons in the vaults below. His fancy was wild and powerful, but gloomy and monstrous, dwelling ever on the vanities of earthly glory, on the nothingness of pomp, not without many terrible hints at the emptiness of our trust, and many bold questionings of human hopes of a hereafter. "His phantasms appear often, and do frequent cemeteries, charnel-houses, and churches, where the devil, like an insolent champion, beholds with pride the spoils and trophies of his victory over Adam." Death is indeed his Muse; not the rose-crowned deity of the ancients, the brother of sleep, the bringer of repose, the winged genius with the extinguished torch, but the hideous skeleton of the monkish imagination, the "grim anatomy," with his crawling blood-worms, and all the loathsome horrors of physical corruption.

His most striking plays are 'The White Devil,' 'The Duchess of Malfy' (Amalfi), 'Guise, or the Massacre of France,' and 'The Devil's Law-case.' In the second of these works, a tragedy in which pity and horror are carried to an intense and almost unendurable pitch, the death of the innocent and beautiful heroine is most powerfully conceived: his simple, direct, straightforward pathos is in the highest degree tragic and affecting; but his plots are totally extravagant, crowded with supernumerary horrors; and if he is occasionally touching and graceful, such passages resemble less the growth of a rich and generous soil, than the pale flowers which sometimes bloom amid the rank and obscene herbage of a crowded burial-ground, springing from fat corruption and watered with hopeless tears. This strange and powerful genius was contemporary in his life and death, as it is supposed, with Dekkar, and these two dramatists wrote many pieces together.

Our space will only allow us to make a brief allusion to Middleton and Marston, the former of whom is remarkable for the use he has made in one of his plays of the popular witch or sorceress of his country's superstition, a circumstance to which some critics have attributed the original conception of Shakspeare's wondrous supernatural machinery in Macbeth. Middleton's witches are, however, nothing more than the traditional mischievous old women, described, it is true, with great vigour and spirit, while those of the greater bard are, as Charles Lamb finely says, "foul anomalies, of whom we know not whence they are sprung, nor whether they have beginning or ending. As they are without human passions, so they seem to be without human relations. They come with thunder and lightning, and vanish to airy music. This is all we know of them. Except Hecate, they have no *names;* which heightens their mysteriousness."

Marston is chiefly remarkable for a fine tone of moral satire: some of his invectives against vice and folly are grand abundant outpourings of Juvenalian eloquence, not without some of Juvenal's grim mirth and grave pleasantry.

We must confess that our favourite among the minor Elizabethan dramatists—that is, after Shakspeare, Jonson, and Fletcher—is John Ford. Of a melancholy and pensive character — witness the strong portrait sketched by a contemporary hand —

"Deep in a dump John Ford alone was got
With folded arms and melancholy hat!"—

sufficiently learned to enrich his scenes with many beautiful images borrowed from the ancients; possessing an ear for the softest harmony, and a heart peculiarly sensitive to pure and elevated emotion, this dramatist has depicted the passions, and particularly the love, of youth and innocence, with a tenderness and force which almost equals Shakspeare himself. Ford's instrument is of no great compass, but its tones are unmatched for softness, and he makes it "discourse most eloquent music." His finest plays are 'The Lover's Melancholy,' 'The Brother and Sister,' 'Love's Sacrifice,' 'The Fancies, Chaste and Noble,' and, above all, the admirable tragedy of 'The Broken Heart.' Do not these exquisite and fanciful titles seem to give earnest of purity, grace, tenderness, chivalrous love, and patient suffering? And the reader will not be disappointed. We do not mean to say that Ford is not sometimes coarse, sometimes licentious, and sometimes extravagant. Unfortunately the audiences of that age required an intermixture of comic scenes, even in the most serious dramas; and Ford's genius was the very reverse of comic. With no humour in his soul, he seems, when trying to write his comic scenes (which are, with few exceptions, base and contemptible in the extreme), to have determined by a violent effort to renounce his own refined and modest character, and like a bashful man, who generally becomes impudent when he attempts to conquer his natural infirmity, he rushes at once from the airiest and most courtly elegance to the vilest and meanest buffoonery. But in his true sphere, what dramatist was ever greater? What author has ever painted with a more delicate and reverent hand the innocence, the timid ardour of youthful passion —

> "le speranze, gl' affetti,
> La data fé, le tenerezze; i primi
> Sgambievoli sospiri, i primi sguardi"? —

and who has ever approached him in the representation of the patience and self-denial of that noblest and most unselfish of passions — of the undying constancy of breaking hearts — in all the more divine and ethereal aspects of the sentiment? In the last play which we have spoken of, the pathos is absolutely carried so far that it oversteps the true limits of dramatic sufferance; nay, almost trangresses the bounds of human endurance. How confident must he have been in his own mastery over every manifestation of the passion which he has so delighted to portray, to have ventured in one drama two such characters as Penthea and Calantha! Ford has also never failed to interest us in a class of personages which it is very difficult to render attractive — the characters of hopeless yet unrepining lovers. We need only mention Orgilus and the noble Malfato.

We now come to the last of these great dramatists, James Shirley. He was a man of learned education, who was at first destined for the clerical profession, but, disappointed in his hopes, took refuge in those two inevitable asylums of indigent erudition, first the school, and afterwards the theatre. His life was full of adventure, for it extended over a most busy period, namely from 1596 till after the Restoration. He had indeed passed through many vicissitudes, for he had fought in the civil wars on the royalist side; and his name forms the connecting link between the two periods of dramatic art, so widely different, one of which is typified in Shakspeare, and the other in Congreve. His works are praised for the elegance, nature, good sense, and sprightliness of their comic language; for the purity of the characters, particularly the female ones; and for the ease and animation of his plots. He has not much pathos, it is true, nor much knowledge of the heart; but there are few dramatists whose works give a more agreeable and unforced transcript of the ordinary scenes of life, conveyed in more graceful language. His humour, though not very profound, is true and fanciful, and his plays may always be read with pleasure, and often with profit. His best dramas are 'The Brothers,' 'The Lady of Pleasure,' and 'The Grateful Servant.'

CHAPTER VIII.

THE GREAT DIVINES.

Theological Eloquence of England and France—The Civil War—Persecution of the Clergy — Richard Hooker — His Life and Character — Treatise on Ecclesiastical Polity — Jeremy Taylor — Compared with Hooker—His Life —Liberty of Prophesying — His other works — The Restoration—Taylor's Sermons—Hallam's Criticism—Taylor's Digressive Style—Isaac Barrow—His immense Acquirements — Compared to Pascal — The English Universities.

In the department of Christian philosophy, and particularly in that subdivision of theological literature which embraces the eloquence of the pulpit, England has generally been considered inferior to many other European nations, and to France in particular. So splendid indeed are the triumphs of reasoning and of eloquence which are recalled to the remembrance of every cultivated mind at the mention of such illustrious names as Pascal, as Bossuet, as Bourdaloue, that the general reader (above all, the Continental one) is apt to doubt whether the Church of England has been adorned by any intellects comparable to these bright and shining lamps of Catholicism. We hope that we shall not be considered presumptuous if we endeavour to show that Great Britain *does* possess monuments of Christian eloquence equal or at least not inferior to the immortal productions of these great men, and, at the same time, if we attempt to explain how it has happened that the triumphs of English divinity are not so generally known and appreciated as those of the great French theologians. This latter circumstance will be found to proceed not only from the much more universal study throughout Europe of the French language as compared to the English (a partiality which, it must be confessed, is now daily wearing away), but also in some measure from the points of difference in many matters of religious belief and ecclesiastical discipline existing between the Anglican Church and that of Rome.

There is, in short, a much greater apparent accordance, in these points, between the opinions of most of the Continental Churches and those of Rome, than exists between Romanism and the Church of England. Add to this, too, the more imposing and dazzling character of the French style, particularly that of the French pulpit, at the splendid epoch so brilliantly adorned by these admirable productions, and we shall not be at a loss to attribute to its real cause the comparative neglect experienced by the works of Hooker, Taylor, Barrow, South, and Stillingfleet.

In instituting a general comparison between the productions of the French and English intellect, few persons have failed to remark one very striking point of dissimilitude, if not even of contrast; and this is, that the former will be found to possess their chief and characteristic beauties *externally*, while those of the latter are not to be perceived or appreciated without a greater degree of study and examination. We do not mean, by the use of the word "external," in any way to imply that the productions of French genius do not possess merits as real and as solid as those which adorn any literature in the world; we wish to express that those merits lie nearer to the surface and are brought more prominently forward in the great trophies of French intellect than in those of the British mind. Whether we examine the drama of the two countries, their eloquence or their poetry, we shall almost invariably find that, while the merits and peculiar graces of the Gallic intellect are conspicuously and prominently placed as it were in the foreground of the picture, the British Muse is of a coyer and more retiring temper, and only yields herself to ardent and persevering pursuit —

> "With sweet, reluctant, amorous delay."

This deep and internal character of our literature arises in a great measure from that Teutonic element which plays so important a part in every development of English nationality — in the literature of the country, in its language, in its social condition, and in its political institutions. The regular and beautiful forms of classical literature —simple, severe, intelligible as the proportions of the Grecian architecture — which the French have generally made their models, are certain at the very first view to strike, to please, and to elevate; while the English literature — and no portion of it more justly than the one now under our consideration—may rather be compared to the artful wildness, the studied irregularity of some Gothic cathedral. Its proportions are less obvious, its outline less distinct; its rich and varied ornaments can only be understood, and its multiplicity of parts can only be harmonized into a beautiful and accordant whole, by the spectator who will pass some time and exert some patience in study.

ing it, and whose eye must first overcome the mysterious gloom which pervades the solemn fabric.

But these remarks will be better substantiated by a comparison of the great works of theologic eloquence which we are about to examine in detail. Those qualities which we have already spoken of as characterising all the literary productions of the period of Queen Elizabeth will be found impressed upon no part of that literature with greater distinctness than upon this. Richness, fertility, universality are stamped upon all the writings of this unequalled era; and richness, fertility, and universality are the distinctive features of the style of the three great divines whom we have selected from a very large multitude as embodying in the highest degree the peculiar merits of their era—an era which, it is proper to remark, extended from the middle of Elizabeth's reign down to the period of the Restoration, and even some time beyond it.

The innumerable discordant sects into which the nation was split during the Commonwealth were much more calculated to encourage wild speculations in doctrine and fantastical innovations in practice than to promote the true interests of religion; and, with that narrow and persecuting bigotry which so strongly contrasted with their professions of universal toleration, the fanatics united all their efforts against the established Church of the country. Bitter as were their enmities towards one another, the thousand sects could at least find one point in which they were all agreed; and this was the annihilation of a Church whose riches and dignity excited at once their envy and their rapacity, while the learning and virtue of its most distinguished defenders must have been felt by them—bigots at once and fanatics as they were — as a tacit reproach upon their own blatant ignorance and plebeian ferocity.

A multitude of the regular clergy were driven from their pulpits, and persecuted with every ingenuity that triumphant malice could devise: many men, venerable for their virtues and illustrious for their learning, were hounded like wild beasts from the tranquil retreats of their universities and the industrious obscurity of their parishes. The Church of England underwent a fierce and unrelenting ordeal, and, in passing through that fiery trial, showed that all the severities of a tyrannical and fanatic government might indeed oppress, but could never humiliate it. It was in imprisonment, in exile, and in poverty that that Church strung its nerves and strengthened itself for its noblest exploits; it was when crushed beneath the armed foot of military fanaticism that it gave out, like the fragrant Indian tree, its sweetest odours of sanctity and its most precious balm of Christian doctrine; and let it be recorded to the glory of these much-tried and illustrious victims, that when the storm of tyranny had passed away, and the Anglican Church was once more restored to its holy places, it used its victory mercifully, as it had supported its affliction patiently. It had suffered persecution, and it had learned forgiveness.

The three great men whose works we propose to examine occupy a period extending between the years 1553 and 1677, or rather more than a century—a century filled with vicissitudes of the gravest import to the fortunes of the English Church. We should not have ventured to take a view of this part of our subject embracing so long a period of time, and necessitating the consideration of so many, so various, and so important works, but from the reflection that these men and their productions bear one stamp and possess a singular resemblance in mode of thought and tone of language; they all belong, intellectually if not chronologically, to the Elizabethan era.

The first of them in point of time is Richard Hooker, born near Exeter in 1553, and enabled, by the wise benevolence of the venerable Jewel, Bishop of Salisbury, to study at the University of Oxford, where he speedily distinguished himself for his vast learning and industry, no less than by a simplicity and purity of character almost angelic.

Having attracted the notice of Bishop Sandys, he was made tutor to that prelate's son, who, together with Cranmer, a descendant of the archbishop, enjoyed the benefit of Hooker's superintendence, and who ever afterwards retained for his wise and simple preceptor the warmest veneration and respect. After occupying for a short time the chair of Deputy Professor of Hebrew, he entered into holy orders, and married. This last important act of life was productive of so much affliction, even to his pious and gentle spirit, and was entered upon with a guileless simplicity so characteristic of Hooker's unworldly temper, that we cannot refrain from giving the anecdote as related by his friend and biographer Walton. Arriving wet and weary in London, he put up there at a house set apart for the accommodation of the preachers who had to deliver the sermon at Paul's Cross. His hostess treated him with so much kindness that Hooker's gratitude induced him to accept a proposition made by her of procuring him a wife. This she accordingly did in the person of her own daughter, "a silly clownish woman, and withal a mere Xantippe,"[*] whom he accordingly married, and who appears to have inflicted upon her simple and patient husband an uninterrupted succession of such penance as ascetics usually exercise upon themselves in the hope of recompense in a future existence. When visited, at a rectory in Buckinghamshire to which he was afterwards presented, by his old pupils Sandys and Cranmer, Hooker was found in the fields tending sheep and reading Horace, possibly contrasting the sweet pictures of rural life painted by the Venusian bard with the vulgar realities which surrounded him. On returning to the house the guests "received little entertainment except from the conversation of Hooker," who was disturbed by his wife's calling him away to rock the cradle. On their departure the next morning Cranmer could not refrain from expressing his sympathy with Hooker's domestic miseries, with his poverty and the obscurity of his condition. "My dear George," replied this Christian philosopher, "if saints have usually a double share in the miseries of this life, I, that am none, ought not to repine at what my wise Creator hath appointed for me, but labour (as indeed I do daily) to submit mine to his will, and possess my soul in patience and peace." Shortly after the event related in this touching anecdote, Hooker received the dignified appointment of Master of the Temple in London, a post in which his learning, genius, and piety were exhibited in all their brightness, but in which his resignation and love of peace were put to a trial not less severe, though certainly less humiliating, than those to which this heavenly-minded man was exposed in his Buckinghamshire rectory. He soon found himself engaged in a controversy with Walter Travers, his colleague in the ministry of the Temple, an eloquent and able man, but professing certain opinions respecting church government with which Hooker could not coincide. In this interminable sea of discussion was now conscientiously embarked the mild and modest Hooker; and though the argument was conducted on both sides with good temper and courtesy, it embittered the existence of our peace-loving divine, and ended in his antagonist being suspended from his ministerial functions by the authority of Archbishop Whitgift. Hooker on this occasion wrote to the prelate a letter imploring deliverance from "that troubled sea of noises and harsh discontents," an element so unfitted to the peculiar character of his mind and temper, and a position which prevented him from proceeding with the great work he was now meditating, his 'Treatise on the Laws of Ecclesiastical Polity.' The letter breathes so noble a spirit of Christian purity, and is withal so characteristic of the man, that we shall, we trust, be pardoned for inserting some passages of it; the rather as it contains the outline and general aim of the work itself.

"MY LORD,—When I lost the freedom of my cell, which was my college, yet I found some degree of it in my quiet country parsonage. But I am weary of the noise and oppositions of this place; and, indeed, God and nature did not intend me for contentions, but for study and quietness. And, my Lord, my particular contests here with Mr. Travers have proved the more unpleasant to me because I believe him to be a good man; and upon that belief hath occasioned me to examine my conscience touching his opinions. And to satisfy that, I have consulted the Holy Scriptures and other laws both human and divine. . . . . . And in this examination I have not only satisfied myself, but have begun a treatise, in which I intend the satisfaction of others, by a demonstration of the reasonableness of our laws of ecclesiastical polity. But, my Lord, I shall never be able to finish what I have begun, unless I be removed into some quiet parsonage, *where I may see God's blessings spring out of my mother earth*, and eat my bread in peace and privacy; a place where I may, without disturbance, meditate my approaching mortality, and that great account which all flesh must give at the last day to the God of all spirits."

His wise and moderate desire was granted; he was transferred, in 1591, to the rectory of Boscomb, in Wiltshire, where he finished the first four books of his treatise, which were printed in 1594. He was in the following year presented, by Queen Elizabeth, to the rectory of Bishop's Bourne, in Kent, whither he removed, and where he spent, in learned retirement and in the faithful discharge of his pastoral duties, the short remainder of his life. Here he completed the fifth book of his great work, published in 1597, and also prepared three others, which did not appear till after his death. This event took place in November, 1600; and it is difficult to conceive any human soul, purified by suffering, elevated by the most vigorous yet meekest intellect, adorned by learning, and inspired by piety, passing through our mortal life with less of stain, and rising into a more glorious existence with less need of change and purifying, than the angelic spirit of the mild and venerable Hooker.

"'Hooker's Ecclesiastical Polity,'" says the excellent and acute historian of the literature of Europe, "might seem to fall under the head of theology; but, the first book of this work being by much the best, Hooker ought rather to be reckoned among those who have weighed the principles, and delineated the boundaries, of moral and political science." No quality is more surely a concomitant of the highest order of genius than its suggestiveness, and what we may call its *expansive* character. Though originally written to determine a particular and limited controversy on certain matters of church discipline, Hooker's immortal treatise is a vast arsenal or storehouse of all those proofs and arguments upon which rests the whole structure of the moral and political edifice. "The first lays open," says D'Israeli, "the foundations of law and order, to escape from 'the mother of confusion, which breedeth destruction.'" Unhappily, however, this great work is incomplete; or at least so much mystery rests upon its publication, that it is impossible to divest the mind of the most fatal of all suspicions which can affect a book—suspicions as to its genuineness. At the death of Hooker his manuscripts fell into the hands of his despicable wife, who, marrying indecently soon after the loss of the good man whose constant penance she had been, at first refused to give any account of the precious literary remains of her deceased husband. It afterwards appeared that she had allowed various Puritan ministers (men professing the very opinions which Hooker had written to refute) to have free access to these papers; and it is to their sacrilegious tampering that we ought doubtless to attribute not only the destruction of many of these papers, but also alterations which have apparently been made in the text. The wretched woman, who had thus betrayed the glory of her departed husband, was found dead in her bed the day after she had been forced to make this humiliating confession. The precious manuscripts now passed through several hands, and an edition of the five books of the 'Ecclesiastical Polity' was published in 1617. "Again, in 1632," continues D'Israeli, who has given us the secret history of Hooker's great work, "the five undoubted genuine books were reprinted. But their fate and their perils had not yet terminated." At the troubled period of the Long Parliament, Hooker's manuscripts were again examined by order of the House of Commons, and the sixth and eighth books were given to the world. It is singular that in this, as well as in subsequent editions, the seventh book is not included; and doubts were even raised as to the genuineness of that book when restored by Dr. Gauden in his edition of the work. It is, however, now generally admitted that the seventh book, though hastily composed, is really genuine; but we must, on the other hand, content ourselves with the mortifying conclusion that the so-called *sixth* book is irrecoverably lost; that which occupies its place being a separate treatise, never intended to form part of the 'Ecclesiastical Polity.' In spite, however, of the loss of an important portion of its argument, in spite of the numerous and often contradictory passages which have been interpolated by unfaithful copyists and disingenuous commentators, the 'Ecclesiastical Polity' will ever remain one of the noblest ornaments of English literature, and one of the mightiest triumphs of human genius and industry. "He had drunk," says Hallam, "at the streams of ancient philosophy, and acquired from Plato and Tully somewhat of their redundancy and want of precision, with their comprehensiveness of observation and their dignity of soul." When a portion of Hooker's preface was translated by an English Romanist to the Pope, his Holiness expressed the greatest surprise at the erudition and acuteness of the book. "There is no learning that this man has not searched into," said the Pontiff; "nothing too hard for his understanding, and his books will get reverence by age." James I. of England, a prince to whom we cannot deny the possession of most extensive learning, inquiring after Hooker, and hearing that his recent death had been deeply lamented by the Queen, paid the following tribute to his genius:—"And I receive it with no less sorrow; for I have received more satisfaction (that is, *conviction*) in reading a leaf of Mr. Hooker than I had in large treatises by many of the learned: many others write well, but yet in the next age they will be forgotten." Hooker's style, though full of vigorous and idiomatic expressions, is much more Latin and artificial than was usual at that time: he does not disfigure his sentences with that vain parade of quotation which distinguishes contemporary writings: his profound learning was, if we may use the expression, chemically and not mechanically united with his mind; it was incorporated not by contact, but by solution. Though the general tone of the work is of course abstract and even dry, the sweet and simple character of the man sometimes makes itself perceptible through the elaborate and brilliant panoply of the orator; or, to use the beautiful words of D'Israeli, "Hooker is the first vernacular writer whose classical pen harmonised a numerous prose. While his earnest eloquence, freed from all scholastic pedantry, assumes a style stately in its structure, his gentle spirit sometimes flows into natural humour, lovely in the freshness of its simplicity."

In purity and meekness of personal character, in immensity of erudition, and in power of eloquence, there is a strong resemblance between the great writer of whom we have just feebly attempted to give a sketch and the sweet orator to whom we are about to turn our attention—Jeremy Taylor. They were both stamped with the majestic impress of that noble age of our literature, when the minds of men seemed to possess something of the simplicity, grandeur, and freshness which we fondly believe characterized (at least physically) the primeval races of mankind. Taylor's learning, indeed, was hardly less vast and multifarious than that of Hooker; but, whether from the poetical and imaginative turn of his mind, or from the greater temptations offered by the more declamatory nature of the subjects of his writings, his erudition appears less under his command than Hooker's. The latter may be compared to the Roman warrior, whose arms indeed were weighty, but not so much so as to impair his strength and agility in the combat; while Taylor reminds us rather of the knight of the Middle Ages, sheathed from plume to spur in shining and ponderous panoply, but his armour is too complicated in its parts to admit of free motion, and the very plumes, and scarfs, and penoncelles which adorn it, are an impediment, no less than a decoration. We find, in short, in the writings of Taylor something of that diffuse, sensuous, and effeminate over-richness which distinguishes the style of many of the Greek and Roman fathers—Tertullian, for instance, or Chrysostom. But in spite of these defects, we cannot conceal our conviction that the works of Jeremy Taylor are, upon the whole, the finest production of English ecclesiastical literature; or, to use the strong but hardly exaggerated language of Parr, "they are fraught with guileless ardour, with peerless eloquence, and with the richest stores of knowledge, historical, classical, scholastic, and theological."

He was born in the humblest rank of life (his father was a barber at Cambridge), in the year 1613, and entered Caius College, in that university, in his thirteenth year. On taking his bachelor's degree in 1631 he entered into holy orders, and made his first step in the career of ecclesiastical advancement, by preaching, for a friend, in

St Paul's Cathedral in London. Here his eloquence, his learning, and what a contemporary calls "his florid and youthful beauty and pleasant air," procured him immediate reputation, and the notice of Archbishop Laud, who made him his chaplain, gave him preferment in the Church, and presented him to a fellowship in All Souls' College, Oxford. He married, in 1639, Phœbe Langdale, by whom he had three sons, all of whom he had the misfortune to survive. But this prosperous and peaceful existence was now overshadowed by the clouds of that tremendous storm which was soon to burst upon England, and in its fury not only to sweep away the altar and the throne, but almost to efface the very foundations of society. At the breaking out of the civil war Taylor sided warmly with the royalist party, and even wrote a defence of episcopacy. In the troubles which followed he was taken prisoner by the parliamentary army in the battle fought under the walls of Cardigan Castle. The royalist cause now met with a long succession of reverses; and Taylor, who had been released by the victorious party, determined to retire altogether from what he probably foresaw was a hopeless struggle, and one in which an ecclesiastic could hardly hope to mingle with much utility to his party or much honour to his professional character. He retired to Wales, and established a school at Newton Hall, in Carmarthenshire, where he remained in tranquillity, without incurring any very violent or persevering persecution at the hands of the dominant party. His own account of this portion of his life is interesting and beautiful. "In the great storm which dashed the vessel of the Church all in pieces I had been cast on the coast of Wales; and, in a little boat, thought to have enjoyed that rest and quietness which in England, in a far greater, I could not hope for. Here I cast anchor, and, thinking to ride safely, the storm followed me with so impetuous violence, that it broke a cable, and I lost my anchor. And here again I was exposed to the mercy of the sea, and the gentleness of an element that could neither distinguish things nor persons; and, but that he He that stilleth the raging of the sea, and the noise of the waves, and the madness of his people, had provided a plank for me, I had been lost to all opportunities of content and study; but I know not whether I have been more preserved by the courtesies of my friends or the gentleness and mercies of a noble enemy."

The passage just quoted is taken from Taylor's dedication to the Liberty of Prophesying,' his first work of a universal and permanent importance. The object of this admirable production is "to show the Unreasonableness of Prescribing to other Men's Faith, and the Iniquity of Persecuting Differing Opinions." It is, in fact, the first complete and powerful vindication that the world had ever seen of the great principle of religious toleration. Proud, indeed, may England justly be in the reflection that it was she who first gave to the world the noble birth of Religious and Civil Liberty—those twin-sisters, eternal and inseparable, the fairest and strongest children of Heaven. With the line of argument taken by Taylor in this production we have nothing to do at present: viewed as a mere work of literature, it is distinguished by all the excellences which mark his style, though at the same time it is more argumentative and less declamatory than his other writings.

His wife having died three years after her marriage, in 1642, Taylor contracted a second alliance during his residence in Wales. His second wife was Mrs. Joanna Bridges, said to have been a natural daughter of Charles I., a lady possessed of a considerable estate in Carmarthenshire. Though thus relieved from the necessity of continuing to be a schoolmaster, he appears at different times to have suffered serious losses from fines and sequestrations, and even to have been imprisoned on one occasion, if not more, for having too freely expressed his sentiments on public and church affairs. His literary activity, however, did not for a moment relax, and will be best proved by the enumeration of some of his principal works:—'An Apology for authorised and set Forms of Liturgy;' 'The Life of Christ, the Great Exemplar,' published in 1648; 'The Rule and Exercise of Holy Living,' and 'The Rule and Exercise of Holy Dying,' two admirable treatises of Christian conduct, which, like the last-named work, have taken a permanent place in the religious literature of the English Church. Besides these, and a great number of sermons, he wrote 'Golden Grove,' a small but admirable manual of devotion, so named after the seat of his friend and neighbour the Earl of Carbery; and a treatise on the subject of Original Sin, which involved him in a controversy with the Calvinists on the one hand, and the High Church party on the other. This is the only occasion on which Taylor's courtesy and gentleness of character appear to have at all deserted him. The Restoration was now at hand, when the long-oppressed Church might look forward to tranquillity and peace, and when the devoted adherents of the monarchy and the constitution might reasonably expect some reward for their sacrifices and their fidelity.

Their hopes, however, were cruelly disappointed: the profligate monarch forgot, in his moment of prosperity, all the lessons which exile and distress might have taught even the most insensible; and it is satisfactory to think that one exception was made to the melancholy uniformity of ingratitude, and that one pious and apostolic clergyman was rewarded for his sufferings and for his virtues. Taylor was made Bishop of Down and Conner, to which see was afterwards annexed that of Dromore, also in Ireland. These well-won and nobly-worn dignities Taylor did not long enjoy, for he died of a fever at Lisburn, in Ireland, on the 13th of August, 1667, in the fifty-fifth year of his age.

His character was truly apostolic, and his was one of those rare and excellent natures which appear equally venerable in prosperity and in adversity; the one not able to swell him with pride, nor the other to humiliate the simple grandeur of his soul.

"The sermons of Jeremy Taylor are far above any that had preceded them in the English Church. An imagination essentially poetical, and sparing none of the decorations which, by critical rules, are deemed almost peculiar to verse; a warm tone of piety, sweetness, and charity; an accumulation of circumstantial accessories whenever he reasons, or persuades, or describes; an erudition pouring itself forth in quotation, till his sermons become in some places almost a garland of flowers from all other writers, and especially those of classical antiquity, never before so redundantly scattered from the pulpit—distinguish Taylor from his contemporaries by their degree, as they do from most of his successors by their kind. His sermons on the Marriage Ring, on the House of Feasting, on the Apples of Sodom, may be named, without disparagement to others which perhaps ought to stand in equal place. But they are not without considerable faults. The eloquence of Taylor is great, but it is not eloquence of the highest class; it is far too Asiatic, too much in the style of Chrysostom and other declaimers of the fourth century, by the study of whom he had probably vitiated his taste; his learning is ill placed, and his arguments often as much so—not to mention that he has the common defect of alleging nugatory proofs; his vehemence loses its effect by the circuity of his pleonastic language; his sentences are of endless length, and hence not only altogether unmusical, but not always reducible to grammar. But he is still the greatest ornament of the English pulpit up to the middle of the seventeenth century; and we have no reason to believe, or rather much reason to disbelieve, that he had any competitor in other languages."

There can be very little doubt of the general justice of the above criticism; and as the passage is calculated to give, as far as it goes, a faithful idea of the peculiarities—and particularly of the faults—of Jeremy Taylor's prose style, we have not scrupled to quote it here; we cannot, however, do so without remarking on what, to us at least, appears to be a defect in the general judgments of the excellent author from whose work we have extracted it.

No one can deny Hallam the praise of perfect acquaintance with the vast subject he has so ably illustrated, of a store of learning equally accurate and profound, and of a singularly clear and lucid style; but at the same time he will be generally found, we think, to have been barely just to the English literature of the sixteenth and seventeenth centuries. Whether from the peculiar bent of his personal tastes, from the particular direction of his reading, or from the habit of periodical criticism, the discriminating faculty in his powerful mind appears to have been developed disproportionately with, nay, even perhaps at the expense of, the admiring or appreciating power: in other words, he exhibits a strong and possibly involuntary tendency to prefer what is consonant with a pure and regular system of rules to that which bears the stamp of vigorous and possibly irregular originality. His mind delights rather in what is negatively than in what is positively beautiful. Without enthusiasm, criticism becomes rather a dogmatic art than an ennobling and productive science; and Hallam will appear, in doing ample justice to the more regular and colder schools of literature in Europe, to have hardly been sufficiently warm in his praise of the great writers of this, the boldest and most impassioned period of his country's intellectual history. In our opinion, the richness, the inexhaustible fertility, the exquisite and subtle harmony, and the fervent and yet gentle piety which distinguish every page of Jeremy Taylor's writings, nay, the mere abundance of new ideas, and particularly the multitude of images drawn by him from the common objects and phenomena of nature, would of themselves be more than sufficient to place this great poet — for a poet he was, in the highest sense of the term — at least on an equality with any orator of the so-called classical school of French pulpit eloquence.

In the peculiarity to which we have just alluded he is indeed Shaksperian; few prose authors in the English language, and certainly none in any other, having surpassed Taylor in the number, the beauty, or the novelty of images drawn from rural life, from the lovely or sublime objects of nature, from the graces of infancy and the tenderest endearments of affection—those images, in short, which we never meet without a gentle flush and thrill of the heart; for they are echoes and emanations from a purer, a more innocent, and a happier existence.

In one respect, indeed, there exists a resemblance between Taylor and Shakspeare so striking as hardly to have escaped any one who has studied the literary physiognomy of this wonderful epoch; we allude to that exulting and abounding richness of fancy which causes them to be lured away at every turn from the principal aim of their reasoning by the bright phantoms which perpetually arise during its pursuit. As, in a country richly stocked with game, the hounds are perpetually drawn off from their chase by the fresh quarry they have started as they run, the minds of these writers seem incapable of resisting the temptation of turning aside to hunt the fancies started by their restless imagination. This is, it is true, often a defect, and sometimes produces confusion, and injures the very effect of the author's reasoning; few readers are able to follow the irregular movements of the poet's inconstant and suggestive imagination; to do that would imply a vivacity of perception resembling the creative energy of the poet himself. This discursive character is indeed perceptible in almost all the writings of this gigantic era — in those of Bacon no less than in those of Shakspeare; it is essentially the peculiarity of a highly creative age; and though, after accompanying the poet or orator through the long and varied maze of his discursive wanderings, we may occasionally find that we have travelled far from the direct road of argument, we ought to be grateful for the many diversified and lovely views he has shown us in the journey, and for the fresh and fragrant flowers which he has plucked for us as we wandered.

"We will venture to assert," says a critic who has written of this period of our literature with a warmth of enthusiasm that renders his judgment more genial, and therefore in our opinion more just, than the colder and more cautious approbation of Hallam—"we will venture to assert that there is in any one of the prose folios of Jeremy Taylor more fine fancy and original imagery — more brilliant conceptions and glowing expressions — more new figures and new applications of old figures—more, in short, of the body and the soul of poetry, than in all the odes and the epics that have since been produced in Europe. There are large portions of Barrow, and Hooker, and Bacon, of which we may say nearly as much: nor can any one have a tolerable idea of the riches of our language and our native genius, who has not made himself acquainted with the prose-writers as well as the poets of this memorable period."

The three great names which we have selected to form the subject of the present chapter have been chosen from different though successive periods in the history of the Anglican Church, in order that the reader might remark in what peculiarities they differ, and in what they resemble one another; and thus that some notion might be formed as to the points of similitude or difference existing in the epochs of which they are the representatives. In Hooker we have seen the legislative, in Taylor the oratorical feature of religious writing most strongly developed; in Barrow we shall remark the deliberate species of eloquence existing in the highest force. If the first of these great men has dug deep into the eternal rock on which is founded the whole edifice of human society, in search of materials with which to build up the frame of ecclesiastical polity; if the second, by a sweet and abundant eloquence, has made religion lovely and amiable in our eyes, hanging on the altar of God the freshest garlands of fancy and imagination, and dedicating the rich products of intellect and poetry to the service of that Being whose most precious gifts they are, even as Abel offered up to the Lord the firstlings of his flock; we shall find that the third in this illustrious triad of great theologians did not fall short of his predecessors, either in the value of the gifts which he brought as tribute to the same altar, or in the fervency and purity of his ministration. There is a very strong resemblance between the characters of Barrow and of Pascal.

A comparison, it is true, between the respective styles of these two writers would be in some measure an injury to the immortal author of the 'Provincial Letters;' for Barrow's writings, vigorous and even admirable as they undoubtedly are, hardly exhibit that wonderful condensation and originality which make every line of Pascal appeal so irresistibly and so instantaneously to the highest powers of our intellect, and make us pause and meditate as each new expression seems to open to us a long vista of deductions, or suggests to us a vast and complex train of reasoning. Nor indeed is the style of Barrow remarkable, in so high a degree at least, for the frequent occurrence of those admirable expressions so abundant in every page of the great French theologian: expressions at once simple and profound, intensely idiomatic, yet perfectly new. Yet if we look for a manly and fervid eloquence, for a mighty and sustained power kept under control by the severest logic, for a peculiar quality of mastery and vigour to which all tasks appear equally easy, we may point with pride to the writings of Barrow. "He is equally distinguished," says an acute and able critic, "for the redundancy of his matter, and for the pregnant brevity of his expression; but what more particularly characterises his manner is a certain air of powerful and of conscious facility in the execution of whatever he undertakes. Whether the subject be mathematical, metaphysical, or theological, he seems always to bring to it a mind which feels itself superior to the occasion, and which, in contending with the greatest difficulties, 'puts forth but half its strength.'"

Like Pascal, Barrow was one of the greatest physical philosophers of his own, or indeed of any, age; he was the friend and the preceptor of Newton, and a fellow-labourer with the most illustrious of modern investigators in many fields of natural science, particularly in the departments of optics and astronomy. He thus brought to the task of demonstrating the nature and necessity of our Christian duties, and of inculcating the precepts of evangelic morality, a mind trained in the investigation of abstract truth, and a severe and majestic eloquence, the handmaid of the strictest and most comprehensive logic. He was a man of vast and multifarious attainments, as a very brief sketch of his life will sufficiently prove. Born in London, in 1630, of humble though not indigent parentage, he early entered, at Cambridge, on that career which ultimately rendered his name one of the brightest ornaments of that university. Finding that the religious dissensions of the period of the Commonwealth, and particularly the predominance during that period of opinions totally at variance with his own, precluded any hope of success in the clerical profession, he turned his attention to medicine, and cultivated with ardour many of the sciences which are subservient to that pursuit, as anatomy, botany, and chemistry. Nor did he neglect the studies which we should consider more peculiarly congenial to the venerable walls of his "Alma Mater;" he became a candidate for the professorship of Greek in 1655, but, failing in his attempt to obtain that dignity, he went abroad, and passed some years in the East, and particularly at Smyrna and Constantinople. Returning to England in 1659, Barrow obtained the professorship for which he had been before an unsuccessful candidate, and to this post were added several others, of less dignity indeed, but sufficiently proving the high reputation enjoyed by Barrow in many different and dissimilar departments of knowledge. In 1663 he resigned these appointments for that of Lucasian professor of mathematics in the university, a post which he filled with increasing glory for six years, at the end of which period he vacated it in favour of his immortal contemporary, Newton. His rise to public distinction was now steady and rapid: he was successively appointed one of the king's chaplains; nominated, in 1672, Master of his college—that of Trinity, which thus possessed within its bosom at one time two of the greatest and most virtuous men who ever dignified humanity—the king paying Barrow, as he conferred upon him this deserved honour, the just compliment of saying that he had bestowed it "on the best scholar in England;" and lastly he was elected, in 1675, Vice-Chancellor of the University, which dignity he enjoyed only two years, as he died of a fever in 1677, at the age of forty-six.

Barrow is an admirable specimen of a class of men who, fortunately for the political, the literary, and the theological glory of England, have adorned her two great seats of learning, Oxford and Cambridge, at almost every period of her history. Possessed of vast, solid, and diversified learning, with practice and experience in the affairs of real life corrected and rendered philosophical by retirement and meditation, with the intense and concentrated industry of the monk guided by the sense of utility of the man of the world, these rigorous scholars seem peculiarly adapted by Providence to become firm and majestic pillars of such an ecclesiastical establishment as the Church of England. "Blessed is she,"—we may venture to apply the words of Scripture,—"for she has her quiver full of them!"

CHAPTER IX.

JOHN MILTON.

Character of the Poet—Religious and Political Opinions—Republicanism—His Learning—Travels in Italy—Prose Works—Areopagitica—Prose Styl—Treatises on Divorce—His Literary Meditations—Tractate of Education—Passion for Music—Paradise Lost—Dante and Milton compared—Study of Romance—Campbell's Criticism—Paradise Regained—Minor Poems—Samson Agonistes.

MILTON says, in one of the most admirable and characteristic of his prose works, that a poet should be in his own life and person a "true poem—that is, a composition of the best and noblest things;" and whatever discrepancy we may find between the works and the characters of inferior writers, we shall never fail to remark, in the case of that small number consisting of the *very greatest* names in the history of the human mind, a certain, perfect, and wonderful accordance between the character of the man and the peculiar excellences of his productions. Of the four great Evangelists of the human mind, Homer, Virgil, Dante, and Milton, each is in some measure, personally as well as intellectually, the type and reflection of the epoch in which he lived; and, as the appearance of these great luminaries of man's spiritual horizon was coincident with great events affecting the social destinies of our race, we may even say that these sublime minds at once guided and followed the direction of the opinions and condition of their times.

Homer is, in fact, a short expression for the heroic or mythic epoch, taken in its sublimer and more lovely manifestation; Virgil is the incarnation of the power, grandeur, and development of the nationality of empire; Dante was no less the literary embodiment of mediæval Christianity—that wild and wondrous phase of humanity which is found petrified, as it were, and presented to us in a tangible form, in the great triumphs of Gothic art; and our great countryman will seem no unapt or imperfect type of the Christianity of the Reformation—that is, of Christianity combined with freedom of opinion and the right of private judgment carried to its extremest consequences.

Wonderful, indeed, and complicated as is the combination of causes and conditions which must conspire to the production of any work of permanent and universal importance, and to the existence, consequently, of a mind capable of creating such a work, in no case in the whole history of mankind does that combination appear to have been so wonderful as in the example of Milton. Born in an age when the

13

great advance of civilization appeared to preclude the possibility of any great work appearing to rival the immortal monuments of ancient literature, and when men despaired—as they always have done—of a great epic being ever again given to the world—as if the fountains of the beautiful were not inexhaustible as the rivers of Paradise—he appears to have had a vast and all-embracing sympathy with whatever was ennobling in the opinions of his times. His mind was profoundly and wonderfully *eclectic*. His political and religious sentiments were of the extremest and even most violent character; he was a devoted republican, with his grand imagination ever dwelling upon the visionary phantoms of antique glory and virtue. In the earthquake which overthrew the regal and hierarchic institutions of his country, his unworldly and heroic soul saw only a beneficent and temporary convulsion, clearing the ground of its load of false temples, and preparing it for the erection of a new and glorious social edifice, with something of the pure proportions of the Roman Capitol or of the Attic Acropolis.

In religion, too, his haughty intellect and pure morals revolted at that admixture of human motives without which, like the baser alloy in metallurgy, the pure gold of Christianity can hardly be formed—at least as society is now constituted—into a practically useful instrument for the improvement of humanity; and he hoped that, by forcibly bringing back the Church to the structural simplicity of the primitive times, he would restore the pure, ardent, and evangelic spirit which characterised those ages. And perhaps, in a world peopled by Miltons and by Harringtons, such schemes and hopes might cease to be Utopian. Visionary as they were, these convictions gave a peculiar character of elevation to Milton's meditations; and it is not too much to say that, had his opinions on government in church and state been other than they were, we could have possessed neither the 'Areopagitica' nor the 'Paradise Lost'—

"And Heaven had wanted one immortal song."

But the profession of these opinions, and the fierce zeal with which he advocated them, could not efface in such a mind as Milton's the impressions made by mediæval art and by the chivalrous history of his country. And thus there appears continually in his works, we will not say a contest, but a contrast, between his convictions and his sympathies—between his logic and his fancy. And this, which in an inferior mind would not have failed to produce an incessant uncertainty and inconsistency, in such a soul as John Milton's was a healthy and vivifying action: it was like the conflicting currents of the galvanic battery, whose opposing poles give out intensest light and heat. Thus, while Milton the polemic was advocating the overthrow of the monarchic institutions of England, and the destruction of the hierarchic edifice of its Church, Milton the poet had his soul deeply penetrated with the enthusiasm inspired by his country's history, and his ear ever thrilling to the majestic services of its half-Roman worship. The man who desired the abolition of all external dignities on earth has given us the grandest picture of such a graduated hierarchy of orders in heaven—

"Thrones, Princedoms, Virtues, Dominations, Powers."

He who would have reduced the externals of Christianity to a simplicity and meanness compared with which the subterranean worship of the persecuted Christians of the primitive times was splendour, has exhibited a deeper and more prevailing admiration than any other poet ever showed for the grandeur of Gothic architecture and the charms of the solemn masses of the ancient cathedrals:—

"But let my due feet never fail
To walk the studious cloisters pale;
And love the high embowed roof,
With antique pillars massy proof,
And storied windows richly dight,
Casting a dim religious light:
There let the pealing organ blow
To the full-voiced quire below,
In service high and anthems clear,
As may with sweetness, through mine ear,
Dissolve me into ecstasies,
And bring all heaven before mine eyes."

In the same way, the learning of this wondrous being helped to give his mind that catholicity of taste which is above all things necessary to the production of an immortal work. His *favourite* reading, it is true, lay chiefly among the sages and tragic poets of ancient Greece: he loved to wander through "the shady spaces of philosophy," as he beautifully calls them, with his beloved Plato, to follow the soaring of Aristotle's eagle intellect, to listen to the chime of Homer's oceanic harmony, and to the more irregular music of Pindar, or "sad Electra's poet." But all this never deadened his ear, or impaired his sensibility, for the wilder poesy of the chivalric age, nor for the more feminine and artificial graces of the Italian Muse. He was perhaps the most learned man who ever lived, and at the same time the man who had his learning the most completely under his command. Like Rabelais, Milton may without exaggeration be said to have traversed every region in the world of knowledge explored down to his age; but at the same time we must not forget the immense difference, not only in point of extent, but in point also of kind, existing between the state of human knowledge in the fifteenth and the seventeenth centuries. The first of these two wonderful men was the type of the infancy of the Reformation, the second the embodiment of its manhood. Milton enjoyed the rare advantage of a purely literary education. The intellect and aptitude for study exhibited by him in his earliest childhood seems to have sealed him — even as the child Samson was set apart from his birth to the ministry — to the services of poesy and learning. Though educated in part in the university of Cambridge, he did not remain long enough within its venerable walls to acquire any particular direction of thought which might have fettered the development of so mighty an intellect; but only long enough to fill his mind with all that is most solid and ennobling in ancient literature and in abstract science. The care with which he has preserved even the most trivial productions of his college career, his Latin verses and his fragments of academic comedies, and the tone of serious pride with which he speaks of his own youthful studies, prove to us what store he set upon the scholastic occupations of his youth; and it behoves us to remember that what in meaner men would appear vanity, in Milton must be attributed to a sense of the importance of what in ordinary cases is little more than an unproductive and boyish accomplishment. On leaving the university, where his political and religious opinions rendered his longer residence disagreeable, if not impossible, the youthful Milton — already a prodigy of learning, with his mental graces fitly enshrined in a form distinguished for that pure and seraphic beauty which his person retained through life, and which is conspicuous in all the portraits of him — travelled over a considerable portion of Europe, and was received with particular distinction in Italy. It was here that he became personally acquainted with one of the greatest of his contemporaries, "the starry Galileo, with his woes," whom he saw, as he describes, "now grown old, a prisoner in the Inquisition, for thinking in astronomy otherwise than as his Franciscan and Dominican censurers would have him." How interesting is it to picture such a meeting as that of Milton and Galileo! Lofty, we may be sure, and sublime was their conversation, and these interviews could not fail to add new intensity to Milton's fervid zeal for liberty of thought. In Italy, too, the poet received great encomiums for his proficiency in the language of the country, a language in which some of his youthful poems are composed; and these — as we have been assured by an Italian — are hardly to be detected as the work of a foreigner, and are, indeed, scarcely inferior to the compositions of contemporary Italian writers. Such encomiums as these, which, as Milton himself proudly remarks, "the Italian is not forward to confer on those beyond the Alps," helped, undoubtedly, not only to gratify his haughty dignity of intellect, but probably tended to fix in his mind that preference for Italian literature which is so strongly perceptible in his works. It may, indeed, be said that, possessed as was his mind, and even saturated, with the spirit of antique poetry and philosophy, and intimate as was his acquaintance with the whole circle of dead and living languages, it was the Italian literature which left the deepest trace upon his mind, and gave the most marked colouring to his writings—particularly to those among them which are the more peculiar offspring of his *taste*. As a proof of this, we need only mention some of those among his minor pieces which were evidently the reflection of his personal sentiments; the beautiful pastoral elegy entitled 'Lycidas,' the 'Comus,' and the numerous sonnets which he has left us. In all these works he has closely followed not only the spirit, but even the forms, of Italian poetry. In the first-mentioned work we have a *canzone*, so exquisitely harmonized, and so full of the sweet and elaborate grace of Italian lyric poesy, that the very language and music of it has the echo of

"Il bel paese, dove 'l si suona;"

and it is not too much to say that 'Lycidas' is *an Italian poem composed in English.* In 'Comus,' and the lovely fragment of the 'Arcades,'—a work in that peculiarly Italian species of composition, the pastoral-romantic drama — he has surpassed Tasso as far as Tasso has outstripped Beccari: and as to the sonnet, Milton was the first man who grafted upon our more rugged language that fairest fruit of the Ausonian Muse. We speak of course particularly of that variety — the noblest — of the sonnet, whose tone and subject is not exclusively devoted to the passion of love, but which has been made a vehicle for the sublimest outbursts of patriotism and religion—the sonnet, in short, not of Petrarch, but of Filicaja. To this list it would be quite unnecessary to add those two exquisite poems, in which the thoughts and the mode of treatment are no less Italian than their titles — 'L'Allegro' and 'Il Penseroso.'

As Milton was born December 9th, 1608, as he retired from the university in 1632, and began to travel in 1638, he was, at the time of his sudden return from Italy (having spent only fifteen months on the continent), about thirty-one years of age, in the full glow and bloom of beauty and accomplishment. It had probably been his intention to remain abroad for a much longer period, but the breaking out of that furious controversy between the royalist and parliamentary parties, which ultimately led to the judicial murder of a king and the abolition of the regal office, was an event appealing far too powerfully to Milton's ardent opinions in religion and politics to permit him to remain in a distant country a cool spectator of the mighty struggle. In all matters of church and state the convictions of the poet were in accordance with the extremest doctrines of the republican and Antinomian party. His dream was a commonwealth on the model of antiquity, in which purity of manners and dignity of national character would, as he fondly hoped, accompany the simplifying of the structure of the political machine; he imagined, like reformers in all ages, that the destruction of a religious hierarchy would necessarily introduce, into the practice and discipline of the Christian church, the purity and simplicity of the primitive times.

These opinions, probably imbibed, at a very early age, from his father (who was himself, in some measure, a sufferer for conscience' sake), and still further exaggerated by his own haughty spirit, the poet now maintained with astonishing eloquence and vehemence in a large portion of his prose works. Though these compositions were in most cases written on local and temporary subjects, and though he fierce and often sophistical character of their argumentation may have contributed to withdraw them from the study of the general reader, the prose works of Milton are so strongly characteristic of their illustrious author, and contain so many passages of sublimity and beauty, that some acquaintance with this portion of his writings is indispensable for any one desirous of forming a true idea of the intellectual physiognomy of England's greatest epic poet. The study of these works presents us with a new and most striking phase of his character and history: we see still the grand, colossal, and seraphic lineaments of that intellectual being which has given us the picture of primeval innocence, of the splendors of Paradise, and the undying agonies of fallen yet immortal spirits; but those lineaments are contracted with indignation, and lurid with fanatic and persecuting zeal; the soul of Milton is still a mighty angel, but it is an angel of wrath and destruction — it is Azrael, the angel of death.

The prose works of Milton possessing such peculiar features, and having occupied, in the composition, a portion of his life which may be considered apart from those epochs in his history which gave birth to his immortal poems, we will devote a few sentences to a rapid notice of their subjects, and an attempt to fix their value. Among the principal of these extraordinary compositions it will suffice to mention, in the first place, 'Areopagitica,' perhaps the noblest of them all: this is a 'Speech for the Liberty of Unlicensed Printing to the Parliament of England.' It is singular enough, and characteristic of the inconsistency which always accompanies the policy of revolutionists, that the fanatic Parliament of England exercised a sway infinitely sterner and more tyrannical than had ever been attempted to be enforced by the government which it had overthrown; and while the thousand wild sects which now wielded with ruthless hands the powers usurped from the British Constitution maintained in its fullest development the right of individual liberty and the privilege of absolute freedom of private judgment, the inquisition on the press was never so severe as under their oppressive domination. Pretending to be the priests and servants of truth, and of free opinion —the nurse of truth—they fettered the expression of all conclusions not in harmony with their own exaggerated doctrines: the press was absolutely manacled, and fine, sequestration, and military law, the dungeon, the pillory, and the scourge were the rewards for the publication of anything not in servile accordance with their notions.

Eternal honour, then, to Milton, that he manfully stood up for that great principle without which all the professions of the republicans were nothing but hypocrisy and inconsistence! It was an object worthy of his lofty and ethereal spirit; and nobly indeed did he fulfil it. 'Areopagitica' is a most eloquent and conclusive exposition of the necessity and advantages of a free press, and, though entitled a "Speech," is rather an "Oration," conceived and executed in the spirit of the great monuments of classic oratory.

None, probably, of our readers are ignorant that the orations of Demosthenes and Cicero were elaborate and previously prepared compositions; and that they in no way resemble that extempore species of eloquence which is specified by the term "speech," a word borrowed from the parliamentary eloquence of that country which has produced the greatest triumphs in this kind of harangue. Milton's style in this noble production, as well as in all his prose works, is in the highest degree majestic, and is a perfect reflex of the character of the man.

The truth is, that Milton's mind was so completely imbued, so saturated, with ancient, and particularly with Greek, literature, that he could not help imitating, often perhaps unconsciously, the involved structure, the complicated arrangement, and the half-rhythmical cadence of the sentences of Plato or of Isocrates.

In his eagerness to engraft upon our more rugged and unpliant tongue something of the delicacy, something of the ever-varying flexibility which characterises the ancient classical languages, he may be pardoned if he sometimes forgets the impossibility of complete success, and the danger of falling into obscurity and affectation, as well as an air of constraint and pedantry. A totally uninflected tongue as the English is can never be forcibly submitted, even by the boldness and the genius of such a mind as Milton's, to the laws which govern a different language. Independently of the tone of learned and scholastic gravity naturally acquired by a proud and retiring student, something of the peculiar Latinisms and Græcisms which distinguish Milton's style in poetry no less than in prose (much less obtrusively, it is true, and offensively in the former than in the latter) may be doubtless attributed to his proud contempt for the mean vulgarity which distinguished the style of many of his contemporaries, and particularly the party with some of whose religious and political opinions the great poet had identified himself. Like a man of noble birth and aristocratic manners accidentally embracing the popular side in a revolutionary movement, Milton appears ever anxious that he should not be confounded with the rude and ignorant mob in whose ranks he for a moment may find himself, and puts on a double portion of stateliness and dignity. Having spoken of what certainly appears the most complete and important of his prose works, and also the one which possesses the most general and intrinsic interest, the 'Areopagitica,' we will say a few words of several other compositions likely to attract the reader's attention by their singularity or by the precious details they give us of the author's personal character, sentiments, and pursuits. Milton composed two celebrated treatises on the law of divorce, which throw a great light upon the poet's opinions respecting the rights and social importance of the female sex, and pretty clearly indicate the almost Asiatic contempt with which he regarded the fairer part of the creation. At the same time these works give us a most extraordinary idea of the boldness, nay, the audacity, which characterises all Milton's speculations. Will it be believed that in one of these works, the 'Tetrachordon,' an exposition of the four places of the Old Testament in which the law of divorce is expressly treated, Milton has endeavoured to establish, from the rules and practice of Hebrew legislation, the lawfulness of allowing not only personal but moral "uncleanness" to form the ground of separation between man and wife; and that in various passages of these books the most extreme latitude in this respect is not only tolerated but approved? It is true that much of this eagerness to facilitate divorce may have arisen from a desire to relax, in his own case, the strictness of the marriage tie; for we know that his first marriage was an unhappy one, and that, his wife (the daughter of a cavalier) having left him and refused to return to his house, probably disgusted by the studious gloom and religious severity of the poet's life, he actually gave proof of the sincerity of his opinions by paying his addresses to another lady, whom he would infallibly have married but for the voluntary return and submission of his rebellious partner.

The other work to which we have alluded is unspeakably precious as giving us an insight into his own studies and literary meditations; and though these most interesting details are scattered irregularly over all his productions, there are two passages so peculiarly rich in these invaluable notices, that they must be, independently of their own intrinsic grandeur and eloquence, among the most striking passages of autobiography which the world has ever seen. In one of them he gives a minute account of his own daily life and occupations, and in the other, after describing his youthful studies, and the grand aspirations of his early ambition, he gravely passes in review before him a number of the sublimest subjects for some future work which should make his name immortal, and, with a serious and sustained enthusiasm than which perhaps the whole history of literature contains nothing more solemn and more sublime, promises to leave "something so writ as future ages shall not willingly let die." In this passage he proposes to himself a number of the mightest events in the history of mankind; he explains the means by which the immortal work could alone be worthily executed; he describes the intense labour, the severe meditation, and "expense of Palladian oil" which such a work would require; and, above all, expresses his conviction that the true inspiration for such an effort of creative energy was to be sought for "not in the invocation of Dame Memory and her Syren daughters, but in devout prayer to that Spirit who can enrich with all utterance and knowledge, and who sendeth out his seraphim with fire from his altar to touch and purify the lips of whom he pleaseth." From hopes so sublime as these, expressed with so fervent and yet so exalted a devotion, and supported by such unequalled powers and so intense and irresistible an industry, we might well expect a 'Paradise Lost.'

In his singular little work, a 'Tractate (treatise) on Education,' Milton sets forth his own peculiar opinions on that all-important subject, and handles it with his usual boldness and originality of view. The book is distinguished by the same grand and organ-like harmony of language, and by the same tone of lofty dignity of thought, that mark all he ever wrote: in the project itself, as the subject under discussion is of a peculiarly practical nature, we find even more than his usual audacity of innovation and visionary sublimity of design. Naturally a despiser of authority and precedent, and living in an age when great political convulsions made all men familiar with the wildest schemes of moral and social regeneration, Milton has drawn in this book a plan for an entirely new system of national education. We are not, therefore, surprised to find that he rejects the whole machinery of the school and the university, considering the defects of each species of institution as in no way counterbalanced by their advantages; and proposes, in place of the ancient method, a system chiefly imitated from the gymnasia of Sparta and of Athens! Grand, noble, colossal, but at the same time (as our readers need hardly be cautioned) totally impracticable and Utopian, Milton's plan of education embraces, like that of the ancient Greeks, as may be collected from the half-fabulous accounts of the antique philosophers and historians, the physical no less than the moral and intellectual development of the human powers: the bodies of the English youth were to be trained in all kinds of corporeal and gymnastic exercises, while their minds were to be occupied with the whole cycle of human knowledge, in which the arts, particularly that of music, were by no means to be neglected. The whole scheme reminds the reader of nothing so strongly as of the half-burlesque description of the education of Pantagruel in the immortal romance of Rabelais: and this will be quite enough to show its almost ludicrously-impracticable character. Visionary, however, as is the general design, there are in this half-forgotten tract of Milton a thousand traces of wisdom, of genius, and of sublimity, such as no hand but his own could have left; and even many of the suggestions are becoming generally adopted in the more complete and generous education of the present day, particularly the more extended and universal study of music.

This was an art of which Milton never speaks without a peculiar and most touching enthusiasm; never does he omit to describe—and assuredly no poet has ever described them more frequently or more admirably—the charms and the virtues of music. Coleridge has called him (rather pointedly than justly, it is true) "less a picturesque than a musical poet;" and not only does the grandeur and the might of music incessantly form the subject of his most willing and most glorious soarings into the empyrean of poesy, but in all his works we find a peculiar and recognisable music, an echo of that celestial and seraphic harmony which rolls for ever before the throne of God—"a sevenfold chorus of Hallelujahs and harping symphonies." It was to music that Milton owed the only moments of relaxation which he permitted himself in the intervals of the severe and incessant studies, the fierce and strenuous controversies of his youth and manhood: the aspirations and the prayers which his proud and haughty spirit deigned not to send up to heaven from the midst of any congregation of Christians, rose, at dawn and eventide, upon the swelling notes of the organ, which he touched with no unskilful hand, or the more modest chords of his lute; and when "fallen on evil tongues and evil days, with darkness and with dangers compassed round," in blindness, in poverty, in neglect, with all his bright hopes and all his romantic visions shattered and crushed for ever, then it was that Music became the consolation and the comforter of her fondest worshipper, and breathed her softest melodies and her sublimest thunderbursts into the marvellous verses of the 'Paradise Lost.'

The political career of England's greatest epic poet has been described by a vast variety of writers; and while some have seen in the whole of his public life nothing but a manifestation of virtue and independence, others have found reigning throughout his political life the malignity of the fanatic and the ferocious arrogance of the revolutionist. It will be the safest, and probably also the most just judgment, to take a middle course between these two extremes; and posterity, we think, will confirm our own conclusion with respect to the character of this admirable genius viewed as a Christian and as a citizen. It is impossible not to agree with the republican critics at least so far as regards the sincerity in the expression of opinion which none have pretended to deny to Milton; but on the other hand we think that this illustrious name may well serve as a beacon to those ardent and aspiring spirits who think that genius, learning, and sincerity will suffice alone to guard human nature from error, from folly, or from crime, and who forget the deep truth of that admirable precept of the Great Founder of our religion, "Be ye as little children." In the case of an inferior and a less pure mind than Milton's, the sincerity of his republican opinions might perhaps be pleaded in excuse for the unfairness and violence of some of his attacks upon the monarchic institutions of his country; and the universal coarseness and brutality of tone then prevalent in the style of controversy may be held as palliating the unchristian and inhuman malignity which characterises much of his polemic writings; particularly in his celebrated controversy with Salmasius; but surely no such excuses will serve to diminish our reprobation for Milton's slanderous attacks on the personal character of Charles I., who appears, as a man, to have been worthy of respect, and even of veneration: who was, besides, an unfortunate and innocent prince, and had paid with his blood for the errors of an administration which, however erroneous, was at least well-intentioned. Nor can any one hope, but by sophistry, to excuse or justify the various acts of submission to arbitrary and usurped power which form so strong a contrast to Milton's perpetual and rather obtrusive assertions of independence—his accepting office, for instance, under the government of Cromwell; his adulation of that wily despot; and above all, the melancholy weakness (if indeed we ought not rather to use a much severer term) which allowed him to profit by the plunder of the unfortunate and martyred sovereign, and to decorate his studious retirement with the pilfered trappings of royal magnificence; for, alas! we still possess the parliamentary order permitting "Mr. John Milton," Latin Secretary of the House of Commons, to "choose and take away such hangings as he thinks fit" from the dismantled palace of Whitehall.

Such facts as these are painful and humiliating, but salutary also; they powerfully demonstrate that the greatest genius and the sublimest virtues can never guard from folly and from error the man who once loses sight of those plain and simple rules of human conduct — "Fear God, *and honour the King.*"

At the beginning of this chapter we presented Milton to our readers in the character of the great epic poet of Christianity, and we expressed in a brief allusion the difference between the tone of thought and conception perceptible in the 'Paradise Lost' and that which pervades the 'Divina Commedia.' There is, indeed, a singular resemblance between the intellectual features of Milton and Dante, and no small similarity also in their lives. Both possessed of all the knowledge of their age, both deeply versed in the loftiest subtleties of theology, both animated by a stern and intense religious enthusiasm, yet with minds susceptible of the softest as well as the sublimest emotions, each of them is the type and embodiment of an age of violent social convulsion. The fierce and bloody struggles of Guelf and Ghibelline which drove the great Florentine to wander and die in exile, and the spirit of faction which infuses the waters of Marah throughout every page of the Divine Comedy, will form a very close parallel with the furious civil conflicts which ended in the Protectorate, and the republican and sectarian haughtiness of Milton's political and polemic writings But the difference is, that

Dante is essentially and peculiarly a Romanist poet, while Milton may be considered as the incarnation of the reformed faith — or rather of that faith in its extremest Calvinistic intensity. In their manner of *treatment* the two poets differ immensely, though grandeur is the distinguishing peculiarity of each; but the grandeur of Dante seems rather to proceed from the intense earnestness with which he realises his terrific or sublime creations, while that of the English poet seems rather to spring from *idealising* the phantoms of his imagination: in the one case it is the concretive, in the other the abstractive power; the one is a painter, the other a sculptor. If we may venture to take our illustration from a sister art, we should rather compare the immortal poem of Dante to some of those extraordinary conceptions of the grim monastic genius of the Middle Ages in which our terror and interest are powerfully excited by representations whose elements are familiar and every-day; while Milton's poetical conceptions recall rather the pure outline, the subdued tints, and the grand and pure simplicity of Raphael or of the classical sculpture. All readers have remarked this wonderful power of realizing in the one, and the perhaps equally wonderful faculty of idealizing in the other. When we follow Dante into the tremendous scenes of eternal punishment, we meet the poet's friends and acquaintance, speaking and acting as in the world; his illustrations are of the same actual character; he compares the stench of Malebolge to the horrible fetor arising from the pest-house in the Val d'Arno; his giants are described as so many cubits in height, and their size is compared to that of some tower familiar to his readers and to himself; his demons are little else than hideous and cruel executioners. Milton, on the contrary, affects us less (at least in his more terrible and sublime delineations) by what he says than by what he leaves unsaid. In his lazar-house you see a dim vision of agonized motion, and you hear a mingled and inarticulate sound of lamentation: —

"Dire was the tossing, deep the groans;"

and where Dante would certainly have intensified, so to say, our feeling of the reality of the scene, Milton at once soars into abstraction: —

"Despair
Tended the sick, busiest from couch to couch;
And over them triumphant Death his dart
Shook — but delay'd to strike."

Again, in his mode of portraying immensity of size: Satan stands

"Like Teneriffe or Atlas, unremoved.
His stature reach'd the sky, and on his crest
Sate Horror plumed" —

a picture which is absolutely Homeric. In Dante, and even more universally in Tasso, the terror or the sublimity is of the physical kind, and the impression is produced upon the imagination of the reader by the dread fidelity with which the picture is copied from some known or fancied reality: their demons have colossal size indeed, but they are furnished with the horns, the hoofs, the tails, and the talons of the monkish demonology of the Middle Ages: Milton's sublimest pictures, on the contrary, have none of this material or earthly horror about them, but are terrible thoughts, grim abstractions, whose lineaments are veiled and undefined, and which are only the more irresistible in the solemn dread they inspire, as they address themselves, so to say, not to the eye, but to the imagination: they are fragments of the primeval dark, passionless, formless, terrible. Speaking of Death, he says,—

> "The other Shape,
> If shape it might be call'd, that shape had none
> Distinguishable, in member, form, or limb:"

and again, in the same passage, which all the critics have agreed in calling one of the most wonderful embodiments of supernatural terror which ever was conceived by poet,—

> "What *seem'd* his head
> The *likeness* of a kingly crown had on,"

In these and many other passages the poet seems perpetually on the point of giving way to that tendency so natural in the human mind, to *describe*; but his genius puts a bridle upon the *realizing* power, and the dread image is left in the awful vagueness of its mystery, becoming, like the veiled Isis, a thousand times more august and terrible from the cloud that shuts it from our eyes. The greatest of all poets, Homer, Æschylus, Shakspeare, not to mention the Hebrew Scriptures, are full of this kind of *reticence*, by which the grandeur of the object is rendered more terrible by the gloom and indefiniteness which surround it: when the Greeks are marching to the battle, glory blazes in their van like an unwearied fire. What tremendous ideas are conjured up by Shakspeare's single line—

> "To be worse than worst,
> Of *those* that lawless and uncertain thoughts
> Imagine howling"!

Everything in nature and in art which is supereminently grand will invariably be found to be at the same time simple in the extreme; and, in looking through the whole history of mankind for a subject worthy of his genius, Milton selected, most fortunately for posterity, the event which of all others was the grandest in itself, and at the same time possessed of the most universal and eternal interest to the whole human race—the Creation and the Fall of Man. We say fortunately, for we know that he long hesitated as to what subject he should choose:—"Time serves not now, and perhaps I

14

might seem too profuse, to give any certain account of what the mind at home, in the spacious circuits of her musing, hath liberty to propose to herself, though of highest hope and hardest attempting. . . . And lastly, what king or knight before the conquest might be chosen in whom to lay the pattern of a Christian hero." From various passages of his works it is clear that he had meditated taking as the subject of a great epic, among others, the half-fabulous adventures of Arthur, and throughout all his poems are scattered numberless allusions exhibiting his profound acquaintance with, and deep admiration for, all the treasures of mediæval romantic literature:—

> "And what resounds
> In fable or romance of Uther's son,
> Begirt with British and Armoric knights;
> And all who since, baptised or infidel,
> Jousted in Aspramont or Montalban,
> Damasco, or Morocco, or Trebisond,
> Or whom Biserta sent from Afric shore,
> When Charlemain with all his peerage fell
> By Fontarabia."

No language that we could use would be sufficiently strong to express the extent and exactness of this writer's learning; a word which we use in its largest and most comprehensive sense: no species of literature, no language, no book, no art or science seems to have escaped his curiosity, or resisted the combined ardour and patience of his industry. His works may be considered as a vast arsenal of ideas drawn from every region of human speculation, and either themselves the condensed quintessence of knowledge and wisdom, or dressing and adorning the fairest and most majestic conceptions. If Shakspeare's immortal dramas are like the rich vegetation of a primeval paradise, in which all that is sweet, healing, and beautiful springs up uncultured from a virgin soil, the productions of Milton may justly be compared to one of those stately and magnificent gardens so much admired in a former age, in which the perceptible art and regularity rather sets off and adorns nature—a stately solitude perfumed by the breath of all home-born and exotic flowers, with lofty and airy music ever and anon floating through its moonlit solitudes, decorated by the divine forms of antique sculpture—now a Grace, a Cupid, or a Nymph of Phidias; now a prophet or a Sibyl of Michael Angelo.

In his delineation of what was perhaps the most difficult portion of his vast picture, the beauty, purity, and innocence of our first parents, he has shown not only a fertility of invention, but a severe and Scriptural purity of taste as surprising as it is rare. His Adam and Eve, without ceasing for a moment to be human, are beings worthy of the Paradise they inhabit. In the portraiture of their primeval beauty—the primeval perfection, fresh from the hand of God—there can be no doubt that the poet has embodied the impressions left on his mind by the contemplation of the great monuments of art which he had seen in Italy, and which he so well knew how to appreciate. The relics of ancient sculpture gave him in all probability something of their severe simplicity of outline, while the pictures of Raphael may have communicated the sweetness, grace, and heavenly expression of his supernatural and earthly personages.

But of all the arts which have left their spirit to live and glow through the undying pages of 'Paradise Lost,' music is the one whose influence is most intensely and uninterruptedly felt. Of the power of music Milton held a most exalted idea; partly, perhaps, because its pure and ethereal pleasures were most in accordance with the heroic and celestial character of his mind; partly because it was the art which he had himself most successfully cultivated; and partly, too, no doubt, because it was the only art which his blindness, during a great portion of his life, left him the possibility of enjoying otherwise than in memory. The Paradise of Dante is composed of the two ideas of light and music; and in Milton, though less *exclusively* brought forward, music may be said to be the living spirit animating and pervading every creation of his genius. It is music which breathes in every changing harmony of his intricate and lofty versification; it is music which composes the noblest passages in his Heaven and his Paradise; it is music, too, which forms the only contrast with the hopeless agonies of his Hell: not the trivial and sensuous music of modern days, but those solemn and majestic harmonies which were so honoured in the religious and philosophical systems of ancient Greece, and which are perhaps not imperfectly reflected in the grand compositions of Paesiello, of Händel, and of Beethoven:—

"The Dorian mood
Of flutes and soft recorders; such as raised
To height of noblest temper heroes old
Arming to battle; and, instead of rage,
Deliberate valour breathed, firm and unmoved;
Nor wanting power to mitigate and 'suage,
With solemn touches, troubled thoughts, and chase
Anguish, and doubt, and fear, and sorrow, and pain,
From mortal or immortal minds."

The noble and reverential criticism of Campbell is at once so complete and so condensed, that it will not, we think, be inappropriate to quote some passages of it in this place: nothing can be better or more discriminating:—

"Milton has certainly triumphed over one difficulty of his subject, the paucity and the loneliness of its human agents; for no one in contemplating the garden of Eden would wish to exchange it for a more populous world. His earthly pair could only be represented, during their innocence, as beings of simple enjoyment and negative virtue, with no other passions than the fear of Heaven and the love of each other. Yet from these materials what a picture has he drawn of their homage to the Deity, their mutual affection, and the horrors of their alienation! * * * *

"In the angelic warfare of the poem Milton has done whatever human genius could accomplish. * * * * The warlike part of 'Paradise Lost' was inseparable from its subject. I feel too strong a reverence for Milton to suggest even the possibility that he could have improved his poem by having thrown his angelic warfare into more remote perspective; but it seems to me to be most sublime when it is least distinctly brought home to the imagination. What an awful effect has the dim and undefined conception of the conflict which we gather from the opening of the First Book! There the ministers of divine vengeance and pursuit had been recalled — the thunders had ceased

"To bellow through the vast and boundless deep;"

and our terrific conception of the past is deepened by its indistinctness.

"The array of the fallen angels in hell, the unfurling of the standard of Satan, and the march of his troops; all this human pomp and circumstance of war—all this is magic and overwhelming illusion. The imagination is taken by surprise. But the noblest efforts of language are tried with very unequal effect to interest us in the immediate and close view of the battle itself in the Sixth Book; and the martial demons, who charmed us in the shades of hell, lose some portion of their sublimity when their artillery is discharged in the daylight of heaven."

Another circumstance of admirable originality and effect in the supernatural delineations of the 'Paradise Lost' is the singular felicity with which Milton has given variety and interest to the personages of his fallen angels, by considering them as the demons afterwards destined to mislead mankind under the guise of the deities of classical mythology. The idea of the ancient oracles being the inspiration of infernal spirits, permitted for a time to delude the world, is not, it is true, originally Milton's; he found it pervading all the chivalrous and monkish legends of the Middle Ages; and though many poets have adopted a notion so admirably calculated to communicate poetical effect, and so well uniting Paganism with Christianity, none of them — not even Tasso, or our own Spenser — have made such noble or such frequent use of this powerful means of exciting interest in a Christian work.

In the companion work to his immortal epic, in the 'Paradise Regained' — the 'Odyssey' to our Christian 'Iliad' — the first thing that strikes the reader is the unfortunate selection of the subject, and the general inferiority and weaker interest which marks the execution. Neither Milton, nor any human being who ever lived, could have done justice to the only subject worthy of forming a *pendant*, or complement, to the tale

> "Of man's first disobedience, and the fruit
> Of that forbidden tree.'

The subject to which we allude is, of course, the Crucifixion of our Saviour—the only event recorded in past, or possible in future times, of an interest sufficiently powerful, universal, and external, to be placed in comparison with the Fall of Man. Much as we may regret that Milton's peculiar and not very well-understood opinions respecting the divine nature of Christ, and the completeness of the sacrifice of the Redemption, induced him to select for the principal action of the 'Paradise Regained,' not the awful consummation of that sacrifice on the Mount of Calvary, but rather a comparatively unimportant incident in the earthly career of the Redeemer—the Temptation in the desert—it may be doubted whether even Milton's sublime genius could have worthily represented to mortal eyes that terrible crisis in the destiny of man. Sublime as were the flights of that eagle genius —and what intellect ever soared

> "With plume so strong, so equal, and so soft,"

into the loftiest empyrean of poetry, the unshadowed glory of heaven's eternal atmosphere, the flower-breathing air of primeval Eden, or the "thick darkness" of hell?—it must have flagged—even that mighty and tireless pinion—in the gloom and thunder-cloud that veiled the more than human agonies of the Cross!

Of some of the minor works of Milton we have already said a few words. On those which we have left unnoticed it will hardly be necessary to dilate much more. The merit of these productions consists so much more peculiarly in the manner than in the matter, and they derive so much of their charm from their tone and mode of treatment, that a mere analysis would utterly fail in giving any idea of their excellences; while the reader may obtain from a single perusal of any of them, a much clearer notion of their style than from the most laboured and critical panegyric. They all bear the stamp of the Miltonic mind—fulness, conciseness, a pure and Scriptural severity and dignity, and the most consummate grace and variety of versification.

In 'Samson Agonistes,' Milton has given us in English a perfect Sophoclean tragedy, in which every minutest peculiarity of the Attic scene is so faithfully and exactly reproduced, that a reader unacquainted with the Greek language will form a much more just and correct notion of classical tragedy from reading the 'Samson' than from studying even the finest and most accurate *translations* of the great dramas of the Athenian theatre. This may appear extravagant, nay, even paradoxical; but we speak advisedly. The Greek tragodies were grand historical compositions, founded upon the traditional or mythologic legends of the people for whom they were written, and whose religious and patriotic feelings were in the highest degree appealed to by what they considered as a sacred and affecting representation; exactly as the rude audience of the Middle Ages had their sensibilities powerfully excited by the mysteries. The Greek dramas were, in fact, the mysteries and miracle-plays of the Pagan world, and differed from those of the thirteenth century only in their greater polish and refinement as compositions. Now, the legends of classical mythology necessarily affect no less than the stories of the Scripture history; and consequently the 'Samson' (being in all points of structure and arrangement an exact *fac-simile* of a Greek tragedy) produces upon us, Christians, an effect infinitely more analogous to that made upon an Athenian by a tragedy of Sophocles than could be produced by our reading the best *mere translation* of a tragedy of Sophocles that the skill of man ever executed.

In 'Comus' Milton has given us the most perfect and exquisite specimen of a masque, or rather he has given us a kind of ennobled and glorified masque. The refinement, the elegance, the courtly grace and chivalry—all is there; but there is something in 'Comus' better, loftier, and grander than all this—something which no other masques, with all their refined, and scholarlike, and airy elegance, have ever approached—a high and philosophic vein of morality:—

> "Divine philosophy,
> Not harsh and rugged, as dull fools suppose,
> But musical as is Apollo's lute;"

deep and grand thoughts fetched from the exhaustless fountains of the great minds of old—his beloved Plato and the Stagyrite—thoughts fresh with the immortality of their birthplace.

CHAPTER X.

BUTLER AND DRYDEN.

The Commonwealth and the Restoration — Milton and Butler — Subject and Nature of Hudibras — Hudibras and Don Quixote — State of Society at the Restoration — Butler's Life — John Dryden — French Taste of the Court— Comedies and Rhymed Tragedies—Life and Works of Dryden—Dramas— Annus Mirabilis — Absalom and Achitophel — Religio Laici — Hind and Panther—Dryden's later Works—Translation of Virgil — Odes—Fables— Prefaces and Dedications — Juvenal — Mac Flecknoe.

THE great productions of literature may be looked at under two different aspects or relations. Every illustrious name in letters may be considered as typifying and expressing some great and strongly marked epoch in the history of man in general, and also as the offspring and embodiment of some particular era, or some peculiar state of feeling existing in the nation of which that name is an ornament: that is to say, criticism may be *general* or particular, cosmopolite or national. Thus Milton, viewed as a colossal intellect, without any reference to his particular century or country, may be looked upon as the type and offspring of the Reformation and of the republican spirit combined; regarded with reference to England and the seventeenth century, he will be found to embody the Commonwealth—that stirring and extraordinary period of British history, when the united influences of those two mighty phenomena were acting on a stage sufficiently limited, and during a period sufficiently short, to enable us to form a clear and well-defined idea of their character. The period at which Milton wrote was, as we have seen, a period of vehement struggle between powerful and opposite principles: and if in the illustrious author of 'Paradise Lost' we find the eloquent assertor of the liberty of the press, and the uncompromising advocate for democratic forms of government, we cannot be surprised if we behold, in the ranks of the royalist party, a mighty champion of monarchy, and an irresistible satirist of the follies and vices of the republicans. This champion, this satirist, is Samuel Butler, perhaps the greatest master who ever lived of the comic or burlesque species of satiric writing—a strange and singular genius, whose powers of ridicule were as incomparable as the story of his life is melancholy. In point of learning, vast, multifarious, and exact, he was no unworthy rival of Milton: in originality of conception and brilliancy of form his work is unequalled; indeed, 'Hudibras' is one of those productions which may be said to stand alone in literature. It is not to be denied that the reputation obtained out of England by this extraordinary work is by no means commensurate with its real merit as an effort of genius and originality, or with the vast store of wisdom and of wit contained in its pages; nor is it even probable that this indifference to its merits will ever at any future period be less than it has hitherto been, or than it is at present. It arises from a very natural cause. The subject of Butler's satire was too local and temporary to command that degree of attention in other countries, without which the highest powers of humour and imagination will have been exerted in vain. It is undoubtedly true that the vices, the crimes, the follies so pitilessly ridiculed in 'Hudibras' are common to mankind in almost every state of civilized society; but we must no less remember that some of the more prominent of them never burst forth into so full a bloom of absurdity and extravagance as they did at the memorable epoch of English history which he has caricatured. The Commonwealth and the Protectorate form a revolutionary epoch, and, like all epochs of revolution, were fertile in strong contrasts of political and social physiognomy. Such periods, acting, as they so powerfully do, upon the *manners* of a people, are admirably suited for the purposes of the satiric poet. At such times the elements of faction, the extravagances of opinion, of sentiment, of manners, of costume, are brought prominently out upon the surface of society, and present themselves, so to say, in a condensed and tangible form, which the satirist has only to copy to produce a vivid and striking picture—fortunate, too, if a future age, free from these violent agitations and strong contrasts, does not charge him with exaggeration, and mistake the grotesque but faithful delineations of his pencil for the sportiveness of caricature. Curious as they are to the moral speculator, and full of matter to the studious searcher into the history of party, the absurdities of that legion of fanatical sects by whom the destinies of England were then swayed are neither sufficiently attractive or picturesque in themselves, nor sufficiently well known to the general European reader, for Butler's admirable pictures of them to be generally studied or understood out of England; for with political satire, no less than political caricature, much of the point of the jest is lost to those who are not able to judge of the likeness.

It may be objected that, to the great body of English readers, the very considerable time that has elapsed since the occurrences took place which Butler has ridiculed, and the total disappearance of the things and the men represented in his poem, must have rendered them as strange and almost as unintelligible as they are to the non-English reader, from remoteness of place as well as distance of time, and dissimilarity of manners, customs, and sentiments. This is undoubtedly true to some extent: but the intensely idiomatic spirit of this excellent writer has given to his work a sap and a vitality which no obsoleteness of subject could destroy. An immense number of his verses have passed into the ordinary everyday language of his countrymen: containing, as they often do, the condensed thought of proverbs, they have fixed themselves on the memory of the people by their proverb-like oddity and humour of expression, and often by the quaint jingle of their rhymes. Thus multitudes of Butler's couplets float loosely in the element of ordinary English dialogue, and are often heard from the mouths of men who are themselves ignorant of the source of these very expressions, and who possibly hardly know that such a poet as Butler and such a poem as 'Hudibras' ever existed. The fundamental idea of 'Hudibras' is, in our opinion, singularly happy. The title of the poem, which is also the name of its hero, is taken from the old romances of chivalry, Sir Hugh de Bras being the appellation of one of the knights (an Englishman, too, according to the legend) of Arthur's fabulous Round Table. Much also of the structure of the poem is a kind of burlesque of those ancient romances; and the very versification itself is the rhymed octosyllable so much employed by the Norman trouvères, a measure singularly well adapted for continuous and easy narrative, and consequently peculiarly fit for burlesque. Of comic poetry, part of whose humour consists in a resemblance or contrast between a ludicrous imitation and a serious or elevated original, there are two principal species. In the one, the characters, events, language, and style of a sublime and pathetic work are retained, but mingled with mean and ludicrous objects; as when the heroes of the 'Iliad' are represented as cowards, gluttons, and thieves: and in the other, trivial or ridiculous personages and events are described with a pomp of language and an affected dignity of style wholly disproportioned to their real importance. The former species of writing, it is hardly necessary to say, is called *burlesque*, and the second *mock-heroic*. Of the first kind are the innumerable *travesties* of the ancient poets; and of the second both the French literature and the English possess excellent specimens, though the 'Lutrin' is not to be compared to the 'Rape of the Lock.' Although both these kinds of comic writing may appear to have been the offspring of a considerably advanced period of literature, it is nevertheless certain that specimens of them are to be found at an exceedingly early epoch — even in the very infancy of poetry in the heroic age, and in its second birth or avatar of the romantic or chivalric period of the Middle Ages. We need only mention, in proof of our first proposition, the 'Battle of the Frogs and Mice,' falsely, it is obvious, ascribed to Homer, but still a work of very high antiquity; and also we may refer to many of the comedies of Aristophanes.

As to our second position—that in which we speak of the existence in the Middle Ages of this kind of comic writing—it will be necessary to refer rather more fully to the literature of that early period, not only because this section of it is less likely to be familiar to our readers, but also because it bears more immediately upon the subject in hand—'Hudibras' being, to a certain degree, a burlesque of the tales of chivalry which form the staple of mediæval literature. We have, then, numberless proofs that the solemn, wonderful, and stately romance of the trouvère was often parodied, and that ludicrous and burlesque poems were frequently written, for the purpose of exciting mirth, in which the stately manners and occupations of the knight were represented in connexion with the ignorance, rudeness, and coarse merriment of the peasant; somewhat in a similar manner as we find in the Attic theatre the terrible and pathetic tragedy made a source of laughter in the satiric drama, which is supposed to have formed a part of the trilogy of the ancients. Of these latter only one example now exists, in the 'Cyclops' of Euripides, an admirable and most laughable *jeu d'esprit*, in which the heroic manners and adventure of Ulysses and Polyphemus are evidently travestied from a serious tragic version (now lost) of the same adventure, which formed one of the members of the same trilogy. Not to speak of the ancient Norman subdivision of the Romanz poetry, we need not look farther than our own country to find several examples of the same kind of humour existing in the chivalrous literature of the Middle Ages. And the thing is natural enough; the taste and feeling of the ludicrous, which seems innate in the human mind, will find a ready food in the serious or elevated productions fashionable in any age or country. Among the early English poems to which we have alluded there are two which are not only admirable for their oddity and humour, but curious as presenting perfect examples of the principle of which we are speaking: these are the 'Tournament of Tottenham' and the 'Hunting of the Hare.' In the former of these singular *jeu d'esprit* the reader will find a very lively parody of the language, sentiment, and usages of the chivalric period. The subject is a solemn tourney, or "passage of arms," in which the actors are clowns and peasants instead of high-born and gentle knights, and in which the peculiar terms and ceremonies of these solemn and splendid spectacles are most ludicrously burlesqued and misapplied. In the 'Hunting of the Hare' the leading idea is nearly similar, with the exception that it is not the language and the usages of the tournament which are burlesqued by their connexion with the lowest order of the people, but the terms and, if we may so style it, the technology of the art of venery—an art which was in those ages considered as only second in importance to the science of war, which possessed a language of its own no less complicated and elaborate, and was, no less than it, the peculiar privilege of the nobles In this curious poem the "baseborn churls" go out to hunt the hare with all the ceremonies of knightly venery: and the poem, which describes their mishaps and their ignorant misapplication of terms and customs, produced its effect in a similar way to the laughable caricature of military and heraldic splendour in the 'Tournament of Tottenham.'

"Cervantes laugh'd Spain's chivalry away,"

says Byron; and though it is an error to suppose that the ludicrous adventures of the Knight of La Mancha can in any sense be said to have destroyed a system which had ceased to exist when Cervantes wrote, yet every reader must feel how much of the comic effect of this immortal work arises from the strong contrast and want of harmony between the Don's peculiar train of ideas and the social condition of the times in which he attempts to realise his hallucination. So completely indeed had knight-errantry ceased to exist at the period when the Don is supposed to set out on his adventures, that Cervantes was obliged to adopt the idea of *insanity* in his hero ere he could bring in contact two states of society—two conditions of sentiment so incompatible as the chivalric age and the real manners of his own day. But every one sees how much the ludicrous effect is heightened, nay, how completely it proceeds from this forcible juxtaposition of discordant periods; for as all true beauty arises, in nature and in art, from harmony, so the ludicrous has ever for its principal element the incongruous and the discordant. Place Don Quixote in the real age of chivalry, surround him with the real customs and ideas which his "fine madness" has conjured up from the past and from the world of imagination, and he ceases to be a ludicrous, or even an extraordinary character.

In 'Hudibras,' the form of the poem, the versification, and the conception of some of the adventures, derive their comic piquancy from their resemblance to the solemn tales of Anglo-Norman chivalry. The age of knight-errantry is indeed far less prominently brought in contrast and opposition with a different period in 'Hudibras' than in 'Don Quixote;' but it is so brought to a certain degree, and with a certain degree of effect: and herein we may perceive a proof of Butler's good sense. The manners of Spain when Cervantes lived were indeed widely different from those of the chivalric age; but they were not so completely changed but that many relics of chivalry still existed in the legends, the songs, and the recollections of the people: these existed then, it is obvious, for they exist, to a certain extent, down to the present day. But England when Butler wrote, England in the civil war and under the Long Parliament, was as perfect and absolute a contrast to the chivalric age as the mind of man can conceive. Butler therefore contented himself with taking from that period certain general outlines for his picture, the principal of which—the idea of representing his hero as setting out, attended by his squire, in a garb and an equipment ludicrously caricatured, knight-errantlike, to destroy abuses—he undoubtedly took from Cervantes. The characters of the Knight of La Mancha and his inimitable squire, it should be observed, grotesque as they are, are in no sense intended to excite, or capable of exciting, any feeling but that of merriment—a merriment which in the case of the former is always tempered with respect and pity. The object of Butler was different: he intended to produce in us a feeling of ridicule and contempt, and of contempt carried as far towards detestation as was compatible with the existence of the ridiculous. And in their respective aims, both so different and so difficult, each of these great wits has wonderfully succeeded. Cervantes makes you laugh at his admirable hero, and yet love him the more you laugh; while Butler causes you to detest Sir Hudibras as much as it is possible to detest him without ceasing to laugh. Pity and abhorrence are both *tragic* passions, and consequently, when carried beyond certain limits, are destructive of the sense of ridicule: and these two great men have each in his peculiar line carried their ludicrous character exactly so far as to touch the brink where the comic ceases, and where the tragic begins. Butler's object in writing 'Hudibras' was to cover the fanatic and republican party with irresistible ridicule, and in that assemblage of odious and contemptible vices which he has, as it were, condensed in the persons of Sir Hudibras and his clerk, it is impossible not to see at once the strong though certainly exaggerated resemblance between the original and the portrait, and the extraordinary genius of the painter. Sir Hudibras, a Presbyterian officer and justice of the peace, sets out, attended by his clerk Ralph (who is the representative of the Independents), to correct abuses, and to enforce the observance of the strict laws lately made by the fanatic parliament for the suppression of the sports and amusements of the people. In moral and intellectual character, in political and religious principles, this worthy pair forms a parallel as just and admirable as in grotesque accoutrement, in cowardice, and in paradoxical ingenuity. The description of their character, dress, equipment, and even their horses, is as complete and finished a picture as can be conceived: not a single stroke of satire is omitted: they live before us a perfect embodiment of everything that is repulsive and contemptible.

Though the lines which distinguish these two personages are drawn with a strong, a learned, and a delicate hand, there is too great a natural resemblance between the two classes of which Hudibras and Ralph are the representatives for us to derive from them the pleasure we find in Don Quixote, and which arises from the happy and humorous contrast between the Don and Sancho. The differences between Presbyterian and Independent, Antinomian and Fifth-Monarchy-man, were much better known and more easily distinguished when Butler wrote than they can be now after so many years have tended to confound in one general indistinctness the peculiar features which gave individual character to the thousand sects then struggling for supremacy, each hating with a fervent hatred the Church and the monarchy of England, but abhorring each other with far greater cordiality. But it was not so when Butler wrote, and we cannot, therefore, justly complain that a work written with a particular and definite purpose of local and temporary satire does not possess a greater universality of design than it was likely, or indeed possible, it should have. We must remember that the vices and follies ridiculed in 'Hudibras,' though they may no longer exist under the same forms, yet are inherent in human nature; and we may accept this sharp and brilliant satire as an attack, not upon the Presbyterian or Independent of 1660, but upon pedantry, hypocrisy, upon political and religious fanaticism.

The plot and adventures of this poem are very slight and unimportant: the butt of the author was the whole Puritan party, and he was more likely to render that party ridiculous by what he makes his personages *say* than by anything he could make them *do*. The numerous dialogues scattered through the work are, in this respect, more powerful means of throwing contempt on the object of the satire than the events; though many of the latter, as the adventure of the bear and fiddle, the imprisonment in the stocks, the self-inflicted whipping of the knight, &c. &c., are recounted with great gaiety and invention. The learning, the inexhaustible wit, the ingenuity, the ever-surprising novelty of the dialogues, forbid us to regret, or rather altogether prevent us from perceiving, that the intrigue is so imperfect and inartificial as hardly to deserve the name of a plot, that the action is inconsistent, and left unfinished at the conclusion—if, indeed, the abrupt termination of the poem can correctly be called a conclusion—in which nothing is concluded.

In the interval between the appearance of the first and last cantos the Restoration had taken place, to which Butler had so powerfully contributed, and from which he was destined to meet with such ingratitude; and consequently many of the topics which he had treated with such admirable humour in the first part had become obsolete; so that it may be doubted whether Butler could have completed his work, or whether the work would have been rendered more valuable had he done so. Its success was immense—addressed as it was to the strongest prejudices of the royalists, and directed against a party whose peculiar vices were unusually well adapted to serve as a butt for the satirist. It immediately became the most popular book of the time, was quoted and admired by all the courtiers, and by the merry king himself, who was certainly able, whatever were his deficiencies in more important points, to enjoy and appreciate the wit of 'Hudibras;' but who, with that ungrateful levity which forms the worst feature of his character, forgot to reward the admirable author to whom he owed so much in more senses than one. Butler was born in 1612, and, as far as the imperfect notices which we possess of his early career permit us to ascertain, he appears to have been recommended (probably by his youthful learning) to the Countess of Kent, under whose protection he remained some time, enjoying the acquaintance and conversation of the wise and excellent Selden. He appears afterwards to have passed some time in the service (as clerk or tutor) of Sir Samuel Luke, one of Cromwell's officers, and this person is supposed to have sat for the portrait of the hero of 'Hudibras.' Butler has hence been accused of ingratitude and an odious betrayal of his benefactor; but so grave a charge as this deserves, particularly when brought against an illustrious genius, a much more conclusive degree of proof than the evidence will supply. We must know, first, whether Butler was really treated in the family of Sir Samuel Luke with kindness sufficient to justify us in giving the name of ingratitude to his satirizing of that personage; and, secondly, we must have better evidence as to the severity and malice of the alleged satire itself than is to be gathered from the very few and not very distinct allusions to Sir Samuel occurring in the poem of

'Hudibras.' The rapid and immediate success of Butler's poem of course brought him under the notice of the court of the Restoration, whose interests the satire had so powerfully served; and Charles presented the author with a sum of 300*l.*, promising to do more for him. This promise, however, the king never fulfilled, and the great wit, after living in poverty and obscurity a few years longer, died in 1680, in a wretched lodging in Covent Garden, then the most miserable and squalid quarter of London. He was even indebted to the charity of a friend for a grave, as he did not possess sufficient property to pay his funeral expenses; and it was not till some time after his death that this great comic geuius received the honour of a monument, which was erected, with a laudatory inscription, at the cost of an admirer. This tardy recognition of Butler's merit gave origin to one of the acutest epigrams in the English language:—

"Whilst Butler, needy wretch, was yet alive,
No generous patron would a dinner give:
See him, when starved to death and turn'd to dust,
Presented with a monumental bust.
The poet's fate is here in emblem shown;
He ask'd for bread, and he received a stone."

But the true type of the principles of taste, and the system, not only of literature, but even—we may almost say—even of morality which were introduced into England at the restoration of the Stuarts, is John Dryden, a poet and critic who, if he does not deserve a place among the very first and greatest lights of his country's literature, yet must always be ranged at the very head of the second class. The great revolution in taste to which we have just alluded modified to a most important extent the whole face and relations of society, and so powerful was its influence that its effects are very plainly traceable over the whole of that long period of history extending from the Restoration to the first French Revolution. In order to appreciate and measure the effects of this change, it will be necessary to throw a glance upon the nature and causes of its occurrence at this particular period; and in so doing we shall find a new opportunity of perceiving how closely and intimately connected are the political and literary career of every civilized nation. We have seen, in the Elizabethan age, the newly-developed energies of national genius bursting forth, under the fostering glow of political grandeur, commercial prosperity, and great social cultivatton, into the most extraordinary fertility and productiveness; it was under the wise and vigorous sway of that great sovereign that the country first took up its position as a prominent member of the great European family. The struggles of the Reformation too, however disastrous may have been their temporary effect, had accustomed the minds of men to habits of inquiry, and fortified their intellectual energies by the greatest freedom of discussion exercised upon subjects of the gravest and most enduring importance, and, at the same time, the literature had not been so far cultivated, nor the principles of taste so far established, as to expose the writers of that period to the fatal influence of precedent and authority, compelling them (as invariably happens in more advanced periods of cultivation) to accept without inquiry any set of models from some particular age or country. The result of all this was, that those writers (of whom Shakspeare in poetry, and Bacon in philosophy, are the most glorious and complete examples) possessed in the highest degree the apparently opposite qualities of originality and good sense. Living as it were in the infancy of literature, they brought to the contemplation of the great productions of other lands and other ages an eye unhackneyed and fresh, enabling them to perceive the beauties of nature and of art with a sensibility and a relish arising from novelty; and at the same time they were cramped and enslaved in their own productions by none of those timid systems which are founded upon the supposed necessity of imitating some particular models. That character of freshness, earnestness, and intensity, which marks the thoughts of childhood, is stamped also upon the productions of the infancy of literature; the thoughts of men at such a period have not lost their bloom — the dew is still upon them.

The English nation, exhausted with incessant agitation, and wearied of endless and unprofitable dissensions in religion, hailed with rapture the return of their exiled king, and foresaw in a re-establishment of monarchy a pledge for stability, for peace, and for prosperity. In the ardour of triumphant loyalty, they looked forward to "Saturnian days," and expected that with a restored throne would be restored also the ancient nationality and modes of thought of the English people. But these hopes were destined, as might indeed have been foreseen, to be disappointed. The exiled king, and the little court which accompanied him in all his wanderings, had lost much of the spirit of nationality. Pensioners on the bounty of foreign states, Charles and his personal adherents had rubbed off, by their friction with the men and the customs of other countries, much of that external shell of habits and manners which, if not the most valuable and essential part of patriotism, is yet an excellent protection and bond to the love of country. The exiled royalists too, no more than their "merry, poor, and scandalous" chief, could not be supposed to entertain feelings of very deep devotion to that country which had banished them for so long, and to which they were restored mainly through foreign interference and intrigues of foreign jealousy; for it may safely be said that most of the nations of Europe had watched with envy and distrust the rapid career, so brilliant and so short, of republican England.

In considering how far these circumstances were likely to affect the merely literary tastes and predilections of the restored court, we must not forget that the great productions of earlier and more splendid epochs of English literary history had grown obsolete, if not even unintelligible; for we find Dryden, an ardent, if not very enlightened admirer of Shakspeare, complaining that the writings of the greatest of our dramatists had become little read from the difficulty and antiquated expression of his style. Moreover, the English literature was at the period of which we are speaking absolutely unknown to the rest of Europe — a circumstance for which it is easy enough to find a reason. The French nation was, at the epoch of Louis XIV., the one which had reached the highest point of civilization then attained by any European state: her influence, not only political and military, but even intellectual also, was predominant; she dictated the fashion, not only in all minor matters of dress, amusement, and behaviour, but in literature and art. Parisian practice, and the court of the Grand Monarque, was a jurisdiction from which there was no appeal, and its decisions were held to be equally irreversible, whether they settled the principles of poetry or the arrangement of a sword-knot, the laying out of a garden or the rules of the drama. Now, of all the European nations which have at any period of their existence attained to some degree of eminence in letters, France is incontestably the one which has the least *catholicity* of taste, the least sympathy with what differs from her received ideas. This arises, in some measure, from the unity which characterises French society, and from the political causes which have always made Paris the centre and focus of French nationality. Some portion of the effect may have been produced, too, by the inherent poverty of the French language, and by the sudden and rapid progress which the literature made towards excellence — the cultivation of the field being in direct proportion to the narrowness of its limits. Lastly, we must not omit from our calculation the restless and insatiable vanity which incontestably forms a prominent feature in the French character; and we cannot, we think, long wonder either at the industry and activity with which all the French critics maintained the supposed superiority of their national literature over that of every other European country, or at the complete success which their efforts so long secured. That, therefore, the English royalists should have returned from exile with all their predilections enlisted in favour of French literature, can be no matter of surprise to us. What could have been the opinion of a gay and ignorant cavalier respecting the 'Comus,' for instance, of Milton, or the 'Paradise Lost?' And if he could in no sense sympathise with or understand (as it was next to impossible that he could) the grave and profound loveliness which characterises the works of the great Puritan poet, how very dim and imperfect must have been his impressions of Chaucer, of Spenser, of Shakspeare! The consequence of all this was, that there was introduced into England at the Restoration, not merely a difference of tone affecting the general character of the literature, but new models and new forms of composition. The court too, and the society of the metropolis, now began to exercise a more powerful influence, particularly on the lighter departments of literature; and the manners of that court being exceedingly corrupt and profligate, a deeply-seated taint of immorality was communicated to the social intercourse of the age, which required no short period of time, and no small exertion of good taste, good manners, and religion, entirely to purge away. Indeed this corruption was not entirely eradicated, either from manners or from literature, till the time of Addison. The court thus giving the tone and key-note to the metropolis, and the metropolis to the nation, we cannot be surprised to see that a gay and witty profligacy characterises the lighter literature of this time; and that a certain worldliness, and a perfect acquaintance with the surface of fashionable society, should be the prevailing spirit of the day. The nation, disgusted with the long faces and longer prayers of the fanatics, and suddenly freed from their absurd and odious restrictions, now rushed to the opposite extreme: debauchery was considered as identified with loyalty, and oaths, and deep draughts, and a gay contempt for all the decencies of social life, were, as it were, the badges and insignia of a good cavalier. Men are but too apt in all cases to find pretexts for their vices in what is in itself laudable and excellent; and in the present case the follies naturally accompanying the triumph of the royalist party were fostered and encouraged by the scandalous example of immorality set by the court itself. The king, to whom proscription and misfortune had taught neither gratitude nor propriety, who had returned from exile, like the members of another royal house in our own days, "without having learned and without having forgotten anything," appears to have possessed no one good quality but that of a certain good-natured easiness of temper; and his reign is equally memorable for internal disorder and for external weakness and pusillanimity. Now what are the literary features which such an epoch as we have been describing, and such a state of society, might naturally be expected to possess? Assuredly we should look for no great manifestations of creative genius, for no delineations of tragic passion, for no profound and immortal embodiments of human nature: but satire would flourish, and that kindred species of composition, the comedy of manners or intrigue — that satire (the Horatian, not the Juvenalian kind) which skims lightly over the surface of society, and rather wittily ridicules bad taste, bad manners, and folly, than sternly lashes vice or crime; and that comedy which confines itself solely to the external absurdities of society, and therefore but a portrait or a caricature of a particular age: not the comedy which penetrates into the profoundest recesses of human character, representing in lively colours, not an epoch, but humanity itself. Tragedy they had, and in abundance; but it was a tragedy in the highest degree artificial — an exaggerated copy of the already exaggerated imitations of Corneille and of Racine. At a period when society had lost all real dignity of manner and all true intensity and earnestness of tone, it had lost also all sympathy with natural feeling, and all sense for simple passion: and as the convulsive distortions of weakness and disease may at first sight be mistaken for the activity of healthy vigour, the dramatic audiences of that time were content to accept fantastic extravagance for sublimity, and an effeminate affectation for tenderness. To sickly and enervated palates, simple food is tasteless and loathsome; and the unnatural rants of a false and impossible heroism were applauded by the countrymen of Shakspeare and of Jonson. This was the age of rhymed tragedies: in the eagerness to imitate the whole form and structure of the French classical tragedy, they copied not only what was unimportant, but also what was defective. They forgot that the English language possessed examples of the highest perfection of harmony as a medium of dramatic dialogue; and they servilely followed the metrical system of their French models, a system essentially based upon the unmetrical character of the French language. Nor did they stop here: they found it necessary to copy also the artificial and exaggerated tone of the sentiments, the supernatural and impossible elevation of the characters, and to throw over the whole composition the tint of courtly and fantastic gallantry, which accords so ill with the real manners of those epochs (the heroic age of antiquity in particular), from which they generally selected the subject of their plays. Their heroes are no longer men and women, but glittering puppets, dressed up in a collection of contradictory virtues, placed upon the stage to declaim long tirades of artificial and exaggerated sentiment: and, possessing no intrinsic claims on the sympathy of the spectator (for who can sympathise with a phantom — an abstraction?) they were represented as performing prodigies of impossible valour, and making sacrifices of not less impossible generosity.

In this degenerate age, however, of our literature, England produced one man who, though deeply tinged with the stains of his age and country, yet deserved and obtained, by the innate nobility and grandeur of his genius, one of the highest places among the great men of his country. This was John Dryden. He was descended from an ancient Northamptonshire family, and was born in August, 1631. Though the father of the poet was a man of rigid Puritan principles, the future critic and satirist received a good and even learned education, first at Westminster School, and afterwards at Trinity College, Cambridge. Though his first poetical efforts were devoted to the celebration of the republican chief of England, he very soon utterly abandoned the party and opinions of the Commonwealth, so uncongenial to the character and ambition of Dryden, who was essentially the poet of the court and of social life; and we find him among those who welcomed with the most enthusiasm the restoration of the monarchy. The stage being, as we have already intimated, the most fashionable, and perhaps also the most lucrative arena for literary ambition at this time, Dryden became an industrious candidate for dramatic glory, and he now began that career of writing for the stage which continued with little interruption during his whole life. Among the first plays which he wrote are 'The Wild Gallant,' 'The Rival Ladies,' and 'The Indian Emperor;' but this department of his works it will be needless to particularize, as they are now little read, in spite of passages of great occasional merit, and even many noble scenes of a highly eloquent and declamatory cast. These remarks, however, apply solely to the tragedies, for Dryden, great as were his powers of *satire*, can hardly be said to have possessed a spark of *humour*; and humour is the essence and life-blood of comedy. The truth is, that his comedies were written less in compliance with the natural bent of his genius than to obey the taste of the day, and, like most men who do not possess the *vis comica*, he seems to have invariably mistaken buffoonery for comic wit, and coarse unblushing profligacy for comic intrigue. His comedies are, in short, equally stupid and contemptible, and it is but a melancholy excuse for the errors of such an intellect as Dryden's to allege the corruption of the society of his day, or the force of poverty, as palliating what is equally an offence against morality and good manners. In his tragedies there is much more to admire and far less to blame — a freedom and vigour of expression, a masculine energy of thought, and an inexhaustible flow of the purest English, harmonized by a versification which, for ease, abundance, richness, and variety, has never been equalled in the language. The characters in his dramas are all reproductions of the scanty repertory of the French scene; his heroes push courage and generosity to the verge of madness and impossibility; his heroines are little else than eloquent viragos; and each class of personages has a tinge of the fantastic and exaggerated gallantry which had its origin in the system of chivalry, and which was carried to its highest degree of absurdity in the interminable romances of the school of Scudéri; and his tyrants rant and blaspheme *secundum artem*, in sounding tirades which nothing could render tolerable but the sonorous and majestic versification. The truth is, that the genius of this great poet was essentially undramatic. As he wanted all perception of true humour in comedy, so in tragedy he was completely deficient in that sentiment (so nearly akin to humour) without which tragedy becomes nothing but declamation in dialogue — pathos. But his real sphere was lyric, didactic, and satiric poetry, and in these kinds of writing the qualities which we have described him as possessing — perhaps no poet ever possessed them in so high a degree — shine out in full and unmingled lustre. In 1667 he published 'Annus Mirabilis,' a poem of considerable length, written to commemorate the events of the preceding year, which were indeed remarkable enough to justify the title; — among the rest, the great fire of London, and a desperate action between the Dutch and English fleets. In this noble work he made use of a species of versification (imitated, it is supposed, from Davenant) which was peculiarly qualified to exhibit his mastery over the language, and his consummate power of expressing ordinary thoughts in varied and majestic numbers. It is written in stanzas of four heroic lines, alternately rhymed, and, though deformed by occasional false thoughts and extravagances, by marks of haste and hurry, and injured (as are most of Dryden's compositions) by a tone of adulation and flattery unworthy a great man, it must ever be considered as a work of extraordinary merit. The publication of this vigorous work immediately placed Dryden in the first rank of the poets of his time; and he made an engagement with the king's players to supply them with three plays a-year — a task for which he possessed few qualifications excepting a remarkable boldness and prolific fluency of mind, and an inexhaustible supply of rich and varied versification. He was about this period appointed poet laureate and historiographer to the king, which office, together with his share in the profits of the theatre, amounting to about 300*l.* a-year, afforded him a fixed revenue of at least 700*l.* This must be considered as the most prosperous and flourishing period of Dryden's existence; but he soon became involved in controversies and squabbles with other literary men, and particularly with Elkanah Settle, a wretched scribbler of that day, placed in opposition to Dryden partly by the bad taste of the time, and partly by the ingenious malice of the witty and profligate Rochester. These literary quarrels embittered the life of the great poet; and though we may in some sense be said to owe to them several of the finest satiric productions of Dryden's muse, we cannot but regret that his powerful energies were in so many instances unworthily employed in consigning to an immortality of scorn names which but for him would have been long forgotten, and thus embalming in the brilliant and indestructible amber of his satire the lice and beetles of contemporary literature.

In 1681 Dryden published the splendid satirical poem of 'Absalom and Achitophel.' In this noble production, under a thin and transparent veil of Biblical names and Scriptural allusions, we have a most powerful description of the political intrigues of the Duke of Monmouth and his party, and admirably drawn characters of the principal public men of that time; indeed it is the force, variety, and comprehensiveness of the characters which give the work its value in the eyes of modern readers—a value which it can never lose. In satire it is obvious that a degree of epigrammatic point in the delineation of characters is as essential an excellence as the same quality of brilliant discriminative opposition would be a defect in the drama or in the romance; and thus Dryden's admirable skill in this kind of moral portrait-painting absolutely rendered his dramatic personages mere abstractions, rather artificial combinations of distinct qualities than real human beings. Not even in the elegant gallery of the Horatian satire, nor in the darker and more tragic pictures of Juvenal, can we find any delineations, admirable though they be, equal in vigour, lifelikeness, and intensity of colouring, to the rich and magnificent collection of portraits given in 'Absalom and Achitophel;' most of them have been impressed indelibly upon the memory of every reader of English poetry: we may mention, among others, the characters of Zimri (the Duke of Buckingham), of Achitophel (the Earl of Shaftesbury), of Corah (the infamous Oates), and in the second part the masterly descriptions of Settle and Shadwell, his chief personal antagonists, under the names of Doeg and Og. It should be remarked, that the second part of this striking poem was written, not by Dryden himself, but by Tate under his direction, and that the former's share in it (with the exception of "several touches in other places") was confined to the two latter characters. It is, however, but just to the much calumniated genius of Tate to say, that his part of the poem is not unworthy of his great collaborator, and that his style is hardly to be distinguished, in this work, from that of the master. It is true that we know not how far the pencil of Dryden may have left its powerful touches on the canvas of the inferior artist. This work, like all Dryden's satires, narrative compositions, and the dialogue of his tragedies, is written in the rhymed heroic couplet of ten syllables: a measure which Dryden must be considered as having carried to the highest perfection of which it was capable. It is a species of versification exceedingly difficult to write with effect, particularly in a long composition, the structure of this metrical system causing a tendency to complete the sense at the end of each pair of lines or couplet, and thus being peculiarly liable to degenerate into monotony. But Dryden, by a diligent study of the great models in this kind of versification, and particularly of the works of Chaucer (one of the most harmonious of our poets), learned to surpass all who had gone before him in the qualities of vigour, sonorousness, and variety; and he knew how, by the occasional introduction of a triplet (or three lines rhyming together) and the skilful use of the Alexandrine (of twelve syllables) at the end of a paragraph, to break the uniformity of the couplet, and to give to his versification that

"Long-resounding march, and energy divine,"

which is the peculiar characteristic of his poetry.

He possessed in a higher degree than all our other poets, as Johnson justly remarks, the "art of reasoning in verse," and he well knew that he possessed this rare faculty: his mind was rather ratiocinative than impressionable; he possessed but feeble sympathy with nature, and no tenderness at all; in poetical argument, therefore, in invective, in the delineation of characters of artificial life, he was inimitable. Nor was he less impressive in a higher sphere—that of moral or religious controversy—what may be called poetical polemics. He has left us two noble works of this nature, the 'Religio Laici,' and 'The Hind and Panther,'—works which neither the unpoetical nature of their subjects, nor the occasional false reasonings and sophistries which may be detected in them, can prevent us from considering as among the noblest efforts of human intellect ever embodied in majestic verse. The first is a defence of the Church of England against the Dissenters; and in spite of the local nature of its theme, and the tone of scepticism as to revealed religion which is but too perceptible in many parts, it contains passages in the highest strain of Dryden's peculiar excellences. The other is an attempt made by Dryden to justify, under the form of a fable, his recent secession from the English Church which he had so powerfully defended, and whose dogmas he now relinquished for those of Romanism. This event took place about the period of the accession of James II., and Dryden was exposed in consequence to great obloquy,—his conversion being attributed, and with no small show of justice, to motives of interest. Nothing can be more absurd and unartificial than the outline and conduct of this fable; in which the principal doctrines of religious politics are discussed by animals, and the chief sects into which the Christian world is divided are represented under the guise of various wild beasts. In the masquerade of

"A milk-white hind, immortal and unchanged,"

the poet means to present the Roman Catholic Church; in that of the Panther, the other interlocutor in this polemical dialogue, the Church of England, depicted as a beautiful but not unspotted creature:—

"The panther, sure the noblest next the hind,
The fairest creature of the spotted kind,—
Oh, could her inborn stains be wash'd away,
She were too good to be a beast of prey,—
How can I praise or blame, and not offend?
Or how divide the frailty from the friend?
Her faults and virtues lie so mix'd, that she
Nor wholly stands condemn'd, nor wholly free."

Under the other animals are expressed the other sects; and in the portraits of many of them we recognise Dryden's usual vigour and compression of thought. We may specify in particular the Bear and the Wolf, the Presbyterians and Independents, which are touched with a master's hand. We may remark in this noble work, as in all that Dryden ever wrote, a multitude of those terse and happy expressions which, like the glances in the modern poet, are

> "New, as if brought from other spheres,
> Yet welcome, as if known for years:"

as, for instance, when Dryden speaks of the "winged wounds."

We now approach the latter part of Dryden's life, a period when the sun of prosperity, which had thrown a transient glow of well-being over his career, was to set, and leave the great poet to finish his day in gloom, poverty, and unrequited labour.

At the Revolution, in 1688, he lost his office of laureate, and the remainder of his life was passed in unremitting toil. But no diminution of splendour or intensity is perceptible in the lustre of "this mighty orb of song;" and his great powers seem to acquire new vigour and activity with his declining age and his decreasing fortunes. His latest works are esteemed his best; and it seems to furnish us with an irresistible proof (if such were needed by those who remember the life of Milton) of the elastic and unconquerable spirit of the higher order of genius. Dryden now undertook the mighty task of translating Virgil—a task for which it cannot be denied he was peculiarly unfitted, not only by the character of his mind, but by the nature of his previous productions. Of all the classical poets, Virgil is the one whose prevailing and most prominent merit is exquisite delicacy of thought and expression; a quality which Dryden, partly from want of sympathy, partly perhaps also from the rapidity with which he usually wrote, was in no way likely either to appreciate or to reproduce. His translation, therefore, though valuable as retaining many of the excellences of the English poet, can hardly be considered a faithful representation of the Roman bard: it is Dryden, and often Dryden in high perfection, but it is seldom or never Virgil.

Among the finest compositions of his latter years, we must now mention the Ode on St. Cecilia's Day, a lyric composition of the elevated and elaborate character, which is absolutely unequalled in the English language, and approaches nearer to the true tone of ancient lyric poetry than any modern production. Its subject is the power of music, which is most happily illustrated and described in the succession of different passions and sentiments supposed to be excited by Timotheus, in the mind of Alexander, feasting, a triumphant conqueror, in Persepolis. Pride, joy, pity, love, terror, and revenge, are successively evoked by the magic of the "mighty master," and chase each other, like sun and shade along a mountain side, over the conqueror's heart. All these passions, it is true, are not described with equal felicity or equal taste; but minor defects are forgotten in the majestic movements, now gay and now sublime, of Dryden's versification. It reminds the reader of some grand and elaborate concerto of Beethoven, in which the softest airs and the most complex harmonies alternate with grand bursts of wild tempest-music, and swelling strains of lamentation or of triumph, like the grief or the joy of some whole people. Dryden wrote another ode of great but inferior excellence, a funeral lyric on the death of Anne Killigrew; but this latter is injured in its effect by various passages rather ingenious and fantastic than either pathetic or sublime.

His last work of any importance was his 'Fables,' a collection of narrative and romantic poems, chiefly modernised from Chaucer or versified from Boccaccio. In these his genius appears in all its plenitude of splendour; and nothing can exceed in intensity the impression they make upon the reader of the poet's consummate *mastery* over the whole mechanism of his language and versification, and a peculiar air of conscious power which, though it strongly characterises all Dryden's compositions, is in none of them so conspicuous as in these.

We must not forget the deep debt of gratitude which the modern English literature owes to Dryden, were it only for his having in his fables disinterred for his countrymen the rich stores of poetry concealed in the then obsolete and unread pages of Chaucer, and thus prepared the way for a renewed and more reverential study of the admirable productions of our elder writers. If Dryden had done no more than this, he would have done an inestimable service to the literature of his country; and we should have been at a loss to speak with sufficient respect of a man all whose earlier works are in their general character so widely different in feeling and spirit from the productions of the Middle Ages, and who yet had sufficient taste and discernment, though living in an age when these works were almost completely unread, and perhaps confounded in one sweeping accusation of unintelligible barbarism, to perceive their beauties, and to disencumber them of the dust and cobwebs of two hundred years. But the fables of Dryden are not by any means to be considered as mere imitations or modernisings of Chaucer; they have a character intrinsically their own, and they might be read with great advantage together with the originals. Of course the simplicity of the old poet, the sly grace of his language, that exquisite tone of *naïveté*, which, like the lispings of infancy, gives such a charm to the early literature of almost every country, the direct and simple pathos coming directly from and going as directly *to* the heart—all this is wanting in the imitations of Dryden; and it is questionable whether, even if he had felt and sympathised with these qualities of his original (qualities possessed by almost all early poets, and most peculiarly by Chaucer), the process of transfusion into more modern language would not have evaporated this aroma of antiquity: for a modern poet, not inferior to Dryden in genius, and certainly superior to him in reverential admiration of Chaucer, has confessed his complete failure in the attempt to modernise these delightful works without losing their *bouquet*. But what he wants in tenderness Dryden amply makes up in grandeur, in variety of diction, and in richness of metrical arrangement. Among the finest of these tales are the admirable stories of Palamon and Arcite, Cymon and Iphigenia, January and May, and Theodore and Honoria. The besetting sin of Dryden was the vice of his age—licentiousness; a defect which stains this no less than his other works. Chaucer is sometimes coarse and plain-spoken, but he is never immoral; his indelicacies are less in the idea than in the language, and arise less from any native pruriency in the poet's mind than from the comparative rudeness and simplicity of his age: Dryden's we must confess with sorrow and humiliation, are deliberate and most reprehensible administerings to the base profligacy of a corrupted society. In these tales, many of which are distinguished, in the original of Chaucer or Boccaccio, for deep and simple pathos, Dryden shows his usual insensibility to the softer and tender emotions. His love is little else than the physical or sensual passion, and he signally fails in exciting pity. Of this latter remark we shall find abundant proofs; we need only mention the weak and cold painting, in Dryden, of the dying scene in Palamon and Arcite—a scene which, in Chaucer, it is scarcely possible to read without tears.

Dryden's prose is such as such a man might naturally be expected to write. It is careless, hasty, and unequal, but vigorous and idiomatic to the highest degree. His unversified compositions consist chiefly of dedications and prefaces. The former was a species of necessary accompaniment to every book at a time when the literary profession occupied a much lower place in the scale of society than it has since attained. It is humiliating to think of the greatest genius and intellect thus begging, in a strain of adulation only the more fulsome as the more elegant, the patronage of some obscure great man to works which were destined to immortalise the age which produced them, and to form the brightest ornament of the country which gave them birth. How painful to see them thus selling their precedency and birthright for "a piece of silver," and stimulating the niggard bounty of a patron with the highest refinements of intellectual flattery! But this deplorable sacrifice of independence literature is no longer compelled to make,—

"The struggling pangs of conscious truth to hide,
To quench the blushes of ingenuous shame,
To heap the shrine of luxury and pride
With incense kindled at the Muse's flame."

These dedications in most cases are absolute models of elegance and style; so much so, that in reading them one almost forgets the grossness of the adulation they convey. In the prefaces, which were generally treatises on various departments of poetry, or critical essays on the characters of poets, Dryden has established for himself a claim, not only to the glory of being one of the most nervous and idiomatic writers in the language, but also to that of having been the first to write in English anything that deserves the appellation of liberal and comprehensive criticism. These prefaces were in general composed with no higher object than that of swelling the size, and consequently augmenting the price, of the pamphlet or volume to which they were appended; and though written to all appearance very rapidly and carelessly, these essays frequently contain the first germs or outlines of a true judgment respecting the merit of ancient or modern authors, and remarks, equally solid and original, concerning many important departments of literature. That Dryden's literary creed is not always orthodox, nor his opinions always tenable, can be matter neither of astonishment nor animadversion; for we must remember that he lived when the fundamental principles of criticism were not yet established, and that he was the first English labourer who drove a plough into that rich and fertile field which was destined to be so assiduously cultivated. In some of these compositions he has given us short but masterly sketches of many of our older authors, whose works, when Dryden wrote, were either not read at all, or were quoted with a species of disparaging and half-contemptuous approbation. He deserves therefore, and he will obtain, everlasting glory for the justice which he has so nobly rendered to the merits of our elder dramatists—authors with whose peculiar excellences he could hardly have been expected (*à priori*) to feel any very deep sympathy, and whom the fashion of his age had apparently consigned to oblivion; and a still higher degree of applause must be assigned to him for the noble testimony he has borne to the transcendent merit of Milton, an author whose works it must have been, were it only from political motives, unfashionable, if not even dangerous to praise.

In the brief account which we have given of the numerous and varied productions of this great man, we think we have omitted few of any importance, if we except his translation, or rather paraphrase, of the satires of Juvenal and Persius, and his imitations of the epistles of Horace. There was so much resemblance between the personal and literary characters of Dryden and Juvenal, that we should expect to find in the English poet a perfect reproduction, not only of the matter, but of the manner, of the Roman bard. And we shall not be disappointed. The declamatory boldness, mingled with frequent touches of sarcastic humour; the rhetorical gravity, relieved by a kind of stern mirth; the inexhaustible richness of invective; and the condensed weight of moral precept; — all these were qualities which Dryden's moral poetry possesses of itself: he had not to go out of his own manner to be a perfect representative of Juvenal.

This is amply proved by his own satire entitled Mac-Flecknoe, perhaps the most vehement, rich, and varied piece of invective in which personal hatred and contempt ever borrowed the language of moral or literary reprobation. It is chiefly directed against Shadwell, whom he represents, in a kind of mock-heroic allegory, admirable for its boldness and vivacity, as the successful candidate for the crown of stupidity, left vacant by the abdication of Flecknoe, a wretched poetaster of that day, and whose Irish origin is wittily indicated in the name *Mac*-Flecknoe conferred upon his worthy successor. This poem is "the sublime of personal satire:" the lines seem to flow on, burning, bright, and irresistible, like the flood of lava bursting from the crater of the volcano, withering, crushing, and blasting all that they approach.

Dryden died in comparative poverty, though universally placed by all his contemporaries at the head of the poets of his age, a position which his name will ever continue to retain. This event took place on the 1st of May, 1700, and his remains were buried with great pomp in Westminster Abbey. The expense of his funeral was defrayed by a public subscription, and a monument was afterwards erected in his honour by the Duke of Buckingham, intended to bear the following dignified and laconic inscription:—

"This Sheffield raised: the sacred dust below
Was Dryden once. The rest who does not know?"

CHAPTER XI.

CLARENDON, BUNYAN, AND LOCKE.

Clarendon's Life—History of the Rebellion—Characters—John Bunyan—The Pilgrim's Progress—Allegory—Style—Life of Bunyan—Locke—The New Philosophy—Practical Character of Locke's Works—Life—Letters on Toleration—Essay on the Human Understanding—Theory of Ideas—Treatises on Government—Essay on Education.

In the same manner as the external character of the scenery of any country is reflected in the fine arts which flourish there, do the great and stirring periods of history tend to produce the talent by which alone they can be worthily commemorated and described: the savage grandeur of the Calabrian mountains and the sunny loveliness of the plains of Romagna are not more certainly the suggestive cause of Salvator's wild sublimity or Claude's romantic grace, than the rout of Xerxes was of the patriotic fervour of the Æschylean tragedy, or the Peloponnesian War of the profound political philosophy of

Thucydides. We cannot therefore wonder that the great Civil War in England, the Republic, the Protectorate, and the Restoration — a period so crowded with events, and so full of intense dramatic interest — should have produced a historian worthy of describing the mighty revolutions which were to exercise so extensive and enduring an influence upon the future fortunes of Great Britain.

These events were sufficiently striking and important to have inspired even an ordinary intellect: a narration tolerably faithful and detailed, and executed by a common hand, could not fail to possess a strong and lasting interest. How fortunate are we, then, to have a history of this busy period, executed by a man not only endowed with extraordinary powers of intellect, but one who was himself a principal actor in the occurrences he describes! This was Edward Hyde, afterwards Earl of Clarendon and Lord Chancellor of England His work is invaluable for more reasons than one. It contains a minute account of a period of peculiar importance in the constitutional history of the country, was the production of a distinguished lawyer and statesman, himself in a position to enjoy unusual opportunities for obtaining accurate and extensive information, and personally acquainted with many of the most distinguished men of the time; it is much more free from partiality and prejudice than could be reasonably expected under the circumstances, and is, above all, written in that easy and colloquial style which is best adapted to recount the events, without depriving them of their natural power of interesting and amusing the reader.

Hyde was born in 1608, and, after studying at Oxford, devoted himself to the profession of the law, in which he soon distinguished himself so far as to attract the notice of the famous Laud. Being a man of considerable fortune, he now abandoned (in 1640) the practice of his profession, entered parliament, and commenced a political and literary career. He appears, after some hesitation, to have joined the royalist party, and became one of the most wise and trusty advisers of the unfortunate monarch, whose contentions with his parliament and people were so soon to end in the destruction of his throne, the loss of his life, and the expatriation of his family. Though professing monarchic and constitutional opinions, Hyde never pushed them to that pitch of extravagance which caused the temporary ruin of the monarchy; and if the vacillating and infatuated Charles had yielded to the advice of his moderate and sensible minister, the fatal catastrophe might perhaps have been avoided; for the English people has ever been distinguished, as a body, for its firm attachment to monarchical institutions; its cry has been, in all ages, when its true sentiments have been able to secure free expression, that of the barons of King John — "Nolumus leges Angliæ mutari." But it was not to be so in the present instance; Charles I. was destined to pursue the fatal path traced out for him by a mistaken (however sincere) notion of his own prerogative; the nation was to be precipitated into twenty years of bloodshed and tyranny, and Providence was to give a terrible lesson to all infatuated kings and to all rebellious peoples.

Hyde, who had been made Chancellor of the Exchequer, and raised to the dignity of knighthood, now quitted the king at Oxford, and accompanied Prince Charles to the west of England, and afterwards to the island of Jersey, where he remained for two years, occupied in writing an account of the events in which he had been engaged. This was probably the happiest and most tranquil period of his life. In 1648 he again joined the prince in Holland, from whence he was sent to Madrid on a mission to the court of Spain. This embassy—the object of which was to induce Spain to interfere actively in behalf of the exiled house of Stuart—was totally ineffectual; so much so, indeed, that Hyde and his companions were ultimately ordered to quit the country. The subject of our remarks now rejoined his wife and family, whom he had left at Antwerp; and after passing some time there in extreme distress, and even destitution, he again returned to his unfortunate master, who was now at Paris. From this period till the Restoration, Hyde continued to perform for the royal exile those services which none but a very wise and faithful adherent could have rendered, which the carelessness, profligacy, and extravagance of the second Charles's character made so necessary, and which no gratitude could repay. He watched over the financial affairs of the king and his ragged little court, gave continual advice, frequently as unpalatable as it was wise, and keeping up by every means in his power the sometimes precarious harmony, and still more precarious respectability, of the little band of gentlemen who surrounded the king.

Charles, to whom Hyde must have appeared in the light in which a dissipated youth of ruined family regards a severe but faithful steward, expressed his gratitude to him by naming him Chancellor, a dignity which at that time was productive rather of danger and annoyance than either profit or power. At the Restoration he began to receive the solid and merited recompense for his services and privations. He was now the first officer of the crown, and had reached the highest dignity which a subject can attain. His daughter, by marrying the Duke of York, became closely allied to the royal family of England; and at the coronation, in 1661, Hyde was created Earl of Clarendon, and presented with 20,000*l.* For some time he continued to be one of the king's chief advisers; and it is allowed by politicians of all parties that his counsels were distinguished for their sagacity and their moderation. But he soon began to incur the dislike not only of the court, but of the nation. The former were jealous of him for the severity of his morals, for his opposition to the extravagance and profligacy of the times, which must have made Clarendon a perpetual contrast and reproach to the society of that day; and the people, still in the fervour of loyalty, and probably jealous of the great wealth and aggrandisement of Hyde and his family, were but too apt to echo the sentiments of the court. He was compelled to resign the Great Seal, and forced, by the ingratitude of the sovereign for whom he had done so much, to leave the country. He retired to France, where he employed the closing years of his life in composing his invaluable history. He died in 1674.

His 'History of the Great Rebellion' was written entirely from personal recollections, and in that style which is best adapted to relate personal recollections with effect. It is perfectly natural and easy; and thus the strange and romantic adventures of the king are recounted in a manner which not only renders them more impressive and amusing, but convinces the reader of the narrator's good faith and accuracy. Absolutely impartial in every case it is not, and it could not be; but it has always been considered, and with justice, as the most faithful and comprehensive account we possess of the interesting events it commemorates. The style has some defects of prolixity and want of clearness; but it is a work to which the reader returns again and again with renewed pleasure and profit, not only from the immense mass of information which it contains, but from the vigorous, sagacious, manly, and honourable tone of thought which pervades it. It abounds in minute and complete characters of public men. We are hardly apt to appreciate all the penetration displayed in these, as we consider them, in the reading, to be simply a recapitulation of the historian's observations; and we do not at first perceive the quiet sagacity with which this great intellectual portrait-painter has concentrated his attention upon those traits which constitute the individuality of the subject, neglecting, or rather judiciously subduing, those features which are not so marked and characteristic. As, in examining the living likenesses of Titian and Vandyke, a spectator unacquainted with the practical details and the practical difficulties of the art will find his impressions of the painter's genius absolutely weakened by the very ease and facility of the execution, so it may be said that the apparent naturalness and simplicity of Clarendon's narrative is apt at first to diminish our feeling of the difficulty of his task, and of the skill with which he has executed it. "Clarendon," says Hallam, "is excellence in everything that he has performed with care; his characters are beautifully delineated; his sentiments have often a noble gravity, which the length of his periods, far too great in itself, seems to befit; but in the general course of his narration he is negligent of grammar and perspicuity, with little choice of words, and therefore sometimes idiomatic without ease or elegance."

Besides his excellent History, Clarendon has left us, not to speak of a great number of state papers, written in a manner seldom equalled for dignity and weight, a few other works, several of which remained unpublished and unknown till a considerable time after his death, when they were printed, and have much contributed to establish his fame as a great writer, and a wise and virtuous man. That which is likely to possess the most universal interest is a dissertation on the comparative happiness and usefulness of an active or a contemplative life. It is an irresistible argument in favour of the former: and Clarendon's own busy and patriotic existence is a complete confirmation of the proposition maintained by his vigorous logic.

We have more than once taken occasion to remark that in every sound, durable, and healthy literature there will always be found a large number of illustrious names, of men sprung from the middle and lower, and even the humblest, ranks of society: and this phenomenon will be more frequent, obviously, in proportion as the literature in question is of a vaster and more all-embracing character, the expression of national sympathies and feelings, and speaking loudly and clearly to the national heart. To the glory of England it must be said, that the vernacular literature of no civilized nation in ancient or modern times can show so long and so splendid a list of men rising from the humbler classes of citizens, and eternising their own age and their country's greatness by triumphs of valour, of wisdom, and of genius. Among these, not the least remarkable is John Bunyan, whose career was as extraordinary as his origin was low, or as his productions are inimitable and original. There is perhaps hardly any European language which does not possess a version or a paraphrase of the 'Pilgrim's Progress'—that wonderful fiction, in which a religious allegory is conveyed with an effect absolutely heightened by the very qualities of style which at first sight we should consider would be most likely to injure its impressiveness, by an unequalled simplicity and even rudeness of language, and by a bold directness of metaphor and a fearless literalness of parable which no other work, we think, exhibits.

The subject of this romance (for it partakes of the elements of romantic fiction) is a delineation of the trials, temptations, struggles, and ultimate triumph of a Christian, in his progress from a life of sin to eternal felicity, typified under the Golden City, or the New Jerusalem of the Apocalypse. These adventures are all parables; and the hero, Christian, his friends and enemies—in short, all the personages of the drama—are more or less of the same character, personifications of abstract qualities, the follies, the vices, the fears, the hopes, the virtues, and the failings of religious humanity. So far we have nothing more than the ordinary materials of apologue or allegory. In what then consists the peculiar charm of this strange and original fiction,—a charm which renders the rude pages of Bun yan as familiar and delightful to a child as they are attractive to the less impressionable mind of critical manhood? It is the homely earnestness, the idiomatic vigour of the style; it is the fearless straightforwardness of the conceptions, and the inexhaustible richness of imagery and adventure. Drawing all his materials from the Scriptures and from the vivid and intense recollections of his own spiritual career, the wonderful tinker seems to recount the adventures of his hero with a simple eagerness and good faith which annihilates our consciousness of the intervention of a book between the author and the reader: we seem to be sitting besid him as he labours at his "tagged laces" in the jail of Bedford, and we listen with the willing attention and the absorbing wonder of a child hearkening to its nurse's fairy-tale. Indeed the very rudeness of the style, with its rough idiomaticism, its picturesque rustic earnestness, and the strong tinge of Scriptural phraseology, brings us involuntarily back to the age of infancy—the age of belief. In the painting of the multitude of characters which crowd the action of his strange drama, we often mark vigorous strokes of observation, sagacity, and even humour. The adventures, too, are varied with a prodigality of conception which appears absolutely unbounded; and though the primary idea of them is often little more than a bold embodiment of some Scriptural phrase or metaphor, yet the author seems, in spite of himself, to have perpetually brought them before us, and home to our senses as it were, by some unexpected and most picturesque touch of description, generally of that *actual* and material kind which forms so great a charm in popular legends. Like these latter productions, the episodes of Bunyan's Christian drama often possess a high degree of what we may call simple ingenuity: they sometimes attain a true natural tenderness and beauty, and not unfrequently an unusual pitch of terrific grandeur and sublimity. What, for instance, can be more simply and therefore more genuinely graceful than the pastoral picture of the shepherds on the Delectable Mountains; what more gloomy and more terrific than the Valley of the Shadow of Death; what more natural, lively, and dramatic than the dialogues with Mr. Hopeful, Mr. Greatheart, and Mr. Littlefaith?

The impressiveness of Bunyan resembles that of the old woodcuts executed in the infancy of the art of engraving: there is in both cases a rude vigour and homeliness of outline, a strange ignorance of costume, and a powerful tendency to realise even the most abstract things by connecting them with the ordinary details of everyday life; there is also the same earnest intensity of purpose, and incessant struggle to bring the objects within the comprehension of the uncultivated minds to which the work was addressed. Above all there is visible, in the rude woodcut of the old German artist, as in the hardly less rude narrative morality of the English tinker, the unmistakable and inimitable originality of genius. It is this quality which prevents the style of Bunyan, though often *coarse*, from ever being *vulgar.*

Southey has excellently remarked, in his preface to the 'Pilgrim's Progress,' "His is a homespun style, not a manufactured one: and what a difference is there between its homeliness and the flippant vulgarity of the Roger L'Estrange and Tom Brown school! If it is not a well of English undefiled, to which the poet as well as the philologer must repair if they would drink of the living waters, it is a clear stream of current English, the vernacular speech of his age—sometimes, indeed, in its rusticity and coarseness, but always in its plainness and its strength. To this natural style Bunyan is in some degree beholden for his general popularity; his language is everywhere level to the most ignorant reader and to the meanest capacity; there is a homely reality about it; a nursery tale is not more intelligible, in its manner of narration, to a child."

In speaking of the causes of the extraordinary attraction which this book possesses, particularly to the young, we must not forget the immense command which Bunyan had over the whole vast store of Scripture language and imagery. He was emphatically a man of one book, a circumstance which was of itself almost sufficient to give his mind and productions a stamp of sincerity, originality, and force. He is a man of one book, and that book was the best. It was religion which first raised Bunyan from the slough of coarse indulgences and brutal ignorance in which, as he relates in his strange autobiography, he was plunged during the early part of his life: it was religion that first stirred up the depths of his honest and enthusiastic soul, and taught him to think as well as to feel: and much as his fanaticism (which was undoubtedly in some degree extravagant, proportioned to the greatness of the change produced in him by the vivifying influence of religious conviction acting on a powerful, imaginative, and uneducated character) may have exaggerated the extent of that transformation, we cannot wonder at his profound and incessant meditations on the instrument that produced it.

His life may be recounted in a few words: he was the son of a tinker in Bedfordshire, and was born in 1628. Having acquired no education beyond reading and writing, he followed his father's less than humble occupation, and travelled about the country, indulging in all manner of profligate and sinful habits, among which that of swearing appears to have been perhaps the most reprehensible, though he speaks himself with almost equal horror of his reprobate taste for dancing, ale-drinking, and bell-ringing. After having been awakened, as he himself imagined (as do all enthusiasts in a similar case), by a direct miraculous interposition of God, to a sense of his lost and wicked state, he appears to have gone through all the phases of transformation, from a careless and debauched peasant—"Christopher Sly, old Sly's son of Burton-heath; by birth a pedler, by education a cardmaker, by transmutation a bearherd, and now by present profession a tinker"—into an eloquent and celebrated preacher, and an author of enduring reputation. His religious convictions having gradually acquired consistence and certainty, he was admitted, in 1655, a member of the sect or congregation of Baptists; and he in time became a distinguished spiritual leader of that society. In this position he remained for five years, when he fell under the provisions of the law enacted against various denominations of Dissenters, and was imprisoned during twelve years in the jail of Bedford. Part of this long reclusion he employed in the composition of his works, the principal of which are the singular and interesting autobiography to which we have more than once alluded, and to which he gave the title of "Grace Abounding to the Chief of Sinners;' the 'Pilgrim's Progress;' and another religious romance or allegory, entitled 'The Holy War made by King Shaddai on Diabolus, for the regaining of the Metropolis of the World, or the losing and regaining of Mansoul.' Under this strange fanatical title it may easily be understood that we have a description of the Fall of Man, typified in the siege of the city of Mansoul, by Immanuel, the son of Shaddai or Jehovah, who ultimately retakes it from the usurper Diabolus. The 'Pilgrim's Progress' is divided into two parts, of which the first is by far the most striking, the latter exhibiting considerable marks of inferior originality and vivacity, and thus following the ordinary course of Second Parts and Continuations. The first part describes the adventures of Christian in his pilgrimage to the Heavenly Jerusalem; and the second goes over the same ground with a manifest and unavoidable diminution of interest, detailing the journey taken by the wife and children of Christian.

In the manner of thinking, in the subjects selected by this singular genius, no less than in the style by which he conveys his conceptions to the reader, we find innumerable traces of that enthusiastical and fanatic spirit which was prevalent in England during the Civil War and the Republic, and which still characterises the opinions and the language of those numerous sects which dissent from the discipline and doctrines of the Church of England. It is an ardent, sincere, and active spirit, and, if not always very philosophical, very reasonable, or very charitable, we must remember that it has generally been lighted up and cherished by proscription and persecution, and consequently is generally found burning most brightly in the hearts of the obscure and the uneducated. It is not surprising, therefore, that the exclusive study of the Scriptures, and incessant meditation upon a topic so mysterious and so all-important as religion, should lead poor and ignorant and persecuted men first into enthusiasm and then into fanaticism and superstition, and make them fall into the error, so universal in all ages, of overrating the importance and misinterpreting the significance of their own internal sensations, and investing the phantoms of their own heated imagination in the sacred character of direct inspirations of God.

Bunyan was liberated from prison by the generous and charitable interference of Barlow, Bishop of Lincoln, and continued to exercise his occupation of itinerant preacher till the proclamation of James II. appeared, recognising the right of the dissenting sects to liberty of conscience and worship. He then was enabled, with the assistance of several friends, to build a meeting-house in Bedford, where he continued to preach with great and increasing reputation, occasionally making visits to his brother nonconformists in London, until his death. This event took place in 1688. Few of his numerous works are now read, with the exception of the 'Pilgrim's Progress,' a book whose admirable originality will ever cause it to retain its place in English literature beside the 'Robinson Crusoe' of De Foe, a fiction to which it bears in many points a very strong resemblance — a resemblance for which we shall endeavour to account in another place, when we come to speak of the last-named production. The two works are equally favourites with the young: they are read with equal interest, and remembered in after life by all who ever read them with equal tenacity.

In speaking of the vast revolution brought about in philosophy by Bacon, we took occasion to remark how fortunate it was for his system, and for the future value of his writings, that their author should have been a man not theoretically alone, but also practically, acquainted with human affairs, and with the ordinary operations and general errors of the human mind. The distinguishing quality of the New Philosophy is precisely this practical spirit; and whatever the speculations of science have lost in our later days in sublimity and abstractness of tone has been more than compensated for by their greater accuracy, usefulness, and fertility. And indeed this superior sublimity of ancient philosophy is much more in appearance than in reality; for the triumphs of modern science, if more modest in their form and mode of acquirement, are incomparably more solid and more productive; and a much truer and therefore sublimer idea of the grandeur and majesty of nature will be obtained from the calm and cautious experimentalism of modern days, than could be acquired from the bold but so often fallacious theorising of the ancient hypothetical and dogmatic method. Indeed it may be said that the older manner of philosophizing drew us rather to admire the genius and invention of the speculator, while the modern way leads us immediately to the contemplation of the subject of the speculation; and fills us with admiration, not for the intellect, displayed in the investigation, but for the wonders of the department of nature which forms the subject of the inquiry. In this respect, therefore, whatever has been lost by the philosopher has been more than regained by philosophy.

Perhaps one of the most striking exemplifications of the Baconian method, in matter as well as in form, is to be found in the writings, so various and so important, of John Locke. Nor was there a less striking resemblance betweeen many principal features of the personal and intellectual character of these two great men. They possessed, both of them, the spirit of the practical — the useful — in the very highest degree: they both declared incessant and unrelenting war against the spirit of obscurity and mystery, the host of arbitrary and technical forms, in which the subjects of their speculations had been obscured and enveloped by the scholastic philosophers: they were both the apostles and the high priests of common sense.

Something of this plain and practical character—the Lutheranism of science — they possibly derived from their being themselves men personally versed in the real affairs of actual life: but we must not on this ground withhold our admiration for that courage, that rare and highest species of intellectual magnanimity, which enabled them to throw aside in the arena of philosophy all the imposing but cumbrous panoply of systems and of schools, and, like the Spartan, "grapple with glory naked" — with no arms but the vigour and flexibility of their own intellect.

Locke was descended from an ancient and respectable family in Somersetshire, and was born in 1632. He was educated first at Westminster School, and afterwards at Christ Church College, Oxford, where he appears to have received that impulse in the direction of metaphysical and educational science which was afterwards to turn to such invaluable account. The years between 1651 and 1664 he spent at Oxford; and it was during this period that he seems first to have become convinced of the imperfection and sterility of the course of metaphysical study pursued in the university, a course which took Aristotle for its compass, chart, and pilot. He appears to have been peculiarly struck with the comparative inefficiency of the old dogmatic method in the investigation of truth, and the insignificance of the results obtained by the employment of so cumbersome and complicated a mechanism. So great was his dissatisfaction, indeed, and so completely convinced was he of the hopelessness of any true acquisitions being made in this path of study, and with so fallible a guide, that he renounced a university career for the profession of medicine, a study in which the application of the experimental method had produced such striking results and opened so vast and hopeful a career. This profession, however, for which the natural penetration and acuteness of Locke's mind so eminently fitted him, and which is so peculiarly founded on common sense and observation, he was soon obliged to renounce from ill health, and we find him, in 1664, secretary to Sir Walter Vane, in Ireland, and sent by Charles II. on a diplomatic mission to Brandenburg. In the same year, 1664, Locke returned to Oxford, and was offered a considerable preferment in Ireland, provided he would enter the Church: this Locke declined to do, alleging for his refusal a reason the more honourable as it is rare—a want of that sentiment of peculiar vocation without which he justly thought no man ought to embrace the ecclesiastical career. In 1666 our philosopher became acquainted with Ashley, Lord Shaftesbury, a circumstance which brought him into familiar intercourse with many of the most distinguished intellects of the time. He became tutor to the son of his patron, and afterwards to his grandson—the famous Earl of Shaftesbury.

In 1674 he went to France, and resided several years in that country, principally at Paris and Montpélier; probably acquiring and consolidating, by an intercourse with learned and enlightened men, those sound and generous, tolerant and rational ideas, which so strongly characterise his writings. Four years after this, Shaftesbury having been recalled to power for a short period, Locke returned to England, and on his patron's second political fall he retired with him to Holland, where he remained till he was recalled by the Revolution of 1688. It was during his stay here that Shaftesbury died (1683), and Locke appears to have alleviated his exile with a great variety of active intellectual occupation. He established, at Amsterdam, a species of literary society, in which assembled many virtuous and learned men, chiefly, like himself, exiles on religious and political grounds, who were then residing in Holland.

While residing under the protection of Holland, that nursing mother of toleration, Locke produced his first important work, a work worthy of its subject; this was his 'Letter on Toleration,' composed in Latin, and forming a solid and unanswerable argument in favour of religious freedom. This subject he further developed in three other Letters which successively appeared, and which were written in reply to the Oxford criticisms on the first Letter. In all these works he follows the same line as had been taken before, not only by Jeremy Taylor, but by so many of those ardent and acute Protestants who had been driven from France and England into exile for the free expression of their opinions. At this time, as in all ages when despotism has prevailed, political and religious authority were falsely supposed to be similar in nature, and to rest upon the same foundations; an error which has caused the greatest oppressions on the one hand, and the most obstinate resistance on the other.

It may easily be conceived with what delight Locke must have hailed the Revolution of 1688, an event which not only restored him to his country and secured to him the free expression of his opinions on matters of church and state, but which was in itself a kind of practical embodiment of his own political convictions.

But it was not till the year 1690 that the genius of Locke appeared in its full vigour. Hitherto he had been combating, as it were, on the outposts of the great battle of human happiness and true philosophy: he now attacked the main position of the hostile array of error and prescription. It was at this time that appeared his great work, the 'Essay on the Human Understanding,'—a book the composition of which had been suggested, as he himself relates, by an accidental conversation, but the composition of which had occupied nearly eighteen years of inquiry and meditation. He relates that, having been once engaged with several of his friends in a discussion respecting some of the more abstract operations of the human mind, he had found that the argument began very soon to lose itself in the clouds of metaphysic uncertainty; and it then occurred to him, that no sound or true conclusions could be hoped for in such speculations until the nature of the human intellect itself had been, to a certain degree at least, examined and defined, and until some measure or limit had been established by which it could be approximately ascertained what ideas were really within the sphere of those operations, and what beyond them. Till this was done, it is plain, all argument respecting the results would be premature, useless, and productive of nothing but confusion. It was, as we should recollect, one of the most important problems proposed by Bacon, as destined to form the basis of all real progress in knowledge, to ascertain what were the paths in which the human intellect could hope to advance safely and profitably, and what were the reverse; a question in no wise easy to resolve, and one which may form the subject of a special science hereafter to be investigated.

One of the errors against which Locke is chiefly sedulous to warn the student is that mania for definition which in the older philosophy produces so fatal a tendency to substitute names for ideas. He had learned from Descartes the great principle of the impossibility of defining simple ideas, a principle the neglect or ignorance of which had substituted an endless word-catching for true productive investigation. 'The Essay on the Human Understanding,' says Stewart, speaking particularly of the two first books, "is a precious accession to the theory of the human mind; the richest contribution of well-observed and well-described facts which was ever bequeathed by a single individual; and the indisputable, though not always acknowledged, source of some of the most refined conclusions, with respect to the intellectual phenomena, which have since been brought to light by succeeding inquirers."

The leading doctrine of Locke is the double origin of our ideas, which are all to be traced to one of two sources, called by him sensation and reflection. This theory, beautiful and simple as it is, may be considered as little more than a different and enlarged form for the non-existence of innate ideas in the human mind. Nothing is a more certain sign of imperfection either in physical or metaphysical science than the necessity for assigning a complex cause to simple phenomena; it is, in fact, of itself an antecedent improbability affecting the validity of any theory; and is, to a certain degree, an inversion of the usual order of nature, in which we perpetually see a complex result produced by a simple cause, but very seldom a simple effect flowing from a complex cause. In the former part of his proposition, Locke has reached the highest degree of clearness and completeness; namely, the investigation of those ideas which have their origin in sensation: in the latter part, or *reflection*, he has sometimes fallen into a certain degree of obscurity and contradiction; but we have only to note the errors into which the greatest of preceding metaphysicians had fallen, some degrading the operations of the mind into mere material mechanism, and others refining them into a mystical and unintelligible transcendentalism. His style and language is everywhere clear, simple, and idiomatic to the highest degree; not always quite elegant, it is true, but invariably addressing itself directly to the understanding of a plain, cautious, and intelligent reader. It should be distinctly remembered that Locke is the steady and professed enemy of all scholastic and learned phraseology; and perhaps the very skill with which he has popularised his difficult and important subject may have tended to diminish our sense of the obligations which science owes to his name: he has himself often furnished us with arms which we have become so dextrous in using, that we forget they were not of our own invention—a fate which awaits almost all who have simplified human knowledge.

That part of his work which has perhaps the greatest practical utility, and which gives this admirable author the strongest claim to our gratitude, is the portion devoted to guard against the imperfections and the wrong use of words. And in this perhaps consists the peculiar originality of the work. In the older philosophy, which pursues the investigation of truth by the instrumentality of certain logical forms, as the syllogism, the inquirer is perpetually warned against fallacies proceeding from the incorrect use of these intellectual instruments; but the older logic is always of a combative or polemic character, and the reasoner is placed in the light of a gladiator, provided with offensive and defensive weapons, whose efforts are to be directed against an antagonist—a combatant like himself. The older method, in short, enables us to overcome an opponent; but it is far less peculiarly qualified to enable us to conquer ourselves.

The object of philosophy is certainly not the silencing of an antagonist, but the ascertaining of truth; and in pursuit of this last object we are infinitely more exposed to error from fallacies arising in our own minds—from our own passions, prejudices, and ignorance, than from anything exterior to ourselves. It was these passions, prejudices, and this ignorance and misapplication or loose employment of language, that perhaps the most valuable portion of Locke's Essay is intended to combat and overthrow. The necessity of doing this before any true progress could be hoped in metaphysical (or indeed in any) science was first clearly and powerfully urged by Bacon: he first showed the mighty sway over the human mind of those *idols* or prejudices which seem almost inherent in our nature: it was Locke who most triumphantly overthrew their wide and fatal dominion.

In 1690 Locke published his two 'Treatises on Civil Government,' which originally sprang out of his refutation of Sir Robert Filmer's once-celebrated book entitled 'Patriarcha,' an elaborate attempt to prove that the royal power is derived from the paternal authority, and is, consequently, like that species of rule from which it sprang, naturally unlimited. Filmer's proposition leads immediately to despotism, or rather to the impossibility of lawfully resisting, on the part of the people, the encroachments of despotism. The refutation of Filmer is more particularly confined to the first part of Locke's essay, in which he treats the question of the original right and origin of monarchical power, and inquires into the foundation of that right.

Having thus cleared the way, he proceeds to investigate and lay down the true principles on which he conceives all human society to be founded. He first discusses the state of nature, and the rights and obligations of men antecedent to the voluntary establishment of society. He then treats, in an admirable and conclusive manner, of the nature and rights of property, exhibiting in this part of his work a striking contrast to those authors whose useless subtleties and unnecessarily refined definitions had obscured a subject on which it is so indispensable for all men to form true and distinct conceptions. Labour he considers to constitute the true source of property, and to establish a natural and indefeasible right of the individual to the produce of his own exertions. He then traces the establishment of all government to the original or implied compact and consent of the members forming the primitive community, or by an uninterrupted adhesion of the members beginning from that period and remaining unbroken. In these reasonings he chiefly follows the arguments of Hooker, in his 'Ecclesiastical Polity.' The remainder of the work goes on to develop Locke's ideas — all of them bold, and some few perhaps untenable — respecting the rights and principles of communities: and though he generally agrees with Hooker, whose noble treatise has left very little to future investigators, at least as far as the limited nature of its subject extends, it is impossible not to be profoundly struck with the clear, acute, solid, and simple manner of his reasonings, or with the vigorous, idiomatic, and unpedantic style in which the arguments are conveyed.

This subject has been so fully and frequently discussed since Locke's time by men who have been able to throw upon it the light derived from practical experience of the real action of principles which in his time had only begun to be investigated in theory, that this work will perhaps in future be rather referred to than studied as embodying all the arguments and proofs adducible on this subject; but however this may be, this portion of Locke's works must ever be considered as sufficient of itself to place his name very high among the ablest expounders and the boldest defenders of human rights and liberties.

In the next work which we have to notice he will be found in a character not less worthy of our gratitude and respect: this is the 'Essay on Education.' "In this work," says Hallam, "which may be reckoned an introduction to that on the 'Conduct of the Understanding,' since the latter is but a scheme of that education an adult person should give himself, he has uttered, to say the least, more good sense on the subject than will be found in any preceding writer. Locke was not like the pedants of his own or other ages, who think that to pour their wordy book-learning into the memory is the true discipline of childhood. The culture of the intellectual and moral faculties in their most extensive sense, the health of the body, the accomplishments which common utility or social custom has rendered valuable, enter into his idea of the best model of education, conjointly at least with any knowledge that can be imparted by books."

Perhaps the most striking and not the least valuable peculiarity of Locke's treatise is the immense influence which he assigns in it to the power of habit in forming and modifying the characters of men. That he has a little over-stated and exaggerated the amount of this influence is incontestable, but we ought to remember that the effects of such an error, if applied in practice, could only be innocent, if not even beneficial. It is, of course, an error into which the theorist on education is always peculiarly liable to fall, and one which hardly a single writer on the subject of education has altogether escaped. Locke had no personal opportunities for studying, in the only way in which it can effectually be studied, the nature and characters of children. Those who have devoted themselves to this deeply interesting subject are unanimous in their opinion that the characters of children will often be found, even where all external circumstances are as far as can be appreciated identically the same, to retain intrinsic differences which can only be explained by the supposition that there exist at every age of life many and important varieties of character and intellectual constitution, in modifying which, education, however great its power, is very inefficient. Locke's system of education has been by many condemned as unreasonably severe; but those who complain of it should bear in mind that he never fails to inculcate the indispensable necessity of the feeling of *disgrace* as an element in all punishment and correction; a condition which effectually excludes the possibility of undue severity on the part of the instructor, for the human mind has so instinctive an appreciation of what is just, that severity pushed beyond a certain limit would infallibly defeat its own object.

Nothing can surpass the soundness and good sense displayed in the infinite multitude of minute observations respecting the physical, moral, and intellectual treatment of children, with which this excellent treatise abounds: so numerous, indeed, are they, and so valuable, that, though few branches of science have been more seduously cultivated, particularly of late years, than education, the best writers on the subject would seem to have done little more than complete and extend the plan laid down by Locke, whose whole work "bespeaks an intense, though calm, love of truth and goodness; a quality which few have possessed more fully, or known so well how to exert, as this admirable philosopher."

Besides these works, Locke was the author of an 'Essay on the Reasonableness of Christianity,' and also of two vindications of the last-mentioned production, which we shall not stop to analyse, as the nature of its subject places it rather in the department of theology; and also because his reputation is rather founded on the works which we have noticed more at length.

The 'Treatise on the Conduct of the Understanding,' to which we have more than once adverted as having been intended to form an introduction to his great work, did not appear till after his death.

It is delightful to reflect that this great writer, whose mind was so acute and so vigorous, and who devoted all his energies to the furtherance of truth and goodness, was as amiable and venerable a man as he was an admirable author. His life was calm, happy, and laborious; and at his death, which happened in 1704, he left behind him, in his immortal works, a monument worthy of the continuer of Bacon, and of the friend of Newton.

CHAPTER XII.

THE WITS OF QUEEN ANNE.

Artificial School—Pope's early Studies—Pope compared to Dryden—Essay on Criticism—Rape of the Lock—Mock-heroic Poetry—Temple of Fame, &c. —Translation of Homer—Essay on Man—Miscellanies—The Dunciad— —Satires and Epistles. Edward Young—English Melancholy—The Universal Passion—Night Thoughts—Young's Style—Wit.

POETRY, in order to address itself with success to the sympathies of the reader, must necessarily speak the language of the class for which it is written; and the more limited that class, the feebler, the more monotonous will be the accents of the poet. Shakspeare wrote for all mankind; and every human being, whatever his age and country, will find in Shakspeare's works matter of interest, of instruction and delight. Pope and Swift wrote for an artificial and conventional society—not exclusively, it is true, for a court, but for what was then emphatically called *the Town;* and their writings speak the language not of the world, but of the city. The reader will find in them incessant strokes of worldly good sense and acuteness, a delicate and polished irony, a consummate neatness and distinctness of diction; but he will look in vain for any of the higher attributes of creative intellect: he will find a good deal of wit and ridicule; but he will find neither true passion, true humanity, true pathos, nor true humour; for humour is to wit what the pertinent, genial, and creative power of the galvanic pile is to the momentary and destructive shock of electricity; it is not the ray which dazzles, but the heat which glows and animates. Thus wit is a quality immeasurably inferior to humour: indeed, humour is itself the fulfilment and completion of wit, and the possession of the former quality necessarily implies the existence of the latter. Of mere wit, a single scene of Shakspeare often contains as much, scattered with a profuse and apparently unconscious hand, as would furnish forth whole libraries of the neat and antithetic literature of this period of Queen Anne: but in Shakspeare we remark not the wit, for its brilliancy is eclipsed by the much higher quality of humour; while in Pope or Swift or Addison the intellectual ingenuity appeals the more directly to our attention because it is unaccompanied by the higher quality.

At the head of this artificial school in poetry long remained Alexander Pope, born in 1688, and sprung, like so many of the most illustrious men of England, from the middle or citizen class. His constitutional ill health, and the weakness and deformity of his frame, precluded him from pursuing any of the usual paths to distinction, and in a manner assisted in giving to his mind its poetical direction. A great part of his youth was spent in the green shades of Windsor Forest, where his father possessed a country-house. Under circumstances so favourable to the development of the intellect—solitude, forced sedentariness, and that delicacy of organisation which so often accompanies physical weakness—Pope very early gave earnest of his future poetical powers. Self-educated, of immense literary industry, and of a character singularly reflective and sensitive, he had obtained literary reputation of no mean value at a period of life when boys in general are thinking of little else than robbing orchards and playing truant from school. Of this precocity of poetical development he often speaks himself:—

> "As yet a child, and all unknown to fame,
> I lisp'd in numbers, for the numbers came."

At the age of sixteen Pope had already tried his strength in various attempts of different kinds of verse, among the rest in the drama—a species of writing for which his genius so little qualified him, that we have probably no reason to regret that his good sense induced him to destroy these youthful essays in scenic composition. Unsuccessful as he probably felt them to be, such attempts could not fail to strengthen and practise him in the art of expression, to educate his ear, and to give delicacy and variety to his versification. Like the young swallow, whose instinct informs it of the period of migration, Pope had already felt the mysterious call of genius; and these uncertain efforts were but the hovering of the bird before it darts away upon its annual course—the balancing of the unpractised pinion, and the fixing of the yet untried flight. His first publication was a small collection of Pastorals, which, as well as a number of imitations and translations of Chaucer, plainly indicated to the public that a new, great, and original author was about to rise upon the literary horizon. A profound and venerating admirer of the genius of his great predecessor, Dryden, it is not surprising that Pope's first literary efforts should have been made in the same direction: his boyish admiration had been gratified by the approbation of the patriarch of poetry, and by his prediction of the young acolyte's future glory; and it is no less natural that Pope's versification and style should be in some degree founded upon the practice of his illustrious predecessor. But there were essential differences between the manner of these two admirable writers—differences which must be accurately appreciated ere we can hope to form a just idea of their respective merits. In Dryden, a vigorous, careless, self-assured dexterity is perceptible, not accompanied with much passion, it is true, nor with much depth of sentiment, appealing only te the more obvious and direct sympathies of the human character, but imposing from the conscious ease which it indicates. In Pope we observe a greater degree of thought and reflection, a more refined acuteness of remark, and an almost fastidious neatness and polish of expression. Both poets are remarkable for the quality of good sense, and both are admirable for perfect clearness and distinctness of meaning; and if they sometimes fall into truisms and commonplaces, these are generally such as in themselves involve principles whose importance will excuse their frequent repetition, and are so adorned by happiness of illustration, that we forget the insipidity of the precept in the beauty of the language in which it is clothed.

Both poets are greater in the delineation of artificial life, in the analysis of human passions, human motives, and human conduct, than in the delineation of external nature, or the sympathy with unsophisticated humanity; but the force of Dryden rather consists in a kind of brave neglect of minuter shades of character, and a broad and manly touch of intellectual portrait-painting, while the figures of Pope are elaborated with the neat and discriminating delicacy of a pencil accurate without timidity, and distinct without coldness. Dryden is a Rubens, and Pope a Greuze or a Watteau. The peculiar species of versification — the rhymed couplet, so exquisitely adapted for satire and for moral declamation — which Dryden had carried to so high a pitch of harmony, variety, and power, was destined to receive from his successor the last finish of which its structure was capable: in the hands of the former poet it is an instrument of infinite compass, energy, and strength; beneath the touch of the latter it became much more limited, it is true, in variety of music, but exquisitely sensitive and delicate. Dryden frequently introduces the triplet, and occasionally the Alexandrine of twelve syllables, in order to wind up the period with a burst of rolling and sonorous music. This is an artifice much more sparingly employed by Pope. Indeed it may be said that this poet gave such perfection to the species of verse which he generally employed, and which became the popular and fashionable measure of his day, that the anatomy and prosodiacal structure of that kind of rhythm became at last familiar to the lowest class of writers, and the very excellence of Pope's verses furnished his rivals with the means of equalling him, at least as far as concerns the mechanical harmony of his metre. The rhymed couplet was balanced and polished and melodised, until its construction became a mere matter of dexterity; and it has been very justly observed that it is not always easy to distinguish — that is, in point of mere *versification* — between the productions of Pope and the meanest effusions of the most contemptible scribblers of his day. The couplet had been refined and elaborated into a feeble and timid propriety; the sense almost invariably ended with the second line; and the antithesis of sound and meaning between the two portions separated by the cæsura, which was considered so great an ornament, frequently degenerated into a mere verbal opposition — a distinction without a difference. From falling into these defects Pope was admirably secured by the acuteness and sagacity of his mind; he is eminently the poet of good sense and reason: and though it is perhaps hardly fair to charge upon him the faults of his incompetent imitators, our conclusion will be that, in communicating an exquisite and almost effeminate grace to the measure which he used so well, he somewhat impaired its vigour and its flexibility.

In 1711 Pope published his 'Essay on Criticism,' a poem which was received with a universal burst of admiration; a feeling rendered stronger by the contrast between the author's age and the character of his production. Though the work of a young man of not much more than twenty-one, this composition is no less remarkable for the finish of its style than for the ripe judgment which it displays, and the extent of reading and reflection which it indicates. It cannot be denied that the principles of art to be gathered from this well-thought and brilliantly-expressed work have little of that depth and comprehensiveness which the modern study of æsthetic science has communicated to criticism: they hardly, in short, penetrate to the "root of the matter;" but, as far as they go (which is, indeed, farther than criticism had gone before Pope wrote), they leave nothing to be desired as true and sparkling thoughts dressed in the most appropriate language.

But as a noble production of Pope's genius, and perhaps the most happy example of a new and original idea executed in a perfectly felicitous manner, we must cite the mock-heroic narrative poem entitled 'The Rape of the Lock.' The occasion of its being written was the somewhat unjustifiable frolic of Lord Petre in stealing a lock of hair from Miss Arabella Fermor, one of the ornaments of the beau monde of the day. This rather familiar and cavalier piece of pleasantry produced a quarrel between the two families, and Pope composed his charming little poem "to laugh them together again," as he phrases it. In this object he was unsuccessful, it is said; but the little mock-heroic epic, though it did not appease the disagreement to which it owed its origin, will secure for its author an immortality among his country's poets, so long as the language in which it is written shall endure. The poem is, as Addison justly characterised it, "merum sal—a delicious little thing." Like the 'Secchia Rapita' of Tassoni, which has preserved from oblivion the war whose insignificant origin it describes, 'The Rape of the Lock' will immortalise, by the mere force of grace and invention, things and persons otherwise entirely devoid of interest. The work, like the poem of Tassoni, or rather like the 'Lutrin' of Boileau, is written in that species of mock-heroic which describes trifling or contemptible events with the pompous elaboration of epic language. It is, in fact, a dwarf epic, with its involution of interest, its supernatural machinery of beings respectively favourable and adverse to the various personages, its episodes, and its catastrophe. This species of poetry has been most cultivated among the Italians, a people whose intense enjoyment of the ludicrous renders them peculiarly sensitive to burlesque and discordant ideas, while the flexibility and richness of their language—and particularly of some of its provincial dialects, as the Genoese, the Neapolitan, and the Venetian—gives them a singular power of comic expression. Thus in the older Italian comedy, to which Molière owed so much, there is a species of unconscious and almost infantine simplicity of language and dialect, which forms the most admirable and appropriate vehicle for the ludicrous extravagance of the characters, and the sly shrewdness of the drollery. In comparing together the 'Lutrin' and 'The Rape of the Lock,' we think no critic could hesitate to give a most decided preference to the latter. In the first place, the sluggish sensuality, ignorance, and squabbling of a parcel of gorbellied priests, forms a much less attractive subject for the comic poet than the elegant frivolities of aristocratic society; and in the second, the species of machinery (supernatural interference) employed by Pope—the exquisite fairy mythology of the sylphs and gnome which he found in the writings of Paracelsus and the Rosicrucian philosophers—is infinitely more attractive, more elegant, more varied, more accordant with the character of the action, than the unreal impersonations of abstract qualities—as, for instance, in the celebrated episode of Sloth—adopted by Boileau in the 'Lutrin.' In reading the Frenchman's mock-heroic, we are struck with the propriety, polish, and neatness of the language; but we feel that the author is perpetually trenching upon the domain of satire—a territory which, though bordering upon the mock-heroic, "for thin partitions do their bounds divide," can never be entered by the mock-heroic poet without a loss of effect; for satire in its essence is tragic, and the moment the comic author forgets to smile he quits his appropriate character. 'The Rape of the Lock' is divided into five short books or cantos, with a delightful mimicry of epic regularity. In the first, after an appropriate invocation, the poet describes the breaking of day, the awaking of his fair heroine, and the various offices and powers of the sylphs—being the protectors of the fair. We have next an enumeration of the omens which presage the catastrophe; and a speech from Ariel, the guardian spirit of Belinda, warning her to admit into her breast no thoughts of beaux. The toilet is then described with a grace and refined elegance absolutely unequalled, we think, in comic poetry. In the second canto, the fair Belinda goes upon the water; and occasion is taken to describe the "adventurous Baron's" determination to carry off the fatal lock or perish in the essay, with an account of the sacrificial ceremonies by which he propitiates the powers to aid his bold emprise. Next follows an exquisite description of the sylphs, and their desponding councils; among them Ariel distributes the guard of the various parts of Belinda's dress, and menaces them with severe and appropriate punishment in case they abandon or neglect their charge. The reader's expectation being now wound up to the true epic state of suspense, the main action begins. The party land at Hampton Court, where, after a game of ombre, described with consummate grace and airy ingenuity, they take coffee, and the Baron executes his fatal purpose; and the canto closes with an admirable picture of the respective despair and triumph of the different parties. In the fourth book the action quits "this visible diurnal sphere," and the gnome Umbriel betakes himself to the enchanted empire of the goddess Spleen, from whom he obtains "a wondrous bag"—

"Like that where once Ulysses held the winds;
There she collects the force of female lungs,
Sighs, sobs, and passions, and the war of tongues;
A vial next she fills with fainting fears,
Soft sorrows, melting griefs, and flowing tears."

By the aid of these the gnome incites the fair unhappy to despatch Sir Plume (Sir George Brown) to the uncourteous ravisher of the lock. The latter refuses to surrender his shining spoil, and Belinda concludes the canto with a lamentation over her hard fate and irreparable loss. The fifth canto opens with an admirable description of a general battle (in metaphor) between the ladies and the gentlemen; the latter of whom, after a contest described with Homeric fire, are routed, and commanded by the fair and indignant victors to restore the lock. It is, however, discovered that this "causa teterrima belli" has disappeared and ascended to the skies, where it is to shine for ever as a constellation: —

> "A sudden star, it shot through liquid air,
> And drew behind a radiant trail of hair;
> Not Berenice's locks first rose so bright,
> The heavens bespangling with dishevell'd light,
> The sylphs behold it kindling as it flies,
> And pleased pursue its progress through the skies."

From the foregoing meagre outline—all that our space will permit—the reader will obtain an idea of the ingenious plan and distribution of this enchanting miniature epic: to form a notion of the exquisite grace and fancy, and variety and delicacy of its execution, he must read it from beginning to end. He will then see to what a degree the English language (generally considered by foreigners as rather adapted to the expression of strong emotion than to the more evanescent delicacies of *poésies de salon*) has been made by the touch of genius a perfect vehicle for the most refined subtleties of artificial life. We cannot better conclude our remarks on this charming production than by observing the watchful dexterity with which Pope in this work has retained throughout a purely comic tone. Fully conscious that his strength lay in satire, and encountering incessant temptations to do what he knew he could do so well, he has never once abandoned the tone of light and good-humored *persiflage*, which his taste informed him was best in harmony with the character of his work.

Subsequently to 'The Rape of the Lock' Pope published 'The Temple of Fame,' an 'Elegy on an Unfortunate Lady,' and (in 1713) his descriptive poem of 'Windsor Forest,' which last work, however, had been composed at least nine years before. It was not to be expected that any poet, whatever might be his genius, could *twice* hit upon an idea so new, so perfect, so original, as the leading subject of the 'Rape of the Lock;' and therefore we cannot be surprised to find that the works just specified are, in conception, no less than in execution, markedly inferior to the enchanting little mock-heroic. Besides this, Pope's genius excelled less in the delineation of romantic scenes of chivalrous and allegoric splendour than in the pointed and satiric sketching of the follies, absurdities, and affectations of artificial society. 'The Temple of Fame' is a development or modernised version, elegant, it is true, harmonious, and polished, of 'The House of Fame,' which we have already spoken of in our account of Chaucer: and it is impossible not to perceive how much of the effect of the old poet's rich and splendid allegoric painting has disappeared in the process of revival. In conceptions of this kind—and in general in all representations of supernatural objects — the quality most indispensable for effect is an air of perfect sincerity and earnestness in the poet. It is this quality which communicates the peculiar interest and splendour to all the poetry of the Middle Ages; and it is precisely in this—the feeling of *faith*—that consists the immense difference between what are generally called the classical and romantic schools in modern literature. The mediæval writers seem to speak from the fulness of belief; the classicists—or at least their modern imitators — appear to use their supernatural interventions (called by them with an unconscious and intense propriety "*machines*") rather as rhetorical contrivances than as articles of faith.

In the 'Elegy on an Unfortunate Lady,' Pope has exhausted all his powers of pathos and tenderness — not very extensive, it is true — to bewail the untimely death of a person who is represented as driven (by causes very obscurely indicated or hinted in the poem) to the commission of suicide. The great defect of this work is want of distinctness, and an uncertainty and inconsistency of aim. It is exquisitely harmonized, and contains many passages which dwell in the reader's memory; but its passion wants intensity and unity of direction, and the poet seems too intent upon eloquence of expression to fill the reader with a belief of the sincerity of the passion to which he gives such elegant utterance. The feeling is true, indeed, but it seems to us neither very intense nor very comprehensive: it is rather an *echo* of the accents of deep grief than the strong and agonised cry of true passion — rather the sorrow of the stage than the half-stifled and convulsive sobbing of a broken heart. This work forms a companion or *pendant* to another excellent poem of a somewhat similar character, the 'Epistle of Eloisa to Abelard.' In this latter work Pope's mastery over the tender and pathetic is exhibited in its highest force. The agonies of a hopeless and condemnable passion undoubtedly form a subject more fertile and more capable of powerful painting than the early death of genius, beauty, and misfortune. But though Pope has made the Epistle immeasurably superior to the Elegy, every candid reader will, we think, agree with us in allowing the enormous space which separates even the Epistle, eloquent, fervid, and brilliant as it is, from the deep, pure, and natural pathos of Chaucer, or of even many inferior writers among our Elizabethan dramatists.

Of 'Windsor Forest,' we have but few words to say. Pope's genius, which comparatively failed in the portraiture of the simpler and more powerful emotions of the human heart, was not likely to succeed in the delineation of external nature. He had, it is true, gazed with the eye of youth—intensely but without understanding—on the foliage and the streams of that woodland scenery which breathed such freshness into the descriptions of Father Chaucer; but Pope's mind wanted that deep love, that intense and quiet sympathy, which has made Chaucer, as it made Homer and Theocritus, and as it made Thomson and Wordsworth, the interpreters and hierophants of the silent oracles of the cloud, and of the leaf, and of the rippling water. He had the eye to perceive, but had not the "deuteroscopic or second sight" to understand the handwriting of God, inscribed like the responses of the Cumæan Sibyl upon the leaves of the forest.

It was at this period of his life—in the full vigour of his extraordinary powers, and in the morning of his glory—that Pope undertook the execution of his gigantic task—the translation into English heroic verse of the Iliad and Odyssey of Homer. This great work, which was published by subscription, and which laid the foundation of the poet's worldly fortune, extended over a period of twelve years, from 1713 to 1725. He relates himself how agitated and depressed his mind was for some time by the reflection of the colossal labour he had undertaken; but practice rapidly conferred facility, and his unremitting industry was perhaps assisted by the weakness of his health, which secured him from the interruptions of ordinary pleasures and amusements. Of the Iliad Pope alone was the translator, but in the execution of the Odyssey he called in the aid of his friends and fellow-poets Broome and Fenton, to whom together was confided the translation of twelve of the twenty-four books. For his Homer Pope received, after deducting 800*l.*, which was shared between his fellow-labourers, a clear sum of above 8000*l.*; a circumstance not only honourable to the poet, but which strongly indicates the immense improvement which had taken place in the social position of literary men, and the movement of advance which had already begun towards the liberation of the highest of all professions from the degradation of dependence and the humiliating necessity of servile adulation. Great was the improvement when Pope was enabled by the profits of a single translation to acquire a permanent competency in the same country where the 'Paradise Lost' had been sold for 23*l.*! With the prudence and good sense which characterized him, Pope invested this sum in the purchase of a house and garden at Twickenham, one of the most beautiful spots on the banks of the Thames. Here he resided till his death, and here he entertained the greatest, the wisest, and the wittiest of his contemporaries; here assembled Atterbury and Gay, Bathurst and Arbuthnot:—

"Granville the polite,
And knowing Walsh, would tell me I could write;
Well-natured Garth inflamed with early praise,
And Congreve loved, and Swift endured, my lays.
The courtly Talbot, Somers, Sheffield read,
Even mitred Rochester would nod the head;
And St. John's self (great Dryden's friend before)
With open arms received one poet more.
Happy my studies, when by these approved!
Happier their author, when by these beloved!"

The version of Homer, like all translations, may be looked a under two distinct points of view—first, as an English poem; secondly, as a revival, in another age and language, of the Greek original. In its character of an English poem (that character under which it will ever be regarded by all those readers for whose behoof it was written—such persons, that is to say, as are unable to compare it with the Greek)—there can be no question as to its high merit. It is a rich, flowing, dignified, brilliant, and exquisitely versified poem, deficient it is true in intensity of feeling, and occasionally disfigured with trivial and meretricious ornament, but a noble monument of genius and taste. But if we judge it in relation to its immortal original; if we examine it as a revival of Homer, or an accurate and spirited copy—as faithful as the difference of nations, dialects, and times will admit—of the great epic of Troy, our decision will be very different, and very much less favourable. Perhaps the best (as it was the shortest) criticism ever made upon the 'Iliad' of Pope was the acknowledgment returned to the translator for his present of the volumes by Bentley, the Greek philologist:—"It is a pretty poem, Mr. Pope; but you must not call it Homer." We do no injustice to Pope when we say that his translation contains nothing Homeric from beginning to end, except the names and the events. The fervid and romantic tone, the Biblical and patriarchal simplicity, the mythologic colouring, neither quite divine nor altogether human, the unspeakable freshness and audacity of the images —all that breathes of an earlier world, and of the sunny shores, and laughing waves, and blue sky of the old Ægean—all this is vanished and obliterated; nay, the very swell and fall of the versification, regular in its very irregularity, like the rolling of the ocean, to which it has been so well compared, even this has found in the English no attempt—even unsuccessful, for perfectly successful no such attempt could ever be—at reproduction and imitation. Instead of this, we have the accurate and never-failing recurrence of the neat, elegant, well-balanced couplet, the timid propriety of modern manners, with all the modern reluctance to name things by their simple names, the substitution of vague and commonplace ornaments—the "curta supellex" of classical French poetry —for the burning and picturelike words of the Greek; and frequently the introduction, particularly in descriptive passages, of ideas not to be found in the original at all, and conveying absolute contradictions and physical impossibilities; as, for instance, in the celebrated description of a moonlight night, so severely yet justly criticised by Wordsworth :—

"As when the moon, refulgent lamp of night,
O'er heaven's clear azure spreads her sacred light;
Around her throne the vivid planets roll,
And stars unnumber'd gild the glowing pole;
O'er the dark trees a yellower verdure shed,
And tip with silver every mountain's head;
Then shine the vales, the rocks in prospect rise,
A flood of glory bursts from all the skies:
The conscious swains, rejoicing in the sight,
Eye the blue vault, and bless the useful light."

In the above verses there are at least a dozen offences against nature and reality, and these contradictions are in no case to be found in the Greek; for Homer, like Shakspeare, is invariably and minutely true to nature. They both knew well that the works of God are more beautiful than those of art. It would be superfluous to insist here upon the observation of the immense degree in which the effect of a work of fiction depends upon and is modified by the tone of the language in which it was written: and this increases the difficulty of producing a successful translation in exact ratio with the antiquity, and consequently with the merit, of the work. It was well remarked by a man of refined taste, who had been obliged, by ignorance of the Greek language, to make acquaintance with the works of Homer first through the medium of translation, that he experienced a much more intense impression of the power and majesty of the great Ionian from the bold and barbarous literal Latin version usually affixed to the school editions of the bard, than from the most elaborate efforts at transfusing Homer into modern poetry; and that when afterwards enabled to compare those early impressions with the effect of the original Greek, he still retained his opinion. And the fact is so. The rude Latin prose is a *cast* of the immortal statue: its grain is coarse, indeed, and its value is insignificant, but it preserves the precise outline of the godlike lineaments of the original. Our modern poetical translations are *copies*, smooth, polished, and elaborate; but feeble, timorous, and cold. These observations will explain the immense inferiority of all poetical imitations and paraphrases of the grander and more oratorical passages of the Scriptures. The rudest taste instantly perceives the infinite superiority of the concise and burning words of the Hebrew, closely and literally rendered in the modern versions, even though thus fidelity be often attained at the expense of the genius and idiomatic character of the language into which such version has been made.

After this great effort of industry and poetical skill, which was received with a degree of enthusiasm, honourable, indeed, to Pope, but often expressed in terms so strong as to prove how little his age really understood or appreciated the peculiar merits of Homer, our poet published his 'Essay on Man,' a work of metaphysical and moral philosophy, intended to form part of a vast poetical system or cycle of those sciences projected by Pope. The philosophy of this work is neither very profound, nor the reasonings and conclusions (except such as are truisms) either very convincing or very just. The poem, in short, furnishes an additional proof of the natural incompatibility between the higher order of poetry and pure abstract ratiocination, and the want of harmony that results from their forcible union; for the reasoning is generally found to injure the effect of the verse, at least as much as the ornament of verse detracts from the vigour and cogency of argument. But if any writer was ever calculated to surmount this natural want of accordance between means and end, with which we have just reproached didactic poetry in general, that writer was Pope. The abundant richness of ideas, the novelty, variety, and appropriateness of illustration, the sparkling point and neatness of expression, and the perfect finish and harmony of versification which the four epistles composing this work so prodigally display, prove that, if he has not succeeded in establishing a model and perfect exemplar of didactic poetry, it was only because such an object can never be perfectly attained by human genius. The argument of this brilliant composition may be briefly stated:— The first Epistle treats of Man in his relation to the Universe, showing the imperfections of our judgment founded upon our limited acquaintance with the order of nature, and suggesting that a higher degree of endowment would only have been productive of pain and misery—a conclusion which, like many other of Pope's deductions, involves a paradox. In the second, Man is treated as an Individual, *i. e.* with relation to himself; and the poet shows that the passions and desires are given him with an evident benevolence of intention, as by them the stock of happiness is augmented—nay, as without them happiness itself would be inconceivable and impossible. The third Epistle views Man in his relation to Society; and in the fourth and last the poet discusses the various notions respecting Happiness. Throughout the whole of this masterly work it is impossible to decide whether we are most to admire the point and neatness of the argument, the abundant wealth of illustration, collected from a wide extent of reading and observation, or the enchanting harmony and finish of the language and versification. The couplet is carried to its highest perfection; and though an instrument of but limited compass, comparatively to the organ-like blank-verse of Milton, or the myriad-voiced and ever-changing dramatic versification of the elder drama, Pope has proved that in the hand of a master even this imperfect instrument could "discourse most eloquent music."

In 1727 there appeared three volumes of Miscellanies, in prose and verse, the composition of that distinguished society of which Pope and Swift in poetry, and Arbuthnot in humorous prose, were the most brilliant ornaments. The associates, all bound together by the closest ties of friendship, and by a perfect similarity of tastes, principles, and prejudices, worked together so completely that it is impossible to assign to each, at least with much certainty, the portions composed by the respective fellow-labourers. The work is throughout sparkling with satire, wit, and humour — at least that humour which consists rather in an acute perception of the ludicrous and contemptible than in a deep sympathy with the human heart. The severity and occasional personality of the satire raised round Pope a storm of literary hatred, in many cases envenomed by religious and political enmity; and on these assailants Pope was afterwards to inflict a memorable vengeance. One article of the Miscellanies was a portion of a prose comic romance, or written caricature, intended to ridicule the vain pursuits of ill-directed erudition, and the solemn puerilities of scientific pedantry. Of this work, entitled the 'Memoirs of Martinus Scriblerus,' the idea was better than the execution; many of the follies ridiculed being such, according to Johnson's excellent criticism, as had long ceased to be prevalent, and there being a general tone of coarseness and farcical exaggeration prevailing throughout the work. Arbuthnot, there can be but little doubt, was the principal author of this not very successful *jeu d'esprit;* but he was much happier in his ludicrous 'History of John Bull,' which, though referring only to temporary politics, and principally directed against Marlborough, has a vein of irresistible drollery which time cannot deprive of its charm. Indeed, highly as almost all the members of Pope's brilliant coterie were endowed with *wit* (and perhaps at no time in the history of English literature was that quality more abundantly displayed), the amiable and learned Arbuthnot was the only person, with the exception of Addison, who exhibited much of the sentiment properly called *humour.* These qualities, so nearly allied in many respects — for Humour bears the same relation to Wit as Imagination does to Fancy — yet are very rarely found much developed in the same period of literature — much more rarely in the same individual. One is the tropical plant, dazzling in colour, but scentless and unfruitful; the other the rich and life-sustaining vegetation of the temperate zone. They are respectively the gem and the flower — or rather, perhaps, the gem and the seed.

Pope, as we have just hinted, took a terrible revenge on those whose envy, whose jealousy, or whose indignation had been aroused by the burning irony and withering sarcasm embodied in numberless passages of the Miscellanies. His wit, keen and polished as was its edge, was not always wielded by the hand of justice; and, as the Chinese proverb pithily expresses it, the dart of contempt will pierce the shell of the tortoise. The obscurest intellects, the coldest and most insensible of souls, will be roused into anger by the point of a sarcasm; and Pope, one of whose chief and very natural errors was the notion that all true virtue, as well as all pure taste and sound morality, was concentrated in the small circle of his friends, raised around him a cloud of enemies, most of them individually insignificant, and many personally contemptible, but all infuriated by the most intense animosity against the reigning wit and his *clique*. This nest of hornets Pope determined to destroy at one stroke, and he composed his admirable satire of 'The Dunciad,'—the Iliad of the Dunces. Taking for his key-note the MacFlecknoe of his great predecessor, Dryden, he has given us in this satire one of the most sweeping, fierce, and brilliant philippics, in which, under the mask of a reprobation of bad writing and bad taste, Genius ever revenged the injuries of Self-Love. The plot or fable of this admirable satire is the election of a new monarch to fill on earth the throne of Dulness, and the various games and trials of skill performed by the bad writers of the day to do honour to the event. In this manner the poet has been enabled to introduce an incredible number of individuals, most of them, indeed, deserving of contempt in a literary point of view, but some of whom are attacked with a ferocity of personality totally indefensible on either merely literary or moral grounds.

In richness of ideas, in strength of diction, and in intensity of feeling, this production surpasses all that Pope had previously done, and is perhaps the finest specimen of literary satire which exists in any language in the world. The whole vocabulary of irony is exhausted, the whole universe of contempt is ransacked. We find the combined merits of the most dissimilar satirists—the wild, fearless, inventive, picturesque extravagance of Aristophanes, the bitter irony and cold sarcasm of Lucian, the elegant raillery of Horace, and Juvenal's strange union of moral severity and grim pleasantry. It is curious to read these brilliant records of literary animosity, and to reflect upon the unenviable immortality which Pope's genius has conferred upon the meanest of scribblers and the most despicable of pamphleteers. Like the straws, the empty shells, and excrements of dead animals, which the lava has preserved for uncounted centuries, and in which the eye of the geologist beholds the records of past convulsions, these names have been preserved uninjured through a period of time when many things a thousand times more valuable have perished for ever; and they exist, and will continue to exist, as long as the English language shall endure, imperishable but valueless memorials—the trash of literature, vitrified by the lightning of indignant genius.

In the fierce contentions which agitated the declining years of Pope there can be no doubt that the satirist suffered far more than his victims, and that the deepest wounds dealt on others by the keen and polished weapon of his sarcasm, were as nothing in comparison with the agonies which nerved his own arm to wield that resistless weapon. Genius, in its very definition, implies a peculiar and exquisite degree of sensibility, or at least sensitiveness; and it is but just that, when the highest gift of God is perverted to selfish ends, to avenge insulted vanity, to humiliate, to blacken, and to crush, the very exercise of that endowment should necessarily entail upon its perverter a bitter and inevitable retribution. God is love; and his highest gift to man can only be fitly employed in deeds of love and charity. Personal invective and personal hate, though masked under the specious pretext of a zeal for good taste, is hardly a less reprehensible employment for high intellectual powers than sensuality or blasphemy; and it is fortunate that in this instance, as in all others, the crime brings its punishment along with it.

Between the years 1733 and 1740 Pope gave to the world his 'Satires, Epistles, and Moral Essays,' addressed for the most part to his distinguished literary friends, Bolingbroke, Arbuthnot, &c. These admirable compositions, considered separately, are in most cases directed against some prevailing vice or folly, and it is perhaps in them that the poet's genius is seen in its fullest splendour. Glowing with fancy and a rich profuseness of illustration, adorned with every splendour which art or industry could confer, they are noble and imperishable monuments of knowledge, of acuteness of observation, of finish, and of facility; for the poet had now attained that mastery in his art when the very elaboration of the workmanship is concealed in the apparent ease of the execution. They abound in happy strokes of description, in exquisite appropriateness of phrase, and a thousand passages from these charming compositions have passed into the ordinary language of the poet's countrymen — a sure test of the value of a work. Having been less exposed in the composition of this work to the evil influences of personal and literary enmity, Pope has avoided that air of malignant ferocity which defiles so much of the 'Dunciad;' and the tone of the Satires is in general far more Horatian; that is, far more in accordance with good taste, good breeding, and good nature. In 1742 Pope added a fourth book to the 'Dunciad,' describing the final advent on earth of the goddess of Dulness, and the prophesied millennium of ignorance, pedantry, and stupidity. In this he has exhibited a gorgeousness of colouring and a fertility of invention which would enable him to claim no mean place among merely picturesque poets. During the following year our indefatigable satirist, moved by the restless caprice of his literary enmity, published a new edition of the four books of the 'Dunciad,' having deposed from the throne of Dulness its former occupant, Theobald, a tasteless pedant and commentator on Shakspeare, whose place in "that bad eminence" was now supplied by

Cibber, a man who had succeeded in attracting Pope's particular hatred. This change, made to gratify a temporary and personal dislike, was in the highest degree injudicious, and as injurious to the poem as it was destructive of the reader's conviction (no unimportant thing for the effect of a satire) of the author's sincerity and good faith. Theobald was one of the worms of literature, a painful antiquarian, devoting his feeble powers to the illustration of obscure passages in Shakspeare's writings; useful, indeed, but certainly humble enough to have escaped the martyrdom of a 'Dunciad' immortality. The truth is, that private pique had animated Pope in placing Theobald at the head of the dunces. The great poet had himself published an edition of Shakspeare, in which his want of that minute antiquarian knowledge which Theobald undoubtedly possessed was glaringly apparent, a defect which the latter was naturally but too willing to point out. The character given to Theobald in the 'Dunciad,' though of course exaggerated with all the ingenuity of a rich imagination and an intense jealousy, was in the main appropriate; but when Cibber took the commentator's place, and the old books, the obscure learning, the peddling pedantry,—

"And all such reading as was never read,"—

the cold creeping industry and tasteless curiosity, which accorded well enough with the character of Theobald, were transferred to Cibber, even the warmest admirers of Pope were obliged to confess that hatred had blunted the great Poet's taste and destroyed his feeling of fitness. Cibber, then an actor of high reputation, and a man who has left us, in his autobiography, one of the most extraordinary combinations ever seen of vivacity, folly, wit, generosity, vanity, and affectation, was a character as little in accordance with that of Theobald as unfit to take his place as King of the Dunces. "The author of The Careless Husband," as Warton justly remarks, "was no proper king of the dunces."

Pope died at Twickenham, on the 30th of May, 1744, after a life passed in incessant industry and intellectual agitation, but adorned with a greater share of contemporary glory than often falls to the lot of poets. The weakness of his frame, and his almost incessant ill-health, which, by precluding his engaging in the more active scenes and occupations of life, undoubtedly favoured the development of his intellectual powers, also tended to make him set too high a value on merely literary triumphs; and his constitutional irritability, though it gave to his mind an exquisite delicacy, an almost feminine acuteness, yet was calculated to increase his tendency to personal satire, and to deprive him of that large and generous spirit of appreciation which finds out what is beautiful, good, and valuable even in things and works most foreign from the usual field of its contemplation. His poetry was the consummation of what is usually called the classical, but which would be much more correctly denominated the French school — perfect good sense, an admirable though somewhat pedantic propriety, polish, point, and neatness, seldom carried away into enthusiasm, not, as Shakspeare expresses it,—

> —— "A muse of fire, that would ascend
> The brightest heaven of invention,"—

but always delicate, impressive, *satisfactory*. In his serious and pathetic pieces, though the passion or the sentiment is generally true and natural, the expression is often unworthy of the thought —not from its homeliness and simplicity, however, but, on the contrary, from the perpetual fear which we seem to perceive in the poet lest he should degrade his art by making it the expression of human feeling in its grand and dignified plainness and straightforwardness. There is always a degree, and often an unnecessary one, of *ornament*, graceful, it is true, and appropriate: but we remember that the *veiled* Venus is the production of an already degenerating art.

Almost exactly contemporary with Pope lived an author whose poetry, singular, original, and strongly individual, enjoyed a high though certainly inferior reputation. This was Edward Young, the ingenious and often sublime melancholy of whose 'Night Thoughts' obtained numberless readers and admirers among the poet's own countrymen, and powerfully contributed at the same time to lead foreigners, and especially Frenchmen, into that false estimate of the national character of the English people, and those false notions of the general tone of English literature, which have been long so absurdly prevalent even among the best informed of continental critics. Madame de Staël, among others, has attempted to derive the alleged melancholy which she supposes to mark the English character, and the supposed gloom and despondency which so many superficial observers have thought they discovered in our literature, from the influence of the poems of Ossian and the mournful contemplations of Young!

The fallacy of such an opinion hardly requires or admits of a serious refutation. Without stopping to show that the impossible caricature embodied in the so-called poems of Ossian — the caricature of a state of manners that never had nor never could have had a real existence in any age or country—that this extravagant caricature, we say, ever exerted on English literature any perceptible influence, or that MacPherson's bold forgery ever excited in society any sentiment beyond that of a passing and transitory wonder, we might allege that Young's poems have never been so extensively read in England as to warrant the critic in considering him as one of the powerful and influential names in English literature. Indeed, it may be affirmed that the peculiar merits of Young are in no sense such as would be relished by a very extensive class of readers, and, appealing rather to the intellect than to the sensibilities, would not be capable of giving their author that hold upon the national mind of his countrymen, without which it is vain to talk of a writer being either the guide or the reflection of the spirit of his country. The fact is, that, when English literature began to be known to foreigners, it was naturally that department of English letters whose tone, form, and spirit was most consonant with the then taste of continental readers, and consequently it was precisely those productions which possessed least of the peculiar idiosyncrasy of national character. Thus the Frenchman, in forming his estimate of the general character of the English muse, imagined as the principal features of its portrait, not the wild richness of the Elizabethan prose and poetry, its unstudied fancy, its playful wisdom, its all-embracing depth of philosophical verity, but the neat elegance of Pope, or the fantastic and epigrammic sadness of Young.

Edward Young was born in 1681, and educated at All Souls' College, Oxford: the greater and earlier part of his long life (for he died at 84) was busily occupied in the pursuit of literary and political distinction, in not very successful struggles after fame as a poet and as a courtier. Having met at the hands of several patrons, and particularly at those of the infamous Duke of Wharton, with many overwhelming disappointments, Young, at the age of fifty, took clerical orders, and passed the remainder of his life in uneasy retirement, satirising those pursuits in which he had failed, and to which he appears to have looked back with unceasing regret, thinly veiled, however, with a somewhat affected tone of moral self-abnegation and philosophic dignity. His first important work was the 'Love of Fame,' which he qualifies as 'The Universal Passion.' This is a keen, vigorous, aud manly satire, divided into seven epistles, and strongly recalling some of the finer peculiarities of Pope, whose style it resembles more than most of Young's other productions, particularly in its being written in the rhymed couplet. But while we find in this work strong traces of Pope's clearness, directness, energy, and point, we shall look in vain for his exquisite propriety of diction, his gay and playful airiness, and that happy tone of good-nature and *badinage* which he possessed, like his master Horace, in so eminent a degree. Young's satire is, to a certain degree, more Juvenalian, but at the same time we are haunted, in reading it, with an uncomfortable consciousness that the moral declamation which so eloquently abounds in it was the offspring rather of disappointed ambition than of the injured dignity of virtue. On entering the Church, Young by no means relinquished all hopes of distinction; he wrote a panegyric on the king, for which he was rewarded with a pension, and is related to have been deeply disappointed at being afterwards refused a bishopric — a favour withheld by the minister on the ground of the devotion to retirement so frequently and emphatically expressed in his works. This is a remarkable instance of the malicious ingenuity of courts: and this refusal, there can be but little doubt, tended to deepen the gloom which pervades all Young's poetry, and particularly his later works.

Young married a lady of rank, daughter of the Earl of Lichfield, and widow of Colonel Lee, to whose two children the poet was tenderly attached. The death of this lady, which was followed, though at considerable intervals, by that of the two children, produced a powerful impression on Young's mind, and had, it is probable, a great influence in suggesting the tone and subject of his last and greatest work, the 'Night Thoughts.' It is this poem upon which his reputation, in England as elsewhere, is principally founded; and we shall endeavour, in giving a short account of its nature and merits, to show the causes of its great popularity. It is a series of reflections on the most awful and important subjects which can engage the attention of the man or of the Christian—on Life, Death, and Immortality—and is in many passages executed in a manner worthy of the tremendous character of the subject. The poem is divided into nine books, or Nights, each of which pursues some train of thought in harmony with the supposed feelings of the poet at the time of composition. These feelings are modified by the deep grief arising from the recent loss of many beloved objects, and from the contemplation of the total ruin of a surviving person, "the young Lorenzo," by some supposed to be the portrait of the poet's own son, but who is probably nothing more than an embodiment of imaginary atheism and unavailing remorse and despair. There can be no doubt that the gloom of these unhappy events was intentionally aggravated and exaggerated by the poet, in order to give greater weight and impressiveness to the reflections which he pursues. Whether this want of good faith be real, or only existing in the reader's imagination, it is singularly injurious to the effect of the poem; for we are of course apt to look upon the deep gloom which Young has thrown over his picture rather as a trick of art than as the terrific thunder-cloud—the "earthquake and eclipse" of nature: and the diminution of sublimity in our minds produced by this want of sincerity is in exact proportion to the impression that would have been made had this eloquent grief been altogether real.

The style, too, of Young in the 'Night Thoughts' is of a kind little capable of keeping alive those awful feelings of wonder and sublimity which his genius is so powerful in evoking. In him the intellect had an undue predominance over the imagination and the sensibility; and hardly does he raise up before us some grand image of death, of power, or of immortality, than he turns aside to seek after remote and fantastic allusions, which instantly destroy the potent charm. Few writers are so unequal as Young, or rather, few writers of such powerful and acknowledged genius were ever so deficient in comparative or critical taste. To him every idea seemed good, provided only it was strong, original, and ingenious; and as his subject was precisely the one least suited to this species of intellectual sword-play, the conceits, unexpected analogies, and epigrammatic turns of which he was so fond, are as offensive and incongruous as would be the placing of the frippery fountains and clipped yews and trim parterres of Versailles among the glaciers and precipices of Alpine scenery. This false taste for ingenious and far-fetched allusions Young may have in some measure acquired from the study of Crowley, Donne, and other writers of what was incorrectly called the "metaphysical" school of English poetry; but it is easy to observe that what in amatory or encomiastic compositions is nothing but false ornament and perverted ingenuity, becomes, when introduced into a work of a sublime and religious character, a great and unpardonable offence against good taste and propriety. It is impossible to open any page of Young without finding something grand, true, and striking: he is full of

"thoughts that wander through eternity."

He "speaks as one having authority;" and his accents are weighty, solemn and awakening, when he exhibits to us the vanity and nothingness of this life, and the nobility of the human soul — its aspirations, its destinies, and its hopes. But the mind of Young was ever on the watch for an opportunity for anything striking and new; his genius has "lidless dragon eyes," a restless, unappeasable vigilance; and no sooner does he perceive the slightest opening for an unexpected and epigrammatic turn, than he turns aside to pursue these butterflies of wit, these "Dalilahs of the imagination." Consequently there are few poets whose works present a greater number of detached glittering apophthegms — none who is so little adapted to give *continuous* pleasure to a reader of cultivated taste. Like the painter, he is sometimes equal to Raphael, sometimes inferior to himself.

It would be unjust were we to refuse our tribute of acknowledgment and admiration to the vast richness and fertility of imagination displayed by this powerful writer: it is the fertility of a tropical climate; or, rather, it is the abundant vegetation of a volcanic region; flowers and weeds, the hemlock and the vine, the gaudy and noxious poppy, and the innocent and life-supporting wheat — all is brought forth with a boundless and indiscriminate profusion. Hence, in spite of the gloomy nature of Young's subject — a gloom yet further augmented by the half-affected tone of his language — his writings are often studied with rapture by the youthful, and by those whose taste is yet unformed; and there are not many works whose perusal is fraught at the same time with more danger and more advantage. His happinesses of diction are innumerable. What can be finer either in images or in sound than his phantoms of past glory and power?—

"What visions rise!
What triumphs, toils imperial, arts divine,
In *wither'd laurels* glide before my sight!
What lengths of far-famed ages, *billow'd high*
With human agitation, roll along
In unsubstantial images of air!
The melancholy *ghosts* of dead renown,
Whispering faint echoes of the world's applause;
With penitential aspect, as they pass,
All point at earth, and *hiss* at human pride"—

or that noble and yet familiar image, so justly praised by Campbell—

"Where final Ruin fiercely drives
Her ploughshare o'er creation"—

or the bold impersonation of Death, who is introduced

"To tread out empires and to quench the stars."

On the other hand, what can be in worse taste than the comparison of the celestial orbs with diamonds set in a ring to adorn the finger of Omnipotence, which ring, by a supererogation of absurdity, is afterwards called a *seal*-ring?—

"A constellation of ten thousand gems,
Set in one signet, flames on the right hand
Of Majesty Divine; the blazing seal,
That deeply stamps, on all created mind,
Indelible, his sovereign attributes."

But perhaps the most easily perceived defect in this extraordinary work is the want of a plan and interest pervading the whole, and producing a natural connection or dependence between the various parts of the poem. Of course it would be too much to expect that a meditative or contemplative composition should contain a fable or narrative of progressive interest; but, at the same time, we have a right in every work consisting of many parts to look for a certain degree of dependence and mutual coherency. This condition is assuredly not fulfilled by the 'Night Thoughts,' the parts of which have no necessary connection, and may be displaced in their order without any injury to the effect of the whole. This blemish, perhaps to a certain degree inevitable, is but too much aggravated by the fragmentary and paroxysmal character of Young's style, producing its effect upon the reader, as Campbell justly and acutely remarks, rather by short abrupt *ictuses* of surprise than by sustained splendour of thought or steady progression of imagery.

CHAPTER XIII.

SWIFT AND THE ESSAYISTS.

Coarseness of Manners in the 17th and 18th centuries — Jonathan Swift — Battle of the Books — Tale of a Tub — Pamphlets — Stella and Venessa — Drapier's Letters—Voyages of Gulliver — Minor Works — Poems—Steele and Addison—Cato — Tatler — Spectator — Samuel Johnson — Prose Style — Satires of 'London' and 'The Vanity of Human Wishes' — Rasselas —Journey to the Hebrides—Lives of the Poets — Edition of Shakspeare — Dictionary—Rambler and Idler.

It can hardly, we think, be denied, that the Revolution of 1688 either produced or was accompanied by certain social effects at least temporarily injurious to society in England, and lowering the tone of sentiment, not only in political matters, but also, which is of much more importance to our subject, in the literary character of the times. Something of the old courtesy, something of the romantic and ideal in social intercourse between man and man, and still more preceptibly between man and woman, the Revolution appears to have annihilated; a more selfish, calculating, and material spirit begins to be perceptible in society, and consequently to be reflected in books. Language becomes a little ruder, more disputative, and more combative — the intellect now plays a more prominent part than either the fancy or the sensibility — the head has overbalanced the heart.

Of the general prevalence of such a tone of society there can be no more conclusive proof than the personal and literary character of Jonathan Swift; a man of robust and mighty intellect, of great and ready acquirements, of an indomitable will, activity, and perseverance, but equally deficient in heart as a man and in disinterestedness as a patriot. The Dean of St. Patrick's was indeed a rarely-gifted, prompt, and vigorous intellect: in his particular line of satire he is unequalled in literature; he did more and more readily what few beside him could have attempted; he played during his life a prominent and important part in the political drama of his country, and established himself by his writings among the prose classics of the world: but he was, as a man, heartless, selfish, unloving, and unsympathising; as a writer, he degraded and lowered our reverence for the divinity of our nature; and as a statesman, he appears to have felt no nobler spur to the exertion of his gigantic powers than the sting of personal pique and the pang of discontented ambition.

He was born in Dublin in the year 1667; a posthumous child, left dependent upon the uncertain charity of relations for support, and the not less precarious favour of the great for protection. This unfortunate entrance into life appears to have tinged with a darker shade of misanthropic gloom a temperament naturally saturnine, and to have inspired something of that morbid melancholy which ultimately deepened into hypochondria, and terminated so terribly in madness and idiotcy. Swift at the beginning of his career received the aid and protection of Sir William Temple, who enabled him to complete his education at Oxford, and in whose house he made that acquaintance with Mrs. Johnson (the daughter of Temple's steward) which became the source, to Swift, of a signal instance of retributive justice, and to the unfortunate lady of such a sad celebrity under the name of Stella. Swift did not begin to write until he had reached the tolerably mature age of thirty-four; and this circumstance will not only account for the extraordinary force and mastery which his style from the first exhibited, but it will prove the absence in Swift's mind of any of that purely literary ambition which incites the student

> "To scorn delights, and live laborious days."

Throughout the whole of his literary career Swift never appears to have cared to obtain the reputation of a mere writer: his works (the greater number of which were political pamphlets, referring to temporary events, and composed for the purpose of attaining temporary objects) seem never to have been considered by him otherwise than as means, instruments, or engines for the securing of their particular object. The ruling passion of his mind was an intense and arrogant desire for political power and notoriety; or, as he says himself, "All my endeavours, from a boy, to distinguish myself, were only for want of a great title and fortune, *that I might be used like a lord by those who have an opinion of my parts*—whether right or wrong, it is no great matter." This was indeed but a low and creeping ambition; and the fruit—at least as far as any augmentation of human happiness is concerned—is worthy of the tree.

The protégé of Temple, Swift was naturally, at the beginning of his public life, a Whig; and his first achievements in the warfare of party were made under the Whig banner. He also exhibited his attachment to his patron by taking part in the famous controversy respecting the comparative superiority of the ancients or the moderns; a controversy of which Temple was the most distinguished champion. Swift wrote the 'Battle of the Books,' a short satirical pamphlet, full of that coarse invective and savage personality which afterwards rendered him so famous and so formidable. Some of the incidents of the battle are worthy of the hand which painted the Yahoos or the Projectors' College of Laputa. The principal object of attack in this fierce and brutal piece of drollery was Bentley.

In 1704 appeared Swift's extraordinary satiric allegory, entitled 'The Tale of a Tub,' in which the author pretends to give an account of the rise and policy of the three most important sects into which Christendom has unhappily been divided — the Romanist, Lutheran (with which he identifies the Church of England,) and Calvinistic Churches.

These events are recounted in the broadest, boldest, most unreserved language of farcical extravagance; the three religions being typified by three brothers, Peter (the Church of Rome, or St. Peter), Martin (that of Luther), and Jack (John Calvin). The corruptions of the Romish Church, and the renunciation of those errors at the Reformation, are allegorised by a number of tassels, fringes, and shoulder-knots, which the three brothers superadd to the primitive simplicity of their coats (the practice and belief of the Christian religion). These extraneous ornaments Martin strips off cautiously and gradually; but poor Jack, in his eagerness, nearly reduces himself to a state of nature. Nothing can exceed the richness of imagination with which Swift places in a ridiculous or contemptible light the extravagances of the three brothers. It must be observed that he invariably sides with Martin, and pursues the fantastic pranks of Jack with a pitiless and envenomed malignity that shows how richly nature had gifted him for the trade of political and religious lampooning. This strange work is divided into chapters, between which are interposed an equal number of what the author calls "digressions," and which latter, like the main work, are absolute treasuries of droll allusion and ingenious adaptation of obscure and uncommon learning.

In 1708 Swift turned Tory; and he was soon found writing as nervously, fluently, and vigorously on the side of his new patrons as ever he had done in support of his former one. He now published successively a number of able pamphlets, under the title of 'Sentiments of a Church-of-England Man,' 'Letters on the Application of the Sacramental Test,' and the admirable 'Apology for Christianity. In this last production, under his usual veil of grave irony, he shows the ill consequences which would result from an abolition of the Christian religion: among the rest, for example, proving what a loss it would be to the freethinker and scoffer and *esprit fort* to be deprived of so fertile a subject of ridicule as is now afforded by the principles and practice of our religion.

About the same time, Swift, in a succession of humorous *jeux d'esprit*, ridiculed the credulity of many classes of persons at that time as to the predictions of astrology, and the gross ignorance of the almanac-makers and other needy and obscure quacks, who administered food to the public appetite for the marvellous.

In 1712 he wrote a species of half-history, half-pamphlet, entitled 'The Conduct of the Allies,' severely reflecting upon the Duke of Marlborough; and nearly at the same time he became acquainted with the beautiful and most unhappy Vanessa, whose real name was Vanhomrigh. This young lady had been in some measure educated by Swift; and the fair pupil conceived for her instructor a passion of that deep, durable, and all-engrossing character, which, for weal or woe, fills and occupies a whole existence, and to whose intensity not even time can apply any real alleviation. It is not certain how far a thoughtless vanity, or an almost incredible hardness of heart, or a taint of that insanity which was to cloud the setting of Swift's bright and powerful intellect, may have led him to sport with the affections of this unfortunate girl; but, at the very time when he was allowing her to indulge in dreams of happiness which he knew were vain, Swift was keeping up with Stella, the former victim of his selfish vanity, the hope of a union which, if it came at all, was certain to be but too tardy a reparation. Vanessa died of a broken heart, on learning the relations in which Swift stood, and had all along remained, with respect to Stella; and Stella appears ultimately to have received a legal right to Swift's protection as a husband. But this act of justice came too late either to restore her ruined happiness or to save her life. For this double act of heartlessness Swift was to suffer a terrible and just retribution.

At the accession to the English throne of the House of Hanover, Swift retired to Ireland; for the Whigs were now in power. But in leaving the more busy stage of English politics, Swift carried with him the greatest powers to annoy and harass the government at a distance; and he soon arrived at a pitch of popularity among his own countrymen which has never been surpassed—perhaps never equalled—even in the heated atmosphere of Irish politics. Taking advantage of a species of monopoly (apparently not much more unjust and oppressive than such privileges usually are) which the government was about to grant to a certain William Wood, and the object of which was to admit into Ireland a considerable sum of copper money to be coined by Wood, Swift succeeded in raising against the government which granted, and the speculator who obtained, the obnoxious monopoly, so violent a storm of Irish indignation, that not only was it found impossible to execute the project, but an insurrection was very nearly excited; or to use Swift's energetic answer to Archbishop Boulter, who once accused him of having excited the popular fury against the government, "If I had lifted my finger, they would have torn you to pieces!" The engine of this vehement movement was the publication (in a Dublin newspaper) of a succession of letters, signed "M. B. Drapier," written by Swift in the character of a Dublin tradesman, and a most admirable specimen of consummate skill in political writing for the people.

In 1726 appeared the satiric romance of "Gulliver," undoubtedly the greatest and most durable monument of Swift's style and originality of conception. 'Gulliver,' being a work of universal satire, will be read as long as the corruptions of human nature render its innumerable ironic and sarcastic strokes applicable and intelligible to human beings; and even were the follies and basenesses of humanity so far purged away that men should no longer need the sharp and bitter medicine of satire, it would still be read with little less admiration and delight for the wonderful richness of invention it displays, and the exquisite art with which the most impossible and extravagant adventures are related — related so naturally as to cheat us into a momentary belief in their reality. The book consists of an account of the strange adventures of the hero in whose person it is written. Nothing can be better than the dexterity with which Swift has identified himself — particularly at the beginning — with the character of a plain, rough, honest surgeon of a ship, and the minute verisimilitude which pervades his relation — a verisimilitude kept up with surprising watchfulness, even in the least details and descriptions of an imaginary world. Lemuel Gulliver, after being shipwrecked, all his companions having perished, finds himself landed in the country of Lilliput, the inhabitants of which are about six inches high, and in which all the objects, natural and artificial, are in exact proportion to the people. We have a most amusing description of the court, the capital, and the government of this pigmy empire; and while exciting our incessant interest by the prodigality of invention exhibited, and the wonderful richness of fancy, all these descriptions, as well as the account of Gulliver's adventures in Lilliput, are made the vehicle of incessant strokes of satire, directed not only against the vices and follies of mankind (thus held up to ridicule in the disguise of these human insects), but against contemporary persons and intrigues. It is hardly necessary to remark, that what is of general application now possesses a much greater interest than many of the sly temporary allusions which probably gave most delight when the book appeared. In the second part of the fiction our honest Gulliver visits a nation of giants, where we find the same carefully calculated proportion between the people of the country (represented as sixty feet high) and the relative size of their trees, animals, houses, utensils, and so on. In Brobdignag the illusion is perhaps even more artfully kept up than it is in the description of Lilliput; the size — so enormous, yet always so perfectly in accordance with the scale pre-established — of the various objects being here generally indicated, or rather hinted in a parenthesis, than elaborately detailed. What can be more richly comic, for instance, than the conflagration of the capital of Lilliput, the court intrigues, the grand review of the army, Gulliver's capture of the entire fleet of Blefuscu, or the terrible schisms of the Big-endians and Little-endians? What can exhibit a more fertile conception, or a more truly Rabelæsian drollery, than many of the adventures at Lorbrulgrud, the metropolis of the gigantic Brobdignagians; the scene in which poor Gulliver is carried up to the palace-roof by the monkey; the enmities and spiteful tricks of the queen's dwarf, "who was of the lowest stature that was ever seen in that country (for I verily think he was not full thirty feet high);" the description of the maids of honour; and the battles of Gulliver with flies, wasps, rats, and linnets? The satiric aim is the same in both parts of the fiction, though attained by different roads. In Lilliput, the author shows us how contemptible would be human passions, war, ambition, and science, were they exhibited by the insect inhabitants of a microscopic country. In Brobdignag, he makes us perceive, by as it were reversing the telescope, the extreme meanness and insignificance which our institutions, pursuits, and actions would exhibit to beings endowed with gigantic powers. In the second part of the romance he represents Gulliver as giving to the king of the giants—a wise and pacific monarch—a description of human warfare, government, and society; and he makes the king conclude, from the little stranger's narrative, "that, by what I have gathered from your own relation, and the answers I have with much pains wringed and extorted from you, I cannot but conclude the bulk of your natives to be the most pernicious race of little odious vermin that nature ever suffered to crawl on the surface of the earth." Now this, we apprehend, which is but a fair specimen of the general conclusions of this satire, and indeed the general drift of most of Swift's writings, is neither just nor useful. To be truly powerful, satire must be discriminating; and this sweeping contempt and reprobation not only defeats its own object, but is *from* the true purpose of satiric painting—that of rendering the species better, wiser, and more innocent. Nor must we omit here to speak of a blemish which disfigures all Swift's writings, though perhaps it is not more prominently offensive in 'Gulliver' than in some of his other works, particularly his poems. It is a stain which appears to have been, from some strange peculiarity of mental constitution, inherent in Swift's character: we allude to the passion which he seems to have had to seek after images of pure physical disgust and loathsomeness. No writer was ever more truly moral and virtuous than Swift, none more studious to hold up vice and folly to the contempt and execration of mankind; so that this defect in no sense partakes of that detestable ingenuity which makes some writers pander to the vilest propensities of our nature, nor even of that exaggerated warmth of invective under whose influence some satirists (as Juvenal, for instance) have drawn too warm and highly-coloured pictures of the vices they attack, and thus, like Jaques, done

"mischievous foul sin in chiding sin."

No; Swift's offences against delicacy are not of this kind: they cannot be said to excite the passions, but they raise the gorge; they make us shudder, not with moral repulsion, but with physical disgust. Of all men of supereminent genius, Swift appears to have had the least sympathy with what is beautiful, the least enthusiasm for what is sublime. The very force and might of his style consists in its being level, plain, prosaic, logical, and unimaginative. But his taste for images of absolute physical filthiness we believe to be peculiar to him : the *physiologist* might discover its cause.

The third part of this celebrated fiction describes the imaginary countries of Laputa, a flying island, inhabited by speculative philosophers, devoted to mathematics and music; which gives Swift the opportunity to ridicule the follies of pedantic science. From thence the traveller descends to Balnibarbi, a land occupied by projectors. The most notable passage of this part of the work is the description of the academy, which is a not very happy imitation of the college of philosophers so admirably depicted in the second part of Rabelais' immortal extravaganza. Besides, Swift's ridicule in this part of the work is often deficient in point and propriety; nor was the author sufficiently versed either in physical science or ancient learning to be able to ridicule with much effect the abuses of the one or the follies of the other. Many of the objects, too, which he has introduced, are altogether too disgusting and offensive to form proper features even in a satiric fiction. Caricature has its decencies and its *bienséances* no less than historic or romantic painting. Rabelais, it is true, abounds in coarse and indecent images, no less than in the wildest extravagance of burlesque; but we should remember the almost frantic tone of animal spirits which pervades his work, so different from the grave simplicity of Swift: and we must keep in mind the period at which the curé of Meudon wrote, obliging him, at the risk of life and liberty, never for one moment to let drop the antic mask of buffoonery under which he so keenly satirises the superstitions of the Church and the vices of the world. Moreover, Rabelais was (due allowance being made for the difference of their respective epochs) a far more learned man than Swift. He was also a far more genial spirit; at least equal in wit, and immeasurably superior in humour. He *knew* more, and he also *loved* more. Swift was admirably characterised by Coleridge as "anima Rabelæsii habitans in sicco," *the soul of Rabelais dwelling in a dry place.*

The next strange country visited is Glubbdubdrib, an island inhabited by a people of magicians, who evoke, for the amusement of the traveller, the spirits of many great men of antiquity; thus giving the author an opportunity to indulge his satiric vein. But this portion of the book is generally found to be exceedingly poor and flat. The idea is excellent, but very little has been made of it; and we neither laugh nor admire when Hannibal is called up from the shades to assure us that, "in passing the Alps, he had not a drop of vinegar in his camp," or Aristotle to predict to Descartes that the Newtonian doctrine would as certainly be exploded as the vortices of the French philosopher.

Gulliver next finds his way to Luggnagg, in which country he has the opportunity of perceiving how miserable would be the consequence of human beings receiving a privilege of eternal life, unaccompanied by corresponding health, strength, and intellect; a reservation which seems rather unnecessary, and a kind of *petitio principii.* In point of description, however, nothing can be finer, more powerful, and Juvenalian in its gloomy energy, than Swift's picture of the wretched Stuldbrugs, the unhappy possessors of "an immortality of woe."

The fourth voyage of Gulliver carries him to the country of the Houyhnhnms; and is remarkable for a deeper, fiercer, intenser flame of satiric fury than any of the three preceding parts. In the voyage to Lilliput he chiefly ridiculed the persons and events of contemporary politics; in the government of Brobdignag he gives us a kind of model of his notions of good government and of a patriot king; in Laputa, &c., he mocks at the abuses of science and learning; but in the last voyage, the current of his satire, deepening and widening as it rolls, envelops, like some vast inundation, all the institutions of civilized society, and all the passions of our human nature. He represents a country in which horses are the ruling and supreme beings, while man is degraded to the rank of a filthy noxious, and untamable brute, retaining, with some relics and rough outlines of the human form, all our villanous passions and base appetites exhibited in complete nakedness. Setting aside the outrageous improbability of the leading idea—viz. that of making horses change place with men in the social system of nature—it cannot be doubted that the ferocity of the satire is excessive and absurd, and appears to have been inspired rather by the rabid instinct of an unreasoning misanthropy, than to have been dictated by the legitimate anger of indignant virtue. "It is an ill bird," says the good old proverb, "that fouls its own nest;" and any man, possessed of so admirable and commanding an intellect as that of Swift, who should give us as the result of observations on human nature, collected through a long life passed in full communion with the greatest and best of his own country, such a picture as that of the Yahoos—a picture whose every tint and line testifies the real, sincere, unaffected hatred and contempt which guided the artist's hand in tracing it—such a man, we repeat, lays himself open to the charge either of having drawn not a portrait but a gross and odious caricature, or of having his eye grievously blinded and perverted by prejudice.

Besides these two great prose satires, the 'Tale of a Tub' and the 'Voyages of Gulliver,' Swift's collected works contain a vast number of smaller ludicrous compositions, all of them bearing the stamp of the author's mind—originality, vigorous plainness of manner, and a perfect acquaintance with all the minutiæ of social intercourse. Among others we may mention his admirable mock-serious treatise called 'Directions to Servants,' in which, under ironical precepts, he has exhibited the profoundest knowledge of all the mysteries of the kitchen and the servants' hall. In his 'Treatise on Polite Conversation' he has given us a similarly ironical compendium of the coarse jokes, the vulgar repartees, the pert and proverbial expressions which at that time formed the staple of fashionable dialogue. The picture is of course exaggerated, but the outlines are true. It was an age when fine gentlemen and ladies absolutely piqued themselves on their ignorance, and when what were called, in the elegant phraseology of the day, "bites" and "selling of bargains," formed the principal enlivenment of fashionable society.

During his whole life Swift continued from time to time to compose pieces of poetry of various kinds; and standing, as he did, upon the very pinnacle of popularity, it is not surprising that he should have obtained a high reputation as a poet. One quality for the art he assuredly possessed in an eminent degree, that of originality; and his verses, generally written on particular occasions, and often as personal or party lampoons, have certainly the merit of perfect ease, fluency, and sincerity. His more important pieces are written in the octo-syllabic rhyme of Prior and Gay; and though they abound in good sense, acute remark, and intense severity of allusion, they possess none of the higher qualities of poetry: not much harmony, no depth of feeling, no (or very rare) splendour of language. They are, like their author, dry, hard, and cold. In 'Cadenus and Vanessa' he has given a rather dull description of the *commencement* of the sad story of the unhappy Hester Vanhomrigh; in the 'Legion Club' the most intense expression of hatred and contempt (directed against the Irish Parliament) that human pen perhaps has ever traced, or human heart conceived; and scattered through his works are a multitude of farcical little compositions, some of them epigrams and political pasquinades, others trifles meant merely to amuse the privacy of a friendly circle; but all of which are marked with as much excellence as the subject would admit—trifling toys of the ingenuity, but toys constructed by a master's hand. His best poems of any length are the verses entitled 'A Rhapsody on Poetry,' in the beginning of which are several passages of great vigour and more warmth of expression than is usually to be found in Swift; and the other called 'Verses on my Own Death, in which, with admirable nature, drollery, and vivacity, he describes the various feelings with which that event would be received among his friends, acquaintance, and enemies.

This event was not now very remote; but ere this great wit arrived at that repose which an excruciating and incurable disease must have made him view with hope, he was destined to pass through the severest ordeal to which our nature can be submitted. He was to travel, *while yet living*, through "the valley and the shadow of death."

During the whole of his life he had been grievously afflicted with attacks of deafness, giddiness, and pain in the head; and his gloomy and despondent spirit seems to have looked forward with prophetic dread to insanity as the probable termination of his existence. An affecting anecdote is related by Dr. Young of Swift having once been found mournfully gazing on a noble oak, whose upper branches had been struck by lightning: "I shall be like that tree," said Swift, "I shall die first a-top." Nor were these melancholy predictions falsified by the event. About the year 1736 he was attacked by repeated fits of pain and loss of memory, and in the composition of that terrific invective the 'Legion Club' he was seized by a species of fit, from which he never recovered sufficiently to finish the poem. The long and melancholy interval (of nine years) intervening between this time and his death was one uninterrupted succession of mental and bodily suffering. He passed from a deplorable and furious mania to a state of idiotcy; and the active politician, the resistless polemic, the satirist, the poet, and the wit, died, as he himself had feared and half predicted, "in a rage, like a poisoned rat in a hole;"—

"Swift expired a driveller and a show."

This event took place, October 19th, 1745, at Dublin, and excited among the lower and middle classes of that city, whose friend, adviser, and defender he had been, the liveliest expressions of grief and lamentation. "The Dean" was buried in his own cathedral of St. Patrick's, and his place of sepulture marked by an epitaph composed by himself, some words of which form the best and most appropriate commentary that the wit of man could have invented upon the writings and the character of this illustrious but most unhappy man:—

"Hic depositum est corpus
Jonathan Swift, S. T. P.
Ubi *sæva Indignatio*
Ulterius cor lacerare nequit."

We have taken occasion in the preceding pages, to advert more than once to the coarse and corrupted state of society which prevailed in England about the accession of William III., and seems to have continued with little modification through the reigns of at least the first two Georges. That this brutal, selfish, and vulgar tone of social intercourse was at once a result and an indication of a deep and general deterioration of morals is more than probable: it partly arose from the unfortunate mixture of politics in the whole texture, so to speak, of society, and may be attributed partly to the increased influence of the popular element in our political constitution, and in some degree doubtless to that roughness and ferocity of manners which a long-continued period of warfare seldom fails to communicate to a nation, and of which we have a signal example in more recent times in the coarse and violent tone of manners introduced in France by the military spirit of the Republic, the Consulate, and the Empire. Gambling was exceedingly prevalent: and drunkenness — so long, alas! the vice of Englishmen — was grossly and universally habitual. Swearing and gross indecency of language were universally indulged in. The amusements of all classes possessed the coarseness of those athletic pastimes of which Englishmen have in all ages been so fond, but in many cases without either the courage which they inspire, or the generous and manly spirit which they cherish. The barbarous and brutalizing sports of the cock-pit and the bull-ring were still pursued with at least as much passion as the nobler amusements of the turf, the river, and the field. As to the pleasures of the intellect and the taste, they were either absolutely unknown, or confined to a few, and those few regarded as pedants or as humorists. "That general knowledge which now circulates in common talk," says Johnson, speaking of this period, "was then rarely to be found. Men not professing learning were not ashamed of ignorance; and in the female world any acquaintance with books was distinguished only to be censured." To combat the national taste for these low and sordid follies, to infuse a more courteous, refined, and Christian tone into the manners of society, was the aim of a number of excellent writers, extending over a considerable period of our literary history, and known under the general appellation of "Essayists." Their aim being so comprehensive, the subjects they had to treat so multifarious, and the public they had to address so numerous, they adopted the expedient of throwing their remarks upon any subject into the form of a paper, publishing at a very cheap rate, and at regular and very short intervals. The originator of this species of work was Sir Richard Steele, a man admirably qualified by vivacity and readiness of intellect, a profound acquaintance with life in all its phases, and an undeniable goodness of heart and of intention, to undertake the office of a periodical censor of manners; but his reputation as a writer was soon surpassed by many succeeding authors of the same kind, and particularly by his fellow-labourer and friend Addison.

This latter person was long considered as a sort of standard or model of all that is most easy, elegant, and natural in English prose — a throne of supremacy from which he has only recently been ejected by the more weighty, more highly-coloured, more thoughtful and profound style of modern times, particularly since the French Revolution. His career was singularly prosperous. He was born in 1672, the son of a country gentleman of very moderate fortune, received at Oxford a good and learned education, and distinguished himself rather for the elegance than the depth of his scholarship. His first appearance in English literature was a poetical panegyric on Dryden, written at twenty-two, and in which he exhibits much more neatness of versification than originality of thought or justness of criticism. He also translated the Fourth Georgic of Virgil, which Dryden printed in his own Miscellanies with warm encomiums on the young poet. But the work which must be considered his first earnest of success, and which first procured him the entrance to the arena of his after political success, was his poem on the King, addressed to Lord Somers, then keeper of the seals. This procured him the warm and lasting favour and patronage of the powerful lawyer, who soon after gave Addison solid proofs of his protection in procuring him a pension of 300*l.* a-year, which enabled him to travel over the most interesting parts of France and Italy.

The death of King William deprived Addison of his pension, but he soon after more than compensated for this loss by the publication of his poem on the battle of Blenheim, which was rewarded by the place of Commissioner of Appeals. The poem is little better than a rhymed gazette, and strongly reminds the reader of the once equally celebrated but now equally unread poem of Boileau, on the passage of the Rhine by Louis XIV. There is in both works the same incessant and ineffectual struggle to appear splendid and animated, but the same stiffness, artifice, and effort. The famous comparison of Marlborough to a destroying angel was as much admired in its day as the often-quoted

"Il se plaint de sa gloire qui l'attache au rivage"

of the courtly and witty Despréaux.

Addison now rapidly and steadily advanced along the path of political distinction: he was made Under-Secretary of State, and accompanied Wharton to Ireland. In 1716 he married the Dowager Countess of Warwick, to whose son he had formerly been tutor; but this union, as might have been expected, was an unhappy one — as such ill-assorted matches between hereditary nobility and intellectual celebrity are generally found to be. Addison was appointed, in 1717, Secretary of State, an office for which his fastidious delicacy of taste, timid character, and total want both of business talents and parliamentary eloquence, rendered him by all accounts singularly unfit. He soon resigned a dignity for which he was so unfitted by nature, and was rewarded for his services with a pension of 1500*l.* a-year. He died on the 17th of June, 1719, leaving behind him a most enviable reputation for purity and integrity of life. After making due allowances for the tone of exaggeration and panegyric in which his biography has been written, it is impossible not to allow him high praise for personal virtue and piety. It would be too much to expect that any man—particularly one who was at the same time a literary man and a politician — should be perfect; and when we reflect how much a ministerial life tends to sour the temper and inflame envy and suspicion, we cannot be surprised that Addison, in spite of a character naturally amiable and benevolent, should have sometimes exhibited a little querulousness and impatience. As an author it is not so easy to draw his character, though its principal outlines will nearly coincide with those of his political portrait. We shall find the same timid propriety, the same universal and unquestionable goodness of aim and intention, with perhaps a little shade of the subdued jealousy of other men's glory which drew from Pope those far-famed and admirable lines —

> "were there one whose fires
> True genius kindles, and fair fame inspires;
> Bless'd with each talent and each art to please,
> And born to write, converse, and live with ease;
> Should such a man, too fond to rule alone,
> Bear, like the Turk, no brother near the throne;
> View him with scornful, yet with jealous eyes,
> And hate for arts that caused himself to rise;
> Damn with faint praise, assent with civil leer,
> And, without sneering, teach the rest to sneer;
> Willing to wound, and yet afraid to strike,
> Just hint a fault, and hesitate dislike;
> Alike reserved to blame, and to commend,
> A timorous foe, or a suspicious friend;
> Dreading e'en fools, by flatterers besieged,
> And so obliging, that he ne'er obliged;
> Like *Cato*, gives his little senate laws,
> And sits attentive to his own applause;
> While wits and Templars every sentence raise,
> And wonder with a foolish face of praise; —
> Who but must laugh, if such a man there be?
> Who would not weep, if Atticus were he?"

Before we speak of that portion of Addison's writings upon which is chiefly based his enduring reputation as a classical English prose writer, it would be unjust not to speak of one or two of his principal productions, by which he attained in his own day the summit of popularity, though they are now comparatively neglected. The chief of these is, undoubtedly, the tragedy of 'Cato.' 'Cato' is a work constructed according to the very strictest rules of the so-called classical propriety. The three unities are exactly and laboriously preserved, the action simple and elevated, the personages few in number, the sentiments and language throughout studiously elevated and imposing. It is, in short, a carefully-carved mask of the neatest workmanship; but the reader at every moment exclaims, with the fox in the fable, "What a pity it hath no brains!" To preserve the vaunted unity of time and place (which, when preserved, is good for nothing), the author sacrifices probability — not only real, but dramatic — in the most extraordinary manner; making conspirators plot against Cato in Cato's own house; making the hero himself commit suicide in an open hall, public to all the world; representing a project made to carry off a lady by means of the disguise not only of her lover but of all her lover's body-guards; and a thousand other such absurdities. For the characters and manners, they are worthy of the plot: they are neither Romans nor Numidians, neither patriots nor conspirators, because they are not human beings. "The virtuous Marcia towers above her sex" indeed, but it is in frigid pedantry of ambitious declamation; the patriotic harangues of Cato are sickly commonplaces, fagoted together out of history; and the celebrated soliloquy of the hero, when he meditates suicide, though certainly not devoid of merit, yet is only valuable as a purely didactic passage. Shakspeare, Jonson, Massinger, Beaumont — these have shown us Roman passions, Roman patriotism, and Roman language; these frigid abstractions bear the same relation to the Romans of Shakspeare, or the Romans *of Rome*, as the waxen dolls in the window of a barber to the living, moving, thinking, passengers that walk by them in the street.

But it is as a periodical essayist that Addison earned his true glory. On the 12th of April, 1709, Steele commenced the publication of a small sheet, issued thrice a-week, at a very low price (each number cost a penny), containing a short essay or disquisition upon some topic connected with the dress, behaviour, morality, amusements, &c., of the upper and middle classes of society. The remaining portion of the half-sheet was devoted to news and general information. This kind of semi-didactic newspaper was chiefly written by its first projector, Steele, under the pseudonym of Isaac Bickerstaff, and was entitled 'The Tatler.' The essays, which formed its prominent feature, were distinguished for that ease, unaffected good-nature, and fluent, though not always very correct, style which characterised the amiable author; and the work met with so much success that no morning tea-table was without this indispensable accompaniment. 'The Tatler' continued its career till it amounted to 271 numbers, when it was transformed or remodelled into a nearly similar publication, still more famous in English literature, under the name of 'The Spectator.' In the composition of 'The Tatler,' Steele had received the occasional assistance of Addison; but in its successor the latter took a much more active part, contributing all the papers marked with any one of the letters composing the word *Clio*. 'The Spectator' began on March 1st, 1713, and, appearing daily, instead of thrice a-week, as 'The Tatler' had done, extended to 635 numbers, each of which contains a complete essay, generally upon some subject of moral importance, and occasionally a disquisition on the principles of criticism, and the application of those principles in judging of some great work of literature or art. The object of these elegant publications was in the highest degree laudable and excellent. "I shall endeavour," says Steele himself, "to enliven morality with wit, and to temper wit with morality, that my readers may, if possible, both ways find their account in the speculation of the day. It was said of Socrates, that he brought philosophy down from heaven to inhabit among men. I shall be ambitious to have it said of me, that I have brought philosophy out of closets and libraries, schools and colleges, to dwell in clubs and assemblies, at tea-tables, and in coffee-houses." Accustomed as we now are to a much more refined and intellectual tone of social intercourse, and to the diffusion, even to the lower order of people, of a degree of general knowledge and information which was then extremely rare even in the highest, we may smile at the somewhat trite and commonplace tone of many of these essays, at the slender parade of scholarship, the little scrap of Latin or Greek prefixed to them as a motto — a sentence of Tully, or a precept of Seneca or Longinus; but we were unjust to forget the excellent morality, the useful and reasonable principles of good-breeding, the Christian and gentle spirit which they inculcate; and we must remember too, that, however narrow, and prejudiced, and exclusive may seem to us the dogmas of Addison's literary criticisms, yet that these were the first *popular* essays in English towards the investigation of the grounds and axioms of æsthetic science, and that even here, in innumerable instances (as, for example, in the celebrated reviews of 'Paradise Lost,' and of the old national ballad of 'Chevy Chase'), we find the author's natural and delicate sense of the beautiful and sublime triumphing over the accumulated errors and false judgment of his own artificial age, and the author of 'Cato' doing unconscious homage to the nature and pathos of the rude old Border ballad-maker.

But the most delightful portions of 'The Spectator' are those in which the "short-faced gentleman," the supposed author, speaks of the imaginary club of which he is a member. The army is represented by Captain Sentry; the fashionable world by an old beau, Will Honeycomb; the city and men of business express their opinions through the mouth of Sir Andrew Freeport; and the country gentlemen are represented by Sir Roger de Coverley. These personages have very little life, humour, or individuality, with the exception of the last, which is one of the most exquisite embodiments of nature which the pencil of fiction has ever drawn. The mixture, in this enchanting portrait, of benevolence, old-fashioned politeness, simplicity, superstition, charity, and a taste for rural sports, is sketched with a light and delicate, yet firm and skilful hand, which makes the picture—though so different in style—well worthy to hang in the same gallery with Don Quixote or with Parson Adams, with the Lismahago of Smollett or the Mr. Shandy of Sterne. The first idea of this sketch, it is most probable, was suggested, and the outline perhaps roughly drawn in, by Steele. Be this as it may, whether first suggested by Steele, and afterwards elaborated by Addison, or one of those happy conceptions which men owe sometimes to accident fully as much as to inspiration, Sir Roger de Coverley is uniformly and unfailingly the delight of every reader—

"A beautiful thought, and softly shadow'd forth;"

and Addison, not unconscious of the beauty of his work, seems to have taken an inexhaustible delight in placing it in new points of view, and drawing forth, with the gentle and quiet touch of humour and genius, all its innocent and attaching oddities. He gives us Sir Roger during his visit to London; he accompanies him (in an enchanting passage) to Westmininster Abbey; he carries us to the country to visit him in his old pinnacled and mullioned hall, deeply embosomed in ancestral trees; he shows us the good knight in his moments of tender pensiveness, or gaily chatting with his ingenious kinsman, Will Wimble, or mildly testifying against the witchcraft of Moll White, the village sorceress. When Sir Roger dies (for Addison is reported to have killed him, as Cervantes did his admirable knight, in order to prevent any grosser hand from continuing, and perhaps spoiling, his creation), we feel as if we had lost a friend.

"Whoever wishes," says Johnson, "to attain an English style, familiar but not coarse, elegant but not ostentatious, must give his days and nights to the study of Addison." We cannot conclude our notice of this excellent writer and estimable man more appropriately than by adopting the words of Chambers, which are warm, just, and comprehensive:—"In Addison the reader will find a rich but chaste vein of humour and satire; lessons of morality and religion, divested of all austerity and gloom; criticism at once pleasing and profound; and pictures of national character and manners that must ever charm from their vivacity and truth. Greater energy of character, or a more determined hatred of vice and tyranny, would have curtailed his usefulness as a public censor. He led the nation insensibly to a love of virtue and constitutional freedom, to a purer taste in morals and literature, and to the importance of those everlasting truths which so warmly engaged his heart and imagination."

But to us, whose eyes have been scaled and purged by the all-curing power of time, the greatest figure in this period of English literary history is undoubtedly Samuel Johnson. As a writer, he is the very incarnation of *good sense*; and as a man, he was an example of so high a degree of virtue, magnanimity, and self-sacrifice, that he has been justly placed by a profound modern speculator among the *heroes* of his country's annals.

He was the son of a poor provincial bookseller, and was born at Lichfield, September 18th, 1709; affording another testimony of that truth so often exemplified in the history of literature, and so pithily expressed by an old writer, "that no great work, or worthy of praise and memory, but came out of poor cradles." He was afflicted, even from his earliest years, with a scrofulous disorder, which disfigured a person naturally awkward and ungainly, and this disorder was probably connected with another and more terrible one, which renders it still more wonderful how he could have ever attained to such a degree of just reputation as he afterwards earned. This was a constitutional tendency to melancholy and hypochondria—a "vile melancholy," to use his own touching words, "which has kept me mad half my life, or at least not sober." What a contrast to the fantastical and intentional gloom of Young, springing from the ignoble source of disappointed ambition, and indulged as the best key in which he could set his ingenious lamentations over the vanity of human things, his sombre conceits, as sadly fantastic as the glittering ornaments on a rich man's coffin! What a contrast to the cynical asperity of Swift, masking a haughty, selfish, and arrogant pride under an affected contempt of human nature, complaining, though at the pinnacle of fame, of neglect and unrewarded exertions! The earlier part—nay, by far the greater portion—of Johnson's career was passed in obscure and apparently hopeless struggles with want and indigence; and however these may have enlarged his knowledge of human life, or fortified his own powers of industry and reflection, they only place in a higher elevation the virtue of the man and the intellectual vigour of the great scholar. He passed some time at Pembroke College, Oxford, but his father's misfortunes compelled him to leave the university without a degree. To the aspirant after literary fame, to him who takes a wise pleasure in tracing the struggles of genius to emerge from a sea of difficulties, few things are more delightful or more salutary than to follow step by step the commencement of Johnson's career:

"Slow rises worth by poverty oppressed."

We find him acting as usher in schools, and afterwards unsuccessfully attempting to conduct a school himself at the little town of Market Bosworth. Poor, independent, ambitious, conscious of his own powers, he now adopted the desperate yet natural resolution of launching on the broad ocean of London society, and he travelled up to the capital in company with his friend and former pupil, David Garrick, who was afterwards destined to obtain, on the stage, a reputation as great as that ultimately acquired in literature by his companion. Johnson now commenced the profession (or rather trade, for at that time it was, alas! hardly more dignified, and certainly not so well remunerated as many mechanical occupations) of author, obtaining a scanty and precarious subsistence by translating and writing task-work for the booksellers, and principally employed as a contributor to the 'Gentleman's Magazine,' then published by Cave.

Johnson's style during the whole of his career was exceedingly peculiar and characteristic both in its beauties and defects, and when he arrived at eminence may be said to have produced a revolution in the manner of writing in English; and as this revolution has to a certain degree lasted till the present day, it will be well to say a few words on the subject. It is in the highest degree pompous, sonorous, and, to use a happy expression of Coleridge, *hyper-latinistic*; running into perpetual antithesis, and balancing period against period with an almost rhythmical regularity, which at once fills and fatigues the ear. Formed upon certain of our elder writers (as Sir Thomas Browne, for instance), whose learning and grave eloquence cannot always save them from the charge of pedantry, it was a style, like theirs, exactly such as might have been expected from a man who had educated himself in solitary study, and whose memory was filled with echoes of the rhetorical sententiousness of Juvenal and Seneca, and the artful and ambitious periods of Sallust or Tacitus. The great deficiency of the style is want—not of ease, as has been unjustly supposed, for Johnson's strong and nervous intellect wielded its polished and ponderous weapon with perfect mastery and freedom—but of that familiar flexibility which is best adapted to the general course of disquisition. It would be unjust to Johnson's good taste not to remark that he appears to have been sensible of the imperfection of his way of writing; for his later works exhibit a marked and progressive diminution of this stiffness and Latinism; and we may also observe that many of the words (generally Latin, as "resuscitate," "fatuity," "germination," &c.), his use of which excited so much criticism at the time, have since been completely naturalized and endenizened in the language. The prevailing defect of Johnson's style is uniformity: the combinations of his kaleidoscope are soon exhausted; his peal of bells is very limited in its changes; and as there is necessarily, in so artificial a style, an air of pretension and ambitiousness, the sameness is more fatiguing than would be the snipped periods and tuneless meanness of a more unostentatious mode of expression.

In 1738 appeared the admirable satire entitled 'London,' a revival of the Thirteenth Satire of Juvenal, in which the topics of the Roman poet are applied with surprising freedom, animation, and felicity to English manners, and the corruptions of modern London society.

After the satire of 'London,' of which we shall speak more anon, Johnson published his 'Life of Savage,' the biography of a poet whose strange and melancholy story formed an admirable subject for Johnson's dignified and moral pen; and in 1749 appeared the *pendant* or companion-picture to the 'London,' in a similar modernisation of the Tenth Satire of Juvenal. Our readers may not perhaps know that the Thirteenth Satire of Juvenal is directed against the corruptions of society in Rome, against the miseries and humiliations which a residence in the great city imposes upon a poor but virtuous man, and the immense riches and influence obtained, by the most unworthy arts, by Greeks and favourite freedmen. The picture is a striking and impressive one, and has lost none of its grandeur in the hands of the English copyist, who has with consummate skill transferred the invectives of Juvenal to the passion for imitating French fashions, and adapted the images of Juvenal to London vices, discomforts, and corruptions. In the Tenth Satire (perhaps the grandest specimen which we possess of this kind of writing) the Roman takes a higher ground, and in an uninterrupted torrent of noble and melancholy eloquence has pointed out the folly and emptiness of all those objects which form the chief aim of human desires. He shows us successively the misery which has accompanied, and the ruin which has followed, the possession of those advantages for which men sigh and pray: he exhibits the vanity of riches, ambition, eloquence, military glory, long life, and beauty, the whole exemplified by the most signal examples, drawn from history, of the folly of human hopes,—

"Magnaque numinibus Diis exaudita malignis."

Many passages of Johnson's satires must be regarded as translations—consummate translations—of the words of Juvenal; but he frequently changes, augments, and strengthens; as, for example, Juvenal has instanced Sejanus as a proof of the instability of political power and the favour of the great; Johnson has added to this impressive picture the fall of Wolsey. Hannibal and Alexander—whose death forms so instructive a moral of the folly of the conqueror and general—are not excluded, but the equally warning story of Charles XII. is made the vehicle for a moral lesson not less admirably expressed, and even more impressive, from its nearness of time, to a modern reader. The lofty philosophical tone of gloomy eloquence, perhaps, is even more uniformly sustained in the English than in the Roman poet; and in the conclusion of the satire, where, after showing the nothingness of all earthly hopes, the voice of reason points out what are the only objects worthy of the wise man's desire—health, innocence, resignation, and tranquillity—the English poet must be allowed to have surpassed in pathetic solemnity even the grandeur of his model, as far as the consolatory truths of Christian revelation are sublimer than the imperfect lights of Stoic paganism.

Between the years 1750 and 1752 Johnson was occupied in the composition of a journal, or series of periodical essays, entitled 'The Rambler,' founded upon the model of the 'Spectators' and 'Tatlers' which Addison and Steele had employed so usefully as a vehicle of moral improvement. But in Johnson's hands this kind of writing was neither so popular nor so delightful as it had been in those of the easy and elegant essayists whom we have just mentioned

Knowledge, good sense, sincerity, he possessed at least in as high a degree as his predecessors, but the reader observes a lack of ease, a want of light and shade, for which not all the imposing qualities of Johnson's mind can compensate: the style is too uniformly didactic, cathedral, and declamatory; he has no *shift* of words, and will describe the frivolity of a coxcomb with the same rolling periods and solemn gravity of antithesis as would be appropriate enough in an invective against tyranny or fanaticism. But the 'Ramblers' are full of weighty and solid sense, and if less amusing, they are certainly neither less useful nor less instructive. Addison and Steele *talk*, Johnson *declaims:* the former address you like virtuous, learned, and well-bred men of the world, whose scholastic acquirements have been harmonised and digested by long intercourse with polished society; Johnson rather like a university professor, who retains, in the world, something of the stiffness of the chair. The above remarks will apply no less to the 'Idler,' another publication on a similar plan, which continued to appear between 1758 and 1760.

In the interval which occurred between the discontinuance of the former and the commencement of the last-mentioned periodical, appeared the celebrated 'Dictionary of the English Language,' on which Johnson had been laboriously engaged during a period of about seven years. This work is a glorious monument of learning, energy, and perseverance; and, when viewed as the production of a single unaided scholar, is perhaps one of the most signal triumphs of literary activity. If we compare with Johnson's Dictionary the great national work of the French Academy, we shall find abundant reason to admire the astonishing courage and diligence of our countryman, who alone, unsupported, in the midst of other and pressing occupations, found means to produce, in seven years, a dictionary certainly not inferior to what was considered as a great national monument, which was produced by the united labour of a royally-endowed and numerous corporation, and which occupied an infinitely longer time in the preparation. We must not forget, either, the immense difference between the two languages in point of richness and copiousness, which renders the task of an English lexicographer immeasurably more onerous. Both Johnson's work and the 'Dictionnaire de l'Académie' are remarkable for the neatness and acuteness of interpretation of words; both give examples of the various meanings from good authors; and in this last respect we conceive that Johnson's work is markedly superior; for the Académie contents itself with any quotation which exhibits with sufficient clearness the particular use of the word in question, but beyond this has no specific value, and often no meaning or interest whatever. The quotations employed by Johnson, on the other hand, to illustrate and exemplify the different significations of words, are not only taken from a vast collection of works of classical authority, but themselves contain something complete and interesting in itself — either a beautiful passage of poetry, a pithy remark, a historical fact, or a scientific definition. The principal defect of this excellent dictionary is the etymological part. When Johnson wrote, the German literature could hardly be said to be in existence, and the northern languages were consequently not studied: the investigator was deprived almost completely of the immense light thrown upon the history of our language by those dialects which form the source of so important a portion of it.

In 1759 appeared the famous oriental tale entitled 'Rasselas,' a work of no great length, but exhibiting all the peculiarities of Johnson's manner. As a representation of Eastern society, or indeed as a picture of society in any sense, it has no claim to our admiration; there is no interest in the plot, if, indeed, it can be said to have a plot — there is hardly any attempt at the delineation of character; but if read as a fine succession of moral remarks, breathing a somewhat desponding tone of feeling, and conveyed in his characteristic pomp of measured declamation — it merits more than one perusal Compared with the descriptions of Oriental manners, which more recent times have given us — 'Rasselas' will seem stiff, vague, and unnatural. The Happy Valley of the Abyssinian prince is as nothing when compared with the Hall of Eblis in the wonderful tale of 'Vathek;' but we repeat, that Johnson's production is not to be read as a novel, but as a series of moral essays on a vast multiplicity of subjects, full of sense, acuteness, and originality of thought.

The last work which we shall mention is 'The Lives of the Poets,' originally composed at the instance of a bookseller, in order to be prefixed to a collection of specimens of this branch of English literature. The plan of this work was very limited, perhaps unavoidably so, excluding nearly all of the very greatest names in our literature, and embracing for the most part only what must be considered as by no means the most brilliant period of the English Muse, *i. e.* from Cowley to Johnson's own time. With the exception of Milton, all the poets whose biographies he has written belong to that school which we have described as having grown up mainly under Latin, French, and Italian influence — in short, the classicists — in whose works the intellect is the predominant power. In judging of this species of poetry, Johnson has shown a might, mastery, and solidity of criticism, perhaps unequalled by any other author; but he moment he enters the enchanted ground of what is called *omantic* poetry, he exhibits a singular and total want of perception. Indeed, his mind, admirably adapted as it was for the *scientific* part of criticism, was impotent to feel or appreciate what is picturesque or passionate. He is like a deaf man seated at a symphony of Beethoven—a sense is wanting to him. How accurately and acutely has he characterised Cowley, Dryden, Pope, and Otway! How justly has he appreciated the more intellectual qualities of Milton! But when he ridicules the 'Lycidas,' or complains of the blank verse of 'Paradise Lost,'—when he charges the lyrics of Gray with absurdity and extravagance, who does not see that Nature, so liberal to him in some respects, had denied to his powerful mind the least sensibility for what is beautiful and enchanting in the airy world of fancy? 'The Lives of the Poets,' when read with due allowance, will undoubtedly remain a classical work in England. We shall not easily find so vast an accumulation of ingenious, solid, and acute observation, so rich a treasury of noble moral lessons, or so fine and manly a tone of writing and thinking, as this excellent volume contains. Let us enjoy what it possesses and can give, without murmuring at what it has not.

Besides the above works, Johnson composed an immense number of detached pieces of criticism, and distinguished himself as a political writer. Many of his pamphlets (which were always in support of extreme Tory or monarchial opinions) obtained great celebrity at the time. In 1762 he received the gift of a pension of 300*l.* a-year—a just though inadequate reward for the utility of his numerous writings, and his unflinching devotion to the cause of virtue, religion, and morality. He also published an edition of Shakspeare, not very valuable in a philological point of view, from his imperfect acquaintance and sympathy with our older and more romantic literature, but useful as embodying a large mass of notes and illustrations of disputed and obscure passages. The character of Shakspeare's genius, given in the preface, is a noble specimen of panegyric; and it is singular to see how far the divine genius of the dramatist almost succeeds in overcoming all the prejudices of Johnson's age and education. As a moralist, as a painter of men and minds, Johnson has done Shakspeare (at least as far as any man could) ample justice; but in his judgment of the great creative poet's more romantic manifestations he exhibits a callousness and insensibility which was partly the result of his education and of the age when he lived, and partly, without doubt, the consequence of the peculiar constitution of his mind—a mind which felt much more sympathy with men than with things, and was much more at home in the "full tide of London existence" than in the airy world of imagination—among the every-day crowds of Fleet Street, than in Prospero's enchanted isle, or the moonlit terraces of Verona. It was this positivism of mind (to borrow a most expressive French word) that gave him such an extraordinary and well-deserved supremacy as a conversationist; and it was this mixture of learning, benevolence, wit, virtue, and good sense that makes the admirable portrait of him, Daguerreotyped in the memoirs of his friend and disciple Boswell, the most interesting and living portrait which literature exhibits of a great and good man—the perfect embodiment of the ideal of the English character, with all its honesty, goodness, and nobility, rather individualised than disfigured by the few and venial foibles and oddities which alloy its sterling gold.

CHAPTER XIV.

THE GREAT NOVELISTS.

History of Prose Fiction — in Spain, Italy, and France — The Romance an the Novel—Defoe—Robinson Crusoe — Source of its Charm — Defoe's Air of Reality — Minor Works — Richardson — Pamela — Clarissa Harlowe — Female Characters — Sir Charles Grandison — Fielding — Joseph Andrews —Jonathan Wild—Tom Jones—Amelia—Smollett—Roderic Random—Sea Characters—Peregrine Pickle—Count Fathom—Humphry Clinker—Sterne — Tristram Shandy and the Sentimental Journey — Goldsmith — Chinese Letters—Traveller and Deserted Village—Vicar of Wakefield — Comedies — Histories.

We are now arrived at that point in the history of British literature where, in obedience to the ever-acting laws which regulate intellectual as they do physical development, a new species of composition was to originate. As in the material creation we find the several manifestations of productive energy following a *progressive* order, — the lower, humbler, and less organised existences appearing first, and successively making way for kinds more variously and bounteously endowed, the less perfect merging imperceptibly into the more perfect, — so can we trace a similar action of this law in the gradual development of man's intellectual operations. No sooner do certain favourable conditions exist, no sooner has a fit *nidus* or theatre of action been produced, than we behold new manifestations of human intellect appearing in literature, in science, and in art, with as much regularity as, in the primeval eras of the physical world, the animalcule gave way to the fish, the fish to the reptile, the reptile to the bird, the beast, and ultimately to man.

Spain, France, and Italy had all possessed the germ or embryo of prose fiction before it can be said to appear as a substantive, independent, and influential species of literature in Great Britain; and in each of these countries it manifested itself under a different form, modified by the character of the respective peoples, the nature of their language, the character of those antecedent types of literature which gave birth to or suggested it, and the state of society whose manners it reflected. In Spain, for example, arising among a romantic, religious, and chivalrous people, whose memory was full of the traditions of Moorish warfare, and possessing the acute, impressible, and yet profound intellect usually resulting from physical well-being, a considerable degree of political freedom, and a delicious climate, we find it taking the form of the romance, full of adventure, and with a splendid prodigality of incident; showing traces of its mixed origin in the European delicacy of its humour and exquisite sense of the ludicrous, and retaining with the numerous episodes (one inserted within the other, as in the 'Thousand and One Nights') much of the peculiar Oriental structure, together with the Oriental richness of imagination, and Oriental profusion and laxity of style. Here we have the union of the Castilian hidalgo and the Abencerrage, the Goth and the Moor, the lofty sierra and the smooth and luxuriant vega. In Italy, again — the Italy of the fifteenth century—we find a people highly civilised, elegant, commercial, exquisitely sensitive to comic ideas, penetrating, questioning everything, applying to their government and their religion the dangerous test of ridicule, yet at the same time in the highest degree sensuous, with a wonderful and petulant mobility of imagination — at once childishly superstitious and audaciously sceptical. Among them arises Boccaccio, immortalising himself by a collection of tales, short and pointed—alternately drawing the deepest tears and moving the broadest laughter—full at once of the grossest indecency and the highest refinements of romantic purity.

In France, again, we find first the lofty chivalric romance — interminable in length, unnatural and exaggerated in sentiments, but bearing a general impress of dignity and magnificence—which cannot but be held as of Spanish origin. Of this the works of Scudéri and D'Urfé are memorable examples. Secondly, we find another variety, no less imitated from the Spanish, in which the meanest persons of ordinary life are put in motion and pass through a long series of amusing though often rather discreditable adventures, having no involution of intrigue, and connected together only by the slender thread of their being supposed to happen to one person. In this species of fiction (founded upon works which the Spaniards call stories "de vida picaresca" — of ragamuffin life — from the general character of the persons and adventures) the French have surpassed their masters; for much as a careful comparison with the Spanish originals will induce us to detract from Le Sage's *originality*, it will be more than compensated by his *genius*, when we reflect how far that admirable writer is superior to Quevedo, Mendoza, and Aleman and others from whom he so freely borrowed.

From the above remarks it results that we can establish two important and distinct forms of prose fiction,—the one treating of elevated persons, either imaginary or historical, and delineating serious or important events; the other dealing with men and actions of a more ludicrous, mean, or everyday character—the romance, in short, or the novel. The former species derives its name from the long narratives which form the bulk of Middle-Age poetry, which were generally written in the Romanz dialect; the other from the short prose tales so popular in Italy and France at the revival of letters. It is obvious that both these designations have almost com pletely lost their original signification. In England, the romance, besides the qualities just assigned, is generally the vehicle of a more artfully constructed and regular plot; while the novel by no means implies a shorter work, though one of a less grave and ambitious character. In a word, though this distinction may be taken as a general guide to the student, and will aid him perceptibly in classing these works of fiction, he must by no means take it in too rigid and invariable an acceptation; or rather, he must not be surprised to find works partake of both characters.

But, in the department of prose fiction, we hope to be able to establish for the English literature a claim to a degree of originality (originality of the highest order, which is exhibited in the separate creation of a distinct type) not inferior to that which our country incontestably exhibited in many other departments of intellectual development—in the romantic drama, for instance. The father of our romance and novel was Daniel Defoe, the son of a London butcher, born in 1661, and educated with considerable care for the profession of a Presbyterian pastor, but which he renounced for trade, having during a long and eventful life unsuccessfully engaged in a great variety of commercial occupations—at one time a hosier, at another a tilemaker, and ultimately a dealer in wool. His real vocation, however, was that of a writer, for he produced an enormous mass of compositions, general pamphlets, either on temporary and local subjects of political interest, or narratives adapted to suit the passing taste of the day—in fact, what would be styled by a French critic "brochures de circonstance." In 1699 he published his 'True-born Englishman,' a vigorous poetical effusion, written in singularly rough and tuneless rhymes, containing a powerful defence of William of Orange and the Dutch nation; and in 1702 appeared his celebrated pamphlet, 'The Shortest Way with the Dissenters,' an inimitable piece of sarcastic irony, in which, to exhibit in a hateful light the unjust and unconstitutional persecution of the dissenting sects, he puts on the mask of an adherent of government, and gravely advises parliament to make a law punishing with *death* any minister convicted of exercising an unorthodox worship. The government, infuriated by the bitter satire, prosecuted the author of the pamphlet, and the uncompromising writer was punished by fine, imprisonment, exposure in the pillory, and the loss of his ears. This suggested to Defoe the strong and excellent poem called 'Hymn to the Pillory,' a powerful expression of the feelings of outraged liberty and patriotism. During a two years' confinement in Newgate, our indefatigable writer conducted a periodical publication entitled 'The Review,' in which he boldly attacks the arbitrary and oppressive conduct of government, and gallantly pleads the cause of liberty and the constitution. That Defoe must have had a high reputation for honesty and ability is established by the fact that he was afterwards commissioned by Queen Anne's government to go to Scotland, in order to influence the Union between that country and England; and he appears to have acquitted himself in this delicate mission with remarkable skill, zeal, and dexterity. Of this event he afterwards wrote a history. Continuing his course as a pamphlet-writer, we cannot be surprised to find him, after this temporary blink of sunshine in his fortunes, again imprisoned and fined 800*l.* This confinement, however, did not last so long as the former, for he was liberated after two months; and he now appears, either disgusted with the dangerous and ill-requited profession of a political writer, or more probably anxious for the welfare of his own family, to have directed his great powers to a different line of literary exertion—one in which he could encounter no such persecution as had so frequently overwhelmed him, and in which present advantage and popularity were more likely to be attained.

In 1719 appeared the first part of 'Robinson Crusoe,' one of the most truly genial, perfect and original fictions that the world has ever seen. It may be said that some of the high and peculiar merits of this tale have been the very cause of our not appreciating its extraordinary qualities as they deserve. It is almost universally put into the hands of the very young, and the avidity with which its pages are devoured by the childish reader, and the never-failing permanency with which its principal scenes, events, and characters remain graven on the memory of all who have ever read it, prevent us from recurring to its perusal, and thus hinder us from applying to the fiction which enchanted our childhood the test of the more critical judgment of after life. Were such a test to be generally applied, and were we to examine into the means by which those intense impressions—among the intensest which the memory of childhood can recall—were produced, Defoe's name would be regarded with veneration, as that of him who gave our infant curiosity its healthiest and sweetest food, and our infant sensibilities their most legitimate and improving action.

Attempts have been made to deprive Defoe of the glory of having invented the subject and outline of 'Robinson Crusoe;' and some have even suggested that the novelist merely expanded the narrative of Alexander Selkirk, a Scottish seaman, left (as was a not uncommon punishment among the rude navigators of that time, technically called "marooning") by his shipmates upon the island of Juan Fernandez, where he passed a long series of years in a solitary existence, somewhat resembling the supposed life of Crusoe. But apart from the circumstance that the leading idea of the work (a shipwrecked solitary in an uninhabited island of the tropics) implies no very great stretch of invention, and that such an event is at all times exceedingly possible, and was then not unfrequent, Selkirk's narrative is extant, and, if compared to the fiction of Defoe, triumphantly disproves the accusation above stated, and shows us the immense difference between a meagre statement of bare facts and the powers of creative genius. Where shall we find in Selkirk's narrative (the most striking circumstances of which are the savage and almost bestial state to which the unfortunate solitary was reduced) the inexhaustible prodigality of contrivance by which Robinson alleviates his long reclusion, his attempts at escape, his hopes, his terrors, his sickness, his religious struggles, his sorrows, and his joys? In Defoe we associate with the persons, places, animals, and things of which he speaks a reality as absolute and intense—nay, often much more so—as we do with the true recollections of things and people which surrounded us in childhood. If we examine our own memory we shall find that the image of Crusoe, of Friday, of Friday's father, of the goats, the cats, the parrots, of the corn which Crusoe planted, of the canoe which he makes and then finds too heavy for him to launch, the cave in which he stows his gunpowder, the creek in which he lands in his raft, and in general the whole topography of the island—we shall find, we repeat, that these images are as strong, as intense (as surely, therefore, as real) as our recollection of the playthings which we broke, the little plot of ground which we cultivated, the nurse who took care of us, or the woods in which we went a-nutting. What then is the artifice by which genius has worked—for even the divinity of genius must work by secondary means—to do this miracle? We reply, the admirable *causality* of Defoe's mind, the courage with which he renounces the supernatural, the extraordinary—the intensity of good sense which fixed the work *in a low key*, as it were, dealing with the most ordinary elements of human character and the most everyday operations of nature. He might have made Crusoe, instead of the plain work-day being that we behold him—the mate of a merchant-man, an ordinary man, neither wise, nor learned, nor ingenious, nor virtuous, beyond the great mass of human beings—he might have made him *intrinsically* (*per se*) more interesting; but would he not have been *relatively* less so? In like manner Defoe might have made his work a vehicle for much more extensive information in natural history, physics, astronomy, &c., than he has done; but would it have been equally interesting? This question has been settled by all the innumerable works which have been written on the model of Robinson Crusoe, with the laudable object of conveying elementary instruction to the young through the medium of fiction: as for example, the little book called 'Le Robinson Suisse,' Marryat's 'Masterman Ready,' 'History of Sir Edward Seaward,' &c. In all these, and they have all much merit, the author has injured the effect of his picture by crowding his canvas with figures, and represented his shipwrecked families as a great deal too ingenious and adroit, and their exertions as too uniformly successful.

In the difficulties encountered by his hero, the author has frequently represented those as most harassing and as most difficult to be surmounted which at first thought we should be apt to consider as trifles: thus, for example, the repeated failures of Robinson to make an earthenware pot which would stand the fire, or a mechanism by which to turn his grindstone, are certainly difficulties which a superficial consideration would by no means suggest, and yet which reflection would show us were both probable, serious, and surmountable only by great exertion of thought and labour. In the same way the oversights, mistakes, and want of calculation in the supposed hero are exactly such as might, and probably would, happen to everybody. Robinson Crusoe cuts down a huge tree, and with immense labour makes a boat which he cannot launch; but Sir Edward Seaward is far too philosophical to do such a thing. Robinson uses all his ink, and knows not how to make a new stock; but the father of the Swiss family would have suggested half-a-dozen ingenious compounds which would serve as well, and possibly would have manufactured paper into the bargain. But Robinson possesses just the *average* amount of invention, ingenuity, courage, and dexterity, and therefore every reader can instantly and unfailingly put himself in Crusoe's place.

The success of this admirable story was instantaneous and immense, and Defoe afterwards published a second part, universally and justly considered as inferior to the first. The island is changed into a colony; and the quarrels and labours of the English sailors and Spaniards, their battles with the savages, though described with Defoe's neverfailing animation, simplicity, and vigour, fail to interest us like the inimitable history of the Solitary. The conclusion of the work, describing Robinson's voyages and return to England, is also comparatively uninteresting, though there are to be found in them several passages and episodes described with impressive power: as, for example, the ship on fire, the dreadful scene of the crew dying of hunger, the battle with the wolves, and so on. They are like extracts from the journals of some of our old navigators, simple, unaffected, picturesque; striking from the natural pathos of the rough but kind and honest narrator.

Defoe now poured forth a profusion of narratives detailing the adventures and exploits of noted robbers, cheats, and malefactors; showing an intimate acquaintance with the habits and thoughts of such persons, and giving to his narratives, by the peculiar magic of his plain style, all the *prestige* of reality, a quality which no author —not even Swift—ever so perfectly attained. Though the persons and actions described in this class of works are generally mean and discreditable, Defoe has not fallen into that base and corrupting error of more recent literature, of holding up to admiration the characters and actions of immoral and dishonest men, and making our admiration of energy, perseverance, and address, minister to the worst propensities of our nature, by showing these high qualities associated with unrestrained passions and the deeds of crime. In his 'Lives' of Moll Flaggon, Colonel Jack, Captain Singleton, &c., Defoe has written to warn, not to attract. Among the list of these minor works we must not omit his 'Journal of the Plague Year,' a pretended narrative of the great pestilence which devastated London in 1665, written in the character of a plain citizen, and eyewitness of the horrors he describes. In this terrific narrative, many of the details of which are probably real, the verisimilitude is so wonderfully maintained, that the book has often been quoted as an authority on the subject. As a work of mere descriptive fiction, nothing can be more awful, more tremenduous, than the hideous phantom of the maniac, Solomon Eagle, flitting through the city like a messenger of death, the Great Pit in Aldgate, the Dead-Cart, the apparitions in the air, or the silent line of ships stretching down the river, "as far as I could see."

To the numerous proofs already alleged of the power, so eminently possessed by Defoe, of what Scott has happily called "*forging the handwriting of nature,*" *i. e.* perfectly imitating the plain and unaffected air of truthful narration, we have only to add that singular triumph of his peculiar skill in this art, his tract describing the 'Apparition of one Mrs. Veal, the next day after her death, to one Mrs. Bargrave, at Canterbury, the Eighth of September, 1705,'—perhaps the boldest and most adroit experiment upon human credulity that ever was made. It is needless to remark that the whole of this admirably-contrived story, the persons, the place, the minute and familiar details, the exquisite solution of the objections to the reality of the apparition, which, with an air of inimitable candour, Defoe mentions and refutes—in short, the whole thing, is a pure creation of the novelist's mind, invented to recommend a dull book on death. It cannot be wondered at that this consummate artifice perfectly succeeded, and that, to use the sly words of the author, "*Drelincourt's book is, since this happened, bought up strangely.*"

This great and original genius closed his long, useful, and agitated existence in 1731, leaving, among the two hundred and ten different works which he composed, many which will serve the literary student with the finest models of fictitious incidents, so naturally and artfully told as to extort the momentary belief of the most sceptical; offering the metaphysician the materials for solving the abstrusest problems of credibility.

In the elaborate and once universally read novels of Samuel Richardson, we shall see evidences of a new advance in the art of fiction. The leading aim of Defoe is to gratify curiosity through the medium of *faith*; and we have just seen that his primary characteristic is the admirable skill and certainty by which the author excites and maintains in the reader's mind an involuntary and irresistible belief in the reality of the things and persons described. We find in Richardson the struggle after reality, and the effort to inspire belief by natural and minute detail, which in Defoe is a primary feature, now become a secondary one; and something superadded, viz., the ideal—the creation of character. We have passed, as it were, from a lower into a higher class of organisation, in which the faculties and functions of the lower are not suppressed or extinguished; but those which were prominent and capital have become secondary, from the addition of a new and more elevated element. We have advanced to another term of our sublime progression—that progression which begins at zero and rises to infinity.

All men of great genius seem to be eminently possessed of the quality of good sense; and of this truth Richardson, both in his life and writings, offers a striking confirmation. He was the son of rustic parents, in the very humblest class, was born in 1689, and was apprenticed at the early age of sixteen to a London printer. In this occupation, not unfavourable (witness Franklin, and other eminent men) to the self-education of an active and well-constituted mind, he gradually rose to respectability, and ultimately to competence and consideration; for he was afterwards appointed printer of the Journals to the House of Commons; chosen, in 1754, Master of the Company of Stationers; and purchased, in 1760, half the patent or monopoly attached to the lucrative office of King's printer. Having thus arrived at what must be considered as the highest point of an active citizen's career, and having by prudence, industry, and probity, accumulated a handsome fortune, he retired, in the noon of life, to his pleasant suburban retreat of Parson's Green, near London, where he passed the remainder of his useful and honourable life. There appears to have been, whether derived from nature or only resulting from circumstances, something *feminine* in his mental organisation; for his works show not only a good deal of that sensitive or rather sentimental melancholy which characterises the female mind, but much of the female timidity of taste, the female appreciation of minute peculiarities, and also, it is but just to say, the female penetration, and the female purity of moral sentiment. Indeed, he appears to have passed much of his life among women; for, being early distinguished for his talents as a letter-writer, he is related to have devoted his pen, at one period of his youth, to the service of three young women in humble life, and to have conducted their respective love-correspondence. Perhaps this is the germ of 'Pamela' and 'Clarissa;" for the female heart, whether bounding beneath the "sad-coloured" gown of the poor maid-servant, or throbbing beneath the diamond stomacher of the duchess, is invariably and eternally the same. It has been observed, too, with great justice, that Richardson's female characters are, generally speaking, incomparably superior in depth of observation, variety, and naturalness to his men; and we know that one of the innocent weaknesses of the great novelist's advanced life, when he was full of years and glory, was to receive, like the woman-worshipped Krishna of the Indian mythology, the delicious incense of admiration and flattery from a circle of female adorers which he had assembled around him.

Richardson did not begin to write till he was almost fifty years of age; when, being urged by two book-sellers to compose a collection of letters likely to be useful to young people of the lower orders, and calculated to purify their taste and inculcate principles of morality, he accepted the task for which he was so well qualified; and in the course of execution he discovered that his work (destined primarily, also, to serve in a great measure as models of an epistolary style) might be rendered more natural, amusing, and instructive by making the letters *tell a story*. The result was 'Pamela,' an admirable and truly original work of fiction, which at once raised its author to an unprecedented height of popularity, and instantly annihilated the vogue of those affected, unnatural, and wearisome romances which till then had formed the sole amusement of our great-grandmothers. 'Pamela' (which appeared in 1741, said to have been written in three months, and five editions of which were exhausted in one year) was, indeed, an unspeakable improvement upon the interminable and stilted productions which it for ever displaced; and we can sympathise with the delight of a female reader of that day, in obtaining a natural story of ordinary life, full of fine perception of character, exquisite pathos and tenderness, instead of the absurd exaggerations, the feeble pomposity of incidents, the puerile uniformity of character, and everlasting hair-splitting of amorous casuistry, which form the substance of the Cyruses and Clelias of the school of Scudéri and D'Urfé. It relates, in letters supposed to pass between the principal personages of the fable—a form of composition from which Richardson never departed—the sufferings and trials of the beautiful heroine, a servant-girl, who is persecuted by malignity and assailed by seduction, but whose virtue and constancy ultimately triumph over all her enemies, and gain for the victim the hand of her repentant master. Nothing can be simpler, more unpretending, more ordinary than such a canvas. The cause of the power over our sympathies is the consummate knowledge of the human heart—and especially the female heart—which this excellent author displays, and his wise boldness in describing, without scruple and exaggeration, even the most trifling incidents (whether external or mental) as such a story naturally suggests.

His first work having been received with a frenzy of admiration by the public, and even solemnly recommended from the pulpit, it was to be expected that Richardson should continue so auspicious a career; and in 1749 appeared 'Clarissa Harlowe,' another fiction, on a similar though more ambitious plan, and dealing with personages in a higher order of society. This work has obtained a European glory for its author, and has been universally lauded and translated on the continent, and even in France; and indubitably, as a grand and impressive moral drama, teaching deep lessons of virtue through the tragic media of pity and terror, it deserves all its fame. In England, however, neither this nor any other of Richardson's novels can be considered as any longer very generally read. Accustomed as we are to a more fiery, rapid, highly-coloured, and *wide-awake* mode of narration, we have in some measure lost our relish for the manner of this accomplished artist, who produces his effect by an uninterrupted accumulation of touches individually imperceptible, by an agglomerative, not a generative process. If our great modern works of creative fiction may be compared to the rapid colossal agency of volcanic fire, the productions of Richardson may resemble the slow and gradual formation of an alluvial continent, the secular accumulation of minute particles deposited by the gentle yet irresistible current of a river. If the volcanic tract—the offspring of fire—be sublimely broken into thunder-shattered mountain-peak and smiling valley, yet the level delta is not less fertile or less adorned by its own mild and luxuriant beauty. In 'Clarissa,' Richardson has drawn with more skill and a firmer pencil than was usual with him the character of a man of splendid talents and attractions, but totally devoid of morality. Lovelace is familiar to millions of readers as an admirably strong and natural combination of the most consummate villany with all that can dazzle and impose. In general, it may be said that Richardson's men, though often marked and individualised by some happy stroke of character, rather resemble men *as seen by women*—that is to say, not as they appear to their own sex, but with something of that involuntary inaccuracy which necessarily accompanies the estimate of one sex by the other. They are men, but seen through a female atmosphere. The pathos in 'Clarissa Harlowe' is carried to an intense and almost unendurable intensity, and the catastrophe is worthy to be compared, for overwhelming and irresistible agony, to the noblest efforts of pathetic conception in Scott, in our elder dramatists, or in the Greek tragedians.

Four years had not elapsed ere Richardson's indefatigable industry gave to the world his third and last great fiction, the 'Sir Charles Grandison.' In this he endeavoured to give us his ideal of the character of a perfect hero—a union of the good Christian and the accomplished English gentleman. But Sir Charles, the model man of Richardson's imagination, is generally found to be exceedingly tiresome and pedantic; and the heroine, Miss Harriet Byron—a similar model of female perfection—is, like her lover, exceedingly cold, tame, and uninteresting. In general, we must reproach this novel, even in a higher degree than the rest of Richardson's fictions, with the fault of inordinate *lengthiness*. It is true that these works, enormous in length as they are, were an immeasurable improvement, in this respect as well as in the more important qualities of naturalness and interest, upon the egregious tomes which they supplanted; and likewise that, Richardson's *manner* depending upon the progressive accumulation of minute incidents and strokes of character, we speedily become involuntarily carried away by the gentle and equable current of his narration, and are compelled, as it were by magic, to read every page of what we began with reluctance and even with disgust; yet this author abuses the liberal concessions of patience which we make, and even the admirable and truly profound picture of despair and madness in the unhappy Clementina cannot reconcile us to the eternal bowing and formal hand-kissing of tiresome Sir Charles, or the minute and detailed description (occupying Heaven knows how many pages) of the wedding-clothes of the happy pair. The fact is, that, with that *feminine* quality which we have suggested as characteristic of Richardson's mind, he possessed also a womanly interest in, and reliance upon, minute and trivial incidents, and a womanly admiration for fine clothes and the externals of human life. Besides this, he was a man who appears never to have mixed in aristocratic society, and the bourgeois tone of his mind is as perceptible in his conceptions as in his style, which, though always what the Parisians expressively call *cossu*, was at first rather mean and vulgarly fine, though he gradually rendered it both more expressive and less affected, for there is a progressive improvement in this respect to be traced through his successive works. He was of course personally unacquainted with that tone of ease and simplicity which always accompanies the intercourse of the higher classes of society, in which, as the persons who compose them have no fear of being mistaken for what they are not, they have no temptation to exhibit themselves other than as they are. With these deductions duly made, Richardson will appear to every candid mind a great, profound, creative, and, above all, truly original genius, devoting a powerful and active intellect to the holy cause of virtue and honour, a bright ornament to human nature, and a prime glory of his country's literature.

Perhaps there never existed a character so eminently attractive—o emphatically *loveable*—as that of Henry Fielding, or "poor Harry Fielding," as one always calls him in one's own mind. As an author, Fielding was at once the complement and contrast to Richardson, and in every feature of their personal and mental portraits an opposition might be traced out so striking, that such a comparison, though perfectly true, would resemble a chapter of La Rochefoucauld, or an antithetical sketch from La Bruyère. He was descended from an ancient and distinguished branch of the higher nobility of England, being the son (born in 1707) of General Fielding, and grandson of the Earl of Denbigh. His father was a man of gay and extravagant habits, and, dying early, left a large family in very embarrassed circumstances. Henry was imperfectly educated, first at Eton, and afterwards at the University of Leyden, where his studies were suddenly interrupted, and he was forced to return home, by absolute want of funds—"money-bound," as he wittily called it himself. His father dying in inextricable difficulties, and leaving his son a *nominal* income of 200*l.* a-year (for there was no fund from whence it was to be paid), young Fielding was compelled, at a very early age, to eke out by his own exertions a very scanty income he inherited from his mother, and partly from the marriage-portion of his wife—Miss Cradock, a beautiful and most amiable person—whom he appears to have loved with an intensity of affection such as such an object was likely to inspire, and so passionate a temperament as Fielding's to feel. But Fielding was an ardent lover of pleasure, and totally incapable of economy, calculation, or self-denial: he lived in a style totally inconsistent with his means, thinking only of the present moment, and in three years found himself completely ruined. During this time he had obtained precarious and scanty subsistence by writing for the stage; and his dramatic compositions form about a third part of his collected works.

They are chiefly *vaudevilles* and light comic or farcical productions, such as were the fashion of the day, and they form a melancholy proof of Fielding's total inaptitude for the stage. It is singular to see that Fielding's creative power, which in the novels has given us such numberless conceptions of human character, should be totally wanting in these pieces, in spite of the bold, careless vivacity with which they are written. To this remark there is but one exception —the admirable burlesque of 'Tom Thumb,' a gay and farcical extravaganza, ridiculing (as 'The Rehearsal' had done before, and as Sheridan's 'Critic' was to do afterwards) the absurdities and affectations of the style of tragedy in vogue at the time.

He was now totally ruined; but, with many other features of the French national character, he possessed much of that versatility of talent for which our continental brethren are so celebrated, and, above all, their contentedness of disposition and gaiety under every change of fortune. "His happy constitution," says Lady Mary Montagu, his kinswoman, "even when he had, with great pains, half demolished it, made him forget every evil when he was before a venison pasty and a flask of champagne; and I am persuaded he has known more happy moments than any prince upon earth. His natural spirits gave him rapture with his cook-maid, and cheerfulness when he was starving in a garret." It was not until 1742, *i. e.* when Fielding had reached his thirty-fifth year, that he began that career of glory as a novelist that will continue till time shall be no more, as long as men shall delight in wit, humour, originality, and art. At this period the 'Pamela' of Richardson was in the full blaze of popularity, and Fielding was exactly the man to appreciate the ludicrous sides of the book which every reader was devouring with rapture. The man of fashion, the gay prodigal, the hunter after pleasure, intimately versed in all the mysteries of human life, who had moved with good-natured careless ease through every orbit of the social system, whose exquisite sense of character must have made him accurately observe every shade of human manners, and whose inexhaustible sympathy with his kind made him share the joys, the distresses, and the humours of every class of society, and whose easy laxity of morals held as venial any trespasses on propriety so long as they were accompanied and excused by a generosity and manly liberality of feeling—such a person must have looked upon Richardson's famous novel as fair game for ridicule and burlesque. The printer's choice of an humble heroine, his vulgarity of style, his citizen-like inculcation of strict morality and the tamer virtues, his homely incidents, and, more than all, perhaps, the atmosphere of sentimental melancholy thrown over the whole, and the elaborate painting of the mental sufferings and the delicate sorrows of a female heart—all this suggested to Fielding the happy idea of a parody or burlesque. Scarron immortalized himself by the 'Roman Comique,' written to parody the effeminate affectations, the romantic fictions of his time; and the 'Joseph Andrews' of Fielding, though written to caricature a particular author, has not only in a great measure tended to render that author obsolete, but must be considered as the foundation of a new species of writing—the addition of a new province to literature—the opening of a new source of intellectual delight. How disproportionate are sometimes effects to their causes! the sight of a soldier scraping his rusty musket was the proximate origin of the art of mezzotint, and the parody of a popular novel was the generating influence of Fielding's admirable fictions! In 'Joseph Andrews' the wicked wit of Fielding gave the public a most irresistible caricature of 'Pamela:' to add to the piquancy of his attack he represents his hero as the brother of the primly virtuous Pamela, and resisting the amatory advances of his mistress, Lady Booby. This picture of virtue triumphant in a young footman, is irresistibly comic; and the after adventures of Joseph Andrews, when turned out of his place, and wandering through England with his friend, the never-to-be-forgotten Parson Adams, give noble earnest of the wonderful fertility, freshness, and vigour of the creative intellect that was to give us so many hours of mirth and amusement. Nothing can be more different than the manner of the two great writers: in reading one you seem to breathe the close and heated atmosphere of a city parlour; in the other you are tramping, a sturdy pedestrian, along an English high-road, inhaling a fresh, bracing, vigorous breeze, and mixing with the ever-varying groups of passengers, or laughing soundly out with the odd vagabonds you encounter, now in a foxhunter's antlered hall, now with the picturesque, if not always very reputable, figures smoking and drinking round an alehouse fire. In Richardson your ear is perpetually filled with the rustle of a petticoat—in Fielding it is struck by the loud roar of the rustic wag, or the lusty knock of a stout crabtree cudgel encountering some peasant's skull. The character of Adams would be enough to immortalise even the grand 'Cyrus' itself; his goodness of heart, poverty, learning, ignorance of the world, combined with his courage, modesty, and a thousand oddities, make it a portrait to be placed beside that of Sancho Pança or My Uncle Toby.

After this excellent and original work, Fielding, who had now found his true literary element, and who must have enjoyed, in tracing his ever-varying scenes and personages, the unspeakable rapture of genius, published his 'Journey from this World to the Next,' a half-narrative, half-satirical production, not deserving of a more than passing allusion. This was succeeded by the 'Life and Adventures of Jonathan Wild the Great'—a fiction in which, under the mask of describing the history of a notorious cheat, robber, and thief-taker, executed about that time, he has given us a fine satiric invective. The principal character is so utterly odious, so mean as well as so atrocious a scoundrel, that the reader can feel no sympathy with him, and therefore no interest in his story; but there are several inimitable scenes and characters—for instance, the Ordinary of Newgate, who prefers punch to wine, "the rather as it is nowhere spoken against in the Scripture," and the inimitable sermon on the text, "To the Greeks, foolishness."

In 1749 appeared his greatest work, 'Tom Jones,' which has been translated into every civilized language. Fielding had a high opinion of the importance of the novel in literature; he placed it on a level with the epic: and we cannot accuse him of indifference to the gravity of that task which he considered so dignified—the profession of the novelist. Perhaps in no other work do we find such a variety of events, each exquisitely probable and amusing, all converging so infallibly to a catastrophe at once inevitable and surprising. A great part of the adventures of this, as of Fielding's other works, take place in inns and on the road; a circumstance to be accounted for by the much greater duration of journeys in those days, when men travelled mostly on foot or on horseback, and consequently spent more of their time in journeys. This has tended to increase the tone of coarseness with which we, accustomed to much more refined habits of society, should be at first liable to reproach the great novelist, whom Byron calls "the prose Homer of human nature." He may also be charged, and justly, with a very low standard of moral rectitude and virtue. His heroes, never deficient in generosity and courage, are generally very coarse in taste, and not over-delicate or scrupulous; as, for example, in that degrading episode of Jones and Lady Bellaston. We always conceive his heroes as stout, fresh, broad-backed young fellows, with prodigious calves; and his heroines are singularly deficient in ladylike attributes. But hardly any author in the world has succeeded in giving interest to the accomplished young lady and charming young gentleman who form the nucleus of their intrigue; the *jeune prémier* and *ingénue* are as insipid in fiction as on the stage and in real life: and if Fielding has failed where few or none have succeeded, he has made ample amends in the vast crowd of admirable impersonations which are recalled to our memory by the mere mention of his name,—Partridge, Towwowse, Adams, Allworthy, Trulliber, Squire Western, Square, Thwackum, Ensign Northerton, and a thousand more. Nor would it be grateful in us to forget the rich and constant stream of animal spirits, fresh and abundant as a mountain spring, sparkling as champagne, ever bubbling up, as it were, from the perennial fount of good nature and humanity which God had created in the generous heart of Fielding; nor his easy command of a vast store of knowledge, both of books and of the world; nor his simple, vigorous, unaffected English; nor the tenderness of his healthy sensibilities.

In 1749 he was appointed, by the patronage of Lord Lyttleton, to the office of a London police magistrate, and however we may regret the necessity which obliged such a man as Fielding to fulfil duties so inconsistent with his literary pursuits, and in an office which at that time was neither very well paid nor over reputable, it not only gave him many opportunities of exhibiting remarkable zeal, activity, and address as a public functionary, but possibly furnished him with some of those strokes of low life and humour which enrich his admirable writings.

The death of his wife plunged the generous and impressionable heart of Fielding for a time into the deepest despair; but, with that facility of temper which so strongly characterized him, he not long after consoled himself by marrying his late partner's favourite maid, with whom it had been his only relief, during the first poignant agonies of his bereaval, "to mingle his tears, and to lament together the angel they had lost." His second wife, however, strange as it may appear, proved a most faithful and excellent partner, and a good mother to his children; and the warm affection of Fielding soon after erected, in honour of his first wife, the companion of his early struggles, the noblest and most enduring monument that genius ever consecrated to love and grief. This was the romance of 'Amelia,' in which the exquisite picture of conjugal virtue and feminine charm in the heroine, the character and even the infidelities of Booth (her husband), and a multitude of minor persons and events, are evidently transcripts from reality, and (there is little doubt) faithful copies of his own early history. 'Amelia' is a delightful and touching work: its interest is intimate and domestic; and whatever diminution of gaiety and movement may be perceptible in it, when compared to either of its two great predecessors, is more than made up by the calmer, tenderer, and more home-speaking tone which reigns throughout its pages. The characters are touched with consummate skill: Colonel Bath is a perfect masterpiece: and many of the scenes—that, for instance, at Vauxhall, the appearance before the magistrate, the adventures in prison, and so on—are drawn with Fielding's usual vivacity and skill.

Fielding's constitution was now quite broken up, partly with his early irregularities of life, and partly by his severe exertions both as a magistrate and as a writer; and having been ordered by his physicians to try a warmer climate, he made a voyage to Lisbon. Of this expedition he has left a journal, in which we see the last faint glow of his admirable genius, and the undiminished gaiety and good-humour of his character, glimmering through the clouds of sorrow and disease. He set out for Lisbon in the spring of 1754; and, after lingering till October of the same year, he expired there of a complication of disorders (among which dropsy was the chief), and was buried in the cemetery of the British Factory in that city. To conclude this notice in the solemn and majestic language of Gibbon: "Our immortal Fielding was of the younger branch of the Earls of Denbigh, who drew their origin from the Counts of Hapsburg, the lineal descendants of Eltrico, in the seventh century Dukes of Alsace. Far different have been the fortunes of the English and German divisions of the family of Hapsburg: the former, the knights and sheriffs of Leicestershire, have slowly risen to the dignity of the peerage; the latter, the Emperors of Germany and Kings of Spain, have threatened the liberty of the Old, and invaded the treasures of the New World. The successors of Charles V. may disdain their brethren of England; but the romance of 'Tom Jones,' that exquisite picture of human manners, will outlive the palace of the Escurial and the imperial eagle of Austria."

The field of prose fiction, so vigorously and productively cropped by Defoe, Richardson, and Fielding, was rather fertilized than exhausted; and put forth another and hardly less luxuriant harvest of novelty and wit in the hands of Tobias Smollett, whose genius, though perhaps of a somewhat lower order than that of his two great and immediate predecessors, was not less rich and inventive, and certainly not less permanently popular, his works appealing to those faculties of the mind which are most universal—the sentiment of the ludicrous and the grotesque, and the avidity for surprising yet natural adventure. This great but unhappy man (for what misfortune is more deplorable than an irritable and querulous temperament?) was born in Dumbartonshire, in Scotland, in the year 1721, and was educated by the kindness of a grandfather. Having passed some time, as an apprentice, in the service of one Gordon, an apothecary of Glasgow, he journeyed up to London, a poor, unfriended, and probably uncouth Scottish lad, with the intention of supporting himself as a literary man, and carrying with him his manuscript of a tragedy entitled 'The Regicide.' This work, the production of an inexperienced youth of nineteen, was totally unsuccessful; and after struggling for some time with failure and distress, which the infallible instinct of genius must have rendered peculiarly bitter, he underwent the examination of surgeon's mate, and accompanied in this capacity the ill-fated expedition to Carthagena. If 'Roderick Random' and 'Peregrine Pickle' could not have existed without their author having mingled in the scenes which he portrays, who can complain of the price at which Smollett purchased his fame? or would Smollett himself have held that glory as bought too dear?

On his return from that disastrous expedition in 1746, our author continued for some time the career of a miscellaneous writer, and generally of political pamphlets of a very fierce and virulent complexion; for Smollett's temperament was almost morbidly irritable, and his numerous changes of party were the results rather of personal feeling than of any very solid convictions on public or abstract grounds. He published a number of satires and other pieces, in which sincerity of invective and great ease of fancy are the most conspicuous merits. The verses, however, entitled 'The Tears of Scotland' are powerful and pathetic; and many of the lines in his 'Ode to Independence' have a fine lyric grandeur of impersonation.

It was not until 1748 that he published his 'Adventures of Roderick Random,' and the world at once perceived that a great and original novelist had appeared, likely to show that the fertility of English genius in prose fiction was not exhausted, and capable of disputing the crown of supremacy with Fielding himself. Nature, the image and shadow of God, is, like Him, infinite; and Art, the idealization of Nature, and the sublimest emanation from the Divinity, is, like its parent, boundless. There can be no doubt that Fielding was a far superior *artist* to his admirable successor. His plots are infinitely finer, more far-reaching in their conception, and carried on with more skill, coherence, and probability. Smollett can hardly be said to have a plot at all: his works are a succession of adventures which have no other connexion than as happening to one hero; they can be no more said to be parts of a whole, conducing to a natural and distant catastrophe, than the successive images of a magic-lantern to form a dramatic series of pictures like the Marriage à la Mode, or the Harlot's Progress, of Hogarth. They are *thrown* together; they do not *grow* together: they are not an organization like Fielding's, but a mere juxtaposition. Indeed, so intense was the objectiveness of Smollett's fancy, so completely was he identified with the specific scene of drollery which was in hand—so "totus in illâ"—that he perpetually sacrifices to their effect the consistency of his characters; never scrupling to represent his hero, for example, as cowardly, ugly, or contemptible, provided by so doing he can augment the comicality of the incident. The view of life to be derived from the fictions of Smollett is not a very consoling nor a very elevating one: the instances of generous feeling and self-sacrifice are chiefly assigned to personages incessantly placed in a ludicrous light; as, for instance, the faithful Strap, who exhibits much more delicacy than his unfeeling and ungrateful master: and if, as seems more than probable, Roderick Random is a true embodiment of Smollett's own London reminiscences, and Strap a real character, the author has indirectly convicted himself of a degree of selfishness which, it is but just to say, the whole tenor of his life disproves. But his great force lies in the vivid and ever-new delineation of comic incidents of a broad and farcical cast, and the outrageous oddities of those numerous characters (or what may be called natural caricatures) which anybody may find swarming in society. In one class of these oddities he is unrivalled—sailors. His own experience in the navy brought him in contact with this class of men (a class still distinguished in England by marked peculiarities, and at that time forming a perfectly distinct and peculiar species, little known to their countrymen), and gloriously has Smollett worked this new and fertile vein of singularity. The rude kindness, the fidelity, the contempt for money, the ignorance of the world, the courage, superstition, and all the habits of the English seaman (a type as strongly individual as the vieux moustache of the Old Guard, or the backwoodsman of the Far West), are described under a dozen different forms with a *verve* and animation showing the author's profound knowledge of the subject, and producing the most intense delight in the reader. What a number of names arise at the mention of Smollett's admirable sailors!—Lieutenant Bowling with his cudgel, the choleric Ap-Morgan with his toasted cheese and family pride, Admiral Trunnion on his wedding expedition, and the ingenious and taciturn Pipes. Nor are sailors the only portraits which attest a master-hand: the low characters of every kind—prostitutes, sharpers, tipstaves, and all the vermin of society—are vividly and amusingly delineated.

The next novel produced by Smollett was 'Peregrine Pickle,' strongly resembling, in its merits and deficiencies, the work which preceded it. If the adventures of Peregrine are still more discreditable than those of Roderick, and the character of the hero even less respectable, ample amends are made by the side-splitting humours of Admiral Trunnion, Hatchway, and Pipes, with their amphibious household, and the drollery of many incidents of the hero's travels in France, not forgetting the irresistible supper in the manner of the ancients, which

"Would move wild laughter in the throat of death."

At two successive intervals of two years he produced his third fiction, entitled 'The Adventures of Ferdinand Count Fathom,' and a translation of 'Don Quixote.' The former work resembles in its plan and execution his previous novels, with the difference, however, that it is pitched in a much higher key of moral impressiveness, and was intended less to amuse by the oddity of the incidents, than to give an impressive picture of the certain degradation and gradual descent of infamy that follow a youthful neglect of honour and generosity. It may in some sense be called a companion-picture to Fielding's 'Jonathan Wild.' But Fathom is far superior in interest to Fielding's hero—not personally, it is true, for he is as base and contemptible a rascal as the other, but from his superior dexterity and address, and from the consequent greater variety of his adventures. He is a heartless scoundrel, who, after becoming a gambler and "*chevalier d'industrie,*" dies in misery and despair. Despite of the gloomy and discouraging tone which prevails through this picture, some of the scenes (as for instance that admirable one in which Fathom is rooked at play in a French coffeehouse by a more adroit sharper disguised as a raw booby English squire) are full of Smollett's usual vivacity. The translation of 'Quixote'—the most untranslatable of all books—is also a failure: it wants that picturesque and romantic tone which is so great a charm in the original—that tenderness of feeling in the midst of, and modifying, the wildest extravagance of gaiety, which forms as it were the atmosphere of the southern humour, and distinguishes alike the frantic wit of the old comedy of Greece, the broad burlesque of the primitive Italian stage, and glows with such a steady and yet subdued radiance through the pages of the gentle Cervantes. Smollett's 'Don Quixote' wants *sun*—the sun of La Mancha.

During a considerable portion of his life Smollett had been unsuccessfully struggling to establish himself as a physician; he was for some time the principal writer in the 'Critical Review,' one of the first progenitors of that class—now so numerous in England and elsewhere—of periodical publications devoted at once to political disquisition and the criticism of books. For this dangerous trade Smollett possessed no qualifications but those of sincerity, learning, and genius; and though his strictures were never dictated by an unworthy motive, they were strongly and involuntarily coloured by personal feelings, and raised around our impatient and thin-skinned author a swarm of hornets—enraged doctors, offended politicians, and, more venomous and implacable still, the insulted vanity of literary pretension. For some severe remarks on the conduct of Admiral Knowles, Smollett was convicted of a libel, imprisoned for a considerable time, and fined 100*l.* During his confinement he composed 'Sir Lancelot Greaves,' a most unfortunate attempt to transfer to the England of the eighteenth century that admirable picture which Cervantes had drawn of Spain in the sixteenth. In such a state of society, and among such a people, as that of Spain in the days of Cervantes, the existence and adventures of the Don were neither impossible nor even at all inconceivable; but what shall we say of a young English squire of good family setting out (in the reign of George II.), attended by an old sea-captain for his Sancho Pança, for the redress of wrongs, with the chivalrous language and even the arms of Quixote? The madness of the Spanish hero, drawn with so delicate and reverent a hand, affects only a particular class of his mental perceptions, and is, besides, perfectly conceivable when taken into consideration with the age, the position, the limited education of a poor country gentleman of Spain; but the madness of Greaves, affecting a mind and body otherwise sound, a handsome, virtuous, and enlightened Englishman (in so unromantic an age and country too), is a mania which renders him fit for Bedlam, and excites our pity rather than our sympathy. Such be the inevitable fate of imitation!

Smollett, after this, composed a continuation of Hume's 'History of England,' said to have been written in fourteen months; and after a journey through France and Italy, in which his splenetic disposition, probably aggravated by ill health, found no language but contempt with which to speak of the great monuments of ancient art, he published 'The Adventures of an Atom,' a satire upon his former patron, Bute. In 1770 ill health again drove him abroad, and he resided some time at Leghorn, where he died, October 21st, 1771. Thus, like his great predecessor Fielding, this admirable novelist expired in a foreign land.

During the year of tranquillity which Smollett passed in the delightful climate of Italy, the genius of this great writer shed its last and most genial ray; it was like the setting sun, pouring forth a calmer and gentler radiance as it sank below the horizon. It was here that he composed 'Humphry Clinker,' the richest and most exquisite picture of English manners which his pen had ever delineated. It is a tale related in letters, supposed to be written by the admirably-contrasted members of a family visiting the then fashionable watering-place of Bath; and the adventures, irresistibly comic in themselves, receive a double power over our laughter, and sometimes over our tears too, when seen, as it were, through the medium of the characters who describe them. The irritable but benevolent Bramble (a portrait of Smollett himself), with his querulous richness of imagination, the never-to-be-forgotten Mrs. Tabitha and Winifred

Jenkins, the simplicity of Humphry Clinker, and the humours of Lismahago—all these make the novel equal, if not superior, to the finest productions of Smollett's meridian genius.

There are few great names in literature whose intellectual and personal character present such a tissue of inconsistencies and paradox as the life and writings of Lawrence Sterne. Both as a man and as n author, there is in this truly original person such a union of apparently incompatible merits and defects, that it is impossible not to feel all our systems of moral and intellectual speculation completely at a loss when applied to him.

Sterne was borne in 1713, at Clonmel, in Ireland; and was the son of a lieutenant of an infantry regiment. But though the future author of the 'Sentimental Journey' came into the world in very poor and unpromising circumstances, his mother's relations (many of whom were rich English clergymen) not only secured him a good education—finished at Jesus College, Cambridge—but also pointed out the ecclesiastical profession as his future path in life. Sterne, on entering orders, obtained the living of Sutton, in Yorkshire, to which he afterwards added a prebendary of the cathedral in the same archbishopric; and he ultimately acquired by marriage the presentation to another preferment in the Church. Neither his life nor his character, however, were more in accordance with his sacred functions than his face or writings—the features of Sterne being strongly comic, marked with a most singular mixture of penetration, gaiety, and an almost morbid sensibility; while his unfeeling conduct to his wife, and his perpetual squabbles with his brother clergymen, were as little in accordance with the susceptibility he vaunted as with the character of a country pastor. It was one of these squabbles that gave Sterne the opportunity of displaying his satiric humour; for his first work was a pamphlet, in which, under a burlesque history of a village uproar about a "good warm watchcoat," he made so droll and severe a reflection on the greediness for reversionary preferment exhibited by one of the Yorkshire clergymen, that the person ridiculed is said to have relinquished his claim on condition that Sterne would suppress the pasquinade. In it one may see the dawn, the embryo, of much of his peculiar manner.

In 1759 our author visited London, carrying with him the two first volumes of 'Tristram Shandy,' which excited, on their appearance, such a tumult of enthusiasm, that the writer immediately ascended to the summit of popularity, and was urged by universal acclamation to continue the book; two more volumes of which were given to the world in 1761, and again two more the year following. This eagerness of the public cannot be attributed to the same cause which made the ladies besiege Richardson with prayers to finish his 'Clarissa,' viz.—intense interest in the story, and eagerness to learn the catastrophe; for in Sterne's fiction there is absolutely neither plot nor catastrophe to learn; and one of the principal oddities of the book, and chief sources of the impression it produced, was that it cannot be called a story at all, seeing that it has not one of the Aristotelian requisites—a beginning, a middle, or an end. Its charm consists in the easy, rambling style, in the exquisite touches of pathos and humour that alternately glow and sparkle through its pages, in the familiarity established between the reader and the fantastic gossiping author, and, above all, in the delicate and masterly delineations of its many admirably conceived characters. In this last respect there is something Shakspearian in Sterne's manner; and he, like the greatest creator of character that the world has ever seen, develops and depicts the personage rather by words than actions—rather by unconscious self-betrayals than by elaborate description. Much of the popularity of the book arose—at least when it appeared—from the fearless novelty of the style, full of breaks and interruptions, abrupt and exclamatory rather than continuous, which, though certainly in part natural, was also in some measure a trick of art. This peculiarity at first gives a great charm and raciness, but soon rather offends than pleases; for we speedily perceive that it is, like the perpetual interruptions and digressions, a piece of mechanical artifice.

The obscure erudition which so astonished the readers of Sterne's time, when the study of the Middle-Age literature was accounted a barbarous pedantry, will now be found neither very accurate nor very extensive; and we now perceive that this author, apparently so original in his form, was one of the most unblushing plagiarists that ever wrote, borrowing incessantly from Rabelais and Burton, and owing, indeed, nearly the whole of his imagery to those authors, even now little, and then never, read. Coleridge has acutely remarked, that the character of Mr. Shandy in this novel is an embodiment of pure intellect, and that of My Uncle Toby an impersonation of unmixed goodness of heart; and an amusing parallel might be made between these two admirable characters and Panurge on the one hand, and Pantagruel on the other—the *chef-d'œuvres* of the immortal romance of the curé of Meudon. Sterne must claim all the merit of individualizing these conceptions, of bringing them down from the airy regions of burlesque to the familiar reality, the flesh-and-blood consistency of common life, of incrusting them in the ordinary incidents and manners of the English society of the day, and of surrounding them with a train of minor personages, as exquisitely real, individual, and varied as ever were imagined by the fancy of genius—Mrs. Shandy, the ideal of nonenity, a character profoundly individual from its very absence of individuality; the choleric and uncharitable Dr. Slop, Yorick, Obadiah, the Widow Wadman, and Susannah. Toby and Corporal Trim are two noble portraits of goodness and gentleness, sketched in with most delicate strokes of Humour's own pencil, and glowing with the iris tints of tenderness and pity. How identical are the chief elements of these two characters, and yet how admirably are they distinguished!

The perpetual digressions, interruptions, blank and marbled pages which abound in Sterne, produce at first an air of oddity and surprise, which soon merges into something like contempt; but the innumerable effusions of true pathos, the exquisite relations of simple and affecting incidents, will remain for ever a deep and peculiar charm, and be his title to a durable glory. At two different periods Sterne made a tour on the continent, first to France, and afterwards to France and Italy; and found no difficulty in appending his impressions of foreign manners to the desultory pages of 'Tristram Shandy.' These impressions are often read separately as 'The Sentimental Journey,' a little volume full of the most charming strokes of tenderness and wit, which has obtained a European reputation. With the exception of some passages of too warmly-coloured description (a defect rendered more dangerous by the delicate and romantic tone of Sterne's writings, and one from which none of his works are free), this volume justifies the author's reputation; and he particularly deserves our praise for the gentle and cosmopolite spirit which makes him perceive and appreciate the peculiar merits of other nations, and do justice not only to their arts and their triumphs, but even to the amiable peculiarities of their national character and manners. This Sterne laboured to do, and both England and France have well rewarded him. Many of the episodes of this singular writer are familiar to all readers, and these are generally the most pathetic passages: the picture of Captivity, the Dead Ass, Maria, the story of Lefevre, the Sermon read by Trim, and a thousand others, immediately recur to the reader's memory: these are the most popular, because they are the most intelligible to all. But he who should confine himself to these would form a very imperfect notion of Sterne's literary and intellectual portrait The comic passages must be read also; and the conversations of Mr. Shandy, Toby, and Trim, the numerous soliloquies and artful betrayals of the minutest shades of character, must be studied ere we can form a true notion of the singularly complex idiosyncrasy of the author, or the delicate brilliancy of his style.

Sterne died in 1768, in London, whither he had gone to superintend the printing of his 'Sentimental Journey;' and it is not to be wondered at that the flattery which he received, acting on an impressible temperament, should have weakened a character naturally neither very virtuous nor very firm. His health had been during nearly his whole life exceedingly precarious; and though his writings show the warmest and tenderest glow of feeling and generosity, his life was by no means in accordance with such sentiments.

If the writings, and particularly the character, of Sterne be found to possess a strong resemblance to the national idiosyncrasy of the French people and genius, Oliver Goldsmith must undoubtedly stand for the most complete embodiment, the *beau idéal*, of the *artist* character. This we see in every act, both good and bad, of his romantic life, so full of vicissitudes, of glory and distress, of folly and generosity, of profound ignorance of the world and deep though transient impressibility, of genius and of shame, of childish vanity and tender wisdom. Much of this arises, doubtless, from his Irish birth; and there is not a greater contrast than between the lives and characters of the two illustrious friends who were at the head of the literature of their day, Johnson and the author of 'The Vicar of Wakefield.' The one is the very personification of the Englishman, the other of the Irishman. Both starting from an obscure and humble origin, both struggling through the early part of their career with every obstacle, Johnson emerged from the "sea of troubles" which threatened to overwhelm him by the simple vigour of moral and intellectual energy; Goldsmith floated above the waves by the innate buoyancy of a careless and happy temperament: one was a strong swimmer; the other was the stormy petrel. Goldsmith was the son of a poor Irish curate, whose utmost exertions could hardly give bread to a large family; and was born in July, 1728, at the village of Lishoy, in Longford—a village afterwards immortalised in one of his most exquisite productions. He was partially and very imperfectly educated by the kindness of his uncle, Mr. Contarine, who sent him to Dublin University, where the youth distinguished himself by a number of freaks evidencing an almost incredible want of prudence and common sense, and proved not only in some instances the romantic generosity of his heart, but a total incapacity to resist the temptation of the moment. After having been ignominiously dismissed from the university, he was again received, obtained, though not without difficulty, his degree, and, having chosen—as far as such a thoughtless person could be said to choose—medicine as his profession, he set out to travel to Leyden, where he did study some time; and wandered nearly over the whole of Europe, principally on foot, supporting himself in some measure by charity and by his flute. In this way he visited nearly all the principal places in France, Germany, Holland, and Flanders. This vagabond and gipsy life was perfectly in harmony with his sensitive and *expansif* character, and may indeed be considered—whatever its bad effects upon the excitable heart and weak moral principles of this child of genius—as singularly fortunate for his glory. It is assuredly in the lower classes of mankind that fiction will find its richest and most accessible materials. The liquid notes of his own flute, had he touched it with the finest finger, breathe not a sweeter air of feeling, a more touching and tenderer melancholy, than do his writings when the theme is the goodness and happiness of the poor.

On returning to England in 1756, he began to write for the booksellers, and obtained a precarious subsistence by contributing to the 'Monthly Review.' With a moderate degree of economy and foresight, Goldsmith's charming style would have soon enabled him gradually to obtain competence as a writer; but economy and foresight were words unintelligible to "poor Goldy," whose Irish heart could never resist the temptation of vanity or pleasure for himself, or of an almost insane liberality to others. He was himself exceedingly fond of fine clothes, had the fatal propensity of the gambler, and his heart was so extravagantly tender, that he perpetually gave his last guinea to the first object which awakened his morbid sympathies. Thus devoid of care for the future, and yielding to present impulses, his benevolence was neither just to himself nor useful to others; and he may be charged with heartlessness and ingratitude to those who had the greatest claims on his assistance and respect. The same cause kept Goldsmith always poor and plunged in debt; and though he remained for many years the most admired and popular writer of his time, he never ceased to be a bookseller's hack, and closed a life of fruitless and severe exertion in indigence and ruin.

In 1758 he attempted to pass the medical examination qualifying him as surgeon's mate in a ship of war, but was rejected; and so poor was he at this time that he was obliged to borrow a suit of clothes from a bookseller to appear in before the court, which suit he afterwards pawned. A letter is still preserved, written by him to the person he had so dishonestly deceived, full of the most passionate expressions of despair.

It was now that he commenced that rapid succession of easy and delightful writings, in prose and verse, which have rendered his name so dear to all who appreciate unaffected grace, delicacy, and humour. We shall specify only the more remarkable. The 'Chinese Letters,' afterwards known under the title of 'The Citizen of the World,' are full of the sweetest touches of character, and are written in a truly attractive and pure style. Goldsmith's manner of writing resembles, at least in those points which are not peculiar to him, at once that of Addison and that of Steele; but possessing a warmer and more genial tone than the writings of the former, and an infinitely greater purity and elegance than those of the latter. It is more *transparent* than Addison, less prim, less formal; and far fuller of sentiment, more ideal, than anything of Steele's, between whose character and Goldsmith's there was a strong resemblance.

Goldsmith then wrote a short and familiar 'History of England;' a mere compilation as to the matter, but related in such exquisitely easy and amusing language, that it is a model of the art of narrative. Johnson said justly that Goldsmith could make even the driest and most repulsive subject "as amusing as a Persian tale." And certainly nothing but his inimitable ease and grace of narration could make us forgive—as we do in spite of ourselves—the shallow crudeness of his learning, and the total want of grasp and system in his views.

It was now that appeared the first of his two memorable poems, 'The Traveller,' a meditative and descriptive work, embodying the mpressions of human life and society which he had felt in his travels and in his early struggles. Neither the ideas nor the imagery are very new or striking, but it is exquisitely versified (in the rhymed couplet); and its ease, elegance, and tenderness have made many passages pass into the memory and language of society. It is peculiarly admirable for the natural succession and connection of the thoughts and images, one seeming to rise unforcedly, and to be evolved, from the other. It is also coloured with a tender haze, so to say, of soft sentiment and pathos, as grateful to the mind as is to the eye the blue dimness that softens the tints of a distant mountain-range. It is a relief to the reader after Pope, in whom the objects stand out with too much sharpness, and in whom we see too much intense activity of the mere intellect at work. Pope is daylight; Goldsmith is moonlight.

In 1766 appeared the immortal tale which all the world has read, translated, and admired—'The Vicar of Wakefield.' The subject is nothing. A worthy, simple country parson is reduced to the deepest and most unmerited distress, and again restored to happiness. But the charming character of the hero—a kind of more refined Parson Adams—the exquisitely drawn portraits of his family, the natural incidents, the true and tender pathos, and the gentle humour—who knows not these? The style is perfection itself; and the adventures, though not always quite probable, are sufficiently so to maintain the reader's interest.

In the following year Goldsmith, as if not contented with the glory of being the most delightful narrator and the finest painter of character of his day, now aspired to the more poignant rapture of theatrical applause. His first comedy was 'The Good-natured Man;' and the hero was undoubtedly a dramatised portrait of the author himself, with his unthinking easiness of temper, and his culpable imprudence and generosity. The piece has the defect chargeable against many similar works, particularly on the French stage, namely, the taking of some mental quality as the subject, around which are grouped the inferior characters and interests, and which the dramatist has an irresistible and incessant temptation to exaggerate and caricature. This is not so injurious to nature and probability (the prime requisites of comedy) when the species of folly chosen is of a graver and more reprehensible kind, when it is a *vice*, in short, instead of a mere absurdity; but when it is a mere obliquity of taste, the more forcible and vivid the delineation, the less interest do we feel in it. Harpagon is always amusing, because we detest as well as laugh at him; but the weakness of Arnolphe in the 'Malade Imaginaire,' though we may laugh heartily at the oddity of the incidents and dialogue, is not of sufficient solidity and consistency to carry the weight of a comic plot. But 'The Goodnatured Man' is lively and gay, and some of the inferior characters, particularly Croaker, are touched with a humour that makes us pardon the rather tiresome uniformity of Honeywood's exaggerated generosity and self-abnegation.

The year 1770 gave to the world the companion poem to 'The Traveller,' 'The Deserted Village,' a work similar in tone, but immeasurably superior in distinctness of aim and felicity of idea. It depicts the sentiments of a wanderer, who, on return to his native place, which he left a smiling pastoral hamlet, finds nothing but ruin and desolation, or relics of former happiness more sad and painful still. "Sweet Auburn" is supposed to have been painted from Goldsmith's own recollections of the village of Lishoy, where his brother had the living; and as 'The Deserted Village' is more distinct and concentrated in its subject, and more homely in its details, than 'The Traveller,' it is incomparably more touching and more beautiful. Goldsmith was one of the first English poets of this age who had taste and feeling enough to rely for effect upon simple and unornamented descriptions of natural, ordinary objects and persons. He threw aside all that false and vulgar affectation which thought it necessary to clothe such objects in a parade of declamatory language; and his poem is exquisitely pathetic. He—and the numerous great men who followed him in this true conception of poetical art—did nothing else but restore the manner of our greater and more ancient writers, who find, in the commonest and most familiar images, an inexhaustible source of the most powerful emotions—the tenderest beauty and the sublimest terror.

Not very long after this poem appeared 'She Stoops to Conquer,' one of the most amusing comedies which the English stage possesses. The action of this piece is exceedingly animated and laughable, and the absence of any moral aim, the renunciation of any attempt to draw, in a principal or leading character, a portrait of some particular folly, is singularly advantageous to its effect, however it may degrade the work as a physiological embodiment. The personages are very numerous, and sketched with felicity; the booby Squire and his pot-house companions, the prosy and hospitable Mr. Hardcastle, his foolish wife, and the equivoques produced by Marlow's extravagant bashfulness—all these, if not of the higher order of comedy, are abundantly laughable and well managed.

In concluding our remarks on this author it will only be necessary to mention a number of histories written merely as booksellers' task-work — mere compilations as regards the matter, but exhibiting Goldsmith's never-failing charm of style: this circumstance, together with the absence of any very oppressive degree of erudition, has rendered them peculiarly well adapted for class-books in schools; a place they will retain till the more accurate and profound method of modern historical investigation shall have been communicated even to the elementary instruction of the young. Besides the 'History of England,' Goldsmith successively published that of 'Rome,' of 'Greece,' and of 'Animated Nature,' the last being for the most part a condensation of Buffon.

Our industrious writer (whose life was embittered, notwithstanding his great reputation, activity, and success, by perpetual debts and difficulties) died in 1774, having hastened, if not produced, his own decease, by injudiciously and obstinately taking a powerful medicine; and left behind him a reputation as well deserved as it is universal. There are very few branches of literature which he had not cultivated, if not with unparalleled, at least with more than ordinary success. In all he was above mediocrity, in some he reached excellence, and in *one* work (the delightful 'Vicar') he has left us a masterpiece of originality and grace.

CHAPTER XV.

THE GREAT HISTORIANS.

David Hume — As Historian—As Moralist and Metaphysician—Attacks on Revealed Religion—William Robertson—Defects of the "Classicist" Historians — Edward Gibbon — The Decline and Fall — Prejudices against Christianity — Guizot's judgment on Gibbon.

THE character of the English people is marked by singular inconsistencies: there is no nation which exhibits so much reluctance to pursue to their utmost consequences the deductions of any new system or chain of arguments. The English temperament is at once bold and timid; at the same time penetratingly far-seeing, yet almost slavishly devoted to prescription and authority. Nowhere is a new theory in legislation or in science more freely and candidly discussed; nowhere the true sifted from the false with a more industrious activity; nowhere does a new truth find a more enlightened and ready acceptance; but, at the same time, nowhere is there a greater dread of innovation, or a more determined adherence to the forms of particular systems or institutions.

Of these remarks the story of David Hume is a striking example.

He was sprung from an ancient and noble Scottish family, and was born in 1711. The greater part of his life was passed abroad, chiefly in France. Hume was happy and tranquil in the possession of an income so small that hardly all his national prudence sufficed to make it a competence. What is still more to his honour, he supported, during the early part of his literary career, a degree of neglect and failure which the consciousness of his talents must have rendered exceedingly bitter—this severe trial he bore, if not without a deep and very pardonable discouragement, yet with great manliness and dignity. His first work, 'A Treatise on Human Nature,' published in 1737, was received with absolute neglect; and though recommended by an exquisite refinement of style, and by great novelty of views, and a bold acuteness of argument, it "fell still-born from the press." Five years after this appeared his 'Essays, Moral and Philosophical,' which contain a great variety of refined and original speculations, often on subjects previously considered as "hedged in" and defended by an insurmountable barrier of sanctity and prescription. During this part of his life he appears to have had most difficulty and discouragement to struggle with; for he was for some time obliged to accept the most painful of human occupations, the charge of a madman. This was the young Marquis of Annandale, in attendance upon whom the future historian remained a year. Hume was soon afterwards appointed to the post of secretary to General St. Clair, whom he accompanied, first to Canada, and afterwards in his embassy to Vienna and Turin. In 1751 was re-published, under the title of 'An Inquiry concerning the Principles of Morals,' much of the substance though now considerably altered and almost recast, of the not very popular or successful treatise which had appeared fourteen years before: and about this time he gave to the world his 'Political Discourses.' Having caused himself to be appointed librarian to the Faculty of Advocates in Edinburgh, an office which he fulfilled gratuitously for the opportunity of making use of the books under his care, he now entered upon a new path, a path in which he was to more than redeem the ill success of his former publications—that of History. In 1754 appeared the first volume of his 'History of Great Britain,' containing the reigns of James I. and Charles I. This new attempt was for a while not more popular than his previous ones, but, in proportion as the succeeding volumes appeared, the public admiration grew ever stronger and stronger, and Hume was soon placed, by the unanimous applause of his countrymen, at the head of all the English historians who had then written. This reputation he deserved for many rare qualities, for his philosophic views, and for his exquisite style: and though History has received in more recent times a very different form, a much wider spirit of inquiry and investigation, a far more comprehensive, minute, and accurate spirit, as well as a more picturesque and striking language, there can be no doubt that Hume's work is of great beauty and value. Its chief defects are want of accuracy in detail, and strong partialities affecting various important principles. A polished and fastidious scholar, a Scotsman of aristocratic birth and sympathies, Hume was tinged not only with those Jacobite tendencies which were so prevalent in the higher classes of his country, but with an exaggerated dread of popular movements, and an indisposition to acknowledge the undeniable advantage which our constitution has so often and so uniformly derived from revolutions. A monarchist in principle, he entertained a somewhat extreme opinion as to the paramount importance of *stability* in any system of polity, forgetting that in the case of the British constitution a gradual and steady progressive movement was inherent in its very essence—was its sap and life-blood; and that, so far from its stability being compromised by popular movements, or even by revolutions, these were its very conditions and vitality. The English character has more in common (at least in its political manifestations) with that of the Roman people than with that of any other great and civilised nation with which history has made us acquainted. The resemblance is overwhelmingly striking when we take into account the immense difference between the political constitutions of the two countries. Both, however, were eminently aristocratic, and in both the principle of stability is surprisingly prominent—a stability so far from being diminished by incessant internal agitations, and even considerable organic changes, that these changes and agitations are its very exponents. Montesquieu has well remarked that movements which in other countries would infallibly involve a complete overthrow and possible reconstruction of the whole political machine, in England are considered, and justly so, as a proof of the vitality of the government. And the same thing is true of Rome, at least during its earlier and more glorious period. Both nations are eminently practical, logical, and calculating, and in both the attachment to old institutions goes only so far as to make the citizens distrust the prospective advantage of any proposed innovation: in other words, never to admit an innovation until forced on them by circumstances. Thus, the perpetual changes which were going on in the body politic were no more destructive to its individuality, nor injurious to its strength, than are the changes of the seasons to the growth of some majestic tree. Its leaves may be strewn by the gales of autumn, the vernal sap may rise within its vessels, incessant deposits of new matter and never-ceasing loss of old may continue, till not a particle of substance in the whole living structure may remain the same after the lapse of a few years, yet the tree is still the same, it is one, and no other and man and beast find shelter under its ever-waving boughs.

We have already given Hume credit for a philosophical spirit

This he undoubtedly possessed, but only to a certain degree. His mind had early accustomed itself to abstract investigations, and his long residence in France had contributed to develop in him a tendency to those barren and endless speculations which characterised the French literature of the period. Acuteness he undoubtedly possessed to a high degree, as well as a sincere love of truth: but his mind was cold and unsympathising; it wanted that profound *humanity*, that deep fellow-feeling with his kind, which is the only vivifying and fecundating principle. In his philosophy he had reached that point at which all is *negative:* he doubted of everything; he doubted even of the conclusions obtained by means of his own refined dialects; and if this species of Pyrrhonism could ever become generally prevalent, nothing would be left to man but the gratification of sense and the prosecution of mere temporary interests. But there is a point beyond this: indeed, a man who stops here halts on the very threshold of the great temple of wisdom. He who has never doubted (at least in matters of human reason) cannot be said properly to believe; and he who believes not can feel no perfect love. In his history Hume has taken too much upon trust from former compilers, and he has consequently fallen into a great many errors in points of fact, and been guilty of strange oversights and misrepresentations. Too indolent to consult, and too falsely refined to appreciate, the authentic sources of history in the writers contemporary with the events he describes, he has given us a work which is indeed a model of easy, fluent, agreeable narration, but a work which, if compared to many more modern productions of history (as for instance the admirable 'Conquête d'Angleterre par les Normands' of Augustin Thierry), will afford an incontrovertible proof of the immense advance made since his time in this branch of literature. His strong predilections in favour of the Stuart race have led him into innumerable errors and contradictions, and the whole of one most important episode in English history, the Civil War, the Republic, and the Protectorate, is full of inconsistency. This great and noble monument of Hume's genius appeared as follows:—the first volume in 1754, the second in 1757, the third and fourth in 1759, the fifth and sixth in 1762. From what we have said above, it may easily be inferred that Hume was unreasonably addicted to paradox and theorising on false or insufficient grounds. Moreover, his hostility to the doctrines and authority of the Christian religion led him to describe in one uniform tone of contemptuous indifference the labours and sufferings of many of those illustrious men who have sealed with their blood the charter of their country's liberty. Religion, so intimately interwoven with the whole tissue of private life in England, is a no less prominent element in all public and political events; and a historian, therefore, who should feel no sympathy with the religious convictions of some section or other (it little matters which) of the English people, might indeed avoid party prejudice, but could never succeed, be his genius what it may, in giving a true picture of events. "He had early in life," says Mackintosh, "conceived an antipathy to the Calvinistic divines, and his temperament led him at all times to regard with disgust and derision that religious enthusiasm or bigotry with which the spirit of English freedom was, in his opinion, inseparably associated: his intellect was also, perhaps, too active and original to submit with sufficient patience to the preparatory toils and long-suspended judgment of the historian, and led him to form premature conclusions and precipitate theories, which it then became the pride of his ingenuity to justify."

As a moralist and metaphysician Hume is less remarkable for any novel or original views in the investigation of fundamental principles than for the admirable clearness and elegance of his mode of reasoning, for the candour with which he admits objections, the acuteness—always tempered with courtesy and good taste—with which he combats them, and above all for the courage which he exhibits in carrying to their ultimate results the arguments which he uses. His chief test for the moral value of an action or a motive is the principle of utility—a principle into which must be, after all, resolved all questions of right and wrong. It is one which has in all ages excited the greatest outcries against every philosopher who has ventured overtly to propound it; and yet it is obvious that all systems professing to assign different foundations for good and evil in human actions are nothing else, when closely examined and carried to their ultimate application, than fruitless attempts to mask under specious forms a doctrine which to an unenlightened mind appears selfish and incompatable with elevated emotion. In stripping off the bandages of error and prejudice which envelop, like some Egyptian mummy, the body of moral truth, ordinary investigators content themselves with stopping at a secondary point. They are afraid to look face to face upon what they think is a corrupted and loathsome corpse; but if we clearly understand the principle, and properly limit its application, we shall find not only that all other modes of accounting for what we so unreasonably consider the invariable sentiment of right and wrong are insufficient, but that this is the only conceivable and possible way of explaining the existence of that sentiment at all.

Hume is considered also as one of the most dangerous and insidious enemies by whom the Christian religion has ever been attacked. The point against which his batteries are chiefly levelled is the credibility of the history of those miraculous events on which the religion founds its claim to be considered as a *revelation*, *i. e.* a supernatural interposition. The ground he takes is broad and simple: the nucleus of his arguments is to be found in the two famous propositions, 1st, that it is contrary to human experience that miracles should be true; 2nd, that it is not contrary to experience that human testimony should be false. This mode of reasoning it was quite natural that he should adopt, inasmuch as his philosophy is altogether of the negative and sceptical character: but at the same time his reasoning lies open to a powerful counter-argument—viz. that, if the essential incompetency of *any* degree of evidence be so great as to overbalance any force of probability, then that the convincing power of any arguments addressed to our minds must labour under an equal degree of uncertainty.

All evidence, whether addressed to our senses (often the most fallacious reporters) or to our reason, is comparative, and never can reach the intensity of abstract certitude, for God alone can be capable of *absolutely* knowing anything: all that remains is the question of comparative weight between the probability of the given event and the degree of evidence before us (an imperfect evidence, but an evidence which is *all that we require* or can appreciate); in short, it is a striking of a balance between two conflicting improbabilities. There is moreover a fallacy in the stating of the two celebrated propositions above quoted, and also something like a *petitio principii*; for, in the first place, the use of the words "experience" and "contrary to experience" would induce us to imply a contradiction fatal to the whole argument; seeing that, if miracles entered into the ordinary operations of nature (*i. e.* were subjects of experience), they would no longer be miracles at all; and it is clear that a revelation cannot be founded, as regards the evidence of its reality, on anything else *but* miracles, that is to say on events which are deviations from the ordinary laws of nature. Whatever of dangerous is contained in these arguments of Hume, whatever of mischief they may have done to the minds of inexperienced investigators, is to be attributed, less to their intrinsic weight and cogency than to the blind and bigot zeal of many of his answerers, who, in fervour of arrogant orthodoxy, have replied to Hume's arguments by reproaches and the ill-simulated language of contempt, combating his cool and skilful attacks with threats, slanders, and childish declamation. Those who have not acuteness enough to overthrow the logician are often content to calumniate the man: the hand which cannot wield the sword can always guide the dagger. Against personal attacks Hume found his best defence in the innocence and benevolence of his life, in the respect of the great and the wise of all countries, and in the affection of his own private friends. He gradually rose to the dignity of Under Secretary of State, and soon retired from public life with a moderate, but to him abundant fortune, and, after living many years in tranquil and lettered ease, he died in 1776 in Edinburgh, his native city.

Our remarks on the life and works of William Robertson, the next celebrated name in the department of History, will be very short. His story is a very simple one: it is the record of a man of pure and virtuous life, interchanging the obscure but arduous duties of a Scottish pastor with the labours of an ardent and enlightened scholar—a career fertile in active benevolence, in the unceasing fulfilment of quiet duties, and in the calm satisfactions of literary usefulness, but presenting little materials for the narrator.

It is singular that two out of the three great historians of this period should have been Scotsmen, that they should have produced extensive works of great and durable value under circumstances apparently very unfavourable to this kind of composition, and that their style should have strong points of general resemblance in its purity, elegance, and clearness. We can warmly agree with the sentiments of Walpole, who expresses his admiration and surprise that Robertson, then an obscure country clergyman, without access to any extensive sources of information, should have produced works equally distinguished for learning and accuracy, written in the purest and most classical English. This excellent historian was born near Edinburgh in 1721, and cannot be said to have acquired much fame until the appearance, in 1759, of his 'History of Scotland during the Reigns of Queen Mary and James VI.' This work not only opened to its amiable author the road to eminence and distinction, but, what is of more advantage to us, encouraged him to persevere in a line so auspiciously begun. In 1769 he published his 'History of the Reign of Charles V.,' and six years afterwards the 'History of America,' the three great pillars of his fame. All these books are distinguished by an elevated and noble tone of feeling, contain many clear and reasonable if not very profound views of the important epochs in human history which they portray, and deserve the highest possible eulogy for the refined elegance and grace of their style. Robertson's mind, though calm and meditative, was full of a sincere and well-regulated enthusiasm for all that is noble and good, and he has related with manly pathos the touching story of the beautiful and unhappy Mary, and the yet sublimer woes of that great navigator whose genius gave a world to ungrateful Spain. But with all this grace of style, with a harmony so liquid and so gentle that its art is occasionally somewhat too perceptible to the reader, we cannot fail to perceive a sort of smooth uniformity—not a monotony of tone, but a uniformity of *treatment*—in works detailing the annals of such different ages and countries. There is no distinction between his handling of these so different subjects; we do not find an *individuality* in his portraitures of such widely-differing states of society—and it is undoubtedly in that individuality that we must seek for the invaluable quality of picturesqueness, whether in literature or art. It would be difficult, almost impossible, for any dulness of narration to deprive of interest such subjects as the story of Mary Queen of Scots, the character and abdication of Charles V., or the discovery of America; and yet we cannot disguise from ourselves an unpleasant feeling that Robertson does not place himself, and consequently the reader, *among* the persons and events which he describes. To sympathise deeply with these, and to appreciate them profoundly, the reader ought to be made to breathe the atmosphere of the particular age and country in question. He ought not to gaze down upon them from the chilly heights of abstract philosophic speculation, he should mingle with them to a certain degree on a level. In the 'History of America,' for example, the author seems to have taken his materials at second hand, preferring (or perhaps obliged by circumstances) to obtain them filtered through the medium of previous compilations—a process in which, even when performed by the most skilful hand, a vast proportion of the raciness and spirit must inevitably evaporate. It is possible that Robertson was afraid of injuring the finish of his execution by admitting, in all their rude and vigorous animation, the picturesque details of old chroniclers and contemporary narrators, as, for example, the narratives of Bernal Dios and the Conquestadors. In Hume this absence of the peculiar tone and spirit of the age arose in a great measure from indolence and a philosophic (a falsely philosophic) indifference to those details of social life, art, religion, and popular feeling, which not only are characteristic of the particular age or people, but are absolutely the only things that we wish to know; for the scaffolding, the skeleton of history is pretty universally the same: what we desire to recall is not the battles, treasons, and coronations, for battles, treasons, and coronations are almost always the same thing; in evoking past ages from the tomb, it is not the bones, but the flesh and blood, the *life*, that we would behold; not a spectre, but

Our fathers in *their habit as they lived.*

The third, and unquestionably the greatest, of our English historical triad was Edward Gibbon. He was a man of good family and easy circumstances, and was born at Putney, near London, in 1737. He received an excellent education, and even passed some time in the University of Oxford; but he employed his early years in desultory and multifarious study, which, though it gave him the materials for future eminence in literature, was useless for any mmediate object. His attachment to the Protestant faith was also o much shaken about this time by controversial reading, that he became a convert to the Popish religion, on which his father sent him to reside with M. Pavillard, a Protestant minister at Lausanne, whose arguments were so conclusive that the young convertite again returned to the bosom of his national Church. A religious faith, however, so subject to change, could not have been very solid, and Gibbon's works afterwards gave abundant proof that his convictions of the truth of the evangelic history were by no means deeply rooted in his mind. Indeed he soon became a confirmed sceptic. While at Lausanne he pursued a regular and steady course of study, and seems to have adopted the opinions which were so prevalent just before the outbreak of the first French revolution. Nor is this to be wondered at: his mind appears to have been strikingly similar in its principal features to the character of the *Encyclopédiste* intellect; the same acuteness and activity, the same confidence in its own powers, the same distrust of the virtue and disinterestedness of mankind, and the same tendency towards the actual and sensuous rather than the abstract and the ideal. In 1758 he returned to England, and gave the first fruit of his reading in a little essay, written in French, on the Study of Literature: and during great part of the war he held the commission of captain in a body of militia. Four years afterwards he again visited the continent, where he passed a considerable time in travelling through France and Italy, and it was during these wanderings that he first conceived the idea of his great work. The incident, so eventful in the annals of English literature, took place at Rome, October 15th, 1764, and is immortalised in his own picturesque words: "As I sat musing," he says, "amidst the ruins of the Capitol, while the barefooted friars were singing vespers in the temple of Jupiter, the idea of writing the decline and fall of the city first started to my mind." But so gigantic a task was not to be executed, or even begun, without immense preparatory labour, and without the author passing through a period of uncertainty and vague agitation when determining upon the plan, the extent, the arrangement, and even the style of the work. He returned to England in 1765, and, on the death of his father, Gibbon, who had come into possession of an embarrassed fortune, ultimately entered upon a political career. During all this time his great plan was working and fermenting in his head, and he underwent those throes and struggles which genius ever feels in giving birth to a mighty and durable offspring. These he has related, and described how long it was ere his subject arranged itself before his mental eye in a definite form and with intelligible order and completeness: he has told us how often he was tempted to abandon in despair the accumulated materials of years of study; how he composed the first chapter three times, and the second and third twice over, ere he was satisfied with their effect. Such is the training of genius, such are the labours by which alone great productions can be created.

Gibbon was elected in 1774 member of Parliament for the borough of Liskeard; but though he sat for many sessions in the House of Commons, he never ventured to take part in the debates: his knowledge and intellectual powers were very great, nor was he unconscious of his own gifts, but his taste was fastidious, and his habits were those rather of the man of letters than of the statesman. He sate, therefore, invariably silent, filled, as he says, by the good speakers with despair of imitation, and by the bad ones with the dread of failure and ridicule. In reward for his adherence to the ministerial party Lord North appointed him one of the Commissioners of Trade, so that this historian, like his illustrious contemporary Hume, occupied a place in the government of his country.

It was in 1776 that appeared the first volume of his History, and the book became instantly so popular that its success rather resembled that of some amusing work of fiction than of a grave and serious history. It was the talk and admiration of the day; the volume was found in the library of every reader, and in the dressing-room and boudoir of the fashionable and the fair. Gibbon was greeted with the warm and generous applauses of Hume, Robertson, and all the distinguished literary men of his day, both in England and abroad; and when we reflect upon the brilliancy and originality of the work itself, we can easily account for the delight with which it was received: even its faults were of a nature to impress and to attract. The period which forms the subject of the work was one which, though fertile in splendid, impressive, and pathetic events, had never been studied or investigated by a genius sufficiently patient and enlightened to disentangle the contradictions and complexities of the barbarous historians in whose works alone the materials were to be found. The antecedent and subsequent epochs had been repeatedly discussed; but the long interval between the commencement of the decadence of Rome and the consummation of its ruin had remained, like some desolate border-country, unvisited and unexplored; it was a region of gloom and darkness—a twilight between the ancient and modern world. His genius was peculiarly calculated to give full effect to the grand but confused details of this astonishing picture, and his solemn, gorgeous, and rhetorical style was in happy harmony with the character of the times which he described. It would seem as if he had studied the writings of the Lower Empire till he had caught, perhaps involuntarily, something of their Asiatic splendour —the "barbaric pearl and gold," which dazzles the imagination though it does not gratify the taste; and of which the writings of the Greek and Latin fathers give a striking example.

We have said that Gibbon, like Hume, is one of the most dangerous enemies by whom the Christian faith was ever assailed—he was the more dangerous because he was insidious. The following is the plan of his tactics. He does not formally deny the evidence upon which is based the structure of Christianity, but he indirectly includes that system in the same category with the mythologies of paganism. The rapid spread of Christianity he explains by merely secondary causes; and in relating the disgraceful corruptions, persecutions, and superstitions which so soon supplanted the pure morality of the primitive Church, he leads the reader to consider these less as the results of human crime, folly, and ambition, than as the necessary consequences of the system itself. He either did not or would not distinguish between the *parceque* and *quoique;* and represents what is in reality an abuse as an inevitable consequence. Byron well describes him as

> "Sapping a solemn creed with solemn sneer,
> The lord of irony, that master-spell."

Moreover, though perpetually warmed by the grand or touching incidents he relates into noble bursts of eloquence and enthusiasm, he has no admiration for the struggles of Christian fortitude and the triumphs of Christian virtue. The same energy and virtue which, appearing in a heathen or a Mahomedan, fills his heart with fervour, and his lofty periods with a swelling grandeur, leaves him cold and impassible, or cavilling and contemptuous, when it is exhibited in the cause of Christianity.

In Gibbon's character there is also a peculiarity which, whether innate and natural or acquired from Voltaire and similar writers of that period, renders his writings dangerous to the young: this is a peculiar filthiness of imagination, which seems to revel in objects and events of gross and sensual immorality. No sooner does he find occasion to relate a scandalous or obscene story (and the corruption of manners during the period which forms the subject of his history gives him but too many opportunities to indulge in this vein) than he seems to delineate it with a peculiar gusto and minuteness which is in the highest degree offensive. He does not hasten rapidly over such scenes, saying, with Dante,

> "Non ragioniam di lor, ma guarda e passa!"

but he seems to take a perverse pleasure in dwelling on degrading images. Voltaire has much of this, and never omits an opportunity to introduce ideas not only sensual, but often physically disgusting; but in Voltaire these images are coloured by wit and sarcastic drollery, and are in harmony with the satiric petulance of his ridicule. In Gibbon the majestic solemnity of style, and the grave earnestness of the tone, render these offences against good taste exceedingly prominent and shocking.

In 1781 were published the second and third volumes, and the three last in 1787. Gibbon, who has with a justifiable pride given us the anecdote of the circumstances attending the origin of his great work, has left us an equally minute and not less interesting record of his feelings at its conclusion:—"It was on the day, or rather night, of the 27th of June, 1787, between the hours of eleven and twelve, that I wrote the last lines of the last page in a summer-house in my garden. After laying down my pen, I took several turns in a berceau or covered walk of acacias, which commands a prospect of the country, the lake, and the mountains. The air was temperate, the sky was serene, the silver orb of the moon was reflected from the waters, and all nature was silent. I will not dissemble the first emotions of joy on the recovery of my freedom, and perhaps the establishment of my fame. But my pride was soon humbled, and a sober melancholy was spread over my mind, by the idea that I had taken an everlasting leave of an old and agreeable companion, and that, whatsoever might be the future fate of my history, the life of the historian must be short and precarious."

From Lausanne Gibbon again returned to England for a short time, but he came back again to Switzerland, where he remained till shortly before his death. Finding the society of Lausanne distracted by parties consequent upon the outbreak of the French Revolution, and induced by the death of Lord Sheffield, his most intimate friend, to return to London, in order to console and counsel the widow, he came back to his own country, and died in London in 1794.

With all its defects, Gibbon's 'Decline and Fall of the Roman Empire' is a noble monument of genius and industry. The style is extraordinarily elevated and ornate, and resembles rather the antithetical tone of the French literature of the eighteenth century than an idiomatic English work. Indeed, so completely was Gibbon's mind saturated with French sympathies, that there is a tradition that he for some time hesitated whether his great work should be written in French or English. His narration is very clear, animated, and picturesque: he brings before the reader's eye the persons and events which he describes; and wherever his scepticism and prejudices do not interfere, he gives a lively, penetrating, and natural account of the characters and motives of men. But his moral susceptibility was not very delicate, and he frequently lavishes on the external splendour of great actions that enthusiasm which should be reserved for the simple dignity of moral grandeur. His sympathies were somewhat theatrical; and though the general current of his narrative is exceedingly clear, his gorgeousness and measured pomp of language becomes fatiguing and oppressive. So great is his dread, too, of repeating the same word or name in the same page or at short intervals, that his expedients of finding a synonym are frequently productive of confusion and uncertainty in the reader. We cannot better conclude our remarks than by quoting the excellent and elaborate judgment of Guizot:—"After a first rapid perusal which allowed me to feel nothing but the interest of a narrative, always animated, and, notwithstanding its extent and the variety of objects which it makes to pass before the view, always perspicuous, I entered upon a minute examination of the details of which it was composed; and the opinion which I then formed was, I confess, singularly severe. I discovered, in certain chapters, errors which appeared to me sufficiently important and numerous to make me believe that they had been written with extreme negligence; in others, I was struck with a certain tinge of partiality and prejudice, which imparted to the exposition of the facts that want of truth and justice which the English express by their happy term *misrepresentation.* Some imperfect quotations, some passages omitted unintentionally or designedly, have cast a suspicion on the honesty of the author; and his violation of the first law of history—increased to my eyes by the prolonged attention with which I occupied myself with every phrase, every note, every reflection—caused me to form on the whole work a judgment far too rigorous. After having finished my labours, I allowed some time to elapse before I reviewed the whole. A second attentive and regular perusal of the entire work, of the notes of the author, and of those which I had thought it right to subjoin, showed me how much I had exaggerated the importance of the reproaches which Gibbon really deserved: I was struck with the same errors, the same partiality on certain subjects; but I had been far from doing adequate justice to the immensity of his researches, the variety of his knowledge, and, above all, to that truly philosophical discrimination which judges the past as it would judge the present; which does not permit itself to be blinded by the clouds which time gathers around the dead, and which prevent us from seeing that, under the toga as under the modern dress, in the senate as in our councils, men were what they still are, and that events took place eighteen centuries ago as they take place in our own days. I then felt that his book, in spite of its faults, will always be a noble work; and that we may correct his errors and combat his prejudices without ceasing to admit that few men have combined, if we are not to say in so high a degree, at least in a manner so complete and so well regulated, the necessary qualifications for a writer of history."

CHAPTER XVI.

THE TRANSITION SCHOOL.

Landscape and Familiar Poetry—James Thomson—The Seasons—Episodes—Castle of Indolence—Minor Works—Lyric Poetry—Thomas Gray—The Bard, and the Elegy—Collins and Shenstone—The Schoolmistress—Ossian—Chatterton and the Rowley Poems—William Cowper—George Crabbe—The Lowland Scots Dialect and Literature—Robert Burns.

"The less man really knows," says an eloquent and acute Russian writer, "the greater his contempt for the ordinary, for what surrounds him. A practical every-day truth appears to him a degradation; what we see *before our eyes and often* were present to ourselves as undeserving of attention; we want the far, the remote; *il n'y a pas de grand homme pour son valet-de-chambre.*" What is true of philosophy in general is applicable to art in particular, and to literature, the highest, completest, and most perfect of the arts. What is the distinction between the tone of literature of the eighteenth and that of the nineteenth century? What but the substitution of the real and the actual for the abstract and the remote? It is true that the real and the actual are idealised, are glorified, in passing into the golden atmosphere of art, no less than were the abstract and the remote, and this is an indispensable condition, for the ideal is the very soul of poetry: but we now find in pictures of ordinary life, in the description of common nature, a source of profound pleasure, emotion, and improvement. What Coleridge has said of old paganism may with more justice be applied to the literature of modern times:—

"Clothing the *palpable and familiar*
With golden exhalations of the dawn."

The full and complete daylight of this new era is to be found in Scott, in Byron, in Shelley, in Wordsworth; but the dawning of the auspicious Aurora was gradual and slow. It was first seen to glimmer (we mean in modern days, for of recent periods only do we speak) in the poetry of Thomson, and then gradually glowed with a stronger light, powerfully hastened in its development by the publication of Percy's 'Reliques of Ancient English Poetry,' by the forgeries of Macpherson, and by the fabrications of Chatterton. Its characteristic was an intense and reverent study of Nature in all her manifestations, whether of physical or intellectual activity; of the one, Thomson is the type—of the other, Cowper and Crabbe.

The early part of Thomson's career somewhat resembles that of Smollett. He was born in Scotland in 1700, and came up to London to push his fortune as a literary man. He carried with him the unfinished poem of 'Winter,' some passages of which he had shown to Mallet, by whom he had been strongly advised to publish the work. Arriving in London at the age of eighteen, he obtained the situation of tutor in the family of the Lord Binning, which he afterwards exchanged for the more powerful protection of Lord Chancellor Talbot. With the son of this distinguished lawyer Thomson had the advantage of travelling over the Continent, and thus feeding his rich imagination with the fairest scenes of natural magnificence, and filling his ardent fancy with recollections of the great and wise of ancient history. The poem of 'Winter' was published in 1726, and in the two succeeding years it was followed by its beautiful companions, 'Summer' and 'Spring,' 'Autumn' not appearing until 1730. The four works together compose a complete cycle of the various appearances of Nature during an English year, and are known to all who feel what is beautiful, as the 'Seasons'—the finest descriptive poem in the English or perhaps in any language. There is no country whose climate affords so great a variety and richness of external beauty as that of Great Britain; none in which the surface of the land is more picturesquely broken into every form and tint of beauty, none more abundant in spots sanctified by memory, none where the changes of climate are more capricious and imposing. The finest art and the most idiomatic literature of England bears testimony to the intensity of feeling for the external loveliness of nature which seems to form a distinctive feature of the national character—a trait more marked perhaps among us than even among the ancient Greeks. In that great and peculiar style, invented and principally cultivated in England—descriptive or landscape poetry—Thomson is by far our greatest artist; though this tendency to study and portray Nature for herself is singularly perceptible in all the greatest works of purely English genius. With what a fond enthusiasm has Father Chaucer, whose verses are modulated to the forest-music of an English landscape, the gurgle of the brook, the multitudinous rustle of leaves, and, above all, to the liquid melody of birds—with what an earnest joy has this divine poet seized every occasion of painting the physiognomy of English scenery! Spenser's fairy glades are full of this deep passion for nature *as* nature—Nature looked at for herself: neither Shakspeare nor Milton has ever written any twenty consecutive lines without giving us, often in a single word, and parenthetically as it were, some touch of natural scenery, some embodiment of a physical object familiar as the cloud or the leaf, ever-varying like them, yet, like them, invariable.

In the 'Seasons' of Thomson, we have a subject unbounded in variety, yet happily limited in extent; and it is no exaggeration to affirm that there is not a possible modification of English scenery, terrestrial or atmospheric, which he has not caught and fixed for ever. Everything appears in its natural light, in its relative perspective and proportion; and though we are of course carried in succession through the various appearances of the year, he always has the art to conceal the *joinings* in his canvas, and to give us the feeling of continuity which produces the charm of a well-executed panorama. Above all, the work is animated throughout with so gentle yet so genial a glow of philanthropy and religious gratitude, that its parts are so to say fused naturally together; the ever-changing landscape is harmonised by this calm and elevated and tender spirit, which throws over the whole a soft and all-pervading glow, like the tint of an Italian heaven.

The language and versification, however, are not always worthy of the subject nor of the sentiment of the work. Though very much purified and simplified in his later works, there is often an ambitious tumidity in Thomson's diction not unaccompanied by vulgar and mean expressions; and though in a thousand places he has exhibited a peculiar felicity in finding those appropriate words which paint almost to the eye.

> "What oft was thought, but ne'er so well express'd,"

he is occasionally deficient in simplicity and chasteness.

His blank verse is sonorous and musical, but he did not possess that fineness of ear which seems involuntarily to echo the wild and ever-changing voices of nature; nor had he the art of concealing, by an inexhaustible flexibility and sensibility of rhythm, the tendency to monotony which is the prevailing defect of descriptive poetry.

To relieve the uniformity of his plan he has introduced a great number of little tales and episodes, generally suggested by the scene which he is describing. Of these the pathetic pictures are undoubtedly the best; as, for example, the episode of the shepherd perishing in the snow, introduced into the "Winter;' and generally, where a mixture of the pathetic with the terrible is the emotion to be excited; but when he attempts to be simply graceful, tender, or facetious, his failure is painful and inevitable. Thomson's imagination was intensely sensuous: his delineations of love are very far from romantic; and when he endeavours to idealize the passion, he becomes pitiably stilted, affected, and vulgarly fine; as, for instance, in the bathing scene of Musidora, and little less, though certainly less offensively so, in the so-often quoted tale of Lavinia.

His comic scenes (as the fox-hunting debauch) are utterly gross, and totally discordant with the tone of the rest of the work. That he was not destitute of a rich and even refined humour, we shall see when we come to speak of the exquisite 'Castle of Indolence.' 'The Seasons' must be undoubtedly considered, all proper deductions made, a truly great and beautiful work. If the poet has sometimes fallen into the affectation of classicism, and drawn from the ancients instead of from nature; if with the majestic accents of his hymn to the Creator—best praised by the glory of his works—he has allowed to mingle some accents of earthly adulation; if he be sometimes tedious, or solemn out of season; if his ornaments be sometimes meretricious, and his language sometimes too heavy for the thought—all this, and much more, we can pardon him, for he has interpreted the book of Nature with a penetrating yet reverent eye; he has made us feel the loveliness of a thousand objects which escape us from their very familiarness; and he has given to his country the glory of originating a new, elevating, and beautiful species of writing, of which the antique literature offers no example.

The success of 'The Seasons' was so great as to enable Thomson (with the assistance of a government sinecure given him by Talbot) to purchase a cottage on the banks of the Thames near Richmond, and pass the rest of his days in comfort and even luxury. During the whole of his career he continued a pretty industrious writer, and composed several tragedies in the false and unhealthy taste of that day, which were neither very successful at that time, nor deserving of any notice since. They are all remarkable for mannerism, sham grandeur, and sham pathos, and no less for a declamatory and noisy emphasis of patriotism. He also composed an eulogistic poem in honour of Newton, which contains one or two fine passages, and a species of lyric entitled 'Liberty,' which deserved the failure it met with, though its subject, as he ought to have foreseen, was too impracticable for any other result to be possible.

In his suburban retirement he appears to have lived much more happily than often falls to the lot of poets, and to have been able to indulge not only in that pardonable and innocent luxury which was congenial to his temper, but also in those acts of benevolence and goodness that won him the love and respect of his contemporaries. So intensely indolent, indeed, was he, that he is said to have been in the habit, when lounging in his dressing-gown along the sunny walks of his garden, of biting a mouthful out of the peaches ripening on his wall, too lazy to lift his hand to pluck them. So self-indulgent a poet was fitted to be the high-priest of Indolence, and he has in one exquisite composition immortalized the very ideal of his failing. This is 'The Castle of Indolence,' an allegorical poem in the style and manner of Spenser, which not only is the best imitation ever made of the great author of 'The Faërie Queen,' but one of the most delightful works in the English language. Spenser was, to a certain degree, an imitator of Ariosto, and the southern temperament of Thomson enabled him to reproduce, even more faithfully than his immediate model, the luxuriant graces of the 'Orlando;' for 'The Castle of Indolence' is, like Ariosto, more tinged with gaiety than the poem of Spenser. In this work the author of 'The Seasons' exhibits a richness of harmony which could hardly have been expected from him, judging by his former poems, and the soft profusion of his lulling and luxurious fancy is most inimitably expressed in the languishing measure of the verse.

The allegorical part, particularly the birth and education of the knight Industry, who liberates the unfortunate captives from the enchanted castle, is not either very striking or well imagined: it is Spenserian, it is true, but not quite Spenser's finest vein. In this individualizing magic Spenser himself does not always succeed; he delights and impresses us, not with the realizing and embodiment of intellectual conceptions, but by the wonderful variety and vividness of his personages, which, though bearing the names of virtues and vices, do not please us by what they pretend to be, but by what they are, *i. e.* men and women, masked and costumed to act in a splendid pageant. We are pleased with them, not as dramatic characters, but as actors. But the charm of 'The Castle of Indolence' lies in the descriptions, in the inexhaustible yet gentle flow of lulling images of calmness and repose. This luxurious dreaminess we sometimes feel in reading Spenser, but it forms the very colouring and key-note of Thomson's poem: let him express it in his own delicious words:—

"A pleasing land of drowsy head it was,
Of dreams that wave before the half-shut eye,
And of gay castles in the clouds that pass,
For ever flushing round a summer sky;
There eke the soft delights, that witchingly
Instil a wanton sweetness through the breast,
And the calm pleasures, always hover'd nigh;
And whate'er smack'd of noyance or unrest
Was far, far off expell'd from that delicious nest."

This excellent man and great poet died of a cold caught on the Thames, August 27, 1748.

Lyric poetry is perhaps the only important subdivision of literature in which the earlier period of the history of English genius had failed to offer models of supereminent excellence. Cowley, indeed, had made noble essays to reproduce in the literature of his country something analogous in spirit and structure to the lyric compositions of Greece; but in imitating Pindar and Anacreon he seems to have forgot the intense mythological fervour which glows throughout these works, which are among the grandest manifestations of Hellenic art.

Italian poetry, too, was abundant in noble lyrics: Petrarch had shown the power and majesty of his country's language, and a multitude of great men, Chiabura, Pindemonte, Filicaja, had given proof that the peculiar energies of the Greek lyric might be revived, with little diminution of effect, and a not dissimilar form of expression, in the splendid *canzoni* of Italy. These works Milton had profoundly studied, and it was from their study too, combined with an intense perception of the beauties of the Greek lyrics whose spirit they so admirably resuscitated, that Gray was able, in the Ode, to dispute the wreath with Milton himself, and to give noble specimens of this kind of writing. Gray, like Milton, was one of the most learned men of his age, and he also had the good taste to avoid, in the subject and imagery of his works, that feeble affectation of exclusive classicism which gives so monotonous and unnatural an air to most of the lyric compositions of his day: and thus his very boldness in rejecting all the over-worn machinery of Greek and Roman mythology actually tended to give his works a greater real and essential resemblance to the spirit of classical poetry. The artifices of his language and the peculiar structure of his verse are reproductions of ancient poetry, particularly of Greece; but the main source of the pleasure he gives is in the truly national sympathies he excites, a merit strongly exemplified in two of his noblest compositions, the 'Ode on Eton College' and the 'Elegy in a Country Churchyard.' These are works which any Greek poet—even the greatest—might have been proud to own; they are saturated with the finest essence of the Attic Muse. Yet Gray has in no sense Hellenised too much or out of place; he is Greek by very force of daring to be English.

Gray was born in 1716, and began his career by travelling over part of Europe with Horace Walpole. Returning to England in 1741, he wisely adopted an academic life, for which he was best fitted by his character and pursuits. He retired to Cambridge, where he continued to reside, with few interruptions, until his death in 1771, devoting himself to incessant but somewhat desultory study, and keeping up with several literary friends a correspondence which gives us a most amusing and lively portrait of a singular character. In his manners and feelings Gray was extremely timid and fastidious, affecting to despise the pursuits and habits of the academic society by which he was surrounded, and perpetually conceiving great literary plans which his indolence and self-indulgent Sybaritism prevented him from realising.

His works appeared at considerable intervals—the 'Ode on Eton College' in 1747, the 'Elegy' four years after, the noble 'Ode on the Progress of Poetry' in 1757, and 'The Bard' (his greatest work) after the lapse of another period as considerable. In the 'Ode to Eton College' he gives melodious expression to that natural and tender feeling of regret with which in after-life we regard the sports of childhood and the scenes of our school-days. It is weighty and rich with thought, and many passages are versified with inimitable delicacy and skill; we see here some of those bold personifications and sparkling felicities of diction—those "thoughts that breathe, and words that burn"—which give such splendour to his after lyrics.

The subject and general treatment of the 'Elegy' is familiar to readers of every nation. The reflections of this poem are certainly not marked by any striking originality, but they are illustrated with such consummate taste, expressed with such a union of impressiveness and grace, that the work is a masterpiece of poetical handling.

The production by which the genius of this poet will be tried is undoubtedly the lyric entitled 'The Bard.' It is suggested by the legend of King Edward I. having given orders that all the bards should be put to death, as to them he attributed the desperate resistance made by the Welsh people to his victorious arms. The poem opens with a splendid and spirited description of one of these national poets beholding, from a rock, the approach of the invader's army—

> "As down the steep of Snowdon's shaggy side
> He wound with toilsome march his long array;"

and the substance of the work is an awful prophetic denunciation of the woe and ruin which was to avenge on the cruel conqueror and his house the miseries he had inflicted on Wales. The picture is a noble and striking one, and possesses much more distinctness than is generally to be found in Gray. In this he has exhausted all the stores of imagery and all the artifices of harmony; and the effect is singularly grand and imposing. But the poem, in spite of all his skill, has somewhat of an artificial and hot-bed air; the imagery, beautiful as it is, inspires the reader with an involuntary feeling of its having been painfully collected from a multitude of sources. It is a piece of rich mosaic; and though the parts of which it is composed are exquisite in themselves and dovetailed together with no ordinary art, the effect of the whole is rather of *construction* than *evolution.* Gray's personifications, whether of single figures or groups of abstract qualities, are often designed with singular felicity and adorned with a gorgeous splendour of colouring; but they are sometimes out of place, as, for example, in 'The Bard,' that beautiful picture :—

> "Fair laughs the morn, and soft the zephyr blows,
> While, proudly riding o'er the azure realm,
> In gallant trim the gilded vessel goes,
> Youth at the prow, and Pleasure at the helm,
> Regardless of the sweeping whirlwind's sway,
> That, hush'd in grim repose, expects his evening prey."

The Welsh poetry is indeed full of the boldest personification—as indeed is that of every rude and warlike people; but the real fragments of the bardic compositions rather give life to inanimate objects than represent under a sensible form the abstract conceptions of the mind.

In 'The Descent of Odin' and some other pieces Gray endeavoured to reproduce in English poetry the wild and savage character of the Runic imagination; but the spirit is not very happily preserved, and there is visible in these (as for example in the celebrated ode entitled 'The Fatal Sisters') a perpetual and not very successful struggle after effect.

Lyric poetry was a department of the art in which this period of English literary history was exceedingly prolific. The two most popular if not most important names which we have to notice are Collins and Shenstone: the one is held by many, and with no small justice, the equal of Gray; and the other may almost be called the inventor of a peculiar style of pastoral ballad writing. The story of both is painful and melancholy: Collins was driven by disappointment into intemperance, and by intemperance into madness; and Shenstone, by the imprudent indulgence in his taste for an elegant art (the art of ornamental gardening, of which he must be considered as almost the inventor), into inextricable embarrassment. If we admire the genius and skill which has compressed into the few pages of Gray's collected poems so many noble images, so many exquisite movements of harmony, and so much splendour and propriety of diction, we shall find that an intense susceptibility for beauty has concentrated into the yet smaller compass of Collins's productions a quantity and depth of loveliness of a kind even more permanently attractive to the reader. If Gray was the more accomplished artist, Collins was the more *born poet.* In Collins the first thing we remark is the inimitable felicity of his expression. Gray's lovely and majestic pictures are careful, genial, artistic paintings of nature; those of Collins are the images of nature in the *camera obscura.* Gray is the light of day; Collins is the Italian moonlight – as bright almost, but tenderer, more pensive, more spiritual,—

"Dusk, yet clear;
Mellow'd and mingling, yet distinctly seen."

The 'Ode on the Passions' is exquisitely felicitous in conception, full of personifications conceived in the true lyric spirit: the changes, too, of imitative harmony with which the poet at once describes and exemplifies the appropriate music of each passion—all these form a noble effort of taste, sensibility, and genius, and may be boldly compared to the somewhat similar picture in the immortal 'Ode' of Dryden; but we must confess that in our judgment some of the minor lyrics of Collins exhibit not only a rarer and more exquisite degree of merit, but are a more faithful impress of the peculiar idiosyncrasy of his mind. The little 'Ode to Evening' consists of but thirteen short quatrains, *without rhyme;* but in its fifty-two lines we have the whole spirit and quintessence of its subject: it is an orient pearl of tender loveliness. All is soft, airy, full of variety, yet harmonized into grace: it is one of those undulating melodies of Schubert, on which the soul floats dreamily, as if on the dewy breath of twilight.

Several of Collins's songs (as for example the beautiful Dirge in 'Cymbeline,' the stanzas 'How sleep the brave,' the 'Elegy on Thomson,' &c.) possess similar but inferior merit, and are not only fuller of the poet's peculiar charm, but more likely to defy future rivalry, than the more elaborate works, such as the 'Ode on the Highland Superstitions,' that to 'Liberty,' or the 'Oriental Eclogues:' these last, though beautiful, and though admired when they appeared as being one of the first attempts to employ in English poetry Eastern imagery, yet have been much surpassed by more recent writers, better acquainted with the real manners and nature of the "Morning-Land."

The 'Pastorals' of Shenstone were singularly popular in their day, and are still admired by the young. Whatever charm they possess is owing to their smooth and easy language, their simple equable fluency, and also to the true but slender vein of natural sentiment, which makes us forget their intolerable mawkishness, and the absurd affectation of the persons and manners of their shepherds and shepherdesses.

Shenstone affirmed that the vicissitudes of hope, despair, jealousy, and sorrow, painted with a faithful though feeble pencil in these emasculated compositions, were records of a real passion: and those who think, with us, that a single touch of nature will give value to the weakest execution, will look with no implacable severity even upon the wearisome *fadeurs* of this "Bucolical Juvenal."

But in spite of the false innocence and querulous monotony of these Pastorals, Shenstone has in one exquisite and original little poem shown that when he had the courage to trust to reality and nature he could produce what was excellent, nay, inimitable in its kind. We have spoken of Thomson's delightful imitation of Spenser in 'The Castle of Indolence;' Shenstone's 'Schoolmistress' is a somewhat similar imitation of the language and versification of the English Ariosto, though with considerable differences of treatment.

Shenstone has taken for his theme the humble character of a village schoolmistress, and the poem (which is very short) is an exquisite specimen of that kind of burlesque which is ludicrous without ceasing to be reverential. Of course there is little or no allegory; and so far this work neither enters into any dangerous rivalry with Thomson, nor provokes any recollection but an agreeable one of Spenser; and the quaintness of the antiquated diction is in delightful unison with the pleasant rustic details, related with enchanting ease and simple homely tenderness.

But perhaps the most remarkable indication of the tendency (obscure at first and uncertain, but rapidly acquiring a definite direction) towards a new and distinct tone of romanticism, is to be observed in the two remarkable forgeries which had so powerful an effect on literature, not only in England but on the Continent—the fabrications of Macpherson, and the Rowley poems of Chatterton. Of these the former had an infinitely wider popularity, particularly abroad; and it is not too much to say that they gave a strong and peculiar colouring to poetry, which was even more durable in France and Germany than in England. The works which formed the favourite and almost only poetical reading of Napoleon, and which Madame de Staël assigned as the proof of that wild and pensive melancholy which foreigners considered as characteristic of the English mind, must certainly deserve our notice. The history of this strange imposition is as follows:—James Macpherson, a vain and needy Scotsman, published, about 1760, a small volume of fragments, purporting to be prose translations of ancient legendary poems still current in the highlands of Scotland, and relating, in the Erse or Gaelic dialect of the Celtic language, the exploits of heroes. These Macpherson pretended to have merely put into

English, adopting for the purpose a peculiar abrupt and declamatory but modulated prose, full of bold metaphor and apostrophe, which was itself a new and striking innovation in poetry, and tended to increase the air of authenticity. The success of this volume was immense: and having obtained a subscription to enable him to travel through the wild and solitary mountain districts of his country, Macpherson soon produced a fresh supply of similar remains, among which were several regular heroic narratives of considerable length. The discovery of such a treasury of new and impressive forms of poetry in a savage region, the singular and complete delineations of a very chivalrous tone of manners and sentiment existing at a very remote age, the recurrence of names and events which still lived in the popular legends of the Celtic tribes—all these gave rise to a violent controversy respecting the authenticity of the poems. This controversy Macpherson could have immediately settled by the production of the Gaelic originals, but this he refused or was unable to do; and after long and furious discussions, in which the national vanity of the Highlanders was irritated by the contemptuous incredulity of southern literary men, the Highland Society made minute and extensive investigations (by addressing a circular letter of questions to the Gaelic pastors of the mountain country) to set at rest a question which had almost become a matter of national importance. From the evidence thus collected it appeared, first, that a great many of the names and events which figure in the Ossianic poems were familiar to the legendary recollections of the Highlanders, and even of the Welsh and Irish Celts; secondly, that, though some of the imagery employed by Macpherson was really to be found in ancient Gaelic poems, yet that nothing like those compositions, or any one of them in particular, was to be found existing in the Celtic language in an independent, complete, and substantive form. A critical examination further showed that such a raised, artificial, and theatrical tone of sentiment could never have existed among such a people and at such an epoch as Scotland in the fourth and fifth centuries; and a still more minute inspection established the fatal fact that Macpherson was one of the boldest, most reckless, unblushing plagiarists who ever existed. Homer, Virgil, the Hebrew Scriptures, even later poets of his own country, as Milton and Shakspeare—all had been ransacked to furnish forth images for this Celtic paradise. Wordsworth has well observed that the conceptions of really ancient poetry are invariably simple, direct, distinct. Nature appears to the yet unidealising eye of primitive genius, as she does to the physical eye, well defined and vivid: but in Ossian all is vague, misty, phantom-like. In the early ages of poetry, as in human infancy, the imagination corporealizes the remote: it is the last refinement of the ideal to spiritualise the near.

The perpetual recurrence of the same images in Ossian, the grass waving in the blast, the mist rolling around the grey rock, the lonely tomb of the warrior, the heath, the voiceful torrent, and the dim watery phantom floating over the moonlit desert,—these undoubtedly give a certain impressive wildness, and breathe over the reader's mind a feeling of vague sadness, vastness, and desolate grandeur; but the charm is soon broken, and, after looking for a short time upon the cloudy exaggeration of Ossian as the very top and consummation of the sublime, we return with renewed ardour to the true simple, unaffected splendour of real poetry.

The experiments made by Chatterton upon public credulity, conceived with such boldness, executed with such genius, and persevered in with such haughty stoicism of pride, present one of the most singular phenomena in the history of the human intellect. Of all men,

> "Chatterton, the marvellous boy,
> The sleepless soul, that perish'd in his pride,"

appears to have been the most precocious; and the whole of his short but melancholy tale is a dread proof of the danger of a too early development of intellect. He was born a *man*, his mind burst at once into full flower, and, like some plant made prematurely to bloom, it faded and withered "with all its blushing honours thick upon it." No eulogy can be more wonder-exciting than the simple recapitulation of his history. He was the son of a sexton and parish schoolmaster, and was born at Bristol in 1752. Left an orphan by the death of his father, he passed his infancy in the deepest poverty, and received no other education than that of a charity-school. And yet this child, one of the humblest natives of a provincial town, wrote, at *eleven years of age*, verses which are not only equal to the early productions of any of the extraordinary poets who ever lived, but will more than bear a comparison with the average compositions of his day. With a mind strongly impressed with the peculiar character of the Gothic architecture, of which Bristol affords some noble examples, and exhibiting a peculiar susceptibility to the impressions of Middle-Age art, this miraculous child conceived the idea of forging, not some detached records of antiquity, but a whole literature—of creating a style, a language, an author, a society of the fifteenth century. In this colossal project he succeeded so far as to deceive almost all the literary men of his own day, and to extort from after-times a wondering admiration, which has been almost driven to deny irrefragable philological proof, rather than to grant the possibility of such poems being the forgery of the uneducated son of a Bristol gravedigger.

At the age of fourteen Chatterton was apprenticed to an attorney, and this occupation, however insupportable it may have been to so haughty and sensitive a character, undoubtedly furnished him with new means for the accomplishment of his future experiments on credulity, by making him acquainted with the barbarous Latin and Norman French—the relics of feudal and mediæval phraseology—which abound in the language of English jurisprudence. His first attempt was suggested by the completion of a new bridge over the Avon, when he sent to a newspaper a minute account of the ceremonies that had solemnised the opening of the old bridge, which he pretended to have copied from an ancient manuscript discovered by himself, containing a rich and gorgeous account of civic and chivalric processions, tournaments, miracle-plays, and solemn church ceremonies, with a sermon or benediction pronounced on the new structure by a saint of whom nobody had ever heard! Nor were these wonderful impositions devoted only to gratify the municipal vanity of the public of his native city; his inexhaustible invention found relics of antiquity adapted to the tastes and failings of his friends and acquaintance: to Mr. Burgum, a pewterer of Bristol, who was fond of heraldry, Chatterton gives a pedigree, deducing the descent of the honest tradesman from the days of William Duke of Normandy, and making him the representative, in a direct line, of "Od, Duke of Blois and Earl of Holderness." To a pious divine the youth presents a fragment of a sermon on the Divinity of the Holy Spirit, pretended to have been preached in the fifteenth century; and another person, enthusiastic for the architectural antiquities of the city, is gratified with a minute account of all the churches, the castle, &c., accompanied by drawings of the principal objects, as made by the "gode preeste Thomas Rowleie." These, and a thousand more parchments on the most multifarious subjects, Chatterton pretended to have discovered in an old chest which had been deposited in the treasury or muniment-room of St. Mary Redcliffe, at Bristol, of which church Chatterton's father had been sexton. It was customary in the Middle Ages to secure deeds and other important documents by placing them under the protection of consecrated walls. In this church there had been preserved a number of these chests, and among them one called "Canyng's coffre," containing the deeds, grants, &c., of one William Canyng, a great merchant of Bristol. "Canyng's coffre" had been broken open by order of the magistrates, and all the parchments considered of any importance (grants and specifications of land, houses, &c.) had been taken away. It was among the parchments which remained in the chest that Chatterton pretended to have discovered the extraordinary productions which he gave to the world; and he invented a complete history to explain their nature and contents. He affirmed that the "gode Willyam Canynge," a great and royal merchant of Bristol in the fifteenth century, who had been a great beautifier and benefactor of his native city, had employed the monk, Thomas Rowley, to travel about and collect curiosities for this mediæval virtuoso. Rowley is represented as an artist, as an architect, as a herald, as a dramatist, as a divine. Among the fragments are a number of pastorals in dialogue; a portion of a tragedy on the subject of Ella, a Bristolian hero; an admirable ballad entitled 'The Death of Sir Charles Bawdin;' a number of heraldic notices, plans and elevations of buildings; accounts of painters and stainers of glass — in a word, a most vast and miscellaneous collection of documents, all of them wonderfully interesting, and all tending to redound to the glory of Bristol and the fame of the accomplished and munificent "Maistre Canynge." Examined, however, by the light of the more accurate knowledge of our days, these pretended relics of the fifteenth century are full of fatal and inevitable errors, inconsistencies, and parachronisms: the heraldic devices, for example, are such as rebel against the most fundamental rules of the art; the architecture could never have existed in any age; the very artful employment of old words, from Chaucer and similar authors, proves that Chatterton did not always understand the old French which formed a chief element in his mosaic of obsolete diction (as, for example, he used the Chaucerian word "mormal" in the sense of a dish, whereas it is really a disease — *mort-mal*). These mistakes are of course fatal to the authenticity of the poems, and are only a proof of the enormous difficulty of forging an ancient composition with any chance of permanent success; but they cannot diminish our wonder and admiration for the boldness, the invention, the ingenuity, and perseverance of Chatterton. The diction and orthography he adopted is such as never could have existed at any period of the English language; and perhaps the chief and most fatal weakness of the poems is the facility, harmony, and variety of the versification.

There can be no doubt of the admirable merit of the poems themselves: they are full of genius, and some of them are in the highest degree dignified and sublime; but this beauty and sublimity is certainly not of the fifteenth century; so that whatever glory Chatterton loses as an antiquarian, he more than recovers as a poet. As a poet alone he would, if he had lived, have been the greatest of his age.

After exciting intense interest in Bristol, and giving rise to a long controversy as to their authenticity, these poems were submitted by Walpole to Gray and Mason, who at once decided them to be forgeries: but there still remained many who believed it impossible tha an uneducated lad could have invented such an astonishing mass ot fabrication. Full of the consciousness of intellect, glowing witl the "indomitable pride" of a haughty, sensitive, passionate, ana meditative mind, this unhappy child of genius came to London, with the intention of living by his pen. On, on he struggled, in the midst of the most dreadful poverty, writing political lampoons and contributing to the newspapers and reviews. His life was laborious, almost stoically self-denying; at one time his proud and ardent spirit was revelling in the hope of fame and near success; and when he sent to the mother and sister he so tenderly loved the largest share of his miserable gains, he would prophesy them wealth, honour, power, and reputation; but soon his spirit was plunged again into despondency and despair. It is truly dreadful to follow even in imagination the struggles and the vicissitudes of such an existence—the agonies for mere life, for bread, the agonies of such a soul as Chatterton's. They were not long. After gaining for a short time a precarious subsistence as a writer, and having gradually descended into the very abyss and depth of poverty, he tore up all his papers, shut himself in his miserable garret, and poisoned himself with arsenic, August, 25, 1770. When he destroyed himself *he was not quite eighteen!* On the day before his death he refused the offer of a dinner from his landlady; the fangs of famine must have been tearing at his very vitals with a burning anguish like that of the morrow's poison, and yet his more than Spartan pride revolted at the idea of alms.

His compositions during the latter part of his career, though vigorous and spirited, are not only coarse and scurrilous, but manifestly inferior to the Rowley poems: like the wonderful mocking-bird of the western forests, his note of mimicry was sweeter than his natural song.

The great poet or artist is not he who feels that the common topics of daily life, the universal interests of mankind, are too vulgar to form the groundwork of his creative energy, and who is ever thirsting after the vast, the distant, and the extraordinary. His creations are not like the far and brilliant stars of heaven, but like the daisies at our feet, rooted in the common earth of our nature, and watered by the universal dews of human sympathy. Of the truth of these remarks the literary character of William Cowper is a strong testimony: he is emphatically the poet of ordinary and intimate life, of the domestic emotions, of household happiness. His muse is a domestic deity, a familiar Lar, and his countrymen have enshrined his verses in the very holiest penetralia of their hearths. Cowper was one of the first poets—even among the English—who ventured to describe those familiar thoughts, feelings, and enjoyments which are imaged by the word *home*—that word which echoes so deeply in the English heart, that word for which so many cultivated languages have neither synonym nor equivalent. The life of this great and truly original poet was singularly unhappy; the greater part of it was clouded with insanity, taking one of the most dreadful forms of that terrible disease — a form unhappily but too common in England, *i. e.* religious melancholy. Few things are more touching than the history of Cowper's life, as it is related, with more than feminine grace, innocence, and tenderness, in his own inimitable letters; and we can understand the devotedness with which so many of his friends sacrificed their whole existence to cherish and console a being so gifted, so fascinating, and so unhappy. The dim shadow, too, of an early and enduring but hopeless love, throws over the picture a soft and pensive tint, like moonlight on some calm landscape. His first attack of insanity was brought on by a morbid timidity; and though the disease must have been long latent in his system, it appears to have been carried to a crisis by the agitation which he felt at the idea of appearing before the House of Lords to be examined touching his appointment to an office connected with that portion of our legislature. He was reduced to such agonies of fear and despair, that, after an unsuccessful attempt to commit suicide, he was removed to a madhouse, where he remained a considerable time. When discharged from restraint, with his whole system shattered and tremblingly irritable, he retired to Huntingdon, where he resided in the family of Mr. Unwin, a clergyman, whose friendship greatly contributed to his recovery and happiness. On Unwin's death, Cowper, with the widow of his deceased friend, changed his residence to Olney, in Buckinghamshire, where he contracted a close intimacy with Mr. Newton, the rector of that parish. The seeds of the dreadful malady from which he had already suffered were of course not eradicated, and they were unfortunately ripened gradually into a fatal growth by the fervours of fanatic enthusiasm. Newton was a man of powerful energies, and undoubtedly animated by good intentions, but he was deeply tinged with that exaggerated and gloomy mysticism which is the reproach of the Calvinistic or Low-Church party. Accustomed to pay an undue attention to internal religious impressions, considering every sensation as the immediate interposition of Divine influence, and consequently fostering that spirit of valetudinarianism which is even more fatal to the mind than to the body, a more unfortunate associate for a man in Cowper's sad condition could not be conceived: rest and cheerfulness was the only treatment proper for such a case.

With the narrow inquisitorial spirit of his sect, Newton soon constituted himself the religious adviser — the confessor, in fact — of Cowper, and kept up in his timid, sensitive, impressionable heart, a morbid irritability which nothing but a mind naturally powerful could have resisted.

It is singular enough that Cowper's poetical genius was not exhibited till an unusually advanced age: he was fifty before he obtained any reputation as a writer. During the early part of his residence at Olney, Cowper's existence had been that of a religious recluse: either dreading the agitations of life, or feeling his heart and brain still sore from the recent lashes of disease, he occupied himself with the most tranquil and innocent amusements, making bird-cages, taming hares, and so on. He was again overwhelmed by a new and severe attack of his malady, and it was in recovering from this that he turned to literature as a pastime rather than a serious occupation. Previous to this moment he had written nothing except a collection of hymns, entirely unworthy of his great though as yet undeveloped powers: and it was at the suggestion of Lady Austen, a member of the little affectionate circle of devoted friends by which he was surrounded, that he roused himself to exertions which were to render his name immortal. This lady, a gay and accomplished person, seems to have possessed over Cowper an influence which would have been in the highest degree salutary; but Mrs. Unwin, who feared that the poet's affections might be transferred to a more attractive rival, seems to have forced upon him the alternative of renouncing either the friendship of Lady Austen or her own. In this dilemma, Cowper's obligations to Mrs. Unwin, of course, rendered it impossible for him to hesitate, and he was deprived of the healthy intercourse which might have served to some extent as an antidote against the intoxicating poison of enthusiastic religion. It was Lady Austen who gave Cowper, as a subject for his verse, her sofa, which the poet afterwards expanded into the admirable 'Task:' it was she who related to him the story of 'John Gilpin;' and, in short, her society, had he been happily removed from the fatal influence of the Newtons and Unwins, might have restored Cowper to the world.

In 'The Task,' the first poem by which he became generally popular, he starts from a mock-heroic introduction, in the manner of Ambrose Philips, giving a ludicrous account of the rise and origin of the sofa, and gradually and easily glides into exquisite descriptions of rural scenery, inimitable pictures of homeborn and domestic happiness, and reflections upon all that is most interesting and important in the moral, religious, and social life of man. What must have been the innate strength and nobility of Cowper's mind, which could rise superior (as he generally does) to the wretched superstitions of a narrow-minded and exclusive sect! His versification (for the most part he wrote in blank verse) was at first intentionally made rough and irregular, partly for the purpose of giving a colloquial air to his works, and partly from a false notion that the solemn truths he inculcated would only have been degraded by the ornaments of art: but this error was afterwards much corrected. His language is in the highest degree easy, familiar, and consequently impressive; there is no author who so completely *talks* to his reader—none whose works breathe so completely of the individuality and personal character of their writer. He abounds in descriptions of scenery; and we hardly regret that he should have passed his life among the dull levels of the Ouse, when we think that the power of his genius has given an unfading grace and interest to landscapes in themselves neither romantic nor sublime. It appears to us that he is greatly inferior to Thomson in comprehensiveness and rapidity of picturesque perception; but then his mode of expression is simpler, less ambitious, and in purer taste, and he surpasses not only the author of 'The Seasons,' but perhaps all poets, in the power of communicating interest to the familiar details of domestic life. His humour was very delicate and just, and his descriptions of the common absurdities of ordinary intercourse are masterly. When rising, as he often and gracefully does, into the loftier atmosphere of moral or religious thought, he exhibits a surprising ease and dignity: his mind was of that rare order which can rise without effort and sink without meanness. He is uniformly earnest and sincere; and though in many passages he has shown traces of the bigoted and exaggerated spirit of Calvinistic theology, that tendency to see judgments in the most ordinary accidents of life, and perhaps somewhat too, of the indecorous mingling of religious impressions with the common concerns of daily existence, it is only wonderful how he could have lived so long in the heated atmosphere of enthusiasm, without losing the candour, benevolence, and good sense of his character.

After 'The Task,' Cowper produced a new translation of the 'Iliad' of Homer. He was fully aware of the defects of Pope's version, and endeavoured to approach nearer to the majestic simplicity, the primeval grandeur, of the original; and for this purpose he used blank verse as his medium. But Cowper has failed almost as signally as Pope had done before him: his version is indeed rather more faithful, but it is tedious and monotonous; it has neither the might and ever-varying splendour of the original, nor the delicate artificial graces of Pope, who, if he could not imitate the peculiar and Scriptural sublimity of the Greek—

"The large utterance of the early Gods"—

at least made up for the want of that quality by elegance and sweetness peculiar to himself. Neither the recluse of Olney nor the skilful satirist of Twickenham has approached the rough energy, the truly Homeric fire, or even the resounding oceanic music of old Chapman. The translation of Homer was published by subscription, and was tolerably successful; and shortly after the poet migrated with all his friends to Weston, a beautiful village near Olney. Here he again fell into a deep and increasing gloom of religious despondency, and the death of Mrs. Unwin, in 1796, was the last blow to the unhappy poet's sanity. He lingered on for three years in misery and despair, and died on the 25th of April, 1800. The last verses he ever wrote, 'The Castaway,' form a most melancholy record of his dreadful state of mind, and may be compared with the somewhat similar composition of Byron, written shortly before his death. Both breathe the very music of sorrow, but Cowper's is without hope, and Byron's sadness is dignified by resignation and manly fortitude. His finest and most popular poems are those which contain a mingling of serious reflection, description, and comic painting of character, in which last he has a truly Addisonian grace and delicacy. Some of his minor and more familiar works, as the exquisite lines to Mary (Mrs. Unwin), the verses on his mother's picture, are perhaps unequalled in their particular manner. It is on these, on the 'Table-Talk,' and on 'The Task,' that his reputation is based: it is a glory that will endure as long as our language. Cowper was born in 1731, and died at the age of sixty-nine.

If Cowper be the poet who with a wise boldness has depicted the joys and woes of domestic and fireside life in rural England, painting what he saw and felt, not in the colours of meretricious ornament, but in the sober hues of truth, Crabbe must be considered as essentially the poet of the poor—of the English poor. Cowper contented himself with turning the telescopic glance of poesy into the quiet retreats of virtuous, refined, and educated retirement, while Crabbe directed it into the squalid dens of plebeian misery, the workhouse, the gaol, and the smuggler's hut. It is very singular to observe that Cowper, the man of exquisite refinement and sensibility, of aristocratic birth and elegant tastes, should exhibit in his style and tone of thinking a frequent air of ruggedness and asperity, while his great contemporary, born in the very depth of poverty, and nursed during his hard infancy amid the very scenes of want, of crime, and wretchedness which he so powerfully described, retained in all his works something of the elaborate finish and antithesis of style which Pope so long caused to prevail in English poetry. He has been aptly and wittily styled "Pope in worsted stockings." He was born in 1754, at the miserable coast-town of Aldborough, in Suffolk, and his earlier years were passed amid the squalor of extreme poverty, rendered still more oppressive by the gloomy and violent character of his father. Virgil had a deep meaning when he placed the fiend Want at the portals of the infernal shades where his hero was to gain insight into futurity; Crabbe's long wrestling with his fate no doubt gave him that profound knowledge of human nature which has filled his works with such solemn lessons of pathos and wisdom. The place of his nativity is situated in the ugliest and most monotonous scenery of a flat and swampy coast, and the inhabitants were in harmony with the nature which surrounded them —fishermen, poachers, and smugglers, a savage and demoralized race. After receiving an education far superior to what could have been expected, young Crabbe made an unsuccessful attempt to establish himself as a country apothecary, and, finding himself on the brink of ruin, he took the desperate resolution of journeying up to London, where he arrived without a friend, and with three pounds and some unfinished manuscripts in his pocket. After battling nobly and valiantly and hopefully with all the horrors of disappointment, and at the moment when his last hope seemed to have deserted him, he was lucky enough to attract the notice of Burke, one of the wisest, greatest, and most benevolent men who have ever done honour to our country. With his assistance he brought out his first successful poem, 'The Library.' This was the turn of the tide for Crabbe, and fortune soon began to shower upon him rewards for his patience and manly fortitude. He found patrons on every side, and entered the Church, performing his sacred functions for the first time in his native town of Aldborough. In 1783 appeared 'The Village,' a work which at once stamped him as a great original poet. The principal charm of this work was its masterly description of real nature and actual humble life, and it was mainly composed of studies or recollections of the men and scenes that had surrounded his infancy. Crabbe saw the fatal defect of all the pastoral poetry which had hitherto appeared—its false decorum and feeble distrust of nature. His object was to show the poor

"As truth *will* paint them, and as bards will *not*."

He trusted to nature, and received immortality as his reward. The singular apparent incapability of the society and scenery he took for his subject is only an additional proof that Crabbe's principle of art was correct. He is in poetry what Hogarth is in painting; and if both poet and painter have been accused, not without a show of justice, of dwelling too exclusively upon what is odious and repulsive in reality, and giving a too gloomy and discouraging view of human society, this fault is more than redeemed by the admirable instinct with which they have penetrated into the heart of man, and shown that its strength and weakness, its wisdom and its folly, its majesty and its degradation, are alike in all ranks and classes. Crabbe has read us deep and terrible lessons of human crime and folly, and his lessons are, like Hogarth's, only rendered more impressive and home-speaking by the familiar language in which they are conveyed. His works are very numerous, and all very much alike in merit, in form, in conduct, and in moral. He generally selects some ground or framework offering him the opportunity for displaying his peculiar and admirable talent for minute description of commonplace, ordinary, and often even repulsive scenes and persons. On this ground he introduces a number of detached or episodic tales, generally of lowly and often of the humblest life—sometimes deeply tragic, sometimes full of a quaint and subdued humour. Each story is complete in itself, and depicts some striking episode of internal and domestic life; they are short but awful extracts from the unread pages of the great book of the human heart. The following is a list of Crabbe's works: 'The Village;' 'The Parish Register' (supposed to be an account of the most remarkable births, marriages, and deaths occurring during a year in a country parish); 'The Borough,' a minute and masterly delineation of some obscure country town like Aldborough, with inimitable portraits and biographies of the most remarkable characters, from the highest to the lowest, which figure on such a stage; the 'Tales in Verse,' containing many of his finest specimens of pathos and character-painting; and, lastly, 'Tales of the Hall,' published after a very long interval, during which the poet seems to have remained indifferent to the fame he had acquired. These consist principally of the narratives of two brothers, who meet in old age after a life's separation, and mutually communicate their history of early struggles and adventure. All these works are written in the rhymed couplet of Pope. Crabbe's humour is very dry and quaint, and is sometimes introduced somewhat out of place; but his powers of minute descriptive painting, and his skill in setting vividly before us a scene or a character which at first sight we should consider hopelessly unattractive, were never equalled in literature. Nor is he inferior when delineating either the grander or more familiar manifestations of external nature: the sea, in storm and calm, has perhaps never been so admirably represented in poetry; and in the depicting of the fen, the marsh, the quay, the pauper lodging-house, Crabbe has a power as peculiar and as individual. Nor is he less great and admirable in his descriptions of moral suffering—the pangs of plebeian guilt, the hopeless sorrow of uncomplaining bereavement, the wild phantoms of insanity, the punishment of lost innocence, the unpitied sorrows of poverty, ignorance and neglect.

It remains to mention two or three remarkable works, written in a more lyrical form and measure than those to which we have just alluded. The finest of these is 'Sir Eustace Grey,' the story of a madman related with tremendous impressiveness by himself; of a similar kind is 'The Hall of Justice;' and it would be unjust to quit Crabbe without saying a word of the admirable and touching songs occasionally interspersed among the purely narrative poems. Crabbe lived honoured and respected to a great age, and died in 1832.

Great Britain has been inhabited at various epochs by so many different races that there still exist an immense number of distinct provincial dialects or *patois*, almost as numerous as the shires into which the country is territorially divided.

None, however, of these numerous dialects have ever been employed as a medium of literature; and though a few of our poets (as Spenser in his Pastorals, and Jonson in 'The Sad Shepherd') have made timid and ill-assured essays to employ a true rural dialect in poetry, yet these essays were so partial in themselves, and must be considered to have met with so little success and found so few imitators, that we must say that the *patois* of England properly so called have never been dignified by literary employment. It is remarkable that the dialect adopted in the above cases was that of the Northern border—the counties of Cumberland and Westmoreland; and this dialect approaches very near to the patois of Scotland. But the patois of Scotland forms an exception to the remarks we have just made; and if the reader keeps in mind the distinction insisted on in the first chapter of this little work, he will easily understand how the Scottish dialect early acquired and uninterruptedly retained the character of a literary tongue. The distinction just alluded to is peculiarly important for the foreign student of our literature to keep in mind, as a neglect of it will cause the greatest confusion in his ideas. He must remember that the Scottish *dialect* is totally different from the Scottish *language*. The former (usually called Lowland Scots) is essentially and absolutely English, containing, it is true, a few words and expressions not to be found in the latter speech, some of which have arisen from peculiarities of climate, manners, and natural appearances, and some, singularly enough, being French. It differs from the English of London chiefly in pronunciation, having a broader and more vocalic sound, and possessing not only an exquisite *naïveté* of sentiment, arising from the rustic and pastoral character of the people, but a much more musical and singing intonation, which renders it admirably adapted to be a dress for those beautiful and plaintive national airs for which Scotland has ever been so celebrated, and which that country possesses in greater number and variety than any nation in the world.

In fact, the Scottish *dialect* bears exactly the same relation to English as the Doric dialect bore to Attic Greek, and we find consequently that Scotland, like Sicily, has possessed many a Bion and Theocritus. But it must not be supposed that this dialect was a mere patois: it was the speech of the fair, the great, the witty, and the wise; and as long as Scotland possessed an independent court this beautiful and picturesque dialect was used by the noblest and the most refined. The union of the two kingdoms has of course tended to throw this dialect into disuse among the higher classes of Scotland; but it has been for so many ages sanctified by associations of glory, nationality, and patriotism, it has been the vehicle for so much of the sweetest and most touching poetry, it is so entwined with all the fondest recollections of the people, that it will never perhaps descend to the degraded and local position which the comparatively barbarous patois of the English counties have always occupied. These were the corruptions of peasant-speech — the Scottish dialect was a distinct and highly-cultivated form of language. The Scottish *language* (spoken only in the Highlands) is the Celtic or Gaelic of the ancient Britons, another variety of which is still spoken in Wales, and is totally different in origin, grammar, and sound from English, and quite as unintelligible to the Lowlander as it is to the Londoner. Of this we have no occasion to speak The Lowland Scottish dialect possesses a literature of its own — a literature as rich, as ancient, as peculiar, and as admirable as can be boasted by many cultivated nations. This vigorous tongue has been made the medium for science, for theology, for history, and, above all, for poetry of a very high order. "In the fourteenth century," says Campbell, himself a Scot, "Barbour celebrated the greatest royal hero of his country (Bruce) in a versified romance that is not uninteresting. James I. of Scotland; Henrysone, the author of 'Robene and Makyne,' the first known pastoral, and one of the best in a dialect rich with the favours of the Pastoral Muse; Douglas, the translator of Virgil; Dunbar, Mersar, and others, gave a poetical lustre to Scotland in the fifteenth century, and filled up a space in the annals of British poetry, after the date of Chaucer and Lydgate, that is otherwise nearly barren." Dunbar, indeed, is an imaginative poet of a very high order, and his 'Dance of the Seven Deadly Sins in Hell' is an allegory of astonishing vigour and terrific sublimity — at once Dantesque and Spenserian. As a satirist and painter of comic character Sir David Lyndsay is a writer of whom any nation might well be proud; and Scotland can trace an uninterrupted succession of truly admirable poets, comic, descriptive, pathetic, or narrative, of a merit well worthy of those admirable ballads which are inseparably associated with all that is gayest, tenderest, and most humorous in sentiment, married to the sweetest music in the world.

One of the most remarkable and truly national Scottish poets is Allan Ramsay, whose 'Gentle Shepherd' is perhaps the only modern pastoral which can be compared to the exquisite creations of Theocritus. It is the first successful solution of that difficult problem, to represent rustic manners as they really are, and at the same time so as to make them attractive and graceful. The difficulty of the task will best be appreciated by reflecting on the innumerable failures, from Virgil down to Shenstone, which crowd the annals of literature. But the rustic pictures of Allan Ramsay breathe the freshness of real country life — they have an atmosphere of nature, the breezy freshness of the fields: he has revived the magic of Theocritus, and given us a glimpse into the interior life of the real shepherds, with their artless vigour and unsophisticated feelings. The immense popularity of this poem among the people whose manners it describes (for no other readers could generally either understand its language or appreciate its delicate and local allusions) as well as the existence of a vast body of very beautiful songs, would diminish our surprise that Scotland should have produced a number of poets who devoted to the vernacular literature of their country powers of genius which would have made them immortal on a larger theatre than the one which they selected. The greatest of these was undoubtedly Robert Burns, the glory of his country, and one of the innumerable instances, in which Britain has been so prolific, of genius springing to immortality from the humblest origin. He was born in 1758, and passed the earlier part of his life in struggling (though with little success) against the toils and distresses of a peasant's life. Having been reduced by misfortunes in his humble career as a farmer, and also in some degree by indulgence in the passions accompanying so excitable and poetical a temperament, to the verge of ruin, he was upon the point of quitting his country in despair and emigrating to the West Indies, when the unequalled pathos, splendour, and originality of some of his lyrics struck many influential members of cultivated society, and the poet was induced to remain in Scotland. He now went to Edinburgh, where he reigned for some time the undisputed *lion*, the wonder of that literary capital. His conversation was as brilliant as his genius was pathetic and sublime, but, unfortunately for himself, the poet could not resist the fascinations of social indulgence, and the intoxication of universal applause. He retired again to the country, and, after fruitlessly struggling for some time as an agriculturist, he was obliged, in order to obtain bread for his family, to accept an humble situation in the office of Excise. This employment, so unfavourable both to habits of temperance and to literary occupation, only tended to precipitate the setting of this bright and comet-like intelligence: his constitution, worn out with excesses, passions, and anxieties, was completely broken up, and he died in 1796.

His works are singularly various and splendid; the greater part of them consists of songs, either completely original, or recastings of such compositions of older date: in performing this difficult task of altering and improving existing lyrics, in which a beautiful thought was often buried under a load of mean and vulgar expression, Burns exhibits a most exquisite delicacy and purity of taste, and an admirable ear for harmony. His own songs vary in tone and subject through every changing mood, from the sternest patriotism and the most agonising pathos to the broadest drollery: in all he is equally inimitable. Most of his finest works are written in his own Lowland dialect, and give a picture, at once familiar and ideal, of the feelings and sentiments of the peasant. It is the rustic heart, but glorified by passion, and elevated by a perpetual communing with nature. But he has also exhibited perfect mastery when writing pure English, and many admirable productions might be cited in which he has clothed the loveliest thoughts in the purest language. Consequently his genius was not obliged to depend upon the adventitious charm and *prestige* of a provincial dialect. There never perhaps existed a mind more truly and intensely poetical than that of Burns. In his verses to a Mountain Daisy, which he turned up with his plough — in his reflections on destroying, in the same way, the nest of a field-mouse, there is a vein of tenderness which no poet has ever surpassed. In the beautiful little poem 'To Mary in Heaven,' and in many other short lyrics, he has condensed the whole history of love, its tender fears, its joys, its frenzy, its agonies, and its yet sublimer resignation, into the space of a dozen lines. No poet ever seems so *sure* of himself; none goes more directly and more certainly to the point; none is more muscular in his expression, encumbering the thought with no useless drapery of words, and trusting always for effect to nature, truth, and intensity of feeling. Consequently no poet more abounds in those short and picturelike phrases which at once present the object almost to our senses, and which no reflection could either imitate or improve. What can be more wonderfully condensed than his picture of a patriot warrior—

"Pressing forward *red-wat-shod*"?

it is absolutely Shakspearian.

But the religion in which Burns is—not perhaps the most supreme, but the most alone, is that of familiar humour, mingled with a kind of sly and quaint tenderness. Scottish external nature is in his poems represented in its every phase, in its every shade of variation; but he is yet more admirable when he delineates the interior life of his own thoughtful and moral countrymen. There have never been traced by the hand of man such full, such tender, such living picture of rustic life as Burns has left us. The half-serious half-humorous tale of 'Tam o'Shanter,' with its fantastically terrific *diablerie*, the satiric gaiety of 'Holy Fair,' the 'Scotch Drink,' the 'Elegy on Matthew Henderson,' the 'Address to the De'il,' all bear witness to the wonderful diversity of his powers, to his deep sympathy with all that is noble and touching in rustic life, and to his intensely national vein of mingled tenderness and humour. The true poet is he who finds the most of beauty and of dignity in the universal feelings and interests of human life: and increased wisdom and sympathy (the infallible attendant on increased wisdom) is rapidly tending to make all mankind echo the exclamation of Burns when he wept at the sight of a lovely and peasant-peopled scene: "The sight," he said, "of so many smoking cottages gave a pleasure to his mind, which none could understand who had not witnessed, like himself, the happiness and the worth which they contained." One of his most admirable poems, 'The Cotter's Saturday Night,' is nothing but an amplification of this profound and beautiful sentiment

CHAPTER XVII.

SCOTT AND SOUTHEY.

Walter Scott—The Lay of the Last Minstrel—Marmion—Lady of the Lake Lord of the Isles—Waverley—Guy Mannering—Antiquary—Tales of my Landlord—Ivanhoe—Monastery and Abbot—Kenilworth—Pirate—Fortunes of Nigel—Peveril—Quentin Durward—St. Ronan's Well—Redgauntlet—Tales of the Crusaders—Woodstock—Chronicles of the Canongate—Anne of Geierstein. Robert Southey—Thalaba and Kehama—Madoc—Legendary Tales—Roderick—Prose Works and Miscellanies.

THERE is no author in the whole range of literature, ancient or modern, whose works exhibit so perfect an embodiment of united power and activity as is to be found in Walter Scott. He is as prolific as Lopé de Vega, as absolutely original as Homer. He was descended from one of the most powerful and ancient houses of Scotland; and though his father (a writer to the signet in Edinburgh) was rather an active and intelligent lawyer than a representative of Middle Age nobility, yet the spirit of clanship which still so strongly pervades Scottish society was enough to unite the poet in sentiment as in blood to the great and powerful family of Buccleugh. Having received in his childhood a slight injury, which rendered him during his whole life a little lame, though it did not ultimately affect the strength of a robust and athletic body, he passed some of his earliest years among the romantic scenery of his own beautiful country—scenery where every spot had been the theatre of warlike or necromantic tradition. Scott afterwards passed through a regular course of education, first at the High School and afterwards at the University of Edinburgh, where he appears, without distinguishing himself by any extraordinary triumphs, to have acquired the good opinion of his teachers, and to have become very popular among his comrades, partly by his stores of old legends, and not less by his frank, bold, and adventurous character. It is not easy to conceive a finer specimen of humanity than Scott. His frame was vigorous and manly, even surpassing the ordinary size and strength; his features, though not classically regular, were animated and attractive; and his character was an admirable union of imagination, of good sense, and of good nature. Power, in short, and goodness were stamped upon the man, both within and without. On completing his education he became a member of the Scottish bar, and was ultimately appointed, through the recommendation of the head of his clan, the Duke of Buccleugh, sheriff of Selkirk, to which appointment were afterwards added one or two others. As a lawyer his success, though not extraordinary, was respectable. The society of Edinburgh was at that time unusually rich in men of literary and philosophical accomplishments, and it was, moreover, enlivened and diversified by many relics of the political struggles of the '45—old Jacobite gentlemen, whose manners supplied the future novelist with many of his most admirable characters, and whose adventures furnished him with many a wild tale of bravery, persecution, and escape—the traditions of a romantic age which was rapidly passing away.

Henry Mackenzie, the author of 'The Man of Feeling,' and one of the ornaments of Edinburgh literary society, had introduced into Scotland a taste for the ballad-poetry of Germany. It was from the study and admiration of Bürger and the minor lyrists that the English began to turn their attention to the Teutonic muse; and Scott translated the 'Lenore' and other small compositions, chiefly of that wild and spectral character which might have been expected to possess so much novelty for the British public. These translations, some of them executed with great spirit and fidelity (as for example the version of Goëthe's 'Erl König'), were contributed by Scott to Lewis's 'Tales of Terror,' the first attempt to give specimens of German literature in England. After having, by the exercise of reason and good sense, recovered from an early love-sorrow, Scott married a young lady of the name of Carpenter, who was possessed of a small fortune, and retired to a cottage, where, in the very flower of his youth and surrounded by domestic happiness, he prepared for future glory by steady and uninterrupted labour.

From very early youth he had exhibited a most intense passion for the ballad-poetry in which his own country is even richer than England itself; and we know that in childhood his imagination had been lighted up by the repeated perusal of Percy's 'Reliques of Ancient English Poetry'—that admirable collection which was not only the germ of the great romantic revolution in literature, but which has perhaps tended more than any book since Homer to inspire the youthful writer with a passion for natural unsophisticated sentiment and vivid description. After translating 'Goetz von Berlichingen,' Scott travelled over the Border district, collecting new stores of ballads from old peasants and wandering rhapsodists, and thus rescuing from oblivion some of the finest pictures of simple pathos and heroism, and many curious documents of the history of that interesting region: these were published in three volumes, entitled the 'Minstrelsy of the Scottish Border.' Nothing could be better calculated as a preparation for the future triumphs of the romantic poet and novelist of Scotland than this task of love; and the necessary antiquarian reading and investigation must have supplied him with an immense store of the materials he so well knew how to use. He afterwards published another work of a similar nature — a commentary on the singular poetical fragments attributed to Thomas of Erceldoune, said to have lived in the thirteenth century.

The first of that long and splendid line of poems whose glory was only to be effaced by the intenser splendour of his novels, was 'The Lay of the Last Minstrel,' published in 1805, and received by the public with rapturous delight. In its plan, its versification, in the whole design and execution, this was a new and perfectly original production; the reader was presented with a picture, fresh, vigorous, vast, and brilliant as Nature herself. It is a tale of sorcery and chivalric adventure, as vivid and bright as a real poem of the Middle Ages, as faithful, as minute, as picturesque in its details; yet at the same time imbued with the finer sensibility of modern literature, and adorned with all the splendours of modern art. The tale is supposed to be related by a wandering minstrel, the last of a profession once so honoured; and the *framing* of the legend is at once exquisitely beautiful in itself, and admirably calculated to set off and relieve the narrative. The description of the aged and wandering minstrel,—the diffidence with which he begins his legend in the presence of the great lady, and tries to recall the inspiration of vanished days,—and the glorious bursts of truly Homeric fire when he gets into the full tide of minstrel inspiration,—all this is as fine as it is original in conception. Each canto is appropriately and artfully introduced with some passage of description or reflection; and these introductions are among the most exquisite specimens of Scott's picturesque and enchanting style. The tale itself is not very well constructed, and, though many of the supernatural events are impressive, the character of the Goblin Dwarf is unnecessary to the plot, and generally felt to be a blemish. The detached scenes — solemn, exciting, or gorgeous — are the real strength of the poem. The night-journey of Deloraine (an admirable embodiment of the rude mosstrooping borderer) to fulfil the command of the Lady of Branksome; the description of Melrose Abbey by moonlight; the scene of the opening of the tomb of Michael Scott, and the taking of the book of gramarie from the dead hand of the mighty wizard; the description of Lord Howard,—all these are absolutely unequalled in their particular manner. Most authors who have attempted to evoke the shades of buried ages raise them before our eyes, as Samuel was raised by the witch of Endor, rather like shadows than with the consistency of reality. Scott *revivifies* them; and, what is a still greater triumph of art, he puts the spectator into the condition of a contemporary: we not only see the things, but we see them as through the eyes of the Middle Ages. The versification of this poem, and of most of its successors, consists principally of the rhymed octosyllabic couplet, founded on the favourite measure of the Norman Trouvères. This measure, peculiarly well adapted to lively narrative, Scott varies, in passages expressive of passion or more violent movement, with an occasional short Adionic verse interposed at irregular intervals among the octosyllabic lines, which in the latter circumstances rhyme together, not uniformly in pairs, but often in threes or fours. This kind of verse he wields with consummate ease; and though he seems always to have written with extraordinary rapidity, and to have been nowise assiduous to polish or correct, yet so exquisite was his ear, that there are few poets whose versification is more varied and flowing, or more infallibly echoes the feeling and sentiment of the moment.

Scott had now fairly begun that wonderful career which produced more of beautiful and wise, and in a more astounding variety, than perhaps the whole history of literature can parallel. His activity was inexhaustible, and he was perhaps more accurately, extensively, and minutely versed in the details of Middle Age art, letters, and social life, than any man of genius who ever existed. In 1808 appeared 'Marmion,' a tale somewhat similar in its scenery and treatment to the 'Lay,' concluding with the fatal field of Flodden. The hero is an English knight, valiant and wise, but profligate and unscrupulous; and his adventures, which principally take place in Scotland, give the poet many opportunities for his inimitable painting of natural scenery, of chivalrous life, and of interesting historic personages, in particular of King James VI. Marmion himself is finely conceived, but the expedient of bringing about the catastrophe by representing such a character, however wicked, as forging documents, is a fatal blemish to the probability of the intrigue in such an age and country. But this defect of *costume* is amply, gloriously redeemed by the splendour, fire, energy, and livingness with which brilliant and varied scenes succeed each other in this magnificent evocation of chivalrous days. The voyage of the nuns is one of the very finest pictures even in Scott's vast gallery: the reader is carried bounding on like the bark; the verses breathe the very freshness of the sea. In the scene describing the immuring of Constance before the grim tribunal in the vaults of Lindisfarn Abbey, Scott has ventured into the lofty regions of terror and pity; and how wonderfully is this awful episode contrasted with the exquisite grace of the Scottish court, when the fair Lady Heron sings the ballad of Lochinvar! The battle-scene with which this poem concludes is indeed, to use the words of Shakspeare,—

> "A fearful battle render'd you in music."

The majestic pomp of preparation, the breathless pause, the roaring onset, the struggle, the carnage,—all is there: the reader feels his teeth setting, his breath held in, his blood rushing backward to the heart: it is as real as anything in the Iliad; and the wail of lamentation and defeat, and the death of the conscience-haunted Marmion, form a most admirable and appropriate conclusion to that woful day

> "Of Flodden's fatal field,
> Where shiver'd was fair Scotland's spear,
> And broken was her shield."

Two years after this noble work, was produced 'The Lady of the Lake,' perhaps the completest and finest poetical conception of this astonishing genius. In this poem the scene is transferred to a region still more new to English readers, and more picturesque in itself: the country surrounding the beautiful Loch Katrine, and situated on the borders between the civilised Lowlands and the mountains inhabited by the Celtic tribes, is the theatre of the action, and the feuds between the two races (ever at enmity) its principal material. The intrigue, though simple enough, is artful and interesting; it consists partly of the adventures of King James, who has lost his way in the chase, and is received with hospitality in the secret retreat of his former favourite, Douglas, now banished and disgraced; and partly of his knight-errant-like encounter (in disguise) with Roderick Dhu, the formidable chief of a Highland clan which has long defied the power of the Lowland monarch. Roderick, the stern and haughty chieftain; Ellen, the daughter of the Douglas line, yet graceful and simple as peasant maiden; old Allan Bane, the harper; Douglas, with his proud heart swelling under the remembrance of his king's ingratitude, — what noble types of character, and how freely and unaffectedly do they move before us! Certainly nothing can be finer than the approach of Roderick along the lake, the duel between him and Fitz-James, or the death of the captive Highland chieftain. Scott appears to have been conscious of his peculiar power of describing battles, for he makes the harper relate to Roderick in prison the combat between the captive's clan and the troops of King James, and perhaps even the noble and stirring description of Flodden does not surpass the battle of Bealan Duine in 'The Lady of the Lake,' and the death of Roderick, in the mid swing and fury of the minstrel's rhapsody, is nobly and touchingly conceived. It would be unjust to speak of the exquisite descriptions of scenery, both lovely and sublime, with which this poem (particularly its earlier portion) is crowded, without mentioning also, and with equal praise, the charming glimpses into private life which the poet takes as he goes along, and the splendid descriptions of customs, superstitions, &c., which form the subordinate decorations of the work. Few things are more truly pathetic than the little episode of the poor maniac, Blanche of Devon, more impressive than the scene of the Fiery Cross, more exciting than the narrative of the rapid flight of that ensign of war and blood to summon the clansmen to the trysting-place.

After this, perhaps his greatest poetical triumph, Scott somewhat changed the direction and form of his productions: his next work, which appeared in 1811, was 'The Vision of Don Roderick,' founded upon a striking legend which relates that Roderick, the last Gothic King of Spain, persisted, in spite of all dissuasion, in descending into a subterranean vault beneath the cathedral of Toledo, where he saw, prefigured in a kind of phantasmagoria, the invasion of the Moors, and all the ills which his own unbridled passions were to inflict upon his house and kingdom. Scott has somewhat enlarged this impressive groundwork, and made to pass before the eyes of the impious monarch, not only the irruption of the Moorish conquerors, but also the dreadful cruelties and oppressions of the armies of Napoleon. It is written in the Spenserian stanza, and with something of the Spenserian richness and cumbrous profusion of ornament and allegory; and it would seem that in quitting the *trouvère* metre, which he wielded so nobly, Scott had lost much of his peculiar nerve and fire.

Two years after this not very successful effort in a new line, Scott returned to his old one, and published 'Rokeby,' and 'The Bridal of Triermain,' which appeared within a single twelvemonth. In the former of these poems he most injudiciously selected a period too modern, and in general there is perceptible in this work a faintness and uncertainty of hand which is not altogether redeemed by a few beautiful passages. In the other work a short adventure, taken from the old books of chivalry, is related with much grace and vigour, but the enchanted castle is too dreamy and unsubstantial to interest us like 'Marmion, or 'The Lady of the Lake;' and our feeling of probability is outraged by the way in which the magical and fabulous is brought in contact with the action of a real knight. The purely fabulous part, describing the amour of King Arthur with the fairy lady, the reappearance of their daughter at the tournament of Carleon, the tourney itself, and the enchanted slumber of the maiden in the castle of the Valley of St. John — all this is in the finest vein of Romanz poetry. Nor is the description of the watching of the knight unworthy of our chivalric Homer, but the adventures which break the spell of this "sleeping beauty" seem to us not in the finest vein of Middle Age conception. They are rather like the chivalry of a ballet than a page from the *Morte Artus.*

In 1814 appeared 'The Lord of the Isles,' a romantic narrative, in which the principal personage is the heroic Robert Bruce, some of whose almost incredible adventures Scott has skilfully and picturesquely recalled. The action is chiefly carried on amid the savage and desolate scenery of the Western Isles, particularly in the castle of Artornish, and afterwards amid the still bleaker and more tremendous deserts of Galloway. The catastrophe is the great battle of Bannockburn, and the poet's patriotism has fired the description of this event, so glorious in the reminiscences of every Scot, with a glow and *œstrum* which recalls the concluding stanzas of 'Marmion.' But the story is rather entangled, and the march of the events is sometimes languishing and sometimes precipitate.

We have but two more poems to mention, 'The Field of Waterloo,' and 'Harold the Dauntless,' of which the former appeared in 1815, and its companion in the following year. 'Waterloo' was written while the impressions of a recent visit to that battle-field were still fresh in the poet's mind; but the work (which is fortunately short) is entirely unworthy of the author's genius and glory In 'Harold the Dauntless' we have the story of a wild and savage Berserkir, who is recalled by love from his fierce idolatry to civilization and Christianity. The principal character is not ill conceived, but the adjuncts and general character of the poem are rather chivalric than Scandinavian; and though some of the events are in character with the wild legends of the Norwegian Sagas, yet the effect of the whole is not in harmony with the design.

Even so early as 1805, at the period when 'The Lay of the Last Minstrel' burst, like a new *avatar* of the beauty and power of mediæval art, upon the public of Great Britain, Scott had commenced a prose tale embodying some of the striking scenes connected with that romantic event of Scottish history, the gallant but disastrous expedition of Prince Charles Edward, *i. e.* the unsuccessful attempt of the Jacobites to replace upon the British throne the house of Stuart. This event (commonly called the Rebellion of the '45) involved a very great number of the most ancient houses of Scotland, and it should be remembered that that country was markedly inclined to prefer the party of the Stuarts to that of the succession of the house of Brunswick. This period of strong passions and vehement contrasts of political feeling was of course fertile in originality of character, singular traits of courage, and surprising vicissitudes of fortune, and Scott was personally acquainted with a multitude of "old '45 men," as they were called, whose adventures he was very fond of relating, and whose feelings he has immortalized in so many of his admirable fictions. The first sketch of this novel was abandoned after a few chapters only had been composed, and the sheets were put away in an old writing-desk with a quantity of fishing-tackle, and almost totally forgotten by the author. On the appearance, in 1813, of 'Rokeby,' and 'The Bridal of Triermain,' poems which were considered by the public as manifestly inferior to his preceding compositions, Scott's admirable common sense suggested to him that his peculiar poetical vein of chivalrous fiction was now almost exhausted, and that there was little hope that he could, by continuing before the public in the same strain of Middle Age revival, vie with the already dazzling poetical reputation of Byron, which had as it were taken England by storm.

He turned his thoughts to prose; and, drawing the unfinished MS. of which we have spoken from its inglorious repose in the writing-desk, he completed the tale, and it appeared in 1814, the same year as 'The Lord of the Isles,' under the title of 'Waverley, or 'Tis Sixty Years since.' This was the first of that illustrious series of prose fictions which have placed Scott, it is hardly too much to say, almost upon a level with Shakspeare. The novel was published anonymously, and the public instantly perceived that a new era in the history of fiction had begun. The plot is exceedingly simple, and not remarkable for any great ingenuity; but the absolute novelty of the scenery, the immense number, richness, and variety of the characters, the brief, picturelike, and inimitable sketches of natural beauty, and the freedom, freshness, and naturalness of the situations, comic as well as elevated, soon excited an universal rapture of admiration.

The *tone* in Scott, like that of Shakspeare, is always an essentially noble and elevated one — *elevated* and *elevating*. All objects are shown, as it were, through a fresh and sunny atmosphere: all is in its true colour, proportion, and perspective, but glorified by a genial glow of goodness and humanity. Many of the characters of 'Waverley' are masterpieces: the brave, gallant, but pedantic old Baron Bradwardine is equally delightful amid the feudal splendours of his ancestral bears, and scribbling his texts of Livy on the walls of his cave. What noble figures are those of the haughty Vich Ian Vohr and his high-souled sister; how full of life and movement the camp of the insurgents; how pathetic the trial of the rebels; how exquisite the thousand minor characters which crowd these living pages—the fantastic "innocent" Davie Gellatlie, with his snatches of song, as pathetic as the ballads of Ophelia herself—the pig-headed Balmawhapple—the faithful Micklewham and Callum Beg! Scott had the true Shakspearian quality of going out of himself to create —of throwing his own mind so completely into the subject immediately before him, that the creator seems successively to be absolutely identified with all his creations.

The universal enthusiasm which greeted the appearance of 'Waverley' had hardly time to subside into calm admiration when 'Guy Mannering' was published (in 1815, the next year). This novel exhibits a still wider range of power than the preceding one. It did not rely upon the prestige which attaches to a romantic episode in history, and to the interest derivable from the introduction of historical personages and adventures so interesting in themselves as those connected with the '45. In 'Guy Mannering' we enter upon a new and more domestic sphere, the family of a simple Scottish country gentleman, and we find ourselves in the midst of characters, common and every-day enough in their definition, but admirably brought out and contrasted. Scott's personal experience and his legal recollections probably supplied him with nearly all the types of common and low life which he has so admirably individualized in this enchanting story: but with what consummate tact has he avoided the tone of exaggeration and romance which their employment would be very apt to inspire! If the highest manifestation of creative genius be the power of inventing scenes and persons which are at once surprising and natural, strongly individual in themselves yet in perfect accordance with the types of reality, then it is impossible to deny Scott the honours due to the highest creative genius Horace says emphatically, "difficile est propriè *communia* dicere;" and his remark, extended in its application so as to embrace the inventive as well as the expressive in art, is a formula of criticism of great value. The union of the abstract and the concrete is the highest triumph of art. It was the boast of Apelles that he used only four primitive colours in his pictures, and the history of all literature proves that the greatest triumphs of genius have ever been attained by the use of the simplest elements of external or moral existence. It is the mere vibration of a stretched chord that speaks the unutterable language of music; and it is from the skilful contrast and genial study of most ordinary human characters that Scott has read us his noblest lessons of wisdom and of love. Dominie Sampson is one of those admirable *hits* of conception which enter, at once and for ever, like Shakspeare's characters, into the sphere of reality. We think of him not as a creation of genius, but as a *man*, we involuntarily place him in our thoughts beside Uncle Toby, Parson Adams, and Lear's Fool. Nor are the minor elements less admirable: the two young ladies (the most difficult of all characters to render interesting) are delicately and charmingly contrasted; Pleydell (supposed to be a sketch from nature), Henry Bertram, the scoundrel Glossin, Mac Morlan, — all, down to honest Jock Jabez the postilion, are living, natural, unforced, unaffected. In this romance the events which bring about the ruin of the rascally Glossin, and restore Bertram to the inheritance of his ancestors, are at once natural and surprising: the funeral of the old Laird, and the sale of his estate; Henry Bertram's wanderings in the wastes of the Northern Border; that breathless episode where he is concealed by the gipsy in the ruined hut of Derncleugh; the visit of Mannering to Edinburgh, and the legal saturnalia of High Jinks; the funeral of the old maid, and the inimitable scene of the opening of her will; and, above all, every passage in which Dinmont makes his appearance,—we may boldly say that all these scenes, and a thousand others, are set before us with astonishing freedom, ease, and power.

In 1816 appeared 'The Antiquary,' which gives us a new and not less interesting glimpse into the interior life of the Scottish people, and gives another proof of the all-embracing and inexhaustible character of the great man's genius. The chief personage in this novel, the Antiquary himself, is a truly genial creation — as complete and as individual as Jaques or Falstaff; and the book abounds, even more wonderfully perhaps than Scott's other works, with perfect and happy strokes of human character: we need only mention the worthy but weak Sir Arthur, Miss Grizel Oldbuck, Hector McIntyre, the warlike Baillie, and, above all, Edie Ochiltree. The passage describing the party caught by the rising tide at the foot of the cliffs is perhaps unequalled; and the mixture here, as well as in others of Scott's works, of familiar and even ludicrous incidents with the most powerful and terrific emotions, is another strong element of the writer's power. In our remarks upon Shakspeare we observed that his mingling of trivial and agitating ideas is one of the peculiar conditions of the *very highest* power of genius.

In the same year with this exquisite work appeared the first series of 'The Tales of My Landlord,' containing the 'Black Dwarf' and 'Old Mortality;' the first of which was much shorter and less powerful than its companion. These tales were preceded by a kind of fictitious introduction, attributing their authorship to Peter Pattieson, an usher in a village school — an expedient (adopted to mislead the public as to these tales being the composition of the now illustrious "Author of Waverley," for which purpose also a new publisher was selected) neither very happy in itself nor very felicitously executed. The presiding genius—the *Deus ex machinâ* — of 'The Black Dwarf' (the deformed misanthrope who gives name to the tale) is one of those irregularities of nature which inspire rather pity than interest; and though — as in this instance, Elshie the Recluse being drawn from a real personage—of occasional occurrence in the actual world, are yet too rare, and too repulsive consequently, to form a proper foundation for a plot of real life. Scott's genius had no need of dwarfs and monsters to set agoing the wheels of his intrigue: these are the resources of inferior inventors. Elliott and his family, and the wolfish mosstrooper, Willie of the Westburnflat — the two poles, so to say, of border character — are contrasted with consummate skill.

The companion-novel to 'The Black Dwarf' was 'Old Mortality,' a fiction of much higher pretensions, greater length, and completer historical interest: indeed this is one of the very finest fictions that the world has ever seen. It describes the adventures of the Scottish Covenanters from the skirmish of Drumclog to the great battle, so fatal to their cause, of Bothwell Brigg. The tale opens just after the murder of Archbishop Sharpe, and the hero of the intrigue, a young gentleman who is led, by conviction no less than by family sympathies, to embrace the cause of the insurrection, is naturally and easily brought in contact with the most remarkable men of both parties, and is involved in the full vortex of events. Thus we have splendid sketches of the famous Claverhouse, of General Dalziel, and other celebrated royalists, and on the other hand a most admirable picture of the fierce, persecuted, and fanatical Covenanters. There has perhaps seldom been a finer example of the difficult feat of mingling in one delineation real and fictitious things and events. Claverhouse, for example, is as individual, and yet as ideal, as Talbot, or Wolsey, or Henry V., in the historical plays of our divine dramaturge.

Of the purely invented characters in this grand creation it is impossible to speak in too high terms; nor of their variety, nor of their truth, nor of the wonderful power with which the author has harmonized them with the solider personages borrowed from history. To the reader, indeed, they appear to have no less consistence, and he cannot refrain from associating them with the authentic events when he afterwards reflects upon the annals of the times. The Lady of Tillietudlem, Mause Headrigg and her son Cuddy, the old Major and his veteran servant Pyke, the mean and griping Milnwood, Serjeant Bothwell, the kind but grumbling housekeeper—all these are almost real existences, as real as the loftier conceptions of the covenanting preachers and their wild followers: Mucklewrath, and the fierce and crafty Burley, advancing gradually from fanaticism to crime, and from crime to religious frenzy. There is also a very deep knowledge of the human heart in the manner in which the character of Morton, the hero, is gradually modified by the stern and agitating scenes which he passes through; and the touches of simple pathos, the exquisite scenes of rustic gaiety, and the innumerable nooks of tranquil domestic life or lovely rural nature into which we glance, as it were, while borne onward by the interest of the story—all these form a picture which has the vastness, the minuteness, the distinctness, and the splendour of life itself.

In 1818 was published the second series of the 'Tales of My Landlord,' comprising 'Rob Roy' and 'The Heart of Midlothian.' In 'Rob Roy' Scott has again ventured, and more boldly, into a region which he had visited with such success in 'The Lady of the Lake' and in one portion of 'Waverley.' The Highlands form the theatre of action, and the exploits of the famous freebooter who gives name to the work the most prominent materials of this fiction. These scenes and manners, then quite new to the English reader, and which even an inferior talent could hardly render uninteresting, are admirably diversified, and connected with characters and events of a much more familiar kind. The sketch of a London merchant in Mr. Osbaldistone, with which the tale commences, is very finely conceived, and no less so the charming character of Owen, the faithful clerk. The scene soon changes to the North of England, where the family of a rude fox-hunting squire is exquisitely contrasted with that most delicate and lovely of all Scott's creations, the beautiful Di Vernon.

Nor can any thing be finer than the Highland scenes and characters which fill the greater part of this book: how romantic and yet how real is Rob Roy himself; with what an atmosphere of wild energy is the far-famed freebooter — the Robin Hood of Scotland — surrounded; and yet how skilfully has the author, by intermingling perpetual details of familiar life and common feeling, brought him, as it were, near to us, giving him flesh and blood, and substituting the genial air of everyday humanity for that misty and unsubstantial grandeur which an inferior author would have left around it! Helen Macgregor is a conception of a very high order of art, and the scene of the defeat of the English detachment and the horrible punishment of the wretched Morris is intensely exciting. The comic incidents, too, mingled here as everywhere in Scott's more tremendous and impressive scenes, only add to the effect, and give a more intense reality to the narrative. Constructively speaking, the chief defect of Scott's romances arises from the hurried manner in which he winds up his narratives. He probably always (as indeed he has told us himself) laid down, when commencing one of his fictions, a plan or ground-plot of the whole intrigue; but the intensity with which the scenes presented themselves to his glorious imagination, and the delight (which to such a mind must have been, and was, unspeakable) of tracing through every ramification such a character as Dalgetty, for instance, or Baillie Nicol Jarvie, or Monkbarns, or Bradwardine, or Dominie Sampson, soon carried him from the outline he had fixed upon, and forced him, at the risk of writing not a novel but a library, to hurry hastily over the conclusion. To a conception like his, joined with so intense and wonderful a perceptive faculty, the delineation of such personages must have given the double delight of the inventor and the historian. What he absolutely created as *ideal*, he must have anatomised as *real*.

In 'The Heart of Midlothian' we have a narrative of humble — nay, the humblest — peasant life of Scotland. We have here the joys and woes, the weaknesses and the heroism of the poor; described with no affected raptures of sentimentalism, with no unreal views of life, neither *suppressio veri* nor *suggestio falsi* — a simple tale of obscure sorrow and unadorned heroism, connected with pictures of society as vast and varied as they are accurate and lively. The Edinburgh riot with which the tale opens is described with a power that even this picturesque author has never surpassed; and the frightful and agitating scenes of popular vengeance are most skilfully made to give way to the calm repose of rustic existence. David Deans is one of those grim, strongly-marked, yet not unattractive portraits which are as characteristic of Scott's pencil as the spectacled rabbis and alchemists and burgomasters of that of

Rembrandt. The two daughters are exquisitely contrasted — the unhappy Effie, with her beauty, her innocent vanity, and the pretty wilfulness of the spoiled child; and when the ploughshare of sin and shame and sorrow drives so ruthlessly over this nook of human life, and the "Lily of St. Leonard's" is crushed to the earth, how artlessly, how sublimely does Jeannie arise to save her erring sister! Among all the tributes which genius has ever paid to the modest heroism of rustic life, this is perhaps the noblest and the most enduring; and when we revere the name of Scott for the glory which he has thrown over human nature by this noble and touching delineation, let us remember that it was not all fictitious, and that the same country which gave birth to him who has recorded this triumph of village heroism was also the fatherland of a real Helen Walker.

The following year witnessed the appearance of 'The Bride of Lammermoor' and the 'Legend of Montrose'—forming the third series of the 'Tales of My Landlord.' The 'Bride' is a work which differs remarkably in its tone from Scott's other productions: it has been well remarked that this touching and most painful story exemplifies in a narrative form the incessant action of Destiny — of that awful and mysterious power which vivifies and pervades the ancient Greek tragedy. We see, even at the very beginning of the tale, the "little cloud, no bigger than a man's hand," which gradually overshadows the whole atmosphere, and at last bursts in ruin, in madness, and in despair over the devoted heads of Ravenswood and his betrothed. The catastrophe is tremendous, crushing, complete; and even the more comic scenes (the melancholy ingenuity of poor faithful Caleb) have a sad and hopeless gaiety, which forms a dismal and appropriate relief to the profoundly tragic tone of the action. One scene in this awful tale is truly terrific — the muttered cursing of the three hideous hags at the ill-omened marriage; nor is the interview between Ravenswood and the gravedigger, or the appearance of the unhappy hero to claim his promise from Lucy Ashton, inferior. They bear the impress of our elder dramatists: they might have been conceived by Ford, by Middleton, or by the sombre genius of Webster.

In the 'Legend of Montrose' Scott returns into his more usual and congenial sphere of bright, vivid, energetic, and picturesque animation. We come forth, saddened and yet elevated, out of the Valley of the Shadow of Death, and we plunge with fresh ardour into the sparkling, buoyant waves of romantic life. The tale is very short and hurried; and though it contains several scenes drawn with Scott's usual power of lively description, it is not generally found in itself one of the most interesting, but derives its principal charm from the humours of "Rittmaster Dugald Dalgetty," a soldier of fortune, one of the most truly rich, admirable, amusing, and natural personages ever drawn by the hand of genius. This character is a masterpiece: the mixture of pedantry, conceit, valour, vulgar assurance, knowledge of the world, greediness, and a thousand other qualities, makes him uniformly and never-failingly delightful whenever he appears, as he does almost constantly, on the scene.

The last series of the 'Tales of My Landlord' were followed by a number of detached romances, more than maintaining the reputation which Scott had already acquired; *in one year*, 1820, appeared 'Ivanhoe,' 'The Monastery,' and 'The Abbot,' the last-mentioned work being a continuation of the second, though at the same time capable of being read as a distinct narrative. In 'Ivanhoe' our magician has evoked a new period of English history, and one which had never before been revived in fiction. This was the romantic age of Richard Cœur-de-Lion; and it offered the occasion not only of showing in strong opposition the sturdy prejudices and rude manners of the Saxons and the warlike and splendid civilization of the Norman race, but of introducing many of the most remarkable characters of our popular history — the Lionheart himself, the abominable John, and our legendary heroes of the bow and quarter-staff, Robin Hood and his "merry men." The rude log-built mansion of the Saxon noble, the frowning battlements of the Norman castle, the glittering lists of Ashby, the dungeon, the hermitage, and the "good green wood,"—every object remains for ever pictured on the reader's memory. And then the characters: Cedric, Wamba, Gurth, Front-de-Bœuf, Locksley, Friar Tuck, Le Noir Fainéant, Rebecca, Isaac the Jew, the stern Master of the Templars—all, down to the humblest, arise before our astonished eyes "in their habit as they lived."

'The Monastery' is principally injured by the introduction of supernatural machinery. The White Lady of Avenel, a kind of tutelary spirit protecting the fortunes of a noble family, is not in accordance with that air of reality which Scott communicates to all his fictions. The appearances of this tricksy spirit are indeed beautifully described, and the poetry which conveys her oracles — "for still her speech was song"—is exceedingly graceful; but her agency is unnecessary, it impedes the story, and some of her pranks are quite unworthy of the dignity of her mission. All that she does could have been effected much better without her; and she is invariably found to jar with the rest of the action. Christie of the Clinthill is a spirited sketch of the lean, wolfish, dissolute Jackman; and the scenes in the castle of Julian Avenel are drawn with a powerful and pathetic hand; but the enthusiast, Sir Piercy Shafton, though amusing, is a caricature of what was already a caricature of Shakspeare's. Generally speaking, this novel is less admired (we think deservedly so) than its successor, 'The Abbot,' in which we resume the adventures of the two brothers whom we left in 'The

Monastery' just entering upon life. The chief personage is the unhappy Mary Stuart, whose character and misfortunes possess in fiction a power of tender and pathetic interest as inexhaustible as the fascination she exerted on all around her during her life, and which no lapse of time seems likely to deprive of its enchantment. The *dramatis personæ* of this great and living work are numerous and splendid: the Regent Murray, the stern and haughty Lady Douglas, Catherine Seton, Adam Woodcock the falconer, Roland Græme,—all are stamped with life and individuality. Nor is the breathless interest of the principal events less worthy of admiration, nor the fresh animation and vivacity of the dialogues, nor the noble spirit of dignity and gentleness that pervades the whole.

The following year, 1821, was signalised by two more productions of this astonishing being, two singularly different, not only from each other, but from all which preceded them, and marked by the same power and beauty: these were 'Kenilworth' and 'The Pirate.' Kenilworth was a gorgeous pageant of a period of our history dear and glorious to every English heart—the reign of Elizabeth. The chief action is the secret marriage of the great and splendid Leicester, Elizabeth's favourite, with a beautiful woman of inferior rank, and the fatal facility with which the haughty courtier, listening to the dictates of ambition and the perfidious advice of a wicked intriguer, sacrifices to the hope of becoming the Queen's husband the happiness and the life of his innocent victim. Much of this romance is founded on fact: the splendid revelries of Kenilworth are copied from authentic documents of the time, only vivified and gilded by the glow of genius; Sussex—the frank and noble Sussex—Raleigh, Leicester himself, Elizabeth, are faithful and glorious reproductions of history; and the manners, costume, and, so to speak, atmosphere of the whole work afford perhaps the noblest instance which literature can show of the power of genius to evoke past ages and persons in the brilliant hues and motion of life. Perhaps, amid the thousand fictions of the so-called romantic school to which the success of Scott gave birth, there are no scenes even approaching in probability, in ease, grace, and splendour, to the audience in this romance where the lion-hearted Queen commands the reconciliation of Leicester and Sussex, to the episode of Raleigh's first court success, to the passages in the country hostelry of the Black Bear, to the entry of Elizabeth into Kenilworth; and assuredly the power of pathetic terror was never displayed more intensely and with a more Shakspearian conciseness than in the murder of Amy Robsart.

In 'The Pirate' we have a new and untrodden region, new manners, a new nature; we are transported to the "stormy Hebrides,"

"Placed far amid the melancholy main,"

and inhabited by a people of ancient Norwegian descent. Even in this barren nook of earth, where human character might be expected to be as monotonous as its starved and storm-lashed herbage, he has found a rich harvest of interest and beauty: the noble old Udaller; his two daughters, each so lovely a picture, yet distinguished with so gentle a touch, like Celia and Rosalind; Norna of the Fitful-head, half-maniac, half-pythoness; Claude Halcro, Mistress Bahie, and the unfortunate Yellowley, Bunce, and the whole company of buccaneers.

The next romance we have to mention is 'The Fortunes of Nigel,' which appeared in the following year, 1822. Here we have a glimpse into the city life of London in the sixteenth century, and the action is as vast, as crowded, and as varied as the theatre. The court and the domestic manners of the weak and pedantic, but well-meaning James I., that crowned humorist; the shop, the street, the tavern, the ordinary, the theatre, and above all, the squalid retreats of crime and misery—Alsatia; everything appears before us in its true colours, with its true light and shade and true proportion, and peopled with figures so varied, so life-like and individual, that after reading the novel we cannot divest ourselves of a firm conviction of the reality of persons, places, and events. So much so, indeed, is this the case with nearly all Scott's historical novels, that, when we afterwards find in authentic history any proofs of occasional incorrectness or even anachronism in these fictions, we deny the evidence of our reason, and cannot be induced to think that the manners, the characters, or the events, *could* have been otherwise than as the artist has represented them. Thus it is hardly a paradox to say, that the creations of sublime genius are more real than reality, more true than truth itself; and that we really know more of the character of Hamlet, for instance, than we do of Napoleon, or even of a man with whom we are in daily personal intercourse. In this novel of 'Nigel' the character of King James is a case in point to our remark; and the numerous other *dramatis personæ* are marked by the same power. The murder of the old usurer in Whitefriars is a most terrific bit of night-painting, and the action flows on with a clear and rapid current.

The year 1823 again gave to the astounded world three excellent nd wonderfully varied fictions—'Peveril of the Peak,' 'Quentin Durward,' and 'St. Ronan's Well.' In 'Peveril' we have a picture of English society soon after the restoration of Charles II., and many pictures of the court and of the various parties which divided the nation at the period of the ridiculous panic of Titus Oates' pretended popish plot. The most interesting characters are Sir Geoffrey Peverel, a stout old Derbyshire cavalier; a finely marked sketch of a fanatical republican, Major Bridgenorth, a relic of the Protectorate; and, above all, Charles himself, the easy, heartless, good-natured libertine.

"Who never said a foolish thing,
And never did a wise one."

Villiers, the profligate Duke of Buckingham, is brought prominently forward; but in attempting to give identity to that extraordinary compound of vices, follies, wit, and inconsistency, our novelist has signally failed. He followed the admirable character given in Dryden's immortal satire, and produced, not a man, but a bundle of epigrams. The plot of this piece is chiefly carried on by Christian, one of those passionless and all-penetrating intriguers whom we so often see in novels, and so seldom in real life; and his principal instrument for the attainment of his purpose (a long-cherished plan of revenging on the Countess of Derby the death of his brother) is the employment of a deaf and dumb girl, who afterwards turns out to be his own daughter, and to have been *shamming* deaf and dumb for a long succession of years. All this is hardly natural, and not worthy, even if it were, of such a genius as that of Scott.

'Durward' carries us to France and Burgundy in the reign of Louis XI., and we follow with unceasing delight and interest the progress of a young Scottish soldier of fortune to fame, riches, and the hand of a fair countess. His first interview with Louis, who is disguised as a mean old merchant, and attended by his abominable minister Tristan l'Hermite, is highly dramatic, and the gradual view we gain of the dark and tortuous character of that cruel and miserable king, and his gloomy retreat in the castle of Plessis, is extremely fine. None of Scott's works is more powerfully conceived than this, nor has he in any other instance displayed a broader and vaster canvas, filled up with more striking and varied groups. The vile instruments which the subtle monarch employs to carry out his perfidious policy—the catlike barber Oliver le Dain, Tristan and his two congenial satellites Petit André and Trois-Echelles, the wretched Bohemian—how finely are these relieved against the nobler characters, historical as well as fictitious, and how admirably are they all grouped around the grand images of the two protagonists—Louis, and Charles of Burgundy, the wolf and the bull of middle-age history, one the emblem and embodiment of Fraud, the other of brutal Force! Dunois, Crèvecœur, Galeotti, Crawford, the rude bravery of the Balafré—it is absolutely impossible to draw any line of distinction between the phantoms of real men evoked by this "mighty magic" from the dusty tomb of history, and those created by its power. The scenes at Peronne are written with a firm hand and a sort of triumphant mastery, which almost makes us forget the terrific impressiveness of the attack on the bishop's castle at Liège, and the murder of the good prelate by the ruffian De la Marck.

In 'St. Ronan's Well' we have scenes and manners of modern society, but the approaching misfortunes of the illustrious novelist seem to have thrown a shade of gloom over the work which its very merits only render more painful to the reader. This contrast of tone is the more perceptible, as Scott's view of life and mankind is in general cheerful and genial. The story is of a deeply painful and tragic kind, and throughout the work we are haunted with the presentiment of ill, hopeless, inevitable, rendered the more insupportable by the meanness, the frivolity, and the baseness of the majority of the persons. This same mournful presentiment of impending fate forms in 'The Bride of Lammermoor' the great charm — the awful fascination of the work; but there it is unmingled with contempt for the personages: it is rendered solemn, dignified by distance; here it is vulgarised by the general tone of the *dramatis personæ*, and we feel the pang of sorrow without the dignity which can half console us. Touchwood, however, is a spirited sketch of a character which Scott had not before attempted to portray; and Meg Dods, the old innkeeper, is a delineation in his happiest vein.

In 1824 appeared 'Redgauntlet,' a novel in which (though the story is somewhat confused and imperfect) we find some admirable studies of character, and some scenes delineated with extraordinary power. Fairford, the old Scottish lawyer, is exquisitely real, and it is more than probable that it is a portrait of Scott's own father; many of the legal scenes and personages are doubtless reminiscences of the author's own personal experience, and Peter Peebles and his trial are as fine as anything in Fielding. We have always considered, too, that Nanty Ewart, the smuggling captain in this novel, is a *chef-d'œuvre* worthy to be placed beside Scott's most admirable creations, and the scene in which he recounts his early life among the most inimitable passages of fiction. Of the art of tale-telling Scott has given in this romance two most consummate examples — this story of Nanty Ewart, and the unsurpassable ghost-story told by the blind fiddler to Darsie Latimer. The two friends are charming and highly-finished delineations; Joshua Geddes, the worthy quaker, is very attractive; and Thomas Turnbull, the hypocritical smuggler, as superlative as Ewart.

The next year brought forth the first series of the 'Tales of the Crusaders,' containing 'The Betrothed' and 'The Talisman.' Of these two the first is so much inferior to the other, that we shall pass very rapidly over it; it contains very few striking scenes, and those chiefly of a warlike character: but in 'The Talisman' we have one of the finest, most glowing, and most enchanting revivals of the days of chivalry, vivified by the introduction of splendid historical personages and exploits dear to the national heart. It is an episode of the crusade in which the Lion-hearted King achieved those exploits which furnished such inexhaustible matter to the rhapsodists of the Middle Ages, and associated his fame with the fondest recollections of chivalric glory. Into this sea of splendid achievement and gorgeous pageantry Scott threw himself with the passion of a Trouvère, with the power of a consummate artist, and the erudition of an antiquarian. We repeat, without fear of contradiction, that we know no work so truly Homeric in its effect as this. How finely conceived, too, are the female characters, Edith and Queen Berengaria; and what a crowd of noble figures are grouped around the heroic person of the king — Saladin himself, Philip of France, the wicked Hospitaller, the Knight of the Leopard! We are here in the very midst of mediæval chivalry; and, what is more wonderful, we do not regard its splendid pageants with mere unlearned and unsympathising curiosity, but the poet's true epic enthusiasm inspires us, in spite of ourselves, with the feelings of contemporaries.

Scott's ruling passion was for the life of a British country gentleman. His sweetest reverie was the hope of transmitting to his descendants, not only a name famous in Border annals, and glorified by intellectual triumphs, but a landed estate sufficient to support its splendour. To attain this object he laboured with an almost superhuman industry; and the immense revenue which he never ceased to derive from his works he devoted to the purchase and augmentation of his landed estate, and to the building of Abbotsford. Here he transformed a small house, situated on the banks of his beloved Tweed, and in the midst of a wild, bare, and dreary scenery, into a fairy castle—a "romance in stone and lime." The natural dreariness of the scene he remedied by vast plantings of trees, and on the house and surrounding estate he employed not much less than 70,000*l.* Here he lived, in the true splendour of a castellan, and here he delighted to receive, with the graceful hospitality he loved to practise, the fair, the noble, and the famous, and here he "did the honours for all Scotland." It is hardly possible to conceive a higher point of happiness than this. In the prime of life, blessed with a promising family to continue his name; loved, venerated, nay, almost adored by his dependants, his friends, his countrymen, Europe — the whole world; in the full flush and vigorour of his powers, for he never relaxed during his whole life his unremitting industry, (managing, by early rising and regularity, to leave his days free for society); this surprising man had not only conferred upon the profession of letters a splendour which it had never before known—he must be held to have attained as near felicity as humanity could aspire. But the blight was already at work at this noble tree; the worm was gnawing at its core; it was soon to fall prostrate, with all its honours thick upon it, and give the world at once a memorable example of the instability of human things, and a most touching proof of fortitude and greatness of mind. Scott's earlier works had been published by his friend John Ballantyne, and the secret of their authorship had been preserved with a constant and surprising fidelity; but in an evil hour the novelist entered into a kind of concealed partnership with him; and the commercial distresses of 1826 involved the firm in the failure of Constable and other great publishing speculators. Some idea of this tremendous crisis may be formed when we state that Scott's liabilities were not under 117,000*l.* From this consequence of unfortunate speculation Scott might have in a great measure escaped by taking advantage of the indulgence of the English law, but with more than the spirit of chivalry, this great man conceived the colossal project of paying off with his pen this huge mountain of debt. This incredible plan he conceived, and, what is more, almost executed! But he perished in the effort: he kept unstained the ancestral honour of his house, and unspotted the pure glory of his name, but he burst his mighty heart in the unequal struggle. On learning the full extent of his frightful losses, he immediately abandoned the rural splendour which he adorned, shut himself up in an humble lodging in Edinburgh, and set valorously to his huge task. In *six years* it was almost accomplished—in six years he had produced new and hardly less splendid works than the long bright series we have been examining; but Scott himself—the martyr of his commercial integrity—was dying in exhaustion, in delirium, and disease. Perhaps the annals of literature do not present so sublime and so touching a fact as this: it is a fact which has a peculiar significancy to an Englishman, as it is a noble instance of that chivalrous delicacy of commerce to which our country owes a mercantile grandeur, power, and supremacy, as peculiar and as unrivalled as the wisdom of her senates or the glory of her arms.

The historical tale of 'Woodstock' was the first result of his indomitable energy in resisting this great disaster: it was published in 1826. Its subject embraces some of the most exciting episodes of the civil war, and the characters of Cromwell and of Charles II. figure in many of its finest scenes. But the gem of the book is the noble old cavalier, Sir Henry Lee of Ditchley, one of the most complete and touching embodiments of highborn loyalty that ever was conceived. The tale is full of movement, variety, and picturesqueness, and the minor personages too are stamped with strong vitality: Wildrake, the three Commissioners, Jocelyn Jolliffe, Cromwell's canting but resistless soldiers—all, even down to Bevis the majestic stag-hound, are such figures as no author but Scott could have drawn. Indeed we may mention here that a peculiar love for *dogs* was one principal mark by which these wonderful novels were ascribed to him, long before the confession of the great man identified beyond all dispute the author of 'Waverley' with Walter Scott. There are very few of this admirable series of works which do not contain some exquisite portrait of a dog. Who can forget Bevis (in this novel)—that truly comic and attractive generation of Mustards and Peppers which the mere mention of Dandie Dinmont conjures up in our minds—or the noble Roswal, lying wounded beside the banner of St. George—ay, or even Wolf, the ragged attendant of

Garth the swineherd? Scott enters into the personality of the dog character—his affection, his courage, even his humours and caprices. This is no weak indication of a great and noble heart. The escape of the King in Woodstock, the ineffectual search of Cromwell for the royal fugitive, and, above all, the deeply touching concluding scene, the good old knight's *euthanasia* at the triumphal moment of the Restoration—all these are in Scott's very finest manner. It was at this period that the great poet threw aside the mask of incognito: at a public dinner at Edinburgh Scott claimed the authorship of all these admirable fictions, which had, however, almost from the first, been universally attributed to him on the simple ground that nobody else *could* have been the author, and no less from a vast mass of internal evidence distinctly pointing at him as the only man whose nation, genius, profession, tastes, and even prejudices, perfectly coincided with the general character of the works.

In 1827 appeared the 'History of Napoleon'—a work of vigour and liveliness, but written too near the gigantic events which it commemorated, and too much tinged with the strong national and political prejudices of the author, to be permanently valuable. Scott's strong Tory and legitimatist principles, and his attachment to the English Episcopal Church, rendered him incapable of justly appreciating the greatest fact of modern history—the French Revolution—and, consequently, of judging fairly (conscientiously as he strove to do so) of the political and legislative character of Bonaparte; and it was hardly to be expected that an enthusiastic patriot in England, at the very moment of his country's triumph, could hold with a steady hand the balance of historical impartiality.

In the following year appeared the two series of the 'Chronicles of the Canongate,' the first containing 'The Highland Widow,' 'The Two Drovers,' and 'The Surgeon's Daughter;' and the second the single novel, 'The Fair Maid of Perth.' The fiction which serves as introduction to this collection is written with great acuteness and knowledge of life, but is tinged with something of that desponding tone which we objected against 'St. Ronan's Well.' Of these tales, the two first, though exceedingly slight, are powerful and pathetic; but the third, particularly the scenes in India, exhibits a marked want of vividness and condensation. In 'The Fair Maid of Perth' this glorious lamp of genius and wisdom seems to give a dying and convulsive flash; for, in spite of a very perceptible languor in the narrative, some of the scenes (as the battle between the Clan Chattan and the Clan Quhele) are delineated with strong touches of the old minstrel fire; and the character of the smith, Henry of the Wynd, is worthy of his most glorious days. What is general in the above remarks may be applied also to "Anne of Geierstein,' published in 1829, though the work met with a more satisfactory success from the circumstance of the scene being a new and hitherto untrodden one, Switzerland. 'Anne of Geierstein' is closely historical in its tone; and the episode concluding with the execution of Pierre de Hagenbach, the tyrannic governor of La Ferette, is vigorous and striking. The Swiss deputies, particularly the noble old Landamman, are contrasted with strong dramatic power to the splendid and haughty Charles; the scene of the reception of the embassy is very fine; though there is in this novel nothing approaching in tragic pathos and majestic intensity of feeling to the death of Lady Witherington in 'The Surgeon's Daughter.' The Alpine storm with which 'Anne of Geierstein' opens is grand and poetical; and the character of the good but childish King Réné is very exquisitely drawn.

The last fictions of this wonderful writer were 'Castle Dangerous' and 'Count Robert of Paris;' the former a chivalric episode in the Border wars, and the latter a scene from Byzantine history. Both works, though received by the public with grateful indulgence, present melancholy evidence that the gigantic task undertaken by Scott was too Herculean even for his untiring energy and heroic courage. A first stroke of paralysis in 1830 was unable to arrest his industry; but a second, in 1831, rendered it necessary for his family to divert him from the incessant literary labour which his mind, though now ruined, still continued to perform. The Government placed at his disposal a ship of war; and he visited Malta, Naples (where he resided about four months), and ultimately Rome. Through these fair regions was carried this venerable and illustrious wreck, and he was brought home to die. He lingered on some little time at Abbotsford, helpless, unconscious, and patient; his mind wandering to his professional employment, and sometimes to that princely hospitality he so nobly exercised, listening to passages from the Bible and his favourite poet Crabbe, but never once referring to those magnificent monuments of genius by which he had immortalised his country and glorified humanity itself. "About half-past one P.M.," says Mr. Lockhart, his son-in-law and biographer, "on the 21st of September, 1832, Sir Walter breathed his last, in the presence of all his children. It was a beautiful day—so warm that every window was wide open—and so perfectly still that the sound of all others most delicious to his ear, the gentle ripple of the Tweed over its pebbles, was distinctly audible as we knelt around the bed, and his eldest son kissed and closed his eyes."

His miscellaneous works are exceedingly numerous and valuable. The 'Tales of a Grandfather,' remarkable episodes of Scottish history related for children, is perhaps one of the most admirable books for the very young that was ever composed, and may be read with delight at any age. The 'Lives of the Novelists,' and his innumerable contributions to the 'Edinburgh Review' and other critical journals, are rich, genial, and full of a fine spirit of learning and wisdom;

their only defect is their too universally laudatory tone; for Scott, who never had an enemy, seems incapable of saying a harsh thing. No man—and certainly no literary man—ever passed so long and so illustrious a life without a single personal enmity. His character was as amiable, generous, manly, and social, as his genius was varied and sublime.

The life of Robert Southey, extending from 1774 to 1843, was a rare instance of unremitting literary activity; and the immense collection of miscellaneous works which he left behind him is highly honourable to his learning and his talents, though it is only as a prose writer that he is likely to descend to posterity. He began life as a violent partisan of the principles of the French Revolution; and in his earlier works—the ridiculous drama of 'Wat Tyler,' and the extravagant and tedious epic, 'Joan of Arc'—he devotes all his powers to the support of extreme liberal opinions. He soon, however, abandoned his early principles, and became one of the most thoroughgoing supporters of monarchical and conservative doctrines; was named, in 1813, laureate, and exhibited in the maintenance of his new political creed as much fervour, virulence, unscrupulousness, and, it is but just to say, sincerity also, as he had shown for the Utopian theories of a republican millennium. To give some idea of the uncompromising and extreme character of his political predilections, we need only mention that in 'Joan of Arc' he has painted as the blackest of tyrants our heroic sovereign Henry V., and placed the Emperor Titus among the "murderers of mankind," while, in the later stage of his political transformation, he has raised the more than almost morbid obstinacy of George III. to the honours of an absolute canonisation!

In 1801 was published 'Thalaba,' and in 1810 the 'Curse of Kehama,' two works of a narrative character, which have many points of resemblance. They are both, in their subject, wild, extravagant, unearthly, full of supernatural machinery, but of a kind as difficult to manage with effect as at first sight splendid and attractive. 'Thalaba' is a tale of Arabian enchantment, full of magicians, dragons, hippogriffs, and monsters. In 'Kehama' the poet has selected for his groundwork the still more unmanageable mythology of the Hindoos—a vast, incoherent and clumsy structure of superstition, more hopelessly unadapted to the purposes of poetry than even the Fetishism of the savages of Africa. The poems are written in an irregular and wandering species of rhythm—the 'Thalaba' altogether without rhyme; and the language abounds in an affected simplicity and perpetual obtrusion of vulgar and puerile phraseology. The works have a most painful air of *laxity* and want of intellectual *bone and muscle.* There are many passages of gorgeous description, and many proofs of powerful fancy and imagination; but the persons and adventures are so supernatural, so completely out of the circle of human sympathies both in their triumphs and sufferings, and they are so scrupulously divested of all the passions and circumstances of humanity, that these gorgeous and ambitious works produce on us the impression of a splendid but unsubstantial nightmare: they are *ægri somnia*, the vast disjointed visions of fever and delirium. In 'Thalaba' we have a series of adventures, encountered by an Arabian hero, who fights with demons and enchanters, and finally overthrows the dominion of the powers of Evil in the Domdaniel caverns, "under the roots of the ocean." It is more extravagant than anything in the 'Thousand and One Nights;' indeed it is nothing but a quintessence of all the puerile and monstrous fictions of Arabian fancy. In the Oriental legends these extravagances are pardonable, and even characteristic, for in them we take into the account the childish and wonder-loving character of the audience to which such fantastic inventions were addressed, and we remember that they are scattered, in the books of the East, over a much greater surface, so to say, whereas here we have them all consolidated into one mass of incoherent monstrosity. We miss, too, the exquisite glimpses afforded us by those tales in the common and domestic life in the East. 'Kehama' is founded upon one of the most monstrous superstitions of Hindoo belief, viz. that a man, by persisting in an almost incredible succession of voluntary penances and self-torture, can acquire a control over the divinities themselves: and in this poem a wicked enchanter goes near to overthrow the dominion of Brahma, Vishnoo, and Seeva. The poem is full of demons, goblins, terrific sacrifices, and pictures of supernatural existence; and the slender thread of human (or half-human) interest is too feeble to unite them into a whole. These poems, like everything of Southey's, exhibit an incredible amount of multifarious learning; but it is learning generally rather curious than valuable, and it is not vivified by any truly genial, harmonising power of originality.

In the interval between the publication of these poems appeared a volume of metrical tales and the historical epic of 'Madoc.' In the tales, as in general in his minor poems, Southey exhibits a degree of vigour and originality of thought for which we look in vain in his longer works. Some of his legends, translated from the Spanish and Portuguese (in which languages Southey was a proficient), or from the obscurer stores of the Latin chronicles of the Middle Ages, or the monkish legends of the saints, are very vigorous and characteristically written. The author's spirit was strongly legendary; and he has caught the true accent, not of heroic and chivalric tradition, but of the religious enthusiasm of monastic times: and some of his minor original poems have great tenderness and simple dignity of thought, though often injured by a studied meanness and creepingness of expression; for the fatal error of the school to which he belonged was a theory that the real everyday phraseology of the common people was better adapted to the purposes of poetry than the language of cultivated and educated men; and thus the writers of this class often labour as industriously to acquire the language of the workshop and the nursery as the poets of Louis XIV. after an artificial dignity and elevation.

'Madoc' is founded on one of the most absurd legends connected with the early history of America. Madoc is a Welsh prince of the twelfth century, who is represented as making the discovery of the Western world; and his contests with the Mexicans, and ultimate conversion of that people from their cruel idolatry, form the main action of the poem, which, like 'Joan of Arc,' is written in blank verse. The poet thus had at his disposal the rich store of picturesque scenery, manners, and wonderful adventure to be found in the Spanish narratives of the exploits of Columbus, Pizarro, Cortes, and the Conquestadors. But the victories which are so wonderful when related as gained over the Mexicans by the comparatively well-armed Spaniards of the fifteenth and sixteenth centuries, are perfectly incredible when attributed to a band of savages little superior in civilization and the art of war to the people they invaded. Though the poem is crowded with scenes of more than possible splendour, of more than human cruelty, courage, and superstition, the effect is singularly languid; and the exaggeration of prowess and suffering produces the same effect upon the mind as the extravagance of fiction in the two Oriental poems. There is nothing that requires so firm and steady a hand to manage as the extraordinary; the modesty of nature, the boundary of the possible, once overstepped, the reader's curiosity grows more insatiable as it is more liberally fed. When we have had a giant twenty feet high, we require one of sixty; if the hero conquers a dragon which vomits poison, we soon want him to overthrow a monster which belches fire; and so on in an infinite series, till all is extravagance, monstrosity, and childish gaping folly.

'Kehama' was followed at an interval of four years, by 'Roderick, the Last of the Goths,' a poem in blank verse, and of a much more modest and credible character than its predecessors. The subject is the punishment and repentance of the last Gothic king of Spain, whose vices, oppressions, and in particular an insult offered to the virtue of Florinda, daughter of Count Julian, incited that noble to betray his country to the Moors. The general insurrection of the Spaniards against their Moslem oppressors, the exploits of the illustrious Pelayo, and the reappearance of Roderick at the great battle which put an end to the infidel dominion, form the materials of the action. The king, in the disguise of a hermit, figures in most of the scenes; and his agonizing repentance for his past crimes, and humble trust in the mercy of God, is the keynote or prevailing tone of the work. Though free from the injudicious employment of supernatural machinery, and though containing some descriptions of undeniable merit, and several scenes of powerful tenderness and pathos, there is the same want of reality and human interest which characterises Southey's poems in general, and the tone is too uniformly ecstatic and agonizing. His personages, like his scenes, have something unreal, phantomlike, dreamy: they are often beautiful, but it is the beauty not of the earth, or even of the clouds, but of the *mirage* and the Fata Morgana. His robe of inspiration sits gracefully and majestically upon him, but it is too voluminous in its folds, and too heavy in its gorgeous texture, for the motion of real existence: he is never "succinct for speed," and his flowing drapery obstructs and embarrasses his steps. He has *power*, but not *force*—his genius is rather passive than active.

On being appointed poet laureate he paid his tribute of court adulation with an eagerness and regularity which showed how complete was his conversion from the political faith of his youthful days. A convert is generally a fanatic; and Southey's laureate odes exhibit a fierce, passionate, controversial hatred of his former liberal opinions which gives interest even to the ambitious monotony, the convulsive mediocrity of his official lyrics. In one of them, the 'Vision of Judgment,' he has essayed to revive the hexameter in English verse. This experiment, tried in so many languages, and with such indifferent success, had been attempted by Gabriel Harvey in the reign of Elizabeth, and the universal ridicule which hailed Southey's attempt was excited quite as much by the absurdity of the metre as by the extravagant flattery of the poem itself. The deification, or rather beatification of George III. drew from Byron some of the severest strokes of his irresistible ridicule, and gave him the opportunity of severely revenging upon Southey some of the latter's attacks upon his principles and poetry.

Southey was a man of indefatigable industry; his prose works are very numerous and valuable for their learning and sincerity, but the little 'Life of Nelson,' written to furnish young seamen with a simple narrative of the exploits of England's greatest naval hero, has perhaps never been equalled for the perfection of its style. In his other works—the principal of which are 'The Book of the Church,' 'The Lives of the British Admirals,' that of Wesley, a 'History of Brazil,' and of the Peninsular War—we find the same admirable art of clear vigorous English, and no less that strong prejudice, violent political and literary partiality, and a tone of haughty, acrimonious, arrogant self-confidence, which so much detract from his many excellent qualities as a writer, and as a man, his sincerity, his learning, his conscientiousness, and his natural benevolence of character.

In his innumerable critical and historical essays, chiefly contributed to the 'Quarterly Review,' in the 'Colloquies' (a book of imaginary conversations composed on a most absurd plan), and in the strange miscellaneous work entitled 'The Doctor,' we see a gross ignorance of the commonest principles of political and economic science, and an arrogant, dictatorial, persecuting tone, which render these works melancholy examples of the truth that intolerance is not always naturally associated with weakness of intellect or with malignity of heart.

CHAPTER XVIII.

MOORE, BYRON, AND SHELLEY.

Moore: Translation of Anacreon, and Little's Poems—Political Satires—The Fudge Family—Irish Melodies—Lalla Rookh—Epicurean—Biographies. Byron: Hours of Idleness, and English Bards—Romantic Poems—The Dramas—Childe Harold—Don Juan—Death of Byron. Shelley: Poems and Philosophy—Queen Mab, Prometheus Unbound, Alastor, &c.—The Cenci—Minor Poems and Lyrics.

We have seen how the name of Walter Scott was the type, sign, or measure of the first step in literature towards romanticism, or rather of the first step made in modern times *from* classicism—from the regular, the correct, the established.

The next step in this new career was made by Thomas Moore, who broke up new and fresh fountains of original life, first in the inexhaustible East, and secondly in his native Ireland. In the former field, indeed, it may be thought that he was perhaps anticipated by Southey, so many of whose poems are on Oriental subjects; but these two poets are sufficiently dissimilar to absolve the author of 'Lalla Rookh' from the charge of servilely copying, or, indeed, of following, the writer of 'Thalaba' and 'Kehama:' in the latter and more valuable quality, of a national Irish lyrist, he stands absolutely alone and unapproachable.

Thomas Moore, the Anacreon and Catullus, perhaps in some sense the Petronius and the Apuleius also, of the nineteenth century, was born in Dublin in the year 1780. Belonging essentially to the middle class, and a Roman Catholic besides, it may be easily conceived how he must have sympathised in the deep discontent which pervaded his country at that agitated period. Moore passed some time at the university of his native city, and soon after gave proof that he had made a more than ordinary progress in at least the elegant department of classical scholarship. His first work was a translation into

English verse of the 'Odes' of Anacreon, in which he exhibits a very great extent of reading, and no mean proficiency in Greek philology. The translation, however, is much more valuable as giving us an earnest of the poet's future powers than as a faithful reproduction of the original: it is more interesting as Moore than as Anacreon: it is Irish rather than Greek.

Canova is said to have exhibited his Venus in a sort of close recess, surrounded by crimson drapery, and lighted by a single lamp; he is even said to have slightly tinged the marble with a faint rosy glow; and this is what Moore has done to Anacreon. He has diffused over his version a rapturous and passionate air not in harmony with the unadorned simplicity of the Greek; he is fanciful where the original is sensuous. The reputation, both as poet and as scholar, which Moore acquired by his Anacreon, combined with his musical and conversational talents, immediately introduced him to the refined and intellectual society then assembled round the Prince of Wales, afterwards George IV.; for the heir apparent had surrounded himself (as naturally happens in a constitutional monarchy) with a strong phalanx of opposition wits and statesmen, and Charles Fox and Sheridan arrayed themselves with the Prince and against the existing government of the King.

In 1803 Moore received an appointment in the island of Bermuda, which he not long afterwards lost through the malversation of a person employed under him, whose dishonesty exposed Moore to the prosecution of the government, and involved him in difficulties from which he did not easily extricate himself. During his absence from England, both in the beautiful Antilles and his subsequent retirement at Paris, he continued to be an industrious author. We must mention a small volume of 'Odes and Epistles,' written in singularly easy and graceful language, with very little pretension to elaborate finish (he calls them himself "prose tagged with rhyme"), but exhibiting the dawning of those powers which were to render him unequalled in a peculiar and very difficult line. The other production of this period was a small collection of poems, almost all of an erotic character, and some translated from Catullus, and other poets, Greek and Latin, of the same class. This volume was published under the pseudonym of "Thomas Little," and the merit of its contents, though occasionally great, was not sufficient to counterbalance the sensual and immoral tone of many of the pieces. In this respect 'Little's Poems' are indeed open to very severe reprehension, and, without affecting any Pharisaical degree of moral severity, we may affirm that they have really done a great deal of harm.

He now commenced a long series of political satires—light arrows of ridicule aimed against men and measures, generally only of a temporary interest, but so sharply pointed with wit, so lightly feathered with grace and *àpropos*, that these slight shafts will retain to remote posterity very high value as perfect masterpieces of their kind. Moore did for the political "squib" what H. B. has done for the political caricature — "he deprived it of half its evil by depriving it of all its grossness." The Chinese are said to exhibit fireworks of exquisite brilliancy and ingenuity so contrived that they can be let off in a room, not only without danger of fire, but with the peculiarity that in exploding they emit a fragrant odour. These light productions of Moore are like the Chinese fireworks: they are wonderfully varied, petulant, and sparkling; and instead of the heavy vapours of personal malignity, they spread around, after crackling and flashing through their momentary existence, a fragrance of good taste, good humour, and classic grace. Though they must have given, as we know they did, the most exquisite pain to their unfortunate victims, they are absolutely the most unanswerable and galling attacks that were ever made; and the only way to conceal the wound must have been by joining in the laugh. They are full of the most happy turns of ingenuity, of the gay exhaustless fancy which seems the peculiar heritage of the Irish intellect, and they show a vast extent of curious and out-of-the-way reading, which no man ever knew better to employ than Moore.

Among the best of Moore's comic compositions are the admirable letters entitled 'The Fudge Family in Paris,' supposed to be written by a party of English travellers at the French capital. It is composed of a hack-writer and spy, devoted to legitimacy, the Bourbons, and Lord Castlereagh; his son, a young dandy of the first water; and his daughter, a sentimental damsel, rapturously fond of "romance and high bonnets and Madame Le Roy," in love with a Parisian linendraper, whom she has mistaken for one of the Bourbons in disguise. In this, as in his other comic productions, Moore shows great skill in introducing his own witty fancies without destroying the probability of the character who is made the unconscious mouthpiece for the author's good things. We ought not to forget O'Connor, the tutor and "poor relation" of this egregious family, who is an ardent Bonapartist and Irish patriot. His letters are all serious, and contain violent declamations against the Holy Alliance, the British government, &c.; but they are not in harmony with the gay and ludicrous tone of the work — to which they were probably intended to act as a foil or relief.

Another delightful collection of (pretended intercepted) letters, supposed to be from eminent persons, is entitled 'The Twopenny Post-Bag.' These, like the preceding, had a most unparalleled success. Before quitting this category of Moore's multifarious writings, we will mention his 'Rhymes on Cash, Corn, and Catholics,' the subject of which is sufficiently indicated by the title; his 'Fables for the Holy Alliance,' a most spirited and ludicrous mockery of the legitimist doctrines; and a number of political squibs written in the slang or *argot* of the prizefighters. These offer a new proof of the elegance and versatility of Moore's talents; for though in them he has adopted a dialect associated with the lowest and most brutalizing of our national sports, he has handled it so that it is not only not offensive, but in the highest degree comic. Moore has used the jargon of the prize-ring so as to lose all its coarseness, and retain only its oddity and picturesque force. The narrative of the great fight between "Long Sandy and Georgy the Porpus" is in true sporting style, and 'Tom Cribb's Memorial to Congress' contains passages of true poetic spirit.

We now approach those works upon which will be founded this poet's widest and most enduring reputation — these are the 'Irish Melodies.' They are short lyrics, written to suit that vast treasury of beautiful national airs which form the peculiar pride, joy, and consolation of the Irish people. "The task which you propose to me," says the poet, in his letter to Sir John Stevenson, the arranger of the music, "of adapting words to these airs, is by no means easy. The poet who would follow the various sentiments which they express must feel and understand that rapid fluctuation of spirits, that unaccountable mixture of gloom and levity, which composes the character of my countrymen, and has deeply tinged their music. Even in their liveliest strains we find some melancholy note intrude — some minor third, or flat seventh — which throws its shade as it passes, and makes even mirth interesting." We have in another place spoken of the Scottish national airs in terms of admiration which will appear exaggerated to those only who are unacquainted with them: the popular airs of Ireland are inferior to those of Scotland neither in pathos, in gaiety, nor in inexhaustible variety. In Ireland the national music had been associated with coarse, rude, and mean words, often indecent and trivial in the highest degree; and thus by degrees many most beautiful airs, naturally expressive of the tenderest emotion, were deprived, by changes in their time, their key, and their accentuation, of their natural sense and meaning. When we see, among the titles by which the airs are known, such gross and vulgar appellations (generally worthy specimens of the pot-house compositions of which they are the beginning) as 'Paddy Snap,' 'The Black Joke,' 'The Captivating Youth,' 'Bob and Joan,' 'Paddy Whack,' 'The Dandy O,' and the like, we shall partly appreciate the service rendered by Moore to the music and poetry of his country.

The 'Irish Melodies,' as songs, have never been surpassed in their particular kind. The versification is so exquisite, and executed with such delicacy of rhythm, that, on hearing them well read, we involuntarily and certainly conceive the tune, even though we may never have heard it.

Viewed as poetry, these songs are among the most beautifu. productions of literature. The diction is invariably perfect for elegance, neatness, and grace: it is truly Catullian, "*simplex munditiis*:" the words are never too big for the thought. They exhibit marks, not so much of labour and effort as of polish and care; and where the author can prevail upon himself to resist his natural and Irish tendency to say something ingenious and conceited, their sentiment is as true and beautiful as their execution is felicitous. The great art in song-writing is to invent something that is original without being far-fetched; and when we reflect upon the difficulty of finding untouched and unhackneyed ideas on the few topics offered by patriotism, love, and pleasure (which compose nearly the whole *curta supellex* of the song-writer), we shall the more easily excuse Moore for having sometimes fallen into the fantastic and epigrammatic.

If we compare Moore, as a lyric poet, with Burns, we shall acquire a much more elevated idea of the Irishman than by looking at him in a distinct point of view. The peasant poet of Scotland had the advantage of using a dialect which was simple and rustic without vulgarity, and all his finest compositions (with perhaps one or two remarkable exceptions) are written in that dialect; and it is difficult for a critic not *practically* acquainted with that dialect, to judge how far its use may have contributed to give Burns's poetry its charm of *naïveté*, slyness, and pathos. Moore has not this advantage: his lyrics are models of the most refined and classical English. Both poets abound in beautiful love-passages; but the passion of the Scottish ploughman is rather too ardent and unscrupulous, while that of the Irish poet is often frittered away in cold and sparkling *concetti*, and thus loses in depth and tenderness more than it gains in ingenuity and elegance.

In 1817 Moore published the celebrated Oriental romance 'Lalla Rookh' (Tulip-Cheek, so entitled from the name of the heroine). The structure of this work is truly original: it consists of a little romantic love-story, in which the beautiful daughter of Aurengzebe, during her journey into Bucharia, where she is to meet her betrothed husband, the prince of that country, falls in love with a young minstrel, who afterwards turns out to be her affianced bridegroom in disguise, and who thus, "having won her love as an humble minstrel, now amply deserved to enjoy it as a king." This slender plot is related in that ingenious and sparkling prose of which Moore is a consummate master; and nothing can exceed the gorgeousness, splendour, and pleasanty with which he describes all the details of Oriental life and scenery during the journey, and the inimitable character of Fadladeen the high chamberlain, a pedantic critic and accomplished courtier. This prose narrative, which, though very short, is one unceasing sparkle of brilliant antithesis and Eastern imagery, forms a kind of framing (like the prologues of Chaucer) for the poems. These are four in number, 'The Veiled Prophet,' 'The Fireworshippers,' 'Paradise and the Peri,' and 'The Light of the Harem;' and are supposed to be sung for the Princess's amusement by the disguised Feramorz. Of the prose portion of this enchanting work it is impossible to speak too highly; it is the very quintessence, the "*fine fleur*," the bloom and *anthos* of the gorgeous and voluptuous genius of the East: indeed its only fault is that it is too incessantly, too fatiguingly dazzling and splendid; it is "more Eastern than the East itself," and is a concentration or condensation of a thousand traits and strokes derived from a vast extent of Oriental reading. Jekyll said that "it was as good as riding on the back of a camel." The tales themselves are of various merit: 'The Veiled Prophet,' the most ambitious and the longest, does not appear to us the most successful. The narrative wants clearness, consistency, and event: the march of the story languishes, and the characters are too conventional and undefined to possess much power of interest. It is written in rhymed couplets, and there is far too incessant a profusion of ornament, which, though rich and appropriate, is so thickly sown that the effect of the whole is like that of some Oriental robe, in which the whole texture is concealed with an unbroken surface of pearl, and ruby, and diamond.

'The Fireworshippers,' which is written in irregular octosyllabic verses, is less oppressive in its splendour, but it reminds the reader, and unfortunately for its success, of the minor Oriental narratives of Byron, as, for example, 'The Bride of Abydos.' On the whole, our favourite of the four poems is 'The Light of the Harem:' the subject is a love-quarrel and reconciliation between the Emperor Jehanghir and his beautiful favorite Nourmahal. In all these poems the songs introduced, and the lyric passages in general, are inexpressibly beautiful; those sung by the fair houris in the artificial Paradise, where Azim is tempted to join the standard of Mokanna; many of the lyric movements in 'The Peri;' and, above all, the delicious incantations in 'The Light of the Harem,' are in Moore's very finest manner, and perhaps have never been equalled, except by himself in the 'Irish Melodies.'

Of 'The Loves of the Angels,' Moore's other Oriental poem, we have but very few words to say: it is generally found to be inferior to his other works; and though many passages of it breathe a rich and graceful perfume of passion, it is in characters and scenery too modern, so to say, too little imbued with a primeval spirit appropriate to the legend, and the personages have lost the pure and celestial lineaments of the angelic nature, without acquiring our sympathy in their punishment as men. How would Milton have maintained the solemn, ethereal, primeval character of those primeval days of Earth's first infancy, "when men began to multiply on the face thereof, and daughters were born unto them, and the sons of God saw the daughters of men that they were fair, and took them wives of all which they chose"! Moore's angels do not so much resemble the angels of the Bible, or those of Raphael, nor even those of Albert Dürer, as the Scripture personages of a ballet at the Porte St. Martin: and indeed it is curious enough that this poem was composed at Paris.

The remarks we have made on the 'Irish Melodies' will equally apply, though of course not always in the same degree, to various other collections of songs which this poet has given to the world: there are many beautiful productions among his 'National Songs,' written for a selection of airs of all countries; and the 'Evenings in Greece,' and other similar works, may be examined by the reader with a certainty of finding many gems of grace, tenderness, and harmony. We have now to say a few words of Moore as a prose-writer. He has distinguished himself both in fiction and in biography—in the former as the author of the beautiful tale of 'The Epicurean,' and in the latter in a variety of works, of which the most important are the 'Lives' of Lord Byron, his intimate friend and brother-poet, and of his illustrious countryman Sheridan, the British Beaumarchais.

'The Epicurean' is a tale of antique manners, the scene being laid among the primitive Christians, chiefly in Egypt, and terminating with the martyrdom of a converted priestess, whose character, as well as that of the hero, a young Athenian, is beautifully sketched. The book contains many striking and poetical episodes, particularly a descent into the subterraneous temples of the Egyptian deities, and a revelation of the arts by which the pagan hierarchy deceived the candidates for initiation in their unholy mysteries. The night voyage on the Nile is also powerful and picturesque, and the style of the work, though still sufficiently gorgeous and fanciful, is not so overloaded with ornament and conceits as the prose parts of 'Lalla Rookh.' It also exhibits a profusion of curious erudition.

The two 'Lives' which we have mentioned are written on that plan which is immeasurably the best for this kind of work. They are not 'Lives,' but 'Memoirs:' the author allows the subject of the biography to tell his own story; and the mass of the book consists of extracts from the journals and correspondence of the person whose life we are reading. Moore has performed his task with the penetration of the critic, and with the gentleness and enthusiasm of the friend: and nothing in it is more admirable than the warm and generous justice rendered to Byron by a contemporary and most popular poet, and the total absence of anything like jealousy or envy.

It is impossible not to confess that Byron was the most extraordinary man of his age, and perhaps the most extraordinary person in the modern history of Europe. Striking and not uninstructive parallels have been drawn between him and Napoleon, and even between him and Goethe. All three were eminently the embodiment of the period of crisis, literary or political, which characterised their age. No sooner is Napoleon installed in the Tuileries than he begins to revive all the ceremonies and exploded offices of the ancient court of France; and, by what would seem (but only to a superficial glance) a similar caprice, Byron, "the young Napoleon of the realms of rhyme," has no sooner mounted with the step of a giant to the uncontested throne of his country's literature, than his first manifestos proclaim his adherence to those canons of taste and principles of criticism, the total and unsparing annihilation of which was the particular mission of his power. Though the greatest of the romanticists, Byron incessantly insisted on the superiority of the classicist school; and, whether from blindness, or from that perverse contempt for received opinions which so strongly coloured his character, the author of 'Childe Harold' and 'Lara' affected to consider Pope as his superior in poetry. "It was all Virgil then," says he; "it is all Claudian with us now:" and he has compared the two classes of literature respectively to a Grecian temple, and to a glittering but barbarous pagoda. He affected to be prouder of his cold and formal 'Imitations of Horace' than of those immortal poems by which he revolutionised the taste of Europe.

This extraordinary man was born in London on the 22nd of January, 1788. His mother was a Scottish heiress, who had in an evil hour married a ruined profligate, from whom she had soon been obliged to separate; and the early days of the young poet were passed chiefly in Scotland, amid the miseries of poverty and neglect, and exposed to all the dangers arising from the almost insane character of his unhappy mother—capricious alternations of frantic fondness and unreasoning rage. He was eleven years old when the death of his grand-uncle put him in possession of the title, and made him the representative of one of the most ancient Norman houses of the English aristocracy. The hereditary estate, Newstead Abbey, not far from Nottingham, was situated in the middle of the most beautiful rural scenery, in a district dignified by the legends of "Robin Hood and Little John" and the fair Forest of Sherwood; but the property was dilapidated by the follies and vices of his ancestors. However favourable may have been all these circumstances to foster that union of passion and sensibility which composes the poetical character, and to inspire and develop that mixture of pride, melancholy, and haughty repining which characterises the poetry of this great man, they were indubitably not favourable either to his happiness or to his virtue. An early and ill-requited passion came, too, to throw an additional tint of gloom over this lofty and mournful heart; and his boyish love for Mary Chaworth was afterwards to be immortalised in verses whose sad and imperishable beauty only renders their sincerity too painfully apparent.

His prospects in life being considerably improved by his accession to the peerage, young Byron passed some time at Harrow School, where he made himself chiefly remarkable by the intensity and almost feminine fervour of his schoolboy friendships; and afterwards at Trinity College, Cambridge, where the tradition goes that he occupied the same rooms as had been formerly inhabited by Newton. At the university his life was neither very happy nor very moral, but both here and at Harrow he continued to indulge the same voracious appetite for all manner of miscellaneous reading which had distinguished him almost from his infancy. It is singular enough that his predilections should have lain, in a great measure, in the department of Oriental history. Of classical learning, at least of an accurate and technical kind, he never possessed a great share; and he has left us, in many passages of his works, strong indications of the weariness and disgust with which a bad system of education had associated, in his mind, the finest passages of ancient literature.

It was in 1807 that Byron first appeared before the public as an author. The 'Hours of Idleness,' a small volume of fugitive poems, of no intrinsic value whatever, and (what is singular enough) giving no indication of his future powers or style of thought, was treated with extreme severity in a memorable criticism of the 'Edinburgh Review.' Byron's rage at this contemptuous and sarcastic article, and the terrific revenge which he afterwards took, has induced many people to consider this famous criticism as a notable instance either of malignity or ignorance. But it seems to us that this is an error and an injustice. The criticism in itself, though not perhaps written in the best possible taste, is fair and reasonable enough; for the poems are exceedingly weak and commonplace. The true culpability of the reviewer lies in the selection, for a subject of his strictures, of a work so trifling and unimportant. The critique threw Byron into a passion of rage and indignation, and he shortly afterwards printed his satire of 'English Bards and Scotch Reviewers,' a fierce and indiscriminate piece of retaliation, in which he revenges his self-love upon nearly the whole of the literary men of that day. This poem, as might have been expected from the sincere anger which dictated it, is in many parts very powerfully written, and exhibits, if not a complete foretaste of *all* the qualities which distinguish his peculiar genius, at least the *earnestness*, intensity, and admirable clearness of expression, which form chief elements in his future productions. It is equally to the honour of the satirist and his victims in this ebullition of youthful indignation, that he afterwards became the warm friend and correspondent of many of the persons whom he had attacked—of Jeffrey, for example (editor of the obnoxious Review), of Scott, of Moore, and many others.

After inflicting this fierce vengeance the poet travelled for two years, and embodied, in the first and second cantos of 'Childe

Harold,' which appeared on his return in 1812, the impressions of beauty, tenderness, and sublimity which the scenes of Spain and Greece were so likely to make upon such a mind. The appearance of this admirable poem placed the author, instantly and for ever, at the head of all the poets of his time. The remainder of 'Childe Harold' appeared at considerable intervals; the fourth (and last) canto not until 1818. For this reason we think it advisable to defer our remarks upon this work till we can discuss the whole of it at once. The first and second cantos were followed in rapid and brilliant succession by those inimitable romantic narratives which form an era in literature, and which proved that Byron's genius had now found a new and vast source of passion, interest, and sentiment. This source was principally the East, and modern Greece in particular. Familiarised as we now are, and chiefly familiarised by the genius of Byron himself, with the scenery and costume of this region, we can hardly form an idea of the impression which must have been made by the first appearance of 'The Giaour' and 'The Bride of Abydos,' 'The Corsair' and 'Lara;' they produced in the public of England, and indirectly throughout Europe, an enthusiasm which was little short of madness. That deep and spiritual perception of beauty, that mixture of pride and tenderness, of fervour and voluptuous softness, the rapid alternation of the fiercest energy with the loftiest and most pathetic meditation—all these made Byron as peculiarly the poet of Greece, as they rendered Greece the just patrimony of Byron's genius. Most of these narrative poems were written in the irregular-rhymed metres which Scott had brought into fashion. They have rarely any pretensions to ingenuity of plot or connected development of incident; and are, indeed, little else than powerful embodiments of terrible *situations*—culminating instants—in Oriental existence. They are not, in short, dramas, nor hardly *scenes*, of the life of man: they are moments of intense and tremendous passion. They have no variety of character: they contain but two figures, sometimes slightly relieved against a few conventional and monotonous characters, but rendered invariably impressive and affecting by the scenery and circumstances which surround them, and by the unequalled intensity, directness, and pathos with which their passions are set before us. The male character is the same as we behold in Childe Harold, in Conrad, in Lara, in Alp, and even in the tragedies—a character unnatural, impossible, and inconsistent in itself, but painted with a terrible force and distinctness. Both Scott and Byron excel in description; but with this difference, that Scott contents himself with the external manifestation of the object, whose most picturesque and striking lines he selects and reproduces with an admirable energy and vividness; or, if these are allowed to acquire any colouring from the poet's mind, that tint is seldom of any unusual or profound character. No passions, indeed, can be said to colour Scott's descriptions, except occasionally the enthusiasm of chivalric daring, the glow of patriotic exultation, or the tenderness of the domestic affections. Byron is the exact reverse of all this. Not only is every manifestation of his sublime genius intimately and inseparately connected with the peculiar moral constitution of the individual, but the very existence of that genius can only be conceived as inseparable from that constitution. In him it is not possible to separate the artist from the man. The fact is, that the character of Byron is *intensity;* that is to say, intense earnestness and sincerity: and this quality is so rare in art or in literature, that we are content to purchase it even at the price of monotony. In the infancy of society—that is, at the periods of great physical agitation—poetry, like art, preserves its external or superficial character: it speaks to the eye, and to the imagination. But as man, or as mankind, grows older, and he "puts away childish things," he turns his eye inward upon the mysterious workings of his own moral nature, and poetry becomes searching, analytic, deeply passionate. Byron's writings are, in this point of view, as complete a manifestation of the nineteenth century, as the 'Iliad' and the 'Odyssey' are of the heroic, or as Scott's poems are a revival of the chivalric age. It is singular how almost all Byron's human characters resolve themselves into moments and situations of intense but stationary interest. Alp gazing on the cloud, whose passage is to decide his everlasting fate; Lara smiling sadly at the dancers; Manfred drinking in the loveliness of nature, which can, however, bring no consolation to his despair—these are delineations which will occur to every one; and the narrative or dialogue in which these conceptions are introduced is of the same stationary, unprogressive character; there is no *evolution,* nothing advances.

'The Corsair' and 'Lara' are two prominent adventures in the life of the same person; for it is evident that Lara and the page Kaled can be no other than Conrad and Gulnare. These two poems are remarkable as being written in the rhymed heroic couplet of Pope and Dryden, instead of the irregular lyric measures of the other romantic tales. Byron has handled the difficult instrument with perfect mastery. In the former of the two poems, the song of the pirates is inexpressibly vigorous, and full of wild, savage energy; but the analysis of Conrad's character is generally considered as the finest passage, and the death of Medora as an unequalled instance of Byron's power

"To ope the sacred source of sympathetic tears."

No author ever possessed so little of the dramatic power—of that *going out of oneself to create*—of that faculty of getting entirely rid of one's own idiosyncrasy, which Shakspeare possessed to a degree in no sense short of supernatural. In fact, it is to this non centration of thoughts in himself, to the very incapacity of going out of the circle of his own moral being, that Byron owes his specific character as a poet.

It was this portion of Byron's life which we might call the happiest, if glory and pleasure were enough to make life happy. He was now the idol of society, considered "facilè princeps" of the living poets of his country, and boldly compared even with the greatest names among the mighty dead; and about this time he contracted his marriage with Miss Milbanke. The tale of this truly melancholy episode is soon told: after living a short time with his lady, between whom and her illustrious husband there seems to have existed no disagreements not to be explained by the very embarrassed state of their fortune, the relations, and particularly the mother, of Lady Byron, appear to have induced her to separate from her husband, not only (as far as appears) without assigning any sufficient cause, but without communicating to Byron himself any plausible pretext; for he solemnly affirmed, until his dying day, that he never knew the cause of separation. He soon hurried away once more from England, with the hope of forgetting or alleviating his pain amid the loveliness of foreign climes, and in those beautiful regions immortalised by ancient glory, but to which his genius had given a new enchantment. But, before his departure, he gave to the world 'The Siege of Corinth' and 'Parisina,'—short, wild, irregular poems, in which his characteristic merits are splendidly perceptible. In the former, the apparition which visits Alp with a last chance of salvation is a scene nobly contrasted with the warlike fury of the storming of the devoted city; and in the second, pathos of the deepest and most hopeless kind is embodied in descriptions and reflection so exquisitely touching that we forget the horror of crime and vengeance shed over the meagre story, and we feel no want of that strong picturesque situation in which this poet's romantic tales are rarely deficient. The opening lines of 'Parisina' are consummate in deep internal beauty, and are worthy of being compared even with the ghost scene of the siege, or the inimitable attack and capture of Corinth by the Turks.

The restless pang of misery which was now fixed for ever to this noble heart again drove him abroad. In six months he sent to England the third canto of 'Childe Harold,' and the exquisite little poem of 'The Prisoner of Chillon.' Respecting the latter of these, we need not make any very detailed remarks. Story or dramatic interest it has none, but the effect of grief and imprisonment upon the characters of the three brothers is painted with a variety of touch as strong as it is delicate, and the death of the youngest is a haunting image of quiet, patient, uncomplaining hopelessness. We behold the captives, we see "the iron entering into their souls;" and the feverish and fantastic imaginings of the survivor, his reflections on his brother's grave, and his welcoming of the bird which comes to visit him, are deeply-imagined indications of that weakening and revulsion of the mind which follows hopeless and irremediable sorrow —the recoil of the o'erstrained spring. The view of happy nature without is exquisitely relieved and contrasted against the cold dull monotony of the prison, and is like a little glimpse of blue sky framed by the grating of a dungeon.

It was about this period of his career (1817) that Byron began to write dramas; and the first work of this nature, and probably the best also, was, as might have been expected, but little removed in form from the contemplative poems which had gained him his greatest fame. This was the drama of 'Manfred.' Byron's genius was singularly ill adapted for scenic writing, principally from that want of variety with which we have reproached all his attempts at the creation of *character*. 'Manfred' is no more a play for the stage than 'Faust,' and the author has repeatedly insisted that this (and many other of his dramas) were never composed "with the remotest view to representation." The truth is, that this work is dramatic only in form; there are no events, properly so called, there are no characters, and there is no dialogue. The so-called play, in short, is little else than a series of grand and majestic soliloquies, and the form of dialogue is only assumed to enable the author to put into the mouth of a few other persons (who have nothing whatever distinctive and characteristic) remarks which give Manfred the occasion of describing and re-describing his own sublime agonies. The work therefore is much less a drama than the 'Prometheus' of Æschylus, and little more so than the 'Paradise Lost.' It bears a strong superficial resemblance in many points to the 'Faust,' but a very slight examination will show the difference between these two awful productions. 'Faust' is a cold, cynical, cruel, deliberate anatomy of the vanities of human virtue and knowledge; the hero is little more than inert matter in the hands of the sneering fiend, who plays with him as a juggler with his balls. Mephistophiles is the real hero of the poem, as Satan is of the 'Paradise Lost;' Faust is but the weak and erring Adam of his vain Eden of human perfectibility. But Manfred is a haughty and regal spirit, whose tremendous agonies have endowed him with power over the powers of Nature, Destiny, and Ahrimanes. The abstract and unworldly features of this awful conception are softened and humanised by his deep and unfailing love for nature and his longing remembrances of the earthly passion of his youth. The character resembles those Alpine solitudes amid which he utters his sublime woes; it is the cold and glittering unfruitful glacier, bordered with the mournful flowers of the mountain rhododendron; it is the icy peak, thunder-shattered and inaccessible, but glowing in the rosy hues of Love's departed sun. All the soliloquies in this immortal work are full of the rarest beauty; that spoken on the summit of the Jungfrau, the evocation of the Witch of the Alps, and that grand and pathetic passage in which the mind of the lofty victim, now calmed by the hope of approaching death, recalls the majestic sadness of ruined Rome. The songs of the Spirits are indescribably beautiful as lyrics; and in *one* overwhelming scene (that in which the phantom of the dead Astarte is called up to answer Manfred before the throne of Ahriman) it cannot be denied that Byron has shown a power *almost* dramatic.

This splendid work appeared with 'The Lament of Tasso,' and was followed in the succeeding year by the fourth and concluding canto of 'Childe Harold,' about which poem we shall now say a few words. In selecting as the medium of a contemplative and descriptive work the nine-lined stanza of Spenser (itself a modification of the ottava rima of Tasso and Ariosto), Byron at first determined to convey something of that quaint and antiquated air which his great master had adopted in 'The Faërie Queene.' This suits well enough with Spenser's subject, a tale of romantic chivalrous adventure; but even in 'The Faërie Queene' the use of old and obsolete language was carried rather too far. Byron attempted (it is not easy to say with what object) to do the same; the very title of the poem—'Childe' signifying, in our old English legendary language, *knight*—is a proof and example of this. But we feel neither surprise nor regret that he soon abandoned this forced masquerade of diction. 'Childe Harold' derives its wonderful power over our sympathies from the admirable variety, splendour, and beauty of its descriptions of scenery, spots of eternal and historical interest, and the great triumphs of human art and genius. These have no natural coherence or connection, and are only united into one complete whole by the grand tone of mournful reflection in which the impressions are embodied, the atmosphere of lofty sadness through which the various objects are viewed. Harold is an exhausted and disappointed libertine, who wanders over the earth, beholding its fairest and most exhilarating scenes with the calm and abstracted glance of one who no longer either hopes or fears, but who is sometimes capable of being roused for a moment by contempt or admiration, by the base or the beautiful, by patriotism, by despair. Neither the English nor assuredly any other literature had produced any passages of description at all comparable to the pictures of nature, man, and society which crowd these four wondrous cantos—the plaintive loveliness of Greece; the stern splendour of Mussulman dominion; the scenes of heroic struggling for Spanish and Portuguese independence; the cataracts and peaks of Switzerland; the phantom splendours of Venice; and all the wonders of antique and mediæval art. It is of course impossible for the reader, in spite of Byron's eager and reiterated declamations, to avoid identifying the hero of this great work with the personal and individual character of its author. The bitter and scornful declamations against military glory and intellectual supremacy, the invectives against the hollowness of modern society, do indeed sometimes wear a somewhat suspicious air not only of sophistry, but of affectation; but it is to the eternal honour of this great genius that his enthusiasm for what is really good, noble, or beautiful is always stamped with an air of deep and fervent sincerity. The mask is that of Mephistophiles, but the features which it conceals are the lineaments of an archangel. The poem begins and ends with the ocean; to whose majestic undulations, to whose changing aspects of gloom and sunshine, of calm and tempest, of melancholy grandeur and immeasurable depth, it bears no faint similitude, and of whose many-voiced harmonies its varied music is no unworthy echo.

Together with the fourth canto of 'Childe Harold' appeared 'Beppo,' a light, half-playful, half-sarcastic tale of modern Italian society, in which Byron gave the first earnest of his powers as a comic writer. It is composed in the easy stanza employed by Pulci and the more ludicrous Italian poets, and is a consummate example of easy familiar grace, occasionally rising into pathos and tenderness. The story is as trifling as possible, being a not very moral carnival adventure; but what an abundant and transparent flow of refined chat and badinage, with only just that slight touch of satire and pathos which suffices to give it pungency! The somewhat lax morality we pardon with a smile, by attributing it to the custom of Venetian society; and we no more think of directing the artillery of moral declamation against the lady and her dilettante cicisbeo, than of levelling a cannon against a pair of sporting butterflies.

For a considerable time, and with various intervals of travelling, even down to 1821, Byron resided in Italy, principally at Venice and Ravenna, steadily and uninterruptedly adding stone after stone to that pyramid of glory in which he has eternised his name. His private life, during the whole latter part of his career, was neither very moral nor very regular. Driven from his own country by his embarrassed circumstances, endowed with even more than the poet's impressibility and passion, this great man plunged into a life of dissipation neither dignified in itself, nor even excusable by the lax tone of Italian manners at that time. His productions however continued to be poured forth with as much variety, splendour, and effect as ever, though one particular department of them (the tragedies) were rather striking, bold, and original in their manner, than in perfect harmony with the peculiar style which had acquired him such fame

The first work of this epoch which we shall mention is the tale of 'Mazeppa,' full of vigour, passion the more impressive from its air of being bridled in and restrained, and rough rapid descriptions of suffering, terror, and revenge. The *mise en scène* of this narrative is admirable: it is a story of his early days told by the fierce and rugged veteran to amuse Charles XII. at a bivouac after the dreadful defeat of Poltava: and the character of the rude old hetman (who, however, in no way resembles the real historical Mazépa) is in perfect harmony with the scene, the circumstances, and the savage nature of his youthful adventures.

The tragedies are six in number, and can be divided into two categories—first, those of a purely abstract and imaginary kind; and, secondly, the dramas more strictly historical: the former class may be considered as productions of the same phase in the poet's intellectual life which produced 'Manfred,' and the latter to have been written under the combined influence of Alfieri and Shelley. In the one class are placed 'Cain,' 'Heaven and Earth,' and 'The Deformed Transformed;' in the other, 'Marino Faliero,' 'Sardanapalus,' Werner,' and 'The Two Foscari.' Of the first-mentioned three, 'Cain' is undoubtedly the finest, whether we consider the tremendous boldness of the sentiments, the pictures of primeval existence, now awful and now exquisitely lovely, which it contains, or the tremendous agencies which are embodied in its personages. It is little else than a fearful piece of special pleading, in which the goodness of God is brought into question: but if we examine the finest (and consequently most dangerous) dialogues in which this terrific thesis is argued between Cain and Lucifer, we shall discover that there is no *real dialogue*, and that the majestic speeches are nothing else but monologues in reality, and all tending to the same result. The argument against Divine goodness is really an argument in which the speakers are both on the same side. But the glimpses of primeval life which we get through the clouds and darkness of Cain's haughty scepticism, the picture of little Enoch's sleeping infancy, and the gloomy grandeur of those tremendous phantoms which Lucifer shows to his questioner in the realms of space peopled with the ghosts of premundane existences—all these are in the loftiest vein of conception, though their merit is far more lyrical than dramatic: perhaps the only really dramatic passage in the mystery is the last line, in which Cain, with a short, simple, and terrific exclamation of remorse and despair, is sent forth to wander miserable and restless over the world. 'Heaven and Earth' is altogether lyric, and is much feebler than either 'Cain' or 'Manfred:' it seems to us a not very happy imitation of Shelley's abstract and cloudy manner, but without his exquisite diction, imagery, and unequalled melody of versification. In 'The Deformed Transformed' Byron has given a bitter and savage expression to his recollections of his own deformity and unhappy childhood. There is much satire and invective too, in the drama, on the folly of mankind, and on the atrocious puerilities of military glory; but the only passage which remains in the reader's memory is the evocation of the forms of the beautiful and wise of the antique world, when the Stranger offers to the Deformed the choice of a new body.

The more purely historical dramas are undoubtedly fine and dignified compositions, on the model, not of Shakspeare but of Alfieri. Between Byron and the great modern reformer of Italian literature there were innumerable points of resemblance, both moral and intellectual; and those classical tendencies of Byron's mind to which we have alluded some pages back doubtless received new food from the strong admiration he felt for the fiery, haughty, sublime author of 'Filippo.' We doubt whether Byron ever felt a very warm or sincere sympathy with Shakspeare, as a *dramatic artist;* there ever lurked in his mind a sort of suspicion that the unaffected and irregular richness of the Elizabethan stage was rather a defect than a merit—that its admirable ease, grace, vivacity, and nature, could not compensate for the stern dignity of classical tragedy; and perhaps a consciousness, too, of his own want of flexibility and animation of dialogue, and of variety and naturalness in the conception of characters, made him voluntarily adopt those severe and rigid forms which might palliate or conceal those defects. Thus his self-love, as an author, was masked under a natural or affected preference of those models which alone he could hope to imitate. This was natural enough, and therefore our wisest proceeding is to admire the beauties of his tragedies, with their monotony of style, their languid march of incident, and their repetition of a few types of character, their unities and their gravity, without making any invidious comparisons between their somewhat formal grandeur and the inexhaustible glories of our elder drama. The man of true taste is always catholic in his admirations—he can find intense pleasure in the regal gardens of Versailles without losing his relish for the dewy glades of a primeval forest.

In 'Marino Faliero' the principal defect is the insufficiency of such an event as the supposed insult offered by Steno to the Doge to excite in such a mind as that of the heroic veteran the tempest of passion which agitates his soul from the first act to the last. The passion is also somewhat monotonous in itself, and Faliero is too often lashed into wrath rather by his own eloquence than by the suggestions or provocations from without. This will be proved by comparing the character with Othello or with Lear. The conversations between the fierce old Doge and his young wife, though languid, are very beautiful; and the conspiracy-scene is a fine specimen of declamation—but declamation is rather the vice than the beauty of the French and Italian drama; and even the noble energy and force of such passages as the famous curse with which the Doge takes leave of life and Venice bear too strongly impressed this air of *rhetoric*, not *passion.* The description of the ball, by the senator Lioni, is exquisitely luxuriant, but totally out of place in a tragedy; there is nothing *scenic* in this play but the scene in which the illustrious conspirator is awaiting the sound of the great bell of St. Mark which is to give the signal for the massacre. In this the interest is really worked up to a breathless intensity of expectation.

On the stage the most successful of Byron's tragedies are 'Sardanapulus' and 'Werner;' but the latter derives all its effect from the interest of the plot, and the uncertainty, so artfully kept up, as to the real assassin of Strahlenheim. The language is throughout little better than dull prose. In fact this play is nothing else but the admirable prose narrative in Miss Lee's 'Canterbury Tales,' entitled 'The Hungarian's Story,' arranged into acts and scenes, and clumsily cut up into phrases of equal length, by courtesy called verse. 'Sardanapulus' has much higher merit: the character of Myrrha, the Ionian slave, is exquisitely and tenderly touched; and though Sardanapalus himself, with his luxurious good-natured effeminacy, and his moments of heroic courage and careless energy, is little else but an expansion of the antithesis of the historian and the satirist, he is striking and interesting on the stage.

Of 'The Two Foscari' we have only to remark the monstrous improbability of the sentiment which is the root of the action—the frantic and unreasonable love of country in Jacopo which drags him back from exile to die by lingering torture in ungrateful Venice. But nevertheless it is impossible not to sympathise with the despair and agony of the Doge, and our heart, though not our reason, takes part in his sorrow when the desolate old man, the victim of the implacable revenge of Loredano, throws himself to die upon the corpse of his unhappy son.

In all these tragedies, though none of them are unadorned with some noble and majestic declamatory passages, or with some description executed with Byron's never-failing intense and inward sentiment of beauty, the general run of the dialogue is singularly prosaic and sober: we perpetually meet with long passages of the plainest prose, and the line frequently ends with *of*, *to*, *with*, or some such wretched monosyllable, while the sense is so often carried, without any pause, into the next line, that it is only when we read that we can perceive it to be intended for metre. This, in a versifier so consummate as Byron was when he pleased, is a great blemish, and shows how little he had studied the admirable class of dramatists whose external forms he imitated in these plays. Corneille and Racine might have taught him, and Alfieri too, that the highest severity was not incompatible with the most finished and elaborate versification.

We have now only to speak of that extraordinary poem which is the most complete embodiment of all the varied discordant elements of this wonderful genius; nay, which is a full expression or reflection of the age in which he lived. In 'Don Juan,' as in a mirror, we see imaged all the features of modern society, its earnestness and its mockery, its scepticism and its faith, its sublimity and its meanness. The prevailing vice of our age—the haunting demon, is *cant:* and of cant Byron was the most implacable, active, and unresting enemy: cant in all its myriad disguises — the cant of religion, the cant of morality, the cant of patriotism, the cant of literature — it was his chief aim and passion to attack and overthrow. The first five cantos of the poem were written at Venice and Ravenna, and ten more were gradually added, chiefly at Pisa. The work is absolutely without plot or intrigue: it is a 'Gil Blas' in easy verse — a series of varied and almost unconnected adventures. Don Juan is a young Spanish grandee, whose early education is described with touches of the sharpest and most resistless satire. These keen razor-strokes, though bearing reference to the hollow hypocrisy and *Tartufferie* of our age, are frequently directed specially against Lady Byron and her family, and never did genius take a more terrible revenge for real or imaginary wrong. The young Don engages in an amour with a married woman somewhat older than himself, and is obliged to leave Spain. The ship founders at sea, and, after dreadful sufferings, the hero is thrown half-drowned and starving on a little island in the Ægean, where he is succoured by Haidée, a Greek girl — one of Byron's sweetest conceptions. In the midst of the wedding festivities, Lambro, the father of Haidée, a pirate, suddenly returns; Juan is disarmed and put on board his vessel, and carried to Constantinople, where he is sold for a slave, and is bought by Gulbeyaz, the haughty and voluptuous favourite of the Sultan. After some admirable but rather warmly-coloured scenes in the seraglio, Juan escapes, and we find him, with Johnson, an Englishman who had been the companion of his captivity, arriving at the Russian camp before Izmail, just as Suvoroff comes to take command of the besiegers; and we have a most vivid and terrific description of the storming of that devoted place. Juan afterwards passes some time at the court of Catherine II., by whom he is sent on a secret diplomatic mission to England. We then have some most severe and lively descriptions of English society, in which all its weak and rotten points are anatomised with merciless severity; and we at last accompany the hero to a *villeggiatura*, or summer-party, at a great country-house (a noble description of Newstead Abbey is introduced here), and we are admitted into the very focus of aristocratic life. Just as we are about to meet with what promises to be a *piquant* adventure, the poem abruptly concludes.

The primary characteristic of this extraordinary creation is a rapid and incessant alternation of the severest satire and the gayest and most comic impressions with images the most solemn or pathetic. The artifice of the poet consists in passing without a moment's preparation, without any intermediate state of transition, from the loftiest to the humblest images, from the most refined to the most vulgar from the bitterest sneer to the tenderest enthusiasm, from the grin of Mephistophiles to the agonised gaze of the Niobe. The critics have all complained of this, but we think without reason, for it is in this that consists the poem:—

"Aliter non fit, Avite, liber."

It is undeniably true that this close apposition of the ridiculous and the sublime, of the beautiful and the hideous, gives an air of heartless mockery to the satire, and of insincerity to the tenderness; but we must remember that such apposition and inconsistency is the very type of our modern society: the moral of the work lies deeper than the surface, and we must not apply to this vast structure of irony and sadness (a sadness deeper for the irony) the mere rules of literary criticism: if we complain, it should not be of the mocking spirit of the poem, but of the hypocrisy, cant, and hollowness of the age.

It is written in a kind of easy ottava rima, as admirably suited to the purpose as the Spenserian harmonies of 'Childe Harold' are to the subject and character of that splendid work; and it is a curious and instructive proof of Byron's admirable skill and exquisite ear, that in two poems so different in tone he should have used a metre nearly alike in form, but so admirably varied in feeling and rhythm, that the effect is perfect in each case. In 'Don Juan' we have the perfection of easy, familiar, lively conversation; the English is as pure and idiomatic as is conceivable—the style, transparency itself. Of humour this wonderful poem contains no trace, but it is throughout sparkling with an exhaustless current of wit—wit of the cold and caustic character of Beaumarchais and Voltaire. Modern Europe, after the frenzy of war and revolution, feels the collapse, the exhaustion, and the weariness, which are the natural consequence and reaction of violent excitement—the headache and nausea which follow the debauch, the cold shuddering indifference which succeeds to the paroxysm of sensuality. Modern society has acquired a smooth varnish of civilized propriety, and the satire of Byron, like a concentrated acid, burned off and ate away this superficial polish, showing the weak and cracked places concealed beneath. Of the richness, abundance, and intensity of the wit in this poem, there can be but one opinion; the absence of humour is, we think, as evident. All his satire is caustic—all is negative, not reconstructive: in the loftiest, the holiest, the tenderest emotions of the mind he shows us a selfish and contemptible ingredient. Such an element there assuredly is in all human feelings; for man is a composite and complicated being, and the taint of self defiles his most elevated sentiments.

"Quidquid agunt homines, votum, timor, ira, voluptas,
Gaudia, discursus, nostri est farrago libelli."

The secret of the *power* of this astonishing work is, as we have said before, the incredible facility with which the poet passes from the most tender or exalted feeling to the bitterest and most sneering mockery The sarcasm is only the more intense from being uttered with a graceful smile and with the epigrammatic polish of refined society. But perpetually as the mocker is at our side, pouring into our ear, with the smooth voice of Mephistophiles, the heart-hardening sophistries and the heart-piercing verities of artificial life, the poet is never absent either; it is impossible to surpass those delineations (so numerous and so beautiful) of the lovely and terrible scenes of nature, of the intoxication of youthful love, and the splendid gallantries of courts and camps. What truly poetical figures in Haidée, in Gulbeyaz, in Aurora Raby, in Lambro, in Donna Inez, in Julia! The picture of the festivities in the Pirate's Isle of the Ægean, and the inopportune return of Lambro, is superlatively rich and vivid, and so is the caustic portraiture of English aristocratic life.

'Don Juan' is a complete expression of Byron's life and genius; capricious, varied, ranging from cynic mockery to the deepest tenderness, it is also a perfect type of the age which produced it—an age at once sceptical and believing, bold and effeminate, shameless and hypocritical, coldly calculating and wildly imaginative; and it was just that this splendid literary career should close with a work which is so full and perfect a type of its marked and inconsistent features.

Among the singular contrasts and inconsistencies which crowd the personal and literary portrait of this man, not the least striking are those of his political existence. Born and bred an aristocrat, and exhibiting a tenacity of the prejudices of rank and manners even more than usually intense, Byron remained all his life a supporter of extreme liberal opinions. The two speeches, neither very successful, and exhibiting rather rhetorical than statesmanlike ability, which he pronounced in the House of Lords, recorded certainly an unequivocal adherence to liberal doctrines; and during his residence in Italy Byron not only expressed the warmest sympathy with the efforts of the Carbonari, but even entered into the unfortunate speculation of 'The Liberal,' a journal which totally failed. But at the end of his life a noble destiny invited him. He determined to take an active part in the Greek war of independence, and, after consecrating to a cause which must have had for him, as a man, as an Englishman, and as a poet, the deepest interest, not only very considerable sums of money, but great exertions also, he landed, January 4th, 1824, at Missolonghi. Europe has hardly yet recovered from the shock of grief and admiration with which she learned that the great poet, whose glory had filled so large a space of the social horizon, had died (April 18th, 1824), after suffering a short but painful illness produced by extreme fatigue and anxiety acting upon a mind and body worn out with all kind of indulgence and emotions.

It was a benevolent destiny which ordained that this great man should die on those shores which owe half their immortality to his genius, and amid a nation whose noble though fallen character he had rendered so interesting. His remains, after being conducted to the sea-shore amid the universal lamentations of the Greek patriots, were carried to England, and interred in the village church of Hucknall, in Nottinghamshire, where many generations of his ancestors repose: and the stupid bigotry which refused his bones a place in the national cemetery of Westminster Abbey, has not long ago crowned its climax of imbecility by denying within the walls of that Pantheon of England's worthies a statue to the memory of him who is the chief among her intellectual glories in the nineteenth century!

The genius of Shelley is the most exceptional and abnormal, the most difficult to classify, of any of the great poetical manifestations of the present age. No author has exerted a more powerful influence on detached and individual minds; there is none, at least of a merit in any way comparable to his, who has exerted so little influence on his *time*. Byron was a consummate *artist*, and always retains a complete consciousness and self-command. His muse is a Pythoness, who, in the fiercest moments of *possession*, remembers to sit gracefully on her tripod. Shelley is the very reverse of this; he does not possess his art, but is possessed *by* it—crushed, overpowered, overwhelmed; and if his works never fail to bear a peculiar ineffaceable stamp of ideal grace and beauty, this is to be attributed to the innate elegance and purity of his mind. His glory has been exposed to a destiny as strange and fantastic as his life; his fame has been equally injured by uncandid enemies and by injudicious admirers. Shelley's biography can be related in a very few words. In many of its chief outlines it bears a striking and melancholy resemblance to the story of his immortal friend, but there is a general vein of difference pervading even the most similar points in the history of the two men. Both were unhappy in their relations with the world, and both sought, and found, oblivion of their personal and social sufferings in the love of nature and in the unspeakable raptures of genial creation. But in Shelley, both the sufferings and the alleviation, both the disease and the remedy, were of the moral sense; in Byron, both the one and the other were of the *heart*. Byron was discontented with the world as it is, Shelley was ever pining after a world which was not. Both were sprung from ancient and noble houses—Shelley was the son of a baronet of old family, and born in 1792; they both received a very similar education, first at one of the great English public schools, and afterwards at the university. From Eton Shelley was removed to Oxford, from whence he was expel'ed for the bold scepticism of his youthful poem 'Queen Mab.'

But the Harrow boy was distinguished among his companions for generous manliness and the warmth of his schoolday friendships: the young Etonian, delicate and almost feminine in frame and manners, was filled with anguish at the foretaste of the world which the republican constitution of a great English school offers to the child yet warm from the soft existence of home. Shelley left Eton with his mind full of terror, disgust, and sensitiveness, and on entering on his Oxford life plunged ardently into a sea of abstract and physical study. The spirit of resistance to authority and dogmatism, so natural to a youthful and enthusiastic temperament, and combined with a vague course of reading, led him to scepticism, and scepticism to atheism—if that system of belief may be called atheism, which, while denying the existence of a Divine Being, such as we conceive the Deity to be, supplies its place by an imaginary existence whose qualities and attributes, at least as far as they are not mere abstractions, correspond exactly with our own conclusions respecting its nature. He published one or two trifling productions, apparently intended to brave the University, was expelled from Oxford, and soon afterwards renounced, when little past his boyhood, by his family. At eighteen he published the wild and fantastic poem 'Queen Mab,' which was at the same time a formal exposition of the doctrines he had adopted in religious and political philosophy, chiefly consisting of the fallacies and paradoxes of the French writers of the eighteenth century. The *sting* of this work lies in the *notes*, which are, however, little more than the often-refuted dreams of the philanthropist humanitarian theorists, but the poem contains many passages of that peculiar and inimitable melody which forms the great charm of Shelley's writings.

At this period of his life, while yet a mere boy, Shelley married a girl of inferior birth and education, and travelled for some time on the continent. His union was unhappy, and, after once more returning for some time to England, he was separated from his wife. During this short residence in his own country, he lived principally amid the beautiful scenery of Windsor; and here he wrote his poem of 'Alastor, or the Spirit of Solitude.' In this work, a wild romantic poem, he describes the early fate of a youth, whose mind, elevated and purified by a lofty and benevolent philosophy, pines after communion with a similar spirit, and who dies desponding at not finding such a being. The strength of the poem consists in the exquisitely rich and ideal descriptions of solitary woodland scenery, for which Shelley had, indeed, a poet's eye. On being separated, by the intervention of the law, from his wife, he soon afterwards contracted a second marriage, with the daughter of Godwin, a man whose opinions were in many respects in harmony with his own; and retiring to a village in Buckinghamshire, produced 'The Revolt of Islam, a rapturous declamatory narrative, exhibiting, under an allegorical form, the triumph of his philanthropic theories over the tyranny, hypocrisy, and hollowness which he considered inseparable from all the religious and political systems adopted by mankind. His health was now so weak—his fortune, in spite of the singular simplicity of his mode of life, so dilapidated—that he could no longer remain in England. He left his country, in 1818, never to return, and went directly to Italy, where he settled in a climate and a country much more congenial to his poetical temperament. He now produced his drama of 'Prometheus Unbound,' in some measure suggested, as far as its pure lyric form and colossal grandeur of outline are concerned, by the 'Prometheus' of Æschylus. In spite of the transcendental reveries of modern, and particularly of German, criticism, which has discovered, in the gigantic drama of the Athenian, an allegorical shadowing forth of primeval struggles between human will and fate, between the good and evil principles of humanity, we are apt to believe that this lyric tragedy had no such esoteric and mysterious meaning, and that Æschylus simply embodied the traditional mythology of his country, just as the rude monkish artist revived on his stage the events of the Christian history. The transcendental exposition, however, was best suited to Shelley's theory and object; and, therefore, in his 'Prometheus Unbound' he has essayed to give us the complement or companion-picture to the wild and phantasmagorial drama of Æschylus. His hero is nothing but a personification of man's indomitable resistance to the tyranny of religions and governments; for to religion and government he attributed all the ills which afflict humanity. It contains passages of the sublimest grandeur, and the most wonderful richness of imagination; but the effect of the whole is so vaporous and unsubstantial, the images which he evokes are so unsolid, that not even the unsurpassable purity of the diction, and the unequalled variety of the lyric music, can preserve us from weariness and a painful sense of dreamy confusion. As to the attacks upon all systems of religion, which he calls priestcraft, and all systems of government, which he styles tyranny, it is hardly necessary to refute them seriously here. Religion and government, the priest and the king, *viewed from the point which Shelley has selected*, are, indeed, open to all the charges he brings against them. But the fallacy precisely consists in his taking that point, and arguing *ex abusu*, the most fatal of all sophistries. It is obvious that false religions and bad kings are great evils, but the portion of human woe and crime which is produced by the most degrading of superstitions and the cruellest of despots is very far indeed from being comparable to the evils traceable to man's own selfishness and passions: and another great error of Shelley, and such reasoners, is the supposition that religion and kingship are something extraneous, foreign to our nature, and imposed by a superior and independent force; whereas all experience and argument show that these institutions, whether good or bad, are essentially the expression of man's own wants and condition, and are modified, not *ab extra*, but *ab intra*.

In Shelley's writings it is very easy to separate the philosophy from the poetry; and the philosophy, though so hostile to existing conditions of society, is so free from any moral impurity, so ethereal, so imbued with deep love for everything noble and elevated, and withal so exceedingly abstract and impracticable, that we do not think it is likely to do much harm; or, rather, the lovely and incessant manifestations of beauty in which it is clothed are calculated to do more good to the mind of a young and enthusiastic reader, than the declamatory sophistries of the reasoning can do injury.

In 1819 Shelley produced a work surprisingly distinct, in form and spirit, from any of his previous poems. This was the tragedy of 'The Cenci,' founded upon one of the most horrible domestic tragedies recorded in the black annals of Italian society in the Middle Ages — annals which seem written with blood and poison, and recalling a mode of existence only the more revolting from the glow of intellectual splendour which art, literature, and civilization throw over corruption and profligacy. This portion of history resembles the terrific picture of Correggio in which the gilded wreathing serpents are twined around the features of Medusa, lovely but infernal. The style of this play is astonishingly intense and nervous, and the character of the unhappy Beatrice contains some strokes of true and profound pathos, particularly the scene before her execution. The father is one of those demons of wickedness which happily are so rare, that our incredulity becomes an antidote to our loathing. Such beings are unfit for dramatic purposes, and it is no defence to say that they have existed: they are foul anomalies.

We have but few words to say of a number of Shelley's subsequent poems—'Hellas,' 'The Witch of Atlas,' 'Adonais' (a lament for the death of Keats), and 'Rosalind and Helen.' In the former two of these works we have a repetition, though in somewhat feebler and more diluted language, of the same wild declamation against the corruptions of society which forms the staple of his earlier poems, and a reiteration of the same fallacies about priestcraft and kingcraft; but 'Adonais' is a beautiful and affectionate tribute to the memory of Keats, whose early death deprived the world of the promise of a great poet, and whose manner of thinking and writing had much in common with that of Shelley. In 'Rosalind and Helen,' we have an exposition (in form of a domestic tale) of the evils which the poet supposes to arise from the institution of marriage. He shows us two beautiful and accomplished beings, one of whom is driven to despair and death by the tyranny and caprices of an old and repulsive husband, while the other lives a life of happiness and innocence in a union not sanctified by the indissoluble tie of marriage. But, in all human affairs, "abusus non tollit usum," and this tie was undoubtedly invented for the general welfare of mankind, to which experience shows that it *in the main* conduces: so the selection of an arbitrary and imaginary case, where misery follows wedlock, and happiness is assured by a kind of philosophical concubinage, proves nothing at all. It would be just as easy, and infinitely more in accordance with ordinary experience, to select an exactly opposite case. Such theorists begin at the wrong end: marriage is not bad because married people are sometimes unhappy together, but people may be unhappy *though* marriage *in the main* is good.

The death of this exquisite poet, and benevolent visionary, was singular and melancholy. He was returning in a small yacht from Ravenna to Rome, when his vessel was caught by a squall in the Bay of Spezzia, and Shelley and his two companions perished. The poet's body was afterwards washed on shore, and burned, after the ancient manner, on a funeral pile, in presence of Byron and several others of his friends. The ashes of Shelley were buried in the Protestant cemetery of Rome, near the pyramid of Cestius—a spot of sad and tranquil loveliness, where repose the remains of many English wanderers.

Shelley died in 1822, and in his end, and even in the manner of his funeral, there was something strangely in accordance with his life and sorrows. In spite of the hostile and revolutionary tone of his philosophy, he was, as a man, mild, benevolent, temperate, refined: his person, almost ethereal in its delicacy, was in apt accordance with the abstract and visionary tone of his writings: the chief characteristic of his poetry is its profusion of imagery, and a spiritual, tender harmony, like the fitful music of the Æolian harp, which no English poet has ever surpassed in variety and sweetness: the images are of a character at once bold and tender in the highest degree; his intensely passionate study of Greek literature (particularly the lyric writings) gives a peculiar air of classical purity and transparency to his conceptions: and from the same inexhaustible source he drew those artifices of metrical arrangement which make the English language, in his hands, as flexible, as musical, as the Greek itself. One peculiarity in his manner is particularly to be noticed: it is what may be called *incatenation*, a linking together of images, each of which is attached to that which precedes it, and which in its turn suggests another which follows it, but which often lead the reader far away from the original generating idea; so that, if we take two images placed even at a short interval from each other, we shall often be astonished that two ideas so different can be connected together by any middle term. Shelley's mind was in the highest degree impressionable—nay, almost feminine; and thus we often perceive a want of *keeping* and relief in the subordinate parts of his diction: the subsidiary or illustrative image is as vivid as that which it is meant to enforce or interpret; and in him we find a perpetual interchange of type and thing typified, as, for instance, in his exquisite 'Ode to the West Wind,' where the dead leaves are compared to ghosts flying before the spell of an enchanter. Shakspeare has innumerable examples of this incatenation of metaphors and images: it is impossible to open his plays without seeing plentiful instances of it: it is, indeed, the characteristic of his manner: but in him the secondary, the illustrative, is always *subordinate;* while in Shelley the ornament perpetually eclipses the thing to be adorned. In short, Shakspeare "writes all like a *man,*" while Shelley writes like a woman. This singular tendency sometimes renders passages otherwise beautiful almost unintelligible, as, for instance, in those wonderful lines 'On a Cloud,' where the illustrations, drawn from animated nature, are so crowded in the delineation of inanimate things, that the effect is rather fantastical and dazzling than beautiful or distinct. Conscious, too, perhaps, of this *feminineness* of mind, so ill in accordance with the haughty and serene tone of philosophy which he struggled to maintain, he was apt to exaggerate the horrible and repulsive, and his struggles to attain energy and a fierce declamatory tone are often rather extravagant than powerful. But with all these deductions made, the genius of Shelley will not fail to be held by posterity as a wonderful manifestation of power, of grace, and sweetness; and the ode we have just quoted, and the lovely 'Lines written in the Euganean Hills,' and that to a 'Skylark,' which is the very warbling of the triumphant bird, and the tender beauty of the 'Sensitive Plant,' and the magical translations of the 'Walpurgisnacht' of Goethe, and a thousand passages in the longer poems, will form for the memory of Shelley a wreath of fadeless flowers worthy of him who was the friend of Byron, and the pure apostle of a noble but mistaken philanthropy.

CHAPTER XIX.

THE MODERN NOVELISTS.

Prose Fiction The Romance: Walpole, Mrs. Radcliffe, Lewis, Maturin, and Mrs. Shelley—James, Ainsworth, and Bulwer—The Novel: Miss Burney —Godwin — Miss Edgeworth — Local Novels: Galt, Wilson, Banim, &c. — Fashionable Novels: Ward, Lister, &c. — Miss Austen — Hook — Mrs. Trollope—Miss Mitford—Warren—Dickens—Novels of Foreign Life: Beckford, Hope, and Morier — Naval and Military Novels: Marryat and R. Scott.

THE department of English literature which has been cultivated during the latter half of the last and the commencement of the present century with the greatest assiduity and success is undoubtedly that of prose fiction—the romance and the novel.

This branch of our subject is so extensive, and it embraces such a multitude of works and names, that the only feasible method of treating it so as to give an idea of its immense riches and fertility will be to classify the authors and their productions into a few great general species: and though there are some names (as that of Bulwer, for example) which may appear to belong to several of these subdivisions, our plan will be found, we trust, to secure clearness and aid the memory. The divisions which we propose are as follows: I. Romances properly so called; *i. e.* works of narrative fiction, embodying periods of ancient or middle-age history, the adventures of which are generally of a picturesque and romantic character, and the personages (whether taken from history, or invented so as to accord with the time and character of the action) of a lofty and imposing kind. II. The vast class of pictures of society, whether invented or not. These are generally novels, *i. e. romans de vie intime*, though some, as those of Godwin, may be highly imaginative, and even tragic. This class contains a great treasury of what may be called pictures of local manners, as of Scottish and Irish life. III. Oriental novels—a branch almost peculiar to English fiction; and originating partly in the acquaintance with the East derived by Great Britain from her gigantic Oriental empire, and partly from th Englishman's restless, inappeasable passion for travelling. IV Naval and military novels; giving pictures of striking adventure, and containing records of England's innumerable triumphs, by sea and land, together with sketches of the manners, habits, and feelings of our soldiers and sailors.

The history of modern prose fiction in England will be found to accord pretty closely with the classification we have just adopted.

We have spoken in another place of the three patriarchs of the English novel—Richardson, Fielding, and Smollett: and the immense class of works we are about to consider may be looked upon as totally distinct from the immortal productions of these great men, though the first impulse given to prose fiction will be found to have been in no sense communicated by 'Clarissa,' 'Tom Jones,' or 'Roderick Random.' This impulse was given by Horace Walpole, the fastidious *dilettante* and brilliant chronicler of the court scandal of his day, a man of singularly acute penetration, of sparkling epigrammatic style, but of a mind devoid of enthusiasm and elevation. Rather a French courtier in taste and habits than an English nobleman, he retired early from political life, veiling a certain consciousness of political incapacity under an effeminate and affected contempt for a parliamentary career, and shut himself up in his little fantastic Gothic castle at Strawberry Hill, to collect armour, medals, manuscripts, and painted glass, and to chronicle with malicious assiduity, in his vast and brilliant correspondence, the absurdities, follies, and weaknesses of his day.

'The Castle of Otranto' is a short tale, written with great rapidity and without any preparation, in which the first successful attempt was made to take the Feudal Age as the period, and the passion of mysterious, superstitious terror as the prime mover, of an interesting fiction. The supernatural machinery consists of a gigantic armed figure dimly seen at midnight in the gloomy halls and huge staircases of this feudal abode—of a colossal helmet which finds its way into the court-yard, filling everybody with dread and consternation —of a picture which descends from its frame to upbraid a wicked oppressor—of a vast apparition at the end—and a liberal allowance of secret panels, subterranean passages, breathless pursuit and escape. The manners are totally absurd and unnatural, the heroine being one of those inconsistent portraits in which the sentimental languor of the eighteenth century is superadded to the female character of the Middle Ages—in short, one of those incongruous contradictions which we meet in all the romantic fictions before Scott.

The immense success of Walpole's original and cleverly-written tale encouraged other and more accomplished artists to follow in the same track. After mentioning Clara Reeve, whose 'Old English Baron' contains the same defects without the beauties of Walpole's haunted castle, we come to the great name of this class, Anne Radcliffe, whose numerous romances exhibit a very high order of genius, and a surprising power (perhaps never equalled) over the emotions of fear and undefined mysterious suspense. Her two greatest works are, 'The Romance of the Forest,' and 'The Mysteries of Udolpho.' The scenery of her predilection is that of Italy and the south of France; and though she does not place the reader among the fierce and picturesque life of the Middle Ages, she has, perhaps, rather gained than lost by choosing the ruined castles of the Pyrenees and Apennines for the theatre, and the dark passions of profligate Italian counts for the principal moving power, of her wonderful fictions. The substance of them all is pretty nearly the same; and the author's total incapacity to paint individual character only makes us the more admire the power by which she interests us through the never-failing medium of suspense. Mystery is the whole spell. Nothing can be poorer and more conventional than the personages: they are not human beings, nor even the types of classes; they have no more individuality than the pieces of a chess-board; they are merely counters; but the skill with which the author juggles with them gives them a kind of awful necromantic interest. The characters are mere abstract algebraical expressions, but they are made the exponents of such terrible and intense fear, suffering, and suspense, that we sympathise with their fate as if they were real. Her repertory is very limited: a persecuted sentimental young lady, a wicked and myterious count, a haggard monk, a tattling but faithful waiting-maid,—such is the poor *human* element out of which these wonderful structures are created. Balzac, in one of his tales, speaks with great admiration of an artist who, by a few touches of his pencil, could give to a most commonplace scene an air of overpowering horror, and throw over the most ordinary and prosaic objects a spectral air of crime and blood. Through a half-opened door you see a bed with the clothes confusedly heaped, as in some death-struggle, over an undefined object which fancy whispers must be a bleeding corpse; on the floor you see a slipper, an upset candlestick, and a knife perhaps; and these hints tell the story of blood more significantly and more powerfully than the most tremendous detail, because the imagination of man is more powerful than art itself:—

> "Over all there hung a cloud of fear,
> A sense of mystery the spirit daunted,
> And said, as plain as whisper to the ear,
> The place is haunted."

A great defect of Anne Radcliffe's fictions is not their tediousness of description, nor even the somewhat mawkish sentimentality with which they may be reproached, nor the feebly-elegant verses which the heroines are represented as writing on all occasions (indeed all these things indirectly conduce to the effect by contrast and preparation); but the unfortunate principle she had imposed upon herself, of clearing up, at the end of the story, all the circumstances that appeared supernatural—of carrying us, as it were, behind the scenes at the end of the play, and showing us the dirty ropes and trap-doors, the daubed canvas, the Bengal fire, by which these wonderful impressions had been produced. If we had supped after the play with the "blood-bolter'd Banquo," or the "majesty of buried Denmark,'' we should not probably be able to feel a due amount of terror the next time we saw them on the stage; but in Mrs. Radcliffe, where the feeling of terror is the principal thing aimed at, this discovery of the mechanism deprives us of all future interest in the story; for, after all, pure fear—*sensual,* not moral, fear—is by no means a legitimate object of high art.

A class of writing *apparently* so easy, and likely to produce so powerful and universal an effect — an effect even more powerful on the least critical minds — was, of course, followed by a crowd of writers. Most of these have descended to oblivion and a deserved neglect. We may say a few words of Lewis, Maturin, and Mrs. Shelley. The first of these, a good-natured effeminate man of fashion, the friend of Byron, and one of the early literary advisers of Scott, was the first to introduce into England a taste for the infant German literature of that day, with its spectral ballads and diablerie of all kinds. He was a man of lively and childish imagination; and besides his metrical translations of the ballads of Bürger, and others of the same class, he published a prose romance called 'The Monk,' full of horrible crimes and diabolic agency. It contains several passages of considerable power, particularly the episode of 'The Bleeding Nun,' in which the wandering Jew—that godsend for all writers, good, bad, and indifferent, of the "intense" or demoniac school—is introduced with picturesque effect; but the book owes its continued popularity (though, we are happy to say, only among half-educated young men and ecstatic milliners) chiefly to the licentious warmth of many of its scenes. Maturin was a young Irishman of great promise and still greater vanity, who carried the intellectual merits and defects of his countrymen to an extreme little short of caricature: his imagination was vivid, and he possessed a kind of extravagant and convulsive eloquence, but his works are full of the most outrageous absurdities. He perpetually mistakes monstrosity for power, and lasciviousness for warmth. His life was short and unhappy, and his chief work is 'Melmoth,' a farrago of impossible and inconceivable adventures, without plan or coherence, in which the Devil (who is represented as an Irish gentleman of good family in the eighteenth century) is the chief agent. Mrs. Shelley is known also, in this department, as the authoress of the powerful tale of 'Frankenstein,' in which a young student of physiology succeeds in constructing, out of the horrid remnants of the churchyard and dissecting-room, a kind of monster, to which he afterwards gives, apparently by the agency of galvanism, a kind of spectral and convulsive life. This existence, rendered insupportable to the monster by his vain cravings after human sympathy, and by his consciousness of his own deformity, is employed in inflicting (in some cases involuntarily) the most dreadful retribution on the guilty philosopher; and some of the chief appearances of the monster, particularly the moment when he begins to move for the first time, and, towards the end of the book, among the eternal snows of the arctic circle, are managed with a striking and breathless effect, that makes us for a moment forget the childish improbability and melodramatic extravagance of the tale.

To this subdivision will belong the works of that most easy and prolific writer, James—the most industrious, if not always most successful, imitator of Scott, in revival of chivalric and middle-age scenes. The number of James's works is immense, but they bear among themselves a family likeness so strong, and even oppressive, that it is impossible to consider this author otherwise than as an ingenious imitator and copyist—first of Scott, and secondly of himself. The spirit of repetition is, indeed, carried so far, that it is possible to guess beforehand, and with perfect certainty, the principal contents, and even the chief persons, of one of James's historical novels. His heroes and heroines, whose features are almost always gracefully and elegantly sketched in, have more of the English than continental character. We are sure to have a nondescript grotesque as a secondary personage—a half-crazy jester, ever hovering between the harebrained villain and the faithful retainer: we may count upon abundance of woodland scenery (often described with singular delicacy and tenderness of language) and moonlight rendezvous of robbers and conspirators. But whereas Scott has all these things, it must be remembered how much more he has *beside.* He looks through all things "with a learned spirit:" James stops short here, unless we notice his innumerable pictures of battles, tournaments, hunting-scenes, and old castles, where we find much more of the forced and artificial accuracy of the antiquary, than of the poet's all-embracing, all-imagining eye. James is particularly versed in the history of France, and some of his most successful novels have reference to that country, among which we may mention 'Richelieu.' His great deficiency is want of real, direct, powerful human passion, and consequently of life and movement in his intrigues. There is thrown over his fictions a general air of good-natured, frank, and well-bred refinement, which, however laudable, cannot fail to be found rather tiresome and monotonous.

This difference between the works of Scott and those among his imitators who have endeavoured to revive the phantoms of past ages with "the very form and pressure of the time," is also perceptible in the works of Ainsworth and Bulwer: of course we allude only to those in which are depicted the manners of by-gone society. Both of these authors have enjoyed a very high degree of popularity; and though it would be an injustice to the author of 'Eugene Aram' to compare him, *in a general sense,* with the writer of 'Rookwood' and 'Jack Sheppard,' yet we may with advantage establish a parallel between these two novelists as far as they are historical. Several of

Ainsworth's earlier and best works were pictures of mediæval manners and society, and they exhibited, together with much of the extravagance, false taste, and melodramatic exaggeration of youthful productions, no small amount of power, picturesqueness, and originality.

It may appear unjust to the genius of Victor Hugo to say so, but to our minds the romances of Ainsworth possess more resemblance to the particular manner of 'Notre Dame de Paris' than any other productions of English literature. If the *romantic* school of modern France was really generated, as some critics maintain, by the unexampled fascination of Scott's historical fictions, the offspring very soon lost all family resemblance to its parent. All that is essential and characteristic in Scott has disappeared—the simplicity, the ease, the natural and unforced pathos, the fresh and manly drollery, the obtaining of the most powerful impressions by the play of ordinary but consistent characters. Instead of this we have, in the modern French school, an intense convulsive energy, proceeding, not by gradual and uninterrupted progression, but by violent and consequently temporary *jerks* of passion and surprise. In Scott there are very few scenes which can be detached bodily from the work so as to lose no portion of their interest and picturesqueness, and capable of forming *gems* or brilliant extracts in a Chrestomathia; whereas, in the other writers, these bright and salient scenes form precisely the merit of the work, and the writers seem to be of the opinion of Bayes in 'The Rehearsal,' who asks "what the plague is the use of the plot, but to bring in the fine things?"

The general tone of Scott (as well as of Fielding, Cervantes, and Shakspeare) is remarkable for its *universality*—for being intelligible to all men, dealing with the ordinary elements of human character, and consequently coming home to all readers. These elements are indeed highly *idealised*, for the ideal is the very essence of art, but everybody can comprehend them in the measure of his own powers and sympathies. The contrary of this takes place in the school of Hugo. Starting from the shallow paradox, that the adaptability of an object to the purposes of art can only be measured by its power of producing strong emotion, they have conceived that hideous and monstrous objects are quite as fit materials for their purpose as what is beautiful and sublime: if it be not true with them that "le laid est le beau," at least they have shown a perfect indifference which they should choose, and have even exhibited a preference for the horrible and the repulsive. They forget that there is a strong line of demarcation between horror and terror, and that it is the former sentiment alone which is a legitimate object of art. The works of Ainsworth possess much of this fragmentary and convulsive character, and the erudition (often great) which he has lavished on his pictures of past ages, bears, like that of Victor Hugo, a painful air of effort

— of having been *read up* for the purpose, and collected for the nonce. The most successful of Ainsworth's romances are 'Rookwood' (the first) and 'Jack Sheppard:' the former owes its success chiefly to the wonderful hurry and rapid vividness of Turpin's ride from London to York in one day, and in the latter the author has broken up what appeared to the public to be new ground — the adventures of highwaymen, prostitutes, and thieftakers. Defoe had done this before, and with astonishing power of invention and probability; but that great moralist has never confounded good and evil, and has shown his squalid ragamuffins as miserable in their lives as they were contemptible and odious in their crimes. Ainsworth, however, has looked upon the romantic side of the picture, and has represented his ruffian hero as a model of gallantry and courage. This, we know, is contrary to universal experience and probability; and while we read with breathless interest the escape of Jack from prison, we forget the monstrous inconsistencies of the story, and the mean and wolfish character of the real criminal, who is here elevated into a hero of romance. To the ignorant and uneducated, who are charmed, like everybody else, with the boldness, dexterity, and perseverance so often exhibited by the worst characters, and which are here dignified with all the artifices of description, but who cannot distinguish between the good and the evil which are mixed up even in the basest characters, this kind of reading is capable of doing, and has done, the greatest mischief; and the very talent — often undeniable — of such works, only renders them the more seductive and insidious.

Bulwer has written in so many different styles, that he almost forms a separate subdivision of our classification of prose fiction. We may, however, view his long and active career under three distinct epochs, the first exampled in 'Pelham,' the second in 'Eugene Aram,' and the third in 'Ernest Maltravers.' In the earliest of these we find him essaying to give a lively and somewhat ironic reflection of the manners of the higher classes, mingled with occasional scenes of low life, sometimes of a broadly comic and farcical, though more often of a gloomy tragic solemnity; in the second we find an attempt at the ideal in his art; and in the third a mixture of the pure ideal with a prevailing tone of philosophic analysis of character, and a metaphysical and abstract investigation into the principles of human passion and human life, their strength and weakness, their health and their disease. 'Pelham' is in general gay and brilliant enough; not very profound, it is true, but lively, sparkling, and effervescent. It contains a great many ingenious paradoxes, clever epigrams, and *good things;* many scattered hints and fragments of character, but not a single personage drawn with consistency and force. Pelham, the hero, is nothing but a compound of two or three affectations which indeed are often found together in an effeminate dandy and wit about town, but which in no sense compose a real human being: Pelham bears the same relation to Tom Jones, for instance, that a painter's lay figure bears to a living man. The same thing may be said of Vincent; and Glanville is nothing but a caricature of the Corsairs, Manfreds, and Childe Harolds, which Byron's poetry brought into fashion. But in Byron these characters, unnatural as they are, are rendered less apparently so by the romantic grandeur and melancholy beauty of the scenery which forms their background, and by the ideal and ecstatic tone which is essential to poetry; Glanville is Lara speaking in the House of Commons, wearing a dress-coat, with a fine house in Grosvenor Square. The scenes, towards the end of the book, among the thieves, are powerfully interesting, from the author's talent of direct, simple, unaffected description—a quality which he possesses in a high degree: but as pictures of the real manners and way of life of such persons, they are totally absurd and impossible. In this novel, as well as in several others (in 'Paul Clifford' for instance, and in some parts of 'Ernest Maltravers'), Bulwer has attempted, like Ainsworth in 'Jack Sheppard,' or Eugène Sue in 'Les Mystères de Paris,' to bring on the scene the interior life of the lowest orders of artisans, malefactors, &c.; but a whole work can never consist entirely of such scenes; and with whatever fidelity these things and persons may be described, we always find these authors at a loss when it comes to the *fitting on* these passages to the descriptions of ordinary life and personages. They are placed separately, detachedly before the reader, like prints taken from a portfolio or pictures in a gallery; they do not melt into each other by just gradations, as they would to a person successively visiting them: we jump from one to the other; there is nothing between. 'Paul Clifford,' the personages of which are almost all members of a band of highwaymen, the chief being the hero, is a notable example of this discord: the characters are alternately philosophers, high-bred gentlemen, and robbers; Clifford himself a mixture of the coxcomb, the brigand, and the satirist of society. The want of harmony to which we have alluded is never to be found in the works of the greatest writers of fiction. Our *curiosity* is gratified, but not a craving after childish wonder; we have thieves and thieftakers in abundance, gipsies, and rioters, and we have also nobles and judges, tradesmen and princes; but we nowhere see sentimental pickpockets, or highwaymen declaiming against the vanity of human wishes. Mere surprise in fiction is as much below the dignity of the art, as optical illusion is degrading to the art of painting. In the next phase of his literary development, Bulwer has given pictures of a more lofty, ambitious, and ideal kind. Of this 'Eugene Aram' is an example. But here he has exhibited not only an ostentatious parade of indigested philosophy, crudely gathered up chiefly from German writers, but a very reprehensible neglect of the distinctions between good and evil, between virtue and crime. Aram, in the true record of his life, gathered from the prosaic but faithful documents of his trial, was a self-educated man of unusual powers of mind, but in a moral point of view a criminal of the most ordinary calibre. He committed under the basest of influences an atrocious and cowardly murder, which was afterwards discovered in a very singular manner; he defended himself with much perverted ability, which only increases our detestation for his character, and perished on a well-merited gallows. Now in Bulwer's story we have nothing of what we should conceive to be the most impressive and dramatic features of this event — the ever-present terror, the fascination of the murderer, his remorse, his struggles in the net of retribution which imprisoned him, the horrid certainty of discovery, and the striking scene of that discovery; we have the robber and murderer of an old man metamorphosed into a romantic enthusiast of the beautiful and the good—a haughty and retiring scholar, who has been led, in spite of himself, into a crime which his soul abhors, and which he almost justifies on his trial by asserting that in robbing and murdering Daniel Clarke he wished to remedy the unjust and unequal distribution of wealth which Providence has made.

This taste for *soi-disant* philosophy Bulwer carries yet farther in his later works; in 'Zanoni' and 'Night and Morning' it forms the staple of the productions. Irritated, perhaps, by the shrewd common sense which characterises the judgment of English critics, and which did not fail, of course, to point out the weak parts and inconsistencies of many of his novels, Bulwer threw himself headlong into the turbid ocean of German metaphysics; and his later works, though still exhibiting his usual flowing style and vivacity of conception, have become a kind of clumsy allegories, generally developing a paradox or an absurdity. The truest and profoundest philosophy of life is to be gathered from the faithfullest representations of its action and passion; the great verities of humanity spring, like wild flowers, by the hedges and waysides of existence; and, to our idea, there is more true depth, true knowledge, true wisdom, in a single, fresh, vigorous, unaffected, strongly-drawn scene of Fielding or of Scott, than in whole libraries of such cloudy raptures as 'Zanoni' or as 'Alice.' His more purely historical novels are much superior, particularly 'Rienzi,' though the character of the hero is rather of the nineteenth than of the fourteenth century. This novel, which is also better constructed than his works usually are in point of plot, was to a certain degree a labour of love, inasmuch as it served the author to embody many of his political convictions. 'The Last Days of Pompeii' is also generally read with great interest; and though there is rather too much parade of not always very accurate antiquarian knowledge, it is written with great *verve* and brilliancy of imagination. In 'The Last of the Barons' he has ventured into the enchanted ground occupied by Scott—English mediæval history; but with exactly the success that was to be expected. The book is a heavy and extravagant caricature, with perhaps not a single page worthy of Bulwer's reputation.

Our second subdivision—the novels of real life and society—is so extensive that we can but throw a rapid glance on its principal productions. To do this consistently with clearness we must begin rather far back, with the novels of Miss Burney. This lady, while yet residing at her father's house, composed, in her stolen moments of leisure, the novel of 'Evelina,' and is related not to have communicated to her father the secret of its having been written by her, until the astonishing success of the fiction rendered her avowal triumphant and almost necessary. 'Evelina' was followed by a number of other novels bearing the same character: their chief defect is vulgarity of feeling—not that falsely called vulgarity which describes with congenial animation low scenes and humble personages, but the affectation of delicacy and refinement. The heroines are perpetually trembling at the thought of *impropriety*, and exhibit a nervous, restless dread of appearing indelicate, that absolutely renders them the very essence of vulgarity. All the difficulties and misfortunes in these plots arise from the want, on the part of the principal personages, of a little candour and straightforwardness, and would be set right by a few words of simple explanation: in this respect the authoress drew from herself; for her lately-published 'Memoirs' exhibit her as existing in a perpetual fever of vanity and petty expedients; and in her gross affectation of more than feminine modesty and bashfulness—literary as well as personal—we see the painful, incessant flutter of her "darling sin"—"the pride that apes humility." Women are endowed by nature with a peculiar delicacy of tact and sensibility; and being excluded, by the now-existing laws of society, from taking an active part in the rougher struggles of life, they acquire much more than the other sex a singular penetration in judging of character from slight and external peculiarities. In acquiring this power they are manifestly aided by their really subordinate, though apparently supreme position in society, by the seductions to which they are exposed, and by the tone of artificial deference in which they are always addressed; men who appear to each other in comparatively natural colours never approach women (particularly unmarried women) but with a mask of chivalry and politeness on their faces; and women, in their turn, soon learn to divine the real character under all these smooth disguisements.

The prevailing literary form, or type, of the present age, is undoubtedly the novel—the narrative picture of manners; just as the epic is the natural literary form of the heroic or traditionary period, and the above remarks will, we think, sufficiently explain the phenomenon of so many women now appearing, in France, Germany, and England, as novel-writers. Our society is highly artificial: the broad distinctions and demarcations which anciently separated one class of men and one profession from another, have been polished away, or filled up by increasing refinement and the extension of personal liberty: the artisan and the courtier, the lawyer and the divine, are no longer distinguished either by professional costume, or by any of those outward and visible signs which formerly stamped their manners and language, and furnished the old comic writer with strongly-marked characters ready made to his hand. We must now go deeper: the coat is the same everywhere; consequently, we must strip the man — nay, we must anatomise him — to show how he differs from his neighbours. To do this well, fineness of penetration is, above all, necessary — a quality which women, *cæteris paribus*, possess in a higher degree than men.

Miss Burney was followed by a number of writers, chiefly women, among whom the names of Mrs. Inchbald and Mrs. Opie are prominent. Their fictions, like those of Miss Edgeworth in more recent times, have a high and never-failing moral aim; and both these ladies have exhibited a power over the feelings, and an intensity of pathos, not much inferior to Richardson's in 'Clarissa Harlowe.' But their works are very unequal, and the pathos of which we speak is not diffused, but concentrated into particular *moments* of the action, and is also obtained at the expense of great preparation and involution of circumstances; so that to compare their genius to that of Richardson, on the strength of a few powerful pictures of intense moral pathos, would be a gross injustice to the admirable and consummate artist, in whose works the pathos, inimitable as it is, forms but one item in a long list of his excellences.

At the head of the second division of our fictions is undoubtedly William Godwin, a man of truly powerful and original genius, who devoted his whole life to the propagation of certain social and political theories — visionary, indeed, and totally impracticable, but marked with the impress of benevolence and philanthropy. With these ideas Godwin's mind was perfectly saturated and possessed, and this intensity of conviction, this ardent *propagandism*, not only gives to his writings a peculiar character of earnestness and thought — earnestness, the rarest and most impressive of literary qualities—but may be considered to have made him, in spite of all the tendencies of his intellectual character—*invitâ Minervâ*—a novelist. Godwin was born in 1756, and appears to have sucked with his mother's milk those principles of resistance to authority, and attachment to free opinions in church and state, which had been handed down from one sturdy Dissenter to another from the days of the civil war and the republic. He was in reality one of those hard-headed enthusiasts — at once wild visionaries and severe logicians — who abounded in the age of Marvell, Milton, and Harrington; and his true epoch would have been the first period of Cromwell's public life. His own career, extending down to his death in 1836, was incessantly occupied with literary activity; he produced an immense number of works, some immortal for the genius and originality they display, and all for an intensity and gravity of thought, for reading and erudition. The first work which brought him into notice was the 'Essay on Political Justice,' a Utopian theory of morals and government, by which virtue and benevolence was to be the "*primum mobile*" of all human actions, and a philosophical republic—that favourite dream of visionaries—was to take place of all our imperfect modes of polity. Animated during his whole life by these opinions, he has embodied them under a variety of forms, among the rest in his immortal romances. The first and finest of these is 'Caleb Williams.' Its chief didactic aim is to show the misery and injustice arising from our present imperfect constitution of society, and the oppression of our imperfect laws, both written and unwritten—the *jus scriptum* of the statute-book, and the *jus non scriptum* of social feeling and public opinion. Caleb Williams is an intelligent peasant lad, taken into the service of Falkland, the true hero, an incarnation of honour, intellect, benevolence, and a passionate love of fame. This model of all the chivalrous and elevated qualities has previously, under the provocation of the cruellest, most persevering, and tyrannic insult, in a moment of ungovernable passion, committed a murder: his fanatic love of reputation urges him to conceal this crime; and, in order to do this more effectually, he allows an innocent man to be executed, and his family ruined. Williams obtains, by an accident, a clue to the guilt of Falkland, when the latter, extorting from him an oath that he will keep his secret, communicates to his dependant the whole story of his double crime, of his remorse and misery. The youth, finding his life insupportable from the perpetual suspicion to which he is exposed, and the restless surveillance of his master, escapes; and is pursued through the greater part of the tale by the unrelenting persecution of Falkland, who, after having committed one crime under unsupportable provocation, and a second to conceal the first, is now led, by his frantic and unnatural devotion to fame, to annihilate, in Williams, the evidence of his guilt. The adventures of the unfortunate fugitive, his dreadful vicissitudes of poverty and distress, the steady, bloodhound, unrelaxing pursuit, the escapes and disguises of the victim, like the agonised turnings and doublings of the hunted hare—all this is depicted with an incessant and never surpassed power of breathless interest. At last Caleb is formally accused by Falkland of robbery, and naturally discloses before the tribunal the dreadful secret which had caused his long persecution, and Falkland dies of shame and a broken heart. The interest of this wonderful tale is indescribable; the various scenes are set before us with something of the minute reality, the dry, grave simplicity of Defoe. But in Godwin, the faculty of the picturesque, so prominent in the mind of Defoe, is almost absent: everything seems to be *thought out*, elaborated by an effort of the will. Defoe seems simply to describe things as they really were, and we feel it impossible to conceive that they were otherwise than so; Godwin describes them (and with a wondrous power of coherency) as we feel they would be in such and such circumstances. His descriptions and characters are masterly pieces of construction; or, like mathematical problems, they are deduced step by step, infallibly, from certain *data*. This author possesses no humour, no powers of description, at least of nature—none of that magic which communicates to inanimate objects the light and glow of sentiment—very little pathos: but on the other hand, few have possessed a more penetrating eye for that recondite causation which links together motive and action, a more watchful and determined consistency in tracing the manifestations of such characters as he has once conceived, or a more prevailing spirit of self-persuasion as to the reality of what he relates. The romance of 'Caleb Williams' is indeed ideal; but it is an ideal totally destitute of all the trappings and ornaments of the ideal: it is like some grand picture painted in dead-colour.

In 1799 appeared 'St. Leon;' in 1804, 'Fleetwood;' in 1817, 'Mandeville;' and in 1830, just before his death, 'Cloudesley.' These four works are romances in the same manner as 'Caleb Williams;' but there is perceptible in them a gradual diminution in vigour and originality—we do not mean of *positive* but of *relative* originality. 'St. Leon' is, however, a powerful conception, executed in parts with a gloomy energy peculiar to this author. The story is of a man who has acquired possession of the great arcanum—the secret of boundless wealth and immortal life; and the drift of the book is to give a terrible picture of the misery which would result from the possession of such an immortality and such riches, when deprived (as such a being must be) of the sympathies of human affection, and the joys and woes of human nature. This novel contains several powerfully-delineated scenes, generally of a gloomy tone, and a female character, Marguerite, of singular beauty and interest.

At the head—facilè princeps—of the very large class of female novelists who have adorned the more recent literature of England, we must place Miss Edgeworth, born about 1768 This place she deserves, not only for the immense number, variety, and originality of her works of fiction, but also, and perhaps in a superior degree, for their admirable good sense and utility.

Most of those who have undertaken the ill-requited but certainly most important task of writing for children have failed, from not having sufficiently considered the nature and character of the child as mind. They are perpetually haunted by the notion that it is indispensable to *write down* to their audience: they think it necessary to place the moral of their story offensively in the foreground: they do not consider this perpetually perking, as it were, of the moral in the face of the reader—so offensive in a work addressed to grown-up persons—is no less disgusting to children, however young. Children hate to be *lectured* at least as much as their elders; and, consequently, the great difficulty in writing for the very young is either entirely to conceal, under an interesting and striking narrative, the nauseous dose of morality which is to be administered, or, at least, to gild the pill as far as possible. The chief defect of Berquin, and other excellent and well-intentioned writers for childhood, is the leaving nothing to be discovered by the intelligence of the little reader; for children, like grown-up people, are exceedingly glad of the opportunity of employing the perceptive and comparative faculties of their minds; nay, take the more pleasure in doing so, because those faculties have in general been but recently called into activity. Therefore they despise those feeble and affected writings in which the characters are either complete embodiments of some virtue or its corresponding vice; and their sense of probability is very much shocked by seeing represented in fiction what even their imperfect experience shows them to be never occurring in real life—*i. e* characters of unmixed good or unmitigated evil, virtue invariably rewarded, and vice as invariably punished. Miss Edgeworth has written a complete literature for infancy and youth. She has had the sense and courage to begin from the very beginning; and the first tale of her admirable series is, if we remember well, a story in words of one syllable, and adapted for the very earliest age. From this she has passed on to the exquisite little tales contained in 'The Parent's Assistant,' a collection to the first perusal of which no one ever looked back but with feelings of gratitude and delight; and then through the various collections under the titles of 'Popular Tales,' 'Moral Tales,' and 'Fashionable Tales,'—a cycle of fictions which, including the novels of 'Patronage,' 'Leonora,' 'Belinda,' 'Helen,' and 'The Absentee,' may boldly be said to contain more sound sense, acute observation of character, and applicability to practical life, than any set of works professing a didactic tendency. In all, the primary qualities just mentioned are equally visible. Even in 'Frank' and 'Rosamond'—little stories for the almost infant mind—we perceive the same infallible and irresistible sense, the same ease and vivacity of narration, and the same exquisite perception of character and the weaknesses of human nature. To those who confound form with matter in literary judgments it may seem preposterous to assign such high praise to a collection of tales for children; but to persons who know from experience the difficulty of writing effectively in this manner, our criticism, laudatory as it is, will not appear extravagantly favourable. There are few failings of the opening character — few of those passions and errors which, being common to all ages of human life, so easily grow from defects into vices, and from vices into crimes—which she has not with penetrating eye pursued into the inmost foldings of the heart, and driven them forth with her gentle satire and admirable logic of good sense. She excels in reducing a folly, or a false virtue, "ad absurdum;" she is truly Socratic, in the manner by which she drives a fallacy to its last defences. She has invariably and perseveringly discountenanced all exaltation and enthusiasm; and this incessant attention to the real and practical, however it may sometimes diminish her glory as a great *artist*, undoubtedly increases her utility as a moral teacher. In one class of characters she is almost unrivalled: no author has, with so much sympathy, penetration, and vivacity, exhibited the national peculiarities of the Irish — a nation which she has studied with peculiar interest and love. Her volume entitled 'Castle Rackrent' is a kind of chronicle of the oddities and humours, the vices and generosity, of a series of Irish landlords, and contains a wonderful amount of acute observation.

Miss Edgeworth's never-failing success in the delineation of this kind of *local* character will warrant us in placing her at the head of a class of novelists almost peculiar to English literature, and which ought to form a subdivision in this part of our subject — we mean, writers whose works are devoted to the delineation of local manners and character. Thus, there are many excellent writers of fiction who have devoted themselves to the painting of the peculiar manners, oddities, and domestic life of Scotland and Ireland exclusively. John Galt, in a long series of novels, has confined himself to the minute delineation—as rich, as original, and as careful as the workmanship of Douw, Mieris, or Teniers — of the interior life of the Scottish peasantry and provincial tradespeople. The 'Annals of the Parish,' the supposed journal of a quaint, simple-minded Presbyterian pastor, give us a singularly amusing insight into the microscopic details of Scottish life in the lower classes. Galt's primary characteristic is a dry, subdued, quaint humour—a quality very perceptible in the lower orders of Scotland, and which in his works, as in the national character of his countrymen, is often accompanied by a very profound and true sense of the pathetic. The more romantic and tragical side of the national idiosyncrasy has been exquisitely portrayed in the touching tales of John Wilson, than whom, it should be remarked, no author has ever shown a finer eye for the beauties of nature, or a profounder feeling for the virtues and trials of humble life. In this department of *local* manners the Irish have peculiarly distinguished themselves; as might, indeed, be expected, when we remember the intense vivacity of the Hibernian character, and the abundance of materials for the novelist afforded by the incessant social, religious, and political discord which for three centuries has never ceased to convulse that country. A long list of names presents itself to our notice, of which, however, it will suffice to say a few words of the principal—Lady Morgan, Banim, Crofton Croker, Carleton, Mrs. Hall, Lever, and Lover. All these persons have devoted themselves, with more or less success, to the depicting the humours or the passions, the bright or dark, the light and shadow, of Irish life. Some—as, for example, Banim—have attached themselves more exclusively to the tragic, or rather melodramic, scenes of Irish society, generally in the peasant class; and though it is impossible not to appreciate in their works a very marked degree of power, picturesqueness, imagination, and eloquence, yet these high qualities are often eclipsed by an exaggerated and ferocious energy which defeats its own object, and renders the work ridiculous instead of sublime. In the Irish character there is no repose, and where there is no repose there can be no contrast — the only element of strong impressions. Other authors, again, as Crofton Croker, have attached themselves more particularly, and with more effect, to the merely romantic and imaginative features of the national legends and superstitions; and the latter gentleman has produced a little collection of fairy tales worthy to be placed beside the delicious 'Haus und Kindermächen' of the brothers Grimm.

Of those who have devoted themselves to the delineation of purely English manners in all ranks of society, the number is so immense that it would be as useless as tedious to give even a catalogue of their names and works. We shall content ourselves with selecting a few of the most prominent, or rather such as appear *typical*, and as consequently will give, in each instance, the general idea of the class at whose head we place them; and first, of the writers of what are called "fashionable novels"—*i. e.* such as pretend to depict the manners, habits, and sentiments of aristocratic life. There is no country in the world, assuredly, in which the middle and lower classes possess so much personal liberty, and consequently so much enlightment and independence, as England; but, at the same time, there is hardly any nation in which, generally speaking, there is such a tendency in each class to admire and ape the manners of the class immediately above it. Our present business is with the *literary* effect of this peculiar admiration of aristocracy. Its tendency has been to flood our literature with a preposterous amount of trashy writings, proposing to give a reflection of the manners and habits of high life. Frequently composed, and as a mere speculation, by persons totally unacquainted with the scenes they essayed to describe, and relying for their interest either on grotesque exaggerations of what they supposed to exist in those favoured regions—the Empyrean of fashion — or on coarse scandal and misrepresentation, these egregious books were either sign-post caricatures of what the authors had never seen, or were clumsy réchauffés of forgotten scandal, without wit, sense, probability, or nature. The more extravagant, however, were these pictures, and the less they resembled the ordinary life of the reader, the more eagerly were they admired; and it is not to be wondered at that the time should come when persons, either themselves members of aristocratic society, or men capable of forming true ideas on the subject, should have taken in hand to give something like a true picture of the life of these envied circles. Among the best of these fashionable novels are those of Lister (perhaps this gentleman's 'Granby' is as good a specimen as can be selected of this class), Lady Charlotte Bury, Mr. Ward, Benjamin D'Israeli, Lord Normanby, and Lady Blessington. The novels of Ward are distinguished by the author's attempt to unite with an interesting story a good deal of elevated philosophical and literary speculation; so that many of his works—as, for instance, 'Tremaine,' 'Le Vere,' 'De Clifford,' &c,—are something which is neither a good narrative nor a collection of good essays. Either the philosophy impedes the narrative, or the narrative destroys the interest and coherency of the philosophy. But the writings of Ward, as well as of Lister, are valuable for the simple and unaffected tone of their language, for the moral truth and elevation of their sentiment, and for the charm that can only be expressed by that most untranslatable of English words—"gentlemanliness." These merits are also in a very high degree possessed by such of James's novels as describe modern manners, many of which have considerable interest, of a gentle and subdued kind. Of Bulwer we have already spoken.

Descending the social scale, we come to a very large and characteristic department of works—the department which undoubtedly possesses not only the greatest degree of value for the English reader, but will have the most powerful attraction for foreign students of our literature. This is that class of fictions which depicts the manners of the middle and lower classes: and here again we shall encounter a singular amount of female names. The first in point of time, and perhaps almost the first in point of merit, in this class, especially among the ladies, is Miss Austen, whose novels may be considered as models of perfection in a new and very difficult species of writing. She depends for her effect upon no surprising adventures, upon no artfully involved plot, upon no scenes deeply pathetic or extravagantly humorous. She paints a society which, though virtuous, intelligent, and enviable above all others, presents the fewest salient points of interest and singularity to the novelist—we mean the society of English country gentlemen. Whoever desires to know the interior life of that vast and admirable body the rural gentry of England—a body which absolutely exists in no other country on earth, and to which the nation owes many of its most valuable characteristics—must read the novels of Miss Austen. In these works the reader will find very little variety and no picturesque ness of persons, little to inspire strong emotion, nothing to excite wonder or laughter; but he will find admirable good sense, exquisite discrimination, and an unrivalled power of easy and natural dialogue. Miss Ferriar has also written a number of novels, generally depicting with great vivacity and truth the oddities and affectations of semi-vulgar life, but her works are far inferior, as artistic productions, to the elegant sketches of Miss Austen.

Of the purely comic manner of fiction there are few better examples than the novels of Theodore Hook. He is greatest in the description of London life, and particularly in the rich drollery with which he paints the vulgar efforts of suburban gentility to ape the manners of the great. There is not one of his numerous novels and shorter tales in which some scene could not be cited carrying this kind of drollery almost to the brink of farce. Many of his works — as 'Sayings and Doings'— consist of short tales, each destined to develop the folly or evil consequences of some particular inconsistency or affectation: thus the work just cited consists of a set of detached stories, each written on the text, as it were, of some common well-known proverb; and though the narratives are of very slight construction, and do not contain very profound views of *character*, they none of them are devoid of some incredibly droll caricatures of *manners*. What, for example, can be more irresistible than the Bloomsbury evening party in 'Maxwell,' or the dinner at Mr. Abberley's in 'The Man of Many Friends?' Hook's more exclusively serious novels are generally considered as inferior to those in which there is a mixture of the ludicrous; and for one of the last works produced by this clever writer before his death, he selected a subject admirably adapted to the peculiar strength of his talent. This was 'Jack Brag,' a most spirited embodiment of the arts employed by a vulgar pretender to creep into aristocratic society, and the ultimate discomfiture of the absurd hero. Hook was a man of great but superficial powers, one of the most amusing conversationists of the day, an inimitable relater of anecdotes, a singer, and an *improvvisatore*; but he was himself afflicted with the same passion for the society of the great as he has so wittily caricatured in Mr Brag, and his life was passed in incessant but desultory literary labour as a novelist and journalist, in frequent disappointments, in debt, and in the empty applauses of the circle he amused. He died in 1842, leaving a large number of works, all of them exhibiting strong proofs of humour, but mostly deprived of permanent value by the haste perceptible in their execution. The best of them are, perhaps, 'Gilbert Gurney,' and its continuation, 'Gurney Married.'

Very similar to Theodore Hook in the subject and treatment of her novels, and not unlike him in the general tone of her talent, is Mrs. Trollope, whose happiest efforts are the exhibition of the gross arts and impudent stratagems employed by the pretenders to fashion.

Mrs. Trollope's chief defect is coarseness and violence of contrast: she does not know where to stop, and is too apt to render her characters not ridiculous only, but odious, in which she offends against the primary laws of comic writing. Moreover, she neglects light and shade in her pictures: her personages are either mere embodiments of all that is contemptible, or cold abstractions of everything refined and excellent. Her best work is, perhaps, 'The Widow Barnaby,' in which she has reached the ideal of a character of gross, full-blown, palpable, complete pretension and vulgar assurance. The widow, with her coarse handsome face, and her imperturbable, unconquerable self-possession, is a truly rich comic conception. Mrs. Trollope's plots are exceedingly slight and ill constructed, but her narrative is lively, and she particularly excels in her characters of goodnatured, shrewd old maids. She first became generally known to the literary world in 1832, by her relation of a residence of some years in the United States, in which she exhibited so unflattering a picture of American society, that our transatlantic neighbours have not yet recovered from the paroxysm of anger into which the rough strictures of Mrs. Trollope threw them.

It would be a great injustice were we not to devote a few words of admiration to the charming sketches of Miss Mitford, a lady who has described the village life and scenery of England with the grace and delicacy of Goldsmith himself. 'Our Village' is one of the most delightful books in the language: it is full of those *home scenes* which form the most exquisite peculiarity, not only of the external nature, but also of the social life of the country. In nothing is our nation so happily distinguished from all others as in the enlightenment, the true refinement, the virtue, and the dignity of her middle and lower classes, and in no position are those classes so worthy of admiration as in the quiet, tranquil existence of the country. She describes with the truth and fidelity of Crabbe and Cowper, but without the moral gloom of the one, and the morbid sadness of the other. Whether it is her pet greyhound Lily, or the sunburnt, curly, ragged village child, the object glows before us with something of that daylight sunshine which we find in its highest perfection in the rural and familiar images of Shakspeare.

Passing over Smith, whose numerous novels are little more than repetitions or imitations of the works which were in fashion at the different periods when he wrote them, we come to Samuel Warren, who obtained an enviable reputation for vigour and originality so early as 1837, when he commenced contributing to 'Blackwood's Magazine' a series of tales entitled 'Passages from the Diary of a late Physician.' The nature of these narratives may easily be guessed from their title, and Warren very skilfully maintained the disguise of a medical man, gained chiefly by his own early introduction into a humble branch of that profession. The tales themselves are of various lengths, and very unequal degrees of merit. They are all, with the exception of one or two (which are not important enough to change the general impression on the reader), of a very tragic and painful nature—dark and agonising pages from the vast book of human suffering. The scenes are taken from almost every gradation of social life; we have the last moments of the condemned forger, the slow martyrdom of a virtuous philosopher, the madness of the lover and the statesman, and two or three most impressive pictures of commercial ruin, and the fatal effect of vice, ill-regulated passions, and a morbid indulgence of imagination. Perhaps the finest of these tales are those entitled 'The Spectre-smitten,' 'The Banker's Clerk,' 'The Statesman,' and 'The Forger.' The style, though occasionally rather too highly coloured, is very direct, powerful, and unaffected; and the too great prevalence of a tone of agony and extreme distress, which certainly injures the effect of the whole, by depriving the work of *relief*, which is, above all, indispensable in painful subjects, is perhaps rather attributable to the nature of the subjects than to any defect of the artist. It is but just to remark, too, that this monotony of gloom and agony is not perceptible in these tales as they at first appeared, separately and at considerable intervals, in the pages of a magazine, though it is certainly objectionable in them when collected into a single publication. Encouraged by this success, Mr. Warren began the tale of 'Ten Thousand-a-Year,' which also appeared in 'Blackwood's Magazine.' This work portrays the unexpected elevation to immense wealth and importance of one of the most contemptible beings that the imagination can conceive, Mr. Tittlebat Titmouse, a vulgar, ignorant coxcomb of the lowest order, a linen-draper's shopman in Oxford-street, and suddenly exalted, through the instrumentality of some rascally attorneys, who have discovered a defect in a pedigree, to the third heaven of English aristocracy. The book is crowded with "scenes of many-coloured life," and with an infinity of personages, all vigorously, and some admirably drawn. The gradual development of the plot is carried on, not only with considerable skill and probability, but with a great deal more attention to detail than is usual in modern fiction; and many of the scenes are highly dramatic and natural—for instance, the dinner at Mr. Quirk's; the trial; the suicide of Gammon at the end of the book, which is as finely worked up as anything in Richardson; and the insanity of Lord Dreddlington. Mr. Warren is a barrister, and a distinguished writer on legal education; and we cannot, therefore, be surprised that he should exhibit great and accurate knowledge, not only of the profession itself, but of the habits of its members. The work is undeniably a production of great skill and genius, and setting aside a little political partiality (for all Mr. Warren's good people are Tories, and his bad ones as invariably Whigs), must be considered as giving a vivid, well-drawn, and impressive picture of modern English society.

The greatest name in the contemporary literature of Great Britain is indubitably that of Charles Dickens, who first appeared before the public some twelve years ago, as the author of a short series of sketches written to fill the vacant columns of a London newspaper. These were very slight but charming descriptions of metropolitan or suburban life, and must be considered as the first breaking up of an entirely new literary vein. The subject is "everyday life and everyday people," and no author ever showed a more delicate skill in appreciating and expressing the almost imperceptible shades of London life. The best sketches were those of a purely descriptive character, such as 'The Marine-store Shop,' 'Seven Dials,' 'The Streets;' in short, those in which some phase of London life, or one of the thousand appearances of London scenery, is set before us. Several of these sketches were little narratives, of which the most ambitious and elaborate are invariably the least effective; while those embodying some slight trait of character and manners exhibited a victorious power of exciting pathetic impressions, and an infallible tact for the various shades of personal or professional oddity. It was easy to see that a perfectly original author had appeared, possessing an inexhaustible knowledge of all the mysteries of London life, particularly in the lower class, and that rare and infallible evidence of genius—the power of extracting novelty and interest from the most ordinary and common details of society, from things which we are so familiar with that we cannot conceive how they can contain materials either for laughter or for tears. In 1837 began the publication, in monthly numbers, each containing about two chapters, of the humorous tale 'The Pickwick Papers,' which may be described as a succession of detached adventures, very slightly connected together by a thread of plot, full of the richest and raciest delineations of London scenery, characters, and oddities. Mr. Pickwick himself, the citizen Don Quixote of the nineteenth century, is a personage as natural, as delightful, and as completely drawn as the inimitable hero of Cervantes. But what praise can be sufficiently enthusiastic for the admirable conception of Sam Weller, that inimitable compound of wit, simplicity, quaint humour, and fidelity! The "gamin de Paris" does not possess a more distinctive and attractive physiognomy than Dickens has here immortalised in this exquisite portrait of the Londoner; perhaps since Parson Adams literature cannot afford an instance of a personage so exquisitely true to nature, so intensely comic, so individual, and at the same time so perfect a type of a class, as this delightful creation. Of the inferior persons and the adventures it will perhaps suffice to say, that those which belong to London life—Boz's peculiar domain—are almost invariably exquisite: but in quitting the streets of the capital Dickens seems to leave behind him much of his characteristic delicacy and power. Not but that many of his descriptions of country and provincial scenery are exceedingly rich and delicate; but he seems ever most at home in the great Babylon, and appears to look upon every other object with the eye of one who, though a painter and a poet of rare merit, is still a Londoner—a "Cockney." Nothing can be more admirably true to nature and humorous than the supper-party of the medical students, the scenes of low life in which most prominently figure Mrs. Bardell, Mrs. Cluppins, and Mrs. Raddle, with her unfortunate henpecked husband. All the passages in which we behold any of the multitudinous variety of attorneys and attorneys' clerks—a most characteristic species in London—are unsurpassable; it is indisputable that since Scott no author has appeared in European literature who has succeeded in producing anything like the impression made by these truly original draughts from nature. The plot or intrigue of this work is absolutely nothing; the personages flit before the reader like the phantoms of the magic-lantern; but we forget all the improbability of the fable in the vivacity and fluent abundance of the incidents. This author is a striking proof of the truth that the same delicacy of mental organization which renders a man susceptible to the impressions of the humorous and the comic, best enables him to command our tears. Many of the defects of this work are to be traced to the manner of its appearance, in detached portions. There is every reason to suppose, not only that it was published, but that it was also composed, in this desultory and fragmentary form; and the increasing practice of giving to the world narratives in this manner is, we think, productive of so much injury to this branch of literature, that we cannot refrain from saying a few words on the subject. The immense development within a few years, both in England and other countries, of periodical literature or journalism, has induced almost all modern authors to publish works (even of continuous fiction) in this form. The consequence is that the writer, whatever be his genius, and however carefully he may have previously arranged the plan and outline of his work, finds himself exposed to a perpetual temptation of over-colouring each particular portion. He knows that the public expects in each monthly or weekly "feuilleton" something highly spiced and intensely interesting; and is thus tempted to neglect that gradation, that proportion, that subordination of the parts to the whole, which is as necessary to the due effect of a novel as of a picture or as of a work of architecture.

'The Pickwick Papers,' the success of which was enormous (100,000 copies having been sold, according to common report), was almost immediately followed by 'Nicholas Nickleby,' a more regular and carefully constructed fiction, exhibiting no diminution of power, originality, and picturesqueness. The events take place chiefly in

London, though one important portion of the work is devoted to giving a most frightful picture of the atrocities perpetrated in cheap schools — a nuisance which Dickens's powerful *exposé* in this novel tended mainly to diminish, if not altogether to abate. Mr. Squeers, the ignorant, cruel, and rapacious schoolmaster, is a *chef-d'œuvre;* and the wanderings of Nicholas, with his broken-spirited protégé Smike, are full of variety and interest; particularly their adventures in Mr. Vincent Crummles's troop of provincial actors. Among the serious characters in this tale are two usurers, Ralph Nickleby and Arthur Gride, which, as striking yet perfectly natural embodiments, have perhaps never been surpassed.

With a fertility like that of Scott, Dickens very speedily appeared again before the public in 'Oliver Twist,' a simple tale of the adventures of a charity-boy, who "falls among thieves" and is initiated, though without his innocence being corrupted, into all the mysteries of the London housebreakers and pickpockets. The "merry old gentleman," Mr. Fagin, a Jew who keeps a kind of boarding-house for a society of young thieves, and the acolytes who are grouped around this venerable professor of the art of appropriation, all these are as fine as anything in Smollett; the Artful Dodger in particular is a gem, an absolute literary type; but not Smollett, nor Fielding, nor perhaps all the romance-writers whose works we possess, could have produced anything equal, in terrific reality and vividness, to the murder of Nancy and the wanderings of the ruffian Sykes. Sykes and his dog alone are enough to establish Dickens's fame as a great original writer. Nothing so prosaic in its subject, yet raised by the mere force of genius to a true intensity of horror, is perhaps to be found in fiction. The adventures of Oliver, the hero, are unnatural; but the true strength of the work consists in the other characters.

The next work of our inexhaustible novelist was 'Master Humphrey's Clock,' in which, under a general fiction not very probable or well imagined, the author intended to unite a number of detached stories. Of these we have two, 'The Old Curiosity Shop' and 'Barnaby Rudge.' The first is a powerful and impressive delineation of the gambler's mania, exhibited in a miserable old being, tottering on the verge of the grave, and a number of subordinate personages, sometimes grotesque, as Quilp, but always stamped with vigour and consistency. Above all these, and in the thick atmophere of misery, hopeless suffering, and privation, floats the exquisite and angelic figure of "Little Nell," one of the most enchanting conceptions of grace and innocence — the more admirable, perhaps, as Dickens is not always very successful in such delineations. 'Barnaby Rudge' is in some sense historical, as its chief action is the dreadful insurrection of 1783, called "Lord George Gordon's Riots," when the refuse of the London population, under the pretext of a dread of Popery, committed, during several days, the most horrible disorders in the capital. These riots, and the chief personages who figure in them, are set before us with great but somewhat exaggerated energy, and this principal action is combined with the detection of a horrid fratricide supposed to have been committed some years before. The long agonies of the unrepentant murderer are described with a power that reminds of the admirable episode of Sykes.

In 1843 Dickens made a voyage to the United States, and described his impressions of the manners, &c., of the Americans in a book which is strangely unworthy of his powers. The impressions themselves are highly unfavourable to the Americans, and in this respect accord with the reports of almost every English traveller who has given to the world his personal observations on the republic. But many of the richest contents of his American note-book were transferred to the pages of 'Martin Chuzzlewit,' a narrative somewhat resembling 'Nickleby,' which appeared in the year just mentioned. This novel is one of the finest of his composition — not the American scenes, perhaps, for these have generally an air of exaggeration which injures them; but the adventures which occur before and after the hero makes his unfortunate and unsuccessful voyage across the Atlantic. Mr. Pecksniff, the architect, is a finished hypocrite—the Tartuffe of morality, a sort of Mr. Squeers without the brutality. This tale contains, too, one of those exquisite personages which Dickens excels in inventing, and placing amidst his *dramatis personæ*, as a kind of embodiment of his own gentle, generous, loving heart. Who can forget Tom Pinch, *old* Tom Pinch, with his guilelessness, his oddity, his exhaustless goodness of heart? Opposed to this truly delightful creation we have Jonas Chuzzlewit, whose mean brutality and small tyranny is finely and consistently sustained. Even in Dickens there are few things finer than the episode of the murder committed by Jonas; and the pangs of remorse acting on a base and wolfish nature have seldom been more powerfully described. Nor are the comic scenes less varied or less excellent; the dinner-party at Todgers's is one of the very finest things in the whole range of comic fiction, and immeasurably superior even to the far-famed "supper after the manner of the ancients" in Smollett's 'Peregrine Pickle.'

Since the appearance of this rich and rapid succession of noble fictions, Dickens seemed to content himself with reposing on the laurels he has gained; having produced no long works, simply reminding us of the existence of his undiminished power by publishing a series of little festival Christmas tales. Of these, four have already appeared, entitled 'A Christmas Carol in Prose,' 'The Chimes,' 'The Cricket on the Hearth,' and 'The Battle of Life.' They are all admirable for the benevolent genial spirit which they express, and display a degree of grace and fancy which is in every way worthy of the object for which they were written — the noble aim of inspiring the rich and happy with sympathy and compassion for the poor. They breathe the very spirit of Christmas-time — the highest praise which can be given. The best of them, as far as the story is concerned, is the first, though 'The Chimes' contains an immense power of fantastic imagination. They are all very short: the 'Carol' describes the conversation, begun by a ghost, and continued by a series of visions, embodying the "Past, Present, and Future," of a coldhearted old miser, to the hearty benevolence so suited to Christmas; the second is a goblin story; and the third one of those delightful glimpses into very humble life which no author can embody like Dickens. Even should he write no more, he has done enough to deserve the love and admiration of posterity; his works possess the highest and rarest of merits — that of complete originality both of matter and of form; his view of life is generous, elevating, genial; he sympathises with what is good and noble in all classes and conditions alike; he makes us love our kind, he makes us love the exercise of the huumbler and more modest virtues, he chronicles the minor accidents and impressions of life; his writings, though describing the manners of the poorest and lowest classes of mankind, contain nothing which can shock the most fastidious taste; and the only things he has held up to ridicule or detestation are vice, hypocrisy, or the pretensions of imbecile vulgarity. He is an author of whom England may be proud.

The immense colonial possessions of Great Britain, and particularly her colossal empire in the East, combined with the passion for travelling so strongly manifested in the nation, have created in our literature a class of works which may be considered as forming almost a separate department of fiction. These are novels which have for their aim the delineation of the manners, scenery, &c., of distant countries; and as among these works the Oriental are naturally the most splendid and prominent, we shall take three which seem the most favourable specimens of this subdivision. They are different from each other in form, in tone, and in scope, but are equally distinguished for their cleverness and individuality. Of these Oriental novels, then, we select, as the most striking examples, 'The History of the Caliph Vathek,' by Beckford; the romance of 'Anastasius,' by Hope; and the inimitable 'Hajji Baba' of Morier. The first of these fictions was as wild, strange, and dreamily magnificent, as the character and biography of its author—a man almost as rich, as splendidly luxurious, and as coldly meditative as the Comte de Montecristo, in Dumas' popular story. 'Vathek' is an Arabian tale, and was originally published in 1784, *in French*, being one of the rare instances of an Englishman being able to write that difficult language with the grace and purity of a native. Being afterwards translated by the author into his mother tongue, it forms one of the most extraordinary monuments of splendid imagery and caustic wit which literature can afford. It is very short, and in some respects resembles (at least in its cold sarcasm of tone and exquisite refinement of style) the 'Zadig' of Voltaire. But 'Vathek' is immeasurably superior in point of imagination, and in its singular fidelity to the Oriental colouring and costume. Indeed, if we set aside its contemptuous and sneering tone, it might pass for a translation of one of 'The Thousand and one Nights.' It narrates the adventures of a haughty and effeminate monarch, led on, by the temptations of a malignant genie and the sophistries of a cruel and ambitious mother, to commit all sorts of crimes, to abjure his faith, and to offer allegiance to Eblis, the Mahommedan Satan, in the hope of seating himself on the throne of the Preadamite sultans. The gradual development in his mind of sensuality, cruelty, atheism, and insane and Titanic ambition, is very finely traced; the imagery throughout is truly splendid, its Eastern gorgeousness tempered and relieved by the sneering sarcastic irony of a French Encyclpédiste; and the concluding scene soars into the highest atmosphere of grand descriptive poety. Here he descends into the subterranean palace of Eblis, where he does homage to the Evil One, and wanders for a while among the superhuman splendours of those regions of punishment. The fancy of genius has seldom conceived anything more terrible than "the vast multitude, incessantly passing, who severally kept their right hands on their heart, without once regarding anything around them. They all avoided each other, and, though surrounded by a multitude that no one could number, each wandered at random, unheedful of the rest, as if alone on a desert where no foot had trodden."

Hope, like Beckford, was a man of refined taste, luxurious habits, and possessed of a colossal fortune accumulated in commerce. His work, though very different in form from that of Beckford, was not unlike it in some points. 'Anastasius,' published in 1819, purports to be the autobiography of a Greek, who, to escape the consequences of his own crimes and villanies of every kind, becomes a renegade, and passes through a long series of the most extraordinary and romantic vicissitudes. The hero is a compound of almost all the vices of his unfortunate and degraded nation; and in his vicissitudes of fortune we see passing before us, as in a diorama, the whole social, political, and religious life of Turkey and the Morea. The style is elaborate and passionate; and this, as well as the character of the principal personage,

> "Link'd with one virtue, and a thousand crimes,

reminds us, in reading 'Anastasius,' very strongly of the manner of Lord Byron. Indeed, this romance is very much what Byron would have written in prose—the same splendid, vivid, and ever-fresh pictures of the external nature of the most beautiful and interesting region of the world, the same intensity of passion, the same gloomy colouring of unrepenting crime.

But if the darker side of Oriental nature be presented to us in 'Vathek' and 'Anastasius,' in the former combined with the caustic irony of Voltaire, in the second with the mournful grandeur of Byron, the 'Hajji Baba' of Morier will make us ample amends in drollery and a truly comic *verve*. This is the 'Gil Blas' of Oriental life. Hajji Baba is a barber of Ispahan, who passes through a long but delightfully varied series of adventures, such as happen in the despotic and simple governments of the East, where the pipe-bearer of one day may become the vizier of the next. The hero is an easy, merry good-for-nothing, whose dexterity and gaiety it is impossible not to admire, even while we rejoice in the punishment which his manifold rascalities drawn down upon him; and perhaps there is no work in the world which gives so vast, so lively, and so accurate a picture of every grade, every phase of Oriental existence. Mr. Morier, who resided nearly all his life in various parts of the East, and whose long sojourn as British minister in Persia made him profoundly acquainted with the character of the people of that country, has most inimitably sustained his imaginary personage. The Hajji is not only a thorough Oriental, but intensely Persian, and a Persian of the lower class into the bargain; a perfect specimen of his nation — the French of the East — gay, talkative, dexterous, vain, enterprising, acute, not over scrupulous, but always amusing. The worthy Hajji, in the continuation of the story, comes to England in the suite of an embassy from "the asylum of the universe;" and perhaps nothing was ever more truly natural and comic than the way in which he relates his impressions and adventures in this country, his surprise at the condition of women among us, his admiration of the "moonfaces," and, above all, his astonished wonder at the "Coompany," the great enigma to all Orientals.

It now remains only to speak of one species of prose fiction—that which has for its subject the manners and personages of marine or military life. It may easily be conceived that, the former service being most entwined with all the sympathies of the national heart, the subdivision of marine novels should be the richest. The contrary might be naturally expected in France; and in France we accordingly find that though, particularly in modern times, numerous novelists have endeavoured to put in a picturesque and attractive light the manners and scenes of a sea-life, yet that it is the army which has supplied popular literature—the novel, the chanson, and the vaudeville — with the types of character most identified with the national feeling and predilection. What the *militaire* is to the French public, the sailor is to the English: in the songs of the people, on their stage, in their favourite books, the "Jack Tar," the "old Agamemnon" who followed Nelson to the Nile, is as perpetually recurring and indispensable a personage as the "vieux moustache," the grogneur de la vieille garde," to the French. And this is natural enough. Each country is peculiarly proud of that class to which it owes its brightest and least disputable glory: as the Frenchman naturally hugs himself in the idea that France is incontestably the first military nation in the world, so the Englishman, no less naturally is peculiarly vain of his country's naval achievements; not that in either case the former at all forgets or undervalues the naval triumphs of his flag, or the latter the military exploits of his; but simply because France is not essentially maritime, and England is, and therefore the natives of each attach themselves to that species of glory which they consider the peculiar property of their nation.

At the head of our marine novelists stands Captain Marryat, one of the most easy, lively, and truly humorous story-tellers we possess. One of the chief elements of his talent is undoubtedly the tone of high, effervescent, irrepressible animal spirits which characterises everything he has written. He seems as if he sate down to compose without having formed the least idea of what he is going to say, and sentence after sentence seems to flow from his pen without thought, without labour, and without hesitation. He seems half tipsy with the very gaiety of his heart, and never scruples to introduce the most grotesque extravagances of character, language, and event, provided they are likely to excite a laugh. This would produce absurdity and failure as often as laughter, were it not that he has a natural *tact* and judgment in the ludicrous; and this happy audacity —this hit-or-miss boldness—serves him admirably well. Nothing can surpass the liveliness and drollery of his 'Peter Simple,' 'Jacob Faithful,' or 'Mr. Midshipman Easy;' what an inexhaustible gallery of originals has he paraded before us! The English national temperament has a peculiar tendency to produce eccentricity of manner, and a sea-life in particular seems calculated to foster these oddities till they burst into full blow and luxuriance. Marryat's narratives are exceedingly inartificial, and often grossly improbable; but we read on with gay delight, never thinking of the story, but only solicitous to follow the droll adventures, and laugh at the still droller characters. Smollett himself has nothing richer than Captain Kearney, with his lies and innocent ostentation; Captain To, with his passion for pig, his lean wife and her piano; or than Mr. Easy fighting his ship under a green petticoat for want of an ensign. This author has also a peculiar talent for the delineation of boyish characters: his Faithful and Peter Simple (the "fool of the family") not only amuse but interest us; and in many passages he has shown no mean mastery over the pathetic emotions. Though superficial in his view of character, he is generally faithful to reality, and shows an extensive if not very deep knowledge of what his old waterman calls "human natur." There are few authors more amusing than Marryat; his books have the effervescence of champagne.

Captains Glasscock and Chamier, Mr. Howard and Mr. Trelawney, have also produced naval fictions of merit; the two last authors have followed a more tragic path than the others mentioned above, and have written passages of great power and impressiveness; but their works are injured by a too frequent occurrence of exaggerated pictures of blood and horror — a fatal fault, from which they might have been warned by the example of Eugène Sue.

The tales called 'Tom Cringle's Log' and 'The Cruize of the Midge' are also works in this kind (though not exclusively naval) of striking brilliancy and imaginative power. In these we have a most gorgeously coloured and faithful delineation of the luxuriant scenery of the West Indian Archipelago, and the manners of the creole and colonist population are reproduced with consummate drollery and inexhaustible splendour of language. They were the production of Mr. Scott, a gentleman engaged in commerce, and personally familiar with the scenes he described; and the admiration they excited at their first appearance (anonymously) in 'Blackwood's Magazine' caused them to be ascribed to the pen of some of the most distinguished of living writers, particularly to that of John Wilson, the editor of the journal.

Of the military novels we have but a few words to say: they are generally inferior to the same class of works in France. Mr. Gleig has recorded in a narrative form many striking episodes of that "war of giants" whose most glorious and terrific scenes were the lines of Torres Vedras, the storm of Badajoz, and the field of Waterloo; and a number of younger authors, chiefly Irishmen, as Messrs. Lever and Lover, have detailed with their national vivacity the grotesque oddities and gay bravery of their countrymen, who never appear to so much advantage as on the field of battle.

CHAPTER XX.

THE STAGE AND JOURNALISM.

Comedy in England — Congreve, Farquhar, &c. — Sheridan — The Modern Romantic Drama—Oratory in England: Burke—Letters of Junius—Modern Theologians: Paley and Butler—Blackstone—Adam Smith—Metaphysics: Stewart — Bentham — Periodicals: the Newspaper, the Magazine, and the Review — The Quarterly, and Blackwood — The Edinburgh, and the New Monthly—The Westminster—Cheap Periodical Literature.

COMEDY is essentially the expression not of *Life*, but of *Society*. It does not deal with the passions, but with the affectations and follies of our nature: it belongs, therefore, particularly to a highly civilized and artificial state of existence. Many of Shakspeare's most humorous creations are comic in the highest degree, but they are not in any sense comedies: they are something infinitely more elevated, more profound, more far-reaching; but they are not comedies. Exquisitely humorous as they are, the humor is not in them the primary element, the unmixed subject-matter of these inimitable delineations; it is united with tenderness, romantic passion, exhaustless poetic fancy; and therefore we call them Plays. Indeed, it may almost be maintained that humour is not the true element of comedy at all — that is, of comedy properly so named. *Wit* is the essence, the life-blood of comedy, and wit is as different from humour as from tragic passion. Wit is the negative, the destructive process — humour the positive, the reconstructive. Wit is an analytic, humour a synthetic operation. The latter indeed is so demonstrably a higher power of the mind, that it includes the former, but with the addition of something more, and something, too, infinitely higher in its source and nature. The humorist must possess wit; but he must also possess tenderness, sympathy, *love*. In the language of algebra we may formulise it thus: wit + sympathy = humour. And in proportion as the affections are an endowment of our nature far more elevated than the mere activity of our comparative or perceptive faculties (in the unusual delicacy and sensibility of which consists that power we call wit), in exactly the same measure is humour superior to wit. We may be proud to remember that humour is the distinguishing feature of the English national intellect, and the peculiar stamp of individuality which marks our literature. This circumstance alone would suffice to account for the undeniable superiority of our national literature over that of all other civilized countries, in every point — of depth, of grandeur, of variety, of indestructible vitality.

This being granted, it will not be difficult to discover what are the social conditions most necessary to the production of a brilliant school of comedy in a given nation. As the stage in general must ever be the reflection of the life, the character, the colouring of the country and epoch in which it appears, comedy must be the offspring of a highly artificial, corrupt, and intellectual era. As its *pabulum*, its ubject-matter, is folly, its aim being

"To feed with varied fools the eternal jest,"

it may be most certainly expected to flourish at a time when civilization has not advanced so far as to obliterate those strong *class-distinctions* which sharply mark the professions, habits, language, and manners of mankind, and at the same time when those elements are upon the point of being mingled into one unvaried mass. We can have no pure comedy now, because the manners of all classes, like their dress, have come to be so uniform that there remains nothing of conventional, of universally intelligible, sufficiently salient for the comic dramatist to lay hold of. The "frac noir"—the true equalized power of the nineteenth century—has levelled all men, like death. The follies, vanities, and eccentricities of course exist as much as ever, but they have been *thrown inward*; and if we seek for oddities now, we shall find not *classes* but individuals, and, if faithfully represented on the stage, they resemble not types familiar to every spectator, but caricatures, often apparently extravagant. The consequence of all this is, that we have no comedy, but we have a vaudeville—an excellent thing in its way, but very different from its predecessor. In England the reign of Charles II. was the period which most completely satisfies the conditions we have just essayed to establish, just as in France the reign of Louis XIV. The first-mentioned epoch produced Congreve, Wycherley, and Farquhar; the second Molière and Regnard. In the writings of the three great English wits there is seldom any trace of humour, and therefore nothing can be more different from Shakspeare. Wit is the reigning element, and witty dialogue perhaps was never so completely exhibited as in these admirable comedies. They are not natural in an absolute, though highly so in a relative sense: they are not true to universal but to local nature; or rather we may say that the nature of their day was an unnatural nature. They were written, not for the court, nor for the people, in the true sense of the word, but for the *Town*; and they are inimitable for intense vivacity of sparkling dialogue, for the richest abundance of odd and extravagant character, for ingenuity of plot (generally, however, a mechanical ingenuity, arising rather from disguises, mistakes of persons, and errors of the senses, than from the play of passion, or the deceptions caused by vanity and self-love), and above all for an air of inexhaustible high spirits and gaiety. In all these works the chief defect is the shocking tone of immorality which pervades them. The characters are nothing but an unvaried crowd of sharpers, seducers, prostitutes, and butts: but it is fair to remark that in reading these dramas we seem to lay aside all our stricter notions of moral duty: as Charles Lamb acutely remarks, we seem to have got into a new world, where the old-fashioned distinctions of right and wrong have no currency. In point of *art*, their chief defect is allied to their principal merits: it arises partly from the restless and incessant sparkle of the dialogue, which ever glitters with an unappeasable activity, like the blinding ripple of a noonday sea; and, secondly, from the want of *intellectual* distinction between the personages; for the fools, dupes, and coxcombs are quite as brilliant and smart in their repartees as the professed and ostensible wits of the piece. Everything is epigram and point; and though in many of these plays there are occasional touches of nature exquisitely true, delicate, and poignant, and even whole scenes which may serve as models of liveliness not inconsistent with probability, the general character of this school is certainly unsolid, and absolutely wearying from excess of sparkle and epigram. Assuredly no nation has produced anything in this artificial vein finer and more complete than the comedies of 'Love for Love,' 'The Way of the World,' 'The Man of Mode,' 'The Country Wife,' 'The Confederacy,' and 'The Provoked Wife.' The popularity of these works was enormous: comedies and pamphlets formed nearly the sum total of the lighter literature of that age; and though, not having their foundation in the deeper recesses of the human heart, they are now comparatively neglected, no man can have a true idea of the perfections of our noble language who has not made acquaintance with this class of writers. What Hazlitt says of Congreve is generally applicable to all the rest: "His style is inimitable, nay, perfect. It is the highest model of comic dialogue. Every sentence is replete with sense and satire, conveyed in the most polished and pointed terms. Every page presents a shower of brilliant conceits, is a tissue of epigrams in prose, is a new triumph of wit, a new conquest over dulness. The fire of artful raillery is nowhere else so well kept up. This style, which he was almost the first to introduce, and which he carried to the utmost pitch of classical refinement, reminds one exactly of Collins's description of wit as opposed to humour,—

'Whose jewels in his crisped hair
Are placed each other's light to share.'"

The first of this remarkable class was Etherege, and the last Farquhar; though Sheridan (after a long interval, during which the comic stage had obtained a quite different direction) seems to have revived it for a moment in all its brilliancy. The chronology of the principal names among them was as follows: Sir George Etherege, born in 1636, died in 1683; his best comedy 'The Man of Mode.'

Wycherley, the author of 'The Plain Dealer,' a comedy somewhat resembling 'The Misanthrope' and 'The Country Wife,' which may be advantageously compared with 'L'Ecole des Femmes,' born in 1640, died in 1715. Congreve, the greatest of them all, celebrated not only as a comic dramatist, but as the author of 'The Mourning Bride,' a tragedy in the dry classical French taste, but a work of great merit, 1670—1729: his finest comedies are 'Love for Love,' 'The Old Bachelor,' and 'The Double Dealer.' Sir John Vanbrugh (1672—1726) comes next, a great architect as well as a dramatic artist, for he designed Blenheim. His plays are of a somewhat coarser texture than those of Congreve, but superior in a certain rich and genial glow: his master-pieces are 'The Relapse,' 'The Provoked Wife,' 'The Confederacy,' and he left unfinished the admirable fragment afterwards completed by Cibber under the title of 'The Provoked Husband.' The last of these authors was Farquhar, born in 1678, and who died at the early age of 29. His best-known comedies are 'The Constant Couple,' 'The Beaux' Stratagem,' and 'The Recruiting Officer,' all of which, though sufficiently immoral, exhibit less of that cool heartless depravity which marks the productions of this class.

By one of those revolutions of taste — regular as the seasons, or as the oscillations of the tide in the physical world — which takes place in literature generally and in every department of literature in particular, comedy in England acquired, after the brilliant period of which we have been speaking, a direction towards *sentimentalism.* The writings of Sterne very much contributed to this tendency, and Colman, Cumberland, and most of the modern writers for the stage, endeavoured to unite the pathetic and the broadly humorous. This class was begun by Steele; and these comedies have lost the peculiar charm of gaiety, refined satire, and wit, without acquiring anything in exchange: the moral and sentimental parts are mawkish, tedious, and affected, and the laughable ones degenerate into gross farce and caricature. But the true old comedy, the admirable English comedy of Congreve and Wycherley, received a bright and momentary resuscitation in the person of Sheridan. This wonderful Irishman — as perfect an embodiment of the intellect of his country as his biographer Moore — was one of the political and literary comets of his day. Without fixity of purpose, without learning, without any of that political influence (the most important of all in a constitutional country like England) which arises from personal and moral respectability, he obtained as a parliamentary orator a brilliant though useless reputation in that age of giants when the eloquence of Chatham was yet ringing in the national ear, giving animation to the struggles of Pitt and Fox. As a dramatic author, Sheridan produced three works which will ever be considered master-pieces in their different styles — the two comedies entitled 'The School for

Scandal' and 'The Rivals,' and the inimitable dramatic caricature of 'The Critic.' The first of these is a regular comedy of intrigue, the persons all of the upper ranks of life: the dialogue is one incessant sparkle of the finest and most polished repartee; and though the moral of the piece—the unmasking of a coldhearted hypocrite and pretender to virtue, and the forgiveness of his brother, a gay goodnatured rake—is not established but at the expense of some dangerous sophistries, and the confounding of virtue with hypocrisy, and the excusing of vice by the plea of generosity, this comedy is one of the triumphs of the English scene. Many of the situations are so exquisitely comic, though a large portion of the piece is passed in talk which does not advance the action, the habit of scandal and talebearing is so admirably ridiculed, and the tone of the whole is so brilliant and refined, that it is equally delightful when read or when acted. It contains much profound satire on the corruptions of society, as brilliantly expressed, though less animated by bitterness, as in the 'Figaro' of Beaumarchais, to which work it bears some little resemblance; but in point of exquisite finish of form, in consummate elegance of manner, it is equal to Congreve himself—the highest possible praise. The other comedy we have mentioned—'The Rivals'—depicts adventures of a broader cast, and characters less exclusively taken from polished society. 'The School for Scandal' seldom excites more than a smile, while 'The Rivals' keeps the spectators in a broad laugh. Nothing can be happier than the light but masterly sketches of character in this exquisite piece · the self-willed, blustering Sir Anthony; the generous Irish fortune-hunter; the sentimental novel-reading Lydia, who can see no happiness but in disguises, persecuted attachments, and elopements; the inimitable Mrs. Malaprop, with her exquisitely good bad English; and the never-to-be-forgotten Bob Acres. 'The Critic' is one of that numerous class of pieces which contains a double action—the scenes between the author, his friends and critics, and the rehearsal of the tragedy. It is impossible to say which is the best or most witty part of this comedy, the dialogue between Dangle, an empty-headed theatrical busybody; Sneer, the very concentrated essence of critical bitterness; Puff, the bold impudent literary quack; and Sir Fretful Plagiary (a portrait of Cumberland), all alive with sore irritable sensibility; or the admirable extravagance of the "tragedy in the Shakspearian manner."

The subsequent history of the English stage is very soon related, and not very exhilarating. In comedy the German sentimental spirit to which we have alluded gradually gained ground: common types of patriotism, generosity, vulgar burlesque, and yet more vulgar elegance, have been reproduced *usque ad nauseam.* We have been sickened with never-failing tirades about the moral dignity of the British merchant, the noble virtue of the British farmer, and the valour of the British soldier and sailor, who is always represented, in order to "tickle the ears of the groundlings" as able to thrash three Frenchmen,—and all this in a style as vulgar and conventional as the ideas. Nevertheless, it would be unjust to suppose that there are not many scenes, and even some characters, in the plays of Cumberland, Colman, Reynolds, &c., exhibiting a power to do better things: but the general tendency of comic drama with us, as in France, has been towards the vaudeville—with this difference, that the vaudeville is essentially and peculiarly a French creation, and therefore a valuable type of French art; whereas in England it is either servilely copied or coarsely caricatured from that charming production of the French theatre.

The most intensely national type of the English drama is the romantic drama—the school of Shakspeare. It may easily be conceived that some attempts should have been made to revive so admirable and national a mode of composition. Perhaps these essays form the only sound, healthy, and at all promising class of modern theatrical writing; but even this class has a forced and hot-bed air, and is kept alive rather by the taste of a few than by the eager sympathy of the public generally. These works are *imitative*, and, however beautiful they sometimes may be, they confer pleasure rather by recalling to us those forms of literature which we look back upon with the greatest pride and veneration, than by their unassisted merits. The romantic plays of Miss Baillie, and particularly of Sheridan Knowles (the most successful of our modern dramatists), are always interesting, and in some passages even excellent; but their invariable adoption of the Elizabethan diction not only produces a painful impression of the writer being afraid to trust purely to his own unassisted powers of poetry and passion, but carries also with it an air of *sham*, of mimicry—a confounding of the accident with the substance. Admirable as is the diction of that wonderful epoch, the diction is not the essential thing: at all events, it was the natural style of that day, only elevated, of course, and glorified by genius; whereas now an imitation of it must ever wear a pitiable air of factitiousness and affectation. Many of Miss Baillie's 'Plays on the Passions,' Knowles's 'Hunchback,' 'Wife,' 'Virginius,' and others, might be cited with great praise, but with an expression of just regret that they should be so injured by the patchwork air of their diction, in which modern words and ideas jar so strangely with the tone of that glorious, easy, fanciful dialogue, so hallowed in our memory. Two or three men of an original and independent way of thinking have written dramas (designed rather for reading than representation) in which this defect has been "reformed," as the player says in 'Hamlet,' "indifferent well." Mr. Talfourd has composed several pieces in which, though the style is a little too perceptibly modelled upon that of Ford and Beaumont and Fletcher, this air of imitation is compensated for by the pure elegance of design, and the simple, direct, elevated pathos, and something too of an ideal severity reflected from the Greek dramatists. His tragedy of 'Ion' is, indeed, a refined and elevated work, of consummate finish in its parts, and breathing the lofty tenderness and all-embracing humanity of sentiment which characterises the philosophic poetry of Wordsworth. Henry Taylor has essayed, and with no mean success, to revive, in a dramatic form, the picturesque and stormy life of the fourteenth century, in his noble work on the subject of 'Philip van Artevelde,' the brewer-king of Ghent. The picture (a vast and animated one) of the struggle between the infant liberties of the burgess class in Flanders and the oppressive and haughty feudalism, is delineated with no ordinary power; and the central figure of this vast panorama is a grand and ideal conception, whose chief fault is its want of accordance with the conceivable existence of such a character in so rude and fierce an age. But 'Artevelde' is not a drama, but a dramatic poem—full of power and beauty, it is true, but totally incapable of representation; and though 'Ion' is interesting and successful on the stage, it is by no means a work addressed (as every *real* drama must infallibly be) to the tastes, sympathies, and comprehension of the multitude.

Political disquisition, whether spoken or written, has in England a very striking peculiarity of tone: it differs from the mode of discussion adopted in other countries at least as markedly as the popular and national character of Great Britain differs from that of any civilized state in ancient or modern history. The German dreams of everything, the Frenchman talks of everything, the Englishman *reasons* of everything. The Frenchman acts often without thinking. the German is too occupied with his theories either to reason or to act, the Englishman thinks deliberately and acts decidedly. In France we find in general strong attachment to what is so expressly designated by the English term "*claptrap.*" There is no country which has so long retained a taste for those worn-out topics of schoolboy declamation, that shallow classicism of allusion, which swells the period with the names of Brutus, of Aristides, and of Themistocles—none where the threadbare pedantry of personification and prosopopœia has become so engrained, as it were, into the national style. This was of course a consequence of the Revolution of 1789, a period of carnival masquing, when

"Mars, Bacchus, Apollo, virorum,"

danced through speeches, pamphlets, and proclamations, "in all the mazes of metaphorical confusion." English public speaking, at the bar or in parliament, is eminently and essentially practical; and a British audience, whether in a public meeting, in the Houses of Lords and Commons, or a jury in a court of justice, while it will listen with patience to a cogent and practical reasoning, however inelegantly expressed, has no mercy upon mere flowery rhetoric or vain general declamation. Nothing is more fatal to eloquence, in its highest sense, than the *air* of being eloquent; and the object of all public speaking and writing being solely and simply to convince or persuade, it is self-evident that that orator or writer must be the best who produces the greatest practical result. The Greeks thoroughly understood this, as the English have done; and there is, consequently, in the oratory of both nations a singular resemblance in point of directness, *muscularity* of expression, and practical application. The speeches of Chatham, Pitt, Fox, and Wyndham are perhaps the finest monuments of our parliamentary eloquence, and those of Erskine of forensic oratory; and when in reading them, imperfectly reported as they often are, we are sometimes at a loss to explain the fact how they could have produced such effect as they really did, we forget that the very simplicity and absence of parade, which strikes us as meagre and colourless, must have been, at the time when they were delivered, a main source of their resistless power. In general it will be found that those speeches which *read* best are by no means those which were most effective when *spoken*. Our forensic oratory is generally marked by a singular sobriety and a careful exclusion of all rapturous and rhetorical enthusiasm; and therefore the pathetic passages, so rarely and sparingly introduced, have all the power over our sympathies derivable from the impressiveness of *subdued*, restrained, involuntary passion. Chatham, Pitt, and Fox, immeasurably superior as they were, as parliamentary speakers, to their illustrious contemporary, Edmund Burke, were undoubtedly inferior to him in vastness of mind and in grandeur of genius; and yet the latter was seldom listened to with even moderate patience in the House of Commons: and the reason is, that the former were consummate *debaters*, practical speakers; while the latter was the eloquent expounder of a philosophy too ethereal, too abstract, too sublime, for that practical and common sense atmosphere. As a political theorist, as a speculator on the history, character, and tendency of the British constitution, as the analyser of its principles, as the historian of its past and the prophet of its future, Burke occupies a place in the political and literary history of England which is quite peculiar. His speeches and pamphlets on the destinies of the first French Revolution, and of the then infant liberties of the United States, are perhaps as wonderful for their sagacity, their penetration, and for that intensity of predictive power—

"the vision and the faculty divine"—

as they are admirable for the splendid eloquence of their expression. They will form for ever the favorite models of style to the student of historical literature, to the orator, to the thinker; and are among the most signal examples of that power by which, under the magic influence of Genius,

> "Old Experience doth attain
> To something like prophetic strain."

But the most remarkable figure in the political drama of this period is that mysterious personage, the "Iron Mask" of modern history, the admirable writer who launched his fierce diatribes under the name of "Junius." The authorship of these letters is one of the few enigmas which time and investigation have not perfectly solved. Internal and circumstantial evidence points so clearly to Sir Philip Francis as the writer of these compositions, that *moral certainty* is undoubtedly arrived at. Perhaps the literature of no country in the world can offer a finer example of intense, unscrupulous, yet always elegant and dignified invective. Every sentence is weighty with meaning, and pointed with the sharpest and most polished sarcasm; and the air of honest indignant patriotism, which the author has so studiously and carefully preserved, makes us forget, as we read, the atrocious venom of party-spirit, and he unjustifiable attacks on private character, which abound throughout this able but flagitious collection of letters.

We have devoted a short chapter to those great divines whose eloquence and learning have made them the fathers of the Anglican church; who are our Chrysostoms and Augustines, or rather our Fénélons, Pascals, and Bossuets. The epoch which we are now treating was fertile in illustrious men, whose writings, consecrated, like those of Barrow, Taylor, South, and Fuller, to the service of Protestantism, were marked with differences proportioned to the age in which they wrote. They are not rich treasuries of faith, eloquence, enthusiasm, and boundless erudition—they are demonstrations of evidence, and answers to objections; they are not the production of the imagination, but of the reason. Among these writers the names of Paley and Butler are the most prominent. The former, in an extensive cycle of works, has investigated, first, the grounds and principles of moral philosophy generally, he has then advanced to the grêat outlines of morality and government, thence to the consideration, of the probabilities for and against the truth of the Christian history, and lastly he has given us a detailed examination of the writings of St. Paul. In these works, the 'Moral Philosophy,' the 'Evidences of Christianity' (chiefly intended as a refutation of Hume's plausible objections to the truth of the evangelic history), and the 'Horæ Paulinæ,' we remark an acuteness of reasoning which has rarely been equalled, combined with a style so easy, familiar, and natural, that we are sometimes blinded to the sophistry which the author's inimitable air of *bonhommie* and good faith is occasionally employed to mask. His theory of moral sentiment is based upon the doctrine of self-interest; a doctrine to which, however reluctantly, all speculators must sooner or later recur: and in his 'Natural Theology,' when he traces, through the whole creation, and particularly in the constitution of organized bodies, the proofs of a presiding wisdom, benevolence, and power in the Creator, it is impossible not to admire the extent of his knowledge of nature (particularly of physiology), the familiar appropriateness of the illustrations he selects, and above all the complete absence of all pedantry and scientific terminology.

Butler, Bishop of Lichfield (who was born in 1692 and died in 1752), confined himself to the investigation of the degree of *anterior* probability which would lead us to assign to such a revelation as that of Christianity such a character as we find it to possess. Given the phenomenon of a natural religion, he demands what might be expected to be the moral character of a revelation from the nature of the case; and he shows it to coincide exactly with the revelation which we do possess. This great work is entitled 'The Analogy of Natural and Revealed Religion;' and is one of the finest examples which literature can produce of close, clear, candid, and almost mathematical demonstration. Of course Butler's work treats only of the preliminary probabilities of the question; and does not enter into the examination, on historical, critical, and philological grounds, of that mass of evidence which the New Testament contains, and which forms the basis of our belief in the facts of the Christian miracles. That task is executed partly by Paley, and partly by that vast cloud of commentators, such as Clarke, Prideaux, Lardner, &c., whose learning, industry, and candour do such honour to the reformed church of England.

Though perhaps they may be considered as scarcely entering into the plan of our work, we think it our duty not to omit altogether the names of Blackstone, Adam Smith, Stewart, and Bentham; Blackstone having been the first to treat in a popular and untechnical manner of the history and nature of the laws of England; Smith, the first systematic investigator of the science of political economy; Stewart, the most distinguished of modern British metaphysicians; and Bentham, the profound searcher into the theory of government and legislation.

Judge Blackstone was the first of our lawyers who possessed a sufficiently strong tincture of letters to be able to give an elegant and readable epitome of the history of English law, rejecting the dry and repulsive technicality which characterises the profound and admirable Institutes of our great legists, Coke, Fortescue, Littleton, and Selden. The enormous mass of information buried, far out of the reach of any but the unwearied professional student, in the ponderous tomes of our old judges and reporters, Blackstone presented, in 1765, in a form elegant, accessible, and interesting: and when we reflect upon the vastness and complication of our legislative and executive system, and the thousand elements, Roman, mediæval, municipal, feudal and parliamentary, which combine to form that wonderful compound, the British constitution, it is impossible to express too warmly the gratitude which not only every Englishman, but every civilized man, should feel towards Blackstone for having placed, in an intelligible and accessible form, the history of what can never be devoid either of philosophical interest, or influence upon the destinies of human liberty.

Adam Smith's famous 'Wealth of Nations' was the first attempt towards laying down, on a great scale, the principles of political economy. He was the first to demonstrate the fundamental axioms of commerce, manufactures, and the division of labour. This great work has been justly reproached with want of systematic order and completeness of arrangement: but it is distinguished for the soundness of its views in many points exceedingly important in themselves, and which, before Smith's time, had never been satisfactorily investigated: as, for example, the division of labour, the theory of rent, and the principles of advantageous international commerce. It is, also, admirable for the singular clearness and appropriateness of the illustrations employed to exemplify the various parts of the argument; and though more recent labourers in the great field of statistics and political economy—such as Malthus, Ricardo, Mill, Senior, MacCulloch—have profitably cultivated many portions of the field, Smith deserves the credit of having first broken up the surface, and shown the extent and fertility of the ground.

In metaphysical science it is, we fear, incontrovertible that Great Britain is less distinguished than in most other branches of human knowledge; at least that she is incontestably inferior to Germany. It is singular enough that metaphysics have been more cultivated in Scotland than in England—nay, that the Scottish intellect appears to possess a peculiar tendency and aptitude to this kind of disquisition. In the present age, at least, it is Edinburgh which has produced the most distinguished of the metaphysicians of Great Britain; though Scotland has no names to show in any degree comparable, we will not say to Leibnitz and Kant, but even to Fichte, Schelling, or Hegel. Perhaps it will not be unjust to take Dugald Stewart as the most marked name among our modern school of metaphysicians—at least since the date of Chillingworth, Hobbes, Locke, and Berkeley.

There remains another and most important branch of knowledge —only the more important from its very difficulty, which has deterred men of adequate powers from concentrating upon it their systematic attention. This is the science of legislation, and the theory of reward and punishment. Jeremy Bentham was undoubtedly the first among us to enter upon this new and unexplored career. The eccentricity of his manners, his simple and unworldly enthusiasm, the boldness and novelty of his theories,—all this, combined with the oddity of his style, the grotesque pedantry of his language, the strange uncouth terminology which he thought it necessary to invent for his science, and, above all, the repulsive dryness and complexity of a multitude of definitions, limitations, divisions, and subdivisions, —all these things tended to blind his countrymen to the importance of his political and juridicial theories and reasonings. England is eminently the country of the *practical*; and the most fatal character which a philosophical investigator can acquire is that of a visionary or an enthusiast. Bentham's writings were distinguished by so much novelty in the matter, and such fantastic oddity in the manner, that they were received by the general public of England with considerable distrust, and even hostility; and his reputation, now deservedly high and every day rising still higher, has met with very curious vicissitudes. His theories, having gradually obtained a great reputation on the Continent, and particularly in France, have been divested of the strange and repulsive peculiarities of their author's manner, and have come back to us embodied in clear and philosophical language. Thus Bentham's fame had made the tour of Europe before it was firmly established in the country of its birth. His deductions are often made with almost geometrical severity: and if men were pieces of mechanism, and subject to no disturbances in their conduct from causes too capricious and irregular to be appreciated by science, his principles would be not only applicable, but would produce the effect which he hoped would result from them, in the annihilation of crime, poverty, and oppression. But we do not calculate so logically as Bentham supposes; and the greater part of our actions are dictated, in the first instance, not by pure reason, or a balancing of the good and evil that will accrue from a particular line of conduct in given circumstances, but rather by passion, prejudice, or an indistinct interest, which we *afterwards* endeavour to harmonise with the deductions of moral logic. Bentham's life was very long, active, and benevolent: he was born in 1748, and lived to the great age of ninety-four. The 'Popular Fallacies,' the 'Essay on Codification,' the 'Defence of Usury,' are deservedly held to be monuments of admirably-combined industry, acuteness, and originality.

Journalism — that remarkable and distinctive feature of modern literature—has been cultivated in England with all the activity that might have been predicted from the general intelligence and civilization of the country, from the perfect freedom of discussion which our nation has so long enjoyed, and also from the popular nature of our government, which gives every citizen a strong personal interest in all political questions. Our journals, of every kind, have been generally distinguished from those of other countries by two or three striking peculiarities. Till recently, every journal, whether newspaper, magazine, or review, was perfectly miscellaneous in its contents, discussing political questions, giving criticisms on books or works of art, reporting the progress of science,— in short, reflecting the multiform interests of society. Our journals were, indeed, what Hamlet tells us actors are—"the abstract and brief chronicles of the time." This was owing in some measure to the expense of books and publications in England, which has always been enormous as compared with other countries, and which rendered it impossible for ordinary readers to subscribe to many periodicals; so that each was obliged to be in some measure encyclopædic. But as the field of curiosity has enlarged, special journals, each devoted to some particular class of information, have become more numerous, and naturally at the same time much cheaper. Another peculiarity of English journalism is the strict incognito which it has always been the fashion for the contributors to preserve. This proceeds, perhaps, from the reserve of the English character; or from the fear of personal interest interfering with the impartiality of the writer: and all the attempts that have been made (with what possible hope of advantage is not quite clear) to introduce among us the practice, so universal in France and Germany, of the writer signing his name at the foot of his composition, have been uniformly unsuccessful. This incognito, however, applies only to criticism and political disquisition; for the writers who contribute poetry and fiction to our journals do not think it necessary to preserve their incognito.

By the word *Newspaper* we understand, in England, a gazette of politics, general information, and advertisements, appearing in a sheet or sheets at intervals, in general not greater than a week. The *Magazine* (a term peculiar to England) is a miscellaneous periodical, published for the most part monthly, containing original disquisitions, prose fiction, or poetry, and generally of an amusing and varied character. The *Review* is a publication of a much more grave and ambitious cast: it contains no admixture of original narrative or poetical matter, but is a series of essays, or *articles*, ostensibly criticisms of the works whose titles are placed at the head of the disquisition. But these articles are by no means, necessarily, mere critiques of the works *apropos* of which they purport to be written. The latter are frequently quite insignificant in themselves; but are taken merely as the peg upon which is hung a general, and often admirably-written, disquisition on the subject in question.

The history of journalism in England coincides, in the date of its origin, in its general characteristics and vicissitudes, and in the causes which have contributed, at particular periods, to advance or retard its development, with the annals of this important branch of activity in other countries of Europe. All the great political parties have their special organs in the periodical press; and perhaps the best way of giving an idea of this kind of writing in England will be by classing the most eminent and popular journals under the respective opinions advocated in their pages. In a constitutional government, composed, like that of England, of three distinct elements, there will naturally be three principal shades of party feeling;—the Tories, or advocates for the *status in quo* of the constitution, who dread the encroachments of popular opinion, and are enthusiastic maintainers of monarchism and aristocracy—Conservatives, in short. The chief organs of this powerful, wealthy, and intelligent party (which, however, is generally deficient in activity, and acts mainly by its weight —its *vis inertiæ*) are, among the reviews, 'The Quarterly,' and, among the magazines, 'Blackwood's' and 'Fraser's.' The first-mentioned work is undoubtedly one of great influence and importance; the contributions are admirably written, and are generally by the most distinguished men of the day. This journal was established at the very agitated period of 1809, to counteract the danger of those liberal opinions which were at that time almost menacing the integrity of the Constitution; and it was for a long time conducted by William Gifford, the translator of Juvenal, and the author of the 'Baviad' and 'Mæviad,' two of the most bitter, powerful, and resistless literary satires which modern days have produced. Gifford was a self-taught man, who raised himself, by dint of almost superhuman exertions and admirable integrity, to a high place among the literary men of his age. Distinguished as a satirist, as a translator of satires, and as the editor of several of the illustrious but somewhat neglected dramatists of the Elizabethan age, his writings, admirable for sincerity, good sense, and learning, were also strongly tinged with bitterness and personality. Many other distinguished supporters of Conservative doctrines were contributors to 'The Quarterly,' —Croker; the witty, brilliant, sarcastic Canning; and, more recently, Southey. This journal is at present conducted by Lockhart, Walter Scott's son-in-law and literary executor.

Advocating the same doctrines, though in language less solemn and dictatorial, 'Blackwood's Magazine' must be considered as having played, and as long likely to play, a very prominent part. It is exceedingly miscellaneous in its contents; and in its pages some of the most distinguished writers of poetry and fiction have made their *débuts*. 'Blackwood' must be held to have done good service to pure taste by the publication of a rich and masterly series of translations (chiefly by Hay, Merivale, &c.) of the Greek epigrams—a very peculiar and exquisite class of productions. It was in 'Blackwood,' too, that Warren made his first appearance before the public, as the anonymous author of the 'Passages from the Diary of a late Physician' and the novel of 'Ten Thousand a-Year.' The sketches of sea-life and West-Indian scenery, mentioned by us in a preceding chapter with very high commendation, first appeared in this periodical under the titles of 'Tom Cringle's Log' and 'The Cruize of the Midge.' It would be tedious were we to attempt to enumerate all the powerful, splendid, or humorous narratives, all the genial and eloquent political biographies (such as those of Pitt and Burke), or all the penetrating and animated reviews of books and systems, which have appeared in 'Blackwood' since its establishment in 1814. We will only advert to a series of contributions so truly original in form, and so happy in execution, that they may be considered as constituting an absolute and peculiar species. We allude to the exquisitely humorous and eloquent 'Noctes Ambrosianæ,' a collection of imaginary conversations between the supposed editor and contributors (real persons under fictitious and exaggerated masks), in which all the topics of the day are passed in review with a singular union of profound speculation, fervid eloquence, and the broadest and most extravagant gaiety. These are supposed to be chiefly the composition of John Wilson, long the editor of the journal, a man of almost universal accomplishment, and celebrated as a moral philosopher, as a poet, a critic, a publicist, a humorist, and a sportsman. In his 'Isle of Palms,' and 'City of the Plague,' Wilson shows himself to be a poet of no mean order, following the peculiar school of Wordsworth: in his 'Margaret Lyndsay,' and 'Lights and Shadows of Scottish Life,' he has given a beautiful and eloquent picture of the peasant existence of his native country; and under his character of "Christopher North" (his pseudonym as editor of 'Blackwood') he has performed the same office for the scenery of Scotland, as in the prose tales, just mentioned, he had done for the joys and woes, the virtues and sufferings, of its inhabitants.

The second great subdivision of public opinion, or what may be called the Constitutional Liberal party, is represented by 'The Edinburgh Review,' established in 1802 by a small party of young men, obscure at that time, but ambitious and enterprising, who were all destined to attain a high degree of distinction. 'The Edinburgh' founded its claim to success upon the boldness and vivacity of its tone, its total rejection of all precedent and authority, and the audacity with which it discussed questions previously held to be "hedged in" with the "divinity" of prescription. 'The Edinburgh' was an absolute literary Fronde; and its founders—Brougham, Jeffrey, Sidney Smith, Hallam, &c.—were soon convinced that they had not erred in calculating upon an extraordinary degree of success. The criticisms (many of which were *retrospective*, that is, discussing the merits of past eras in the history and literature of England and other countries) were marked by a singular boldness and pungency and in contemporary and local subjects the 'Review' exhibited power and extent of view which made its appearance, in some sense, an era in journalism. The critical articles are supposed to have been chiefly contributed by Jeffrey, many by Scott (though the total variance of his political sentiments with those advocated in the work may make us more surprised that he should have contributed at all than that he should have confined his labours to merely literary subjects), whilst Smith and Brougham, and more recently Macaulay, have united history, politics, and literature. The latter has produced many noble articles on these subjects (for example, those on Machiavelli, on Cromwell, &c.), and Smith treated political questions with a richness of comic humour, and irresistible dry sarcasm, employed generally in *exhaustive* reasoning—in the *reductio ad absurdum*—which is not only exquisitely amusing, but is full of solid truth as well as pleasantry.

With reference to the Liberal party, 'The New Monthly Magazine' occupied at one time a similar position to that which 'Blackwood' does in relation to the Tory opinions. This journal (the continuation of one of the earliest of English periodicals) is exceedingly inferior in general literary talent to any of those which we have mentioned: it is pitched altogether in a lower key, both as regards politics and belles-lettres; but at the same time it cannot be accused of gross partiality and misrepresentation; a charge from which none of the journals above described can be said to have been always free. Its strength consists in the novels which have from time to time appeared, in its pages, in the manner of the *feuilleton*, and in the gay pleasantry which is generally to be found in its articles. It has been conducted by a succession of distinguished humorists and novel-writers—Theodore Hook, Thomas Campbell, Capt. Marryat, and Thomas Hood—and contains a large mass of excellent fiction.

The two great parties of Tory and Whig, monarchical and popular, which we have been speaking of, are strictly constitutional. The remaining one, the youngest in point of origin, but which is rapidly gaining strength and consistency, by no means scruples to advocate what are called organic changes in our form of government. This party—the ultra-liberal, the democratic, the Radical, as it has been nicknamed—is possessed rather of intelligence, restlessness, and ambition than, as yet at least, of influence or weight; but it has its organ like its great rivals. This is 'The Westminster Review,' a journal sustained with very considerable power and energy: but it is rather in certain departments of antiquarian and artistic literature that 'The Westminster has created itself a section of admirers: the educated classes in England sympathise too little with the doctrines advocated in this journal for it to obtain a very general circulation. The 'Quarterly,' 'Edinburgh,' and 'Westminster' (like the generality of reviews) appear every three months: the magazines, in almost all cases, are monthly.

Besides these, there are of course innumerable publications of a local or special kind, devoted to the furtherance of some particular interest or of some science of art. Thus theology, law, history, medicine, physics and their separate branches, commerce, colonies, agriculture, manufactures, and even the most apparently limited sciences, geology, palæontology, numismatology, even railroads, mines, and the art of galvano-metallurgy, have each their separate journal or journals. Each art, each pursuit, each whim or amusement is represented by some periodical, generally of merit and possessing a considerable circulation.

But we have, also, a large and increasing mass of information given to us in a variety of other periodical works, many of which are sold at a price inconceivably small, if we consider the ordinary costliness of books in England: such, for example, as the publications by Constable and Chambers in Scotland, and the prolific brood of 'Family Libraries,' 'Cabinet Cyclopædias,' and penny journals. These works, by which a great extent of useful, if not very profound, knowledge is placed at the disposal of the labouring classes, have in most cases been exceedingly successful, and are calculated to give a foreigner a high idea of the intellectual activity and enterprise of the English people;—an impression which will become still stronger when he finds the contents of these collections to be, in almost every case, well selected, well arranged, decorous and moral, written always with respectable, and often with extraordinary ability.

CHAPTER XXI.

WORDSWORTH, COLERIDGE, AND THE NEW POETRY.

Wordsworth and the Lake School—Philosophical and Poetical Theories—The Lyrical Ballads — The Excursion — Sonnets—Coleridge—Poems and Criticisms—Conversational Eloquence—Charles Lamb—The Essays of Elia—Leigh Hunt—Keats—The Living Poets—Conclusion.

THE throne of English poetry, left vacant by the early death of Byron, is now unquestionably filled by Wordsworth. It was a species of revolution which seated the author of 'Childe Harold' upon that throne: it is a counter-revolution which has deposed "the grand Napoleon of the realms of rhyme." The 'English Bards' was Byron's 18th Fructidor; the publication of 'The Excursion' was his Waterloo. But in the fluctuation of popular taste, in the setting of that current, which, flowing from the old classicism, has carried us insensibly, but irresistibly, first through Romanticism, and has now brought us to a species of metaphysical quietism, there have been many temporary changes of direction; nay, some apparent stoppages. Despite the effort and impulsion of the Byronian poetry—the poetry of *passion*—there were writers who not only retained many characteristics of the forms that had to appearance been exploded, but even something of the old tone of sentiment; modified, of course, by the æsthetic principles which were afterwards to be completely embodied in such a cycle of great works as constitutes a school of literature. Thus Crabbe, with his singular versification (a kind of *mezzo-termine* between the smart antithetic manner of Pope and the somewhat languid melody of Goldsmith), combined a gloomy analysis of crime and weakness with pictures of common life delineated with a Flemish minuteness of detail; and the traditions of the purely classic school survived in the diction of Rogers and the exquisite finish of Campbell. These poets are the connecting links between the two systems so opposite and apparently so incompatible: and it is not surprising that these writers, both of whom have deservedly become classics in our language, should exhibit, in the difference of feeling and treatment perceptible when we compare their first works with their last, a perfect image of the gradual transition of public taste from the one style of writing to the other. They both began, the former in 'The Pleasures of Memory,' and the latter in 'The Pleasures of Hope,' as imitators of Akenside (himself an imitator of Milton) and of Goldsmith; while in their later works we trace a gradually increasing tendency towards the more passionate and lyric tone of modern poetry. In Rogers's exquisite poem of 'Human Life,' in his 'Italy,' in his charming songs and fugitive pieces, we find him gradually receding farther and farther from his first models: and in examining the works of Thomas Campbell we perceive a still stronger proof of the same transition. 'The Pleasures of Hope,' published at the very early age of twenty-four, was absolutely a reproduction of the tone and feeling of 'The Traveller:' but if we follow Campbell through his tender and pathetic narrative poem of 'Gertrude of Wyoming' and his admirable lyrics — national and patriotic, and among the finest in any language — we shall see that in him, as in the general state of literary feeling reflected in his works, a complete and vast change had taken place. In literature nothing can ever be perfectly destroyed or obliterated, nothing can exist without producing an influence on remote times; and poetry therefore will ever bear something of an eclectic character.

It is the philosophy of Wordsworth—his theory, religious, social, and moral—that has most deeply coloured the poetry of the present day in England. He has exercised upon the literature of his country an influence far more permanent and powerful than that which was communicated to the mind of Europe by the splendid innovations of Byron, although it was not so intense and rapid in its first development. The Lake School (so called because its founders resided chiefly among the picturesque scenery of the lakes of Cumberland and Westmoreland, and have described with enthusiastic fondness not only that beautiful mountain region, but also the simple virtues and pastoral innocence of its inhabitants) was founded by Wordsworth, Coleridge, and Southey; of whom the former must be considered as the most industrious apostle and expounder of its doctrines. These doctrines are not of a mere æsthetic character: so far from it, indeed, that their æsthetic deductions are simply an application to art, of principles of faith and reasoning of the most elevated and all-embracing character. Their poetry is, in short, nothing but an embodiment, in a particular form, of a theory which, whether true or false, involves the highest concernments of man in his relation to God, to nature, to his fellow-creatures, and to himself. These writers are in some sense the Quietists, the Mystics, the Quakers of the poetic fraternity. As critics, the chief object of their attacks was the conventional language, so long considered as inseparable from poetry. They considered that the ordinary speech of the common people, being founded on the most general and universal feelings of the mind, and expressive of the most extensive class of wants and ideas, was a more faithful, philosophical, and durable vehicle for thought than the ornamented and ambitious phraseology heretofore deemed essential to poetry, although subject, as it was, to every caprice of fashion and taste. Nor were their ethical doctrines less bold. Strong passions, splendid and striking actions, revenge, ambition, unbridled love, all that had hitherto been considered as the very stuff and material of poetical impressions, they held to be wanting in the higher attribute of dignity and fitness for the artist's purposes. All in our nature, that either indicates, generates, or proceeds from a selfish motive, they held to be demonstrably less sublime than the tranquil virtues, the development of the affections, and the incessant effort of the soul to unite itself by meditation and reverent aspiration with God himself. Thus, casting down, at the feet of the Divinity, the passions of our nature, they of course were the iconoclasts also of the idols of human reason. For the acute speculator, the pryer into the material creation, the philosophaster, the quack and empiric of science, they express the most intense contempt; being too apt to confound the legitimate exercise of our intellect and curiosity with the petty, unfeeling, irreverent spirit of the

"Philosopher, a fingering slave,
One that would peep, and pry, and botanise
Upon his mother's grave."

In proportion as the world becomes more civilized, the *splendida vitia* will, so to say, sink in value in our moral exchange; and the day may come when courage and military energy, for example, will be considered as the necessary barbarism of a savage state, and the exploits of a Charles XII. and a Napoleon will be looked back upon with a half-pitying, half-incredulous wonder. That the human race is yet arrived at this point of philosophy and civilization does not very evidently appear; but the doctrines of Wordsworth's school are an attempt to anticipate this millennium of innocence and virtue. In the same way as the ordinary *sentiments* of poetry are rejected by the Lake School, the ordinary subjects of it have no less been changed. The materials of many of their works, particularly of the earlier ones, are the adventures and sentiments of the very humblest class of human life, and such as, in themselves, would appear to defy any power of rendering them interesting and attractive. Thus the heroes of 'Peter Bell' are a cruel carrier and his ass; an idiot boy forms the whole subject of another poem; and an old pedlar is the chief personage in the noble fragment of 'The Excursion.' The diction is, of course, characterized by similar singularities. Peculiarly awake to the defects of that brilliant and ingenious poetry which was introduced into England from France at the Restoration, and whose chief representatives are Prior, Waller, and Pope, the Lakists appear to have shut their eyes to its incontestable merits; or, if they allow the existence of those merits, they consider them as of so low an order, and purchased so dearly, that they prefer the simple pathos, the rude picturesqueness, of the old English ballads to all the sparkle and ingenuity of the Poets of the Intellect. Wordsworth's earlier diction was marked by a humility and even meanness of phrase; and the ballads, published in 1798, excited an universal uproar of ridicule. Both the system, and the ridicule it gave birth to, were naturally somewhat exaggerated: it is not, therefore, surprising that those very journals, such as 'The Quarterly,' 'The Edinburgh,' and 'Blackwood's Magazine,' which overwhelmed the 'Lyrical Ballads' on their first appearance with ridicule, should have gradually become admirers, if not warm supporters, of Wordsworth's poetical and moral opinions. There can, however, be no question that, in his first publications, he carried his system much too far; and the Lake School, in their eagerness to escape the Idols of the Theatre, have sometimes manifestly fallen under the influence of the Idols of the Den. One thing, however, is incontestable; the new school of poetry draws its inspiration from a truly elevated source. With these writers, poetry is but an embodiment and expression of faith. Their works are not the productions of mere intellectual dexterity; but are monuments of the profoundest conviction, of the sublimest aspirations after what is good and beautiful and true. Poetry, with them, is a *religion;* and they, like the bards of the heroic age, are not artists only, but priests and hierophants. In Wordsworth, poetry, which is but another name for the reverent study of nature, embraces all knowledge, all sanctity, all truth. With him it is

"The anchor of my purest thoughts, the nurse,
The guide, the guardian of my heart; and soul
Of all my moral being."

The prominent feature in Wordsworth's system, of mingled aesthetics and ethics, is the belief that external nature is not the mere lifeless echo of the voice of God, but the voice itself: and that the stream, the cloud, the leaf are not altogether inanimate and feelingless; but that they have a consciousness and a language of their own, audible and intelligible to all who will reverently listen; but most audible, most intelligible to the poet; whose only difference from other men consists in his greater fineness of ear for that universal hymn of nature. This leading idea will be found, also, in the more lofty meditations of the Platonic dialogues. These ideas Plato obtained, we know, from his master Socrates; and they came originally, in all probability, from the East; for Oriental poetry bears much of this peculiar stamp of mysticism. A great deal of this platonism is to be found embodied in the poetry of the Elizabethan era; not only in the great work of Spenser, where it is indeed peculiarly perceptible; but even in the productions of men whose reputation, then very great, has not been able to resist the destroying power of time — in the poems, for instance, of Sir John Davies, of Phineas Fletcher, and of Silvester. In the Indian poetry this diffusion, through all nature, of consciousness and of feeling, tends directly to a species of sublime pantheism: in Wordsworth, the same dogmas made subservient to the doctrines of the Christian revelation, acquire a still more pure and ethereal character. If we examine the whole collection of Wordsworth's poems, we shall find that, while he has remained faithful to the ethical part of his theory, he has involuntarily been obliged to renounce a great deal of what was peculiar in his art; that is, its peculiar language. That extreme simplicity of diction and imagery, which he formerly seemed to consider the only true vehicle of poetical impressions, was obviously too little in accordance with his elevated and abstract doctrines to be retained, for any length of time, as his poetical language. Thus, while an unlearned peasant would have found nothing in Wordsworth's early narratives and songs which he would not have perfectly understood, *as far as the words were concerned*, the deductions, the *drift*, the moral results would have remained, and ever will remain, as unintelligible to such a reader as if they were couched in the most artificial and ornamented rhetoric. Many of Wordsworth's finest productions—as, for example, the admirable 'Laodamia,' his Sonnets, and nearly all 'The Excursion'—are, as far as the diction and versification are concerned, written in strong discordance with the poet's own theory of poetical expression: and are so far from exemplifying an extreme simplicity, and the use of the most popular or even rustic phraseology, that they are absolutely among the most highly finished and elaborate specimens of artificial diction which the English language can show. Milton, Spenser, Akenside, Thomson, are undoubtedly among the most scholastic of our poets; and yet we do not think it too much to say that the language of these learned writers is more intelligible to the great body of readers than the contemplative style of 'The Excursion:' and hence it is that the poets we have just mentioned are really more *popular*—that is, read by a greater number of persons, particularly of the humbler classes —than Wordsworth is now, or is ever likely to be. The really great benefit which he has conferred upon his art, is that of showing future writers the necessity of thinking, and seeing, and describing for themselves; and not accepting at second-hand, from any model however admirable, any set of words or images to which a conventional idea of beauty is attached, and hoping that thereby any strong impressions can be excited.

Many of the smaller detached poems to be found in the 'Lyrical Ballads' are absolutely unequalled. What renders them so remarkable is the pure and lofty tone of philosophical morality, which gives a weight and dignity to apparently the most trivial subjects. Nothing seems inserted in them for the sake of the mere words; and the result is that the diction has that exquisite directness, simplicity, and grace which forms the indefinable charm of the Greek epigrams. The Odes have, perhaps, something in them rather too mystical; and may be censured for a certain want of clearness and intelligibleness: but there is not one of them which does not contain some passage, some phrase, such as no poet but Wordsworth could have produced. The smaller poems in the ballad measure are those which are perhaps most universally known. Who has not read 'The Fountain,' 'Matthew,' 'We are Seven'?

But Wordsworth's great work is indubitably 'The Excursion.' This is a fragment of a projected great moral epic, discussing and solving the mightiest questions concerning God, nature, and man, our moral constitution, our duties, and our hopes. Its dramatic interest is exceedingly small; its structure is very inartificial; and the characters represented in it are devoid of life and probability. That an old Scottish pedlar, a country clergyman, and a disappointed visionary should reason so continuously and so sublimely on the destinies of man, is in itself a gross want of verisimilitude; and the purely speculative nature of their interminable arguments

"on knowledge, will, and fate,"

are not relieved from their monotony even by the abundant and beautiful descriptions and the pathetic episodes so thickly interspersed. It is Wordsworth, too, who is speaking always and alone; there is no variety of language, none of the shock and vivacity of intellectual wrestling: but, on the other hand, so sublime are the subjects on which they reason, so lofty and seraphic is their tone, and so deep a glow of humanity is perceptible throughout, that no reader, but such as seek in poetry for mere food for the curiosity and imagination, can study this grand composition without ever-increasing reverence and delight. Christianity is here exhibited under its most divine aspect; and the oracles of truth are pronounced in words of more than mortal sweetness.

In 1815 appeared 'The White Doe of Rylstone,' the only narrative poem of any length which Wordsworth has ever written. The incidents are of a simple and exceedingly mournful kind, turning chiefly on the complete ruin of a north-country family in the civil wars: but the atmosphere of mystical and supernatural influences in which the personages move, the superhuman purity and unearthliness of the characters, and above all the part played in the action by the white doe, which gives name to the work,—all these things contribute to communicate to the production a fantastic, unreal, and somewhat affected air. In a narrative, clearness, directness, simplicity are, above all things, necessary; and no beauty of imagery and versification, no purity of ideas will suffice to please us where these are wanting. In some of his shorter narratives, 'Hartleap Well,' the beautiful tale of 'The Boy of Egremont,' and above all the unsurpassable 'Laodamia,' Wordsworth has amply shown his power of uniting, to his unequalled grandeur of meditation, all the charms of a rapid and natural narrative. Perhaps the last of these is the finest tale of the kind in any language: and in many other little works—as 'Michael,' 'Ruth,' and 'The Female Vagrant'—the diffuseness of the manner is more than compensated by the beauty and verity of the matter.

A very large proportion of this author's more recent works (he has been all his life a most industrious author, and has now reached his seventy-sixth year) consists of sonnets. Of this difficult, and, at first sight, ungrateful species of composition, apparently so little suited to the peculiar genius of our language, we have in English literature many admirable examples. Its merits are thus insisted upon by Wordsworth himself in the following beautiful lines:—

"Scorn not the Sonnet: Critic! you have frown'd,
Mindless of its just honours: with this key
Shakspeare unlock'd his heart; the melody
Of this small lute gave ease to Petrarch's wound;
A thousand times this pipe did Tasso sound;
Camöens sooth'd with it an exile's grief:
The Sonnet glitter'd a gay myrtle-leaf
Amid the cypress with which Dante bound
His visionary brow: a glowworm lamp,
It cheer'd mild Spenser, call'd from Faëry-land
To struggle through dark ways; and when a damp
Fell round the path of Milton, in his hand
The thing became a trumpet, whence he blew
Soul-animating strains—alas! too few."

The sonnets of Wordsworth are in no sense inferior to the finest examples, we will not say of Shakspeare, Sidney, and Milton only, but of Petrarch or Filicaja. He has perfectly appreciated the true aim and rule of this kind of writing. Whether the prevailing emotion be patriotic enthusiasm, religious fervour, or the tenderer influences of beautiful scenery, historic spots of national interest, or the impressions of art, he never fails to give that unity of feeling, that gradual swell of gentle harmony — rising, like a summer wave, till it softly breaks into melody in the last line—which is the peculiar charm and merit of this most difficult kind of composition. Many of his sonnets are connected together by a predominant tone or key-note; and thus form complete works—a treasury of every charm of thought and grace of execution.

The literary character of Samuel Taylor Coleridge resembles some vast but unfinished palace: all is gigantic, beautiful, and rich; but nothing is complete, nothing compact. He was all his days, from his youth to his death in 1834, labouring, meditating, projecting: and yet all that he has left us bears a painful character of fragmentariness and imperfection. His mind was eminently dreamy; he was deeply tinged with that incapacity of *acting* which forms the characteristic of the German intellect: his genius was multiform, many-sided; and for this reason, perhaps, could not at once seize upon the right point of view. No man, probably, ever existed who thought more, and more intensely, than Coleridge; few ever possessed a vaster treasury of learning and knowledge; and yet how little has he given us! or rather how few of his works are in any way worthy of the undoubted majesty of his genius! ***Materials***, indeed, he has left us in enormous quantity — a store of thoughts and principles, particularly in the department of æsthetic science — golden masses of reason, either painfully sifted from the rubbish of obscure and forgotten authors, or dug up from the rich depths of his own mind; but these are still in the state of raw materials, or only partially worked. Of complete and substantive productions, all that we have of Coleridge are the following.—A small number of odes and lyrics, doubtless of extraordinary splendour and brilliancy, but still too much marked by a perceptible straining after grandeur and energy, as if the poet were lashing up his indolent enthusiasm by convulsive efforts; an admirable translation, or rather paraphrase, of the 'Piccolomini' and 'Death of Wallenstein,' executed under Schiller's own eye; a volume of miscellaneous prose essays, entitled 'The Friend;' the tragedy of 'Remorse' and 'Zapolya;' the 'Lectures on Shakspeare;' and two or three lyrical poems, of which we shall give a somewhat more detailed criticism. During the greater part of his life, too, he was exceedingly poor: and his perpetual struggles to obtain bread by his pen obliged him, in many instances, to engage in tasks for which his peculiar mental constitution was completely unfit; — as, for example, the occupation of a political journalist. He began life as an Unitarian and republican; his intellectual powers were chiefly formed in the transcendental schools of Germany;

but he ultimately became from conviction a most sincere adherent to the doctrines of the Anglican church, and an enthusiastic defender of our monarchical constitution. Though the lyrics to which we have alluded (the finest of which are the odes 'On the Departing Year,' and that supposed to be written "at sunrise in the Valley of Chamouni") are somewhat injured by their air of effort, they are indubitably works of singular richness, and exquisitely melodised language. The translations of the two members of Schiller's Trilogy of 'Wallenstein' are so admirable that they are worthy of being compared with original poems of no mean order. Nothing can be more free from stiffness, coldness, or any sign of the ideas being those of another poet. It is true that Coleridge's mind was in no degree dramatic; and therefore the variations (which are exceedingly numerous, and often exquisitely happy) which he has made from the text of the German, are generally rather beautiful developments of some train of reflection, only hinted at in the original, than any new strokes of character or increased vivacity of action. Coleridge's variations from his original are all of augmentation, or of evolution, never of condensation; for he was great rather as an observer, a describer, and a meditator, than as an embodier. No reader can fail to remark, as an example of this, the beautiful verses in which he describes the ancient popular mythologies and superstitions. This lovely passage is the expansion of a mere hint of Schiller's, conveyed in a couple of lines.

That Coleridge had no power of true dramatic creation is strongly proved by his tragedy of 'The Remorse;' in which, in spite of very striking features of character (as in Ordonio), and a multitude of incidents of the most violent kind, he has not produced a drama which either excites curiosity or moves any strong degree of pity. What is most beautiful in the work is all pure description, and in no sense advances the action or exhibits human passions. It is strange, perhaps, but yet by no means unintelligible, that a man who was so unsuccessful in creating emotions of a theatrical kind should have been a most consummate critic of the dramatic productions of others. Till he wrote, deep and universal as had been the admiring love—almost the adoration — of the English for Shakspeare, there still remained, in their judgments, something of that *de haut en bas* tone which characterises all the criticisms anterior to Coleridge's 'Lectures on Shakspeare.' Coleridge first showed that the creator of 'Hamlet' and 'Othello' was not only the greatest genius, but also the most consummate artist, who ever existed. Nothing can give us a higher opinion of the nobility of Coleridge's mind than that he was the first to make some approach to the discovery of those laws which, expressly or intuitively, governed the evolutions of the Shakspearian drama — that he possessed a soul vast enough, deep enough, multiform enough, to give us some faint idea of the dimensions, the length, and breadth, and depth, of that huge sea of truth and beauty.

Of the poems by which Coleridge is best known, both in England and abroad, the most universally read is undoubtedly 'The Rime of the Auncient Marinere,' a wild, mystical, phantasmagoric narrative, most picturesquely related in the old English ballad measure, and in language to which is skilfully given an air of antiquity in admirable harmony with the spectral character of the events. The whole poem is a splendid dream, filling the ear with the strange and floating melodies of sleep, and the eye with a shifting vaporous succession of fantastic images, gloomy or radiant. The wedding-party stopped on their way to the feast by the "bright-eyed marinere," the awful fascination by which the guest is obliged to hear and the wanderer to tell his tale, the skeleton ships and the phantoms which play at dice for the soul of the mariner, the punishment and repentance of the man who "shot the albatross,"—all this is wound up into one splendid tissue of cloudy phantoms. We read on, with that kind of consciousness of half-reality, that sensation of indistinct surprise, with which we are carried onward in our dreams. Extravagant and unreal as it all is, that important quality of harmony of tone is scrupulously kept up; and hence the pleasure we experience: we are placed in a new unearthly atmosphere, and all glimpses of the real world are carefully avoided.

The poem of 'Christabel,' and the fragment called 'Kubla Khan,' are of the same mystic, unreal character: indeed, Coleridge asserted that the latter was actually composed in a dream—an affirmation which may well be believed, for it is a thousand times more unintelligible than the general run of dreams. It is a dream, perhaps; but it is an *opium-dream*—"ægri somnium"—without so much as that faint coherency which even a dream must have to give pleasure in a picture or in a poem. Like 'The Mariner,' like the odes, like everything that Coleridge ever wrote, it is exquisitely versified. In the hands of a great sculptor marble and bronze seem to become as soft and as elastic as living flesh; and Coleridge seems to possess a similar dominion over his language. It puts on every form, it expresses every sound: he almost writes to the eye and to the ear our rough, pithy English, in his verse, breathes all sounds, all melodies:—

> "And now 'tis like all instruments,
> Now like a lonely flute;
> And now it is an angel's song,
> That makes the heavens be mute."

But in 'Christabel,' which has some slight pretensions to be an intelligible narrative, or, at least, part of an intelligible narrative—for we have a maiden who meets in a forest with a fiend disguised as an earthly damsel, and who apparently defeats the evil spirit's machinations — the mixture of two realities (both *dream-realities*, but one as it were within the other, like a tragedy within a tragedy, as in 'Hamlet,' or as the picture of a picture *in* a picture) is not harmoniously subordinated; and the effect is, of course, fatal to the poem as a work of art.

In point of completeness, exquisite harmony of feeling, and unsurpassable grace of imagery and language, Coleridge has left nothing superior to the charming little poem entitled 'Love, or Genevieve.' Perhaps the English language contains nothing more perfect: the very gentleness, ardour, and timidity of youthful passion — the "purple light of love"— is breathed throughout.

Coleridge's chief reputation, during his life, was founded less upon his writings than upon his conversation; or rather, what may be called his conversational oratory. Possessing, in a degree very unusual in modern society, and particularly rare in England (where this kind of display is little in accordance with the laconism, the reserve, the *positivisme*, and the extreme bashfulness of the national character), a most inexhaustible flow of eloquent imagery, and a ready command of the harmony of speech, Coleridge's conversation — if it could be called conversation, where he had all the talk to himself — must have resembled those disquisitions of the Greek philosophers of which the dialogues of Plato are merely a literary embodiment. Starting from a casual observation on any subject, Coleridge would wander on through the whole infinitude of knowledge with a profuseness of illustration, a profoundness of theory, and a rich and soothing melody of language, which those who knew him describe as having produced a kind of fascination in his hearers; and would scatter, as he went, such stores of reading, such new and sublime ideas on art, literature, and history, that, although his hearers often found themselves, at the end of the disquisition, enormously far from the point of departure, their journey had been so delightful, had given them such glimpses into the sunny realms of the ideal and the pure heaven of truth, and had enriched them with such treasures of thought and sentiment, that they felt neither weariness nor surprise. They were carried, like the knight of Ariosto on his hippogriff, upon the sublime wings of Coleridge's imagination; and gave free way to the magic of the hour. Of this wonderful discourser might be said what Homer tells us of Nestor, that "From his tongue his speech streamed on, like silent flakes of ever-falling snow."

It is in his innumerable fragments, in his rich but desultory remains (published posthumously under the title of 'Table-Talk')—in casual remarks scribbled like Sibylline leaves, often on the margins of borrowed books, and in imperfectly reported conversations, that we must look for proofs of Coleridge's immense but incompletely recorded powers; it is from these alone that we can gather the *disjecta membra poetæ*; and reconstruct, however imperfectly, the image of this great thinker and imaginer. From a careful study of these we shall conceive a high admiration of his genius; and a deep regret at the fragmentary and desultory manifestation of his powers. We shall, also, appreciate the vastness and multiform character of a mind to which nothing was too difficult, or too obscure; a noble tone of moral dignity "softened into beauty" by the largest sympathy; and, above all, an admirable catholicity of taste, which could unerringly pitch upon what was beautiful and true, and find its *pabulum* in all schools, all writers; perceiving, as it were intuitively, the value and the charm of the most unpromising books and systems.

Charles Lamb is one of the most admirable of those *humorists* who form the peculiar feature of the literature, as the ideas they express are the peculiar distinction of the character, of the English people. He was born in 1775, and died in 1835; and forms a bright light in that intellectual galaxy of which Wordsworth is the centre. He was essentially a *Londoner:* London life supplied him with his richest materials; and yet his mind was so imbued, so saturated with our older writers, that he is original by the mere force of self-tranformation into the spirit of the elder literature: he was, in short, an old writer, who lived by accident a century or two after his real time. Wordsworth is peculiarly the poet of solitary rural nature; Lamb drew an inspiration as true, as delicate, as profound, from the city life in which he lived; and from which he never was for a moment removed but with pain and a yearning to come back. In him the organ of *locality* must have been enormously developed: "his household gods planted a terribly fixed foot; and were not to be rooted up without blood." During the early and greater part of his life, Lamb, poor and unfriended, was drudging as a clerk in the India House; and it was not till late in life that he was unchained from the desk. Yet in this, the most monotonous and unideal of all employments, he found means to fill his mind with the finest aroma of our older authors; particularly of the prose writers and dramatists of the sixteenth and seventeenth centuries: and in his earliest compositions, such as the play of 'John Woodvil,' and the 'Essays of Elia,' although the world at first perceived a mere imitation of their quaintness of expression, there was, in reality, a revival of their very spirit. The essays, contributed by him at different times to one of the magazines, are the finest things, for humour, taste, penetration, and vivacity, which had appeared since the days of Montaigne. Where shall we find such intense delicacy of feeling, such unimaginable happiness of expression, such a searching into the very body of truth, as in these unpretending compositions? A chance word, dropped half by accident, a parenthesis, an exclamation, often lets us into the very mechanism of the sentiment—admits us, as it were, behind the scenes. The style has a peculiar and most subtle charm; not the result of labour, for it is found in as great perfection in his familiar letters—a certain quaintness and antiquity, not affected in Lamb, but the natural garb of his thoughts. This arises partly from the saturation of his mind with the rich and solid reading in which he delighted; and partly, but in a much higher degree, from the sensibility of his mind. The manure was abundant, but the soil was also of a "Sicilian fruitfulness." As in all the true humorists, his pleasantry was inseparably allied with the finest pathos: the merry quip on the tongue was but the commentary on the tear which trembled in the eye. He possessed the power, which is seen in Shakspeare's Fools, of conveying a deep philosophical verity in a jest—of uniting the wildest merriment with the truest pathos and the deepest wisdom. It is not only the easy laugh of Touchstone in the forest of Arden, but the heart-rending pleasantry of Lear's Fool in the storm. The inspiration that other poets find in the mountains, in the forest, in the sea, Lamb could draw from the crowd of Fleet-street, from the remembrances of an old actor, from the benchers of the Temple. In his poems, also, so few in number, and so admirable in originality, we have the quintessence of familiar sentiment, expressed in the diction of Herbert, Wither, and the great dramatists.

Lamb was the school-fellow, the devoted admirer and friend of Coleridge; and perhaps there never was an individual so *loved* by all his contemporaries, by men of every opinion, of every shade of literary, political, and religious sentiment, as this truly great wit and amiable man. The passionate enemy of everything like cant, common-place, or conventionality, his writings derive a singular charm, a kind of fresh and wild flavour, from his delight in paradox. The man himself was full of paradox: and his punning repartees, delivered with all the pangs of stuttering, often contained a decisive and unanswerable settlement of the question. In his drama of 'John Woodvil' he endeavoured, though of course unsuccessfully, to revive the forms of the Elizabethan drama; and the work might be mistaken for some woodland play of Heywood or Shirley. But it was his 'Specimens of the Old English Dramatists' which showed what treasures of the richest poetry lay concealed in the unpublished, and in modern times unknown, writers of that wonderful age, whose fame has been eclipsed by the glory of some two or three names of the same period. In the few lines, often only the few words, of criticism in which Lamb sketched the characters of the dramatists (with whose writings, from the greatest to the least, from Shakspeare down to Broome or Tourneur, no man was ever more familiar), we see perpetual examples of the delicacy and penetration of his critical faculty.

Lamb's mind, in its sensitiveness, in its mixture of wit and pathos, was eminently Shakspearian; and his intense and reverent study of the works of Shakspeare doubtless gave a tendency to this: the glow of his humour was too pure and steady not to have been reflected from the sun. In his poems, as for instance the 'Farewell to Tobacco,' the 'Old Familiar Faces,' and his few but beautiful sonnets, we find the very essence and spirit of this quaint tenderness of fancy, the naïveté of the child mingled with the learning of the scholar: they are like "that piece of song" in 'As You Like It,'—"old and plain,"

> "And dally with the innocence of love
> Like the old age."

Among the 'Essays of Elia' are several little narratives, generally visions and parables, inexpressibly simple and beautiful. That named 'Dream-Children,' and that other 'The Child-Angel' are worthy of Jean Paul himself: while the little tale 'Rosamond Gray' is perhaps one of the most inimitable gems ever produced in that difficult style.

Leigh Hunt and John Keats are two of the most distinguished names among the modern minor poets. The former, however, wrote rather under the inspiration of Lord Byron, and the latter under that of Shelley. Hunt endeavoured to revive something of the freshness, fluency, and vivacity of the old English and old Italian poets; while Keats carried to excess the peculiar manner of his model. Both wrote "upon a system," as Byron remarked upon the former; and, therefore, both of them will descend to posterity with an imperfect and unsatisfactory reputation. Hunt's best production, of any length, is the poem entitled 'A Story of Rimini;' an expansion, into a pretty narrative, of the tale of 'Francesca da Rimini' condensed by Dante, with such intensity of pathos, into a few lines of his 'Inferno.' This work, which is written in the rhymed couplet founded upon Dryden's admirable modernizations of Chaucer and the old Italian novelists, is full of a delicate and refined fancy: but the diction is often deformed by a peculiar and intolerable coxcombry of language, to which has been given the significant appellation of *cockneyism.* It is a mixture of the *concetti* of second-rate Italian poetry with the smug arcadianism of a London citizen masquerading as a shepherd. Hunt, like his friend and contemporary Hazlitt, has done good service to his country as a miscellaneous critic and essayist on various detached portions of our literature, particularly that of the sixteenth and seventeenth centuries; and in the 'Indicator' of the former there is much agreeable chat on literature and art; seldom very profound perhaps, but always sparkling with a singular effervescence of animal spirits, and filled (the greatest charm in writing of this nature) with a sincere and lively admiration for the beauties under examination. The more ambitious tone of Hazlitt's writings, and the more scientific exposition and investigation of æsthetic principles, may seem to claim for him a place rather nearer to that occupied by Coleridge: but we are not sure that Hunt's easy, pleasant, good-humoured chat has not done more than Hazlitt's graver tone to disseminate a taste for rich and healthy literature.

Keats, whose short life was embittered by the contemptuous reception his first poems met with from the critics, was born in 1796, and died at the age of 24. What is most remarkable in his works is the wonderful profusion of figurative language, often exquisitely beautiful and luxuriant, but sometimes purely fantastical and far-fetched. The peculiarity of Shelley's style, to which we gave the name of *incatenation*, Keats carries to extravagance—one word, one image, one rhyme suggests another, till we quite lose sight of the original idea; which is smothered in its own sweet luxuriance, like a bee stifled in honey. Shakspeare and his school, upon whose manner Keats undoubtedly endeavoured to form his way of writing, have, it is true, this peculiarity of language: but in them the images never run away with the thought; the guiding master-idea is ever present. These poets never throw the reins on the mane of their Pegasus, even when soaring to "the brightest heaven of invention." With them, the images are produced by a force acting *ab intra;* like wild flowers springing from the very richness of the ground. In Keats the force acts *ab extra;* the flowers are forcibly fixed in the earth, as in the garden of a child, who cannot wait till they grow there of themselves. Keats deserves high praise for one very peculiar and original merit: he has treated the classical mythology in a way absolutely new; representing the pagan deities not as mere abstractions of art, nor as mere creatures of popular belief; but giving them passions and affections like our own, highly purified and idealised, however, and in exquisite accordance with the lovely scenery of ancient Greece and Italy, and with the golden atmosphere of primeval existence. This treatment of a subject, which ordinary readers would consider hopelessly outworn and threadbare, is certainly not Homeric; nor is it Miltonic; nor is it in the manner of any of the great poets who have employed the mythologic imagery of antiquity: but it is productive of very exquisite pleasure; and must, therefore, be in accordance with true principles of art. In 'Hyperion,' in the 'Ode to Pan,' in the verses on a 'Grecian Urn,' we find a noble and airy strain of beautiful classic imagery, combined with a perception of natural loveliness so luxuriant, so rich, so delicate, that the rosy dawn of Greek poetry seems combined with all that is most tenderly pensive in the calm sunset twilight of romance. Such of Keats's poems as are founded on more modern subjects—'The Eve of St. Agnes,' for example, or 'The Pot of Basil,' a beautiful anecdote versified from Boccaccio—are to our taste inferior to those of his productions in which the scenery and personages are mythologic. It would seem as if the severity of ancient art, which in the last-mentioned works acted as an involuntary check upon a too luxuriant fancy, deserted him when he left the antique world; and the absence of true, deep, intense passion (his prevailing defect) becomes necessarily more painfully apparent; as well as the discordant mingling of the *prettinesses* of modern poetry with the directness, and the unaffected simplicity, of Chaucer and Boccaccio.

Depth and intensity of feeling, which we have denied to Keats, form the great secret of the power of Thomas Hood; an author long known chiefly as an admirable punster, and a writer of the most broadly comic character; but whose reputation, as an admirable poet and profound humourist, is growing day by day. For several years he published a volume called 'The Comic Annual,' a species of burlesque upon the gift-books then so popular in England; and the droll prose and verse, illustrated by still droller woodcuts executed by himself, supplied Christmas parties with a never-failing annuity of laughter. He also produced, principally as contributions to 'The New Monthly Magazine,' of which he was for some time editor, a large number of tales, generally turning upon some minute but grotesque incident, and treated in a manner so perfectly original, that Hood must absolutely be considered as constituting an era in the history of comic literature. Like Lamb, he was a consummate punster; and, like Lamb's, his puns and wildest friskings of humour not only excite a momentary laugh, but frequently contain an inner and esoteric sense, often wonderfully beautiful and profound. Like Lamb, too, Hood possessed a sort of intuitive perception of truth and beauty: and, like him, his heart was warm and his sympathy boundless. In the little prose tales, where he talks to his reader in a strain at once wonderfully imaginative, profound, and ludicrous—in his admirable imaginary correspondences, generally between servants, or peasants, who distort the English language so as to produce truly Rabelæsian double and triple meanings—in his comic poems, as the story of Miss Kielmansegg—in his graver letters on the rights of the literary profession, and on the condition of the poor, he shows an inexhaustible richness of invention, a power over words and combinations, which never fails not only to gratify our curiosity and sense of the ludicrous, but even to supply us with ideas new, tender, and sometimes sublime. But Hood is also a great original poet of a serious and romantic cast. His 'Dream of Eugene Aram,' his 'Elm Tree,' are works of powerful conception and permanent interest; his 'Plea of the Midsummer Fairies,' his 'Two Swans,' and 'Lycus the Centaur,' are exquisite pieces of airy and fantastic imagery, nothing inferior to Keats's happiest productions; while he must be considered as the originator of a very peculiar and powerful species of songs, equally admirable for the force and simplicity of their diction, the harmony and novelty of their metrical construction, and above all for the fervid and vigorous spirit of humanity which they breathe. The beautiful stanzas called

'The Bridge of Sighs,' and the painfully touching 'Song of the Shirt,' were the means of exciting for an unhappy and neglected class of his countrywomen the pity, the interest, and even the active benevolence of the nation. Such things are not only good *works*, but good *actions*; and the triumph of having made genius a minister to philanthropy is a glory worthy of the friend of Lamb and the first humorous writer of his age.

It now remains to pass rapidly over a few names of contemporary writers; less remarkable, in general, for originality of genius than for elegance of taste, happy selection of subject, or novelty of treatment. In the department of poetry women have shown as great an activity as in most other fields of modern literature. The rich and fervid tone of Mrs. Hemans would deserve a more detailed mention than our space will afford; and Mrs. Norton, L. E. L., and other ladies have shown no mean mastery over the tenderer moods of the modern lyre. Of the distinguished but less important *men*—our Dii minorum gentium—it will suffice to specify Mr. Barham, who has written, under the pseudonym of Thomas Ingoldsby, a series of comic tales in easy verse;—wild and wondrous legends of chivalry, witchcraft, and diablerie, related in singularly rich and flexible metre; and in language in which the intermixture of the modern cant phrase of society with antiquarian pedantry produces a truly comic effect. Tennyson, Alford, and Milnes may be considered as the poetical disciples of Wordsworth. Thomas Babington Macaulay, celebrated as a brilliant critic and essayist in 'The Edinburgh Review,' having been struck with Niebuhr's theory, that the early history of Rome was compiled by Livy and other historians from popular metrical legends since lost, conceived the bold and happy idea of *reconstructing* some of these vanished ballads in rough picturesque plebeian metre; and producing in English some such fierce republican lays as might have been sung by the peasant heroes of ancient Rome. He has executed in this manner the stories of 'Horatius Cocles,' 'The Battle of Lake Regillus,' 'The Death of Virginia,' with a fire and animation which eclipsed even his own powerful ballads on events in the History of France; and has shown himself to be not merely a master of all the strength and muscular power of our early language, but also intimately penetrated by the spirit of antiquity and the rugged independence of old Rome.

In thus investigating, however cursorily, the course of English iterature from its remote origin in Chaucer—himself an emblem of the confluence, so to say, of three different streams of art and nationality—the original Saxonism, the Italian spirit of the Renaissance, and the free spirit of the Reformation—no one can fail to be struck with one singular and noble peculiarity;—a peculiarity which it has in common with the nationality it reflects; and one which, though perceptible in the character of every branch of the Teutonic race, was never possessed so completely as by the English nation. We mean that intense and ever-present sap and vitality, which allowed no interval to interfere between the most gigantic and dissimilar exertions of creative energy. No sooner does any class of composition, any school of literature, decline from its period of highest fertility, than another springs up, as rich, as living, and as energetic as the former. The English intellect, thanks to the happy freedom of our institutions, and the strong virility of the national character, has no dull, dead, periods of feeble imitation and languid servility. The moment it has duly developed itself in one direction, it instantly takes and steadily maintains another: and our literature —essentially the literature of a nation of men—rich in the finest and most unequalled models of every kind and class of excellence —is in every sense worthy of the greatest, freest, and most thoughtful people that the world has ever seen. So glorious a past can promise nothing but a future as illustrious. The same powers and influences which have enabled England to produce more and greater things than any other community can boast, are still at work; and will enable her to produce others, different in kind perhaps, but as durable, as splendid, as sublime.

A SKETCH

OF

AMERICAN LITERATURE.

A SKETCH

OF

AMERICAN LITERATURE.

CHAPTER I.

Literature in the Colonies imitative—Relation of American to English Literature—Gradual Advancement of the United States in Letters—Their first Development theological—Writers in this Department—Jonathan Edwards—Religious Controversy—William E. Channing—Writings of the Clergy—Newspapers and School Books—Domestic Literature—Female Writers—Oratory—Revolutionary Eloquence—American Orators—Alexander Hamilton—Daniel Webster and others—Edward Everett—American History and Historians—Jared Sparks—David Ramsay—George Bancroft—Hildreth—Elliot Lossing—William H. Prescott—Irving—Wheaton—Cooper—Parkman.

LITERATURE is a positive element of civilized life; but in different countries and epochs it exists sometimes as a passive taste or means of culture, and at others as a development of productive tendencies. The first is the usual form in colonial societies, where the habit of looking to the fatherland for intellectual nutriment as well as political authority is the natural result even of patriotic feeling. The circumstances, too, of young communities, like those of the individual, are unfavourable to original literary production. Life is too absorbing to be recorded otherwise than in statistics. The wants of the hour and the exigencies of practical responsibility wholly engage the mind. Half a century ago, it was usual to sneer in England at the literary pretensions of America; but the ridicule was quite as unphilosophical as unjust, for it was to be expected that the new settlements would find their chief mental subsistence in the rich heritage of British literature, endeared to them by a community of language, political sentiment, and historical association. And when a few of the busy denizens of a new republic ventured to give expression to their thoughts, it was equally natural that the spirit and the principles of their ancestral literature should reappear. Scenery, border-life, the vicinity of the aborigines, and a great political experiment were the only novel features in the new world upon which to found anticipations of originality; in academic culture, habitual reading, moral and domestic tastes, and cast of mind, the Americans were identified with the mother country; and in all essential particulars, would naturally follow the style thus inherent in their natures and confirmed by habit and study. At first, therefore, the literary development of the United States was imitative; but with the progress of the country, and her increased leisure and means of education, the writings of the people became more and more characteristic; theological and political occasions gradually ceased to be the exclusive moulds of thought; and didactic, romantic, and picturesque compositions appeared from time to time. Irving peopled 'Sleepy Hollow' with fanciful creations; Bryant described not only with truth and grace, but with devotional sentiment, the characteristic scenes of his native land; Cooper introduced Europeans to the wonders of her forest and sea-coast; Bancroft made her story eloquent; and Webster proved that the race of orators who once roused her children to freedom, was not extinct. The names of Edwards and Franklin were echoed abroad; the bonds of mental dependence were gradually loosened—the inherited tastes remained, but they were freshened with a more native zest,—and although Brockden Brown is still compared to Godwin, Irving to Addison, Cooper to Scott, Hoffman to Moore, Emerson to Carlyle, and Holmes to Pope, a characteristic vein, an individuality of thought, and a local significance is now generally recognised in the emanations of the American mind; and the best of them rank favourably and harmoniously with similar examplars in British literature; while, in a few instances, the nationality is so marked, and so sanctioned by true genius as to challenge the recognition of all impartial and able critics. The majority, however, of our authors are men of talent rather than of genius; the greater part of the literature of the country has sprung from New England, and is therefore, as a general rule, too unimpassioned and coldly elegant for popular effect. There has been a lamentable want of self-reliance, and an obstinate blindness to the worth of native material, both scenic, historical, and social. The great defect of our literature has been a lack of independence, and too exclusive a deference to hackneyed models; there has been and is no deficiency of intellectual life; it has thus far, however, often proved too diffusive and conventional for great results.

The intellect of the country first developed in a theological form. This was a natural consequence of emigration, induced by difference of religious opinion, the free scope which the new colonies afforded for discussion, and the variety of creeds represented by the different races who thus met on a common soil, including every diversity of sentiment, from Puritanism to Episcopacy, each extreme modified by shades of doctrine and individual speculation. The clergy, also, were the best educated and most influential class; in political and social as well as religious affairs, their voice had a controlling power; and, for a considerable period, they alone enjoyed that frequent immunity from physical labor which is requisite to mental productiveness. The colonial era, therefore, boasted only a theological literature, for the most part fugitive and controversial; yet sometimes taking a more permanent shape, as in the Biblical Concordance of Newman, and some of the writings of Roger Williams, Increase and Cotton Mather, Mayhew, Cooper, Stiles, Dwight, Elliot, Johnson, Chauncey, Witherspoon, and Hopkins. There is no want of learning or reasoning power in many of the tracts of those once formidable disputants; and such reading accorded with the stern tastes of our ancestors; but, as a general rule, the specimens which yet remain in print, are now only referred to by the curious student of divinity or the antiquarian. One enduring relic, however, of this epoch survives, and is held in great estimation by metaphysicians for its subtlety of argument, its originality and vigor, and masterly treatment of a profound subject. I allude to the celebrated Treatise on the Will, by Dr. Edwards, a work originally undertaken to furnish a philosophical basis for the Calvinistic dogmas; and, in its sagacious hardihood of thought, forming a characteristic introduction to the literary history of New England.

Jonathan Edwards was the only son of a Connecticut minister of good acquirements and sincere piety. He was born in 1703 in the town of Windsor; he entered Yale College at the age of thirteen, and at nineteen became a settled preacher in New York. In 1723, he was elected a tutor in the college at New Haven; and after discharging its duties with eminent success for two years, he became the colleague of his grandfather, in the ministry, at the beautiful village of Northampton, in Massachusetts. Relieved from all material cares by the affection of his wife, his time was entirely given to professional occupations and study. An ancient elm is yet designated in the town where he passed so many years, in the crotch of which was his favorite seat, where he was accustomed to read and think for hours together. His sermons began to attract attention, and several were republished in England. As a writer, he first gained celebrity by a treatise on 'Original Sin.' He was inaugurated President of Princeton College, N. J., on the 16th of February 1785; and on the 22d of the ensuing March died of small-pox, which then ravaged the vicinity.

"This remarkable man," says Sir James Mackintosh, "the metaphysician of America, was formed among the Calvinists of New England, when their stern doctrine retained its vigorous authority. His power of subtle argument, perhaps unmatched, certainly unsurpassed among men, was joined, as in some of the ancient mystics, with a character which raised his piety to fervor. He embraced their doctrine, probably without knowing it to be theirs. Had he suffered this noble principle to take the right road to all its fair consequences, he would have entirely concurred with Plato, with Shaftesbury and Malebranche, in devotion to 'the first good, first perfect, and first fair.' But he thought it necessary afterwards to limit his doctrine to his own persuasion, by denying that such moral excellence could be discovered in divine things by those Christians who did not take the same view with him of their religion."*

Although so meagre a result, as far as regards permanent literature, sprang from the early theological writings in America, they had a certain strength and earnestness which tended to invigorate and exercise the minds of the people; sometimes, indeed, conducive to bigotry, but often inciting reflective habits. The mental life of the colonists seemed, for a long time, identical with religious discussion; and the names of Anne Hutchinson, Roger Williams, George Fox, Whitfield, the early field-preacher, and subsequently those of Dr. Hopkins, and Murray the father of Universalism in America, were rallying words for logical warfare; the struggle between the advocates of quakerism, baptism by immersion, and other of the minority against those of the old Presbyterian and Church of England doctrine, gave birth to a multitude of tracts, sermons, and oral debates which elicited no little acumen, rhetoric, and learning. The originality and productiveness of the American mind in this department has, indeed, always been a characteristic feature in its development. Scholars and orators of distinguished ability have never been wanting to the clerical profession among us; and every sect in the land has its illustrious interpreters, who have bequeathed, or still contribute, written memorials of their ability. Davies, Bellamy, Robinson, Stuart, Tappan, Williams, Bishop White, Dr. Jarvis, Dr. Hawkes, Hooker, Cheever, and others, have materially adorned the literature of the church; the diversity of sects is one of the most curious and striking facts in our social history, and is fully illustrated by the literary organs of each denomination, from the spiritual commentaries of Bush to the ardent Catholicism of Brownson.† About the commencement of the present century, a memorable conflict took place between the liberal and orthodox party; and among the writings of the former may be found more finished specimens of composition than had previously appeared on ethics and religion. Independent of their opinions, the high morality and beautiful sentiment, as well as chaste and graceful diction, of the leaders of that school, gave a literary value and interest to pulpit eloquence which soon exercised a marked

* Progress of Ethical Philosophy.

† The clergy have been among the prominent laborers in the field of useful literature. The names of Dehon, Payson, Potter, Abbott, Bedeli, Knox, Todd, Woods, Sprague, Baird, Barnes, Alexander, Tyng, Bacon, Stewart, of the Orthodox and the Episcopal denomination; and of Buckminster, William and Henry Ware, Dewey, Whitman, Osgood, Greenwood, Frothingham, Brooks, Furness, Peabody, Stetson, and many others of the Unitarian, are identified with current educational and religious literature.

influence on the literary taste of the community. Religious and moral writings now derived from style a new interest. At the head of this class, who achieved a world-wide reputation for genius in ethical literature, is William Ellery Channing.

"Half a century ago, there might have been seen threading the streets of Richmond, a diminutive figure, with a pale attenuated face, eyes of spiritual brightness, an expansive and calm brow, and movements of nervous alacrity. An abstraction of manner and intentness of expression denoted the scholar, while the scrupulously neat, yet worn attire, as clearly evidenced restricted means and habits of self-denial. The youth was one of those children of New England braced by her discipline, and early sent forth to earn a position in the world, by force of character and activity of intellect. He was baptized into the fraternity of Nature by the grandeur and beauty of the sea as it breaks along the craggy shore of Rhode Island; the domestic influences of a Puritan household had initiated him into the moral convictions; and the teachings of Harvard yielded him the requisite attainments to discharge the office of private tutor in a wealthy Virginian family. Then and there, far from the companions of his studies and the home of his childhood, through secret conflicts, devoted application to books, and meditation, amid privations, comparative isolation, and premature responsibility, he resolved to consecrate himself to the Christian ministry. Illness had subdued his elasticity, care shadowed his dreams, and retirement solemnized his desires. Thence he went to Boston, and for more than forty years pursued the consistent tenor of his way as an eloquent divine and powerful writer, achieving a wide renown, bequeathing a venerated memory, and a series of discourses, reviews and essays, which, with remarkable perspicuity and earnestness, vindicate the cause of freedom, the original endowments and eternal destiny of human nature, the sanctions of religion and 'the ways of God to man.' Sectarian controversy, the duties of the pastoral office, journeys abroad and at home, intercourse with superior minds and the seclusion made necessary by disease,—the quiet of home, the refining influence of literary taste, and the vocations of citizen, father and philanthropist, occupied those intervening years. He died, one beautiful October evening, at Bennington, Vermont, while on a summer excursion, and was buried at Mount Auburn. A monument commemorates the gratitude of his parishioners and the exalted estimation he had acquired in the world. A biography prepared by his nephew, recounts the few incidents of his career, and gracefully unfolds the process of his growth and mental history.

"It is seldom that ethical writings interest the multitude. The abstract nature of the topics they discuss, and the formal style in which they are usually embodied, are equally destitute of that popular charm that wins the common heart. A remarkable exception is presented in the literary remains of Channing. The simple yet comprehensive ideas upon which he dwells, the tranquil gravity of his utterance, and the winning clearness of his style, render many of his productions universally attractive as examples of quiet and persuasive eloquence. And this result is entirely independent of any sympathy with his theological opinions, or experience of his pulpit oratory. Indeed, the genuine interest of Dr. Channing's writings is ethical. As the champion of a sect, his labours have but a temporary value; as the exponent of a doctrinal system, he will not long be remembered with gratitude, because the world is daily better appreciating the religious sentiment as of infinitely more value than any dogma; but as a moral essayist, some of the more finished writings of Channing will have a permanent hold upon reflective and tasteful minds. His nephew has compiled his biography with singular judgment. He has followed the method of Lockhart in the Life of Scott. As far as possible, the narrative is woven from letters and diaries,—the subject speaks for himself, and only such intermediate observations of the editor are given as are necessary to form a connected whole. Uneventful as these memoirs are, they are interesting as revelations of the process of culture, the means and purposes of one whose words have winged their way, bearing emphatic messages, over both hemispheres,—who, for many years, successfully advocated important truths; and whose memory is one of the most honored of New England's gifted divines.

"To Dr. Channing's style is, in a great degree, ascribable the popularity of his writings; and we are struck with its remarkable identity from the earliest to the latest period of his career. A petition to Congress, penned while a student at the University, which appears in these volumes, has all its prominent characteristics — its brief sentences, occasionally lengthened where the idea requires it—its emphasis, its simplicity, directness, and transparent diction. This is a curious evidence of the purely meditative existence he must have passed; for it is by attrition with other minds and subjection to varied influences, that the style of writing as well as the tone of manners undergoes those striking modifications which we perceive in men less intent upon a few thoughts. His character is, therefore, justly described as more indebted to 'the influences of solitary thought than of companionship.' Such is the process by which all truth becomes clearly impressed and richly developed to consciousness; on the same principle that, according to Mary Wollstonecraft, reflection is necessary to the realization even of a great passion. 'I derive my sentiments from the nature of man,' says one of Channing's letters. Perhaps it would have been more strictly true if he had said one man; for an inference we long ago derived from his writings, we find amply confirmed in his memoirs — that he was a very inadequate observer. Some of his attempts to portray character are as complete fancy sketches as we ever perused. They show an utter blindness to the real traits even of familiar persons. Beautiful in themselves, it is usually from the graceful drapery of his imagination that the charm is derived. Indeed, Dr. Channing hardly came near enough to see the features in their literal significance. He drew almost exclusively from within. His subjects were what the lay-figure is to the artist — frames for his thoughts to deck with effective costume. When he reasoned of a truth or an idea, he was more at home; for in the abstract he was at liberty to expatiate, without keeping in view the actual relations of things — the stern facts and bare realities of life and character. Indeed, nothing can be more delightful to a refined and thoughtful mind, than to follow Channing in his exposition of a striking idea or truth—so clearly and dispassionately stated, then gradually unfolded to its ultimate significance, with, here and there, a striking illustration; and then wound up, like a fine strain of music, which seems to raise us more and more into light and tranquillity on invisible pinions!" *

Of all the foreign commentators on our political institutions and national character, De Tocqueville is the most distinguished for philosophical insight; and although many of his speculations are visionary, not a few are pregnant with reflective wisdom. He says in regard to the literary development of such a republic as our own, that its early fruits "will bear marks of an untutored and rude vigor of thought, frequently of great variety and singular fecundity." What may be termed the casual writing and speaking of the country, confirms this prophecy. The two most prolific branches of literature in America, are journalism and educational works. The aim in both is to supply that immediate demand which, according to the French philosopher, is more imperative and prevailing than in monarchial lands. Newspapers and school-books are, therefore, the characteristic form of literature in the United States. The greatest scholars of the country have not deemed the production of the latter an unworthy labor, nor the most active, enterprising, and ambitious failed to exercise their best powers in the former sphere. An intelligent foreigner, therefore, who observed the predominance of these two departments, would arrive at the just conclusion, that the great mental distinction of the nation is two-fold—the universality of education and a general, though superficial intellectual activity in the mass of the people. There is, however, still another phase of our literary condition equally significant — and that is the popularity of what may be termed domestic reading: a species of books intended for the family, and designed to teach science, religion, morality, the love of nature, and other desirable acquisitions. These works range from a juvenile to a mature scope and interest, both in form and spirit; but are equally free of all ex-

* Characteristics of Literature. First Series.

travagance—except it be purely imaginative—and are unexceptionable, often elevated, in moral tone. They constitute the literature of the fireside, and give to the young their primary ideas of the world and of life. Hence their moral importance can scarcely be overrated. Accordingly, children's books have not been thought unworthy the care of the best minds: philosophers like Guizot, poets like Hans Andersen, popular novelists like Scott and Dickens, have not scorned this apparently humble but most influential service. The reform in books for the young was commenced in England by Maria Edgeworth and Mrs. Barbauld; when the 'Parent's Assistant,' and 'Original Poems for Infant Minds,' superseded 'Mother Goose' and 'Jack the Giant-Killer;' and with the instinct of domestic utility, so prevalent on this side of the water, this impulse was caught up and prolonged here, and resulted in a class of books and writers, not marked by high genius or striking originality, yet honorable to the good sense and moral feeling of the country. These have supplied the countless homes scattered over the western continent, with innocent, instructive, and often refined reading, sometimes instinct not only with a domestic but a national spirit; often abounding with the most fresh and true pictures of scenery, customs, and local traits, and usually conceived in a tone of gentleness and purity fitted to chasten and improve the taste. These writers have usually adapted themselves equally to the youngest and to the most advanced of the family circle—extended their labor of love from the child's story-book to the domestic novel.*

Oratory is eminently the literature of republics. Political freedom gives both occasion and impulse to thought on public interests; and its expression is a requisite accomplishment to every intelligent and patriotic citizen. American eloquence, although not unknown in the professional spheres of colonial life, developed with originality and richness at the epoch of the revolution. Indeed, the questions that agitated the country naturally induced popular discussions, and as a sense of wrong and a resolve to maintain the rights of freemen, took the place of remonstrance and argument, a race of orators seems to have sprung to life, whose chief traits continue evident in a long and illustrious roll of names, identified with our statesmen, legislators and

---

* It is creditable to the sex that this sphere has been filled, in our country, chiefly by female writers; the list of whom includes a long array of endeared and honoured names, at the head of which stands Hannah Adams, with her once popular histories, Catharine M. Sedgwick, with her moral and graphic illustrations of New England life, and Lydia M. Child, with her poetic and generous suggestiveness. Among others may be mentioned Mrs. Lydia H. Sigourney, Miss Leslie, sister of the artist, Eliza Robbins, Mrs. Gilman, of Charleston, S. C., Mrs. Lee, of Boston, Mrs. E. Oakes Smith, Miss Beecher, Mrs. Kirkland, Mrs. Ellett, Mrs. S. J. Hale, and such *noms de plume* as Fanny Forrester and Grace Greenwood; also Mrs. Embury, of Brooklyn, L. I., Miss McIntosh, Mrs. Neal, Alice Carey, Mrs. Farrar, Mrs. Willard, Mrs. Hall, and Miss Wetherel.

divines. From the stripling Hamilton, who, in July 1774, held a vast concourse in breathless excitement, in the fields near New York, while he demonstrated the right and necessity of resistance to British oppression, to the mature Webster, who, in December 1829, defended the union of the States with an argumentative and rhetorical power ever memorable in the annals of legislation, there has been a series of remarkable public speakers who have nobly illustrated this branch of literature in the United States. The fame of American eloquence is in part traditionary. Warren, Adams, and Otis in Boston, and Patrick Henry in Virginia, by their spirit-stirring appeals, roused the land to the assertion and defence of its just rights; and Alexander Hamilton, Governeur Morris, Pinkney, Jay, Rutledge, and other firm and gifted men gave wise and effective direction to the power thus evoked, by their logical and earnest appeals.

"At the time the contest began," says Guizot, "there were in each colony some men already honored by their fellow-citizens, already well known in the defence of public liberty, influential by their property, talent, or character; faithful to ancient virtues, yet friendly to modern improvement; sensible to the splendid advantages of civilization, and yet attached to simplicity of manners; high-toned in their feelings, but of modest minds, at the same time ambitious and prudent in their patriotic impulses." Foremost among these remarkable men was Alexander Hamilton; by birth a West Indian, by descent uniting the Scottish vigor and sagacity of character with the accomplishment of the French. While a collegian in New York, his talents, at once versatile and brilliant, were apparent in the insight and poetry of his debates, the solemn beauty of his devotion, the serious argument of his ambitious labors, and the readiness of his humorous sallies; with genuine religious sentiment, born perhaps of his Huguenot blood, he united a zest for pleasure, a mercurial temperament, and grave aspirations. In his first youth the gentleman, the pietist, the hero, and the statesman alternately exhibited, sometimes dazzled, at others impressed, and always won the hearts of his comrades. His first public demonstration was as an orator, when but seventeen; and notwithstanding his slender figure and extreme youth, he took captive both the reason and feeling of a popular assembly. Shortly after he became involved in the controversy then raging between whigs and tories; and his pamphlets and newspaper essays were read with mingled admiration and incredulity at the rare powers of expression and mature judgment thus displayed by the juvenile antagonist of bishops and statesmen. But his arm not less than his tongue was dedicated to the cause he thus espoused with equal ardor and intelligence. He studied the military art, gained Washington's notice in the retreat of the American forces through New Jersey; and from that moment became his intimate coadjutor. His next intellectual labor was devoted to explaining and enforcing the principles of finance

—a subject of which his countrymen were practically ignorant. To his zeal and sagacity in this department, combined with the noble efforts of Robert Morris, the country was indebted for the pecuniary means of carrying on the war of the revolution, and finally for a regulated currency and established credit.

As first secretary of the treasury, Hamilton may be said to have laid the foundation of our national prosperity. His mind, even at a period most burdened with official cares, was given to the successful advocacy of a neutral course in regard to France; after honorable service attaining the rank of lieutenant-general, when the army disbanded, Hamilton resumed the legal profession. The idol of the Federal party, and a candidate for the Chief Magistracy, he became entangled in a duel planned by political animosity, and fell at Weehawken, opposite the city of New York, by the hand of Aaron Burr, on the eleventh of June, 1804. The impression caused by his untimely death was unprecedented in this country; for no public man ever stood forth "so clear in his great office," more essentially useful in affairs, courageous in battle, loyal in attachment, gifted in mind, or graceful in manner. During a life of such varied and absorbing occupation, he found time to put on record his principles as a statesman; not always highly finished, his writings are full of sense and energy; their tone is noble, their insight often deep, and the wisdom they display remarkable. His letters are finely characteristic; his state-papers valuable, and the 'Federalist' a significant illustration both of his genius and the age.*

The historical and literary anniversaries of such frequent occurrence in this country, and the exigencies of political life, give occasion for the exercise of oratory to educated citizens of all professions — from the statesman who fills the gaze of the world, to the village pastor and country advocate. Accordingly a large and, on the whole, remarkably creditable body of discourses, emanating from the best minds of the country, have been published in collected editions, to such an extent as to constitute a decided feature of American literature. They are characteristic also as indicating the popular shape into which intellectual labors naturally run in a young and free country, and the fugitive and occasional literary efforts which alone are practicable for the majority even of scholars. The most solid

* No small part of the political writing of the United States is fugitive in its character; but the State papers, including the correspondence of the chief actors in the revolutionary war, and the adoption of the Constitution, form a mine of political ideas and principles. After these, the speeches of the leading statesmen contain, in themselves, a history of the political opinions and crises of the nation; and an armory of logical weapons, of more or less value, may easily be drawn from the works of Franklin, Hamilton, Morris, Jay, Quincy, Dickinson, Paine, Jefferson, Madison, Livingston, Ames, Freneau, Noah Webster, Rawle, William Sullivan, Leggett, and other political essayists. The 'Federalist,' the joint production of Hamilton, Madison, and Jay, is a standard book of this class.

of this class of writings are the productions of statesmen; and of these, three are conspicuous, although singularly diverse both in style and cast of thought—Webster, Calhoun, and Clay. The former's oration at Plymouth in 1820; his address at the laying of the corner-stone of the Bunker Hill Monument, half a century after the battle; his discourse on the deaths of Adams and Jefferson, the following year; and his reply to Hayne, in the U. S. Senate, in 1829, are memorable specimens of oratory, and recognised everywhere as among the greatest instances of genius in this branch of letters in modern times. These are, however, but a very small part of his speeches and forensic arguments, which constitute a permanent and characteristic, as well as intrinsically valuable and interesting portion of our native literature.

Daniel Webster is the son of a New Hampshire farmer. He was born in 1782, graduated at Dartmouth College, and began the practice of law at a village near Salisbury, his birth-place, but removed to Portsmouth in 1807. He soon distinguished himself at the bar, and as a member of the House of Representatives; retired from Congress and removed to Boston in 1817; and, by his able arguments in the Supreme Court, as well as his unrivalled eloquence on special occasions, was very soon acknowledged to be one of the greatest men America had produced. His career as a senator, a foreign minister, and secretary of state, has been no less illustrious than his professional triumphs; but, as far as literature is concerned, he will be remembered by his state-papers and speeches. His style is remarkable for great clearness of statement. It is singularly emphatic. It is impressive rather than brilliant, and occasionally rises to absolute grandeur. It is evidently formed on the highest English models; and the reader conjectures his love of Milton, from the noble simplicity of his language, and fondness for sublime rather than apt figures. Clearness of statement, vigor of reasoning, and a faculty of making a question plain to the understanding, by the mere terms in which it is presented, are the traits which uniformly distinguish his writings, evident alike in a diplomatic note, a legislative debate, and an historical discourse. His dignity of expression, breadth of view, and force of thought, realize the ideal of a republican statesman, in regard, at least to natural endowments; and his presence and manner, in the prime of his life, were analogous. Independent of their logical and rhetorical merit, these writings may be deemed invaluable from the nationality of their tone and spirit. They awaken patriotic reflection and sentiment, and are better adapted to warn, to enlighten, and to cheer the consciousness of the citizen, than any American works, of a didactic kind, yet produced.

In the speeches of Clay there is a chivalric freshness, which readily explains his great popularity as a man; not so profound as Webster, he is far more rhetorical, and equally patriotic. Calhoun is eminently individual; his mind has that precise energy which is so effectual in debate; his style of argument is concise; and in personal aspect he was quite as remarkable—the incarnation of intense purpose and keen perception. These and many other eminent men have admirably illustrated that department of oratory which belongs to statesmen.

Fisher Ames, William Wirt, John Quincy Adams, Hugh S Legaré, and others, famed as debaters, have united to this distinction the renown of able rhetoricians on literary and historical occasions; and to these we may add the names of Verplanck, Chief Justice Story, Chancellor Kent, Rufus Choate, Randolph, Winthrop Burgess, Preston, Benton, Prentiss, Bethune, Bushnell, Dewey, Birney, Hillhouse, Sprague, Wayland, A. H. Everett, Horace Binney, Dr. Francis, Sumner, Whipple, Hillard, and other authors of occasional addresses, having by their scope of thought or beauty of style, a permanent literary value. The most voluminous writer in this department, however, is Edward Everett. His two large and elegant volumes not only exhibit the finest specimens of rhetorical writing, but they more truly represent the cultivated American mind in literature, than any single work with which we are acquainted. Oratory has always flourished in republics; it is a form of intellectual development to which free political institutions give both scope and inspiration; and we hesitate not to declare that Edward Everett's Orations are as pure in style, as able in statement, and as authentic as expressions of popular history, feeling and opinion in a finished and elegant shape, as were those of Demosthenes and Cicero in their day. Let not the frequency of public addresses, and the ephemeral character they so often possess, blind our countrymen to the permanent and intrinsic merits of these Orations. They embody the results of long and faithful research into the most important facts of our history; they give "a local habitation and a name" to the most patriotic associations; their subjects, not less than their sentiments, are thoroughly national; not a page but glows with the most intelligent love of country, nor a figure, description, or appeal but what bears evidence of scholarship, taste, and just sentiment. If a highly-cultivated foreigner were to ask us to point him to any single work which would justly inform him of the spirit of our institutions and history, and, at the same time, afford an adequate idea of our present degree of culture, we should confidently designate these Orations. The great battles of the Revolution, the sufferings and principles of the early colonists, the characters of our leading statesmen, the progress of arts, sciences, and education among us—all those great interests which are characteristic to the philosopher—of a nation's life—are here expounded, now by important facts, now by eloquent illustrations, and again in the form of impressive and graceful comments. History, essays, descriptive sketches, biographical data, picturesque detail, and general principles, are all blent together with a tact, a distinctness, a felicity of expression, and a unity of style, unexampled in this species of writing. Mr. Everett has made the art of oratory his peculiar study; again and again his beautiful elocution has charmed audiences composed of the most intelligent and fairest of our citizens. Many of these occasions have a traditional renown. Indeed, whoever has heard one of these addresses delivered, has enjoyed a memorable gratification; not one of them but has to every true American heart and mind a sterling value, as well as an enduring fascination. They include the most salient points in our annals; they consecrate the memories of some of the noblest spirits who have blessed our country; they celebrate events hallowed by results which, at this hour, are agitating the world; and all these attractions are independent of the rare and invaluable literary merit which distinguishes them. No public or private library should be without them; the old should grow familiar with their pages to keep alive the glow of enlightened patriotism; and the young, to learn a wise love of country and the graces of refined scholarship.

There is no branch of literature that can be cultivated in a republic with more advantage to the reader, and satisfaction to the author, than History. Untrammelled by proscription, and unawed by political authority, the annalist may trace the events of the past, and connect them, by philosophical analogy, with the tendencies of the present, free to impart the glow of honest conviction to his record, to analyse the conduct of leaders, the theory of parties, and the significance of events. The facts, too, of our history are comparatively recent. It is not requisite to conjure up fabulous traditions or explore the dim regions of antiquity. From her origin the nation was civilized. A backward glance at the state of Europe, the causes of emigration, and the standard of political and social advancement at the epoch of the first colonies in North America, is all that we need to start intelligently upon the track of our country's marvellous growth, and brief, though eventful career. There are relations, however, both to the past and future, which render American history the most suggestive episode in the annals of the world; and give it a universal as well as special dignity. To those who chiefly value facts as illustrative of principles, and see in the course of events the grand problem of humanity, the occurrences in the New World from its discovery to the present hour, offer a comprehensive interest unrecognised by those who only regard details. Justly interpreted, the liberty and progress of mankind, illustrated by the history of the United States, is but the practical demonstration of principles which the noblest spirits of England advocated with their pens, and often sealed with their blood. It is as lineal descendants in the love of freedom and humanity, of Milton, Locke, and Sidney, that the intelligent votaries of American liberty should be considered. It is easy to trace in the municipal regulations, the tone of society, and in the press of the colonists, a recognition of and familiarity with the responsibilities and progressive tendency of liberal institutions. Their minds were fed upon the manly nutriment of English letters; they knew by heart the bold sentiments of those intellectual benefactors who adorned the age of Elizabeth, and the times of Cromwell; they gloried in the best triumphs of the Commonwealth; and with the earnest reflection and generous knowledge thus derived from their ancestral country, they united the adventurous spirit of the pioneer, and the enthusiasm of the colonist having a new and open field for experiment both of thought and action; accustomed to the elective franchise, imbued with attachment to freedom, and enlightened by sympathy with those who had nobly pleaded and bravely suffered in her cause at home, we cannot but perceive that the colonists achieved a revolution in the manner, rather than in the spirit, of their institutions; they carried out what had long existed in idea; and, as it were, actualised the views of Algernon Sydney and his illustrious compeers. It is through this intimate and direct relation with the past of the Old World, and as initiative to her ultimate self-enfranchisement, that our history daily grows in value and interest, unfolds new meaning, and becomes endeared to all thinking men. It is a link between two great cycles of human progress; the ark that, floating safely on the ocean-tide of humanity, preserves those elements of national freedom which are the vital hope of the world.

Glorious, however, as is the theme, it is only within the last quarter of a century that it has found any adequate illustration. The labors of American historians have been, for the most part, confined to the acquisition of materials, the unadorned record of facts; their subjects have been chiefly local; and, in very few cases, have their labors derived any charm from the graces of style, or the resources of philosophy: they are usually crude memoranda of events, not always reliable, though often curious. In a few instances care and scholarship render such contributions to American history intrinsically valuable; but, taken together, they are rather materials for the annalist than complete works, and as such will prove of considerable value. It is to collect and preserve these and other records, that historical societies have been formed in so many of the states. A storehouse of data is thus formed, to which the future historian can resort; and probably the greater part of the local narratives are destined either to be re-written with all the amenities of literary tact and refinement, or, cast in the mould of genius, become identified with the future triumphs of the American novelist and poet. In the meantime, all honor is due to those who have assiduously labored to record the great events which have here occurred, and to preserve the memories of our patriots. Jared Sparks, now president of Harvard University, has labored most effectually in this sphere. In a series of well written biographies, and in the collected letters of Washington and Franklin, which he has edited, we have a rich fund of national material.*

Among the earliest and most indefatigable laborers in the field of history was Ramsay. His "Historical View of the World, from the earliest Record to the Nineteenth Century, with a particular Reference to the state of Society, Literature, Religion, and Form of Government of the United States of America," was published in 1819; a previous work early in 1817; and more than forty years during intervals of leisure in an active life, were thus occupied by a man not more remarkable for mental assiduity than for all the social graces and solid excellencies of human character.

---

* Among the local and special histories, all more or less valuable as books of reference, and some having both literary and authentic merit, are 'Belknap's New Hampshire,' 'Sullivan's Maine,' 'Morton's New England Memorial,' 'Trumbull's Connecticut,' 'Smith's New York,' 'Watson's Annals of Pennsylvania,' 'Williams's Vermont,' 'Stephens's Georgia,' 'Minot's Massachusetts,' 'Stithe's Virginia,' 'Winthrop's Journal,' 'Thatcher's Journal,' 'Flint's Western States,' 'Gayerre's Louisiana,' 'O'Callahan's New York,' 'Proud's Pennsylvania,' 'Moultrie's Revolution in North and South Carolina and Georgia,' 'Bishop White's History of the Episcopal Church,' 'Jefferson's Notes on Virginia,' 'Barton's Florida,' 'Young's Chronicles of the First Planters of Massachusetts Bay' and 'Chronicles of the Pilgrim Fathers of New Plymouth,' in N. E. Cheever's 'Journal of the Pilgrims,' Frothingham's 'History of the Siege of Boston,' 'Hammond's Political History of New York,' 'Holmes's Annals,' 'Kip's Early Jesuit Missions in North America,' 'Upham's History of the Salem Witchcraft,' 'Mayer's History of the Mexican War,' 'Miner's History of Wyoming,' 'Marmette's History of the Valley of the Mississippi,' 'Newell's History of the Revolution in Texas,' 'Smith's Virginia,' 'Sprague's History of the Florida War,' J. T. Irving's 'Conquest of Florida,' 'Thomas's Historical Account of Pennsylvania,' 'Thompson's Long Island,' 'Buckingham's Reminiscences,' 'Upham's History of the Salem Witchcraft,' 'Whittier's Supernaturalism in New England,' 'Pickett's Alabama,' 'Thomas's History of Printing,' 'Morton's Louisiana,' 'Macy's Nantucket,' 'Sewell's Quakers,' 'Drake's Indians,' 'Camther's Cavaliers of Virginia,' 'Alden's Collections,' 'Francis Baylies' Colony of Plymouth,' 'Bradford's History,' and 'Green's Historical Studies.'

There are also many interesting volumes of American biography. Those of revolutionary and colonial times are embodied in the series edited by Sparks; and among other pleasing and valuable works in this department, are the following:—'Marshall's Life of Washington,' 'Tudor's Otis,' 'Austin's Gerry,' 'Wirt's Patrick Henry,' 'Wheaton's Pinckney,' the 'Life of Josiah Quincy' by his son, 'Colden's Fulton,' the 'Life of John Adams,' by his grandson, 'Tucker's Jefferson,' 'Knapp's American Biographies,' 'Biddle's Cabot,' the 'Life of Alexander Hamilton,' by his son, the 'Life of Washington,' 'Franklin,' 'John Jay,' 'Governeur Morris,' by Sparks, 'Gibbs's Life of Wolcott,' 'Kennedy's Life of Wirt,' 'Life of Judge Story,' by his son, 'Life of William E. Chauncey,' by his nephew, 'Life of Margaret Fuller Ossoli,' 'Dunlap's American Theatre and History of the Arts of Design,' 'Lives of Generals Putnam, Greene, Marion, and Captain Smith,' by W. Gilmore Simms, Col Stone's 'Life of Brant and Red-Jacket,' 'Davis's Life of Aaron Burr,' 'Life of Reed,' 'Life of Stirling,' 'Sabine's American Loyalists,' 'Wynne's Lives of Eminent Americans,' 'Osgood's Studies in Christian Biography,' 'Mrs. Lee's Huguenots,' 'Mrs. Ellett's Women of the Revolution,' 'Sherburne's Paul Jones,' and 'MacKenzie's Decatur and Perry.'

Dr. David Ramsay, a native of Lancaster county, Pennsylvania, was the son of an Irish emigrant. After graduating at Princeton College, and, according to the custom of the period, devoting two years to private tuition, he studied medicine, and removed to Charleston, South Carolina, where he soon became a distinguished patriotic writer. He was a surgeon in the American army, and active in the councils of the land, suffering, with other votaries of independence, the penalty of several months' banishment to St. Augustine. He earnestly opposed, in the legislature of the state, the confiscation of loyalist property. In 1782, he became a member of the Continental Congress; he three years after represented the Charleston district; and for a year was president of that body, in the absence of Hancock. He died in 1815, in consequence of wounds received from the pistol of a maniac. Remarkable for a conciliatory disposition and ardent patriotism, he was a fluent speaker, and a man of great literary industry. Besides a history of the revolution in South Carolina, which was translated and published in France, a history of the American revolution, which reached a second edition, a life of Washington, and a history of South Carolina, he left a history of the United States, from their first settlement to the year 1808,—afterwards continued, by other hands, to the Treaty of Ghent, and published in three octavo volumes,—a monument of his unwearied and zealous research, and patient labor for the good of the public and the honor of his country.

The most successful attempt yet made to reduce the chaotic but rich materials of American history to order, beauty, and moral significance, is the work of George Bancroft.* The inadequate history of Judge Marshall, and the careful one relating to the colonial period, by Grahame, were previously the only works devoted to the subject. Our revolution, in its most interesting details, was known in Europe chiefly through the attractive pages of Carlo Botta. With the ground thus unoccupied, Mr. Bancroft commenced his labors. He was prepared for them not only by culture and talent, but by an earnest sympathy with the spirit of the age he was to illustrate. Having passed through the discipline of a brilliant scholastic career at the best university in the country, studied theology, and engaged in the classical education of youth, he had also visited Europe, and become imbued with the love of German literature; he was for two

---

* George Bancroft was born in Worcester, Massachusetts, in the year 1800; he is the son of Rev. Aaron Bancroft, for more than half a century minister of that town, a man highly venerated, and devoted to historical research, particularly as regards his native country. Thus under the paternal roof, and from his earliest age, the sympathies and taste of the son were awakened to the subject of American history. He graduated in the first rank of Harvard College in 1817. In 1834 appeared the first volume of his History of the Colonization of the United States; in 1837 the second, in 1840 the third, and in 1852 the fourth, being the introductory History of the Revolution.

years a pupil of Heeren, at Gottingen, and mingled freely with the learned coteries of Berlin and Heidelberg. His two first published works, after his return to the United States, are remarkably suggestive of his traits of mind, and indicate that versatility which is so desirable in an historian. These were a small volume of metrical pieces, mainly expressive of his individual feelings and experience; and a translation of Professor Heeren's "Reflections on the Politics of Ancient Greece;" thus early both the poetic and the philosophic element were developed; and although, soon after, Mr. Bancroft entered actively into political life, and held several high offices under the general government, including that of Minister to Great Britain, he continued to prosecute his historical researches, under the most favourable auspices, both at home and abroad, and from time to time put forth the successive volumes of his "History of the United States." To this noble task he brought great and patient industry, an eloquent style, and a capacity to array the theme in the garb of philosophy. Throughout he is the advocate of democratic institutions; and in the early volumes, where, by the nature of the subject, there is little scope for attractive detail, by infusing a reflective tone, he rescues the narrative from dryness and monotony. Instead of a series of facts arranged without any unity of sentiment, we have the idea and principle of civic advancement towards freedom, as a thread of gold upon which the incidents are strung. He is remarkably assiduous in unfolding the experience of the first discoverers, and the political creeds of the early settlers; many curious and authentic details of aboriginal habits are also given; there are everywhere signs of careful research and genuine enthusiasm. Owing, perhaps, to the unequal interest of the subject, the same glow and finish are not uniformly perceptible in the style, in which we occasionally discern an obvious strain after rhetorical effect; and sometimes the influence of the author's political opinions is too apparent; but these are incidental defects; the general spirit, execution, and effect of the work is elevated, genial, and highly instructive. Mr. Bancroft has, at least, vindicated his right to compose the annals of his country, by giving to the record that vitality, both of description and of thought, which distinguishes a genius for history from the mere ability to collate facts. His manner and reflection rise, too, with his subject; the outline becomes firmer, and the inferences clearer, as he emerges from the colonial and enters the revolutionary era. Combining apparently in his own mind, the traits of his two-fold culture, we have the speculative tendency of the German, and the graphic delineation of the English writers; in a word, he gives us pictures like the one, and arguments and suggestions like the other; carefully stating the fact, and earnestly deducing from it the idea; he is more comprehensive as a philosopher than a limner; and yet no tyro in the latter's art, for here and there we encounter a character as tersely drawn, and a scene as vividly painted as any of those which have rendered the best modern historians popular. But it is the under-current of thought, rather than the brilliant surface of description which gives intellectual value to Bancroft's History, and has secured for it so high and extensive a reputation. In sentiment and principles, it is thoroughly American; but in its style and philosophy, it has that broad and eclectic spirit appropriate both to the general interest of the subject, and the enlightened sympathies of the age. Perhaps the best way to appreciate the literary merits of Bancroft's History is to compare it with the cold and formal annals, familiar to our childhood. Unwearied and patient in research, discriminating in the choice of authorities, and judicious in estimating testimony, Bancroft has the art and the ardour, the intelligence and the tact required to fuse into a vital unity the narrative thus carefully gleaned. He knows how to condense language, evolve thought from fact, and make incident and characterization illustrate the progress of events. This bold, active, concentrated manner is what is needed to give permanent and living interest to history. Portraits of individuals, scenes pregnant with momentous results and philosophic inferences, alternate in his pages. The character of Pitt, the death of Montcalm, and the rationale of Puritanism, are very diverse subjects, yet they are each related to the development of the principle of freedom on this continent; and accordingly received both the artistic and analytical treatment of the American historian.

Hildreth's "History of the United States" will probably become a standard book of reference. Rhetorical grace and effect, picturesqueness and the impress of individual opinion, are traits which the author either rejects or keeps in abeyance. His narrative is plain and straightforward, confined to facts which he seems to have gleaned with great care and conscientiousness. The special merit of his work consists in the absence of whatever can possibly be deemed either irrelevant or ostentatious. A "History of Liberty" by S. A. Elliot, is the work of scholarship and taste, but not of poetic inspiration or philosophy; it is, however, an elegant addition to our native writings in this sphere. In a popular form, the most creditable performance is the "Field-Book of the Revolution," by Benson J. Lossing, a wood-engraver by profession, who has visited all the scenes of that memorable war, and, with pen and pencil, delineated each incident of importance, and every object of local interest. His work is one which is destined to find its way to every farmer's hearth, and to all the school libraries of our country.

The freshness of his subjects, the beauty of his style, and the vast difficulties he bravely surmounted, gained for William H. Prescott*

* William H. Prescott is the grandson of Colonel William Prescott, who commanded the Americans at the battle of Bunker Hill. He was born in Salem, Massachusetts, on the 4th of May, 1796. Educated in boyhood by Dr.

not only an extensive but a remarkably speedy reputation, after the appearance of his first history. Many years of study, travel, and occasional practice in writing, preceded the long-cherished design of achieving an historical fame. Although greatly impeded at the outset by a vision so imperfect as to threaten absolute blindness, in other respects he was singularly fortunate. Unlike the majority of intellectual aspirants, he had at his command the means to procure the needful but expensive materials for illustrating a subject more prolific, at once of romantic charms and great elements of human destiny, than any unappropriated theme offered by the whole range of history. It included the momentous voyage of Columbus, the fall of the Moorish empire in Spain, and the many and eventful consequences thence resulting. Aided by the researches of our minister at Madrid,* himself an enthusiast in letters, Mr. Prescott soon possessed himself of ample documents and printed authorities. These he caused to be read to him, and during the process dictated notes, which were afterwards so frequently repeated orally that his mind gradually possessed itself of all the important details; and these he clothed in his own language, arranged them with discrimination, and made out a consecutive and harmonious narrative. Tedious as such a course must be, and laborious in the highest degree as it proved, I am disposed to attribute to it, in a measure at least, some of Mr. Prescott's greatest charms as an historian: the remarkable evenness and sustained harmony, the unity of conception and ease of manner as rare as it is delightful. The 'History of Ferdinand and Isabella' is a work that unites the fascination of romantic fiction with the grave interest of authentic events. Its author makes no pretension to analytical power, except in the arrangement of his materials; he is content to describe, and his talents are more artistic than philosophical; neither is any cherished theory or principle obvious; his ambition is apparently limited to skilful narration. Indefatigable in research, sagacious in the choice and comparison of authorities, serene in temper, graceful in style, and pleasing in sentiment, he possesses all the requisites for an agreeable writer; while his subjects have yielded so much of picturesque material and romantic interest, as to atone for the lack of any more original or brilliant qualities in the author. 'Ferdinand and Isabella' was followed by 'The Conquest of Mexico,' and 'The Conquest of Peru.' The scenic descriptions and the portraits of the Spanish leaders, and of Montezuma and Gautimozin, in the former work, give to it all the charm of an effective romance. Few works of imagination have more power to win the fancy and touch the heart. The

Gardiner, a fine classical teacher, he entered Harvard College in 181. He studied law, and passed two years in Europe. In 1838 was published his 'History of Ferdinand and Isabella,' which met with almost immediate and unprecedented success. It was soon translated into all the modern European languages.

* Alexander H. Everett.

insight afforded into Aztec civilization, is another source of interest. The moral qualities of considerate reflection and frankness are memorable characteristics of Prescott. He has added to the standard literature of the age, and to the literary fame of his country, by his graceful, judicious, and attractive labors in a field comparatively new, and abounding in artistic material.

Prescott is said to be engaged on a history of 'Philip of Spain.' In his previous efforts, he had the advantage of subjects not identified with the prejudices and passions of the present age; and not demanding for their just display any great reach of thought. His well-balanced periods, quiet and sustained tone, and agreeable manner, therefore, had their full effect. Perhaps, had he thus discussed historical themes nearer the sympathies of the hour, this absence of earnestness and reflection would have been more consciously felt by his many delighted readers.

Another of the few standard works in this department, of native origin, is the 'Life and Voyages of Columbus,' by Washington Irving. Ostensibly a biography, it partakes largely of the historical character. As in the case of Prescott, the friendly suggestions of our minister at Madrid greatly promoted the enterprise. The work is based on the researches of Navarette; and it is a highly fortunate circumstance that the crude, though invaluable data thus gathered, was first put in shape and adorned with the elegances of a polished diction, by an American writer at once so popular and so capable as Irving. The result is a life of Columbus authentic, clear, and animated in narration, graphic in its descriptive episodes, and sustained and finished in style. It is a permanent contribution to English as well as American literature;—one which was greatly needed, and most appropriately supplied.

Henry Wheaton, long our minister at Berlin, is chiefly known to literary fame by his able 'Treatise on International Law;' but, while Chargé d'Affaires in Denmark, he engaged with zeal in historical studies, and published in London, in 1831, a 'History of the Northmen;' a most curious, valuable, and suggestive, though limited work.

Cooper's 'Naval History of the United States,' although not so complete as is desirable, is a most interesting work, abounding in scenes of generous valor and rare excitement, recounted with the tact and spirit which the author's taste and practice so admirably fitted him to exhibit on such a theme. Some of the descriptions of naval warfare are picturesque and thrilling in the highest degree. The work, too, is an eloquent appeal to patriotic sentiment and national pride. It is one of the most characteristic histories, both in regard to subject and style, yet produced in America.

One of the most satisfactory of recent historical works is 'The Conspiracy of Pontiac,' by Francis Parkman, of Boston. During a tour in the Far West, where he hunted the buffalo and fraternized with the Indians, the author gained that practical knowledge of aboriginal habits and character, which enabled him to delineate the subject chosen with singular truth and effect. Having faithfully explored the annals of the French and Indian war, he applied to its elucidation the vivid impressions derived from his sojourn in forest and prairie, his observation of Indian life, and his thorough knowledge of the history of the Red-men. The result is not only a reliable and admirably planned narrative, but one of the most picturesque and romantic yet produced in America. Few subjects are more dramatic and rich in local associations; and the previous discipline and excellent style of the author, have imparted to it a permanent attraction.

CHAPTER II.

Belles Lettres—Influence of British Essayists—Franklin—Dennie—Signs of Literary Improvement—Jonathan Oldstyle—Washington Irving—His Knickerbocker—Sketch-Book—His other Works—Popularity—Tour on the Prairies—Character as an Author—Dana—Wilde—Hudson—Griswold—Lowell—Whipple—Ticknor—Walker—Wayland—James—Emerson—Transcendentalists—Madame Ossoli—Emerson's Essays—Orville Dewey—Humorous Writers—Belles Lettres—Tudor—Wirt—Sands—Fay—Walsh—Mitchell—Kimball—American Travellers—Causes of their Success as Writers—Fiction—Charles Brockden Brown—His Novels—James Fenimore Cooper—His Novels—their Popularity and Characteristics—Nathaniel Hawthorne—His Works and Genius—Other American Writers of Fiction.

THE colloquial and observant character given to English literature by the wits, politicians, and essayists of Queen Anne's time—the social and agreeable phase which the art of writing exhibited in the form of the 'Spectator,' 'Guardian,' 'Tattler,' and other popular works of the kind, naturally found imitators in the American Colonies. The earliest indication of a taste for belles-lettres is the republication in the newspapers of New England, of some of the fresh lucubrations of Steele and Addison. 'The Lay-Preacher,' by Dennie, was the first successful imitation of this fashionable species of literature; more characteristic, however, of the sound common sense and utilitarian instincts of the people, were the essays of Franklin, commenced in his brother's journal, then newly-established at Boston. Taste for the amenities of intellectual life, however, at this period, was chiefly gratified by recourse to the emanations of the British press; and it is some years after that we perceive signs of that native impulse in this sphere which proved the germ of American literature. "If we are not mistaken in the signs of the times," says Buckminster (in an oration delivered at Cambridge and published in the 'Anthology,' a Boston magazine, which, with the

Port Folio issued at Philadelphia, were the first literary journals of high aims in America) "the genius of our literature begins to show symptoms of vigor, and to meditate a bolder flight. The spirit of criticism begins to plume itself, and education, as it assumes a more learned form, will take a higher aim. If we are not misled by our hopes, the dream of ignorance is at least broken, and there are signs that the period is approaching when we may say of our country, *tuus jam regnat Apollo.*" This prophecy had received some confirmation in the grace and local observation manifest in a series of letters which appeared in the New York Chronicle, signed Jonathan Oldstyle, Gent.—the first productions of Washington Irving, the Goldsmith of America, who was born in New York, April 6, 1783. Symptoms of alarming disease soon after induced a voyage to Europe; and he returned to the island of Manhattan, the scene of his boyish rambles and youthful reveries, with a mind expanded by new scenes, and his natural love of travel and elegant literature deepened. Although ostensibly a law-student in the office of Judge Hoffman, his time was devoted to social intercourse with his kindred, who were established in business in New York, and a few genial companions, to meditative loiterings in the vicinity of the picturesque river so dear to his heart, and to writing magazine papers. The happy idea of a humorous description of his native town, under the old Dutch governors, was no sooner conceived than executed with inimitable wit and originality. Not then contemplating the profession of letters, he did not take advantage of the remarkable success that attended this work, of which Sir Walter Scott thus speaks, in one of his letters to an American friend: "I beg you to accept my best thanks for the uncommon degree of entertainment which I have received from the most excellently jocose history of New York. I am sensible that as a stranger to American parties and politics, I must lose much of the concealed satire of the piece, but I must own that, looking at the simple and obvious meaning only, I have never read anything so closely resembling the style of Dean Swift as the annals of Diedrich Knickerbocker. I have been employed these few evenings in reading them aloud to Mrs. S. and two ladies, who are our guests, and our sides have been absolutely sore with laughing. I think, too, there are passages which indicate that the author possesses power of a different kind, and has some touches which remind me much of Sterne." 'Salmagundi,' which Mr. Irving had previously undertaken, in conjunction with Paulding, proved a hit, and established the fame of its authors; it was in form and method of publication imitated from the 'Spectator,' but in details, spirit, and aim, so exquisitely adapted to the latitude of New York, that its appearance was hailed with a delight hitherto unknown; it was, in fact, a complete triumph of local genius. From these pursuits, the author turned to commercial toil, in connection with which, he embarked for England in 1815, and while there, a reverse of fortune led to his resuming the pen as a means of subsistence. In his next work, the 'Sketch-Book,' Sir Walter's opinion of his pathetic vein was fully realized; 'The Wife,' 'The Pride of the Village,' and 'The Broken Heart,' at once took their places as gems of English sentiment and description. Nor were the associations of home inoperative; and the 'Legend of Sleepy Hollow' first gave "a local habitation," in our fresh land, to native fancy. His impressions of domestic life in Great Britain, were soon after given to the public in 'Bracebridge Hall,' and some of his continental experiences embodied in the 'Tales of a Traveller.' Soon after, Mr. Irving visited Spain to write the 'Life of Columbus,' to which we have before alluded. His sojourn at the Alhambra, and at Abbotsford and Newstead Abbey, are the subjects of other graceful and charming volumes; while 'Astoria, or Anecdotes of an Enterprise beyond the Rocky Mountains,' and the 'Life of Mohammed,' proved solid as well as elegant contributions to our standard literature.

There are writers who have so ministered to our enjoyment as to become associated with our happiest literary recollections. The companionship of their works has been to us as that of an entertaining and cherished friend, whose converse cheers the hours of languor, and brightens the period of recreative pleasure. We are wont to think and to speak of them with quite a different sentiment from that which prompts us to speculate upon less familiar and less endeared productions. There is ever within us a sense of obligation, an identification of our individual partiality with the author, when the fruits of his labors are alluded to, his merits discussed, or his very name mentioned. The sensitiveness appropriate to the writer's self seems, in a manner, transferred to our own bosoms; his faults are scarcely recognised, and we guard his laurels as if our own efforts had aided in their winning, and our own happiness was involved in their preservation. Such feelings obtain, indeed, to a greater or less extent, with reference to all the master spirits in literature, whose labors have been devoted, with signal success, to the gratification and elevation of humanity. But the degree of permanency for such tributary sentiment in the general mind, depends very much upon the field of effort selected by the favorite author, and his own peculiar circumstances and character. Subjects of temporary interest, however admirably treated, and with whatever applause received, are obviously ill calculated to retain, for any considerable length of time, a strong hold upon human regard; and, notwithstanding the alleged inconsistency between an author's personal character and history and the influence of his works, the motives adduced by Addison for prefacing the Spectator with an account of himself, are deeply founded in human nature. Not merely contemporary sentiment, but after opinion in relation to literary productions, will be materially affected by what is known of the author. The present prevailing tendency to inquire, often with a truly reprehensible minuteness, into whatever in the most distant manner relates to the leading literary men of the age, affords ample evidence of this truth. Indeed, we may justly anticipate that literary, if not general biography, will, ere long, from the very interest manifested in regard to it, attain an importance, and ultimately a philosophical dignity, such as shall engage in its behalf the sedulous labors of the best endowed and most accomplished minds.

The occasion which first induced Geoffrey Crayon to delineate, and those which have suggested his subsequent pencillings, were singularly happy; and the circumstances under which these masterly sketches were produced, nay, the whole history of the man, are signally fitted to deepen the interest which his literary merits necessarily excited. In saying this, we are not unmindful of the prejudices so ungenerously forced upon the attention of the absentee, and so affectingly alluded to in the opening of his first work after returning from Europe; but do we err in deeming those prejudices as unchargeable upon the mass of his countrymen, as they were essentially unjust and partial? Nay, are we not, in this volume, with our author's characteristic genuineness of feeling and simplicity, assured of his own settled and happy sense of the high place he occupies in the estimation and love of Americans?

The 'Tour on the Prairies' appeared in 1836. It is an unpretending account, comprehending a period of about four weeks, of travelling and hunting excursions upon the vast western plains. The local features of this interesting region have been displayed to us in several works of fiction, of which it has formed the scene; and more formal illustrations of the extensive domain denominated *The West*, and its denizens, have been repeatedly presented to the public. But in this volume one of the most extraordinary and attractive portions of the great subject is discussed, not as the subsidiary part of a romantic story, nor yet in the desultory style of epistolary composition, but in the deliberate, connected form of a retrospective narration. When we say that the 'Tour on the Prairies' is rife with the characteristics of its author, no ordinary eulogium is bestowed. His graphic power is manifest throughout. The boundless prairies stretch out illimitably to the fancy, as the eye scans his descriptions. The athletic figures of the riflemen, the gaily arrayed Indians, the heavy buffalo and the graceful deer, pass in strong relief and startling contrast before us. We are stirred by the bustle of the camp at dawn, and soothed by its quiet, or delighted with its picturesque aspect under the shadow of night. The imagination revels amid the green oak clumps and verdant pea vines, the expanded plains and the glancing river, the forest aisles and the silent stars. Nor is this all. Our hearts thrill at the vivid representations of a primitive and excursive existence; we involuntarily yearn, as we read, for the genial activity and the perfect exposure to the influences of nature in all her free magnificence, of a woodland and adventurous life; the morning strain of the bugle, the excitement of the chase, the delicious repast, the forest gossiping, the sweet repose beneath the canopy of heaven —how inviting, as depicted by such a pencil!

Nor has the author failed to invigorate and render doubly attractive these descriptive drawings, with the peculiar light and shade of his own rich humor, and the mellow softness of his ready sympathy. A less skilful draftsman would, perhaps, in the account of the preparations for departure (Chapter III.), have spoken of the hunters, the fires, and the steeds—but who, except Geoffrey Crayon, would have been so quaintly mindful of the little dog, and the manner in which he regarded the operations of the farrier? How inimitably the Bee Hunt is portrayed; and what have we of the kind so racy, as the account of the Republic of Prairie Dogs, unless it be that of the Rookery in Bracebridge Hall? What expressive portraits are the delineations of our rover's companions. How consistently drawn throughout, and in what fine contrast, are the reserved and saturnine Beatte, and the vain-glorious, sprightly, and versatile Tonish. A golden vein of vivacious, yet chaste comparison — that beautiful, yet rarely well-managed species of wit; and a wholesome and pleasing sprinkling of moral comment—that delicate and often most efficacious medium of useful impressions—intertwine and vivify the main narrative! Something, too, of that fine pathos which enriches his earlier productions, enhances the value of the present. He tells us, indeed, with commendable honesty, of his new appetite for destruction, which the game of the prairie excited; but we cannot fear for the tenderness of a heart that sympathises so readily with suffering, and yields so gracefully to kindly impulses. He gazes upon the noble courser of the wilds, and wishes that his freedom may be perpetuated; he recognises the touching instinct which leads the wounded elk to turn aside and die in retiracy; he reciprocates the attachment of the beast which sustains him, and more than all, can minister even to the foibles of a fellow-being, rather than mar the transient reign of human pleasure.

It has been said that Mr. Irving, at one period of his life, seriously proposed to himself the profession of an artist. The idea was a legitimate result of his intellectual constitution; and although he denied its development in one form, in another it has fully vindicated itself Many of his volumes are a collection of sketches, embodied happily in language, since thereby their more general enjoyment is insured, but susceptible of immediate transfer to the canvas of the painter. These are like a fine gallery of pictures, wherein all his countrymen delight in many a morning lounge and evening reverie.

Until within the last half century, not only the standard literature but the critical opinions of America were almost exclusively of trans-atlantic origin. But within that period a number of writers, endowed with acute perceptions and eloquent expression, as well as the requisite knowledge, have arisen to elucidate the tendencies, define the traits, and advocate the merits of modern writers. By faithful translations, able reviews, lectures and essays, the best characteristics of men of literary genius, schools of philosophy, poetry, and science have been rendered familiar to the cultivated minds of the nation. Thus Richard H. Dana has explored and interpreted, with a rare sympathetic intelligence, the old English drama; Andrews Norton, the Authenticity of the Gospels; Richard H. Wilde, the Love and Madness of Tasso; Alexander H. Everett, the range of contemporary French and German literature; Professor Reed, the Poetry of Wordsworth; Norman H. Hudson, the Plays of Shakspeare; John S. Hart, the Faery Queen; Russell Lowell, the Older British Poets; and Edwin P. Whipple, the Best Authors of Great Britain and America. W. A. Jones, Hoffman, Duykinck, and others, have also illustrated our critical literature.

For the chief critical and biographical history of literature in the United States, we are indebted to Rufus W. Griswold, whose two copious and interesting volumes, so popular at home and useful abroad, give an elaborate account of what has been done by American writers from the foundation of the country to the present hour. These works are the fruit of great research, and an enthusiasm for native literature as rare as it is patriotic. Our numerous "Female Prose Writers" have also found an intelligent and genial historian and critic in Professor Hart.

The philosophic acuteness, animated and fluent diction, and thorough knowledge of the subjects discussed, render Mr. Whipple's critical essays among the most agreeable reading of the kind. His reputation as an eloquent and sagacious critic is now firmly established. Both in style and thought these critical essays are worthy of the times; bold without extravagance, refined yet free of dilletantism, manly and philosophic in sentiment, and attractive in manner. The most elaborate single work, however, in this department, is George Ticknor's History of Spanish Literature, the result of many years' research, and so complete and satisfactory, that the best European critics have recognised it a permanent authority; it is both authentic and tasteful; the translations are excellent, the arrangement judicious, and the whole performance a work of genuine scholarship. It supplies a desideratum, and is an interesting and thorough exposition of a subject at once curious, attractive and of general literary utility. James Walker and Francis Wayland, although of widely diverse theological opinions, are both expositors of moral philosophy, to which they have made valuable contributions. Henry James, of Albany, is the most argumentative and eloquent advocate of new social principles in the country; and Waldo Emerson, by a certain quaintness of diction and boldly speculative turn of mind, has achieved a wide popularity. It is, however, to a peculiar verbal facility rather than to any philosophic genius that he owes the impression he creates. He is regarded as the leader of a sect, who, some years since, from the reaction of minds oppressed and narrowed by New England conventionalism and bigotry, and, in some instances, kindled by the speculations of German literature, broke away from the ultra rational and sought freedom in the transcendental school. In the Memoir of Margaret Fuller Ossoli, recently published, the movement is described and the principles of its disciples hinted rather than explained. "The rise of this enthusiasm," says her biographer, "was as mysterious as that of any form of revival; and only they who were of the faith could comprehend how bright was this morning-time of a new hope. Transcendentalism was an assertion of the inalienable integrity of man, of the ordinances of Divinity in instinct. In part it was a reaction against Puritan orthodoxy; in part an effect of renewed study of the ancients, of Oriental Pantheists, of Plato, and the Alexandrians, of Plutarch's Morals, Seneca and Epictetus; in part the natural product of the place and time. On the somewhat stunted stock of Unitarianism—whose characteristic dogma was trust in individual reason as correlative to Supreme Wisdom,—had been grafted German idealism as taught by masters of most various schools."

Whoever turns to Emerson's 'Essays,' or to the writings of this transcendental sibyl (whose remarkable acquirements, moral courage, and tragic fate, render her name prominent among our female authors) for a system, a code, or even a set of definite principles, will be disappointed. The chief good thus far achieved by this class of thinkers has been negative; they have emancipated many minds from the thraldom of local prejudices and prescriptive opinion, but have failed to reveal any positive and satisfactory truth unknown before. Emerson has an inventive fancy; he knows how to clothe truisms in startling costume; he evolves beautiful or apt figures and apothegms that strike at first, but when contemplated, prove, as has been said, usually either true and not new, or new and not true. His volumes, however, are suggestive, tersely and often gracefully written; they are thoughtful, observant, and speculative, and indicate a philosophic taste rather than power. As contributions to American literature they have the merit of a spirit, beauty, and reflective tone previously almost undiscoverable in the didactic writings of the country. A writer of more consistency in ethics, and a sympathy with man more human, is Orville Dewey, whose discourses abound in earnest appeals to consciousness, in a noble vindication of human nature, and a faith in progressive ideas, often arrayed in touching and impressive rhetoric.

We have not been wanting in excellent translators, especially of German literature; our scholars and poets have admirably used their knowledge of the language in this regard. The first experiment was Bancroft's translation of Heeren already referred to; and since then, some of the choicest lyrics and best philosophy of Germany have been given to the American public by Professor Longfellow, George Ripley, R. W. Emerson, John S. Dwight, S. M. Fuller, George H. Calvert, Rev. C. T. Brooks, W. H. Channing, F. H. Hedge, Samuel Osgood, and others. Dr. Mitchell, of New York, translated Sannazario's Italian poems, Mrs. Nichols the 'Promessi Sposi' of Manzoni, and Dr. Parsons, of Boston, has made the best metrical translations into English of Dante's great poem.

The most elaborate piece of humor in our literature has been already mentioned—as Irving's facetious history of his native town. The sketch entitled 'The Stout Gentleman,' by the same genial author, is another inimitable attempt in miniature, as well as some of the papers in 'Salmagundi.' The letters of 'Jack Downing' may be considered an indigenous specimen in this department; and also the 'Charcoal Sketches' of Joseph C. Neal, the 'Ollapodiana' of Willis G. Clarke, the 'Puffer Hopkins' of Cornelius Matthews, and many scenes by Thorpe, and in Mrs. Kirkland's 'New Home.' The original aspects of life in the West and South, as well as those of Yankee Land, have also found several apt and graphic delineators; although the coarseness of the subjects, or the carelessness of the style, will seldom allow them a literary rank.

That delightful species of literature which is neither criticism nor fiction — neither oratory nor history — but partakes somewhat of all these, and owes its charm to a felicitous blending of fact and fancy, of sentiment and thought—the Belles-Lettres writing of our country, has gradually increased as the ornamental has encroached on the once arbitrary domain of the useful. Among the earliest specimens were the 'Letters of a British Spy,' and the 'Old Bachelor' of William Wirt, and Tudor's 'Letters on New England;' in New York, this sphere was gracefully illustrated by Robert C. Sands and Theodore S. Fay, by tale, novelette, and essay; in Philadelphia, by Robert Walsh, who gleaned two volumes from his newspaper articles; and at present, by the 'Reveries of a Bachelor' of Mitchell, and in a more vigorous manner in the 'St. Leger Papers' of Kimball. Professors Frisbie, Caldwell, Henry, and others, have contributed to the taste and culture of the Belles Lettres in America.*

* There are a few American books which cannot be strictly classified under either of these divisions; which not only have a sterling value, but a wide and established reputation; such as the 'Legal Commentaries of Chancellor Kent,' the 'Dictionary' of Noah Webster, Dr. Rush's 'Treatise on the Philosophy of the Human Voice,' 'Lectures on Art,' by Washington Allston; the 'Classical Manuals' of Professor Anthon; Dr. Bowditch's translation of the

The literature of no country is more rich in books of travel. From Carter's 'Letters from Europe,' Dwight's 'Travels in New England,' and Lewis and Clark's 'Expedition to the Rocky Mountains,' to the 'Yucatan' of Stephens, and the 'Two Years before the Mast' of Dana, American writers have put forth a succession of animated, intelligent, and most agreeable records of their explorations in every part of the globe. In many instances, their researches have been directed to a special object, and resulted in positive contributions to natural science; thus Audubon's travels are associated with his discoveries in ornithology, and those of Schoolcraft with his Indian lore. Stephens revealed to our gaze the singular and magnificent ruins of Central America; Sanderson unfolded the hygiene of life in Paris; Flint guided our steps through the fertile valleys of the West, and Irving and Hoffman brought its scenic wonders home to the coldest fancy.*

"Americans are thought by foreign critics to excel as writers of travels; and the opinion is confirmed by the remarkable success which has so often attended their works. Indeed, in scarcely any other field of literature has the talent of this country been so generally recognised abroad; and this superiority appears to be a natural result of American life and character. With few time-honoured customs or strong local associations to bind him to the soil, with little hereditary dignity of name or position to sustain, and accustomed, from infancy, to witness frequent changes of position and fortune, the inhabitant of no civilized land has so little restraint upon his

---

'Mecanique Celeste' of La Place; the 'Ornithology' of Wilson and Audubon; Catlin's and Schoolcraft's works on the Indians. The ethnological contributions of Squier, Pickering's philological Researches, and the 'Essays on Political Economy' by Albert Gallatin, Raguet, Dr. Cooper, Tucker, Colton, Wayland, Middleton, Raymond, A. H. Everett, and Henry C. Carey. Francis Bowen has published able lectures on metaphysical subjects. James D. Nourse, of Kentucky, has published a clever little treatise, the 'Philosophy of History;' Dr. Palfrey, of Massachusetts, a series of erudite lectures on 'Jewish Antiquities;' J. Q. Adams a course on 'Rhetoric;' Judge Buel and Henry Colman valuable works on 'Agriculture,' and A. J. Downing, on 'Rural Architecture and Horticulture.'

* It is difficult to enumerate the works in this department; but among them may be justly commended, either for graces of style, effective description, or interesting narrative—and, in some instances, for all these qualities combined —the 'Year in Spain' of Mackenzie, the 'Winter in the West' of C. F. Hoffman, the 'Oregon Trail' of Francis Parkman, the 'Pencillings by the Way' of Willis, the 'Scenes and Thoughts in Europe' of George H. Calvert, Longfellow's 'Outre-mer,' the 'Typee' of Melville, the 'Views A-Foot' of Taylor, 'Fresh Gleanings' by Mitchell, 'Nile-Notes' by George Curtis, Squier's 'Nicaragua,' and the writings of this kind by Robinson, Long, Melville, Jewett, Spencer, Gregg, Townsend, Fremont, Lanman, Bryant, Thorpe, Kendall, Wilson, Webber, Colton, Gillespie, Headley, Dewey, Kip, Silliman, Bigelow, Cushing, Wise, Warren, Mitchell, Cheever, Catlin, Norman, Wallis, Shaler, Ruschenberger, King, Breckenridge, Kidder, Brown, Fisk, Lyman, the Exploring Expedition by Wilkes, the Dead Sea Expedition by Lynch, and the voyages of Delano, Cleveland, Coggeshall, and others.

vagrant humor as a native of the United States. The American is by nature locomotive; he believes in change of air for health, change of residence for success, change of society for improvement. Pioneer enterprise is a staple of our history. Not only do the economy of life and the extent of territory in the New World, train her citizens, as it were, to travel; their temperament and taste also combine to make them tourists. Their existence favors quickness of perception, however inimical it may be to contemplative energy. Self-reliance leads to adventure. The freedom from prejudice incident to a new country, gives more ample scope to observation; and the very freshness of life renders impressions from new scenes more vivid. Thus free and inspired, it is not surprising that things often wear a more clear and impressive aspect to his mind, than they do to the jaded senses and the conventional views of more learned and reserved, but less flexible and genial travellers. The sympathetic grace of Irving, the impersonal fidelity of Stephens, the Flemish details of Slidell Mackenzie, the picturesque and spirited description of Hoffman, and the De Foe-like narratives of Melville and Dana, are qualities that have gained them more readers than fall to the lot of the herd of travellers, who have lavished on pictures of the same scenes more learning and finish, perhaps, but less of integrity of statement and naturalness of feeling."*

Romantic fiction, in the United States, took its rise with the publication of 'Wieland' by Charles Brockden Brown, in 1798; attained its most complete and characteristic development in the long and brilliant career, as a novelist, of James Fenimore Cooper; and is now represented, in its artistic excellence, by Nathaniel Hawthorne. The parents of Brown were Philadelphia Quakers, and he was born in that city on the 17th of January, 1771. An invalid from infancy, he had the dreamy moods and roaming propensity incident to poetical sympathies; after vainly attempting to interest his mind in the law, except in a speculative manner, he became an author, at a period and under circumstances which afford the best evidence that the vocation was ordained by his idiosyncrasy. With chiefly the encouragement of a few cultivated friends in New York to sustain him, with narrow means and feeble health, he earnestly pursued his lonely career, inspired by the enthusiasm of genius. His literary toil was varied, erudite, and indefatigable. He edited magazines and annual registers, wrote political essays, a geography, and a treatise on architecture, translated Volney's 'Travels in the United States,' debated at clubs, journalized, corresponded, made excursions, and entered ardently into the quiet duties of the fire-side and the family. His character was singularly gentle and pure; and he was beloved, even when not appreciated. It is by his novels, however, that Brown

* Characteristics of Literature, 2d series.

achieved renown. They are remarkable for intensity and supernatu ralism. His genius was eminently psychological; Godwin is his English prototype. To the reader of the present day, these writings appear somewhat limited and sketch-like; but when we consider the period of their composition, and the disadvantages under which they appeared, they certainly deserve to be ranked among the wonderful productions of the human mind. Brown delighted to analyse the phenomena of consciousness, to bring human nature under mystic or extraordinary influences, and mark the consequences. In 'Ormond,' 'Arthur Mervyn,' 'Jane Talbot,' 'Edgar Huntley,' and 'Wieland,' we have such agencies as pestilence, somnambulism, rare coincidence, and ventriloquism, brought to act upon individuals of excitable or introspective character, and the result is often thrilling. The descriptions are terse and suggestive, the analysis thorough, and the feeling high-strung and reflective. The pioneer of American fiction was endowed with rare energy of conception, and a style attractive from its restrained earnestness and minute delineation. He died at the close of his thirty-ninth year. Had his works been as artistically constructed as they were profoundly conceived and ingeniously executed, they would have become standard. As it is, we recognise the rare insight and keen sensibility of the man, acknowledge his power to "awaken terror and pity;" and lament the want of high finish and effective shape visible in these early and remarkable fruits of native genius.

The first successful novel by an American author was the 'Spy.' A previous work by the same author, entitled 'Precaution,' had made comparatively little impression. It was strongly tinctured with an English flavor, in many respects imitative, and, as it afterwards appeared, written and printed under circumstances which gave little range to Cooper's real genius. In 1823, he published 'The Pioneers.' In this and the novel immediately preceding it, a vein of national association was opened, an original source of romantic and picturesque interest revealed, and an epoch in our literature created. What Cooper had the bold invention to undertake, he had the firmness of purpose and the elasticity of spirit to pursue with unflinching zeal. Indeed his most characteristic trait was self-reliance. He commenced the arduous career of an author in a new country, and with fresh materials; at first, the tone of criticism was somewhat discouraging; but his appeal had been to the popular mind, and not to a literary clique, and the response was universal and sincere. From this time, he gave to the press a series of prose romances conceived with so much spirit and truth, and executed with such fidelity and vital power that they instantly took captive the reader. His faculty of description, and his sense of the adventurous, were the great sources of his triumph. Refinement of style, poetic sensibility, and melo-dramatic intensity, were elements that he ignored; but when he pictured the scenes of the forest and prairie, the incidents of Indian warfare, the vicissitudes of border life, and the phenomena of the ocean and nautical experience, he displayed a familiarity with the subjects, a keen sympathy with the characters, and a thorough reality in the delineation, which at once stamped him as a writer of original and great capacity. It is true that in some of the requisites of the novelist, he was inferior to many subsequent authors in the same department. His female characters want individuality and interest and his dialogue is sometimes forced and ineffective; but, on th other hand, he seized with a bold grasp the tangible and characteristic in his own land; and not only stirred the hearts of his countrymen with vivid pictures of colonial, revolutionary, and emigrant life, with the vast ocean and forest for its scenes; but opened to the gaze of Europe, phases of human existence at once novel and exciting. The fisherman of Norway, the merchant of Bordeaux, the scholar at Frankfort, and the countess of Florence, in a brief period, all hung with delight over Cooper's daguerreotypes of the New World, transferred to their respective languages. This was no ordinary triumph. It was a rich and legitimate fruit of American genius in letters. To appreciate it we must look back upon the period when the Spy, the Pioneers, the Last of the Mohicans, the Pilot, the Red Rover, the Wept-of-the-Wish-ton-Wish, the Water Witch, and the Prairie, were new creations; and remember that they first revealed America to Europe through a literary medium. In the opinion of some critics, the unity and completeness of Cooper's fame has been marred by those novels drawn from foreign subjects and induced by a long residence in Europe; by his honest but injudicious attempts to reform his countrymen in some of their particular habits and modes of thought or action; and also by his persistency in issuing volume after volume of fiction, less directly inspired by observation, and comparatively devoid of interest. Whatever truth may exist in such a view of his course, it is to be considered that all temporary defects are soon forgotten in those memorials of individual genius which have the stamp of the author's best powers, and the recognition of the world. Leather-Stocking and Long Tom Coffin are standard characters; the woodland landscapes, the sailing matches of men-of-war, the sea-fight, wrecks, and aboriginal heroes, depicted, as they are, by Cooper to the very life, and in enduring colors, will be identified both with his name and country; and ever vindicate his claims to remembrance. His youth was passed in a manner admirably fitted to develope his special talent, and provide the resources of his subsequent labors. Born in Burlington, N. J., on the 15th of September, 1789, he was early removed to the borders of Otsego Lake, where his father, Judge Cooper, erected a homestead, afterwards inhabited and long occupied by the novelist. He was prepared for college by the Rector of St. Peter's Church, in Albany, and entered Yale in

1802. Three years after, having proved an excellent classical student, and enjoyed the intimacy of several youth afterwards eminent in the land, he left New Haven and joined the United States Navy as a midshipman. After passing six years in the service, he resigned, married, and soon after established himself on his paternal domain, situated amid some of the finest scenery and rural attraction of his native state. Thus Cooper was early initiated into the scenes of a newly-settled country and a maritime life, with the benefit of academical training, and the best social privileges. All these means of culture and development his active mind fully appreciated; his observation never slumbered; and its fruits were industriously garnered.

His nautical and Indian tales form, perhaps, the most characteristic portion of our literature. 'The Bravo' is the best of his European novels; and his 'Naval History' is valuable and interesting. He was one of the most industrious of authors; his books of travel and biographical sketches are numerous, and possess great fidelity of detail, although not free from prejudice. Cooper represents the American mind in its adventurous character; he glories in delineating the "monarch of the deck,"—paints the movements of a ship at sea as if she were, indeed, "a thing of life;" follows an Indian trail with the sagacity of a forest-king; and leads us through storms, conflagration, and war with the firm, clear-sighted, and all-observant guidance of a master-spirit. His best scenes and characters are indelibly engraven on the memory. His best creations are instinct with nature and truth. His tone is uniformly manly, fresh, and vigorous. He is always thoroughly American. His style is national; and when he died in the autumn of 1851, a voice of praise and regret seemed to rise all over the land, and a large and distinguished assembly convened soon after, in New York, to listen to his eulogy—pronounced by the poet Bryant.

Hawthorne is distinguished for the finish of his style, and the delicacy of his psychological insight. He combines the metaphysical talent of Brown with the refined diction of Irving. For a period of more than twenty years he contributed, at intervals, to annuals and magazines, the most exquisite fancy sketches and historical narratives, the merit of which was scarcely recognised by the public at large, although cordially praised by the discriminating few. These papers have been recently collected under the title of 'Twice-told Tales,' and 'Mosses from an Old Manse;' and, seen by the light of the author's present reputation, their grace, wisdom, and originality are now generally acknowledged. But it is through the two romances entitled 'The Scarlet Letter,' and 'The House of the Seven Gables,' that Hawthorne's eminence has been reached. They are remarkable at once for a highly finished and beautiful style, the most charming artistic skill, and intense characterization. To these intrinsic and universal claims, they add that of native scenes and subjects. Imagine such an anatomiser of the human heart as Balzac, transported to a provincial town of New England, and giving to its houses, streets, and history, the analytical power of his genius, and we realize the triumph of Hawthorne. Bravely adopting familiar materials, he has thrown over them the light and shadow of his thoughtful mind, eliciting a deep significance and a prolific beauty; if we may use the expression, he is ideally true to the real. His invention is felicitous; his tone magnetic; his sphere borders on the supernatural, and yet a chaste expression and a refined sentiment underlies his most earnest utterance; he is more suggestive than dramatic. The early history of New England has found no such genial and vivid illustration as his pages afford. At all points his genius touches the interests of human life, now overflowing with a love of external nature as gentle as that of Thomson, now intent upon the quaint or characteristic in life with a humor as zestful as that of Lamb, now developing the horrible or pathetic with something of John Webster's dramatic terror, and again buoyant with a fantasy as aerial as Shelley's conceptions. And, in each instance, the staple of charming invention is adorned with the purest graces of style. Hawthorne was born in Salem, Massachusetts, educated at Bowdoin College, and after having filled an office in the Boston custom-house, and the post-office of his native town, and lived a year on a community farm, is now settled in a pleasant country town and become an author by profession; and one who has already proved his ability to create standard exemplars of American romantic fiction.

"What we admire in this writer's genius is his felicity in the use of common materials. It is very difficult to give an imaginative scope to a scene or a topic which familiarity has robbed of illusion. It is by the association of ideas, by the halo of remembrance and the magic of love, that an object usually presents itself to the mind under fanciful relations. From a foreign country our native spot becomes picturesque; and from the hill of manhood the valley of youth appears romantic; but that is a peculiar and rare mental alchemy which can transmute the dross of the common and the immediate into gold. Yet so doth Hawthorne. His 'Old Apple Dealer' yet sits by the old South Church, and 'The Willey House' is inscribed every summer-day by the penknives of ambitious cits. He is able to illustrate, by his rich invention, places and themes that are before our very eyes and in our daily speech. His fancy is as free of wing at the north end of Boston, or on Salem turnpike, as that of other poets in the Vale of Cashmere or amid the Isles of Greece. He does not seem to feel the necessity of distance either of time or space to realize his enchantments. He has succeeded in attaching an ethereal interest to home subjects, which is no small triumph. Somewhat of that poetic charm which Wilson has thrown over Scottish life in his

'Lights and Shadows,' and Irving over English, in his 'Sketch Book,' and Lamb over metropolitan in his 'Elia,' has Hawthorne cast around New England, and his tales here and there blend, as it were, the traits which endear these authors. His best efforts are those in which the human predominates. Ingenuity and moral significancy are finely displayed, it is true, in his allegories; but sometimes they are coldly fanciful, and do not win the sympathies as in those instances where the play of the heart relieves the dim workings of the abstract and supernatural. Hawthorne, like all individualities, must be read in the appropriate mood. This secret of appreciation is now understood as regards Wordsworth. It is due to all genuine authors. To many whose mental aliment has been exciting and coarse, the delicacy, meek beauties and calm spirit of these writings will but gradually unfold themselves; but those capable of placing themselves in relation with Hawthorne, will discover a native genius for which to be grateful and proud, and a brother whom to know is to love. He certainly has done much to obviate the reproach which a philosophical writer, not without reason has cast upon our authors, when he asserts their object to be to astonish rather than please."*

There is a host of intermediate authors between the three already described in this sphere of literature, of various and high degrees, both of merit and reputation, but whose traits are chiefly analogous to those of the prominent writers we have surveyed. Some of them have ably illustrated local themes, others excelled in scenic limning, and a few evinced genius for characterization. Paulding, for instance, in 'Westward Ho,' and 'The Dutchman's Fireside,' has given admirable pictures of colonial life: Richard H. Dana, in the 'Idle Man,' has two or three remarkable psychological tales; Timothy Flint, James Hall, Thomas, and more recently M'Connell of Illinois, have written very graphic and spirited novels of Western Life; John P. Kennedy of Baltimore, has embalmed Virginia life in the olden time in 'Swallow Barn,' and Fay that of modern New York; Gilmore Simms, a prolific and vigorous novelist, in a similar form has embodied the traits of Southern Character and Scenery; Hoffman the early history of his native State; Dr. Robert Bird of Philadelphia, those of Mexico; William Ware has rivalled Lockhart's classical romance in his 'Letters from Palmyra' and 'Probus;' Allston's artist-genius is luminous in 'Monaldi;' Judd in 'Margaret' has related a tragic story arrayed in the very best hues and outlines of New England life; and Edgar A. Poe, in his 'Tales of the Grotesque and Arabesque,' evinces a genius in which a love of the marvellous and an intensity of conception are united with the wildest sympathies, as if the endowments of Mrs. Radcliffe and Coleridge were partially united in one mind. In adventurous and descriptive narration we have Melville and Mayo. John Neal struck

* Leaves from the Diary of a Dreamer.

off at a heat some half-score of novels that, at least, illustrate a facility quite remarkable; and, indeed, from the days of the 'Algerine Captive' and 'The Foresters' the first attempts at such writing in this country, to the present day, there has been no lack of native fictions. The minor specimens which possess the highest literary excellence are by Irving, Willis, and Longfellow; but their claims rest entirely on style and sentiment; they are brief and polished, but more graceful than impressive.

CHAPTER III.

POETRY.

Its essential Conditions—Freneau and the early Metrical Writers—Mumford—Cliffton—Allston, and others—Pierpont—Dana—Hillhouse—Sprague—Percival—Halleck—Drake—Hoffman—Willis—Longfellow—Holmes—Lowell—Boker—Favorite Single Poems—Descriptive Poetry—Street—Whittier, and others—Brainard—Song-Writers—Other Poets—Female Poets—Bryant.

'It has been well observed by an English critic, that poetry is not a branch of authorship. The vain endeavor to pervert its divine and spontaneous agency into a literary craft, is the great secret of its decline. Poetry is the overflowing of the soul. It is the record of what is best in the world. No product of the human mind is more disinterested. Hence comparatively few keep the poetic element alive beyond the period of youth. All that is genuine in the art springs from vivid experience, and life seldom retains any novel aspect to those who have long mingled in its scenes, and staked upon its chances. A celebrated artist of our day, when asked the process by which his delineations were rendered so effective, replied that he drew them altogether from memory. Natural objects were portrayed, not as they impressed him at the moment, but according to the lively and feeling phases in which they struck his senses in boyhood. For this reason it has been truly observed, that remembrance makes the poet; and, according to Wordsworth, "emotions recollected in tranquillity," form the true source of inspiration. A species of literature depending upon conditions so delicate, is obviously not to be successfully cultivated by those who hold it in no reverence. The great distinction between verse-writers and poets is, that the former seek and the latter receive; the one attempt to command, the other meekly obey the higher impulses of their being.'*

* Thoughts on the Poets.

The first metrical compositions in this country, recognised by popular sympathy, were the effusions of Philip Freneau, a political writer befriended by Jefferson. He wrote many songs and ballads in a patriotic and historical vein, which attracted and somewhat reflected the feelings of his contemporaries, and were not destitute of merit. Their success was owing, in part, to the immediate interest of the subjects; and in part to musical versification and pathetic sentiment. One of his Indian ballads has survived the general neglect to which more artistic skill and deeper significance in poetry, has banished the mass of his verses; to the curious in metrical writings, however, they yet afford a characteristic illustration of the taste and spirit of the times. Freneau was born in 1752, and died in 1832. The antecedent specimens of verse in America, were, for the most part, the occasional work of the clergy, and are remarkable chiefly for a quaint and monotonous strain, grotesque rhymed versions of the Psalms, and tolerable attempts at descriptive poems. The writings of Mrs. Bradstreet, Governor Bradford, Roger Williams, Cotton Mather, and the witty Dr. Byles, in this department, are now only familiar to the antiquarian. Franklin's friend Ralph, and Thomas Godfrey of Philadelphia, indicate the dawn of a more liberal era, illustrated by Trumbull, Dwight, Humphreys, Alsop, and Honeywood; passages from whose poems show a marked improvement in diction, a more refined scholarship, and genuine sympathy with nature; but, although in a literary point of view they are respectable performances, and for the period and locality of their composition, suggestive of a rare degree of taste, there are too few salient points, and too little of an original spirit, to justify any claim to high poetical genius. One of the most remarkable efforts in this branch of letters, at the epoch in question, was doubtless William Mumford's translation of the Iliad — a work that, when published, elicited some authentic critical praise. He was a native of Virginia, and his great undertaking was only finished a short period before his death, which occurred in 1825. The verses which have the earliest touch of true sensibility and that melody of rhythm which seems intuitive, are the few bequeathed by William Cliffton of Philadelphia, born in 1772. After him we trace the American muse in the patriotic songs of R. T. Paine, and the scenic descriptions of Paulding, until she began a loftier though brief flight in the fanciful poems of Allston.

"In the moral economy of life, sensibility to the beautiful must have a great purpose. If the Platonic doctrine of pre-existence be true, perhaps ideality is the surviving element of our primal life. Some individuals seem born to minister to this influence, which, under the name of beauty, sentiment, or poetry, is the source of what is most exalting in our inmost experience and redeeming in our outward life Does not a benign Providence watch over these priests of nature? They are not necessarily renowned. Their agency may be wholly social and private, yet none the less efficient. We confess that, to us, few arguments for the benevolent and infinite design of existence are more impressive than the fact that such beings actually live, and wholly unfitted as they are to excel in or even conform to the Practical, bear evidence, not to be disputed, of the sanctity, the tranquil progress and the serene faith that dwell in the Ideal. Washington Allston was such a man. He was born in South Carolina in 1779, and died at Cambridge, Mass., in 1843. By profession he was a painter, and his works overflow with genius; still it would be difficult to say whether his pen, his pencil, or his tongue chiefly made known that he was a prophet of the true and beautiful. He believed not in any exclusive development. It was the spirit of a man, and not his dexterity or success, by which he tested character. In painting, reading, or writing, his mornings were occupied, and at night he was at the service of his friends. Beneath his humble roof, in his latter years, there was often a flow of wit, a community of mind, and a generous exercise of sympathy which kings might envy. To the eye of the multitude his life glided away in secluded contentment, yet a prevailing idea was the star of his being—the idea of beauty. For the high, the lovely, the perfect, he strove all his days. He sought them in the scenes of nature, in the master-pieces of literature and art, in habits of life, in social relations, and in love. Without pretence, without elation, in all meekness, his youthful enthusiasm chastened by suffering, he lived above the world. Gentleness he deemed true wisdom, renunciation of all the trappings of life, a duty. He was calm, patient, occasionally sad, but for the most part happy in the free exercise and guardianship of his varied powers. His sonnets are interesting as records of personal feeling. They eloquently breathe sentiments of intelligent admiration or sincere friendship; while the 'Styles of the Season' and other longer poems show a great command of language and an exuberant fancy.

On his return to America, the life of our illustrious painter was one of comparative seclusion. The state of his health, devotion to his art, and a distaste for promiscuous society and the bustle of the world, rendered this course the most judicious he could have pursued. His humble retirement was occasionally invaded by foreigners of distinction, to whom his name had become precious; and sometimes a votary of letters or art entered his dwelling, to gratify admiration or seek counsel and encouragement. To such, an unaffected and sincere welcome was always given, and they left his presence refreshed and happy. The instances of timely sympathy which he afforded young and baffled aspirants, are innumerable.

Allston's appearance and manners accorded perfectly with his character. His form was slight and his movements quietly active.

The lines of his countenance, the breadth of the brow, the large and speaking eye, and the long white hair, made him an immediate object of interest. If not engaged in conversation, there was a serene abstraction in his air. When death so tranquilly overtook him, for many hours it was difficult to believe that he was not sleeping, so perfectly did the usual expression remain. His torch-light burial harmonized, in its beautiful solemnity, with the bright and thoughtful tenor of his life."*

John Pierpont, a Unitarian clergyman of Massachusetts, has written numerous hymns and odes for religious and national occasions, remarkable for their variety of difficult metres, and for the felicity both of the rhythm, sentiment, and expression. His 'Airs of Palestine,' a long poem in heroic verse, has many eloquent passages; and several of his minor pieces, especially those entitled 'Passing Away,' and 'My Child,' are striking examples of effective versification. The most popular of his occasional poems is 'The Pilgrim Fathers,' an ode written for the anniversary of the landing at Plymouth, and embodying in truly musical verse the sentiment of the memorable day.

Richard H. Dana is the most psychological of American poets. His 'Buccaneer' has several descriptive passages of singular terseness and beauty; although there is a certain abruptness in the metre chosen. The scenery and phenomena of the ocean are evidently familiar to his observation; the tragic and remorseful elements in humanity exert a powerful influence over his imagination; while the mysteries and aspirations of the human soul fill and elevate his mind. The result is an introspective tone, a solemnity of mood lightened occasionally by touches of pathos or beautiful pictures. There is a compactness, a pointed truth to the actual, in many of his rhymed pieces, and a high music in some of his blank verse, which suggest greater poetical genius than is actually exhibited. His taste evidently inclines to Shakspeare, Milton, and the old English dramatists, his deep appreciation of whom he has manifested in the most subtle and profound criticisms. Of his minor pieces, the 'Intimations of Immortality' and 'The Little Beach-Bird,' are perhaps the most characteristic of his two phases of expression.

James A. Hillhouse excelled in a species of poetic literature, which, within a few years, has attained eminence from the fine illustrations of Taylor, Browning, Horne, Talfourd, and other men of genius in England. It may be called the written drama; and however unfit for representation, is unsurpassed for bold, noble, and exquisite sentiment and imagery. The name of Hillhouse is associated with the beautiful elms of New Haven, beneath whose majestic boughs he so often walked. His home in the neighborhood of this

---

* Artist-Life, or Sketches of American Painters.

rural city was consecrated by elevated tastes, and domestic virtue. He there, in the intervals of business, led the life of a true scholar; and the memorials of this existence are his poems 'Hadad,' 'The Judgment,' 'Percy's Masque,' 'Demetria,' and others. In the two former, his scriptural erudition and deep perceptions of the Jewish character, and his sense of religious truth, are evinced in the most carefully finished, and nobly-conceived writings. Their tone is lofty, often sublime; the language is finely chosen, and there is about them evidence of gradual and patient labor rare in American literature. On every page we recognise the Christian scholar and gentleman, the secluded bard, and the chivalric student of the past. 'Percy's Masque' re-produces the features of an era more impressed with knightly character than any in the annals of England. Hillhouse moves in that atmosphere quite as gracefully as among the solemn and venerable traditions of the Hebrew faith. His dramatic and other pieces are the first instances, in this country, of artistic skill in the higher and more elaborate spheres of poetic writing. He possessed the scholarship, the leisure, the dignity of taste, and the noble sympathy requisite thus to "build the lofty rhyme;" and his volumes, though unattractive to the mass of readers, have a permanent interest and value to the refined, the aspiring, and the disciplined mind.

Charles Sprague has been called the Rogers of America; and there is an analogy between them in two respects,—the careful finish of their verses, and their financial occupation. The American poet first attracted notice by two or three theatrical prize addresses; and his success, in this regard, attained its climax in a 'Shakspeare Ode' which grouped the characters of the great poet with an effect so striking and happy, and in a rhythm so appropriate and impressive, as to recall the best efforts of Collins and Dryden united. A similar composition, more elaborate, is his ode delivered on the second centennial anniversary of the settlement of Boston, his native city. A few domestic pieces, remarkable for their simplicity of expression and truth of feeling, soon became endeared to a large circle; but the performance which has rendered Sprague best known to the country as a poet, is his metrical essay on 'Curiosity,' delivered in 1829 before the literary societies of Harvard University. It is written in heroic measure, and recalls the couplets of Pope. The choice of a theme was singularly fortunate. He traces the passion which "tempted Eve to sin" through its loftiest and most vulgar manifestations; at one moment, rivalling Crabbe in the lowliness of his details, and at another, Campbell in the aspiration of his song The serious and the comic alternate on every page. Good sense is the basis of the work; fancy, wit, and feeling, warm and vivify it, and a nervous tone and finished versification, as well as excellent choice of words, impart a glow, polish, and grace, that at once gratify the ear, and captivate the mind.

James G. Percival has been a copious writer of verses, some of which, from their even and sweet flow, their aptness of epithet and natural sentiment, have become household and school treasures; such as 'The Coral Grove,' 'New England,' and 'Seneca Lake.' His command both of language and metre is remarkable; his acquirements have been very extensive and various, and his life eccentric. Perhaps a remarkable power of expression has tended to limit his poetic fame, by inducing a diffuse, careless, and unindividual method; although choice pieces enough may easily be gleaned from his voluminous writings, to constitute a just and rare claim to renown and sympathy.

The poems of Fitz-Greene Halleck, although limited in quantity, are perhaps the best known and most cherished, especially in the latitude of New York, of all American verses. This is owing, in no small degree, to their spirited, direct, and intelligible character; the absence of all vagueness and mysticism, and the heartfelt or humorous glow of real inspiration; and in a measure, perhaps, it can be traced to the *prestige* of his youthful fame, when, associated with his friend Drake, he used to charm the town with the admirable local verses that appeared in the journals of the day, under the signature of Croaker and Co. His theory of poetic expression is that of the most popular masters of English verse — manly, clear, vivid, warm with genuine emotion, or sparkling with true wit. The more recent style of metrical writing, suggestive rather than emphatic, undefined and involved, and borrowed mainly from German idealism, he utterly repudiates. All his verses have a vital meaning, and the clear ring of pure metal. They are few but memorable. The school-boy, and the old Knickerbocker, both know them by heart. In his serious poems, he belongs to the same school as Campbell; and in his lighter pieces reminds us of Beppo and the best parts of Don Juan. 'Fanny,' conceived in the latter vein, has the point of a fine local satire gracefully executed. 'Burns' and the lines on the death of Drake, have the beautiful impressiveness of the highest elegiac verse. 'Marco Bozzaris' is perhaps the best martial lyric in the language; 'Red Jacket' the most effective Indian portrait; and 'Twilight' an apt piece of contemplative verse; while 'Alnwick Castle' combines his grave and gay style with inimitable art and admirable effect. As a versifier, he is an adept in that relation of sound to sense which embalms thought in deathless melody. An unusual blending of the animal and intellectual with that full proportion essential to manhood, enables him to utter appeals that wake responses in the universal heart. An almost provoking mixture of irony and sentiment is characteristic of his genius. Born in Connecticut, his life has been chiefly passed in the city of New York, and occupied in mercantile affairs. He is a conservative in taste and opinions, but his feelings are chivalric, and his sympathies ardent and loyal; and these, alternating with humor, glow and sparkle in the most spirited and harmonious lyrical compositions of the American muse.

"Centuries hence, perchance, some lover of 'The Old American Writers' will speculate as ardently as Monkbarns himself, about the site of Sleepy Hollow. Then the Hudson will possess a classic interest, and the associations of genius and patriotism may furnish themes to illustrate its matchless scenery. 'The Culprit Fay' will then be quoted with enthusiasm. Imagination is a perverse faculty. Why should the ruins of a feudal castle add enchantment to a knoll of the Catskills? Are not the Palisades more ancient than the aqueducts of the Roman Campagna? Can bloody tradition or superstitious legends really enhance the picturesque impression derived from West Point? The heart for ever asserts its claim. Primeval nature is often coldly grand in the view of one who loves and honors his race; and the outward world is only brought near to his spirit when linked with human love and suffering, or consecrated by heroism and faith. Yet, if there ever was a stream romantic in itself, superior from its own wild beauty, to all extraneous charms, it is the Hudson. Who ever sailed between its banks and scanned its jutting headlands,—the perpendicular cliffs,—the meadows over which alternate sunshine and cloud,—umbrageous woods, masses of grey rock, dark cedar groves, bright grain-fields, tasteful cottages, and fairy-like sails; who, after thus feasting both sense and soul, through a summer day, has, from a secluded nook of those beautiful shores, watched the moon rise and tip the crystal ripples with light, and not echoed the appeal of the bard?

'Tell me—where'er thy silver bark be steering,
By bright Italian or soft Persian lands,
Or o'er those island-studded seas careering,
Whose pearl-charged waves dissolve on coral strands:
Tell if thou visitest, thou heavenly rover,
A lovelier scene than this the wide world over?'*

"It was where

'The moon looks down on old Cro'nest,
And mellows the shade on his shaggy breast,'

that Drake laid the scene of his poem. The story is of simple construction. The fairies are called together, at this chosen hour, not to join in dance or revel, but to sit in judgment on one of their number who has broken his vestal vow. Evil sprites, both of the air and water, oppose the Fay in his mission of penance. He is sadly baffled and tempted, but at length conquers all difficulties, and his triumphant return is hailed with 'dance and song, and lute and lyre.'

"It is in the imagery of the poem that Drake's genius is pre-emi-

* Hoffman's "Moonlight on the Hudson."

nent. What, for instance, can be more ingenious than the ordeals prescribed had any 'spot or taint' in his ladye-love deepened the Fay's sacrilege? Most appropriate tortures, these, for a fairy inquisition! Even without the metrical accompaniment, how daintily conceived are all the appointments of the fairies! Their lanterns were owlet's eyes. Some of them repose in cobweb hammocks, swinging, perhaps, on tufted spears of grass, and rocked by the zephyrs of a midsummer night. Others make their beds of lichen-green, pillowed by the breast-plumes of the humming-bird. A few, whose taste for upholstery is quite magnificent, find a couch in the purple shade of the four-o'clock, or the little niches of rock lined with dazzling mica. The table of these minnikin epicureans is a mushroom, whose velvet surface and quaker hue make it a very respectable festal board at which to drink dew from buttercups. The king's throne is of sassafras and spice-wood, with tortoise-shell pillars, and crimson tulip-leaves for drapery. But the quaint shifts and beautiful outfit of the Culprit himself, comprise the most delectable imagery of the poem. He is worn out with fatigue and chagrin at the very commencement of his journey, and therefore makes captive of a spotted toad, by way of a steed. Having bridled her with silk-weed twist, his progress is rapid by dint of lashing her sides with an osier thong. Arrived at the beach, he launches fearlessly upon the tide, for among his other accomplishments, the Fay is a graceful swimmer; but his tender limbs are so bruised by leeches, star-fish, and other watery enemies, that he is soon driven back.

"The *materia medica* of Fairy-land is always accessible; and cob-web lint, and balsam dew of sorrel and henbane, speedily relieve the little penitent's wounds. Having refreshed himself with the juice of the calamus root, he returns to the shore, and selects a neatly-shaped muscle shell, brightly painted without, and tinged with pearl within. Nature seemed to have formed it expressly for a fairy-boat Having notched the stern, and gathered a colen bell to bale with, he sculls into the midst of the river, laughing at his old foes as they grin and chatter around his way. There, in the sweet moon-light, he sits until a sturgeon comes by, and leaps, all glistening, into the silvery atmosphere; then balancing his delicate frame upon one foot, like a Lilliputian Mercury, he lifts the flowery cup, and catches the one sparkling drop that is to wash the stain from his wing. Gay is his return voyage. Sweet nymphs clasp the boat's side with their tiny hands, and cheerily urge it onward. His next enterprise is of a more knightly species; and he proceeds to array himself accordingly, as becomes a fairy cavalier. His acorn helmet is plumed with thistle-down, a bee's nest forms his corselet, and his cloak is of butterflies' wings. With a lady-bug's shell for a shield, and wasp-sting lance, spurs of cockle-seed, a bow made of vine-twig, strung with maize-silk, and well supplied with nettle-shafts, he mounts his fire-fly

Bucephalus, and waving his blade of blue grass, speeds upward to catch a 'glimmering spark' from some flying meteor. Again the spirits of evil are let loose upon him, and the upper elements are not more friendly than those below. Fays are as hardly beset, it seems, as we of coarser clay, by temptations in a feminine shape. A sylphid queen of the skies, 'the loveliest of the forms of light,' enchants the wanderer by her beauty and kindness. But though she played very archly with the butterfly cloak, and handled the tassel of his blade while he revealed to her pitying ear 'the dangers he had passed,' the memory of his first love and the object of pilgrimage kept his heart free. Escorted with great honor by the sylph's lovely train, his career is resumed, and his flame-wood lamp at length rekindled, and before the 'sentry elf' proclaims 'a streak in the eastern sky,' the Culprit has been welcomed to all his original glory.

"It will be observed that the materials—the costume, as it were—of this fairy tale, are of native and familiar origin. The effect is certainly quite as felicitous as that of many similar productions where the countless flowers and rich legends of the East, furnish the poet with an exhaustless mine of pleasing images. It has been remarked that the dolphin and flying-fish are the only poetical members of the finny tribes; but who, after reading the Culprit Fay, will ever hear the plash of a sturgeon in the moon-lit water, without recalling the genius of Drake? Indeed, the poem which we have thus cursorily examined, is one of those happy inventions of fancy, superinduced upon fact, which afford unalloyed delight. There are various tastes as regard the style and spirit of different bards; but no one, having the slightest perception, will fail to realize at once that the Culprit Fay is a genuine poem. This is, perhaps, the highest of praise. The mass of versified compositions are *not* strictly poems. Here and there only the purely ideal is apparent. A series of poetical fragments are linked by rhymes to other and larger portions of commonplace and prosaic ideas. It is with the former as with moon-beams falling through dense foliage—they only chequer our path with light. 'Poetry,' says Campbell, 'should come to us in masses of ore, that require little sifting.' The poem before us obeys this important rule. It is 'of imagination all compact.' It takes us completely away from the dull level of ordinary associations. As the portico of some beautiful temple, through it we are introduced into a scene of calm delight, where Fancy asserts her joyous supremacy, and woos us to forgetfulness of all outward evil, and to fresh recognition of the lovely in Nature, and the graceful and gifted in humanity."*

For some of the best convivial, amatory, and descriptive poetry of native origin, we are indebted to Charles Fenno Hoffman. The woods and streams, the feast and the vigil, are reflected in his verse with a graphic truth and sentiment that evidence an eye for the pic-

* Thoughts on the Poets.

turesque, a sense of the adventurous, and a zest for pleasure He has written many admirable scenic pieces that evince not only a careful, but a loving observation of nature; some touches of this kind in the 'Vigil of Faith' are worthy of the most celebrated poets. Many of his songs, from their graceful flow and tender feeling, are highly popular, although some of the metres are too like those of Moore not to provoke a comparison. They are, however, less tinctured with artifice; and many of them have a spontaneous and natural vitality.

The Scripture pieces of N. P. Willis, although the productions of his youth, have an individual beauty that renders them choice and valuable exemplars of American genius. In his other poems there is apparent a sense of the beautiful and a grace of utterance, often an exquisite imagery, and rich tone of feeling that emphatically announce the poet; but in the chastened and sweet, as well as picturesque elaboration of the miracles of Christ, and some of the incidents recorded in the Bible, Willis succeeded in an experiment at once bold, delicate, and profoundly interesting. 'Melanie' is a narrative in verse, full of imaginative beauty and expressive music. The high finish, rare metaphors, verbal felicity, and graceful sentiment of his poems are sometimes marred by a doubtful taste that seems affectation; but where he obeys the inspiration of nature and religious sentiment, the result is truly beautiful. A native of Maine, he has been an extensive traveller, and has gathered his illustrations from a wide range of observation and experience.

Henry W. Longfellow has achieved an extended reputation as a poet, for which he is chiefly indebted to his philological aptitudes and his refined taste. Trained as a verbal artist by the discipline of a poetical translator, he acquired a tact and facility in the use of words, which great natural fluency and extreme fastidiousness enabled him to use to the utmost advantage. His poems are chiefly meditative, and have that legendary significance peculiar to the German ballad. They also often embody and illustrate a moral truth. There is little or no evidence of inspiration in his verse, as that term is used to suggest the power of an overmastering passion; but there is a thoughtful, subdued feeling that seems to overflow in quiet beauty. It is, however, the manner in which this sentiment is expressed, the appositeness of the figures, the harmony of the numbers, and the inimitable choice of words that gives effect to the composition. He often reminds us of an excellent mosaic worker, with his smooth table of polished marble indented to receive the precious stones that are lying at hand, which he calmly, patiently, and with exquisite art, inserts in the shape of flowers and fruit. Almost all Longfellow's poems are gems set with consummate taste. His 'Evangeline' is a beautiful picture of rural life and love, which, from the charm of its pictures and the gentle harmony of its sentiment, became popular although written in hexameters. His 'Skeleton in Armor' is the most novel and characteristic of his shorter poems; and his 'Psalms of Life' and 'Excelsior' are the most familiar and endeared. He is the artistic, as Halleck is the lyrical and Bryant the picturesque and philosophic, of American poets.

The most concise, apt, and effective poet of the school of Pope, this country has produced, is Oliver Wendell Holmes, a Boston physician and son of the excellent author of the 'Annals,' long a minister of the parish of Cambridge, at which venerable seat of learning this accomplished writer was born. His best lines are a series of rhymed pictures, witticisms, or sentiments, let off with the precision and brilliancy of the scintillations that sometimes illumine the northern horizon. The significant terms, the perfect construction and acute choice of syllables and emphasis, render some passages of Holmes absolute models of versification, especially in the heroic measure. Besides these artistic merits, his poetry abounds with fine satire, beautiful delineations of nature, and amusing caricatures of manners. The long poems are metrical essays more pointed, musical, and judicious, as well as witty, than any that have appeared, of the same species, since the 'Essay on Man' and 'The Dunciad.' His description of the art in which he excels, is inimitable, and illustrates all that it defines. His 'Old Ironsides'—an indignant protest against the destruction of the frigate Constitution — created a public sentiment that prevented the fulfilment of that ungracious design. His verses on 'Lending an old Punch Bowl' are in the happiest vein of that form of writing. About his occasional pieces, there is an easy and vigorous tone like that of Praed; and some of them are the liveliest specimens of finished verse yet written among us. His command of language, his ready wit, his concise and pointed style, the nervous, bright, and wise scope of his muse, now and then softened by a pathetic touch, or animated by a living picture, are qualities that have firmly established the reputation of Dr. Holmes as a poet; while, in professional character and success, he has been equally recognised.

James R. Lowell, also the son of a clergyman and a native of Cambridge, unites, in his most effective poems, the dreamy, suggestive character of the transcendental bards with the philosophic simplicity of Wordsworth. He has written clever satires, good sonnets, and some long poems with fine descriptive passages. He reminds us often of Tennyson, in the sentiment and the construction of his verse. Imagination and philanthropy are the dominant elements in his writings; some of which are marked by a graceful flow and earnest tone, and many unite with these attractions that of high finish.

George H. Boker, the author of 'Calaynos,' 'Anne Boleyn,' and other dramatic pieces, is a native and resident of Philadelphia. "The glow of his images is chastened by a noble simplicity, keeping them within the line of human sympathy and natural expression. He has followed the masters of dramatic writing with rare judgment. He also excels many gifted poets of his class in a quality essential to an acted play—spirit. To the tragic ability he unites aptitude for easy, colloquial, and jocose dialogue, such as must intervene in the genuine Shakspearian drama, to give relief and additional effect to high emotion. His language, also, rises often to the highest point of energy, pathos, and beauty."*

A casual dalliance with the muses is characteristic of our busy citizens, in all professions; some of these poetical estrays have a permanent hold upon the popular taste and sympathy. Among them may be mentioned Frisbie's 'Castle in the Air,' Norton's 'Scene after a Summer Shower,' Henry Ware's 'Address to the Ursa Major,' Pinkney's verses entitled 'A Health,' Palmer's ode to 'Light,' Poe's 'Raven' and 'The Bells,' Cooke's 'Florence Vane,' Parson's 'Lines to a Bust of Dante,' Wilde's 'My Life is like a Summer Rose,' Albert G. Greene's 'Old Grimes,' and Woodworth's 'Old Oaken Bucket.'

Extensive circulation is seldom to be hoped for works which appeal so faintly to the practical spirit of our times and people, as the class we have thus cursorily examined. Yet, did space allow, we should be tempted into a somewhat elaborate argument, to prove that the cordial reception of such books agrees perfectly with genuine utilitarianism. As a people, it is generally conceded that we lack nationality of feeling. Narrow reasoners may think that this spirit is best promoted by absurd sensitiveness to foreign comments or testy alertness in regard to what is called national honor. We incline to the opinion founded on well established facts, both of history and human nature, that the best way to make an individual true to his political obligations, is to promote his love of country; and experience shows that this is mainly induced by cherishing high and interesting associations in relation to his native land. Every well-recorded act, honorable to the state, every noble deed consecrated by the effective pen of the historian, or illustrated in the glowing page of the novelist, tends wonderfully to such a result. Have not the hearts of the Scotch nurtured a deeper patriotism since Sir Walter cast into the furrows of time his peerless romances? No light part in this elevated mission is accorded to the poet. Dante and Petrarch have done much to render Italy beloved. Beranger has given no inadequate expression to those feelings which bind soldier, artisan and peasant to the soil of France. Here the bard can draw only upon brief chronicles, but God has arrayed this continent with a sublime and characteristic beauty, that should endear its mountains and streams to the American heart; and whoever ably depicts the natural glory of the country, touches a chord which should yield responses of admiration and loyalty. In this point of view alone, then, we deem the minstrel who ardently sings

* Characteristics of Literature. Second Series.

of forest and sky, river and highland, as eminently worthy of recognition. This merit may be claimed for Alfred B. Street, of Albany, who was born and reared amid the most picturesque scenery of the state of New York. That he is deficient occasionally in high finish — that there is repetition and monotony in his strain — that there are redundant epithets, and a lack of variety in his effusions, is undeniable; and having frankly granted all this to the critics, we feel at liberty to utter his just praise with equal sincerity. Street has an eye for Nature in all her moods. He has not roamed the woodlands in vain, nor have the changeful seasons passed him by without leaving vivid and lasting impressions. These his verse records with unusual fidelity and genuine emotion. I have wandered with him on a summer's afternoon, in the neighbourhood of his present residence, and, stretched upon the greensward, listened to his woodland talk, and can therefore testify that he observes *con amore* the play of shadows, the twinkle of swaying herbage in the sunshine, and all the phenomena that makes the outward world so rich in meaning to the attentive gaze. He is a true Flemish painter, seizing upon objects in all their verisimilitude. As we read him, wild flowers peer up from among the brown leaves; the drum of the partridge, the ripple of waters, the flickering of autumn light, the sting of sleety snow, the cry of the panther, the roar of the winds, the melody of birds, and the odor of crushed pine boughs, are present to our senses. In a foreign land his poems would transport us at once to home. He is no second-hand limner, content to furnish insipid copies, but draws from reality. His pictures have the freshness of originals. They are graphic, detailed, never untrue, and often vigorous. He is essentially an American poet. His range is limited, and he has had the good sense not to wander from his sphere, candidly acknowledging that the heart of man has not furnished him the food for meditation, which inspires a higher class of poets. He is emphatically an observer. In England we notice that these qualities have been recognised. His 'Lost Hunter' has been finely illustrated there, thus affording the best evidence of the picturesque fertility of his muse. Many of his pieces also glow with patriotism. His 'Grey Forest Eagle' is a noble lyric, full of spirit; his 'Forest Scenes' are minutely, and at the same time, elaborately true. His Indian legends and descriptions of the seasons have a native zest we have rarely encountered. Without the classic refinement of Thomson, he excels him in graphic power. There is nothing metaphysical in his tone of mind, or highly artistic in his style. But there is an honest directness and cordial faithfulness about him that strikes us as remarkably appropriate and manly. Delicacy, sentiment, ideal enthusiasm, are not his by nature, but clear, bold, genial insight and feeling he possesses in a rare degree, and his poems worthily depict the phases of nature, as she displays herself in this land, in all her picturesque wildness, solemn magnificence, and serene beauty.

To the descriptive talent as related to natural scenery, which we have noted as the gift of our best poets, John G. Whittier unites the enthusiasm of a reformer and the sympathies of the patriot There is a prophetic anathema and a bard-like invocation in some of his pieces. He is a true son of New England, and, beneath the calm, fraternal bearing of the quaker, nurses the imaginative ardor of a devotee both of nature and humanity. The early promise of Brainard, his fine poetic observation and sensibility, enshrined in several pleasing lyrics, and his premature death, are analogous to the career of Henry Kirke White. John Neal has written some odes, carelessly put together, but having memorable passages. Emerson has published a small volume of quaint rhymes; Croswell wrote several short but impressive church poems, in which he has been ably followed by Cleveland Cox; Bayard Taylor's California ballads are full of truth, spirit, and melody; Albert Pike of Arkansas, is the author of a series of hymns to the gods, after the manner of Keats, which have justly commanded favorable notice; Willis G. Clarke is remembered for his few but touching and finished elegiac pieces. Epes Sargent's 'Poems of the Sea,' are worthy of the subject, both in sentiment and style. F. S. Key of Baltimore was the author of the 'Star-Spangled Banner,' and Judge Hopkinson of Philadelphia, wrote 'Hail Columbia.' George P. Morris, among the honored contributors to American poetry,* whose pieces are more or less familiar, is recognised as the song-writer of America.

A large number of graceful versifiers, and a few writers of poetical genius, have arisen among the women of America Southey has recorded, in no measured terms, his estimation of Mrs. Brooks, the author of 'Zophiel.' The sentiment and melody of Mrs. Welby have made the name of 'Amelia' precious in the west. Mrs. Sigourney's metrical writings are cherished by a large portion of the New England religious public. The 'Sinless Child of Mrs. Oakes Smith is a melodious and imaginative poem, with many verses of graphic and metaphysical significance. The occasional pieces of Mrs. Embury, Mrs. Whitman, Mrs. Hewitt, and Miss Lynch, are

* Among them are Hill, Godwin, Mellen, Griffin, Ware, Doane, Colton, Rockwell, Sanford, Ward, Gallagher, Aldrich, J. F. Clark, Hormer, Burleigh Noble, Hirst, Read, Matthews, Lord, Wallace, Legaré, Miller, Walter, East burn, Barker, Schoolcraft, Tappan, Jackson, Meek, Seba Smith, Thacher, Peabody, Ellery, Channing, Snelling, Murray, Fay, C. C. Moore, J. G. Brooks, A. G. Greene, Bethune, Carlos Wilcox, Frisbie, Goodrich, Clason, Leggett, Fairfield, Dawes, Bright, Conrad, Prentice, Simms, John H. Bryant, Lawrence, Benjamin, Vesy, Cutter, Cranch, Peabodie, Matthews, Huntington, Saxe, Dewey, Fields, Hoyt, Stoddard. For biographical notices and a critical estimate of these metrical writers, with specimens of their verse, the reader is referred to Griswold's 'Poets and Poetry of America,' last edition.

thoughtful, earnest, and artistic. The facility, playfulness, and ingenious conception of Mrs. Osgood rendered her a truly gifted *improvisatrice*. Miss Gould has written several pretty fanciful little poems, and Miss Sara Clark's 'Ariadne' is worthy of Mrs. Norton. The Davidsons are instances of rare, though melancholy precocity in the art. The moral purity, love of nature, domestic affection, and graceful expression which characterize the writings of our female poets, are remarkable. Many of them enjoy a high local reputation, and their effusions are quoted with zeal at the fire-side. Taste rather than profound sympathies, sentiment rather than passion, and fancy more than imagination, are evident in these spontaneous, gentle, and often picturesque poems. They usually are more creditable to the refinement and pure feelings, than to the creative power or original style of the authors. Among a reading people, however, like our own, these beautiful native flowers, scattered by loving hands, are sweet mementoes and tokens of ideal culture and gentle enthusiasm, in delightful contrast to the prevailing hardihood and materialism of character.*

In the felicitous use of native materials, as well as in the religious sentiment and love of freedom, united with skill as an artist, William Cullen Bryant is recognised as the best representative of American poetry; and we cannot better close this brief survey of native literature than by an examination of his poems; in which the traits of our scenery, the spirit of our institutions, and the devotional faith that proved the conservative element in our history, are all consecrated by poetic art.

"The first thought which suggests itself in regard to Bryant, is his respect for the art which he has so nobly illustrated. This is not less commendable than rare. Such an impatient spirit of utility prevails in our country, that even men of ideal pursuits are often infected by it. It is a leading article in the Yankee creed, to turn every

* For a very complete and interesting survey of this class of writings, the reader is referred to 'Griswold's Female Poets of America.' His list comprises nearly a hundred names; the biographical sketches afford a good insight into the domestic culture of the nation; and the specimens are various, and often beautiful, including, besides the writers of colonial and revolutionary times, and those already mentioned, the names of Miss Townsend, Mrs. Gilman, Mrs. Hale, Mrs. Wells, Miss James, Mrs. Ward, Mrs. Ware, Mrs. Gray, Mrs. Little, Mrs. Child, Mrs. Hall, Mrs. Follen, Mrs. Green, Miss Taggart, Mrs. Canfield, Miss Bogart, Mrs. Mary E. Brooks, Mrs. Loud, Mrs. Chandler, Mrs. Barnes, Mrs. Kinney, Mrs. Ellett, Mrs. Scott, Mrs. Dinnies, Mrs. Stephens, Mrs. St. John, Mrs. L. P. Smith, Mrs. Oliver, Miss Mary E. Lee, Mrs. Esling, Mrs. Sawyer, Mrs. Bailey, Mrs. Thurston, Miss Day, Mrs. Dodd, Mrs. Judson, Mrs. Eames, Mrs. Emeline Smith, Miss Fuller, Mrs. Pierson, Mrs. Worthington, Mrs. Lewis, Mrs. Mowatt, Mrs. M'Donald, Lucy Hooper, Mrs. Mayo, Miss Jacobs, Mrs. Case, Mrs. Bolton, Miss Woodman, Mrs. Nichols, Mrs. Wakefield, Miss E. Lee, Miss Susan Pindar, Caroline May, Mrs. Neal, Mrs. Sproat, Mrs. Winslow, Miss Campbell, Miss Bayard, Mrs. Lascom, Edith May, Alice and Phœbe Carey, Miss Dawson, Mrs. Lowell, and Miss Phillips.

endowment to account: and although a poet is generally left 'to chew the cud of sweet and bitter fancies,' as he lists, occasions are not infrequent when even his services are available. Caliban's lowly toil will not supply all needs. The more 'gentle spiriting' of Ariel is sometimes desired. To subserve the objects of party, to acquire a reputation upon which office may be sought, and to gratify personal ambition, the American poet is often tempted to sacrifice his true fame and the dignity of Art to the demands of Occasion. To this weakness Bryant has been almost invariably superior. He has preserved the elevation which he so early acquired. He has been loyal to the Muses. At their shrine his ministry seems ever free and sacred, wholly apart from the ordinary associations of life. With a pure heart and a lofty purpose, has he hymned the glory of Nature and the praise of Freedom. To this we cannot but, in a great degree, ascribe the serene beauty of his verse. The mists of worldly motives dim the clearest vision, and the sweetest voice falters amid the strife of passion. As the patriarch went forth alone to muse at eventide, the reveries of genius have been to Bryant, holy and private seasons. They are as unstained by the passing clouds of this troubled existence, as the skies of his own 'Prairies' by village smoke.

"Thus it should be, indeed, with all poets; but we deem it singularly happy when it is so with our own. The tendency of all action and feeling with us, is so much the reverse of poetical, that only the high, sustained, and consistent development of the imagination, would command attention or exert influence. The poet in this republic, does not address ignorance. In truth, the great obstacle with which he has to deal, so to speak, is intelligence. It is not the love of gain and physical comfort alone, that deadens the finer perceptions of our people. Among the highly educated there is less real enjoyment of poetry than is discovered by those to whom reading is almost a solitary luxury. No conformity to fashion or affectation of taste influences the latter. They seek the world of imagination and sentiment, with the greater delight from the limited satisfaction realized in their actual lot. To them Poetry is a great teacher of self-respect. It unfolds to them emotions familiar to their own bosoms. It celebrates scenes of beauty amid which they also are free to wander. It vindicates capacities and a destiny of which they partake. Intimations like these are seldom found in their experience, and for this reason,—cherished and hallowed associations endear an art which consoles while it brings innocent pleasure to their hearts. It is, therefore, in what is termed society, that the greatest barriers to poetic sympathy exist, and it is precisely here that it is most desirable the bard should be heard. But the idea of culture with this class lies almost exclusively in knowledge. They aim at understanding every question, are pertinacious on the score of opinion, and would blush to be thought unacquainted with a hundred subjects with which they have not a particle of sympathy. The wisdom of loving, even without comprehending; the revelations obtained only through feeling; the veneration that awes curiosity by exalted sentiment—all this is to them unknown. Life never seems miraculous to their minds, Nature wears a monotonous aspect, and routine gradually congeals their sensibilities. To invade this vegetative existence is the poet's vocation. Hazlitt says all that is worth remembering in life is the poetry of it. If so, habits wholly prosaic are as alien to wisdom as to enjoyment; and the elevated manner in which Bryant has uniformly presented the claims of poetry, the tranquil eloquence with which his chaste and serious muse appeals to the heart, deserves the most grateful recognition. There is something accordant with the genius of our country, in the mingled clearness and depth of his poetry. The glow of unbridled passion seems peculiarly to belong to southern lands where despotism blights personal effort, and makes the ardent pursuit of pleasure almost a necessity. The ancient communities of northern latitudes have rich literatures from whence to draw materials for their verse. But here, where Nature is so magnificent, and civil institutions so fresh, where the experiment of republicanism is going on, and each individual must think, if he do not work, Poetry, to illustrate the age and reach its sympathies, should be thoughtful and vigorous. It should minister to no weak sentiment, but foster high, manly and serious views. It should identify itself with the domestic affections, and tend to solemnize rather than merely adorn existence. Such are the natural echoes of American life, and they characterize the poetry of Bryant.

Bryant's love of Nature gives the prevailing spirit to his poetry. The feeling with him seems quite instinctive. It is not sustained by a metaphysical theory as in the case of Wordsworth, while it is imbued with more depth of pathos than is often discernible in Thomson. The feeling with which he looks upon the wonders of Creation is remarkably appropriate to the scenery of the New World. His poems convey, to an extraordinary degree, the actual impression which is awakened by our lakes, mountains, and forests. There is in the landscape of every country something characteristic and peculiar. The individual objects may be the same, but their combination is widely different. The lucent atmosphere of Switzerland, the grouping of her mountains, the effect of glacier and water-fall, of peaks clad in eternal snow, impending over valleys whose emerald herbage and peaceful flocks realize our sweetest dreams of primeval life—all strike the eye and affect the mind in a manner somewhat different from similar scenes in other lands. The long, pencilled clouds of an Italian sunset—glowing above plains covered with brightly-tinted vegetation, seem altogether more placid and luxuriant than the gorgeous masses of golden vapour, towering in our western sky at the close of an autumnal day. These and innumerable other minute features are not only perceived, but intimately felt by the genuine poet. We esteem it one of Bryant's great merits that he has not only faithfully pictured the beauties, but caught the very spirit of our scenery. His best poems have an anthem-like cadence, which accords with the vast scenes they celebrate. He approaches the mighty forests, whose shadowy haunts only the footsteps of the Indian has penetrated, deeply conscious of its virgin grandeur. His harp is strung in harmony with the wild moan of the ancient boughs. Every moss-covered trunk breathes to him of the mysteries of Time, and each wild flower which lifts its pale buds above the brown and withered leaves, whispers some thought of gentleness. We feel, when musing with him amid the solitary woods, as if blessed with a companion peculiarly fitted to interpret their teachings; and while intent in our retirement upon his page, we are sensible as it were, of the presence of those sylvan monarchs that crown the hill-tops and grace the valleys of our native land. No English park formalised by the hand of Art, no legendary spot like the pine grove of Ravenna, surrounds us. It is not the gloomy German forest with its phantoms and banditti, but one of those primal, dense woodlands of America, where the oak spreads its enormous branches, and the frost-kindled leaves of the maple glow like flame in the sunshine; where the tap of the woodpecker, and the whirring of the partridge, alone breaks the silence that broods, like the spirit of prayer, amid the interminable aisles of the verdant sanctuary. Any reader of Bryant, on the other side of the ocean, gifted with a small degree of sensibility and imagination, may derive from his poems the very awe and delight with which the first view of one of our majestic forests would strike his mind.

The kind of interest with which Bryant regards Nature is common to the majority of minds in which a love of beauty is blended with reverence. This in some measure accounts for his popularity. Many readers, even of poetical taste, are repelled by the very vehemence and intensity of Byron. They cannot abandon themselves so utterly to the influences of the outward world, as to feel the waves bound beneath them "like a steed that knows his rider;" nor will their enthusiasm so far annihilate consciousness as to make them "a portion of the tempest." Another order of imaginative spirits do not greatly affect the author of the Excursion, from the frequent baldness of his conceptions; and not a few are unable to see the Universe through the spectacles of his philosophy. To such individuals, the tranquil delight with which the American poet expatiates upon the beauties of Creation is perfectly genial. There is no mystical lore in the tributes of his muse. All is clear, earnest, and thoughtful. Indeed, the same difference that exists between true-hearted, natural affection, and the metaphysical love of the Platonists, may be traced between the manly and sincere lays of Bryant, and the vague and artificial effusions of transcendental bards. The former realize the definition of a poet which describes him as superior to the multitude only in degree, not in kind. He is the priest of a universal religion; and clothes in appropriate and harmonious language sentiments, warmly felt and cherished. He requires no interpreter. There is nothing eccentric in his vision. Like all human beings, the burden of daily toil sometimes weighs heavily on his soul; the noisy activity of common life becomes hopeless; scenes of inhumanity, error, and suffering grow oppressive, or more personal causes of despondency make "the grasshopper a burden." Then he turns to the quietude and beauty of Nature for refreshment. There he loves to read the fresh tokens of creative beneficence. The scented air of the meadows cools his fevered brow. The umbrageous foliage sways benignly around him. Vast prospects expand his thoughts beyond the narrow circle of worldly anxieties. The limpid stream upon whose banks he wandered in childhood, reflects each fleecy cloud and soothes his heart as the emblem of eternal peace. Thus faith is revived; the soul acquires renewed vitality, and the spirit of love is kindled again at the altar of God. Such views of Nature are perfectly accordant with the better impulses of the heart. There is nothing in them strained, unintelligible, or morbid. They are more or less familiar to all, and are as healthful overflowings of our nature as the prayer of repentance, or the song of thanksgiving. They distinguish the poetry of Bryant, and form one of its dominant charms.

Nothing quickens the perceptions like genuine love. From the humblest professional attachment to the most chivalric devotion, what keenness of observation is born under the influence of that feeling which drives away the obscuring clouds of selfishness, as the sun consumes the vapour of the morning! I never knew what varied associations could environ a shell-fish, until I heard an old oyster-merchant discourse of its qualities; and a landsman can have no conception of the fondness a ship may inspire, before he listens, on a moon-light night, amid the lonely sea, to the details of her build and workings, unfolded by a complacent tar. Mere instinct or habit will thus make the rude and illiterate see with better eyes than their fellows. When a human object commands such interest, how quickly does affection detect every change of mood and incipient want — reading the countenance as if it were the very chart of destiny! And it is so with the lover of Nature. By virtue of his love comes the vision, if not "the faculty divine." Objects and similitudes seen heedlessly by others, or passed unnoticed, are stamped upon his memory. Bryant is a graphic poet, in the best sense of the word. He has little of the excessive detail of Street, or the homely exactitude of Crabbe. His touches, like his themes, are usually on a grander scale, yet the minute is by no means neglected. It is his peculiar merit to deal with it wisely. Enough is suggested to convey a strong impression, and often by the introduction of a single circumstance, the mind is instantly enabled to complete the picture. It is difficult to select examples of his power in this regard. The opening scene from 'A Winter Piece' is as picturesque as it is true to fact.

Bryant is eminently a contemplative poet. His thoughts are not less impressive than his imagery. Sentiment, except that which springs from benevolence and veneration, seldom lends a glow to his pages. Indeed, there is a remarkable absence of those spontaneous bursts of tenderness and passion, which constitute the very essence of a large portion of modern verse. He has none of the spirit of Campbell, or the narrative sprightliness of Scott. The few humorous attempts he has published are unworthy of his genius. Love is merely recognised in his poems; it rarely forms the staple of any composition. His strength obviously consists in description and philosophy. It is one advantage of this species of poetry that it survives youth, and is, by nature, progressive. Bryant's recent poems are fully equal if not superior to any he has written. With his inimitable pictures there is ever blended high speculation, or a reflective strain of moral command. Some elevating inference or cheering truth is elicited from every scene consecrated by his muse. A noble simplicity of language, combined with these traits, often leads to the most genuine sublimity of expression. Some of his lines are unsurpassed in this respect. They so quietly unfold a great thought or magnificent image, that we are often taken by surprise. What a striking sense of mortality is afforded by the idea,—

"The oak
Shall send his roots abroad and pierce thy mould."

How grand the figure which represents the evening air, as

"God's blessing breathed upon the fainting earth."

In the same poem he compares

"The gentle souls that passed away,

to the twilight breezes sweeping over a churchyard,—

"Sent forth from heaven among the sons of men,"
And gone into the boundless heaven again."

And what can be more suggestive of the power of the winds, than the figure by which they are said to

"Scoop the ocean to its briny springs"?—

He would make us feel the hoary age of the mossy and gigantic forest-trees, and not only alludes to their annual decay and renewal, but significantly adds,

"The century-living crow
Whose birth was in their tops, grew old and died."

To those who have never seen a Prairie, how vividly does one spread before the imagination, in the very opening of the poem devoted to those "verdant wastes."

The progress of Science is admirably hinted in a line of 'The Ages,' when man is said to

> "Unwind the eternal dances of the sky."

Instances like these might be multiplied at pleasure, to illustrat the efficacy of simple diction, and to prove that the elements of real poetry consist in truly grand ideas, uttered without affectation, and in a reverent and earnest spirit.

A beautiful calm like that which rests on the noble works of the sculptor, breathes from the harp of Bryant. He traces a natural phenomenon, or writes in melodious numbers, the history of some familiar scene, and then, with almost prophetic emphasis, utters to the charmed ear a high lesson or sublime truth. In that pensive hymn in which he contrasts Man's transitory being, with Nature's perennial life, solemn and affecting as are the images, they but serve to deepen the simple monition at the close.

In 'The Fountain,' after a descriptive sketch that brings its limpid flow and flowery banks almost palpably before us, how exquisite is the chronicle that follows! Guided by the poet, we behold that gushing stream, ages past, in the solitude of the old woods, when canopied by the hickory and plane, the humming-bird playing amid its spray, and visited only by the wolf, who comes to "lap its waters," the deer who leaves her "delicate foot-print" on its marge, and the "slow-paced bear that stopt and drank, and leaped across." Then the savage war-cry drowns its murmur, and the wounded foeman creeps slowly to its brink to "slake his death-thirst." Ere long a hunter's lodge is built, "with poles and boughs, beside the crystal well," and at length the lonely place is surrounded with the tokens of civilization.

Thus the minstrel, even

> "From the gushing of a simple fount,
> Has reasoned to the mighty universe."

The very rhythm of the stanzas "to a Waterfowl," gives the impression of its flight. Like the bird's sweeping wing, they float with a calm and majestic cadence to the ear. We see that solitary wanderer of the "cold thin atmosphere;" we watch, almost with awe, its serene course, until "the abyss of heaven has swallowed up its form," and then gratefully echo the bard's consoling inference.

But it is unnecessary to cite from pages so familiar; or we might allude to the grand description of Freedom, and the beautiful "Hymn to Death," as among the noblest specimens of modern verse. The great principle of Bryant's faith is that

"Eternal Love doth keep
In his complacent arms, the earth, the air, the deep."

To set forth in strains the most attractive and lofty, this glorious sentiment, is the constant aim of his poetry. Gifted must be the man who is loyal to so high a vocation. From the din of outward activity, the vain turmoil of mechanical life, it is delightful and ennobling to turn to a true poet,—one who scatters flowers along our path, and lifts our gaze to the stars,—breaking, by a word, the spell of blind custom, so that we recognize once more the original glory of the Universe, and hear again the latent music of our own souls. This high service has Bryant fulfilled. It will identify his memory with the loveliest scenes of his native land, and endear it to her children for ever."*

* Thoughts on the Poets.

THE END.

www.ingramcontent.com/pod-product-compliance
Lightning Source LLC
LaVergne TN
LVHW020927110826
845150LV00004B/785

* 9 7 8 1 4 2 5 5 5 3 6 2 3 *